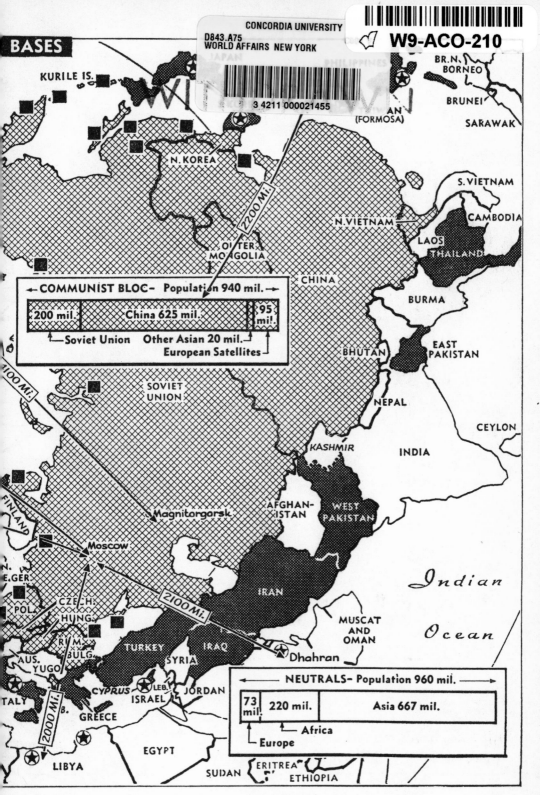

BASES

KURILE IS.

JAPAN

PHILIPPINES

BR.N. BORNEO

BRUNEI

SARAWAK

N. KOREA

(FORMOSA)

2200 MI.

S. VIETNAM

N. VIETNAM

CAMBODIA

OUTER MONGOLIA

LAOS

THAILAND

CHINA

BURMA

EAST PAKISTAN

COMMUNIST BLOC— Population 940 mil.

| 200 mil. | China 625 mil. | 95 mil. |

↑Soviet Union   Other Asian 20 mil.⤶
European Satellites⤶

BHUTAN

NEPAL

CEYLON

1100 MI.

SOVIET UNION

KASHMIR

INDIA

FINLAND

Magnitorgorsk

AFGHAN-ISTAN

WEST PAKISTAN

Moscow

N. E.GER.

Indian

POL.

CZECH.

HUNG.

RUM.

BULG.

IRAN

Ocean

AUS.

YUGO.

TURKEY

IRAQ

MUSCAT AND OMAN

ITALY

B.

SYRIA

CYPRUS   LEB.

ISRAEL

JORDAN

2100 MI.

Dhahran

GREECE

2000 MI.

NEUTRALS— Population 960 mil.

| 73 mil. | 220 mil. | Asia 667 mil. |

↑Africa
↑Europe

EGYPT

LIBYA

SUDAN

ERITREA

ETHIOPIA

By permission of The New York Times

World Affairs

PROBLEMS and PROSPECTS

POLITICAL SCIENCE SERIES

Edited by TAYLOR COLE

WORLD AFFAIRS

Problems and Prospects

Elton Atwater
William Butz
Kent Forster
Neal Riemer

The Pennsylvania State University

NEW YORK

APPLETON-CENTURY-CROFTS, INC.

PRINTED IN THE UNITED STATES OF AMERICA

Preface

53704

This book is a response to the need for a challenging and stimulating approach to the study and teaching of world affairs. Designed to provide an introduction to the nature of international problems and an appreciation of their complexity, it has been written not only for students beginning their majors in international relations, political science, economics, and history, but also for students in the more technical fields, like engineering, chemistry, agriculture, business, education, and home economics. Students in the more specialized curricula—frequently outside the college of liberal arts—are as much in need of an introduction to world affairs as their brethren in the college of liberal arts.

Today, unfortunately, a large proportion of university students are graduating from college without such an introduction; yet, they become citizens of a nation which has assumed unprecedented responsibilities and which is faced by truly momentous problems in world affairs. Among such problems are the challenges of Soviet power, the revolution of rising expectations in the underdeveloped areas of the world, and the harnessing of the tremendous power of the atom; foremost among the responsibilities is mature and farsighted leadership of the free world. Both problems and responsibilities urgently call for liberally educated college graduates. Such graduates—as actual and potential leaders in public affairs, as favorable and adverse critics of public policies, as technical, cultural, economic, and social representatives of their nation abroad —need a meaningful introduction to international affairs as part of their general education.

Guided by these reflections, we have sought to achieve the following objectives: (1) *to create a continuing interest in world affairs;* (2) *to foster an appreciation of key international problems;* (3) *to develop a conceptual, interdisciplinary framework which the student can continue to apply to world affairs after leaving the university;* and (4) *to challenge the imagination and creative intelligence of the student so that he acquires a genuinely critical commitment to the principles underlying a free, just, and peaceful world.*

It was our belief that the most effective way to achieve these objectives would be through the "problems approach." Instead of attempting to cover, superficially, a field as vast as international relations and world affairs, we have concentrated on a limited number of fundamental and representative problems. We believe that the study of key problems affords a more intelligible introduction to world affairs than does the traditional survey course.

The "problems approach," an educational device at least as old as Socrates, is based upon the premise that a student is stimulated to think most fruitfully when he is confronted with a situation that requires a choice or decision. Accordingly, the first portion of each chapter is devoted to setting forth the background of each problem. This background material is designed to set the stage for a critically intelligent and meaningful discussion of the central prob-

v

lem from several points of view. These varying positions on the problem are
then presented in the second part of each chapter. Frequently they are controversial; sometimes they are conflicting and mutually exclusive; sometimes
they are incompatible only in part. Occasionally the alternative positions are
fundamentally compatible, differing only in emphasis. Often they are pitched
to different levels of discourse. Ideally—when relevant subject matter is respected, when pertinent concepts like power and national interest are investigated, when the consequences of principles and policies are explored, and
when cogent argumentation is used to obtain light rather than generate heat—
the "problems approach" is well adapted to knowledgeable, disciplined debate
at a high level.

Three years of experimentation with the method indicate that this approach
may at first produce in students a sense of frustration at the complexity of world
affairs. This is followed, however, by a growing capacity for sober reflection
and a tendency to be wary of quick solutions and plausible panaceas. Finally,
there emerges a modest sense of discrimination in selecting the evidence and
logic that buttress a student's own more independent conclusions. In this
evolutionary process lies the greatest promise for attaining the objectives
previously listed.

Questions at the end of each chapter have been added to enable the student
to ascertain whether he understands the major points in the background material. They also measure the student's grasp of the arguments supporting the
alternative positions in the second part of each chapter. Primary emphasis, it
will be noted, has been placed upon critical and analytical evaluation of the
positions rather than upon mere acquisition of facts and ideas by rote.

The select bibliography at the conclusion of each chapter is intended to
refer the student to additional literature relevant to the particular problem
treated. The annotations may also help to crystallize and clarify the problems
themselves. Obviously, the development of good reading habits should be a
primary objective in any course of study.

The appendix contains a suggested outline for the preparation of a model
"position paper" on some foreign-policy problem. This "position paper" is
similar to those prepared in the United States Department of State. We believe
that the student will find it stimulating to select some current problem of
American foreign policy, analyze its background, suggest three or four alternative policies which the United States might follow in dealing with the problem, and recommend which course of action he considers it wisest to adopt.
This project will not only be a useful means of integrating and applying much
of the material studied in the book, but will also give the student a very realistic
idea of the problems involved in the actual formulation of a foreign policy.

In this book we have utilized the values of the interdisciplinary approach to
world affairs more fully than in most standard texts on international relations.
Whenever relevant to the problems at hand, we have emphasized the pertinent
contributions that philosophy, religion, science, economics, geography, biology,
social psychology, anthropology, and education have made to the study of
world affairs. Consequently, we have examined the influence of science and
economic resources on world problems. We have also devoted attention to
selected nonwestern cultures of the world, and we have probed the nature of

man himself and analyzed the ideologies that contend for man's allegiance in the modern world.

Our appreciation of the importance of this method has been heightened by our colleagues on The Pennsylvania State University Committee on International Understanding. This committee was appointed in 1951 by Milton S. Eisenhower, then President of The Pennsylvania State University, for the purpose of developing university-wide programs of international understanding for the students and faculty in all curricula. We feel especially indebted to Dr. Eisenhower whose vigorous support made it possible to start the work which culminated in this book.

To the following members of the original University Committee on International Understanding, who helped us launch this study, we owe far more than a simple listing can indicate: R. Wallace Brewster, Department of Political Science; Henry S. Brunner, Department of Agricultural Education; Arnold J. Currier, Department of Chemistry; Lawrence E. Dennis, Vice President in Charge of Academic Affairs; William H. Gray, Department of History and Director of International Student Affairs; Hazel M. Hatcher, Department of Home Economics Education; John D. Lawther, Assistant Dean of the College of Physical Education and Athletics; J. Campbell Lester, Department of Mechanical Engineering; Richard C. Maloney, Associate Dean of the College of Liberal Arts; Vaclav Mares, Department of Economics; Hugh G. Pyle, Division of Informal Instruction, General Extension; David W. Russell, Department of Education; Amos J. Shaler, Department of Metallurgy; and Palmer C. Weaver, Dean of Summer Sessions.

We also wish to express our gratitude to the following members of the University Committee on International Understanding who in succeeding years gave us encouragement and criticisms as our work progressed: Frank Anthony, Department of Agricultural Education; Vernon V. Aspaturian, Department of Political Science; Gerald K. Gillan, Department of Civil Engineering; Franklin B. Krauss, Department of Romance Languages; Lawrence J. Perez, Department of Civil Engineering; Werner F. Striedieck, Department of German; Helen Webb, Department of Physics; and Eugene Wettstone, Department of Physical Education.

Our list of acknowledgments would not be complete without mentioning those students of The Pennsylvania State University who, at their September, 1954 Encampment, first expressed a need for an approach like this to world affairs and requested that such a course be made available to students in all colleges of the University.

Finally, we wish to convey deep appreciation to our many professional friends whose interest, support, and suggestions have helped make this a better book.

E.A.
W.B.
K.F.
N.R.

University Park, Pennsylvania

Contents

Contents

Part I

THE INDIVIDUAL
and the
CONTEMPORARY CRISIS

What Is the Nature of the World Crisis?

THE PROBLEM
AND ITS BACKGROUND

SYMPTOMS AND SYMBOLS
OF OUR AGE OF CRISIS

The Atom at Hiroshima: "Hot War"

At exactly 8:15 A.M., August 6, 1945, Japanese time, an atomic bomb exploded over Hiroshima. To many of the survivors the explosion appeared as a great light: like a sheet of sun, a white or brilliant yellow flash, a blinding light. Light, and then darkness—and a city of 344,000 became a gigantic hospital-morgue of buried bodies, bloody heads, chests, backs, broken bones; a nightmare of collapsed, blasted, and burning buildings; literally a shower of timber, tile, and glass.

Fifty thousand people were killed outright. Eventually, the fatalities were to rise closer to 100,000. Direct burns from the bomb killed approximately one out of every four. One out of every two died from injuries received at the time. The effects of radiation were fatal for one out of every five.

Of the 90,000 buildings in the city, 62,000 were destroyed. An additional 6,000 were damaged beyond repair. Indeed, in the heart of the city only five modern buildings remained that could be used again without major reconstruction. Two hundred ninety thousand people were left homeless.

The "great light," the darkness, the bare statistics of destruction cannot, however, begin to reveal the physical and mental impact of the bomb upon the human beings who lived and died amidst the holocaust caused by the first use of the atomic bomb against a military foe.[1]

And Hiroshima, it should not be forgotten, was only one incident, though a tremendous one, in a world-wide war which raged for six years and claimed a toll in death and destruction that defies man's understanding.

It is difficult really to grasp these facts about World War II:

1. Approximately 15½ million men and women in the military forces of the Allied and Axis powers were killed.
2. More than twice that number were wounded.
3. More civilians died as a result of the war than did soldiers; estimates of civilian deaths range up to 30 million.
4. Reliable estimates put the monetary cost of the war at $1,348,000,000,000 (approximately 1⅓ trillion dollars).[2]

The immensity of the war's fatalities can only be glimpsed with the realization that 1 out of every 500 Americans was killed; 1 out of every 150 British; 1 out of every 46 Japanese; 1 out of every 25 Germans; 1 out of every 22 Russians.

For a more graphic accounting of the number of soldiers killed or missing in World War II, we would have to picture a parade lasting over 12 weeks (89 days), with a row of ten soldiers passing the reviewing stand every five seconds, day and night.

To begin to conceive the astronomical cost of World War II, we would have to imagine a man, born in the same year as Jesus, and blessed with long life, spending $10,000 a week, year in and year out, from the date of the birth of Jesus to the present day. At this rate, he would have just passed the billion mark by 1957—and this expenditure would be roughly a thousandth of the estimated cost of World War II.

The costs of war, however, in terms of battle casualties and dollar expenditures present only a partial and inadequate account of the meaning of war. How are we to measure the losses occasioned by the displacement and dislocation of whole populations? What about the long-term effects of devoting major portions of the world's over-all capabilities for six years to the objective of military, economic, political, and intellectual destruction? Or the tragedy of death and injury in war, war's cruelty and privation, war's violence to the human spirit—how are these to be measured in terms of numbers and dollar signs?

[1] See John Hersey, *Hiroshima* (New York, Knopf, 1946).
[2] See the articles "World War II" and "War" in the *Encyclopaedia Britannica* (Chicago, Encyclopaedia Britannica, 1954), Vol. 23, pp. 793Q-R and 334.

The atomic bomb, which brought light and darkness to Hiroshima, is a truly vivid symbol of our age of crisis, as it, like war itself, is also a vivid symptom of the same age. Yet, atomic power is a paradoxical symbol, for it symbolizes both war and peace, destruction and creativity, evil and good.

The atomic bomb was justified by those who used it, or supported its use, on the ground that it would save lives and bring peace more quickly, both to the nations that had withstood the onslaught of rampant militarism and to Japan itself, which sealed its military defeat when it unleashed its surprise attack on Pearl Harbor. Yet the bomb's use in war and war itself still disturb the moral conscience of mankind. Many people are troubled; they recognize that, at Hiroshima, the creative genius which went into the discovery and exploitation of the secret of nuclear fission was used to destroy a civilian city, not a military fortress.

The paradox remains as nations have added hydrogen bombs to atomic bombs, the discovery of nuclear fusion to nuclear fission, have penetrated outer space, and have been feverishly developing rockets and intercontinental missiles, with potentialities for either peace, life, and creative construction or war, death, and devastating destruction.

The meaning of a hydrogen-bomb war has become increasingly clear to Americans as a result of H-bomb tests in the Pacific and mock H-bomb attacks over the United States. The blast at the Pacific Proving Grounds at Bikini on March 1, 1954, polluted 7,000 square miles with lethal fallout. In the hypothetical enemy attack on the United States in June, 1955, "Operation Alert," it was assumed that nuclear bombings had wrecked 61 cities, killed over 8 million persons, injured over $8\frac{1}{2}$ million, and dislocated uncounted millions more. Val Peterson, Federal Civil Defense Administrator, estimated that $1\frac{1}{2}$ million fatalities and $2\frac{3}{4}$ million nonfatal casualties were prevented by simulated evacuation of 35 key cities. No "casualties" were announced in the mock attack staged on July 20, 1956, but it was known that the five imaginary 1-megaton bombs, each equivalent to 1 million tons of TNT, dropped over New York City could have theoretically blown the city off the map.[3]

War, however, may take many forms. A "hot" military war against an enemy nation is only one form of war—only one kind of symptom of our age of crisis. Another type of war, again symptomatic, is a war of systematic extermination of a whole people, not because they are members of an enemy nation but because, for example, they happen to be members of a particular religious group.

[3] See the *New York Times*, July 21, 1956, pp. 1 and 6, for coverage of the 1956 mock attack and a recapitulation of vital facts concerning the Bikini test and the 1955 mock attack.

The Concentration Camp in the Third Reich: Genocide [4]

Man's memory is short. He tends to forget the shocking stories of the Nazi concentration camps, first revealed in all their savage brutality when Allied armies broke into Germany and liberated such notorious camps as Belsen, Auschwitz, Maidanek, and Dachau. Man's inhumanity to man—in the twentieth century! It is hard to believe! Yet the documentary evidence of tyranny and terror, of crimes against humanity—in pictures, confessions, eye-witness accounts, Nazi records—is incontrovertible. Here Hitler's crimes against the Jews (which started with prejudice, were inflamed by propaganda, led on to persecution, and ended in mass murder) parallel those he perpetrated against civilian Germans, Austrians, Poles, Czechoslovaks, Frenchmen.

It is difficult to describe genocide, the planned, calculated, systematic extermination of a racial, religious, or ethnic group. It seems incredible. It is hard to believe that the leaders of a "civilized" nation in the twentieth century could set out to exterminate a whole people and succeed in killing 6 million of them, 4 million in extermination camps. Extermination—not in battle, not by frenzied mob action in the heat of revolution, but by deliberate and systematic gassing, burning, shooting, and poisoning.

Yet, the cumulative shock of 6 million dead cannot be felt unless one attends a murdering party of a small fraction of that unimaginable number. Here is a summary description of the operation of a gas chamber in Auschwitz, based on an eye-witness account.

The railroad train arrives at Auschwitz with 6,000 persons, 1,450 of whom are dead upon arrival. Here are children, scared half to death, women, men. They are driven out of the railroad cars with leather whips. They are ordered to undress completely, to give up false teeth, and glasses. Then clothing and valuables are collected. The women and girls are sent to the hairdresser, who shears their hair in one or two strokes. The severed hair vanishes into huge potato bags, to be used for special submarine equipment and door mats.

All are reassured by an SS man that nothing will happen to them; that all they have to do is breathe deeply; that the "disinfectant" will strengthen their lungs and protect them against contagious diseases. Mothers, nursemaids, with babies at their breasts, naked, children of all ages, naked, men—all are pushed or driven with whips into the gas chambers. Their curses are rewarded with whip lashes. Many say their

---

[4] For the full record, see Nürnberg Military Tribunals, *Trials of War Criminals* (Washington, D.C., Government Printing Office, 1950), especially Vol. V, pp. 1128–1131. The commentary here follows closely the wording of the author of the publication and attempts to express his spirit of unbelief and indignation, shared by so many about the record of the war crimes. The episode at Auschwitz related here is based largely upon an eye-witness account by an SS lieutenant.

prayers. Within the chamber they are packed tightly together. Outside the death chambers, in the winter weather, the balance await their turn to enter.

Finally, after thirty-two minutes all are dead. Like stone statues the dead still stand; bodies press against other bodies; there is no space for them to fall or bend over. The families can still be recognized; their hands are clasped. It is difficult to separate them in order to clear the chamber for the next load.

Mouths are opened by means of iron hooks. Dentists with chisels tear out the gold teeth, bridges, or caps. The police captain in charge hands the SS lieutenant a large tin full of teeth and says, "Estimate for yourself the weight of the gold!"

For most, death was sweet, in comparison to the living hell of the concentration camp—the horror, brutality, starvation, degradation. Again and again survivors could only say: Unless you have lived through it yourself, you could never understand. All the photographs and documents in the world, even seeing the piles of corpses with your own eyes, would never explain what it was like.

Here then is another type of warfare, an evil manifestation of totalitarian tyranny, and as symptomatic of our age of crisis as was the Second World War, which Hitler unleashed with his blitzkrieg against Poland on September 1, 1939. The concentration camp still stands as a symbol of totalitarian tyranny.

Hitler is dead, and the leaders and tyrannical achievements of the Third Reich are discredited. The free world would like to forget the monstrous crimes of Nazi Germany—crimes involving, in addition to genocide, the imprisonment of hundreds of thousands of other persons in concentration camps, the killing of thousands of war prisoners. The free world has sought to welcome a liberty-loving Germany once again into the community of free nations.

Adolf Hitler is dead, but has his passing brought an end to tyrants or to despotism? To totalitarianism? To warfare in its many forms?

Stalin's Struggle Against the Kulaks:
The Liquidation of a Class

One form of warfare may be directed against another nation, another form at a race, still another at a religion. Warfare, however, may also be waged against a class, and may under the guise of Marxist class struggle add up to the elimination of the capitalistic class and its allies—whether in the factory or on the farm, the church or the university, the government or the professions, transportation or the trade union. It may lead to forced or slave labor on a scale dwarfing even the Nazi effort. It may culminate in the liquidation of nationality groups, which in its immensity rivals the Nazi campaign against the Jews.

The *kulak* (a landowning or relatively better-off peasant) is symbolic of other liquidated classes or groups within the Soviet Union. The *kulak's* story, as briefly sketched here, is indicative of the Soviet government's maltreatment of its own people, a maltreatment which is symptomatic of our age of crisis. *Kulak* originally meant a relatively rich, tough-fisted, hardhearted, landowning peasant. With the Bolshevik Revolution, however, its meaning changed. *Kulak* became a term to describe the relatively well-to-do, more prosperous, more energetic peasant or farmer who was able to hire some help for his farm or to purchase farm machinery. Frequently it was extended to include any recalcitrant peasant who opposed the Soviet government's agricultural policy of forced collectivization.

By 1929, the Soviet government had in large measure succeeded in socializing (that is, in achieving government or public ownership and control of) the major means of industrial production and exchange. However, the collectivization of agriculture lagged behind. To Joseph Stalin, it was the *kulak* class (which numbered over 5½ million people) which blocked the path to collectivization.[5]

In 1929, therefore, Stalin announced the policy of "liquidating the *kulaks* as a class on the basis of total collectivization." By 1934 Stalin could declare that the "policy of liquidating the *kulaks* and of mass collectivization has conquered."[6]

Again, man's inhumanity to man is hardly believable. Here the world lacks the kind of authentic and copious detail that was unearthed in the trial of Nazi war criminals. Nevertheless, the general record is substantially clear.

The official *History of the Communist Party of the Soviet Union* (*Bolsheviks*) admits that "solid collectivization was not just a peaceful process." The history indicates also what the Soviet government did to achieve the liquidation of the *kulaks*. "It permitted the peasants to confiscate cattle, machines, and other farm property from the *kulaks* for the benefit of the collective farms. The *kulaks* were expropriated."

The landless peasants expropriated the *kulaks*, "driving them from the land, dispossessing them of their cattle and machinery and demanding their arrest and eviction from the district by the Soviet authorities."[7]

However, these accounts scarcely begin to reveal the full human story

[5] See Julian Towster, *Political Power in the U.S.S.R., 1917–1947* (New York, Oxford University Press, 1948), p. 42.
[6] *Ibid.* See also Samuel Kucherov, "Communism vs. Peasantry in the Soviet Union," *Political Science Quarterly*, Vol. LXX (June, 1955), pp. 181–196. Kucherov points out that, of the 5,618,000 *kulaks* registered in 1928, only 149,000 remained in 1934, according to the 1935 agricultural yearbook of the U.S.S.R.
[7] *History of the Communist Party of the Soviet Union* (*Bolsheviks*), (New York, International Publishers, 1939), pp. 303–304.

of a "liquidation" involving, at the very least, a million families, and probably more.[8]

Even more sympathetic observers of Soviet communism, writing in 1936, were disturbed by the "summary ejection . . . of something like a million families"; by the "enforced diaspora"; by the "manner in which it appears to have been carried out"; by the "unsatisfactory conditions of life into which the victims seem to have been" "arbitrarily deported" "without judicial trial or any effective investigation"; and by the unhappy fate of those who were sent to prison or to lumber camps or coal mines, or to other industrial projects to labor.[9]

Again, to appreciate the human impact of the liquidation of the kulaks, one must read a book like Maurice Hindus' Red Bread and hear the personal story related to him by an old Russian peasant who had been "dekoolackized." Why? Because of his possession of three cows, two horses, a wool-carding machine, a newly built house, and because of his refusal to join a kolkhoz (collective farm)![10]

Even more revealing perhaps as an illustration of what has been called the world's iron age was the Soviet government's use of famine to complete the liquidation of the kulaks and other recalcitrant peasants. The famine afflicted the southern and southeastern sections of European Russia in 1932–33. It had been caused by a poor crop attributable to unfavorable weather and, in part, to a productive failure by a disaffected peasantry. The Soviet government contributed indirectly to the death of millions from hunger and disease by continuing heavy governmental requisitions for grain before and during the famine, by failing to im-

---

[8] Winston Churchill's conversation with Stalin on this subject is illuminating. The following appears in Churchill's *The Hinge of Fate* (Boston, Houghton Mifflin, 1950), pp. 498–499:

"Tell me," I asked, "have the stresses of this war been as bad to you personally as carrying through the policy of the Collective Farms? . . ."

"Oh, no," he said, "the Collective Farm policy was a terrible struggle."

"I thought you would have found it bad," said I, "because you were not dealing with a few score thousands of aristocrats or big landowners, but with millions of small men."

"Ten millions," he said, holding up his hands. "It was fearful. Four years it lasted. It was absolutely necessary for Russia, if we were to avoid periodic famines, to plough the land with tractors. . . . We took the greatest trouble to explain it to the peasants. It was no use arguing with them. . . ."

"These were what you call Kulaks?"

"Yes," he said, but he did not repeat the word. After a pause, "It was all very bad and difficult—but necessary."

"What happened?" I asked.

"Oh, well," he said, "many of them agreed to come in with us. Some of them were given land of their own to cultivate . . . [elsewhere] but the great bulk were very unpopular and were wiped out by their labourers."

[9] Sidney and Beatrice Webb, *Soviet Communism: A New Civilisation?* (New York, Scribner, 1936), Vol. II, pp. 563, 566, 571–572, 567.

[10] Maurice Hindus, *Red Bread* (London, Jonathan Cape and Harrison Smith, 1931), Chap. 13.

port sufficient food for the starving or even to acknowledge the existence of the famine.[11]

The reader may say: "Enough of past history! The atomic bomb at Hiroshima, the Auschwitz gas chamber, the liquidation of the *kulaks*— all this is past history!" True, this may be past history, but war is not! Nor is totalitarian tyranny! Nor are the lesser tyrannies of lesser despots than Hitler and Stalin! And man has by no means succeeded in eradicating man's inhumanity to man! For the cold war has replaced the "hot war." And according to many keen observers, global civilization itself is in peril.

The Present Bipolar Struggle: The Cold War

Men continue to live in an armed, anxious, unsettled, disturbed, and tense world. A cold war now divides the world into hostile blocs—a cold war which began to chill hopes for peace when World War II was barely over; a cold war which broke out into "little hot wars" in Greece (1944–49 or 1950); in Korea (1950–53); in Indochina (1946–54); a cold war which has left Germany, Korea, and Vietnam bitterly divided; a cold war tremendously complicated by a gigantic colonial revolution; a cold war which at the worst might lead to open nuclear conflict and its devastating consequences; a cold war in which the "best" to be expected was portrayed in the following words of President Dwight D. Eisenhower: [12]

. . . a life of perpetual fear and tension; a burden of arms draining the wealth and the labor of all peoples; a wasting of strength that defies the American system or the Soviet system or any system to achieve true abundance and happiness for the peoples of this earth. . . .

Every gun that is made, every warship launched, every rocket fired signifies, in the final sense, a theft from those who hunger and are not fed, those who are cold and are not clothed.

This world in arms is not spending money alone.

It is spending the sweat of its laborers, the genius of its scientists, the hopes of its children.

The cost of one modern heavy bomber is this: a modern brick school in more than 30 cities.

It is two electric power plants, each serving a town of 60,000 population.

It is two fine, fully equipped hospitals.

It is some 50 miles of concrete highway.

We pay for a single fighter plane with a half million bushels of wheat.

We pay for a single destroyer with new homes that could have housed more than 8,000 people. . . .

This is not a way of life at all, in any true sense. Under the cloud of threatening war, it is humanity hanging from a cross of iron. . . .

Is there no other way the world may live?

[11] See William H. Chamberlin, *Russia's Iron Age* (Boston, Little Brown, 1934), pp. 82–87. See also his *Collectivism: A False Utopia* (New York, Macmillan, 1937), pp. 29 and 91. Kucherov, *op. cit.*, estimates that approximately 3 million starved to death during the famine in the Ukraine in 1931–33.

[12] *New York Times*, April 17, 1953.

Despite expressions by leaders in the U.S. and the U.S.S.R. on behalf of peace, freedom, and justice, and despite the enunciation of hopes for the end of aggression, the reduction of the burden of armaments, and the achievement of peaceful coexistence, both the U.S. and the U.S.S.R. seem committed to a many-sided struggle for a good many years to come.[13]

Each side blames the other for the cold war. Each insists that it maintains military power for defensive purposes only. Each condemns war, highlights its dangers, and bemoans its costs.

How does this many-sided struggle, the cold war, which is both a symbol and a symptom of the contemporary crisis, affect the individual American citizen?

THE INDIVIDUAL AND THE CONTEMPORARY CRISIS

First, the American citizen feels the effect of the draft or military service. Men are needed to maintain the defensive strength of the nation. This strength called for a military establishment in 1959 of approximately 2,375,000 persons: an army and an air force of almost a million each, and a navy of more than half a million.[14] Military service thus takes a "bite" out of the life of the individual male citizen between $18\frac{1}{2}$ and 26, who is

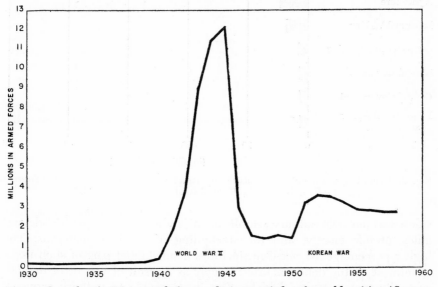

Fig. 1. Growth of U.S. armed forces during periods of world crisis. (*Sources: Statistical Abstract of the United States, 1955*, p. 226, and *1956*, p. 236; *The Federal Budget in Brief, Fiscal Year 1956, 1957, 1958.*)

[13] See, for example, former Premier Bulganin's and President Eisenhower's statements on the eve of their departures for the "summit" meeting at Geneva in late July, 1955, *New York Times*, July 16, pp. 2 and 3.

[14] See *The Budget of the United States for Fiscal 1959* (Washington, D.C., Government Printing Office, 1958), pp. 450, 504, 468.

called upon to serve his country. It affects his education, his family, his marriage, his career. Nothing could be more direct and personal. If he is concerned about spending two to three years in military service, about the postponement or interruption of his education, marriage, and career, he will probably be concerned about the state of world affairs that requires his government to call upon him for military service.

Figure 1 illustrates in graph form how the American military establishment has grown in periods of international crisis and war.

Second, the individual citizen feels the "bite" in taxes. Approximately 62 to 81 per cent of President Eisenhower's recommended $73.9 billion budget in fiscal year 1959 was for purposes of defense or national security. The lower percentage, 62 per cent, holds if only such items are con-

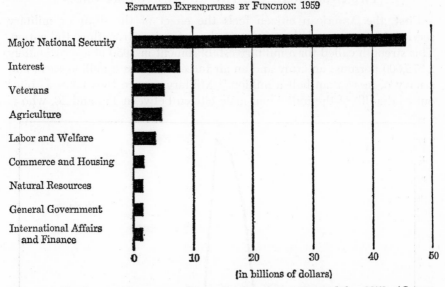

ESTIMATED EXPENDITURES BY FUNCTION: 1959

Fig. 2. Federal government expenditures by function, estimated for 1959. (*Source: The Federal Budget in Brief, Fiscal Year 1959*, p. 14.)

sidered as our own military establishment, military aid to our friends and allies, atomic energy, and the stockpiling of strategic materials. The higher percentage, 81 per cent, includes a substantial part of such items as interest on the debt (incurred largely as a result of war or of defense expenditures), veterans' benefits (again, traceable to military service), and foreign economic and technical aid. The bulk of this money, of course, comes from taxes.[15]

Figure 2 charts the estimated expenditures by function for fiscal year

[15] *The Federal Budget in Brief, Fiscal Year 1959* (Washington, D.C., Government Printing Office, 1958), pp. 54, 16, 18, 24, 30. "Major National Security" alone ac-

1959. Figure 3 illustrates where the money comes from and where it will go in fiscal year 1959, in terms of major sources and purposes. The visual relationship between the world situation and taxation levels in the United States is given in Fig. 4.

It should also be noted that, in 1939, two years before the United States entered World War II, defense expenditures were a little over a billion.

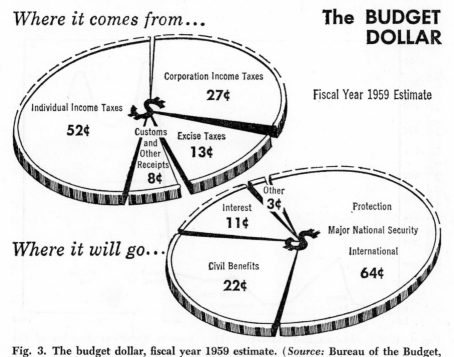

Where it comes from... **The BUDGET DOLLAR**

Corporation Income Taxes
27¢

Fiscal Year 1959 Estimate

Individual Income Taxes
52¢

Customs and Other Receipts
8¢

Excise Taxes
13¢

Other **3¢**

Interest
11¢

Protection

Major National Security

International

Where it will go...

Civil Benefits
22¢

64¢

Fig. 3. The budget dollar, fiscal year 1959 estimate. (*Source:* Bureau of the Budget, Executive Office of the President.)

At the peak of World War II, defense expenditures had risen to over 80 billion. After World War II, expenditures tapered off again, only to rise with the Korean War to a 1953 height of over 50 billion, declining to over 40 billion by 1957, and then rising again in fiscal 1959 to almost 46 billion in response to the Soviet sputnik.[16]

More meaningful, however, than total defense expenditures is the actual individual tax load. For example, before World War II, a single person

counts for 62.0 per cent of the 1959 budget. "International Affairs and Finance" add up to 1.8 per cent. "Veterans Services and Benefits" total 6.8 per cent. The interest on the debt comes to 10.6 per cent. See also the *New York Times,* January 14, 1958, p. 17.

[16] *The Federal Budget in Brief, op. cit.,* p. 54, *New York Times, op. cit.,* and U.S. Bureau of the Census, *Statistical Abstract of the United States, 1955,* 76th ed. (Washington, D.C., Government Printing Office, 1955), p. 224.

with no dependents and a net income of $3,000 paid only $68 in federal income taxes. The same individual's federal income tax rose to a World War II peak of $585, dropped after the war, and rose again, post-Korea, so that in 1953 he was required to pay $542.

In 1953, taxes for such an individual earning $5,000 (net) was $1,052; for someone earning $8,000 (net) the federal income tax was $1,992. Here at the pocketbook level, the impact of world affairs comes home meaningfully.[17]

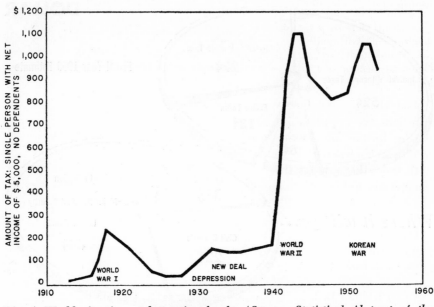

Fig. 4. World situation and taxation levels. (*Source: Statistical Abstract of the United States, 1955*, p. 359.)

Third, the present world situation affects almost every one of the individual citizen's governmental principles and domestic institutions. The disturbed and tense state of world affairs poses a real challenge to the successful maintenance of democratic and constitutional government, a form of government that Americans hold more dearly than monetary income or a draft-free life. Democratic and constitutional government is based upon popular, controlled, and limited government. Such a government is increasingly difficult to maintain in a cold war atmosphere. This atmosphere —a hypertense, heavily armed, and bitterly divided world constantly threatening to erupt in armed violence—seems likely to remain a part of the world's climate for a long time to come.

The fact that democratic and constitutional government is not geared to its best functioning amidst crisis and external danger has long been

[17] U.S. Bureau of the Census, *op. cit.*, p. 359.

recognized. The problem is real and momentous: how can the United States prevent successful aggression by a totalitarian dictatorship without itself becoming transformed in the process into a garrison prison, dominated by soldiers and police?

Certainly, there is ample evidence to support the view that the possibility of a garrison-police state in America is real. According to Harold Lasswell's "preview of the serious possibilities for the loss of freedom if the crisis continues and intensifies," here are the significant factors that highlight the possible threats of the garrison-police state in America: [18]

. . . rising defense expenditures, expansion of government, centralization of government, withholding of information, police investigation, decline of the press and public opinion, weakening of the political parties, decline of the Congress, decline of civilian administrators (except the political police), weakening of the courts.

The changes involved here, Lasswell argues,[19] "imply that free institutions are crippled, not alone in the government, but in the market, in the forums of public enlightenment, and in the laboratories and libraries of science and scholarship."

If, then, the individual citizen has a vital stake in the maintenance of democratic and constitutional government at home, he will be affected by the cold war crisis as it threatens the successful retention of popular and limited government.

Of course, at present the President of the United States is not a dictator, Congress is not dead, public opinion and the parties remain vigorous, the courts still function, the military have not displaced the civilian heads of governments, the forty-eight states have not dried up and blown away, the FBI has not become a Gestapo. Yet the crisis has already put democratic and constitutional government to the test, and there is sufficient evidence of dangers to make the individual citizen aware of how intimately the international crisis touches and often adversely affects all the major democratic institutions and principles of the country.

Also, of course, if the cold war breaks out into a "hot war," the trials and tribulations of democratic and constitutional government, as evidenced by two past world wars, will increase in severity.

Woodrow Wilson's anguished fears on the eve of United States' entry into World War I (not all of which were realized) may well be pondered.

Once lead this people into war [Wilson told Frank Cobb, editor of the New York *World*] and they'll forget there ever was such a thing as tolerance. To fight you must be brutal and ruthless, and the spirit of ruthless brutality will enter into the very fibre of our national life, infecting Congress, the courts, the policeman on the beat, the man in the street.

[18] Harold D. Lasswell, *National Security and Individual Freedom* (New York, McGraw-Hill, copyright 1950, reprinted with permission), p. 46.
[19] *Ibid.*

According to Cobb, the President thought that "the Constitution would not survive it; that free speech and the right of assembly would go." Cobb wrote: "He said a nation couldn't put its strength into a war and keep its head level; it had never been done." [20]

If, then, the international crisis has a direct, immediate, personal effect upon the individual American citizen, how does he look at the world?

THE MIND OF AMERICA

According to a fairly recent public-opinion survey, most Americans are not terribly concerned about world problems, even war. For example, world problems, including the threat of war, did not evoke a spontaneous response from more than 8 per cent of the survey's sample.[21] Here is the "box score" on the question: "What kinds of things do you worry about most?" [22]

	PUBLIC, % *
Personal and family economic problems	43
Personal and family health problems	24
Other personal and family problems	30
World problems, including war	8
Other national and local problems	6
Communists or civil liberties	1
Never worry	9

* Percentages add up to over 100% because each person could give many answers.

Of course, it was to be expected that most people would be worried about personal and family problems. The response is still disquieting, however, particularly in view of the answer to the more direct follow-up question: "Are there other problems you worry or are concerned about, especially political or world problems?" (Fifty-two per cent said they had nothing to add.[23])

Some of the open replies to the question: "What kinds of things do you worry about most?" are quite revealing. For example, a furnace maker from Michigan declared:

How to make a living for my family is my biggest worry. We've got the new house now if we can ever get it paid for. I don't worry about things like politics, because we have people who are paid to do that kind of worrying.

A textile worker from North Carolina replied:

I've served my time on Guadalcanal and now I'm home minding my own business. I work graveyard shift and put in a crop besides. The plant has cut

[20] Cobb's account is related in Arthur S. Link, *Woodrow Wilson and the Progressive Era* (New York, Harper, 1945), p. 277.

[21] Samuel A. Stouffer, *Communism, Conformity, and Civil Liberties* (New York, copyright © 1955 by Samuel A. Stouffer, reprinted by permission of Doubleday & Co., Inc.), p. 59.

[22] *Ibid.*, p. 73.

[23] For this quotation and those following, see Stouffer, *ibid.*, pp. 60–70.

down to a four-day week. That's what bothers me. I don't worry about world problems. When trouble gets here, I can take it. I'm paying taxes for someone to do my worrying for me.

The wife of a glass blower in Pennsylvania commented:

Husband hasn't worked since January, but I really don't worry like I did when my son was missing in Burma. I depend entirely on God.

The wife of a brewery bottler in Missouri retorted:

I worry about my health. Other worries I leave to Papa. He's got the brains in the house.

A maintenance worker's wife in Wisconsin stated:

I worry about getting pregnant. My doctor tells me not to worry, but I do.

Among those who initially expressed worry about world problems, including war, responses were generally couched in such terms as: "I don't like what is happening in Asia," or "I worry about what Russia is up to," or "When will the international situation settle down?" Only half the 8 per cent who did express initial concern about world affairs directly used the word *war*. The more usual comments were of the following pattern: "I worry quite a bit about the atom bomb." "Oh, why can't we live in peace like we used to?" "I hate to think about carrying off our home boys and they being slaughtered up."

Roughly one person in ten who did express anxiety about world affairs put his or her worry in personal terms. Thus, a purchasing agent in New York declared:

The biggest worry is about our boy in R.O.T.C. We wonder if they take him in the Army, that will mean the end. Will he have any future? War would ruin his future.

A milk delivery man in Pennsylvania said:

I worry about war, as I'm still of age. I don't know where I stand. I don't like wars and I wouldn't want to leave my family either.

Of course, it is unrealistic to expect every American to be as concerned about world problems as the Secretary of State. Still, sound public opinion on world affairs is of great importance, and a greater awareness of world problems is a prerequisite for that public opinion.

At this point a few pertinent questions are in order:

1. If Americans are primarily, and perhaps naturally, concerned with personal, family, and economic problems, can they develop adequate international understanding and be alerted to the contemporary crisis in world affairs?

2. Are college students and potential community leaders more interested in international understanding and more sensitized to world affairs than the average American?

Here the Stouffer public-opinion study, already mentioned, if it is reliable, sheds some light.[24] Most pertinent is the fact, according to Stouffer's public-opinion study, that a higher percentage (22 per cent) of community leaders showed concern for world problems, including war, than did the national cross section (8 per cent). Also relevant is the conclusion that community leaders are more tolerant than is the cross section of people in their own cities or in the nation as a whole. Similarly, it may also be significant that the younger generation and the more educated are more tolerant than the older generation and the less educated.

These conclusions of the Stouffer study (although not all relating directly to international understanding and world affairs) are encouraging and suggestive, if not startlingly new.

If sound, they suggest, first, that education may be effective in the area of international understanding and world affairs.

They indicate, second, that community leadership may be relied upon, relatively speaking, to "give sober second thought" to problems and controversies in the field of world affairs—the kind of "sober second thought" that is so important to the intelligent, wise, and prudent resolution of almost all issues.

There would seem, then, to be some basis for confidence in a basic assumption of this book: that education, in general, and education for potential leadership, in particular, can serve in some degree to advance the critical international understanding that is so crucial to the kind of free, peaceful, and creative world most people want to live in.

WHAT DO WE MEAN BY "CRISIS"?

The word *crisis* has been used here several times without being defined. It might be gathered that a crisis is something to worry about; that it is a serious matter; and that it embodies an unhappy, disturbed, alarming, uneasy, unsettled, critical state of affairs.

We need only raise our sights a little to recognize some of the crises beyond our immediate national ken, the crises in the field of world affairs:

1. The crisis of subjugation that faced Britain as, alone and ill-prepared, after the fall of France in 1940, she awaited the savage Nazi onslaught;
2. The American crisis at Pearl Harbor on December 7, 1941, when the American fleet and therefore U.S. defense were dealt a shattering blow;
3. The crisis of American and United Nations arms when, in the late summer of 1950, United Nations forces were almost driven off the Korean peninsula;
4. The crisis of tyrannical rule that faces so many peoples behind the Iron and Bamboo Curtains today.

[24] *Ibid.*, pp. 57, 73, 107–108.

An international or world crisis, then, seems to be a threatening situation, a menacing state of affairs in which the health, safety, welfare, preservation of a nation or the world itself are adversely, gravely, and vitally affected.

What is perhaps most striking about international crises is that they seem less clear and real the further they are removed from us. The rise of fascism and Hitler's dominance on the continent of Europe in the 1930's seemed a remote danger to many Americans as late as the Munich Pact (1938), and possibly up to the fall of France in 1940. For some, it was not until German submarines began attacking American vessels that the significance of the crisis first became clear. So, too, the dangerous implications of the activities of militaristic Japan in the 1930's—Japan's conquest of Manchuria (1931 to 1933) and her undeclared war against China after mid-1937—were not fully grasped by many Americans until Pearl Harbor. So, too, the civil war in China, which ended in the defeat of the Nationalist forces of Chiang Kai-shek, did not assume the proportions of a crisis situation for many Americans probably until the Chinese Communists intervened in the Korean War against the United Nations forces in 1950. It must be noted, however, that the relationship between the clarity and the proximity of an international crisis in the foregoing examples has perhaps been less true for Americans in the post-World War II crisis growing out of Russian pre-eminence on the continent of Europe. This may be attributed to two factors: first, that the security of Western Europe has been closer to American hearts than the security of Asia, or even of central Europe, and, second, that Americans learned a lesson in World War II.

The historically minded critic may ask why we get so excited about the contemporary crisis. Examining history, we might conclude that the world's present troubles are not as great or as unique as the alarmists of gloom and doom would have us believe. Furthermore, men everywhere always tend to magnify their own time of troubles. If we look at other crisis situations in history—in western civilization, in other civilizations—we might conclude that people today are unduly alarmed at their own time of troubles.

Turning to the first book of the Bible, Genesis, we see the beginning of troubles for mankind as a whole. At least, this is a view which has influenced the Judaic-Christian world. Let man today compare his troubles, for example, with those which faced Adam after he had been thrust from the Garden of Eden. Consider Milton's words in *Paradise Lost:* "Of Man's First Disobedience, and the Fruit Of that Forbidden Tree, whose mortal taste Brought Death into the World, and all our woe."

Consider the ancient Hebrews of the Old Testament: the slavery and attempted genocide of the Egyptian captivity, or the Babylonian captivity.

Consider the eloquent testimony of the observant Greek historian Thucydides about the Peloponnesian War (431 to 404 B.C.), the war which (according to one school of thought) symbolizes the time of troubles of Hellenic civilization:

> The Peloponnesian War was prolonged to an immense length, and long as it was it was short without parallel for the misfortunes that it brought upon Hellas. Never had so many cities been taken and laid desolate. . . . Never was there so much banishing and blood-shedding, now on the field of battle, now in the strife of faction. . . . There were great droughts in sundry places and consequent famines, and that most calamitous and awfully fatal visitation, the plague.[25]

Modern troubles? Contemporary crisis? Compare them with the Peloponnesian War which set Greek against Greek, and which resulted in the disintegration of this marvelous Hellenic civilization.

Consider the testimony of the renowned historian, Edward Gibbon, deploring the decline and fall of the Roman Empire, which constituted, for Gibbon, the "greatest, perhaps, and most awful scene in the history of mankind."

Reflect upon the Thirty Years' War in the seventeenth century which was "the most horrible military episode in western history prior to the twentieth century." It was accompanied by "orgies of wanton destruction and violent crime." It bred famine, pestilence, and even cannibalism. In this war one out of every three German-speaking peoples perished—7 million in all.[26]

Thus, the historically minded critic might call attention to other critical periods in world history, many of which involve other civilizations and other peoples, and his central point would be: Viewing history broadly, man today can see, all too clearly, similar troubles and difficulties involving war and revolution, slavery and genocide, starvation and the plague, moral decay and loss of nerve, personal insecurity and mass psychosis.

Is there then nothing unique in the contemporary crisis? Are there not distinguishing features which set it apart from other times of troubles?

The uniqueness of the contemporary international crisis, many would reply, lies in man's capacity for world-wide suicide, or world-wide enslavement, or the world-wide crippling of civilization, or world-wide degeneration.[27]

Wars today are global wars. War today is total: of, by, and against

---

[25] Thucydides, *History of the Peloponnesian War,* Book i, Richard Crawley, transl. (New York, Everyman's Library volume, Dutton, 1910), pp. 15–16.

[26] See the brief account in the *Encyclopaedia Britannica, op. cit.,* Vol. 23, pp. 330–331.

[27] See, among others, Hans Morgenthau, *Politics Among Nations,* 2nd ed. (New York, Knopf, 1954), Chap. 12; Bernard Brodie, ed., *The Absolute Weapon* (New York, Harcourt Brace, 1946); Harold Lasswell, *op. cit.*

total populations, and for total stakes! In today's war, man has the power, as a result of modern scientific development, to destroy himself. Similarly, nations now have the scientific know-how, in terms of military force, control of communications, organizational techniques, to enslave each other on a world-wide scale. Furthermore, even if civilization were not destroyed in a "hot war" it might be gravely crippled, and if one group does not succeed in enslaving the rest of the world in a cold war, a cold war might generate such tensions as to lead to the breakdown of civilization.

Never before in the recorded history of mankind has this been the situation because never before were the nations and peoples of the world in such close and potentially deadly contact with each other.

What Do We Mean by "Contemporary"?

With this brief glance at the meaning of *crisis,* it might be wise now to consider a little more carefully what is meant by *contemporary.* The reader may then be better able to place the contemporary crisis in historical perspective. It might be well, however, to preface the views on *contemporary* with the remarks of a former Secretary of State, Dean Acheson. Before speaking to a group of publishers, in 1951, on the present world situation, he had some research done to see what light would be thrown on the meaning of *present* and on the common or outstanding characteristic of the present, as distinct from the past or future.

When is "present"? One writer says the present situation began in 1905 with Japanese victory over the Russians in the Russo-Japanese War. Another writer says it began with the conference at Yalta. Another says it began with General Marshall's mission to China in 1945–46. Another says it began with the invention of the airplane. Another says it began with the great upsurge of population which took place when modern medicine checked the death rate of the last century. Another one, who is not quite so modern, says it began with the Protestant Reformation. Another says it began with the collective action taken against aggression in Korea. Another, a medievalist, says it began with the Portugese exploring the Senegal River 500 years ago. Another says the "present" began with the dropping of the atom bomb.[28]

What, then, is the fundamental or common or outstanding characteristic of the present? Here again, Acheson noted, a number of theories have been advanced.

One is that the fundamental quality of the present situation is that it is a contention between great powers over the control of territory and that in this contention between great powers ideological differences not only are secondary but really obscure the real meaning of the present time. Another writer says that the fundamental characteristic of the present is that it is a conflict between

[28] Dean Acheson, "The Measure of Today's Emergency," June 29, 1951, Dept. of State Publ. 4311, *General Foreign Policy Series 63,* pp. 3–4.

ideologies and that the old conflicts of states about territories have nothing to do with the present. Another says that it is fundamentally a struggle between the rule of law, imposed in the classic conception of the state, and a conspiracy, on the other hand, which is the revolt of men against the state. Another says that it is the struggle between the awakened peoples of Asia and the decadent peoples of the West. Another says that the fundamental quality of the present situation is that nations have tended to renounce the healthy interest in national self-interest and have run off after the will-o'-the-wisp of collective security. Another one says that the quality of the present is that nations have not renounced their interests in national security and have failed to set up collective security in a world commonwealth.

Acheson's conclusions as to the dating and quality of the present both agree and disagree with the views that follow. Perhaps for this very reason they provide a stimulating introduction to the meaning of *contemporary*.

Said Acheson:

All we know is that we are in the present, but when it began we cannot tell. . . . All that we get out of these analyses of the quality of the present is that struggle is at the heart of the times in which we live, that the times in which we live are onerous, but there is hope for mankind if we keep our minds on the heart of the problem.

A Short View

Many people take a short view of the contemporary crisis: the current or present crisis. They believe that the current crisis has its origin in World War II (1939–45) and its immediate aftermath. At this time, so they argue, the Allies defeated the two historic enemies of Russia in the twentieth century: Germany and Japan. Furthermore, the Allies insisted upon the unconditional surrender of these two barriers to Soviet expansion. In addition, a victorious and mighty United States rapidly demobilized its powerful armed forces. The consequence of these actions, so this argument runs, was to create a power vacuum in Germany and Japan and related areas of the world, east and west, into which it was inevitable that Soviet power would flow. The complete destruction of German and Japanese power together with United States demobilization was, in fact, an open invitation to communist aggression.

The communists accepted the invitation and began to exert pressure at all weak points on the periphery of the Soviet Union. Communist power in the so-called satellite states of central and southeastern Europe —Poland, East Germany, Bulgaria, Hungary, Rumania, Yugoslavia, Albania—was consolidated. A successful internal coup brought Czechoslovakia under native communist rule. The pattern varied from state to state, but, with the exception of Yugoslavia, the results were the same: Soviet-supported communist governments in control of the so-called "people's democracies."

Internal revolt was fanned in Greece. Pressure was exerted on Turkey. Soviet troops lingered on in the northern province of Iran.

Communist forces in China, Korea, and Indochina were encouraged and were shortly to consummate their respective bids for power.

The Communist Parties in Italy and France, riding on the peak of Soviet popularity and on the crest of respect for the role of native communists in the wartime resistance movements of both countries, anxiously sought a popular mandate which would enable them to come to power via the ballot box.

In the United States there came a rude awakening, which is perhaps best symbolized by the Truman Doctrine (military and technical aid to Greece and Turkey), by the Marshall Plan (initially for the economic reconstruction of war-devastated Europe), and by hasty remobilization. This is the period of history that we commonly call the beginning of the cold war. The North Atlantic Treaty Alliance (binding the nations of Western Europe in common defense against aggression) was to follow. So was the Korean War which caused an even sharper increase in the military budget of the United States. Finally the launching of the Soviet sputnik profoundly shocked and challenged the American public.

Central to the argument of this short view of the contemporary crisis is the contention that the problem has sprung largely out of the threat of communist expansion and out of the mistakes of the western peacemakers at the end of World War II.

A Slightly Longer View

Others contend that the roots of the contemporary crisis go back somewhat further. They argue that World War I (1914–18) is the starting point of the current crisis, because it clearly marks the decline of the West. It unmistakably marks the beginning of the end of Western Europe's dominance in the world.

This school of thought maintains that Western Europe never really recovered from World War I. France and Britain were both dealt blows as great powers, from which they never fully recovered. The war demonstrated clearly, for example, that Britain's historic role as a generally constructive arbiter of the European balance of power was over. Mastery of the seas was now shared with the United States and Japan. The very safety and preservation of the British Empire became increasingly dependent upon American strength and support. France, still suffering from the shock of her valiant effort in World War I, tried desperately to hold a potentially stronger Germany in check by means of the military and economic restrictions of the Versailles Peace Treaty. She was successful in this attempt for only a little over a decade.

Furthermore, so this school of thought runs, World War I created the European seedbed out of which were to emerge the dynamic and aggressive ideologies of communism (U.S.S.R.), fascism (Italy), and Nazism (Germany). Given this situation in their own back yard, Britain and France were unable to cope effectively with the rise and challenge of Japanese power in the Far East, particularly in the light of America's isolationism after World War I. It would only be a question of time until the totalitarian and/or militaristic ideologies would be strong enough to challenge the status quo. Similarly, it would only be a question of time until the colonial and underdeveloped peoples would emerge to challenge the already weakened hegemony of the once clearly dominant nations of Western Europe, Britain and France.

A Much Longer View

People in still another group say that we must go much further back than World Wars I and II in order to understand the contemporary crisis. Adherents of this view stress the importance of several major developments of the past three or four hundred years. These developments, they maintain, lay bare the origin and real manifestations of our crisis today.

The rise of the sovereign nation-state. The basic character of world problems today, it may be argued, can only be understood if we turn back at least to the sixteenth and seventeenth centuries when the comparative unity of medieval Europe was replaced by the gradual emergence of a number of sovereign nation-states. International tensions since that time have been largely due to the rivalry and competition of those independent nation-states.

The advent of the sovereign nation-state was perhaps clearly recognizable as early as 1648 (Treaty of Westphalia) in countries like England and France. Although of earlier origin, the phenomena of the nation-state began to assume a more distinct form in the seventeenth century, becoming clearer in succeeding centuries, reaching an historical peak in the nineteenth century with the national unification of Italy and Germany, achieving a delayed crescendo in the Wilsonian principle of self-determination in World War I, and bursting out in new fury in the nationalistic upsurge of colonial peoples during and after World War II. Those who defend this view insist that nationalistic warfare explains both World Wars I and II. They contend that, until we learn to live in peace as a family of free and respected nations, we shall continue to live in a world-in-crisis, now over several centuries old.

The Reformation. Adherents of this viewpoint may also point to the Reformation (in sixteenth century Europe) as an event which shattered the unity of Western Europe in several ways. First, the Reformation destroyed the older Catholic unity of Western Christendom. Second, it unleashed bitter and savage wars of religion which divided rulers and ruled, peoples within a given country, and countries themselves. Third, the Reformation encouraged the forces of the sovereign national state (operating usually through the king, prince, or ruler) to strengthen their own secular grip on the state.

The Industrial Revolution. Another factor relevant to the contemporary crisis is industrialism, whose origins also precede the twentieth century. The key point, according to advocates of this much longer view, is that industrialism intensifies conflict and creates problems both within a given national state and between nation-states.

Industrialism and the growth of world commerce have made the world economically interdependent. Yet the political framework of the world is still based largely on the sovereignty and independence of a large number of nation-states. The frequent conflict between a nation's preoccupation with its domestic economy and the economic interdependence of all nations in the world has intensified the problem of nations living together harmoniously in the modern world.

Industrialism also makes society more dynamic. It raises living standards by increasing a nation's productivity. It makes possible an increase in the world's population. It may whet the appetite of materialism. Through its quest for raw materials and markets, it may contribute to imperialistic rivalry.

Furthermore, the development of the Industrial Revolution was not always accompanied by social and economic justice. Injustice, in turn, led to protest and often to an intensification of the ideological and political struggle for the control of power within a given nation. Protest also led to demands for the end of colonialism and imperialism throughout the world. Karl Marx and his followers constituted only one wing of critics of the modern industrial society and its evils. Marx emphasized class conflict (between the proletariat and the capitalists or bourgeoisie) and urged the social, instead of private, ownership of the means of production. Others criticized the ruthless way in which the Industrial Revolution was destroying older ways of life, principles, and institutions; uprooting man and his ancient loyalties; setting him adrift without moorings in large, bleak cities, corrupted by crime, vice, and other pernicious influences.

The democratic revolution. Finally, mention should be made of democracy as another factor pertinent to the contemporary crisis. Democracy, whose beginnings in Western Europe antedate the twentieth century, also serves to accentuate and intensify the contemporary crisis. The battle to achieve popular self-determination, self-rule, or freedom creates a powder keg in every country chafing under undemocratic or alien rule. Popular demands for liberty, equality, and fraternity (in a world which denies them to hungering millions) do not make for a static world or unchallenged foreign rule. This was made clear by the French Revolution which broke out in 1789. This revolution shattered both a French and a

European feudal status quo and brought the demise of European absolutism. The French Revolution itself had followed closely in the wake of
a fairly mild and essentially conservative American Revolution, which
was, nevertheless, the first major colonial revolt against the British
Empire.

However, democracy may not be an unmixed blessing. If a new,
democratic, and constitutional order does not replace the system that has
been overthrown, the promise of the democratic revolution may be lost.
Dictators, like Napoleon in France, may claim to represent the French
people and nation and lead them—on behalf of liberty, equality, and
fraternity—into disastrous military adventures. Certain modern dictatorships, for example, those of Hitler and Perón, have been based on the
support of the masses, and have illustrated the dangers of demogogic
appeals to the masses when they are unprepared for the responsible
exercise of freedom. Also, of course, modern communists claim to be in
the democratic tradition and to draw their strength from the working
masses and their aspirations for freedom. The vital consideration here is
that the democratic revolution is fundamentally a revolution of rising
expectations, of hopes that life can be better politically, socially, economically. This revolution has generally been associated with the use of
state power to advance a better life in those respects. The power or the
struggle for power may sometimes dissolve the bonds that tie peoples together in freedom and a more harmonious union.

The "intolerable frying-pan of our time of troubles." Arnold Toynbee,
an historian, with whom not all historians agree, maintains "that we are
already far advanced in our own time of troubles." [29] If we ask, he writes,

. . . what has been our most conspicuous and specific trouble in the recent
past, the answer clearly is: nationalistic internecine warfare, reinforced . . . by
the combined "drive" or energies generated by the recently released forces of
Democracy and Industrialism. We may date the incidence of this scourge from
the outbreak of the French Revolutionary wars at the end of the eighteenth
century.

However, according to Toynbee, our time of troubles precedes even
the French revolutionary wars:

But, when we examined this subject before, we were confronted by the
fact that, in the modern chapter of our Western history, this bout of violent
warfare was not the first but the second of its kind. The earlier bout is represented by the so-called Wars of Religion which devastated Western Christendom from the middle of the sixteenth to the middle of the seventeenth century, and we found that between these two bouts of violent warfare there in-
tervenes a century in which warfare was a comparatively mild disease, a
"sport of kings," not exacerbated by fanaticism in either the religious sectarian
or the democratic national vein. Thus, in our own history too, we find that we

[29] Arnold J. Toynbee, *A Study of History,* Abridgement of Vols. I–VI, by D. C.
Somervell (New York, Oxford University Press, 1947), pp. 552–553.

have come to recognize as the typical pattern of a time of troubles: a break-down [recognizable in the sixteenth-seventeenth century], a rally [eighteenth century], and a second relapse [nineteenth and twentieth centuries].

Thus, for Toynbee, whether we agree or disagree with his interpretation, the contemporary crisis is to be viewed in the total perspective of our western civilization; so viewed, the contemporary crisis (what Toynbee calls our time of troubles) is of pretty long duration. Western civilization is only a stage away from the "steady fire of a universal state where," if western civilization follows the same pattern as other civilizations, it "shall in due course be reduced to dust and ashes." The latter stage is not, however, inevitable. Modern man is not compelled to leap from the frying pan into the fire.

The essential point, made by those who argue that our contemporary crisis is not simply a twentieth century crisis, is that men can't come to grips with the present crisis if they operate on the assumption that all would have been well if the democratic nations had prevented the rise of Germany and Japan in the 1930's or if they could destroy Soviet communism today. Rather, the contemporary crisis is three or four centuries old. It is rooted in the character of the sovereign nation-state; in the bitter wars of religion which followed the Reformation; in the cruel nationalistic wars which followed the French Revolution and have continued in the twentieth century; in the dynamic energies and problems released by industrialism and democracy; and in the substitution of earthly idols (like the nation-state or communism) for a truly common superior, God, to whom men might truly pay allegiance.

These views of *contemporary* (which by no means exhaust the possibilities) may stimulate the reader to think more clearly and critically about this key word and the temporal roots of the international crisis.

In the next section of this chapter, three viewpoints will be presented on the nature of the contemporary world crisis. The purpose is to make the reader more aware of the complicated, many-sided character of current world problems. Some readers may, of course, feel that they could better resolve such problems at the end of this book rather than at the beginning. The authors believe there is something to be said for tentatively coming to grips with them early in the course of study. The student thereby is able to realize more quickly the difficulty of the subject and the need to bring to the problem qualities of mind that emphasize knowledge of relevant and accurate facts, use of good logic, and critical analysis of values. Such an approach to key problems is difficult, but it may prove exciting as an intellectual adventure in which fact, logic, and value are pitted against fact, logic, and value in the search for truth and in the quest for a free, peaceful, and creative life among peoples and nations.

The three viewpoints do not, of course, exhaust the positions that might be taken on the nature of the contemporary crisis. Rather, they represent divergent and provocative views held by important sections of opinion throughout the world. The first position may serve to illuminate a view frequently encountered in the western world. The second may help the student understand the outlook of the communist world. The third may explain, at least in part, the philosophic orientation of the India of Gandhi and Nehru.

The three positions, it should be understood, express the point of view of those who believe in them, and not necessarily the point of view of the authors of this book. The authors, of course, are not neutral on the great issues of war and peace, freedom and slavery, democracy and communism. They have, however, endeavored to present the positions in the next section as they might be made by persons who actually advocate them. It is the authors' hope that the presentation of these positions will stimulate genuine intellectual controversy and more independent, critical analysis.

In question form the three views or positions may be put as follows: Is the contemporary crisis the result of the threat of totalitarian expansion? Is the contemporary crisis attributable to capitalism and capitalistic imperialism? Is it the commitment by East and West alike to false values that is the basic cause of the contemporary crisis?

POSITIONS
ON THE PROBLEM

1. THE CONTEMPORARY CRISIS ARISES
FROM THE THREAT OF TOTALITARIAN EXPANSIONISM

(The following position, prepared by the authors of this book, incorporates the ideas of a number of critics in the West. This position, it should be clear, does not necessarily represent the point of view of the authors. It is presented here solely to stimulate a critical examination of the nature of the contemporary crisis. The ideas embodied in this position provide, in part at least, a more fundamental rationale for the foreign policy of nations in the western world. The more exact reference to specific critics who have best articulated these ideas will be found in the footnotes.)

The Threat: The Intent, Power, and Actions *53704* of the Totalitarian State

Despite the existence of many complicated factors which make any single-factor analysis of world affairs dangerously superficial, it is primarily the menace of totalitarian expansionism that is responsible for the contemporary world crisis. Although the threat today comes chiefly from communist totalitarianism, it has not been exclusively associated with the Soviet Union and its communist allies. In the 1930's it was the coalition of Nazi Germany, Fascist Italy, and militaristic Japan which threatened to engulf the world. Both forms of totalitarianism, the communist and the fascist, have been characterized by a driving passion, pseudo-religious in its fervor and fanatical in its dedication. Such an ideological conviction, backed up by militant power, threatens the fundamental values and free peoples of both western civilization and the world. Such a totalitarian state, dedicated as it is to revolution, expansion, subversion, and conquest, is incompatible with world peace or with that international consensus which has moderated and restrained the struggle for power in world politics.

The Basis for a Free, Peaceful, and Creative World

The basis for a relatively free and peaceful world has been the presence in Western Europe—the cockpit of world politics until very recently—of a certain moral, intellectual, and political consensus.[30] At rock bottom this consensus has rested upon the common moral standards and interests of western Christian civilization. It has frequently been expressed in phrases like the "community of Christian princes" or "the republic of Europe" or "the political system of Europe."[31] There was, then, at least theoretical agreement upon accepted standards of conduct, domestic and international. They were based on a fundamental moral order, ordained by God or prescribed by natural law or, at least, generally recognized by rulers and ruled alike. Furthermore, such standards were buttressed by widespread acceptance of established institutions like the sovereign nation-state and private property and by a widespread demand for law and order within the nation-state. The result of this consensus was substantial intellectual, religious, and political tolerance, compatible with the rights of people and nations to differ religiously, intellectually, and politically, so long as their quarrels did not threaten the safety of the state or the fabric of the international community of sovereign nation-states. Europe, then, was viewed as "one great republic" with "common standards of 'politeness and cultivation' and a common 'system of arts, and

[30] See Hans Morgenthau, *op. cit.*, "Restraining Influence of a Moral Consensus," pp. 194–197, and "Moral Consensus of the Modern State System," pp. 197–201.
[31] *Ibid.*, p. 196.

laws, and manners'." "The common awareness of these common standards restrained" the "ambitions" of the nation-state " 'by the mutual influence of fear and shame', imposed 'moderation' upon their actions, and
instilled in all of them 'some sense of honour and justice'." [32]

This consensus was present, by and large, between 1648 when the
fanatical wars of religion ended and 1789 when the French Revolution
occurred. It was also present between 1815, the end of the Napoleonic
Wars, and 1914, the beginning of World War I. It served to moderate
and restrain the struggle for power in world politics, and to make warfare itself more temperate and indecisive. Monarchs and governmental
leaders who shared this consensus had no desire, despite the rivalry of
their respective nations, to destroy completely the social order of their
opponents.

The danger confronting the whole world today, now gravely intensified, also confronted Western Europe in the fanatical religious wars that
racked Germany and Europe between 1546 and 1648, and in the wars of
the French Revolution which plagued the European continent between
1789 and 1815. It is posed by those who are convinced that they and
their nation or rulers have a mission to spread the *true* ideology everywhere in the world, by nonviolent means if possible, by force if necessary. This is also to say that the moral, intellectual, and political consensus which had hitherto moderated and restrained the struggle for
power has been dangerously weakened and perhaps lost. In its absence,
the "stops" are out! The door to universal dominion is open. International
tolerance and an international policy of "live-and-let-live" are impossible. Hence, nations and peoples determined to preserve their values
and interests, their safety and security against the world-wide crusade
of an aggressive, powerful, fanatical totalitarianism must arm in self-
defense or perish. The primary blow to the older moral consensus has
been struck by the aggressive totalitarian state, which expresses the
spirit of "universal nationalism." Such a state "not only does not recognize any moral obligations above and apart from it, but even claims
universal recognition from all the world." [33] The totalitarian state is
driven to repudiate the old moral consensus not only in theory but also
in practice: first within its own borders and then in international politics.
It is this drive, backed by militant power, which has produced the contemporary crisis in world affairs.

Conclusion

One final point should be made clear. The contemporary crisis is not
attributable to the fact that one ideology is opposed to another, or even

[32] *Ibid.*, p. 199.
[33] *Ibid.*, p. 312.

to the existence in the world of dictatorial or totalitarian regimes per se. Peoples and nations may differ in ideology or other questions related to a nation's vital interests. Similarly, dictatorships per se do not necessarily constitute a menace to international peace and freedom; some may lack the intent or will or power to destroy the international moral, intellectual, and political consensus that has, in the past, moderated the struggle for power. It is only when an intolerant and crusading ideology becomes the fuel firing the motor of a nation-state (a nation-state with the power of imposing its will or values on other nations) that the challenge of the totalitarian state assumes the proportions of a world crisis. The crisis today, then, is attributable to the insistence by a powerful communist state on imposing its influence, will, and values on a whole world, a world in which free nations would rather remain free in a cold war or take the calculated risk of a "hot war" than submit to enslavement or domination by another nation and its ideology.

2. The Contemporary Crisis Is Attributable to Capitalism and Capitalistic Imperialism

(The following position is a Marxist viewpoint which has provided a rationale for communists and the communist bloc. Specific quotations are identified in the footnotes.)

The Immediate Danger: The Reactionary Forces of Capitalism

The immediate danger that confronts the world is a war unleashed by the capitalistic, imperialistic countries against the countries of socialism. "While capitalism remains on earth the reactionary forces representing the interests of the capitalist monopolies will continue to strive for war gambles and aggression and may try to let loose war." [34] The essence of the contemporary crisis is the bitter but futile struggle on the part of imperialistic, capitalistic nations to perpetuate their ill-gotten profits and power in the modern world.

The Immediate Danger in Perspective: Class Struggle and Private Property

This crisis is not of recent origin. Actually, the immediate danger is merely a current manifestation of a long series of class struggles centering upon the ownership and control of private property, or more accurately the means of production and exchange. To be properly understood, the immediate danger must be viewed in the light of the primary factor in all history, the class struggle. Similarly, the danger of an im-

[34] Nikita S. Khrushchev, Speech to the Twentieth Congress of the Soviet Communist Party, *New York Times*, February 15, 1956, p. 10.

perialist, capitalist war must be viewed in the light of the refusal by those who own the means of production and exchange peacefully to give up their exploitive power and position.

What is meant by the class struggle? What did Marx and Engels mean when they said, in *The Communist Manifesto*, that "the history of all hitherto existing society is the history of class struggles"? [35] Marx was simply calling attention to a "fundamental proposition," which Engels enunciated as follows: [36]

That in every historical epoch, the prevailing mode of economic production and exchange, and the social organization necessarily following from it, form the basis upon which is built up, and from which alone can be explained, the political and intellectual history of that epoch; that consequently the whole history of mankind (since the dissolution of primitive tribal society, holding land in common ownership) has been a history of class struggles, contests between exploiting and exploited, ruling and oppressed classes; that the history of these class struggles forms a series of evolutions in which, nowadays, a stage has been reached where the exploited and oppressed class, the proletariat, cannot attain its emancipation from the sway of the exploiting and ruling class, the bourgeoisie, without at the same time, and once and for all, emancipating society at large from all exploitation, oppression, class distinctions, and class struggles.

It is, thus, against the background of an uninterrupted fight between "oppressor" and "oppressed," this class struggle of long duration, that the immediate danger must be appraised. The contemporary crisis must be considered within the framework of the communist struggle for freedom for the exploited masses.

In the modern world the two great camps or classes in this struggle are the oppressive bourgeoisie or capitalist class, and the oppressed proletariat or working class. In other words, the struggle is between those who privately own or control the means of production and exchange, and those who produce value by their labor; between capitalism and scientific socialism (or communism).

The present crisis is, then, but a high watermark in a series of crises involving the clash of old and new modes of production. Central to the crisis in the modern world has been the institution of private property or, more exactly, the bourgeois property involved in the private ownership of the means of production and exchange. An earlier crisis was the conflict between the feudal system of production and the capitalistic, industrial system of production. Out of the struggle between feudal property and bourgeois (capitalist) property, that is, between feudalism and capitalism, capitalism emerged victorious. Feudalism died. Now capitalism is struggling for its life against communism. As feudalism died,

[35] *Capital, The Communist Manifesto, and Other Writings,* Modern Library ed. (New York, copyright by Random House, 1932), p. 321.
[36] *Ibid.,* pp. 318–319.

so will capitalism. Whether capitalism will die wthout engulfing the world in another horrible world war is the key question that now confronts mankind. Of one thing the world can be sure: capitalism is doomed. It is doomed by the same laws of historical development which tell us that, as capitalism emerged out of feudalism, so communism will emerge out of capitalism. The danger is that, fearing its inevitable downfall, the capitalistic world may not give up without a bloody fight.

This struggle is one between the working masses everywhere and the bourgeois propertied classes everywhere. It pits the worker against the bourgeois employer in all countries where bourgeois property and capitalism dominate. It pits the natives in the colonial areas of the world against the imperialistic forces of capitalistic nations. The working men of the world are in revolt against the same capitalistic, imperialistic policies that deprive the colonial peoples of political, economic, and social freedom. Capitalism exploits the toiling masses, subjecting them (the overwhelming majority) to the domination of the bourgeoisie (the employing and owning minority). This exploitation of the majority of workers by the bourgeois capitalist, with his minions in government, law, religion, education, permeates all of life. Real freedom—economic as well as social, and genuine political freedom for all—is impossible under capitalism, based as it is on pervasive exploitation.

Nevertheless, capitalism will fall, for it is not a stable system. It contains inherent contradictions or difficulties which will bring about its downfall. Capitalism engenders enmity between workers and employers; it produces inevitable depressions and mass unemployment; it increases the misery of the workers; it breeds rivalries between capitalistic nations and leads to war. Thus, sooner or later, it will destroy itself.

The Culmination of the Crisis

The long-standing crisis of the capitalistic world is now coming to a head. World War I marked a significant step in the culmination of this crisis, for it was World War I which severely weakened the capitalistic world and provided the opportunity for the emergence of the Soviet Union. The Soviet revolution first broke the united capitalist front. The rise and consolidation of Soviet power created a mighty bastion of Soviet socialist strength, a mighty base for world-wide communist victory. World War II further weakened the capitalist world and further strengthened the communist world. It is only a matter of time until capitalism, where it survives, will crumble and fall.

The new post-World War II alignment of political forces is, therefore, now as follows: the imperialist, capitalist, antidemocratic camp (led by the U.S.A. and including countries like Britain, France, and many nations in NATO, SEATO, and comparable military alliances), versus the anti-imperialist, socialist, democratic camp (based on the U.S.S.R., China, and the peoples' democracies). In the struggle for peace, certain countries not aligned militarily with either East and West are, however, working with the Soviet Union to advance the "zone of peace." "The cardinal purpose of the imperialist camp is to strengthen imperialism, to hatch a new imperialist war, to combat Socialism and democracy, and to support reactionary and anti-democratic pro-fascist regimes and movements everywhere." [37]

In view of the growing strength of the socialist world the inevitable breakdown of capitalism (as predicted by Marx and Lenin) will not be put off by false prosperity caused by military expenditures, or by American imperialism and domination (of former foes and long-standing allies), or even by war.

Conclusion

The contemporary crisis is but the culmination of an age-old struggle against private ownership of the means of production and exchange: for freedom and against exploitation. In the modern world this struggle is as old as the capitalistic system, which dominated the world scene from the demise of the feudal system until the advent of the Union of Soviet Socialist Republics. With capitalism, the age-old class struggle became one between the bourgeoisie and the proletariat; it became a world-wide struggle with the world-wide spread of capitalism; it became a world-wide crisis with the development of capitalistic imperialism; it became an even more fearful crisis for the peace-loving peoples of the world with United States' possession of the atomic and hydrogen bombs. The violence that threatens the world with a nuclear war is the outcome of the refusal of monopolistic and imperialistic forces in such capitalistic countries as the United States peacefully to concede the inevitability of the socialist triumph: the abolition of bourgeois private property (private ownership of the means of production and exchange), the end of exploitation of man by man, the termination of class struggle, the achievement of genuine freedom for all peoples everywhere.

3. FALSE VALUES OF EAST AND WEST
HAVE DRIVEN THE WORLD TO THE PRESENT IMPASSE

(The following position, taken from the literature of the American Friends Service Committee and from the writings and speeches of India's Jawaharlal Nehru, may serve to illuminate a pacifist philosophy of nonviolence and, to some extent, India's philosophy of noninvolvement in the military alliances of the rival great powers.)

[37] These are the views of Andrei Zhdanov. The speech from which these quotations were taken may be found in U.S. Congress, House Committee on Foreign Affairs, *The Strategy and Tactics of World Communism*, 80th Congr., 2nd sess., House Doc. 609, Suppl. 1, pp. 212–230. The reference to "zone of peace" may be found in Khrushchev's speech, *op. cit.*

Our Real Enemy: False Values [38]

The real evils that have driven the world to the present impasse, and which we must struggle to overcome, spring from the false values by which man has lived in East and West alike. Man's curse lies in his worship of the work of his hands, in his glorification of material things, in his failure to set any limit on his material needs. This idolatry leads him to lust for power, to disregard human personality, to ignore God, and to accept violence or any other means of achieving his ends. It is not an idolatry of which the communists alone are guilty. All men share it, and when it is examined, the global power struggle is given a new perspective.

The Perspective of Man's Idolatry

1. *Lust for power.* One of the things that the United States fears most about the Soviet Union is its expansionism. The communist revolution proclaims itself as a global revolution, and in its seemingly insatiable lust for power has already brought much of the world within its orbit. Americans see this expansionism as something that must be halted at any cost and by whatever means.

But no less an historian than Arnold Toynbee has pointed out that a dominant factor in world history from about 1450 on was *the expansionism of the West.* It was the peoples of Western Europe, driven by their lust for power and possessions, who pushed out in all directions, subjugating or exterminating those who blocked the path, and resorting in their colonial operations to bloodshed and slavery and humiliation whenever it appeared necessary. Nor can the United States escape responsibility. Our history has also been marked by a dynamic, persistent, and seldom interrupted expansionism.

Less than two centuries ago the nation was a string of colonies along the Atlantic seaboard. Now it straddles the continent, and its military bastions are found in over half of all the nations in the world. Its navies cruise the coasts of Russia and China, and its bombers are based in Germany and Japan. It is easy for Americans to regard this as normal, though they would be outraged and terrified if Russian warships cruised our coasts and Russian bombers were based on Canada or Guatemala. It is also easy for Americans to forget that this expansionism was often as ruthless as that which we fear in others. The Indian was almost exterminated, the Negro and later the flood of European immigrants were cruelly exploited; violence was threatened or provoked with Mexico, with Spain, with Colombia, with Nicaragua—all in the name of expanding the power and influence of the United States.

To point out such things is not to justify either Russian or Western expansionism, nor is it to underestimate the human suffering and the social cost that are involved in new embodiments and contests of power. But it suggests that the disease is not geographical and that to build ever greater instruments of power is not to end the disease but to spread it until it destroys the whole organism of civilization.

2. *Denial of human dignity.* Another of the fundamental evils in modern totalitarian regimes that is often cited is the degradation of the human being into an impersonal object to be manipulated in the interests of the state. Men become mere cogs in the machinery of a monolithic party which recognizes no higher authority than its own. The concept of man as a child of God, possessing dignity and worth, and vested with inalienable rights, is patently denied.

[38] The source of the quotations in this section and that which follows is American Friends Service Committee, *Speak Truth to Power,* 1955, pp. 28–31.

It is clear on the other hand that this noble concept of man, and the limits it imposes on the power of government, still has vitality in the West. But the West has been quick to ignore it when the situation demanded. The tendency toward centralization of power, toward subjugation of men to the demands of an impersonal technology, did not originate in modern Russia or the Orient, or in the minds of Marxist theoreticians. It was, and is, a part of the process of industrialization and technical development of the West. The tragedy of material progress is that nowhere in the world, any more than in Russia today, has enough original capital been accumulated for both industrial development and military expansion without subjecting men to some degree of exploitation and indignity. Indeed, the process of Western Industrialization made virtual slaves of vast multitudes of peasants and laborers in underdeveloped countries and often imposed on them in addition the humiliation of "white supremacy." There is obviously room for much freedom and material well-being to flourish in the more highly developed countries, but . . . even these blessings are endangered as the demands of military preparedness make inroads on liberty and accelerate the drive toward centralized authority.

Again, this is in no sense to condone the invasion of human personality wherever it may occur, but only to indicate that the virus is not localized. The elimination of communism would not eliminate the evil we see in communism. Indeed, it may safely be predicted that the waging of atomic war against the Soviet Union, far from providing a cure, would itself be a virulent, if not final, instrument for the destruction of liberty and the dehumanizing of man.

3. *Atheism.* A third charge against Soviet communism is its atheism. Religion is rejected as the "opiate of the people" and in its place is put the Marxist doctrine of materialism. However tragic and blasphemous this denial may seem to us, it is relevant to remember that it, too, is a product of the West. Karl Marx denounced religion on the basis of his observation of Western, not Russian, society. Arnold Toynbee, in *The World and the West*, points out that Western culture has become in recent centuries ever more materialistic and secular, and has steadily moved away from its Christian or spiritual origin. More recently the Evanston Assembly of the World Council of Churches recognized the "practical atheism" of much of life in the so-called Christian countries.

Communism has simply carried to its logical conclusion, and expressed in theoretical form, what the West has practiced. "It seems in many ways," says William Hordern, in his *Christianity, Communism, and History,* "to be nothing but one particularly unruly expression of the modern view of life. While condemning communist 'materialism' in theory, the rest of the world has lived by materialistic motives. The communists have been hated primarily because they have dragged the skeleton from the closet of Western culture." This is a harsh judgment, but we believe it is an accurate one, for the power of Hydrogen is clearly trusted among us more than the power of Love. Like the communist East, therefore, the Christian West is secular, and that secularism that unites all men in its bondage will not be ended by the simple expedient of destroying those nations where the disease is most virulent at the moment.

4. *The cult of violence.* Finally, we come to the acceptance of violence as the essential means of social revolution, and the corollary doctrine that the end justifies the means. Here again for many Americans are decisive reasons for citing Soviet communism as an absolute evil, which must at all costs be destroyed.

Violence has, indeed, reached unsurpassed proportions in our time. The outbreak of the first World War marked the beginning of this modern orgy of uncontrolled violence, and it has continued ever since. But no reputable historian has ventured the ideas that either the first or the second World War was spawned by communism. Nor are the Russians responsible for the concept of blitzkrieg, or obliteration bombing, or for the first use of atomic weapons. These have all been loosed upon the world by the very nations which now profess outrage at the cynical Soviet concept of the role of violence and the validity of *any* means. Western theory is indeed outraged, but Western practice has in this area, too, belied Western theory. We have, in fact, been prepared to use any means to achieve *our* ends. Here again, as in so many other points in the exposure of the devil theory, we are reminded of the words Shakespeare put into the mouth of Shylock: "The villainy you teach me, I will execute, and it shall go hard, but I will better the instruction."

Moreover, military leaders are apparently ready now to use any means, even the ultimate immorality of hydrogen bombs, to stop communism. Is it not clear that to resort to immoral means in order to resist what is immoral is not to preserve or vindicate moral values, but only to become collaborators in destroying all moral life among men? Especially if the issue is a moral one, we must renounce modern war. If we say that any means are justified, we adopt a completely amoral position, for there is then no ethical line that can be drawn anywhere. All morality has been discarded. Only if we ourselves reject the doctrine that the achievement of *our* ends justifies any means is there any hope that we may be able to bring healing to a world caught in the fearful dilemma of our time.

The Proper Perspective for a Just and Peaceful World

An integrated, peaceful, creative, and just community can only be built on love, trust, and confidence. It can never be built on hate, distrust, and fear. Man will not be able to come to grips with the salient characteristics of his time of troubles (violence, totalitarianism, social revolution), and he will not be able to contribute most fully to the solution of the vital problems of modern times (the peaceful resolution of conflict, the liberation of the human spirit, the conquest of physical poverty) until he appreciates the following points: that peace will not be for the strong but for the just; that there will be neither peace until men learn to be just, nor justice until men determine to renounce violence.

If men in the major nations of the world want to live and not die, "if they want to lead the way toward a world where peace prevails, and the miracles of science are put to work for man's benefits, and not his destruction, they must face individually the need for an ultimate and fundamental break with violence. There is . . . no other way to eliminate the scourge of war." If this choice is accepted, men can resolve most meaningfully the real paradoxes of our age of violence: "Poverty and wealth, hunger and food, insecurity and power, bondage and freedom, war and peace. . . ." [39]

Some persons will argue that the foregoing position is idealistic, unreal, naïve; that it has no relevance and applicability in the world of

[39] *Ibid.*, especially pp. 3, 53, 51.

power politics; that nations, which must be guided by national self-interest, would be endangered if they formulated their foreign policy on the basis of this point of view. Advocates of the preceding point of view are aware of such criticisms. Yet they would remind critics in both East and West alike that there is a large sector of the world which finds the "idealistic" point of view "realistic." This area is India. Although not a perfect illustration of the philosophy of love and nonviolence, India has come closer than any other nation in advocating and practicing this philosophy. This may well be due to the teaching and influence in India of Mahatma Gandhi. As the Prime Minister of India, Pandit Jawaharlal Nehru, declared on November 19, 1955: [40] "We in India have been conditioned by the master spirit of the present age, Mahatma Gandhi, who told us to get rid of hatred and violence and to make friends with all, at the same time holding to our convictions and principles."

Gandhi insisted that love was "the source and end of life," and the highest form of nonviolence. He exalted the life of the spirit and criticized the corrupting materialism of much of modern life. Gandhi argued that we must be on guard against other forms of hatred than that which leads to killing. We must also be aware of and conquer "harsh words, harsh judgments, ill will, anger, and spite, and the lust of cruelty." Similarly, we must recognize and triumph over "selfish greed" which can lead to the exploitation, torture, and starvation of men. We must also guard against the "wanton humiliation and oppression of the weak, and the killing of their self-respect." [41] Gandhi was convinced that only in love, nonviolence, and peace (what the Indians call *ahimsa*) could the way out of the contemporary crisis be found. "It is my unshakable belief," Gandhi wrote, "that India's destiny is to deliver the message of nonviolence to mankind. It may take ages to come to fruition. But so far as I can judge, no other country will precede India in the fulfillment of that mission." [42]

This philosophy—which also rejects the lust for power, condemns the denial of human dignity, repudiates the brutal and soulless materialism of the modern world, and excoriates the cult of violence—underlies the outlook of India under the leadership of Nehru, one of Gandhi's disciples.

[40] *Indiagram*, No. 827. This is an information release from the Indian Embassy, Washington, D.C.
[41] Quoted from *The Gandhi Sutras*, arranged by D. S. Sarma, published 1949 by The Devin-Adair Co., New York, copyright 1949 by Devin-Adair, pp. 54–55.
[42] *Ibid.*, p. 172.

An Indian View of Our Contemporary Crisis

Nehru has written that "we live in an age of crises." He continues: [43]

In the multitude of crises, political and economic, that face us, perhaps the greatest crisis of all is that of the human spirit. Till this crisis of the spirit is resolved it will be difficult to find a solution for the other crises that afflict us.

Gandhi's teachings may enable us to resolve this crisis of the human spirit, Nehru believes. As he states it: [44]

In India during the last quarter of a century and more, Mahatma Gandhi made an outstanding contribution not only to the freedom of India but to that of world peace. He taught us the doctrine of non-violence, not as a passive submission to evil, but as an active and positive instrument for the peaceful solution of international differences. He showed us that the human spirit is more powerful than the mightiest of armaments. He applied moral values to political action and pointed out that ends and means can never be separated, for the means ultimately govern the end. If the means are evil, then the end itself becomes distorted and at least partially evil. Any society based on injustice must necessarily have the seeds of conflict and decay within it so long as it does not get rid of that evil.

All this may seem fantastic and impractical in the modern world, used as it is to thinking in set grooves. And yet we have seen repeatedly the failure of other methods and nothing can be less practical than to pursue a method that has failed again and again. We may not perhaps ignore the present limitations of human nature or the immediate perils which face the statesmen. We may not, in the world as it is constituted today, even rule out war absolutely. But I have become more and more convinced that so long as we do not recognize the supremacy of the moral law in our national and international relations, we shall have no enduring peace. So long as we do not adhere to right means, the end will not be right and fresh evil will flow from it. That was the essence of Gandhi's message and mankind will have to appreciate it in order to see and act clearly. . . .

Today fear consumes us all—fear of the future, fear of war, fear of the people of the nations we dislike and who dislike us. That fear may be justified to some extent. But fear is an ignoble emotion and leads to blind strife. Let us try to get rid of this fear and base our thoughts and actions on what is essentially right and moral, and then the dark clouds that surround us may lift and the way to the evolution of world order based on freedom will be clear.

It is this philosophy which has led Mr. Nehru to condemn military alliances and blocs, reliance on armaments for security, and the arms race. Men and nations will not, Mr. Nehru has argued, achieve peace and security in a militarized world. What is more, we will never develop an atmosphere of trust and confidence, until we also pluck from our hearts the immoral atom bombs that lurk therein.

Gandhi's philosophy also helps to explain Nehru's estimate of the root

[43] Jawaharlal Nehru, *Independence and After* (New York, copyright, 1950, by The John Day Company), p. 302.
[44] *Ibid.*, pp. 302–303.

causes of war: imperialism or political subjugation, racial superiority based on the false belief in racial inequality, and misery and want or economic inequality. Because India's and Asia's fight has, in the past, been directed at the West, Nehru's criticism tends to strike harder at the West than at the Soviet Union. Thus, Nehru's criticism may serve to underline the thought that the evil faced by the world resides not simply and solely in Soviet man and the Soviet world, but also in western man and the western world.

Here is how Mr. Nehru puts it: [45]

If we seek to ensure peace we must attack the root causes of war in the modern world.

One of the basic causes is the domination of one country by another or an attempt to dominate. Large parts of Asia were ruled till recently by foreign and chiefly European powers. Much of Asia . . . is subject to foreign powers, some of whom still attempt to enlarge their dominions. It is clear that all remaining vestiges of imperialism and colonialism will have to disappear.

Secondly, there is the problem of racial relations. The progress of some races in knowledge or in invention, their success in war and conquest, has tempted them to believe that they are racially superior and has led them to treat other nations with contempt. . . . In Asia and Africa, racial superiority has been most widely and most insolently exhibited. . . . This is one of the great danger points of our modern world; and, now that Asia and Africa are shaking off their torpor and arousing themselves, out of this evil may come a conflagration of which no man can see the range of consequences. . . . The world cannot long maintain peace if half of it is enslaved and despised. . . .

The third reason for war and revolution is the misery and want of millions of persons in many countries and, in particular, in Asia and Africa. . . . If they [the necessities of life] are lacking, then there is the apathy of despair or the destructive rage of the revolutionary. Political subjection, racial inequality, economic inequality and misery—these are the evils that we have to remove if we would ensure peace. If we can offer no remedy, then other cries and slogans make an appeal to the minds of people.

Conclusion

The conclusion seems to us to be clear that the real evils at the root of the tragic conflicts which threaten to destroy mankind are those that flow from man's Idolatry: the lust for power and the inability of power to set limits to itself; the violation of human personality and infringements on its freedom and dignity; the "practical atheism" of a pervading materialism and secularism; the spreading cult and practice of violence and the poisonous doctrine that *our* ends justify any means. These evils will not be rooted out, or so much as disturbed, even if we succeed in cutting off all their heads in one geographical area or another. On the contrary, the recent experience of two victorious world wars for democracy, with the subsequent decline of the democratic spirit in the world, is evidence which all who run may read that resistance to evil, when evil is attributed exclusively to the occupants of this or that geographical or ideological area, is futile.[46]

[45] Jawaharlal Nehru, *Visit to America* (New York, copyright, 1950, by The John Day Company), pp. 31–33.
[46] American Friends Service Committee, *op. cit.*, pp. 31–32.

The time is now rapidly drawing to a close when the philosophy of violence and the philosophy of man's innate worth and dignity can dwell together on this globe. Now war and preparations for war "require total effort and involve total destruction, not only of life and property, but of spiritual integrity as well." [47]

Coexistence without war and without resolving the conflict—this policy is certainly preferable to war, but it is only a temporary expedient, which may not permanently forestall war.

A more fundamental solution is needed. Such a fundamental solution is love and nonviolence.

QUESTIONS

1. Are the symptoms and symbols presented in this chapter really symptomatic and symbolic of the contemporary crisis? Why? Why not? What others would you add in order to underscore the nature of the contemporary crisis in world affairs?

2. How is the individual American citizen affected by the cold war? Which of these impacts do you think is most disturbing? Why? How is the American citizen affected in comparison, say, to the Soviet citizen?

3. What kind of things do you worry about most? How does your response compare to the box score on worries presented in this chapter?

4. Are we living in a world of crisis or crises? Explain.

5. Which of the three views of *contemporary* ("A Short View," "A Slightly Longer View," "A Much Longer View"), described in this chapter, is most meaningful to you? Why?

6. According to the advocates of Position 1, what is the nature of the consensus which in the past in Western Europe has moderated and restrained the struggle for power in world politics? Why do they believe that this consensus has been gravely weakened or lost? On what grounds do you agree or disagree with the analysis in Position 1?

7. According to Marxists of communist persuasion, how is the class struggle related to the contemporary crisis? Why do you agree or disagree with this analysis?

8. Do you agree with the authors of *Speak Truth to Power* that the "real evils that have driven the world to the present impasse . . . spring from the false values by which man has lived in East and West alike"? First, state what these "false values" are; then indicate the grounds for your agreement or disagreement with this argument.

9. What is Prime Minister Nehru's view of the contemporary crisis? Does Nehru fully reflect Gandhi's teachings? How does India's behavior with regard to Kashmir and Pakistan square with the teachings of Gandhi? Is India's policy of noninvolvement in the military alliances of the U.S. and the U.S.S.R. based upon a shrewd appraisal of India's national interest rather than upon Gandhi's philosophy of love and nonviolence? Explain.

10. Which of the three positions do you agree with most fully? Why?

[47] *Ibid.*, p. 33.

SELECT BIBLIOGRAPHY

ARON, Raymond, *The Century of Total War* (New York, Doubleday, 1954). A French writer's historical and analytical examination of the dilemma of Europe and the world. Concludes that no one knows whether the third world war can be won without becoming total. Contends that in a limited war, more than in a total one, courage and faith count as much as material resources.

CONANT, James Bryant, *Modern Science and Modern Man* (New York, Columbia University Press, 1952). Readable account for laymen of the cultural significance of developments in science. Perceptive presentation by an outstanding scientist, educator, and public servant of the relation of modern physics and chemistry to our present-day intellectual revolution.

FINER, Herman, *America's Destiny* (New York, Macmillan, 1947). A discussion by a British political scientist propounding the "bitter truth" that, in the absence of an over-all world power and a common world morality, peace and justice can be sustained by intimidatory force and mingled persuasion supplied by such a strong power as the U.S.

HERSEY, John R., *Hiroshima* (New York, Knopf, 1946). A human account by an American journalist and novelist of the atomized city which has become a symbol of our crisis.

HUXLEY, Aldous L., *Brave New World* (New York, Harper, 1932). Antiutopian novel by the well-known British satirist, dramatizing some logical implications of utilizing modern science to advance a materialistic, hedonistic, and soulless culture.

MULLER, Herbert J., *The Uses of the Past* (New York, Oxford University Press, 1952). Brilliantly written series of profiles of former societies by a perceptive philosopher-historian in the mature liberal tradition. Places both past and present in critical perspective. A healthy corrective for Toynbee and Sorokin. Available in pocket edition.

NIEBUHR, Reinhold, *The Irony of American History* (New York, Scribner, 1954). Deals with the position of America in the present world situation. The author, a Protestant theologian who has greatly influenced American realists in foreign affairs, is critical of some key presuppositions of religious and secular idealists.

NORTHROP, F. S. C., *The Taming of the Nations* (New York, Macmillan, 1953). A study by the philosopher-author of *The Meeting of East and West* of the cultural bases of international policy. Argues that diverse, yet united, moral and cultural principles, rather than power politics, constitute the basis for peacefully resolving suicidal conflicts.

ORTEGA Y GASSET, José, *The Revolt of the Masses* (New York, Norton, 1932). A Spanish philosopher's elaboration of the theme that modern civilization is threatened by the triumph and dominance of the crude, ignorant materialistic masses.

ORWELL, George, *Nineteen Eighty-four* (New York, Harcourt Brace, 1949). An Englishman's thought-provoking novel of the totalitarian world which we may reach by 1984.

SOROKIN, Pitirim A., *Social Philosophies of an Age of Crisis* (Boston, Beacon, 1950). A Russian-born American sociologist sees our age of crisis in terms of the dominance of a sensate culture which has led to war, totalitarianism, absolutistic government, the withering of individual and civic freedom, the decline of capitalism and true democracy.

TOYNBEE, Arnold J., *A Study of History* (New York, Oxford University Press, Abridgement of Vols. I–VI, by D. C. Somervell, 1947). An abridgement of the British historian-philosopher's view of the geneses, growths, breakdowns, and disintegrations of civilizations. Valuable for its multi-civilization perspective. Volume IX of the same study, published in 1954, contains Part XII, "The Prospects of the Western Civilization." Difficult for beginner, but stimulating and rewarding.

Is There a Key Outlook
on World Affairs?

THE PROBLEM
AND ITS BACKGROUND

DIFFERENT VANTAGE POINTS ON WORLD AFFAIRS

The positions presented in the last part of Chapter 1 illustrate three widely divergent interpretations of the present world crisis. It would not be difficult to bring together other interpretations, for example, the views of Pope Pius XII as expressed in his Christmas messages to the world, the views of such a noted historian-philosopher as Oswald Spengler, or the views of the American Socialist leader, Norman Thomas.

Although the divergencies of such interpretations may confuse the average citizen, it is nevertheless possible for him, with a little patience, to see how they originate. Some understanding is gained when one realizes that world affairs can be viewed from at least four different vantage points: the vantage point of a nation-state, the vantage point of an ideological system, the vantage point of religious idealism, and the vantage point of critical scholarship.

The Vantage Point of a Nation-State

Viewing world affairs primarily through the eyes of a nation-state or national government will produce great varieties in the interpretation of world problems. There are today over eighty nation-states in the world. Each has its own concept of how best to achieve its national security and welfare. Each consequently views world affairs in the light of how its own national interests are affected.[1] The official policies of each foreign office reflect these views, and frequently wide sections of public opinion will also take this approach.

Thus the United States government and its various West European allies see the world crisis today largely in terms of the expansion of Soviet power and the intolerant, totalitarian character of this power. Alliances like the North Atlantic Treaty Organization (NATO), and the Southeast Asia Treaty Organization (SEATO), have consequently been organized to check the threat of Soviet expansion in different parts of the world. The Soviet Union, on the other hand, sees these alliances and the establishment of American military bases throughout the world as a threat to its position and power. The United States regards NATO as defensive, and the Soviet Union continually calls it aggressive.

The government of India has still a different view of the situation. It regards the existence of rival military alliances on both the Soviet and the western sides as dangerous and likely to lead ultimately to World War III. Although India is basically sympathetic to western democratic ideals, and the United States has tried to persuade it to join in the collective defense of the free world, the Indian government has decided that its national security will be best assured if it does not join any system of alliances but tries to act as a mediator between the two major power blocs. This position may reflect in part India's exposed geographic position adjacent to the Soviet Union. It is also undoubtedly influenced by Gandhi's philosophy of nonviolence.

The case of the British-French intervention in Egypt in the fall of 1956 in connection with the Suez Canal dispute also illustrates strikingly different national viewpoints of an international crisis. Normally, the United States, Great Britain, and France work together harmoniously in the United Nations and other international activities because they have common interests on almost all major issues except the colonial question. With the Suez crisis, however, there was a serious breach in this common front, stemming from divergent national concepts of what was at stake and what should be done.

Britain, which had in the past relied heavily on the Suez Canal for vital imports of oil from the Middle East, felt that its national economic welfare would be at the mercy of Egypt's President Nasser if the latter controlled the Canal. Since the British also felt, rightly or wrongly, that

---

[1] By *national security* is meant the preservation of the independence of a nation-state and the protection of the state and its citizens from external attack or intervention in its domestic affairs. This is a basic objective of the foreign policy of every nation-state. Another basic objective of foreign policy is to promote the "general welfare" of the state and its people. This includes the fostering of conditions that add to the economic, social, cultural, educational, scientific, and political well-being of the national community.

The term *national interest* refers to what is deemed important to the maintenance of national security and the promotion of national welfare.

they could not trust President Nasser's promise to keep the Canal open, they decided upon armed intervention in the fall of 1956, in the hope that the Nasser Government would be overthrown and that some kind of international operation of the Canal would be established.

The French were also convinced, though for somewhat different reasons, that their national interest required the overthrow of the Nasser Government. Like the British, they desired international rather than Egyptian operation of the Canal, but their main grievance against Nasser seems to have been their belief that he had been inciting the Arabs in North Africa, particularly in Algeria, to oppose the French position there. If Nasser were allowed to go unchecked, the French believed their stake in Algeria and North Africa would be gravely threatened.

The United States was much more removed from the direct impact of the Suez Canal crisis. Although aware of the dependence of its NATO allies on Middle Eastern oil, the United States itself did not rely upon this oil for its own needs, and its own general economy was not as contingent upon continued access to the Suez Canal as was that of Britain. Moreover, the United States had become primarily concerned with checking deeper Soviet penetration into the Middle East, and to this end had been seeking to develop friendlier relations with the Arab countries of that region. Armed intervention against Egypt, in the view of the United States, would run the grave risk of alienating the entire Arab world from the West and of giving the Soviet Union an unparalleled opportunity for enhancing its influence in that area. The United States therefore felt that armed force should not be used but that alternatives should be attempted. Hence when the British and French did intervene with armed force against Egypt, without the approval of the United Nations, and without previously consulting the United States, the latter reacted sharply and joined with the overwhelming majority of United Nations members in calling on Britain and France to halt their action.

One of the first points then in understanding world affairs is to be able to recognize the existence of different national viewpoints among the nation-states of the world. Nation-states have divergent concepts of their national security, and sometimes, in the competition for power and advantage, the security of one state comes to mean the insecurity of another. When the security concepts of one major power overlap those of a rival major power, a serious international crisis can easily develop. Figure 5 attempts to illustrate how the security concepts of the United States and the Soviet Union overlap in Europe and Asia. The circles roughly represent certain geographic areas which each of the two powers seems at present to regard as vital to its national security. Thus one of the American "perimeters of defense" runs through Central Europe on one side of the world, and embraces on the other side of the world areas like South Korea, Japan, Formosa, as well as certain portions of Southeast Asia. Any communist threat to the independence of these areas would be regarded at the present time as a serious threat to the security of the United States. Although exact limits of the Soviet "perimeters of defense" may not be easily or sharply defined, they seem clearly to overlap the American perimeters in such areas as Germany, Korea, and Japan. The Soviet Union has shown great sensitivity toward the presence of American air bases and the increase of armaments in these areas. It is in such regions, where the vital security interests of the two powers have overlapped, that the most serious crises of the cold war have arisen.

The circles do not include all the areas where the security interests of the two powers have overlapped. Other areas would be Greece and Turkey (Truman Doctrine) and more recently the Middle East (Eisenhower Doctrine).

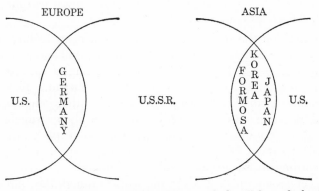

Fig. 5. Overlapping security concepts of the U.S. and the U.S.S.R.

A study of the character of the nation-state and of its underlying concepts of nationalism and national interest is therefore essential to an understanding of world affairs. A grasp of the role of power in conducting foreign affairs is equally important.

The Vantage Point of an Ideology

Viewing world affairs primarily from the standpoint of an ideology will produce still further differences in the interpretation of international problems. Is the world crisis today primarily a struggle between "democracy" and "communism," "freedom" and "slavery," or is it essentially a conflict between rival nation-states with ideology only a secondary factor?

This is one of the really confusing questions in a study of world affairs. Many Americans feel that the United States has a real mission to further the cause of freedom throughout the world. Often, official American statements reflect this viewpoint. Secretary of State John Foster Dulles, for example, declared in an address entitled "Freedom's New Task," on February 26, 1956: [2]

This nation was conceived with a sense of mission and dedicated to the extension of freedom throughout the world. President Lincoln . . . said of our Declaration of Independence that there was "something in that Declaration giving liberty, not alone to the people of this country, but hope for the world for all future time. It was that which gave promise that in due time the weights should be lifted from the shoulders of all men and that all men should have an equal chance."

That has been the spirit which has animated our people since they came together as a nation. . . .

Let me conclude with the words which Benjamin Franklin wrote from Paris on May 1, 1777:

"It is a common observation here that our cause is the cause of all mankind, and that we are fighting for their liberty in defending our own. It is a glorious task assigned us by Providence; which has, I trust, given us spirit and virtue equal to it, and will at last crown it with success."

Communists, on the other hand, also have a deep feeling of mission. To them, western democracy is simply the political ideology of capitalism. As was pointed out in Position 2 of the preceding chapter, communists believe that capitalism will inevitably collapse because they believe it engenders class struggle and war. They also feel that genuine peace and individual freedom will come only when the class struggle has been ended by the abolition of private ownership of capital and when the new classless society is sufficiently economically productive to provide goods according to the needs of all its members.

The sincere communist, viewing the world through the eyes of his own ideology, feels that time is on his side and that the ultimate establishment of communism is certain because the "laws of historical development" as he understands them are moving in this direction. He sees confirmation of this in the fact that in 1939 some 170 million people were living under communism whereas in 1957 over 900 million people were doing so.

Lazar M. Kaganovich, one of the top Soviet leaders until his demotion in 1957, summarized this official ideological confidence in the following words: [3]

Revolutionary ideas know no frontiers. They travel throughout the world without visas and fingerprints.

If the nineteenth century was a century of capitalism, the twentieth century is a century of the triumph of socialism and communism.

If world affairs are viewed exclusively from the standpoint of democratic and communist ideologies, the emerging interpretations are so contradictory and incompatible that permanent peaceful accommodation between the two views seems almost impossible. Neither democracy

---

[2] *Dept. of State Bull.*, March 5, 1956, p. 367.
[3] *New York Times*, November 7, 1955, p. 8.

nor communism, it would appear, can feel secure as long as the other exists. Because this ideological conflict is so strong, it leads some individuals to justify extreme proposals such as "preventive war," "wars of extermination," or "wars of liberation."

At this point, however, many people recoil and question whether their country should become involved in war simply to further their ideology in other parts of the world. Unless their own national security seems threatened, most citizens are not disposed to resort to war for purely ideological reasons. Hence, governments in practice usually give priority to considerations of national security, although at the same time professing devotion to the furtherance of ideological principles.

When the Hungarians in 1956–57 rebelled against Soviet domination of their country, Americans generally were deeply moved by this struggle for freedom. Many Americans were subsequently frustrated to find that nothing happened except moral protests and resolutions of condemnation by the United Nations. Yet most Americans reluctantly concluded that the cost of trying to uphold the cause of freedom in Hungary in the face of a Soviet army was too great for the interests of American national security. The western powers, wisely or unwisely, had since World War II tacitly recognized what amounted to a Soviet sphere of influence in Hungary. With the Soviet Union determined in 1956 to maintain this sphere, the western powers felt they would be risking World War III if they gave military support to the Hungarian revolution. Active support of the revolution, they concluded, was too dangerous to undertake in an area of Eastern Europe which they had not previously regarded as vital.

American policy toward the French colonial position in North Africa also illustrates the difficulty of balancing ideological interests against national-security interests. When an American views the Arab struggle for independence in North Africa, his deep-rooted instincts of freedom will probably lead him to sympathize with the Arabs. Ideologically, the United States is naturally drawn to support any people striving to be free of foreign control. However, this ideological sympathy leads to a serious dilemma, for France, which has had a dominant position in North Africa for many years, is one of the important West European allies of the United States. Effective French participation in NATO and the defense organization of Western Europe seem very vital to American national security. To alienate France by championing Arab claims in French North Africa might have run the risk of splitting the West European defense coalition. The United States, therefore, in its official utterances never felt free to support the North Africans as against the French, although it did urge the French to move as rapidly as possible toward granting some measure of independence to the North Africans.

When the Arabs on several occasions endeavored to have the problems of Tunisia, Morocco, and Algeria discussed in the United Nations Security

Council or General Assembly, the French argued that these were strictly domestic questions, exclusively within French jurisdiction, and that the United Nations had no business discussing them. The United States— torn between devotion to its principles of freedom, on the one hand, and loyalty to its important French ally, on the other—tried to take a middle-of-the-road course. Usually it voted with the French, although on one occasion in April, 1952, it abstained from voting on whether or not to have United Nations discussion.[4] Since 1956, the French have acquiesced in United Nations discussion of the Algerian question, but the United States' official position has continued to be a cautious, middle-of-the-road attitude on the merits of the case.

Thus it can be seen that *viewing world affairs primarily through the eyes of ideological principles will not only produce sharply divergent interpretations but will often pose the dilemma of whether ideology and national security can always be pursued simultaneously in the conduct of foreign policy.*[5] Our study of international understanding must therefore include an analysis of the conflict of ideologies and the impact of this conflict on world affairs.

The Vantage Point of Religious Idealism

Other interpretations of world affairs appear if the situation is considered from the vantage point of religious principles and idealism. Here the approach is to examine the world scene and the foreign policies of various governments in terms of the extent to which government actions conform to specific principles of religious belief. The effort is frequently made to define the national interest in a way that will seem consistent with certain religious principles. The attempt to put religious principles first in formulating foreign policy often leads to adverse criticism of actions appearing to be based primarily on reasons of political or military expediency or strategy. This, in turn, has been criticized as naïve and un-

---

[4] United Nations, Security Council, *Official Records,* 7th year, 576th meeting, 14 April, 1952, p. 28.

[5] Hans J. Morgenthau, in his book *In Defense of the National Interest* (New York, Knopf, 1951), presents a thought-provoking argument that American foreign policy has on many occasions been overly preoccupied with "crusading" on behalf of ideological and moral principles, and has been neglectful of what Morgenthau considers to be American national-security interests. In the zeal to further democratic ideology, American policy, according to Morgenthau, has from time to time made moral or legal commitments which it did not have the power to enforce, and which it could not honor without gravely jeopardizing the security of the United States.

Thomas I. Cook and Malcolm Moos, in a book entitled *Power through Purpose* (Baltimore, Johns Hopkins Press, 1954), criticize Morgenthau's concept of national interest, and suggest that America's strongest asset in world affairs is its reputation as a practitioner and defender of democratic freedom. They contend that the real interest of the United States lies in vigorously furthering these democratic principles throughout the world, and in trying to sow seeds of discontent within communist and other undemocratic countries.

realistic because it subordinates considerations of expediency and strategy to the dictates of religious principles.

There are obviously different concepts of religious idealism. One such outlook was presented in Position 3 in Chapter 1. There it was suggested that the principal cause of the present world crisis lay in the competitive lust for power and expansion by all major nations, and in the resort to violence to achieve these materialistic ends. According to this viewpoint, only the substitution of love for violence in human relations can provide a sound basis for international peace.

Another example of a religious or moral approach to world affairs is seen in the following quotation from an article, entitled "Foreign Policy and the Law of Charity," by a Jesuit writer, James L. Vizzard: [6]   .

In this nation founded by men who spelled out clearly the moral basis of our political society, it is strange and discouraging to have to insist that our national interest is a much broader concept and reality than mere military security, political stability or economic advantage. Unless this nation has interests and responsibilities which are rooted in moral principles, how do we differ from the arbitrary "legality" of totalitarian states? Unless "national" interest is based upon moral interest, our objectives can claim no superiority over those of the Communist nations. If our foreign economic policy fails to recognize that the very fact of our abundance creates opportunities and obligations which far transcend any narrowly conceived selfish and temporary interest, then we deserve to be weighed and judged by the world and by God in the same balance as Russia.

In public debate and private discussion a great variety of reasons are given to justify programs of international aid: we have smothering farm surpluses; our expanding industrial economy demands overseas markets and raw materials; we need to win friends and bolster our national security; if *we* don't, the Communists will.

But the moral reasons for these programs, if they are mentioned at all, are

[6] *World Alliance Newsletter,* June, 1956, p. 1. This was published by the World Alliance for International Friendship through Religion. (Since January, 1958, the *Newsletter* has been entitled *Worldview,* and is distributed by the Church Peace Union, 170 East 64th St., New York 21, N.Y.) Father Vizzard is Assistant to the Executive Director of the National Catholic Rural Life Conference. The quotation is part of a policy statement of this organization.

Many Christian spokesmen and theologians would probably not go so far in suggesting that love of neighbor is a workable standard for formulating a government's foreign policy. Reinhold Niebuhr, for example, is an outstanding Christian theologian who regards the Christian ethic of love as not immediately applicable to the problem of securing justice in a sinful and selfish world. Without denying that Jesus' ethic of love and nonviolence is absolute and uncompromising, Niebuhr contends that it represents a form of ultimate perfectionism rather than an immediate alternative to political strategies for achieving justice. He conceives of man as a basically sinful creature, and therefore argues that some form of coercion and power must be exercised in order to restrain man's tendencies to do evil. His argument is that the ethic of love and nonviolence, if applied absolutely in the face of the rise of tyranny, would result in the extension of the tyranny rather than its destruction. See, for example, his *Christianity and Power Politics* (New York, Scribner, 1952). Niebuhr's views are set forth in greater detail in Position 3 at the end of this chapter.

brought in only parenthetically, or with embarrassed apology. Patronizing "realists" clearly imply that charity and justice have no pertinence to the issues, that they represent only the sentimental idealism of international "do-gooders."

Yet, in fact, love of neighbor and justice not only have validity, even in terms of national interest, but are motives for programs of aid which are more urgent, more far-reaching, and of greater value than any other motives. Moreover, these motives, if properly explained, could win much more sincere and practical approval here and abroad. Finally, programs undertaken for these motives are more likely to achieve, as by-products, the aims of our foreign policy.

Certain church bodies, since World War I, have taken an increasingly active interest in world affairs, and have attempted to encourage their members to appraise and criticize government policies in terms of their religious and moral principles. One of the most active of these organizations is the National Council of the Churches of Christ in the U.S.A., representing a large number of Protestant denominations as well as Orthodox Christian churches. It was formerly known as the Federal Council of Churches of Christ in America. Through a Department of International Justice and Good Will, the National Council and the Federal Council have for many years encouraged wide study and discussion of the problems of peace and war.[7] The reports and pronouncements of these bodies have consistently reflected a religious and moral approach to world affairs.

During World War II, the Federal Council of Churches created a special commission to study the bases of a just and durable peace. This commission prepared a statement of guiding principles, which it felt should be followed if the postwar organization of peace were to be effective. Excerpts from three of these principles follow: [8]

1. We believe that moral law, no less than physical law, undergirds our world. There is a moral order which is fundamental and eternal, and which is relevant to the corporate life of men and the ordering of human society. If mankind is to escape chaos and recurrent war, social and political institutions must be brought into conformity with this moral order.

3. We believe that it is contrary to the moral order that nations in their dealings with one another should be motivated by a spirit of revenge and retaliation. Such attitudes will lead, as they always have led, to renewed conflict.

10. We believe that, in bringing international relations into conformity with the moral law, a very heavy responsibility devolves upon the United States. For at least a generation we have held preponderant economic power in the

---

[7] See, for example, Sidney Gulick, *The Christian Crusade for a Warless World* (New York, Macmillan, 1922). This was one of the early studies published by the Federal Council of Churches to develop a public opinion that would support international policies of "righteousness and goodwill."

[8] The Commission to Study the Bases of a Just and Durable Peace, "A Message from the National Study Conference on the Churches and a Just and Durable Peace," Delaware, Ohio, 1942, pp. 10–14. This publication is available at the National Council of Churches, 120 East 23rd St., New York 10, N.Y.

world, and with it the capacity to influence decisively the shaping of world events. It should be a matter of shame and humiliation to us that actually the influences shaping the world have largely been irresponsible forces. Our own positive influence has been impaired because of concentration on self and on our short-range material gains. Many of the major preconditions of a just and durable peace require changes of national policy on the part of the United States. Among such may be mentioned: equal access to natural resources, economic collaboration, equitable treatment of racial minorities, international control of tariffs, limitation of armaments, participation in world government. We must be ready to subordinate immediate and particular national interests to the welfare of all. If the future is to be other than a repetition of the past, the United States must accept the responsibility for constructive action commensurate with its power and opportunity.

The chairman of the commission which prepared this statement was John Foster Dulles, who later became Secretary of State.

Other examples of religious views of world affairs might be cited,[9] but enough has been said to indicate that certain religious principles, as a point of departure, may easily lead to a different concept of national interest and welfare than when international problems are considered primarily from the point of view of the political or strategic position of the nation-state. As with the vantage point of ideology, questions are often posed: "Do religious and moral principles play a role in the shaping of foreign policy?" "Can they have a real influence if they seem to conflict with the political or strategic requirements of national security?" A meaningful understanding of world affairs must include the study of such questions.

The Vantage Point of Critical Scholarship

The three previous vantage points on world affairs reflect the views of those who are seeking to advance particular interests of certain nation-states, ideologies, or religious principles. The conflicting interpretations arising from these points of view may discourage the reader who is seeking an understanding of all sides of a problem. He may ask: "Is it possible to obtain a 'true' picture of world affairs, a view not vitiated by national, ideological, or religious bias? Can one rise above the interests of his nation, ideology, or religion and obtain an 'objective,' impartial picture of the international situation?"

These very natural questions are much easier to ask than to answer. The physical scientist can approach the problems of the natural world in a relatively detached, objective manner, and can often isolate in his

---

[9] In 1953, the National Council of the Churches of Christ in the U.S.A. issued a report, entitled "Christian Faith and International Responsibility." Pope Pius XII and many of his predecessors have frequently dealt with the international situation in terms of religious principles, similar to those quoted here. See, for example, Robert C. Pollock, *The Mind of Pius XII* (New York, Crown, 1955), and Francis J. Powers, *Papal Pronouncements on the Political Order* (Westminster, Md., Newman Press, 1952).

laboratory all elements involved in a particular problem. After observing and measuring all pertinent elements in a scientific manner, he may be able to reach certain conclusions which can be verified as "true." That the same approach can be applied to the problems of human and social behavior, and especially to the problems of international relations, seems more questionable. Can the student of world affairs, for example, remain detached and objective when he feels that his country's national security or way of life is threatened, or when he is confronted with a sharp challenge to his religious, moral, or ideological loyalties? Unlike the physical scientist who is able to separate himself from the physical phenomena he is studying in his laboratory, the student of world affairs himself is one element in the problem and therefore cannot so easily detach himself from what he is studying.

Although complete objectivity in studying world affairs seems therefore to represent an almost impossible ideal, there may be certain scholarly standards which, if followed, will produce a more complete and accurate picture of world problems than might otherwise be true. This approach might be called the vantage point of critical scholarship.

The critical scholar, for example, can guard against outright falsehoods, clear-cut distortions, and incomplete accounts. Thus he may give the lie to certain atrocity stories which circulated in Europe and the United States during World War I.[10] He may correct the distortion, popular in the 1930's, that the United States was pushed into World War I solely by bankers and munitions-makers concerned primarily with financial profits.[11] He may also give a more complete picture of the origins of World War I by a careful study of the archives of all the major nations involved.[12]

Critical scholarship, furthermore, can make us aware of the ways in which history and other textbooks have often reflected strong nationalist

[10] See, for example, James M. Read, *Atrocity Propaganda 1914–1919* (New Haven, Yale University Press, 1941), and James R. Mock and Cedric Larsen, *Words That Won the War* (Princeton, Princeton University Press, 1939).

[11] A convenient summary of the main viewpoints of scholars on America's entrance into World War I may be found in Thomas A. Bailey, *A Diplomatic History of the American People* (New York, Appleton-Century-Crofts, 6th ed., 1958), Chaps. 38–39. Although economic pressures may have made it easier for the United States to fight Germany rather than the Allies, many scholars do not conclude that these reasons were decisive in the American decision. More influential reasons were: (*a*) Germany's resumption of unrestricted submarine warfare in January, 1917; (*b*) Germany's interest in preventing the United States from continuing as a major base of supplies for the Allies; (*c*) the belief that a German victory would so upset the European balance of power as to threaten the future security of the United States and the freedom of shipping on the Atlantic Ocean.

[12] See, for example, Sidney B. Fay's book *The Origins of the World War* (New York, Macmillan, 1928 and 1930), which sheds considerable new light on the diplomatic background of World War I through the study of extensive collections of documents released by the German, Austrian, and Russian governments at the end of the war.

prejudices, and have thereby reinforced popular suspicions and antagonisms. German and French textbooks, for example, present different versions of relations between their countries, especially in regard to the major wars fought. German children have been told many times about the burning of the castle at Heidelberg by the French, and French children have been told about the burning of the castle at Saint Cloud by the Germans. In like fashion, American schoolboys are invariably told about the burning of the White House by the British in the War of 1812, but not about the burning of the Canadian Parliament building at Toronto by the Americans.[13]

History textbooks in western countries still give very superficial and inadequate treatment to Asia and Africa. Although the peoples of Asia comprise over one-half of the world's population, surprisingly few pages of most standard public school textbooks are devoted to this part of the world. The wide variations in Asian cultures have often been submerged in uniform generalities. The great personages of recent Asian history have been virtually ignored. The backwardness of Asians in industrial development is often portrayed as meaning backwardness in every aspect of development. Stereotyped phrases such as "natives," "uncivilized," and "white man's burden" are common.[14] Critical scholarship can obviously do much to provide school children with a more complete and accurate understanding of this vast portion of mankind.

In dealing with the more controversial problems of current international affairs such as disarmament, the reunification of Germany, or the increase of communist influence in the Middle East and Asia, the critical scholar cannot be content simply with the American national viewpoint on these problems, nor with an interpretation based solely upon democratic ideology and hypotheses. He must also examine the Soviet national outlook and the interpretation based upon communist ideology and hypotheses. In addition, the viewpoints of our principal allies, as well as of other

[13] See D. W. Brogan, "Deodorized History," in UNESCO Courier, May, 1956, pp. 20–21. Carlton J. H. Hayes, France; a Nation of Patriots (New York, Columbia University Press, 1930), analyzes the impact of nationalism on French textbooks and presents many excerpts from them to illustrate the discussion.

The United Nations Educational, Scientific and Cultural Organization has been much concerned about correcting the biased, inaccurate, and incomplete accounts in public school textbooks. Teachers of various countries have been encouraged to sit down together and examine their respective textbooks with a view to agreeing on how the books might be made more accurate. As a result of discussions among German, French, British, and American historians, for example, progress has been made in agreeing on more accurate accounts of the background of World Wars I and II. See the United Nations Educational, Scientific and Cultural Organization, A Handbook for the Improvement of Textbooks and Teaching Materials as Aids to International Understanding (Paris, 1949), and "Bilateral Consultations for the Improvement of History Textbooks," in the series Educational Studies and Documents, July, 1953, No. IV.

[14] Ronald Fenton, "Asian History through Western Glasses," UNESCO Courier, May, 1956, p. 12.

interested countries such as India, Pakistan, Egypt, and Israel, may need to be considered. With such an approach, the critical scholar not only gains a fuller understanding of the central issues of each problem but also lays a better basis for discovering whether or not areas of compromise and agreement are possible among the interested governments. By a critical examination and appraisal of various proposals for meeting each problem, more prudent conclusions can be reached.

Finally, the critical scholar is conscious of his own limitations as an observer, and of his own framework of values and methods which to a greater or lesser degree will color his account. Frequently, he will also be aware of the inadequacy of his own store of factual information for drawing valid conclusions. To the extent that he is aware of his own limitations, he ceases to be a blind captive of the view of others, for he realizes that they, too, have their limitations.

Conclusion

Four vantage points on world affairs have now been discussed. They help to explain why so many different interpretations of world affairs exist. Undoubtedly, the reader could think of other vantage points to add to the ones already considered. The ability to recognize them should enable him to cut through some of the maze and confusion that often seem to surround international affairs. Such a vast amount of material on all phases of world affairs is now available that the student may find it helpful to classify the various items at his disposal according to the particular vantage point each seems to reflect. Identification of the approaches of various writers or speakers will enable the student better to appraise the usefulness and validity of the different materials, and to arrive at a more reasoned judgment and conclusion of his own.

The Role of International Understanding

In a world which has shrunk and become increasingly interdependent, peoples and nations have been brought into contact with one another to an extent scarcely conceivable three or four generations ago. More than ever before, the conduct of foreign affairs involves the complicated task of seeking harmonious adjustments between countries of widely divergent cultures, philosophies, and aspirations. Indeed, one frequently encounters the assumption that international conflict and war are, in part at least, a result of the failure to understand other peoples, their cultures, interests, and needs. This viewpoint is seen very clearly in the preamble to the Constitution of the United Nations Educational, Scientific and Cultural Organization (UNESCO), which states: [15]

[15] Dept. of State, *Basic Documents: UN Educational, Scientific and Cultural Organization,* 4th ed., 1956, Dept. of State Publ. 6364, p. 7.

that since wars begin in the minds of men, it is in the minds of men that the defences of peace must be constructed;

that ignorance of each other's ways and lives has been a common cause, throughout the history of mankind, of that suspicion and mistrust between peoples of the world through which their differences have all too often broken into war; . . .

Implicit in this assumption regarding international misunderstanding is the belief that man often suspects and fears that which he does not know. From these suspicions and fears, tensions and conflict may arise. Foreigners in a country are often distrusted or looked down upon because they are different. They sometimes even seem peculiar because their dress, eating habits, religion, language, and customs are in striking contrast to the manner of living of the inhabitants of that country. Under the impact of a strong nationalistic loyalty, a person may easily come to regard his own national institutions and customs as superior to those of other nations. If, in addition, his schoolbooks have presented one-sided or grossly biased accounts of the foreign policies of his government and its neighbors, serious misunderstanding may ensue, which can easily intensify international conflict. Under the influence of such factors as these, the people of one country often form prejudiced and inaccurate stereotype-impressions of the people of other countries.

A study made in 1948 by UNESCO illustrates rather dramatically the wide variety of stereotype-impressions that various nationalities have of one another.[16] The study was based on a public-opinion poll in nine countries, in which a representative sample of approximately 1,000 persons in each country was interviewed. Each person interviewed was given a list of twelve adjectives [17] and was asked to indicate which he thought applied to the people of certain countries, including his own. A partial summary of the results of the survey in four countries appears on page 58.

The figures in each table indicate the percentage of respondents who felt that each adjective applied to the nationality being described. The totals do not equal 100 per cent because the same adjective could be applied to more than one nationality. It should be remembered that this survey was made in the summer and early fall of 1948, when the Marshall Plan had been in operation for a few months, when the Berlin blockade had started, and when the preliminary negotiations for NATO had just got underway.

These findings may be of some value in helping nations to see themselves as others see them. Americans, for example, may be understand-

[16] UNESCO, *International Social Science Bulletin,* Autumn, 1951, Vol. II, No. 3, pp. 515–528.
[17] The twelve adjectives were: hard-working, intelligent, practical, conceited, generous, cruel, backward, brave, self-controlled, domineering, progressive, and peace-loving.

Country in which
   survey was made:
   Great Britain

| | People Described | | | | |
Adjectives:	American	Russian	French	Chinese	Self
Intelligent	38%	12%	32%	17%	52%
Practical	38	21	20	11	47
Generous	52	3	14	7	48
Backward	4	36	9	37	6
Domineering	37	42	11	2	6
Peace-loving	39	6	21	22	77

Country in which
   survey was made:
   West Germany
   (British Zone)

| | People Described | | | | |
Adjectives:	American	Russian	French	Chinese	Self
Intelligent	34%	4%	22%	6%	64%
Practical	45	8	5	3	53
Generous	46	2	5	1	11
Backward	1	41	10	12	2
Domineering	10	12	12	1	10
Peace-loving	23	5	12	5	37

Country in which
   survey was made:
   France

| | People Described | | |
Adjectives:	American	Russian	Self
Intelligent	37%	15%	79%
Practical	81	11	17
Generous	34	7	62
Backward	2	56	4
Domineering	46	49	4
Peace-loving	26	10	69

Country in which
   survey was made:
   United States

| | People Described | | |
Adjectives:	Russian	British	Self
Intelligent	12%	49%	72%
Practical	13	32	53
Generous	3	13	76
Backward	40	11	2
Domineering	49	33	9
Peace-loving	7	42	82

ably surprised to see that only 39 per cent of the British and 26 per cent of the French respondents regarded the Americans as peace-loving, or to see also that as many as 37 per cent of the British and 46 per cent of the French respondents felt that Americans were domineering.

Although the UNESCO survey did not suggest that favorable or unfavorable stereotypes had a causative effect upon the relations between nations, the results did indicate that the prevalence of complimentary or uncomplimentary stereotypes was a good index of friendly or unfriendly relations between nations. This is evidenced in the generally uncomplimentary adjectives applied by the West Germans to the French and by all four nationalities to the Russians.

Government officials, as well as private citizens who travel or work abroad, play a significant role in the formation of foreign public opinion toward their own country. By their conduct and attitudes, they can do much to create or destroy good will between their own country and the countries where they travel. The American who travels abroad, for example, has been known to judge the culture of other peoples by the material conveniences it provides similar to those he enjoys in the United States—modern plumbing and heating, paved roads, electric refrigerators, telephones, and television; too often his conclusion has been that, if it does not provide these physical comforts, the culture is inferior to his own. Such attitudes are obviously not conducive to friendly relations and may easily lead to anti-American feeling abroad.[18]

American officials who are sent to Asian or African countries on technical-assistance missions sometimes become impatient and frustrated because the tempo or pattern of the native culture is not such that American techniques in agriculture or industry can be readily adopted. They seem especially inclined to assume that what succeeds in the United States will work anywhere. When they therefore encounter local cultural or religious barriers to rapid adjustment to American techniques, they may demand that the local traditions be set aside in order to move ahead quickly with the program. Technical success is sometimes accomplished in this way, but usually a high cultural price in terms of misunderstanding is paid for it, and the impression is reinforced that Americans are ingenious but uncouth.

In view of this, there is increasing emphasis on the importance of a

[18] It is of special interest to note that the Department of Defense in recent years has prepared a series of attractive pocket guides for American armed forces overseas. These booklets, dealing with the culture and history of the various countries in which the American armed forces may be stationed, are designed to prepare the Americans to expect different ways of life in these countries and to avoid actions that might be misunderstood abroad, thereby diminishing or discrediting American standing in the eyes of the people in other lands. U.S. Dept. of the Army Pamphlets #20, Pocket Guide Series. See, for example, *A Pocket Guide to Japan*, DA Pam 20-177; *A Pocket Guide to Germany*, DA Pam 20-179.

broader knowledge of other cultures as a means of reducing international tension and improving the effectiveness of international co-operation and negotiation. This has been stressed on various occasions by President Dwight D. Eisenhower. In an address at Trinity College, Hartford, Connecticut, on October 20, 1954, he said: [19]

If we are to develop the kind of understanding that will avoid the great catastrophe of war, we must know about the cultures of these other countries, the history of them, and above all why . . . they react to certain actions, certain considerations and circumstances in this world in a different way from which we do.

Again on November 8, 1954, before the National Council of Catholic Women, President Eisenhower said: [20]

And let us remember this: war and peace, struggle and resolution, hatred and concord are not merely the concerns of government and diplomacy. They well from the emotions and impulses in the hearts of individual men and women, in every nation of the world.

These emotions, from generation to generation, are passed on from parent to child. The problems these emotions create are incredibly complex. Why must a country fight to the death to hold seemingly worthless territory? Why must a nation passionately strive to maintain an apparently meaningless boundary? Why must the people of one nation continue to hate or fear the people of another, for reasons lost in the dimness of the past?

Solution of these problems requires more than skillful diplomacy. Essential to lasting peace is a genuine desire of the individual citizens of each nation to understand the traditions and hopes and desires of the citizens of all other nations. We in America must strive to understand the emotions and attitudes, instilled in other people from childhood, which lie at the heart of vexing international difficulties.

Above all we need the religious quality of compassion—the ability to feel the emotions of others as though they were our own. If the mothers in every land could teach their children to understand the homes and hopes of children in every other land—in America, in Europe, in the Near East, in Asia—the cause of peace in the world would indeed be nobly served.

The promotion of international understanding and friendship appeals to many persons because it fits easily into an educational or civic program and often leads to visible and tangible results. The increasing number of international student and teacher exchanges provides countless opportunities for schools and communities to become better informed on a personal basis with many countries of the world.[21] The revision of history textbooks in various countries, with a view to making them more objective and unbiased, also seems practical. The United Nations Educational, Scientific and Cultural Organization, with a budget of only a

[19] *New York Times,* October 21, 1954, p. 1.
[20] *New York Times,* November 9, 1954, p. 14.
[21] According to the Institute of International Education, nearly 42,000 foreign students and teachers came to the United States in the academic year 1956–57, and over 11,000 American students and teachers went abroad.

few million dollars a year, seeks in a variety of ways to promote greater exchange of educational, scientific, and cultural knowledge among the peoples of the world.

A contrasting view is that it is naïve and even dangerous to devote major efforts to the increased understanding of other peoples and cultures. It is naïve, according to this view, because it assumes that conflict and war arise primarily out of failure to understand other countries, rather than out of fundamental clashes of political, economic, and strategic interests. It is dangerous because it may give the impression that it is the causes of war that are being dealt with, when in reality only surface symptoms and manifestations of war are being tackled. In "Positions on the Problem," the next section of this chapter, these viewpoints regarding the significance of understanding other peoples and their ways of life will be presented more fully.

In subsequent chapters, other factors will be examined which, in the judgment of various observers, contribute to international war and tension: human nature, nationalism and the struggle for power, the uneven distribution of natural resources, and modern scientific development.

THE NATURE OF PEACE

Any understanding of world affairs must sooner or later come to grips with the nature of peace. There is nothing on which the governments of the world seem to be in more complete agreement than their professed desire for peace. Soviet and American leaders, for example, vie with each other in proclaiming their devotion to peace; yet the actual state of world affairs does not evidence much actual agreement between Soviet and American spokesmen on what peace really means. Both governments belong to the United Nations, the first purpose of which is "to maintain international peace and security." However, the record of their relations within the United Nations indicates that peace and security mean different things to the two governments.

To the communist, peace may mean the condition in which the class struggle has been abolished, and he therefore concludes that revolutionary activity to overthrow capitalism and eliminate the class struggle is the only way of establishing peace. The ardent democrat, on the other hand, may feel that peace involves the extension of freedom and democracy throughout the world. The communist and the democrat might in this way use the same term *peace* but attach entirely different meanings to it. The meaning here takes on a highly subjective character and becomes equated closely with the national and ideological outlooks of different states. It is indeed a moot point whether a single definition of peace would be acceptable to all governments.

A less subjective approach may lead one to define peace simply as the absence of military hostilities. This definition, however, is largely negative and could include many situations, such as an armed truce or a cold war, which seem far removed from conditions of genuine peace and might easily erupt overnight into a full-scale war. The mere absence of military hostility, furthermore, can sometimes be purchased only by a nation's submitting to the demands of a powerful neighbor and accepting considerable restrictions or the complete loss of freedom and liberty. Witness the "peaceful" occupation of Denmark by the Nazis in 1940.

A more satisfactory definition of peace therefore seems desirable—one which implies more than the mere absence of war and which involves the existence of a state of affairs in which nations do not feel that war is the only method on which they can ultimately rely to defend their territories and promote their interests. It would imply the creation of conditions and institutions capable of assuring settlement of all international disputes in an orderly and constitutional manner without resort to violence or hostilities. Within this framework of peace, nations must feel confident that their respective interests and claims can be fairly considered and adjusted, either through the processes of negotiation and conciliation or through impartial arbitration and judicial settlement if negotiation and conciliation break down. There must be effective peaceful procedures for bringing about the inevitable changes in a particular status quo, for whenever change cannot take place by peaceful means there is real danger that the change will be effected by force or by violence.

This definition assumes not only the availability of certain procedures for adjusting international differences but also adequate agreement or consensus among nations as to certain fundamental principles governing their relations with one another. Without a general consensus or agreement on fundamentals, the procedures of peaceful international adjustment will have great difficulty operating. The willingness to compromise or accept the procedures of impartial judicial process can exist on a broad scale only within a framework of agreement on certain fundamental principles underlying society.

This consensus might go so far as to include agreement on common ideals and expectations, common standards of law and morality, common principles of political and economic ideology, and common concepts of mutual defense. The relations between the United States and Canada illustrate such a consensus at a very advanced stage of development. As such, they represent a good example of peace as it has been defined in the preceding two paragraphs. The relations between the United States and the other members of the North Atlantic Treaty Organization also are grounded on a considerable amount of agreement, although not as much so as are Canadian-United States relations. The members of the British Commonwealth likewise evidence a broad consensus in their relations with one another.

Although a broad consensus of the type characterizing United States-Canadian relations or British Commonwealth relations can scarcely be expected in the near future among all or even a majority of the nations of the world, a more limited one embodying general toleration of different political systems and noninterference in one another's internal affairs may be possible for many nations. The relations between the United States and the various countries of Latin America might be cited as an example, or the relations between the western powers and the new independent states of Asia like India, Burma, or Indonesia. To some extent, a limited consensus characterizes even the relations between Yugoslavia and the western powers. So long as nations are ready to accept this "live-and-let-live" basis for their relations with one another, there is considerable room for harmonizing the conflicts of national interest through the techniques of peaceful adjustment.

When there is little or no consensus between nations, the procedures of peaceful settlement can operate only with extreme difficulty, as is apparent from the seemingly endless and often frustrating negotiations between the Soviet Union and the western powers since World War II. Although some important agreements have been reached as a result of such negotiations,[22] the relations between the Soviet Union and the western powers at present scarcely reflect a condition of genuine peace. They might be more accurately characterized as simply the absence of military hostilities or the condition of cold war. For the large part of the world, therefore, genuine peace represents an objective still to be achieved rather than a condition already in existence. It is in the establishment of the conditions of genuine peace that mankind seems, unfortunately, to be making extremely slow progress.

Various techniques for achieving peace and adjusting international differences will be analyzed in Part IV of this book. Particular attention will be given to diplomatic negotiation, balance-of-power policies, and United Nations procedures, as well as to proposals for transforming the United Nations into a stronger organ of world government. Careful study of these techniques should enable the reader to understand better how a framework of international relations can be established within which competition and rivalry can take place peacefully rather than in the form of war and violence.

[22] The post-World War II peace treaties with Italy, Hungary, Rumania, Bulgaria, and Finland, which were signed in February, 1947, took fifteen months to negotiate because of sharp differences between the Soviet and western viewpoints. The peace treaty with Austria was not signed until May, 1955, ten years after the defeat of Germany. Approximately four hundred sessions between the Soviet and western delegates were held before final agreement was reached. The negotiations with Communist China for a truce in the Korean War lasted two years, from July, 1951, to July, 1953.

THE NATURE AND ROLE OF POWER

The techniques for promoting peace and resolving international differences do not operate in a vacuum but are influenced very markedly by the relative strength and power of the states involved. When we look closely at the operation of these techniques, we quickly realize that states vary tremendously in their capacity to promote and defend their respective interests. One of the strange ironies of international relations is the fact that states, although theoretically and legally equal, are actually exceedingly unequal in their power and influence in world affairs. The designations *great powers* and *small powers* attest to this inequality. International organizations such as the United Nations pay theoretical tribute to the legal equality of their members by according each member one vote, regardless of population, size, or economic development. However, in the discussions and bargaining leading up to the actual voting, the discrepancies in power and influence are more apparent. The United States and Costa Rica, for example, may each have only one vote in the United Nations, but this is the extent of their actual equality in the workings of the United Nations.

In negotiating the settlement of international disputes, the relative equality or inequality of the disputants may be an important factor in reaching an agreement that seems reasonable to both sides. Negotiations between the United States and Panama regarding the Panama Canal, or between the Soviet Union and Finland over mutual trade problems, illustrate very well the implications of the actual inequality between sovereign states which are legally equal. This is not to say that a powerful state always seeks to place its weaker neighbors at a disadvantage, but the possibility of its doing so at any time must always be kept in mind.

The role of power, therefore (including the relative inequalities of power potential among nation-states), is another pertinent factor in any realistic understanding of the techniques of adjustment in world affairs. Scarcely any experienced observer of the world scene would deny that power and the struggle for the accumulation of power have an influence on international relations. The exact extent of this influence, however, is more difficult to determine, and is therefore a more debatable matter. Can all international relations, for example, be explained primarily in terms of the struggle for power? Or are there important phases of international relations in which there is no conspicuous power struggle? How much do international disputes yield to the influence of reason, education, or moral principles, and how much only to the pressure of political, economic, or military power? Can permanent and mutually satisfactory settlements of disputes be expected when power has been the primary factor?

The Elements of National Power

The basic elements on which the power or potential power of a nation-state rests include such tangible factors as geography, population, raw materials, economc development, and military preparedness, as well as certain less tangible qualities: national morale, national character, quality of diplomacy, and the international appeal of a nation's ideological principles. These elements, especially the tangible ones, are not evenly distributed among the states of the world, thus causing the inequalities in power mentioned previously. The same unevenness also leads frequently to competition and rivalry for additional elements of power, thereby contributing to international tension and conflict.

In gauging a nation's relative power in world affairs, many questions must be considered. Some, arranged according to the various elements of national power, are suggested in the following paragraphs. The questions are left unanswered at this point in order to stimulate the reader to work out his own answers regarding the relative power of various states of the world.

Geography. Does the state have an exposed or an isolated location? Is it, like Poland, situated between two powerful rivals and thereby exposed to attack from two sides? Or is it, like the United States, separated by vast distances or bodies of water from the principal areas of struggle and conflict? Does it have ready access to the sea for trade and commerce, or is it landlocked and thus more dependent on its neighbors for outlets to overseas trade? Is it physically large enough to permit the dispersion of its vital industries and population centers over considerable areas, and to provide the advantages of defense in depth? Does it have frontiers that can be easily crossed, such as open plains, making it more vulnerable to attack? Or does it have frontiers like mountains, rivers, oceans, or deserts which constitute strategic barriers? Does it have a climate suitable for good agricultural production and conducive to the health and energy of its population?

Geography constitutes one of the most stable of all the elements of power. Because geographic elements are not in themselves susceptible to much change, the struggle for possession of the more favorable ones is often permanent and relentless. History is full of examples of rivalries for strategic frontiers, warm water ports, and control of major trade routes.

Population. Here a state's power is affected by the size and character of its population. Is its population large enough to support both an extensive economy and an adequate military establishment? Is the rate of its population growth increasing or decreasing? Does it have a larger population than can be supported adequately by its level of economic development and productivity; in other words, does it suffer from the pressure of overpopulation? Is the population sufficiently trained to be able to utilize the techniques of modern industry and agriculture and thereby develop an efficient economy and a relatively high standard of living? Is the population made up of a homogeneous nationality group, as in France or Germany, or does it have sizable national minorities, as in Czechoslovakia or Poland, which may embroil it in minority disputes with its neighbors?

Possession of a large population or of a sizable territory does not, in itself, mean that a nation will be powerful. Nations like China and India have large populations and vast territories but are still relatively weaker powers than the United States or the Soviet Union. This illustrates the fact that national power generally rests on a combination of several elements rather than on any single one.

Raw materials. Does the state have reasonably adequate supplies of foodstuffs and grains for its population? (No state, of course, is completely self-sufficient.) Does it possess the raw materials for modern industry such as coal, iron, oil, tin, rubber, the ferroalloys, and, more recently, uranium? If these resources are present in the state, are they readily accessible and are they being mined, produced, and utilized at a level that will assure economic strength? Or are they still in a relatively undeveloped condition and, therefore, more of a potential source of future power than a base of actual power today? If a state is poorly endowed with these materials, as are Great Britain, Italy, and Japan, does it have dependable access to other areas where such materials can be obtained? Or is it vulnerable to blockades or embargoes by rival states, which by virtue of their geographic location can control the various trade routes of the world? Can the state deficient in raw materials develop synthetic products to relieve any of its deficiencies?

Economic development. Does the nation have a high level of industrial and agricultural productivity? How does its production of steel, which is a good index of industrial development, compare with that of the United States (104,500,000 metric tons in 1956), the Soviet Union (48,600,000 metric tons in 1956), West Germany (23,200,000 metric tons in 1956), France (13,400,000 metric tons in 1956), or Communist China (4,000,000 metric tons in 1956)?[23] Is the nation's industry reasonably well balanced, as in the United States, between capital-goods and consumer-goods production? Is it developed sufficiently to support a substantial armament program without cutting seriously into its consumer-goods production? Or has its development of heavy capital-goods and armaments industry been largely at the expense of consumer-goods industry, as in the Soviet Union?

[23] United Nations Economic Commission for Europe, *Quarterly Bulletin of Steel Statistics for Europe,* Vol. VIII, No. 4. Figures for Communist China are cited in Edmund Stevens, "Inside Red China," *Look,* April 16, 1957, p. 36.

Economic development is a crucial element of power in the modern world in both a military and an economic sense. When combined with favorable geographic, population, and raw-material factors, as in the United States and the Soviet Union, it provides a solid base for economic and military strength. Even in countries that lack many geographic, population, and raw-material advantages, such as Belgium or Switzerland, a high level of economic development and foreign trade has brought relatively high living standards to the populations. The eagerness with which the countries of Asia and Africa are today undertaking programs of economic development is eloquent witness to the significance of this element of power.

Military preparedness. This is one of the most obvious elements of power, upon which nations rely to defend and promote their interests and security. The extent to which it can become a formidable asset to a state depends, however, on the existence of other more basic elements of power such as manpower and industrial development. The strongest military powers are those which have the most advantageous combination of geographic, population, raw-material, and economic-productivity factors. Military strength is also bolstered by some intangible elements of power such as national morale and character.

National morale. This intangible is most apt to show up in time of national danger or crisis. A component part is the loyalty and devotion of a nation's population to its institutions and ways of life. Do they, for example, stand vigorously behind the policies of their government in peace and war? Are they likely to buckle down and work harder when faced with economic difficulties or crisis? Will their determination weaken or collapse in the face of military threats or defeat? How susceptible will the people be to the influence of psychological warfare and propaganda from a hostile state? Is a dictatorship, which maintains its power primarily through violence and coercion, more apt to have a lower level of national morale than a democratic state where the government rests on popular consent and the people have a greater voice in public affairs? Can a high degree of morale be expected in a state like France which, although democratic, has sharp internal divisions between rightist and leftist political groups? Or is national morale likely to be stronger in states like Great Britain and the Scandinavian countries, where political institutions are more stable than in France? Can the remarkable resistance of Britain in 1940 at the height of the "blitz" be explained in any other terms than high national morale?

National character. Like national morale, this is another intangible element of power. Although there are obvious hazards in generalizing about a whole people or even attributing certain characteristics to certain national groups, the question does occur as to whether the power and strength of some nations do not indicate the presence of varying amounts of initiative, adaptability, organizational and methodical efficiency, discipline, endurance, thoroughness, respect for individual rights, and willingness to submit to authority. Sociologists would remind us that, though national groups appear to vary in these traits, the qualities are not inherent in the people themselves but are a product of the cultural environment in which they have lived. Yet the very fact that people in different countries are conditioned differently means that there will be variations in characteristics, and it is not inconceivable that the variations may affect the relative power of different states.

To what extent, for example, has the spectacular economic recovery of Germany since World War II been facilitated by the reputed German methodical efficiency, organization, and industry? Has the absence of large standing armies until recently in the United States and Great Britain developed a national aversion to military service, which has placed these countries at some military disadvantage in their rivalry with states like Germany and Japan, where the army has enjoyed a position of greater prestige and influence? On the other hand, have not certain other traits—such as inventiveness, adaptability, and capacity for tremendous expansion of output when challenged—helped Americans offset whatever initial disadvantages were caused by a lack of military preparedness? In a country like India, will the traditional and widespread philosophy of nonviolence have a significant influence in restricting the potential power of that country in world affairs? Or is it likely to provide India with a different and more effective kind of power, particularly among the peoples of Asia with whom it has much in common?

The international appeal of a nation's ideological principles. Reference was made earlier in this chapter to the vantage point of ideology in interpreting world affairs. It is suggested that a nation's ideological principles also may constitute an important element of power. For example, is not the influence and strength of the United States enhanced throughout the world because it is looked upon as a citadel of freedom? Do freedom-loving people naturally turn to the United States for sympathy and assistance in attempting to achieve and maintain their independence? Do we strengthen our position whenever we actively support the freedom of the colonial and other "captive" peoples? Do we correspondingly weaken our position whenever we compromise these principles?

How much advantage, on the other hand, accrues to the Soviet Union because of its constant propaganda against western colonialism in Asia, Africa, and the Middle East? Does the Soviet Union have an advantage in appealing to the peoples of these areas because it criticizes the system of private enterprise so often associated with western capitalism and imperialism?

To the extent that this ideological "struggle for men's minds" has a bearing on the relative power of the democratic and the communist states, it illustrates clearly the fact that power cannot be measured exclusively in terms of military or economic might.

Quality of diplomacy. Professor Hans Morgenthau has suggested that the quality of a nation's diplomacy is its most important element of power.[24]

All the other factors that determine national power are, as it were, the raw material out of which the power of a nation is fashioned. The quality of a nation's diplomacy combines those different factors into an integrated whole, gives them direction and weight, and awakens their slumbering potentialities by giving them the breath of actual power. The conduct of a nation's foreign affairs by its diplomats is for national power in peace what military strategy and tactics by its military leaders are for national power in war. It is the art of bringing the different elements of national power to bear with maximum effect upon those points in the international situation which concern the national interest most directly.

Diplomacy, one might say, is the brains of national power, as national morale is its soul. If its vision is blurred, its judgment defective, and its determination feeble, all the advantages of geographical location, of self-sufficiency in food, raw materials, and industrial production, of military preparedness, of size and quality of population will in the long run avail a nation little. . . . By using the power potentialities of a nation to best advantage, a competent diplomacy can increase the power of a nation beyond what one would expect it to be in view of all the other factors combined. Often in history the Goliath without brains or soul has been smitten and slain by the David who had both.

In the interest of surviving in an age of nuclear warfare, it may well be asked whether nations will not have to resort increasingly and skillfully to other elements of power than that of military might. If war is now "unthinkable," as many seem to feel, will diplomacy become increasingly important as a technique of adjustment? If so, will not the quality of it be a major factor in defending and advancing its interests?

Conclusion

An attempt has been made in the first section of this chapter to suggest some useful clues to a better understanding of world affairs and the divergent outlooks on the subject. In the next section, three specific positions are presented which are sufficiently divergent to provoke a stimulating discussion of whether any one viewpoint can be regarded as a "key outlook" on world affairs. The first position suggests that understanding other peoples and cultures is a most essential foundation of international peace. The second position sharply criticizes the first outlook and suggests that understanding the conflict of power and interest among nation-states is more realistic. The third position criticizes both

[24] Reprinted from *Politics Among Nations*, 2nd ed., by Hans J. Morgenthau, by permission of Alfred A. Knopf, Inc., copyright 1954 by Alfred A. Knopf, Inc., pp. 128–129.

the so-called "idealists" and the "realists," and calls for a better understanding of the relationship between morality and power as the most
sensible outlook on world affairs.

POSITIONS
ON THE PROBLEM

1. UNDERSTANDING OTHER PEOPLES AND CULTURES

(This viewpoint is well represented by the philosophy and program of
the United Nations Educational, Scientific and Cultural Organization,
popularly known as UNESCO. UNESCO was organized in November,
1945, for the purpose of promoting greater mutual knowledge and understanding among the peoples of the world. One of the basic assumptions
of UNESCO is that ignorance of other peoples breeds mistrust, and mistrust in turn creates a climate of international suspicion in which differences between nations easily degenerate into war.

The organizers of UNESCO felt that the advent of atomic weapons had
the most serious implications for the future survival of civilization. International mistrust and fear had now become conditions so dangerous to
mankind that they could no longer be tolerated. By the same token,
international trust and confidence could no longer be regarded as vision-
ary ideals to be attained in some distant future but were inescapable
necessities to be realized here and now by every available means. Without
questioning the urgent necessity of removing the economic and political
causes of misunderstanding, UNESCO proposed an organized international onslaught on ignorance and prejudice, with a view to developing
a climate of mutual understanding and trust which alone could assure
the survival of civilization.

The following passages from the preamble and Article I of the
UNESCO Constitution set forth clearly the premises and purposes of the
organization.[25])

That since wars begin in the minds of men, it is in the minds of men that
the defences of peace must be constructed;
That ignorance of each other's ways and lives has been a common cause,
throughout the history of mankind, of that suspicion and mistrust between the
peoples of the world through which their differences have all too often broken
into war;
That the great and terrible war which has now ended was a war made

[25] Dept. of State, *Basic Documents: UN Educational, Scientific and Cultural Organization, op. cit.*, pp. 7–9.

possible by the denial of the democratic principles of the dignity, equality and mutual respect of men, and by the propagation, in their place, through ignorance and prejudice, of the doctrine of the inequality of men and races;

That the wide diffusion of culture, and the education of humanity for justice and liberty and peace are indispensable to the dignity of man and constitute a sacred duty which all the nations must fulfil in a spirit of mutual assistance and concern;

That a peace based exclusively upon the political and economic arrangements of governments would not be a peace which could secure the unanimous, lasting and sincere support of the peoples of the world, and that the peace must therefore be founded, if it is not to fail, upon the intellectual and moral solidarity of mankind. . . .

Article I. Purposes and Functions

1. The purpose of the Organization is to contribute to peace and security by promoting collaboration among the nations through education, science and culture in order to further universal respect for justice, for the rule of law and for the human rights and fundamental freedoms which are affirmed for the peoples of the world, without distinction of race, sex, language or religion, by the Charter of the United Nations.

2. To realize this purpose the Organization will:

a. collaborate in the work of advancing the mutual knowledge and understanding of peoples, through all means of mass communication and to that end recommend such international agreements as may be necessary to promote the free flow of ideas by word and image;

b. give fresh impulse to popular education and to the spread of culture; by collaborating with Members, at their request, in the development of educational activities; by instituting collaboration among the nations to advance the ideal of equality of educational opportunity without regard to race, sex or any distinctions, economic or social; by suggesting educational methods best suited to prepare the children of the world for the responsibilities of freedom;

c. maintain, increase and diffuse knowledge; by assuring the conservation and protection of the world's inheritance of books, works of art and monuments of history and science, and recommending to the nations concerned the necessary international conventions; by encouraging cooperation among the nations in all branches of intellectual activity, including the international exchange of persons active in the fields of education, science and culture and the exchange of publications, objects of artistic and scientific interest and other materials of information; by initiating methods of international cooperation calculated to give the people of all countries access to the printed and published materials produced by any of them.

3. With a view to preserving the independence, integrity and fruitful diversity of the cultures and educational systems of the States Members of this Organization, the Organization is prohibited from intervening in matters which are essentially within their domestic jurisdiction.

In carrying out these purposes and functions, UNESCO has, among many other things, stimulated the exchange of students, teachers, and technical experts; encouraged studies of various national cultures and ideals; promoted research on the causes of international tension; facilitated the exchange of books, music, films, and other works of art representative of various cultures; sponsored seminars to stimulate the voluntary elimination of nationalistic bias and prejudice from history and other textbooks of different countries. It has also aided several countries in postwar educational expansion and in strengthening their programs of fundamental education in the basic fields of literacy, health, sanitation, and community development.

In view of the fact that there are more than 1 billion adult illiterates in the world, and that more than half the world's children have no schools, the significance of UNESCO's work can be readily appreciated. UNESCO's annual budget at present is only about 10 million dollars, yet it has already made an important start in developing greater understanding and knowledge among the peoples of the world. If its budget and program could be multiplied one hundred times (a 1-billion dollar budget, for example, instead of 10 million dollars) a real dent might be made in the problem of ignorance, prejudice, and suspicion. The cause of international peace would thereby, according to this view, be immeasurably strengthened.[26]

2. UNDERSTANDING THE CONFLICTS OF POWER AND INTEREST AMONG NATION-STATES

(The underlying premises of UNESCO have been vigorously criticized by Professor Hans J. Morgenthau of the University of Chicago. Although he is not opposed to the dissemination and improvement of culture and education as ends in themselves, Professor Morgenthau does not believe that these activities deal with the most important factors in international affairs. In his judgment, the most important factors relate to the struggle for power. He emphasizes the primacy of power in these words: [27])

International politics, like all politics, is a struggle for power. Whatever the ultimate aims of international politics, power is always the immediate aim. Statesmen and peoples may ultimately seek freedom, security, prosperity, or power itself. They may define their goals in terms of religious, philosophic, economic, or social ideal. They may hope that this ideal will materialize through its own inner force, through divine intervention, or through the natural development of human affairs. They may also try to further its realization through nonpolitical means, such as technical co-operation with other nations or international organizations. But whenever they strive to realize their goals by means of international politics, they do so by striving for power.

It is naïve and dangerous, according to Professor Morgenthau, to assume that in dealing with international problems we will not ultimately

[26] For further details regarding the operation of UNESCO, see UNESCO in Brief (Paris, UNESCO, 1956); Brenda M. H. Tripp, "UNESCO in Perspective," International Conciliation, March, 1954. Current activities are reported in UNESCO Courier, a monthly periodical published by UNESCO.

[27] Reprinted from Politics Among Nations, 2nd ed., by Hans J. Morgenthau, by permission of Alfred A. Knopf, Inc., copyright 1954 by Alfred A. Knopf, Inc., p. 25.

have to come to grips with the awkward but very real conflicts of interest between nation-states—with their rivalry for control of strategic territories, trade routes, or sources of raw materials. To assert that men have a choice between international power politics, on the one hand, and a different, better kind of international relations, on the other, is to promulgate a serious misconception of the world as it actually exists. UNESCO, unfortunately, contributes to the misconception by suggesting that the key to international peace lies in the development of greater mutual understanding between peoples.

UNESCO's Erroneous Assumptions [28]

The philosophy of UNESCO starts with the assumption that education (especially when it aims at international understanding), cultural interchange, and in general all activities that tend to increase contacts among members of different nations and to make them understand each other are factors in the creation of an international community and in the maintenance of peace. Implicit in this assumption is the supposition that nations are nationalistic and go to war with each other because they do not know each other well enough and because they operate on different levels of education and culture. Both assumptions are erroneous.

Cultural Development and Peace

There are primitive peoples, completely lacking in institutionalized education, who are generally peace-loving and receptive to the influence of foreign cultures to the point of suicide. There are other peoples, highly educated and steeped in classical culture, such as the Germans, who are generally nationalistic and warlike. The Athenians under Pericles and the Italians of the Renaissance created cultures not equalled in the history of Western civilization, and both were at least as nationalistic and warlike in that period of their history as at any time before or after.

Furthermore, in the history of some nations, such as the British and the French, periods of nationalistic exclusiveness and warlike policies alternate with cosmopolitan and peaceful ones, and no correlation exists between these changes and the development of education and culture. The Chinese people have a tradition of respect for learning superior to that of any other people, and they can look back upon a history of cultural attainments longer than any other and at least as creative. These high qualities of education and culture have made the Chinese look with contempt on the profession of the soldier as well as upon the members of all other nations, which at the beginning of the nineteenth century were still regarded as barbarian vassals of the Chinese emperor. Yet all this has not made the Chinese people less nationalistic and more peaceful. Russian education in our time has reached a higher level of achievement than ever before, especially in the fields of literacy and technical education. Its excellence has had no influence upon the receptiveness of the Russian people to foreign ideas nor upon the foreign policies of the Russian government. . . .

These examples taken at random show that the quantity and quality of

[28] Reprinted from *Politics Among Nations*, 2nd ed., by Hans J. Morgenthau, by permission of Alfred A. Knopf, Inc., copyright 1954 by Alfred A. Knopf, Inc., pp. 488–491.

education and culture as such is obviously irrelevant to the issue of a world community. That issue hinges not upon knowledge and upon the creation and appreciation of cultural values, but upon a moral and political transformation of unprecedented dimensions.

Cultural Unity and Peace

What has been said of education and culture as such holds true also of educational and cultural activities aiming at the interchange of the products of different national cultures. The existence of a multitude of interpersonal relations transcending national boundaries is no answer to our problem. More particularly, the existence of intellectual and esthetic ties across national boundaries proves nothing in favor of a world community. A world community with political potentialities is a community of moral standards and political action, not of intellect and sentiments. That an intellectual elite in the United States enjoys Russian music and literature and that Shakespeare has not been banned from the Russian state has no relevance at all for the problem with which we are concerned. This sharing of the same intellectual and esthetic experiences by members of different nations does not create a society, for it does not create morally and politically relevant actions on the part of the members of different nations with respect to each other which they would not have undertaken had they not shared in those experiences.

It should be remembered that on a much higher plane than the intellectual and the esthetic, and with the objective of clearly defined action, most members of most politically active nations have shared the same experiences for more than a thousand years. They have prayed to the same God, have held the same fundamental religious beliefs, have been bound by the same moral laws, and have had the same ritual symbols in common. That community of religious experiences, much more intimately related to the whole personality of the individual and to his actions than anything that supranational intellectual and esthetic experiences have to offer, has been able to create an international community of sorts, but not an international community sufficiently integrated to make a world state possible. How, then, can we expect that the melodies of Tchaikovsky, the profundities of Dostoevski, the insights of *The Federalist*, and the imagery of *Moby Dick*, which might be shared by all Americans and Russians alike, could create not only a fleeting community of feeling but a community of moral valuations and political actions overthrowing old loyalties and establishing new ones?

To that question history has given an unmistakable answer. Cultural unity, much closer than anything UNESCO can plan and achieve, has coexisted with war in all periods of history. We are not speaking here of civil wars, which by definition are fought by members of the same national culture. The wars among the Greek city-states, the European wars of the Middle Ages, the Italian wars of the Renaissance, the religious wars of the sixteenth and seventeenth centuries, even the wars of the eighteenth century in so far as the elite was concerned, were fought within the framework of a homogeneous culture. These cultures had all the essentials in common: language, religion, education, literature, art. Yet these cultures did not create a community, coextensive with themselves, that could have kept disruptive tendencies in check and channeled them into peaceful outlets. How, then, can one expect that such a community will be created through interchange among cultures, so diverse in all the respects in which those historic ones were homogeneous?

International Understanding and Peace

It is in the third purpose of UNESCO, international understanding, that the basic fallacy of UNESCO's conception of international affairs comes to the fore. International conflicts, it is believed, are the result of an intellectual deficiency, of ignorance and lack of judgment as to the qualities of other peoples. If Americans could only come to understand the Russians, and vice versa, they would realize how much they are alike, how much they have in common, and how little they have to fight about. The argument is fallacious on two counts.

Individual experience, which anybody can duplicate at will, shows that increased friendship is not necessarily a concomitant of increased understanding. There are, of course, numerous instances in which A has misunderstood the character and the motive of B and in which clarification of the facts will remove the source of conflict. Such is not the case when A and B are engaged in a conflict in which their vital interests are at stake. A does not fight B for economic advantage because he misunderstands the intentions of B; it is rather because he understands them only too well. Many an American GI went to France full of sentimental friendship for the French people whom he did not know. His friendly feelings did not survive the shock of understanding. The similar experiences of many friendly visitors to Russia are too typical to need elaboration.

Among those who from the beginning were most firmly opposed to the foreign objectives of the Nazi regime, even at the risk of war, were some who had a profound understanding of German culture. It was exactly that understanding that made them implacable enemies of the Nazi regime. Similarly, the students of Russian history and culture, those who really understand Russia and the Russians, have as a rule been equally unaffected by the pro- and anti-Russian hysteria. They have known the traditional objectives of Russian expansionism as well as the traditional methods of Russian diplomacy. If their understanding had had an influence upon the conduct of foreign affairs in the Western democracies, that conduct would certainly have been more intelligent and successful than it actually was. Whether or not such understanding would have made for better relations with the Soviet Union is an open question. An intelligent and successful foreign policy depends upon the Americans' and the Russians' understanding what both nations are and want. Peace between the United States and the Soviet Union depends in the last analysis upon whether what one of them is and wants is compatible with what the other one is and wants.

This observation points up the other fallacy in UNESCO's conception of international affairs. In the conception that international conflicts can be eliminated through international understanding, there is implicit the assumption that the issues of international conflicts, born as they are of misunderstandings, are but imaginary and that actually no issue worth fighting about stands between nation and nation. Nothing could be farther from the truth. All the great wars that decided the course of history and changed the political face of the earth were fought for real stakes, not for imaginary ones. The issue in those great convulsions was invariably: Who shall rule and who shall be ruled? Who shall be free and who, slave?

Was misunderstanding at the root of the issue between the Greeks and the Persians, between the Athenians and the Macedonians, between the Jews and the Romans, between emperor and pope, between the English and the French in the late Middle Ages, between the Turks and the Austrians, between Napoleon and Europe, between Hitler and the world? Was misunderstanding of the other side's culture, character, and intentions the issue, so that those wars were fought over no real issue at all? Or could it not rather be maintained that in many of these conflicts it was exactly the misunderstanding of the would-be conqueror's culture, character, and intentions that preserved peace for a while, whereas the understanding of these factors made war inevitable? So long as the Athenians refused to heed the warnings of Demosthenes, the threat of war remained remote. It was only when, too late for their salvation, they understood the nature of the Macedonian Empire and of its policies that war became inevitable. That correlation between understanding and the inevitability of conflict is one of the melancholy lessons history conveys to posterity: the more thoroughly one understands the other side's position, character, and intentions, the more inevitable the conflict often appears to be.

Irrespective of its great intrinsic merits, the program of UNESCO is irrelevant to the problem of the world community because its diagnosis of the bars to a world community so completely misses the point. The problem of the world community is a moral and political and not an intellectual and esthetic one. The world community is a community of moral judgments and political actions, not of intellectual endowments and esthetic appreciation. Let us suppose that American and Russian education and culture could be brought to the same level of excellence or completely amalgamated, and that the Russians would take to Mark Twain as Americans could take to Gogol. If that were the case, the problem of who shall control Central Europe would still stand between the United States and the Soviet Union as it does today. So long as men continue to judge and act in accordance with national rather than supranational standards and loyalties, the world community remains a postulate that still awaits its realization.

3. Understanding the Relationship Between Morality and Power

(The following position is drawn from the writings of Professor Reinhold Niebuhr of Union Theological Seminary. According to Professor Niebuhr, a distinction must be made between the personal morality of individuals and the collective morality of social groups. An individual may observe very high standards of morality in his personal life, but social groups seem incapable of achieving similarly high levels of conduct. Nation-states, which are very complex social groups, cannot, in Niebuhr's opinion, approach the moral and ethical standards that may characterize the behavior of individuals. Since nations often resort to power to advance their interests, power has to be used by other nations to assure some semblance of order and stability.

Professor Niebuhr is consequently very critical of those who feel that international peace and justice depend primarily on the extension of morality, reason, and education. However, as a theologian, he also warns against the dangers of extreme cynicism and egoism which are often associated with the pursuit of power. Finding a balanced relationship between the claims of morality and power is therefore advanced as the most important factor in dealing with world affairs.

Professor Niebuhr presents his argument in the following words: [29])

The thesis to be elaborated in these pages is that a sharp distinction must be drawn between the moral and social behavior of individuals and of social groups, national, racial, and economic; and that this distinction justifies and necessitates political policies which a purely individualistic ethic must always find embarrassing. The title "Moral Man and Immoral Society" suggests the intended distinction too unqualifiedly, but it is nevertheless a fair indication of the argument to which the following pages are devoted. Individual men may be moral in the sense that they are able to consider interests other than their own in determining problems of conduct, and are capable, on occasion, of preferring the advantages of others to their own. . . . But all these achievements are more difficult, if not impossible, for human societies and social groups. In every human group there is less reason to guide and to check impulse, less capacity for self-transcendence, less ability to comprehend the needs of others and therefore more unrestrained egoism than the individuals, who compose the group, reveal in their personal relationships. . . .

Inasfar as this treatise has a polemic interest it is directed against the moralists, both religious and secular, who imagine that the egoism of individuals is being progressively checked by the development of rationality or the growth of a religiously inspired goodwill and that nothing but the continuance of this process is necessary to establish social harmony between all the human societies and collectives. Social analyses and prophecies made by moralists, sociologists and educators upon the basis of these assumptions lead to a very considerable moral and political confusion in our day. They completely disregard the political necessities in the struggle for justice in human society by failing to recognize those elements in man's collective behavior which belong to the order of nature and can never be brought completely under the dominion of reason or conscience. They do not recognize that when collective power, whether in the form of imperialism or class domination, exploits weakness, it can never be dislodged unless power is raised against it. If conscience and reason can be insinuated into the resulting struggle they can only qualify but not abolish it.

The most persistent error of modern educators and moralists is the assumption that our social difficulties are due to the failure of the social sciences to keep pace with the physical sciences which have created our technological civilisation. The invariable implication of this assumption is that, with a little more time, a little more adequate moral and social pedagogy and a generally higher development of human intelligence, our social problems will approach solution. . . .

What is lacking among all these moralists, whether religious or rational, is an understanding of the brutal character of the behavior of all human collectives, and the power of self-interest and collective egoism in all intergroup relations. Failure to recognize the stubborn resistance of group egoism to all moral and inclusive social objectives inevitably involves them in unrealistic and confused political thought. They regard social conflict either as an impossible

[29] From *Moral Man and Immoral Society*, by Reinhold Niebuhr, copyright 1932 by Charles Scribner's Sons, reprinted by permission of the publishers, pp. xi–xiii, xx, xxii–xxiv, and 20–22.

method of achieving morally approved ends or as a momentary expedient which a more perfect education or a purer religion will make unnecessary. They do not see that the limitations of the human imagination, the easy subservience of reason to prejudice and passion, and the consequent persistence of irrational egoism, particularly in group behavior, make social conflict an inevitability in human history, probably to its very end. . . .

Teachers of morals who do not see the difference between the problem of charity within the limits of an accepted social system and the problem of justice between economic groups, holding uneven power within modern industrial society, have simply not faced the most obvious differences between the morals of groups and those of individuals. The suggestion that the fight against disease is in the same category with the fight against war reveals the same confusion. Our contemporary culture fails to realise the power, extent and persistence of group egoism in human relations. It may be possible, though it is never easy, to establish just relations between individuals within a group purely by moral and rational suasion and accommodation. In inter-group relations this is practically an impossibility. The relations between groups must therefore always be predominately political rather than ethical, that is, they will be determined by the proportion of power which each group possesses at least as much as by any rational and moral appraisal of the comparative needs and claims of each group. The coercive factors, in distinction to the more purely moral and rational factors, in political relations can never be sharply differentiated and defined. It is not possible to estimate exactly how much a party to a social conflict is influenced by a rational argument or by the threat of force. . . .

Whatever increase in social intelligence and moral goodwill may be achieved in human history, may serve to mitigate the brutalities of social conflict, but they cannot abolish the conflict itself. That could be accomplished only if human groups, whether racial, national or economic, could achieve a degree of reason and sympathy which would permit them to see and to understand the interests of others as vividly as they understand their own, and a moral goodwill which would prompt them to affirm the rights of others as vigorously as they affirm their own. Given the inevitable limitations of human nature and the limits of the human imagination and intelligence, this is an ideal which individuals may approximate but which is beyond the capacities of human societies. Educators who emphasize the pliability of human nature, social and psychological scientists who dream of "socialising" man, and religious idealists who strive to increase the sense of moral responsibility, can serve a very useful function in society in humanising individuals within an established social system and in purging the relations of individuals of as much egoism as possible. In dealing with the problems and necessities of radical social change they are almost invariably confusing in their counsels because they are not conscious of the limitations in human nature which finally frustrate their efforts. . . .

The fact that the coercive factor in society is both necessary and dangerous seriously complicates the whole task of securing both peace and justice. History is a long tale of abortive efforts toward the desired end of social cohesion and justice in which failure was usually due either to the effort to eliminate the factor of force entirely or to an undue reliance upon it. Complete reliance upon it means that new tyrants usurp the places of eminence from which more traditional monarchs are cast down. Tolstoian pacifists and other advocates of non-resistance, noting the evils which force introduces into society, give themselves to the vain illusion that it can be completely eliminated, and society organised upon the basis of anarchistic principles. Their conviction is an illusion, because there are definite limits of moral goodwill and social intelligence beyond which even the most vital religion and the most astute educational programme will not carry a social group, whatever may be possible for individuals in an intimate society. The problem which society faces is clearly one of reducing force by increasing the factors which make for a moral and rational adjustment of life to life; of bringing such force as is still necessary under responsibility of the whole of society; of destroying the kind of power which cannot be made socially responsible . . . ; and of bringing forces of moral self-restraint to bear upon types of power which can never be brought completely under social control. Every one of these methods has its definite limitations. Society will probably never be sufficiently intelligent to bring all power under its control. The stupidity of the average man will permit the oligarch, whether economic or political, to hide his real purposes from the scrutiny of his fellows and to withdraw his activities from effective control. Since it is impossible to count on enough moral goodwill among those who possess irresponsible power to sacrifice it for the good of the whole, it must be destroyed by coercive methods and these will always run the peril of introducing new forms of injustice in place of those abolished. . . .

The future peace and justice of society therefore depend upon, not one but many, social strategies, in all of which moral and coercive factors are compounded in varying degrees. So difficult is it to avoid the Scylla of despotism and the Charybdis of anarchy that it is safe to hazard the prophecy that the dream of perpetual peace and brotherhood for human society is one which will never be fully realised. It is a vision prompted by the conscience and insight of individual man, but incapable of fulfillment by collective man. It is like all true religious visions, possible of approximation but not of realisation in actual history.

Regarding the establishment of international peace and a world community, Niebuhr says: [30]

All these difficulties are sufficiently apparent to prompt the emergence of realistical as well as idealistic interpretations of the global task which faces our age. While America has produced more idealistic plans for world order than realistic ones, the realistic approach has also been attempted in both Britain and America. It is indicative of the spiritual problem of mankind that these realistic approaches are often as close to the abyss of cynicism as the idealistic approaches are to the fog of sentimentality.

The realistic school of international thought believes that world politics cannot rise higher than the balance-of-power principle. The balance-of-power theory of world politics, seeing no possibility of a genuine unity of the nations, seeks to construct the most adequate possible mechanism for equilibrating power on a world scale. Such a policy, which holds all factors in the world situation in the most perfect possible equipoise, can undoubtedly mitigate anarchy. A balance of power is in fact a kind of managed anarchy. But it is a system in which anarchy invariably overcomes the management in the end. Despite its defects, the policy of the balance of power is not as iniquitous as idealists would have us believe. For even the most perfectly organized society must seek for a decent equilibrium of the vitalities and forces under its organiza-

[30] From *The Children of Light and the Children of Darkness*, by Reinhold Niebuhr, copyright 1944 by Charles Scribner's Sons, reprinted by permission of the publishers, pp. 173–176 and 186.

tion. If this is not done, strong disproportions of power develop; and wherever power is inordinate, injustice results. But an equilibrium of power without the organizing and equilibrating force of government, is potential anarchy which becomes actual anarchy in the long run.

The balance-of-power system may, despite its defects, become the actual consequence of present policies. The peace of the world may be maintained perilously and tentatively, for some decades, by an uneasy equilibrium between the . . . great powers. . . .

While a balance between the great powers may be the actual consequence of present policies, it is quite easy to foreshadow the doom of such a system. No participant in a balance is ever quite satisfied with its own position. Every center of power will seek to improve its position: and every such effort will be regarded by the others as an attempt to disturb the equilibrium. There is sufficient mistrust between the great nations, even while they are still locked in the intimate embrace of a great common effort, to make it quite certain that a mere equilibrium beween them will not suffice to preserve the peace.

Thus a purely realistic approach to the problem of world community offers as little hope of escape from anarchy as a purely idealistic one. Clearly it has become necessary for the children of light to borrow some of the wisdom of the children of darkness; and yet be careful not to borrow too much. Pure idealists underestimate the perennial power of particular and parochial loyalties, operating as a counter force against the achievement of a wider community. But the realists are usually so impressed by the power of these perennial forces that they fail to recognize the novel and unique elements in a revolutionary world situation. . . .

A view more sober than that of either idealists or realists must persuade us that,

> "If hopes are dupes,
> Fears may be liars." . . .

The field of politics is not helpfully tilled by pure moralists; and the realm of international politics is particularly filled with complexities which do not yield to the approach of a too simple idealism. On the other hand the moral cynicism and defeatism which easily results from a clear-eyed view of the realities of international politics is even more harmful. The world community must be built by men and nations sufficiently mature and robust to understand that political justice is achieved, not merely by destroying, but also by deflecting, beguiling and harnessing residual self-interest and by finding the greatest possible concurrence between self-interest and the general welfare. They must also be humble enough to understand that the forces of self-interest to be deflected are not always those of the opponent or competitor. They are frequently those of the self, individual or collective, including the interests of the idealist who erroneously imagines himself above the battle.

Professor Niebuhr continues on the question of idealists and realists: [31]

The idealists naturally believe that we could escape the dilemma if we made sufficiently strenuous rational and moral efforts. . . . [However] all the arguments of the idealists finally rest upon a logic which derives the possibility of an achievement from its necessity. . . .

The realists on the other hand are inclined to argue that a good cause will hallow any weapon. They are convinced that the evils of communism are so great that we are justified in using any weapon against them. Thereby they closely approach the communist ruthlessness. The inadequacy of both types of escape from our moral dilemma proves that there is no purely moral solution for the ultimate moral issues of life; but neither is there a viable solution which disregards the moral factors. Men and nations must use their power with the purpose of making it an instrument of justice and a servant of interests broader than their own. Yet they must be ready to use it though they become aware that the power of a particular nation or individual, even when under strong religious and social sanctions, is never so used that there is a perfect coincidence between the value which justifies it and the interest of the wielder of it.

We cannot expect even the wisest of nations to escape every peril of moral and spiritual complacency; for nations have always been constitutionally self-righteous. But it will make a difference whether the culture in which the policies of nations are formed is only as deep and as high as the nation's highest ideals; or whether there is a dimension in the culture from the standpoint of which the element of vanity in all human ambitions and achievements is discerned. But this is a height which can be grasped only by faith; for everything that is related in terms of simple rational coherence with the ideals of a culture or a nation will prove in the end to be a simple justification of its most cherished values. The God before whom "the nations are as a drop in the bucket and are counted as small dust in the balances" is known by faith and not by reason. The realm of mystery and meaning which encloses and finally makes sense out of the baffling configurations of history is not identical with any scheme of rational intelligibility. The faith which appropriates the meaning in the mystery inevitably involves an experience of repentance for the false meanings which the pride of nations and cultures introduces into the pattern. Such repentance is the true source of charity; and we are more desperately in need of genuine charity than of more technocratic skills.

QUESTIONS

1. Do you regard the present world crisis primarily as a struggle between competing ideologies or as a conflict between rival nation-states with ideology only a secondary factor? Cite specific examples from the current news to support your conclusions.

2. To what extent can or should religious idealism be a major guide in the formulation of a government's foreign policy?

3. Select two or three articles from current newspapers or periodicals which seem to you to reflect the approach of critical scholarship. Select two or three not written from this vantage point.

4. Read again President Eisenhower's statement on page 60. Do you think that national emotions and fears inculcated from childhood lead nations to fight for "seemingly worthless territory" or "apparently meaningless" boundaries? Can you cite examples to support your opinion?

5. Which adjectives would you choose to describe the people of the Soviet Union, Great Britain, France, West Germany, Japan, and the United States (see pages 57–58)?

6. What is your own definition of the nature of peace?

7. Compare the relative power positions of the United States and the Soviet Union in terms of the various elements of national power that the two countries possess.

8. How might a supporter of UNESCO answer Professor Morgenthau's criticisms of the UNESCO approach to international peace?

9. Do you agree or disagree with Professor Niebuhr that the "realist" view of international affairs is often too cynical, and that the "idealist" or "moralist" view is apt to be too optimistic or naïve? Why?

10. From what you have read thus far, would you say that there is a key outlook on world affairs?

SELECT BIBLIOGRAPHY

BERNARD, L. L., *War and Its Causes* (New York, Holt, 1944). A sociologist's analysis of war as a special institution and of its causes.

CARR, Edward H., *The Twenty Years' Crisis, 1919–1939* (London, Macmillan, New York, St. Martin's, 1949). A stimulating analysis by a British scholar of the basic issues behind the crisis of the period between World Wars I and II. Attempts to assay the appropriate roles of power and morality in international relations.

COOK, Thomas I., and Moos, Malcolm, *Power through Purpose* (Baltimore, Johns Hopkins Press, 1954). A vigorous criticism of Morgenthau's concept of the national interest and of efforts to conduct American foreign policy on the basis of expediency rather than of principle. Authors contend that American power in world affairs is best developed by vigorously prosecuting the principles of democratic freedom throughout the world, rather than by making expedient arrangements with undemocratic governments which may compromise our basic principles of freedom.

DUNN, Frederick S., *War and the Minds of Men* (New York, Harper, 1950). A study of the basic premises of UNESCO by a professor of international relations at Yale and Princeton. Explores the possibilities of influencing political behavior and minimizing the danger of war by altering men's attitudes toward one another.

FOSDICK, Dorothy, *Common Sense and World Affairs* (New York, Harcourt Brace, 1955). An extremely readable book, designed to give the layman something of the "feel for foreign policy" and the "knack for judging things." The author worked for several years in the top offices of the U.S. Dept. of State, and therefore writes from extensive personal experience. Can be read profitably alongside the present book.

KLINEBERG, Otto, *Tensions Affecting International Understanding* (New York, Social Science Research Council, 1950). A social psychologist analyzes the factors of human behavior that contribute to tensions and misunderstanding between nations. Prepared at request of UNESCO.

MORGENTHAU, Hans, *In Defense of the National Interest* (New York, Knopf, 1951). A thought-provoking argument that American foreign policy, particularly in recent years, has often tended to "crusade" on behalf of ideological and moral principles, rather than to base itself on a realistic and honest appraisal of American national-security interests.

PADELFORD, Norman J., and LINCOLN, George A., *International Politics* (New York, Macmillan, 1954). An excellent survey of the basic factors in international relations.

SPROUT, Harold, and SPROUT, Margaret, *Foundations of National Power*, 2nd ed. (New York, Van Nostrand, 1951). Stimulating readings from a wide variety of sources dealing with the basic factors in international politics and the international struggle for power. Several chapters deal with the politics of major regions of the world and the foreign policies of each of the principal world powers. Reference to even a few of these readings will prove rewarding.

WRIGHT, Quincy, *A Study of War* (Chicago, University of Chicago Press, 1942), 2 vols. A monumental study of the nature and causes of war throughout human history. Volume II deals especially with the causes of war and the problem of controlling and preventing it.

Part II

FACTUAL and FICTIONAL
SOURCES of TENSION

THE PROBLEM
AND ITS BACKGROUND

MAN: "THE UNKNOWN"

The contemporary world crisis has been surveyed on a broad, exploratory plane in Part I of this book. Now, in Parts II and III, more specific and detailed consideration will be devoted to a selected number of possible roots of the crisis.

First, what is the "nature" of the creature Linnaeus classified as Homo sapiens? Since the dawn of history, man has hated and loved, warred on his neighbor and then sent him bread. He has devised horrible deaths and developed life-saving drugs. Is man a sinner or a saint? How valid is the argument that the contemporary crisis in world affairs stems directly from man himself—man the soulless, man the godless, man the materialist, man the brute? Is a free, peaceful, and creative world impossible until man returns to God and recovers his soul?

Or is man basically good but the victim of a corrupt and evil society? If we remove the evils in society, will man's noble qualities shine forth, lighting the way to an epoch of perpetual peace and progress?

Just what kind of a being is man? What is known, or unknown, about the factors that influence his behavior? Specifically, do these motivating influences tend to make human warfare inevitable?

According to Winston Churchill: [1]

[1] Winston Churchill, from a speech in the House of Commons, March 28, 1950.

Man in this moment of history has emerged in greater supremacy over the forces of nature than has ever been dreamed of before. He has it in his power to solve quite easily the problems of material existence. He has conquered the insects and the microbes. There lies before him, if he wishes, a golden age of peace and progress. All is in his hands. He has only to conquer his last and worst enemy—himself. With vision, faith and courage, it may still be within our power to win a crowning victory for all.

Is this "crowning victory for all" really within man's reach? After all, has not man been the object of scientific inquiry of biologists, philosophers, political scientists, psychologists, sociologists, and economists since, and even before, the time of Greek civilization? Why have these inquiries not been more productive in bringing about man's victory over himself? Do modern instances of man's inhumanity to man suggest the presence of irresistible forces in man's nature which drive him toward self-destruction? This is the query to be considered in this chapter.

Human Nature Defined

There are several interpretations of the term *human nature*. To some, human nature refers specifically to the innate biological characteristics of man, such as the number of toes and fingers or the number of sexes. Others also include the learned attributes that man acquires from the particular society of which he is a part. The second and more inclusive interpretation has been adopted in this book. Briefly, then, *human nature*, as referred to here, consists of both the inherited and the environmental influences on man's make-up. In this context, the argument that "human nature cannot be changed" is only a partial truth, for, though genetic or biological characteristics are, normally, extremely stable, man's learned or acquired behavior can be altered relatively easily. Man's dynamic character, as reflected in the changes occurring in human nature in response to varying environmental conditions, has often been observed.

Hadley Cantril writes: [2]

"Human nature," then, is anything but static and unchangeable. It can and does change with conditions. In fact, it is always changing. And not only is there gradual change, but frequently there is the sudden emergence of new qualities and characteristics formed when a single individual or group of individuals find themselves in a new set of conditions.

It is possible to examine man from a number of perspectives: that of biology, sociology, psychology, philosophy, religion, political science, economics, to mention a few. In this chapter, main attention will be paid to the first four. Those of political science and economics are developed in later chapters.

[2] Hadley Cantril, "Don't Blame It on Human Nature," *New York Times,* magazine section, July 6, 1947, p. 32.

VARIOUS PERSPECTIVES OF MAN

"Biological and Physiological" Man

To the biologist, man is the product of millions of years of evolution. He is one of many animal species which have emerged in this evolutionary process. The biological classification places man in the mammal class, the highest category in the vertebrate group. Anatomically, man stands at the top of mammals in the primate series, which includes such nonhuman animals as apes, monkeys, marmosets, and lemurs.

Similarities between man and other animals. Homo sapiens shows rather close physiological similarities to other primates, especially anthropoid apes, in blood chemistry and in the structure of the skeleton, teeth, and sex organs. Despite these similarities, biologists are certain that man did not descend from the anthropoid ape existing today. Over a million years ago, during the branch-swinging era, the anthropoid and human lines divided, the biologists claim. Ancestors of the anthropoids stayed in the trees; those of Homo sapiens took to the ground. In the biological classification, then, the anthropoid ape is not the ancestor but merely a cousin of man.

Several behavioral characteristics of apes indicate the rather close relationship to humans. For instance, the ape, like man, may breed at any time; anthropoids are capable of making a variety of facial movements to express emotions; they have been found to have family life and to care for their offspring; and they have shown evidence of working and playing co-operatively. More important than the similarities, however, are the unique characteristics of man, attributes that have enabled him to rise above other animals.

Man's uniqueness among animals. In a physical sense, an important difference between man and other primates is the size and complexity of the brain and central nervous system. In relation to body weight, the brain of a human is three to four times as large as the "gray matter" of an ape. The larger and more highly organized brain has provided an opportunity for man to develop a mental capacity far beyond that of other vertebrates.

A second physiological characteristic that distinguishes Homo sapiens from other high-order vertebrates is upright posture. A few other mammals can assume an upright posture temporarily, but man alone habitually carries himself upright. Biologists assert that man's unique posture can be traced directly to his terrestrial environment, for only a land animal could acquire a completely erect posture. More important, the upright posture freed the arms and hands as locomotor limbs and permitted their conversion to manipulative appendages.

Longevity is another biological characteristic unique to man. Although the life expectancy of humans varies significantly around the globe, under favorable conditions man's life span averages considerably longer than five decades. Few other animals can claim a longer span.

The most distinctive attribute of man, however, is his capacity for conceptual thought. Man's capacity for articulate speech—having words for objects and using these words as tools—has had a most significant effect upon his development. Commenting upon the contribution of speech to man's progress, Julian Huxley writes: [3]

> This basic human property has had many consequences. The most important was the development of a cumulative tradition. The beginnings of tradition, by which experience is transmitted from one generation to the next, are to be seen in many higher animals. But in no case is the tradition cumulative. Off-spring learn from parents, but they learn the same kind and quantity of lessons as they, in turn, impart: the transmission of experience never bridges more than one generation. In man, however, tradition is an independent and potentially permanent activity, capable of indefinite improvement in quality and increase in quantity.

This ability to transmit cumulative experience from generation to generation, to bridge generations, has enabled man to become a "time-binder," in the language of Raymond Pearl. The telescoping of the past into the present through the spoken and written word has probably been man's most significant achievement. Each generation begins where the former generation ended, without having to discover for itself everything accumulated in previous generations.

From these four physiological attributes—complex brain and nervous system, upright posture, longevity, and conceptual thought—man has been able to develop three abilities, which in other animals are either completely absent or only rudimentarily developed. First, articulate speech permitted development of a language, by which man could communicate knowledge and ideas to his fellow man. Second, the larger and more complex brain has been at least partly responsible for man's superiority in thinking and reasoning. Achieving their highest development in man, they enable him to interpret his environment and to alter his behavior in subsequent, similar environmental circumstances if he desires. The skillful use of tools is the third great ability unique to man, which emerged and developed from the freeing of the forefeet as locomotor limbs in man's upright posture. Man's pre-eminence in the use of tools is related also to the other abilities, communication and reason. In brief, then, man's control of himself and his environment, his ability to transcend nature, stems directly from the unique development of these three abilities.

Biologists have been able to isolate another fateful characteristic that separates man from other nonhuman animals. Man is the only member of

[3] Julian Huxley, *Man in the Modern World* (New York, Mentor Books, 1948), pp. 8–9.

the primate series who engages in war. In fact, only one other species, the harvester ant, among the whole animal kingdom, wages war. By war is meant organized physical conflict among groups of the same species. Disputes between individuals of the same species do not constitute war. Nor does war include organized conflict between groups of two different species, such as man's "war" against the European cornborer or the fox's "war" on hares. War is a specific kind of conflict involving: (1) physically violent methods, (2) organized, not individual, efforts, and (3) groups of the same species.

The foregoing has demonstrated how man differs biologically from non-human animals. The differences are the same for all men, yet all men are not alike in all respects. What is the nature of the differences among men? How important are they in international relations?

Diversities among mankind. When physical or social scientists refer to the unity or oneness of mankind they do not imply that all men are biologically identical. That man differs from man is a truism. Men are different in terms of color of skin, hair, or eyes. Men have different forms or shapes of body, head, nose, and ears. What the scientists mean by the unity of mankind is that all men have probably originated from a single ancestral line. A group assembled by UNESCO from among the world's leading scientists, representing anthropology, biochemistry, biology, education, embryology, genetics, sociology, and psychology prepared a statement in 1950 setting forth their views regarding mankind's common heritage. The group reported: [4]

Scientists have reached general agreement in recognizing that mankind is one: that all men belong to the same species, Homo sapiens. It is further generally agreed among scientists that all men are probably derived from the same common stock; and that such differences as exist between different groups of mankind are due to the operation of evolutionary factors of differentiation. . . .

The scientists are thus reaffirming the Bible story of Adam and Eve in the sense that all Homo sapiens belong to the same family, with a common origin.

Despite the scientific evidence demonstrating the biological unity and commonality of mankind, 6 million people, principally Jews, were put to death during the 1940's because it was alleged that they were members of an inferior race. What bases exist for such an allegation? Is one race "better" than another? Just what does the term *race* mean, and what characteristics serve to classify men into different races?

Unfortunately, the term *race* has been too often misused. Race has been used to distinguish between national groups (such as American, French, Turk, Japanese), between religious groups (Christians, Jews, Moslems), between linguistic groups (English, Hindustanic, or Spanish-speaking).

[4] Ashley Montagu, *Statement on Race* (New York, copyright 1951 by Henry Schuman, Inc., reprinted with permission of Abelard-Schuman Limited), p. 21.

Not one goes to constitute a race of people. A race has been defined as "a sub-group of peoples possessing a definite combination of physical characters, of genetic origin." [5] Thus, race is a classification determined by characteristics or traits that are hereditary. Much of the inaccuracy stems from a confusion of hereditary traits with socially or culturally acquired traits. The anatomy of our ancestors determines our racial traits, such as skin color, body stature, head form, color and form of eyes, and color and form of hair. Acquired traits are determined, on the other hand, by the group or culture into which we are born. Acquired traits are products of learning, not of inheritance.

The attitude of a given group toward war, for instance, is not racially derived. National aggressiveness or national nonaggressiveness is a culturally determined, learned form of behavior. Thus nonaggressors at a given moment in history can become the aggressors of a later period. The race of this group has not changed; their behavior has. A careful review of the past 600 years' history reveals clearly that all major nations have had their periods of aggressive and nonaggressive behavior, and that this behavior has not been the result of factors peculiar to the people of any one race.

One of the most frequent excuses for conflict between so-called races is racial "superiority." One race, it is alleged by racists, is better in some respects than another race. In the modern era, Hitler proclaimed the supremacy of the Aryan "race" over non-Aryans (primarily Jews in Hitler's racial classification). Aside from other errors in the "Aryan-supremacy" thesis, neither ethnic group—Aryan or Jew—constitutes a race. Aryans are people who speak Indo-European languages. Jews are people who belong to the Jewish religion or share a common cultural heritage. As Hitler used the word *Aryan* (to refer to Nordics, Germans, to blond Europeans, or to persons who shared his political beliefs) the term had no meaning in either a racial or linguistic sense. "Aryan supremacy," which frequently manifested itself in anti-Semitism, was primarily Hitler's pretext for rallying and uniting the German people.

Claims of enhanced mental ability of a given race are frequently offered as a basis for racial superiority. This belief is widespread, according to the results of a survey conducted in the United States immediately before World War II. In the survey, respondents were asked: "Do you think Negroes now have generally higher intelligence than white people, lower, or about the same?" In every section of the country, the majority of persons interviewed regarded the Negro as inferior in intelligence. The figures for separate sections ranged from 60 to 77 per cent. Respondents who believed Negroes had lower intelligence than whites were then asked: "Do you think this is because: (1) they have lacked opportunities,

<hr>

[5] Wilton M. Krogman, "The Concept of Race," in *The Science of Man in the World Crisis*, Ralph Linton, ed. (New York, Columbia University Press, 1945), p. 49.

or (2) they are born less intelligent, or (3) both?" The figures for those who believed Negroes were born less intelligent ranged from 29 to 55 per cent among the different regions of the country. The proportions who thought inherited factors were either completely or partially responsible (that is, those who checked the second or third answer) totaled from 56 to 79 per cent among the different regions of the country.[6] How valid is this popular belief in the innate differences in mental abilities between races? Is it founded on scientific fact?

In measuring intelligence, scientists recognize that they are measuring innate ability *plus* the development of it through the experiences of the individual since birth. In other words, both inherited ability and environmental factors influence intelligence. Scientists have demonstrated this fact over and over. Among the most comprehensive studies aimed at measuring differences in intelligence between ethnic groups was that conducted among members of the American Expeditionary Force in World War I. A comparison of the intelligence of whites and Negroes showed that: (1) Negroes made a lower score on intelligence tests than whites, but that (2) white and Negro persons from the northern states made higher scores on intelligence tests than whites or Negroes from southern states. Scientists did not conclude from these results that whites were innately superior in mental ability to Negroes, nor did they conclude that Northerners (white and Negroes) were born more intelligent than Southerners. Such conclusions would have been untenable because the findings demonstrated also that northern Negroes achieved higher average scores on intelligence tests than did southern whites.

The scientists did conclude that the principal explanation for the differences stemmed from variations in educational background of the respondents. Before World War I, educational expenses per pupil among most southern states were only a fraction of the amounts expended per student in most northern states. Children in the North, white and black, had a better opportunity to develop their innate mental abilities than did the children of the South. This, the scientists concluded, was the crucial factor in explaining differences on intelligence tests. As Ruth Benedict and Gene Weltfish wrote, interpreting the results: [7]

The differences did not arise because people were from the North or the South, or because they were white or black, but because of differences in income, education, cultural advantages, and other opportunities.

The UNESCO group of scientists, cited previously, made the following statement regarding the relation between race and mental ability: [8]

[6] Otto Klineberg, "Racial Psychology," in *The Science of Man in the World Crisis, ibid.*, p. 63.

[7] Ruth Benedict and Gene Weltfish, *The Races of Mankind,* Public Affairs Pamphlet 85 (New York, Public Affairs Pamphlets, 1951), p. 18.

[8] Ashley Montagu, *op. cit.*, p. 119.

According to present knowledge there is no proof that the groups of mankind differ in their innate mental characteristics, whether in respect of intelligence or temperament. The scientific evidence indicates that the range of mental capacities in all ethnic groups is much the same.

With all the accumulated evidence, it would be presumed that the myth regarding differences in inherited mental abilities among races would have been demolished. That proclaimers of racial superiority still exist merely reflects a complete disregard of biological facts by those who seek an excuse for persecution or by those who attempt to protect the socioeconomic status quo. For valid explanations of tension and conflict between ethnic groups we must turn to sciences other than biology. The biologist, demonstrating the common biological heritage of all mankind, has thoroughly and effectively undermined the racist's argument that aggressiveness is racially derived.

"Sociological" Man

The sociologist views man as a member of a group or a society. Sociology, consequently, focuses on the origin and evolution of human groups, including the form, institutions, and functions of social groups.

Society and culture defined. Among the larger groups of humans studied by sociologists is a society which is defined by Elgin Hunt as "a group of people who have lived together long enough to get themselves organized and to think of themselves as a social unit." [9]

In simpler terms, Clyde Kluckhohn and William Kelly define society as "a group of people who have learned to work together." [10] Man, of course, is not the only social animal. The trait of living in groups is present among many subhuman animals, including ants, bees, and birds. Nevertheless, man is generally considered to be unique in a sociological sense, for he is the only creature who achieves and builds culture. The term *culture* has been adopted by social scientists to designate a way of life of a group of humans. Thus, distinguishing between the terms *society* and *culture*, M. J. Herskovits states: [11]

A culture is a way of life of a people, while a society is the organized aggregate of individuals who follow a given way of life. In simple terms a society is composed of people; the way they behave is their culture.

A more specific interpretation of culture is offered by Ralph Linton, who writes: [12]

---

[9] Elgin F. Hunt, *Social Science* (New York, Macmillan, 1955, reprinted with publisher's permission), p. 11.

[10] Clyde Kluckhohn and William H. Kelly, "The Concept of Culture," in *The Science of Man in the World Crisis, op. cit.,* p. 79.

[11] Melville J. Herskovits, *Man and His Works* (New York, Knopf, 1952), p. 29.

[12] Ralph Linton, "Present World Conditions in Cultural Perspective," in *The Science of Man in the World Crisis, op. cit.,* p. 203.

The culture of a society is the way of life of its members; the collection of ideas and habits which they learn, share, and transmit from generation to generation. Culture provides the members of each new generation with effective ready-made answers to most of the problems with which they are likely to be confronted.

Culture, a way of life, represents learned or acquired behavior and is distinct from the biological capacities of man. It is, however, related to man's biological needs or drives. The culture of a society reflects the ways by which biological needs are satisfied within a society. For instance, the need for food is of biological origin, but whether a society habitually eats one, two, three, or four meals a day is determined primarily by cultural forces. Likewise, other biological needs—clothing, shelter—are shared by all humans, yet the responses to these needs vary among societies. Human needs are, of course, not limited to the biological; "social" needs, as they are frequently called by sociologists and psychologists, influence human behavior in all societies and cultures. Education, family organization, system of political control, and methods of organizing economic activities are illustrative of social needs.

Universals of culture. Herskovits has labeled the biological and social needs common to all societies as the universals of culture. Economic system, kinship structure, political control, philosophy of life, and aesthetic satisfaction are cited by Herskovits as typical cultural universals.[13] Each society, for example, has devised methods for producing, distributing, and exchanging goods and services. Some economic systems are very simply organized. Methods of production are crude, and goods are produced primarily for the individual's own use. The distributive and exchange functions may be completely absent or may exist in very simplified forms, as in a barter economy. Other economic systems are highly organized. Specialization, mechanization, and automation characterize the productive process. A monetary system serves to facilitate exchange of goods and services, and a complex network of distributive agencies evolves to transport goods. Each type of system, however, whether simple or complex, facilitates the particular group need of getting a living.

Similarly, each society must provide some system of family organization and control. Monogamy is the most common pattern of family life, but polygamy (one husband and two or more wives) and polyandry (one wife and two or more husbands) are socially acceptable family patterns in certain cultures.

Each society, each group of people who have learned to work together, experiences a need for political control. No group is completely devoid of mechanisms to regulate affairs that relate to the whole society. Systems to meet this universal need vary from the anarchical, in which political control is extremely limited, to governmental systems in which the life

---

[13] *Op. cit.,* p. 19.

of the individual is almost completely regimented by the political body.

A society of humans likewise feels a need for explaining the nature of the world, and the place and role of man in the universe. Man, the world over, follows diverse patterns in attempting to satisfy the common need for establishing a relationship between himself and supernatural beings. Despite the differences in customs, man's religious devotions seek, as the primary objective, a favorable response to his petitions from supernatural beings.

The desire for aesthetic satisfaction in the various forms of art is another facet of culture which finds expression in all human groups. Similarly, language, which represents the "vehicle of culture" in the words of Herskovits, and a system of education are universals of culture.

Elgin Hunt would add another characteristic which he asserts is common to all cultures: "Defense and aggression. It is said that some primitive groups never engaged in warfare, but the culture of most societies include patterns of behavior for carrying on war." [14]

In essence, this description of cultural universals demonstrates that each group of humans faces the same basic problems. Responding to natural and social habitat, each group learns or acquires—by trial and error, by copying from another group, or by accident—acceptable ways of meeting these problems. Each new generation learns the "correct" responses from previous generations. Correct or acceptable responses can become so well learned and such an integral part of the culture that the responses *appear* to be inborn or instinctive in man. The readiness and adaptability with which new members learn the traits and customs of a culture led some social scientists to embrace the "instinct theory" of human behavior. This theory will be discussed later in the chapter. Suffice it to say here that the "instinct theory" has been discarded by most contemporary psychologists.

Cultural diversity and cultural change. Despite the commonality or universality of problems or needs faced by human groups the world over, a fundamental characteristic of mankind is its variability. Man has established and built different ways of life. Responses to specific needs, biological or social, vary among groups according to social and cultural conditions. Thus, the physical growth of a child to manhood is determined primarily by biological forces, but the specific kind of man emerging depends on what he learns from other members in his society. Commenting on the process and effects of cultural learning, Otto Klineberg states: [15]

This learning process may itself occur according to laws which are very similar for all human beings, perhaps even for all biological organisms. . . . *What* he learns will, however, vary enormously, and the consequent effect on his behavior will be correspondingly great.

[14] *Op. cit.*, p. 30.
[15] Otto Klineberg, *Social Psychology*, rev. ed. (New York, Holt, 1954), p. 64.

Cultural conditioning in food habits, for instance, sets distinct limits on the kinds of foods that are deemed acceptable by a particular society. In our culture, milk is considered essential for a nutritious diet. In Southeast Asia, milk is widely rejected as a food. Conversely, our culture excludes insect larvae, grasshoppers, and locusts (raw or roasted) as acceptable foodstuffs. To the Arab nomad, these insects are delicacies to be enjoyed at every available opportunity.

Similarly, each culture establishes ways of expressing anger or aggressiveness. Among several cultures of the South Pacific islands, for example, children are trained to remain impassive to provocation. American culture, on the other hand, permits the anger impulse to be actively expressed.

A significant factor in cultural groups is the process of change that occurs in responses of a particular culture. Cultures are dynamic, or as Herskovits has said,[16] ". . . the only completely static cultures are dead ones." As has been indicated, the impetus for cultural change may stem from invention, borrowing from another culture, or accidental discovery. Whatever the origin of the change, traditional ideas and established methods are modified and replaced as better ideas and methods of doing things become known to a culture. In this context, culture appears as the "precipitate of history."[17] In other words, modifications of existing ways of meeting situations, of responding to the universal biological and sociological problems, are introduced and become an integral part of the fabric of a culture, so far as the "new way" proves to have "survival value," that is, proves to be an improved way of answering some need.

Changes in culture are possible because human nature is not fixed or immutable. Man's responses to his natural and social environment can be altered because cultural traits represent learned rather than inherited characteristics.

"Psychological and Social-Psychological" Man

The science of psychology developed originally as a branch of philosophy. It is not surprising, therefore, that many problems studied by contemporary psychologists and social psychologists were also considered by the early philosophers. Among the Greek philosophers, for instance, Plato (427–347 B.C.) and Aristotle (384–322 B.C.) pondered and deliberated on "human nature" and presented their hypotheses on human behavior. Thus speculation concerning the effects of biological and social forces on human nature is not new.

Psychologists now define their field of inquiry as the scientific study of the behavior of the individual. Social psychology, which represents a synthesis of the sciences of sociology and psychology, customarily serves

[16] *Op. cit.*, p. 20.
[17] Clyde Kluckhohn and William H. Kelly, *op. cit.*, p. 85.

to designate the science of the individual as influenced by the behavior of other persons. Since our concern is primarily with human nature as it relates to conflict and war (war has previously been described as organized conflict between groups), the social psychological implications of human behavior have greater significance for our inquiry than does general (individual) psychology.

"Since wars begin in the minds of men. . . ." If this excerpt from the preamble to the UNESCO Constitution is valid, psychological investigations should be able to advance our understanding of human tensions and war. For example, what does psychology have to say about the presence of a combative or warlike "instinct" in man? What is the psychological process by which the people of one group or nation frame their opinions of other groups or nations? How do prejudices and stereotypes originate, and what is their relation to war? Can group attitudes be modified to bring about a decrease in international tension? These questions reflect only a few of the problems that psychologists have been investigating in recent years in order to appraise more accurately the potential contribution of psychology to human behavior in world affairs.

The "instinct theory" of war. The explanation of human behavior as a series of instincts reached its peak early in the twentieth century, with William McDougall as its principal advocate. According to this theory, instincts are the fundamental determinants of human behavior. Thus, the roots of war are to be found in the "combative" or "fighting" instinct in man. Writing during World War I, McDougall asserted [18] that the combative instinct ". . . makes of Europe an armed camp occupied by twelve million soldiers"; "we see how, more instantly than ever before, a whole nation may be moved by the combative instinct."

The all-inclusive, oversimplified instinct theory of human behavior has been largely discarded by modern psychologists. Accumulated evidence demonstrates that the behavior of humans cannot be accurately predicted *solely* on the basis of an innate or inborn disposition. How quickly the instinct theory of war was discredited is reflected in a poll conducted in 1932 among nearly 400 psychologists.[19] Asked whether man's nature instinctively makes for war, over 90 per cent replied in the negative. Only 3 per cent answered "Yes," and 6 per cent were undecided.

A more recent statement of the psychologist's explanation of war is offered by Mark A. May, who asserts: [20]

The modern view is that while behavior, including mass action such as war, has a broad biological foundation, the factors that determine what acts

[18] William McDougall, *An Introduction to Social Psychology* (Boston, John W. Luce, 1915, reprinted with permission of Methuen & Co., Ltd., London), p. 280.

[19] J. M. Fletcher, "The Verdict of Psychologists on War Instincts," *Scientific Monthly*, Vol. 35 (August, 1932), p. 142.

[20] Mark A. May, *A Social Psychology of War and Peace* (New Haven, Yale University Press, 1943), pp. 3–4.

will occur in specific situations are for the most part products of learning. According to this view, war is not inevitable because man has a fighting nature, but is a direct result of habits, attitudes and beliefs that he has acquired.

With the refutation of the instinct hypothesis, psychologists chose more promising roads for exploring and explaining human behavior. A few more important factors relating to international tensions will be reviewed briefly.

In-groups as a source of tension. A concept fundamental to an analysis of human behavior is the development of what psychologists call an *in-group*, which Allport defines [21] as "any cluster of people who can use the term 'we' with the same significance." The existence of an in-group al-

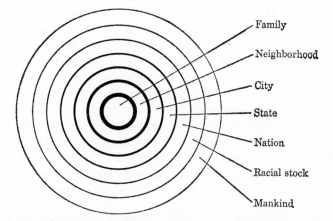

Fig. 6. Decline in potency of membership with increase in size of in-group. (*Source:* Allport, *The Nature of Prejudice*, Reading, Mass., Addison-Wesley, 1954, p. 43.) Note that circular lines become progressively less distinct, moving outward from center.

ways implies the presence of an out-group. An in-group may be a family, citizens of a nation, or persons of a given ethnic stock. Correspondingly, out-groups would be all other families, citizens of all other nations, people of all other racial stocks. Our patterns of behavior, attitudes, and opinions are shaped primarily by in-group or reference-group membership, the psychologists say.

The ties that bind groups together, that create a sense of "belonging" or "loyalty" to the group, are referred to as "social nearness" or "group solidarity." There is, of course, great variation in the amount of group solidarity, the individual's sense of belonging generally being inversely related to the size of the in-group. Figure 6 illustrates how, as inclusiveness of membership widens and distance from personal contact grows

[21] Gordon W. Allport, *The Nature of Prejudice* (1954, Addison-Wesley, Reading, Mass.), p. 37.

larger, the bonds of oneness or solidarity become less distinct, that is, a person feels a much greater loyalty or sense of belonging to his family than to mankind in general. The extent to which an individual is identified with a group can be estimated by the sacrifice he will make and the risks he will accept to protect the group. The closer personal identification of family than that of nation can be demonstrated by the immediate response a man will make to protect his family from criminal attack, as compared with what may be termed a delayed response: an invitation from a draft board when his nation is attacked.

A psychological device for improving the solidarity of a group is the creation of a "common enemy." This technique can be applied at any level of group organization—family, community, nation, specific group of nations. Thus, Hitler created the Jewish and communist menaces, not primarily to exterminate Jews and Communists, but to unite the people of Germany behind the Nazi policies in general and their anti-Semitic and anti-communist policies in particular. The Soviet Union refers to the capitalistic states as its "common enemy"; conversely, a unifying force among western democracies is the common danger of communism.

Allport's diagram indicates that a world loyalty, unity of all mankind, will be the most difficult to attain since the ties binding mankind are weakest. Is it conceivable that the "family of man" can develop a loyalty and group solidarity comparable to that achieved by individual ethnic groups and individual nation-states? Allport states that psychologically, at least, such a world loyalty can be developed. He argues: [22]

> There is no intrinsic reason why the outermost circle of membership needs to be the weakest. In fact, race itself has become the dominant loyalty among many people, especially among fanatic advocates of "Aryanism" and among certain members of oppressed races. It seems today that the clash between the idea of race and of One World (the two outermost circles) is shaping into an issue that may well be the most decisive in human history. The important question is, can a loyalty to mankind be fashioned before inter-racial warfare breaks out?
>
> Theoretically it can, for there is a saving psychological principle that may be invoked if we can learn how to do so in time. The principle states that *concentric loyalties need not clash*. To be devoted to a large circle does not imply the destruction of one's attachment to a smaller circle. *The loyalties that clash are almost invariably those of identical scope*. . . . A traitor who serves two nations (one nominally and one actually) is mentally a mess and socially a felon. Few people can acknowledge more than one alma mater, one religion, or one fraternity. On the other hand, a world-federalist can be a devoted family man, an ardent alumnus, and a sincere patriot. The fact that some fanatic nationalists would challenge the compatibility of world-loyalty with patriotism does not change the psychological law. Wendell Willkie and Franklin Roosevelt were no less patriots because they envisioned a United Nations in One World.

[22] *Ibid.*, p. 44.

Despite the presence of an alleged "saving psychological principle," additional psychological forces deter the fashioning of an in-group of all mankind. The attitudes and opinions of one group toward another, for instance, are frequently so unfavorable that harmonizing of interests and unity of purpose seem almost impossible to achieve.

Attitudes and opinions: formation and effects. Although the two terms *attitudes* and *opinions* frequently occur as interchangeables it is wise, as Klineberg observes,[23] ". . . to reserve the word *attitude* to indicate what we are prepared to do and *opinion* to represent what we believe or regard to be true." From analysis of formation of attitudes, psychologists suggest that one of the most important determinants of an individual's attitude is the prevailing, ready-made attitude of the group of which he is a member. Other factors such as the particular experiences of the individual are significant, but essentially our attitudes, how we are prepared to act, are shaped by the adoption and imitation of the attitudes of other in-group members.

The study of the formation of opinions is crucial to an understanding of human affairs, for our actions are influenced by our beliefs. According to psychologists, our concepts of persons or objects consist of two elements: an immediate or real sensory impression and a "stored" impression. This stored impression or opinion is called a *stereotype*. Perhaps the most descriptive phrase for stereotypes is that suggested by Walter Lippmann, who first referred to these fixed mental images humans have as "pictures in our heads." [24] Quite frequently the stored image is a false impression, developing with little or no objective basis. A stereotype may not be completely false. The danger, however, lies in forming opinions or images of others on fragmentary, inconclusive evidence. Warning against the hazards of stereotyping others, Klineberg says: [25] "The safest conclusion . . . is that every stereotype must be examined in order to determine its relation to objective reality, and that no stereotype may be regarded as even partially true simply because it exists."

A very common kind of stereotype is the image of members of one nation held by members of another nation. An extremely comprehensive study of national stereotyping was undertaken by UNESCO during 1948. Persons in nine countries (Australia, Britain, France, Germany, Italy, Netherlands, Norway, Mexico, and the United States) were asked identical questions involving their opinions of people of foreign lands.[26]

The major conclusions of this study may be summarized in four observations, according to Hadley Cantril, director of the research investiga-

---

[23] Otto Klineberg, *Social Psychology*, rev. ed. (New York, Holt, 1954), p. 482.

[24] Walter Lippmann, *Public Opinion* (New York, Macmillan, 1922), p. 3.

[25] *Loc. cit.*, p. 486.

[26] See Chap. 2, p. 58, for the characteristics assigned to people of several countries by people of other nations.

tion. First, each of the nation-groups interviewed demonstrated a tendency to assign certain characteristics to people of foreign lands. Second, the respondents, taken as a group, tended to be in greater agreement on the characteristics ascribed to Russians than on those ascribed to Americans. Third, the stereotypes or mental pictures that a person has of his own countrymen are consistently flattering. For instance, 68 per cent of the American respondents described the American as "hard-working"; only 49 per cent of the same respondents used "hard-working" in describing the Russians; and only 43 per cent characterized the British as hard workers. Similarly, 59 per cent of the respondents living in Great Britain described the British as "brave." Only 31 per cent termed the Russians "brave," and even less, 19 per cent, thought that "bravery" characterized Americans. The fourth conclusion was that the friendliness between nation-states could be fairly well measured by the "prevalence of complimentary over derogatory terms in a national stereotype." [27] Commenting on the formation of national stereotypes, Buchanan and Cantril write: [28]

> Once a people or government has come to our attention, and we have reacted positively or negatively toward that people or government, we then select the images that support and fill out the stereotype until a credible picture of that unreal concept—a "people"—is before us.
>
> Thus we can account to ourselves in familiar everyday terms for otherwise inexplicable events and actions. We are also able to act ourselves . . . since we are now confronted by a "real" and reasonable phenomenon. We know what to do with "Backward" people—educate them; we know what to do with "Generous" people—thank them and return the courtesy; we know what to do with "Cruel" and "Arrogant" people—obliterate them. Thus these stereotypes permit us, especially in a war situation, to act, where we might hesitate if we continued to hold the thought that across the border were individuals as varied and as human as we.
>
> The danger of stereotypes is not so much that nations are hostile to other "peoples" because they have unfavorable stereotypes; it begins to appear that they have unfavorable stereotypes *because they are hostile.* The greater danger is that we will act irrationally on the basis of these single, satisfying, realistic, but entirely fanciful images.

The impact of these "pictures in our heads" on our relations with others, especially our attitudes and opinions toward people of foreign lands, can scarcely be overestimated. Stereotypes, for instance, can provide a fertile breeding ground for ethnic and national prejudices. Stereotypes can lead to harmful and hostile action that objective and factual information would have negated. Stereotypes can be deadly. Buchanan and Cantril, for example, suggest that "Hiroshima" was the result of our stereotyping the Japanese. They report: [29]

[27] William Buchanan and Hadley Cantril, *How Nations See Each Other* (Urbana, University of Illinois Press, 1953), p. 57.
[28] *Ibid.,* p. 96.
[29] *Ibid.,* pp. 96–97.

. . . the Foreign Morale Analysis Division of the U.S. Office of War Information concluded in May, 1945, on the basis of a statistical analysis of Japanese prisoner-of-war interviews, confiscated diaries, and similar intelligence data:
1. that loyalty to the Emperor could not be shaken; but
2. that home front morale was badly weakened and that surrender by the Japanese was a possibility.

At that time neither conclusion coincided with the opinions prevailing in American policy circles and among the public as well. The current view, based on a particular stereotype of the Japanese "people" as fanatics who would never surrender, was that war would last until 1946.

These preconceptions were not revised until after Hiroshima. Had they been revised before, that holocaust might have been avoided; had they not been revised when they were, the war might have continued until invasion and attrition, costly to both sides, had completely shattered the Japanese nation. . . . The important observation is that, in this latter case, the *stereotype would have been proved to be correct.*

If a false "picture in our head" was even partly responsible for the human destruction wrought at Hiroshima, is further proof required to demonstrate the importance of stereotypes in their influence on human behavior?

Can prejudiced opinions and stereotypes be changed? The psychologist's answer to this is: "If prejudice can be learned, it can also be unlearned." [30] Although reduction and elimination of prejudices are not easy, numerous investigations have demonstrated that attitudes (dispositions to act) and opinions (beliefs) can be altered. Legislation, personal contact, formal education, mass media, and psychoanalysis—all have proved of value in reducing group tension by lessening prejudices.

Despite the cliché that "you cannot legislate against prejudice," civil rights and fair employment laws have clearly lessened discrimination against minority groups. When discrimination is lessened, prejudice is reduced.

Numerous examples might be cited of the effect of formal education in reducing prejudices. Several studies have demonstrated that white children in southern schools had a favorable change in attitude toward Negroes after receiving information about the Negro. Such studies point out, however, that the direction and magnitude of attitude change can be influenced significantly by the teacher. Klineberg reports a study by Manske, who investigated the effects of high school courses on minority-group problems.[31] Each of the courses contained factual information, and all the teachers used the same material. The results demonstrated conclusively that students instructed by a teacher who was tolerant and friendly toward minority-group problems showed an attitudinal change of greater friendliness toward minority groups. No such change occurred among students taught by prejudiced instructors. Manner of presentation,

[30] Otto Klineberg, *loc. cit.,* p. 541.
[31] *Ibid.,* p. 525.

thus, is of crucial significance in effecting changes of attitudes. Also, psychologists assert that the effectiveness of the technique—whether legislation, formal education, or mass media—depends primarily upon the extent to which the individual sees the *personal* implications. Failure of the technique to induce personal involvement can lead to sterile results in attitude changes. Buchanan and Cantril report an unfortunate experience of a few years ago, in which the residents of Cincinnati were "bombarded" by radio, posters, meetings, and sermons concerning the objectives of the United Nations in working toward peace. The slogan for the campaign was: "Peace begins with the United Nations—the United Nations begins with you." The net result of the campaign, according to the authors, was typified by the response of a woman who, when asked about the slogan, replied, "Why yes. I heard it over and over again —but I never did find out what it means." [32]

On the other hand, some evidence indicates that opinions, especially stereotypes, can change even though no directed effort is being made. This can be seen by a comparison of the opinions of Americans toward Russians in a study made in 1942, by the Office of Public Opinion Research, with the opinions held by Americans of Russians in the previously mentioned UNESCO study of 1948. Proportions of the respondents who ascribed a given characteristic to the Russians in 1942 and in 1948 are indicated in the accompanying table.[33]

Adjective	Proportion of Respondents, %	
	1942	1948
Hard-working	61	49
Intelligent	16	12
Practical	18	13
Conceited	3	28
Cruel	9	50
Brave	48	28
Progressive	24	15

Invariably, unfavorable opinions (Conceited, Cruel) had increased whereas favorable stereotypes had declined. In 1942, with the Soviet Union allied with the West against the Axis powers, 48 per cent of the respondents (American) had labeled the Russians as Brave. By 1948, in the midst of the cold war, the percentage had declined to 28. In the earlier year, when the United States and the Soviet Union were partners in the struggle against common enemies, only 9 per cent of the respondents described the Russians as Cruel; in 1948, after the Iron Curtain had been dropped, 50 per cent considered them Cruel.

[32] Buchanan and Cantril, *op. cit.*, pp. 99–100; S. A. Star and H. M. Hughes, "Report on an Educational Campaign—the Cincinnati Plan for the United Nations," *American Journal of Sociology,* Vol. LV, No. 4 (January, 1950), p. 397.

[33] Buchanan and Cantril, *op. cit.*, p. 55.

The principal force behind the change in opinions was presumably the worsening of United States-Soviet Union relations after World War II and the accompanying division of most major powers of the world into two opposing blocs. Each bloc has adopted what it considers the most effective techniques for informing its members of the threat posed by the "enemy" bloc. Thus the changes in the opinions of Americans toward Russians should not be surprising; the altered opinions merely attest to the effectiveness of the techniques applied to inform and persuade.

Changes in these stereotypes demonstrate, however, that "pictures in our heads" may not be as inflexible as at first presumed. In-group images appear to be modified so as to reflect the current state of relations between nations: During periods of friendly relations, favorable pictures of members of the other nation are formed; during periods of enmity, unfavorable attributes dominate the image.

The flexibility or plasticity of stereotypes suggests also that these "pictures in our heads" are the *effects*, not the *causes*, of liking or disliking a group. As Buchanan and Cantril postulate: [34]

Rather than summing up the characteristics of a people as "pictured in his head" and deciding whether this is a portrait of a "nice" or a "bad" person . . . it seems the individual is first brought to a feeling of like or dislike, after which he refocuses his mental image to correspond.

Stereotyping may not be a direct cause of tension, but once a dislike for a group is formed, the "pictures in our heads" fill out and reinforce our impressions. When the stereotypes are based upon "kernels of truth," as frequently happens, our expectations of future relations with out-groups are influenced. For instance, some psychologists assert that, if the people of the United States expect war with the Soviet Union, war is more likely to occur than if it is not expected. Regarding the impact of expectancy on actions, Klineberg maintains that: [35]

Expectancy—real expectancy—of war means that we no longer do everything in our power to avert it; we are discouraged from looking for peaceful alternatives . . . if we spoke less of the probability of war and more of the possibility of peace, less about the routes by which we or the Soviet Union could be attacked and more of our faith in the United Nations—these things too would reduce by a little the threat of war. Obviously, the same would have to be done from the other direction. Talk of the "American capitalistic Wall Street imperialist fascist warmongers" is hardly conducive to an atmosphere in Russia which could be characterized as an expectancy of peace.

In short, our expectations of future events, which can be influenced by what is done now, condition our present actions so as to increase the probability of the expectation. Since expectations stem directly from beliefs, it is significant to note what the various national groups believe

[34] *Ibid.*, p. 56.
[35] *Loc. cit.*, p. 557.

concerning the immutability of human nature and their opinions concerning the possibility of world peace.

Beliefs about human nature and peace: a world summary. The results of the UNESCO study cited previously indicate that slightly less than one-half the respondents, 46 per cent, believe that human nature can be changed (see accompanying table). An even smaller proportion, 43 per cent, believe that world peace is possible.

Relationship Between Beliefs Concerning Human Nature and Peace

Response	Proportion of Respondents in Each Country							Unweighted Average for 9 Countries *
	Fr.	W. Ger.	Italy	Mex.	Nor.	U.K.	U.S.	
Human nature:								
can be changed	59	54	34	32	56	40	50	46
cannot be changed	22	30	43	55	31	48	40	40
don't know	19	16	23	13	13	12	10	14
World peace:								
is possible	47	58	30	18	43	47	49	43
is not possible	41	35	59	74	52	44	45	50
don't know	12	7	11	8	5	9	6	7

* Includes responses from residents of Australia and the Netherlands in addition to nations shown.

Source: Buchanan and Cantril, *op. cit.*, p. 62.

Comparison of the data for individual countries indicates a general relationship between those who believe "world peace is possible" and those who believe "human nature can be changed." In the four countries having the largest proportions of people who believe that "world peace is possible" (West Germany, United States, France, and the United Kingdom) are included three of the four countries (France, Norway, West Germany, and the United States) in which the belief that "human nature can be changed" is greatest.

The tabulation also indicates wide variation among countries with regard to beliefs about human nature and peace. Less than one-third of the respondents in Mexico believed that human nature could be changed whereas nearly three-fifths of those in France held this belief. The proportion of respondents who considered world peace possible varied from 18 per cent in Mexico to 58 per cent in West Germany, the only country with a majority of the respondents in this category.

The results must be interpreted with reference to the status of international relations at the time the study was conducted (1948 and 1949). It is unlikely, however, that changes would be significant in a current poll, since most of the basic causes of the East-West stalemate of 1948–49 remain unresolved.

Of greater importance is the conclusive demonstration by the UNESCO survey of the controversial beliefs that prevail, in this country as well as in other nations, concerning human nature and its relation to an enduring peace.

"Philosophical-Spiritual" Man

One of man's most perplexing philosophical problems is how to think of himself. Reinhold Niebuhr describes this dilemma as follows: [36]

If man insists that he is a child of nature and that he ought not to pretend to be more than the animal, which he obviously is, he tacitly admits that he is, at any rate, a curious kind of animal who has both the inclination and the capacity to make such pretensions. If on the other hand he insists upon his unique and distinctive place in nature and points to his rational faculties as proof of his special eminence, there is usually an anxious note in his avowals of uniqueness which betrays his unconscious sense of kinship with the brutes.

The problem emerges also in man's philosophical reflections on human warfare. The modern view of man, that is, since the Renaissance, has developed primarily from two distinct interpretations: the classical (Graeco-Roman) and the Biblical. Each will be sketched briefly to demonstrate their separate contributions to contemporary philosophical-religious views about man. It should be noted that they focus on western man, and represent the views that have developed from western philosophy.

Classical man. The classical interpretation of man, largely derived from the teachings of Plato, Aristotle, and the Stoics, held that war was rooted in the nature of things—in the nature of men and the nature of city-states with their limited resources. Aristotle, for instance, argued in these words: [37]

. . . The whole of life is divided into two parts, business and leisure, war and peace. . . . There must be war for the sake of peace, business for the sake of leisure, things useful and necessary for the sake of things honourable. . . . For men must engage in business and go to war, but leisure and peace are better; they must do what is necessary and useful, but what is honourable is better.

That war was deemed a necessary prerequisite of peace is evident also in the postclassical teachings of St. Augustine, one of the fathers of the Christian church. In the fifth century St. Augustine wrote: [38]

. . . What, then, men want in war is that it should end in peace. Even while waging a war every man wants peace. And even when men are plotting to disturb the peace, it is merely to fashion a new peace nearer to the heart's desire; it is not because they dislike peace as such. It is not that they love peace less, but that they love their kind of peace more.

[36] Reinhold Niebuhr, *The Nature and Destiny of Man,* Vol. I, *Human Nature* (New York, Scribner, 1941), p. 1.

[37] *Aristotle's Politics,* Benjamin Jowett, transl. (Oxford, Clarendon Press, 1905), pp. 288–289.

[38] St. Augustine, "The City of God," Book 19, Chap. 12, in *The Fathers of the Church,* G. G. Walsh and D. J. Honan, transl. (New York, Fathers of the Church, 1954), pp. 212–213.

In these words, St. Augustine is enunciating the classical doctrine of the harmony of man with nature: Peace between men exists when each is in harmony with the other, and all men in harmony with natural laws. Thus, Augustine concludes that the peace of all things is dependent upon the tranquillity of order.

St. Thomas Aquinas, philosopher of the scholastic period, suggested that envy and greed were the principal sources of discord among men. He believed that peace among men came primarily from peace within men. Man had to be at peace with himself before peace among men and nations could be achieved, and ". . . man's heart is not at peace," continued Aquinas, "so long as he has not what he wants, or if, having what he wants, there still remains something for him to want." [39] Peace, however, is more than apparent harmony or concord among men, argued Aquinas, for a man may enter into an agreement with another counter to what he prefers. Then, men will resort to war ". . . to break this concord, because it is a defective peace, in order that they may obtain peace, where nothing is contrary to their will. Hence, all wars are waged that men may find a more perfect peace than that which they had heretofore." [40]

Biblical man. The Christian view of man rests ultimately upon two theses: Man is made in the "image of God," [41] and man is a "fallen creature." [42]

In the Judaic-Christian tradition, man is not only a special creature made in the image of God; he has also been made by God. The world "and all that dwell therein" have been made by God. God did not transform the world from some previously existing state of matter. God *made* the world. The world is not God, but it is not that the world is evil because it is not God. Since the world was a creation of God, the world was good, but man through his sin has corrupted it.

The effect of this interpretation of the world upon the Christian view of human nature is, as Niebuhr states: [43]

. . . to allow an appreciation of the unity of body and soul in human personality which idealists and naturalists have sought in vain . . . it prevents the idealistic error of regarding the mind as essentially evil . . . it also obviates the romantic error of seeking for the good in man-as-nature and for evil in man-as-spirit or as reason. Man is, according to the Biblical view, a created and finite existence in body and spirit.

This Christian interpretation of man as an image of God means that man is on an entirely different level of creation than are all other animals.

---

[39] *The "Summa Theologica" of St. Thomas Aquinas*, Part II, Second Part, Fathers of the English Dominican Province, transl. (London, Burns Oates and Washbourne, 1916), Question 29, Art. 1, p. 382.

[40] *Ibid.*, p. 384.

[41] Genesis, 1:27.

[42] Romans, 5:12–14.

[43] *Op. cit.*, p. 12.

It means also that man is "a responsible being called by God to free obedience but capable of resisting the call." [44]

That man can resist the "call" of God is exemplified in Christianity's second affirmation that man is a "fallen creature" as a consequence of Adam's sin. Christian theologians have developed varying interpretations of the doctrine of original sin. To some, Adam's "fall" is an historical fact. To others, the "fall" is interpreted primarily "as man's failure to answer the call of his higher nature, or as man's departure from his true spiritual type." [45] Although Christian views differ in their interpretation of man as a fallen creature, Christian theology is optimistic about what God can do for man if man chooses to identify his will or desire with the will of God. In the Christian view, consequently, "the essence of man is his freedom. Sin is committed in that freedom." [46] Man's sin stems, therefore, from the unwise use of his freedom. By following the divine commandments and by adhering to God's will, man could erase sin. That man chooses to do otherwise does not deny his relationship to God. On the contrary, man's "freedom to fall" and his frequent inclination to do so merely attest to his imperfections in contrast to the perfect God. This is the Biblical view of man. What has been the impact of this interpretation upon the modern view of man?

Modern man. The term *modern man,* as indicated previously, refers to the interpretation of man that has emerged during the last 500–600 years, that is, since the Renaissance. The chief concepts from which the modern view of man derives are reason, experience, and faith; each has its roots in classical and/or Biblical tradition.

With the Enlightenment (the latter part of the seventeenth century and the eighteenth century), reason became a dominant element in man's attempt to explain himself and his place in the world. Men evidenced supreme confidence in the power of reason to develop the truths about the natural world and to lead man to the meaning of nature's laws. This reliance upon reason assumed that nature itself must be rationally ordered—otherwise man would have little success in probing its secrets. In modern naturalism, then, man is regarded as part of materialistically conceived nature, and human nature is to be understood best through the application of natural laws and principles. Eugene G. Bewkes and his colleagues offer this description of modern naturalism: [47]

. . . naturalism seeks to find general principles in man's external world and to interpret man as part of the world . . . and . . . seeks to include man and his mind as products of nature. It tends to interpret the inner life of man, his emotions and his knowledge, in terms of the outer world, as though the gar-

[44] John C. Bennett, *Christian Realism* (New York, Scribner, 1943), p. 52.
[45] H. Shelton Smith, *Changing Conceptions of Original Sin* (New York, Scribner, 1955), p. 196.
[46] Niebuhr, *op. cit.,* p. 17.
[47] Eugene G. Bewkes, and others, *Experience, Reason, and Faith: A Survey in Philosophy and Religion* (New York, Harper, 1940), p. 517.

ment of humanity were cut out of the cloth of nature, spun with matter as its woof and with mathematical law as its warp.

Another dominant philosophy of man in the modern world is idealism, which could more aptly be labeled "idea-ism" or "mental-ism" in that its interest and concepts revolve primarily about ideas. The human mind is the center or starting point in idealism. Reality, according to this philosophy, "is ultimately made up of such stuff as mind is made of." [48] The roots of idealism, developing as a reaction against the rationalistic-materialistic view of man of the eighteenth century, can be traced in part at least to the English philosopher, John Locke, who in the late seventeenth century taught that experience was the source of all that man knows, of man's ideas. According to Locke, man's mind was a blank slate upon which experiences were tabulated or imprinted. In this context it was possible to write "peace" (or "war") on man's mind. Locke's philosophy was further developed by early eighteenth century empiricists such as Bishop Berkeley and David Hume. In essence, Berkeley challenged eighteenth century materialism by suggesting that the natural *thing* is mental, whereas Hume challenged eighteenth century rationalism by arguing that the natural *law* is mental.

Immanuel Kant (1724–1804), following in the footsteps of both the rationalists and the empiricists, attempted to harmonize the two philosophies. Kant's contribution was the postulation of an "idealistic interpretation of natural law." Natural law was transferred from being inherent in reality to being inherent in mind; thus the Kantian philosophy held that reason was innate in experience.

These differing interpretations of man and his world have presented modern man with numerous perplexities. As Niebuhr states,[49]

Modern man . . . cannot determine whether he shall understand himself primarily from the standpoint of the uniqueness of his reason or from the standpoint of his affinity with nature, and if the latter whether it is the harmless order and peace of nature or her vitality which is the real clue to his essence. Thus some of the certainties of modern man are in contradiction with one another. . . .

Another philosophical conflict is how to consider evil. Niebuhr believes that modern man has largely rejected the Christian tradition that man is a fallen creature, that the focus of man's personality or will is evil. The consequence of this rejection is to "make the Christian gospel simply irrelevant to modern man." [50]

These brief glimpses of "philosophical-spiritual" man have traced the development of some of the major bodies of thought in man's inquiries about himself and his world. The real significance lies not in "what is asked" but in the "asking," for in the asking man gives evidence of two

[48] *Ibid.,* p. 518.
[49] *Op. cit.,* p. 21.
[50] *Ibid.,* p. 23.

principal qualities of human nature: knowledge and ignorance, greatness and misery. As Pascal, seventeenth century philosopher, commented: [51]

For, in fact, what is man in nature? A Nothing in comparison with the Infinite, an All in comparison with the Nothing, a mean between nothing and everything. . . .

It is dangerous to make man see too clearly his equality with the brutes without showing him his greatness. It is also dangerous to make him see his greatness too clearly, apart from his vileness. It is still more dangerous to leave him in ignorance of both. But it is very advantageous to show him both. Man must not think that he is on a level either with the brutes or with the angels, nor must he be ignorant of both sides of his nature; but he must know both.

In summary, the philosophical-spiritual perspective confronts man with his greatest challenge. For if man's will is free, we can hope that he will not unendingly lend himself to violence and aggression.

Conclusion

From the biological, sociological, psychological, and philosophical perspectives of man have arisen numerous views concerning human nature and its relation to war. Three views are presented in the next section. The first represents a biological argument that war is rooted in the inborn fierce nature of man. The second position represents an attempt to refute the biological determinist by stating that war is not a product of man's biological nature. The argument set forth in the third point of view has a social-psychological origin and contends that the causes of war are to be found in society, not in the biological nature of man.

POSITIONS
ON THE PROBLEM

1. WAR MUST BE ATTRIBUTED TO MAN'S INBORN FIERCE NATURE

(The following passages are from *Evolution and Ethics*, by Sir Arthur Keith.[52] The author, an anthropologist, wrote *Evolution and Ethics* in England during World War II.)

[51] Charles W. Eliot, ed., *Blaise Pascal*, The Harvard Classics (New York, P. F. Collier, 1910), pp. 27, 136.
[52] Sir Arthur Keith, *Evolution and Ethics* (New York, Putnam, 1946), pp. 105, 109, 113, 116–119, 125, 192, 193. Reprinted with permission of Watts & Co., London, publishers of the original *Essays on Human Evolution*.

There is another very important factor which forms part of the machinery of evolution—namely, man's inborn competitive spirit or nature. Man is by nature competitive, combative, ambitious, jealous, envious, and vengeful. These are the qualities which make men the slaves of evolution. We are all familiar with the rivalry between man and man in civil life; but is not the competition, the rivalry between the nations of Europe even more intense? The "struggle for survival"—I think it would be more accurate to say, the "struggle for integrity"—often reaches such an extremity that decisions can be reached only by the use of force—by resorting to war. Here again I bracket evolution and war together.

I come now to the crucial question put to me by my correspondent: "Is evolution of mankind the correct method of procedure?" No one with a spark of humanity in him could approve of the bloody spectacle which meets his eye in all parts of the earth today. If war be the progeny of evolution—and I am convinced that it is—then evolution has "gone mad," reaching such a height of ferocity as must frustrate its proper role in the world of life—which is the advancement of her competing "units," these being tribes, nations, or races of mankind.

There is no way of getting rid of war save one and that is to rid human nature of the sanctions imposed on it by the law of evolution. Can man, by taking thought, render the law of evolution null and void? . . . I may say that I have discovered no way that is at once possible and practicable. "There is no escape from human nature" . . . my main theme [is]—namely, that a double code of morals (the ethical and cosmical) are entrenched in man's nature or mentality, and that without this duality there could have been no organized and effective evolution of humanity. . . . There can be no clear thinking about war or any other matter bearing on the relationships of one nation to another until we draw a sharp distinction between the twofold code under which the nations of the world live, move and have their being—the ethical code of civilized behavior and the cosmical code of savage behavior. In war we are under the domination of the cosmical code.

I . . . look on the brain mechanism which subserves the dual code as of extreme antiquity, for it is obeyed instinctively by social animals low in the animal scale; it is deeply entrenched in human nature. Man's emotions, his feelings, and his inherited predispositions are so contrived as to make him responsive to its behests. . . .

We shall obtain some light on the "ethical confusion with which the popular mind is perplexed" if we scan for a moment the writings of those who, applying only the ethical code to the problem of war, denounce it as a crime or as a monstrous vice. "War," said Seneca, "is a glorious crime." Condorcet: "It is a heinous crime." "Great generals," exclaimed Mencius, "are great criminals." All of which verdicts are true, on the basis of an ethical code. When Thomas Hobbes states, in Leviathan (1651), that "in war, force and fraud are cardinal virtues," he is basing his judgment on the cosmical code. When he affirms that "by nature man is both faithful and false," he evinces his belief in the duality of man's mental constitution. The popular saying, "All is fair in love and war," is a recognition of the cosmical code. Napoleon was cosmically minded: "In war," he said, "all things are moral." So was Hindenburg: "War," he declared, "suits me like a visit to a health resort." So was Bismarck. . . . And yet under Hitler, as under Bismarck, Germany was ruled by the dual code; her own folk by the ethical, and all others (save her satellites) by the cosmical code.

Sir Henry Maine, in Ancient Law, writes as a lawyer when he informs us that "sovereign states live in a state of nature." This means that each state is ruled within by the ethical code, and that their external affairs are controlled by the cosmical code. The cosmical code is based on compulsion—on force, and in the last resort, on war. A state applies the cosmical code not only to enemies outside its frontier, but also to enemies—such as criminals and rebels—which are in its midst. . . . The criminal, because of his nefarious activities, has been excluded from the ethical code of his country and has his life or liberty taken from him so that his nation may enjoy internal peace. The soldier, on the other hand, gives his life in order that his country may have security and external peace; the moment he shoulders arms he passes from the ethical to the cosmical code. Under that code it becomes his duty to reverse every item of the ethical code—to kill, to deceive, to lie, to destroy, to damage the enemy by every means in his power. Particularly noticeable is the reversal of his sense of justice: "home" justice is no longer valid. In war, said David Hume, "we recall our sense of justice and sympathy and permit injustice and enmity to take their place." My readers may remember that famous Piraeus party of ancient Greece when Socrates asked his companions for their definition of justice. "Justice," answered Polemarchus, "is helping friends and harming enemies." This answer, which conformed to the cosmical code, was rejected by Socrates; he and his pupil, Plato, were in search of an ideal justice, a justice which had a quality which was both universal and eternal. Yet ancient Greece, like the modern world, was divided into a multitude of political fields, each swayed by the dual code. Justice, under the ethical code, is one thing—under the cosmical code it is quite another. Under the cosmical code justice is that which is enforced by political measures or by the might of arms. Here I take no note of what "ought" to be, but only of what has been and now is.

. . . later . . . I shall have occasion to deal with the evidence on which Elliot Smith based his conception of human nature as having been originally peaceful. Meantime it may be stated that it is possible to hold this conception of human nature only by concentrating attention on its ethical or peaceful side and overlooking the equally old side—the cosmical or warlike. There is evidence of strife in the world long before civilization came to it. . . .

My readers will have perceived by now that the thesis I am seeking to prove is that fierce war must be attributed to an inborn fierce nature which has developed in tribes long subjected to the rigors of competitive evolution. Such a view will be strenuously opposed by scientists such as Professor W. C. Allee, who regards war as an acquired habit; and by Dr. Carr-Saunders, who traces war, not to the inheritance of warlike qualities, but to the handing on of a warlike tradition. Now, I agree with both of them that if a Mongol child or a German child had been removed from tribal surroundings during infancy and brought up in a home in China, or within the confines of an Indian caste, those children would have grown into peaceful, law-abiding citizens. But this admission does not imply that these children would have lost their warlike aptitudes; only that the conditions which call out such qualities would be lacking. We have still to explain how such a fierce tradition arose along the vast tribal zone of the Old World and endured over thousands of years. I cannot conceive that a tribe, be it Mongolian or German, could tolerate over a long period of time a tradition which was antagonistic to its true nature. Tradition is molded to fit the mentality which fashions it, not the other way around.

2. WAR IS NOT AN INEVITABLE PRODUCT
OF MAN'S BIOLOGICAL NATURE

(The following are excerpts from an essay entitled "War as a Biological Phenomenon," by Julian Huxley.[53] Dr. Huxley, an eminent biologist, has served as director of many learned societies, as a governmental adviser, and as Director-General of UNESCO.)

How does war look when pinned out in the biologist's collection? In the first place, he is able to say with assurance that war is not a general law of life, but an exceedingly rare biological phenomenon. War is not the same thing as conflict or bloodshed. It means something quite definite: an organized physical conflict between groups of one and the same species. Individual disputes between members of the same species are not war, even if they involve bloodshed and death. Two stags fighting for a harem of hinds, or a man murdering another man, or a dozen dogs fighting over a bone, are not engaged in war. Competition between two different species, even if it involves physical conflict, is not war. . . . Still less is it war when one species preys upon another, even when the preying is done by an organized group. A pack of wolves attacking a flock of sheep or deer, or a peregrine killing a duck, is not war. Much of nature, as Tennyson correctly said, is "red in tooth and claw"; but this only means what it says, that there is a great deal of killing in the animal world, not that war is the rule of life.

In point of fact, there are only two kinds of animals that habitually make war—man and ants. Even among ants war is mainly practiced by one group, comprising only a few species among the tens of thousands that are known to science. They are the harvester ants, inhabitants of arid regions where there is little to pick up during the dry months. Accordingly they collect the seeds of various grasses at the end of the growing season and store them in special underground granaries in their nest. It is these reserve supplies which are the object of ant warfare. . . .

Harvesters are the only kind of ants to go in for accumulating property, as well as the chief kind to practice war. This association of property with war is interesting, as various anthropologists believe that in the human species war, or at any rate habitual and organized war, did not arise in human evolution until man had reached the stage of settled civilization, when he began to accumulate stores of grain and other forms of wealth. . . .

So much then for war as a biological phenomenon. The facts speak for themselves. War, far from being a universal law of nature, or even a common occurrence, is a very rare exception among living creatures; and where it occurs, it is either associated with another phenomenon, almost equally rare, the amassing of property, or with territorial rights.

Biology can help put war in its proper perspective in another way. War has often been justified on biological grounds. The progress of life, say war's apologists, depends on the struggle for existence. This struggle is universal, and results in what Darwin called "Natural Selection," and this in its turn results in the "Survival of the Fittest." Natural Selection, of course, works only

[53] Julian S. Huxley, "War as a Biological Phenomenon," in *On Living in a Revolution* (New York, Harper, 1944, copyright 1944 by Julian S. Huxley, and reprinted with permission). Essay is now available in *Man in the Modern World* (New York, Mentor Books, 1948), pp. 183–191.

in a mass way, so that those which survive in the struggle will merely have an average of fitness a little above those which perish or fail to reproduce themselves. But some of the qualities which make for success in the struggle, and so for a greater chance of survival, will certainly be inherited; and since the process continues generation after generation not merely for thousands but for millions of years, the average fitness and efficiency of the race will steadily and continuously be raised until it can be pushed no higher. In any case, say the believers in this doctrine, struggle is necessary to maintain fitness; if the pressure of competition and conflict is removed, biological efficiency will suffer, and degeneration will set in.

Darwin's principle of Natural Selection, based as it is on constant pressure of competition or struggle, has been invoked to justify various policies in human affairs. For instance, it was used, especially by politicians in late Victorian England, to justify the principles of laisser-faire and free competition in business and economic affairs. And it was used, especially by German writers and politicians from the late nineteenth century onwards, to justify militarism. War, so ran this particular version of the argument, is the form which is taken by Natural Selection and the Struggle for Existence in the affairs of the nations. Without war, the heroic virtues degenerate; without war, no nation can possibly become great or successful.

It turns out, however, that both the laisser-faire economists and the militarists were wrong in appealing to biology for justification of their policies. War is a rather special aspect of competition between members of the same species—what biologists call "intra-specific competition." It is a special case because it involves physical conflict and often the death of those who undertake it, and also because it is physical conflict not between individuals but between organized groups; yet it shares certain properties in common with all other forms of intra-specific struggle or competition. And recent studies of the way in which Natural Selection works and how the Struggle for Existence operates in different conditions have resulted in this rather surprising but very important conclusion—that intra-specific competition need not, and usually does not, produce results of any advantage to the species as a whole.

A couple of examples will show what I mean. In birds like the peacock or the argus pheasant, the males are polygamous—if they can secure a harem. They show off their gorgeous plumage before the hen birds in an elaborate and very striking display, at definite assembly grounds where males and females go for the purpose of finding mates. . . . Individual male birds meet with different degrees of success in this polygamous love business: some secure quite a number of mates, others one or a few, and some get none at all. This puts an enormous biological premium on success: the really successful male leaves many times more descendants than the unsuccessful. Here, then, is Natural Selection working at an exceedingly high pitch of intensity to make the display plumage and display actions more effective in their business of stimulatng the hens. Accordingly, in polygamous birds of this kind, we often find the display plumage and display actions more effective in their business of stimulating the species as a whole. Thus the display organ of the peacock, his train or enormously over-grown tail-covert feathers, is so long and cumbersome that it is a real handicap in flight.

On the other hand, intra-specific competition and struggle need not always lead to results which are useless to the species. The competition between individuals may concern qualities which are also useful in the struggle of the species against its enemies, as in deer or zebra or antelope—the same extra turn of speed which gives one individual an advantage over another in escaping from wolf or lion or cheetah will also stand the whole species in good stead. Or it may concern qualities which help the species in surviving in a difficult environment; an extra capacity for resisting drought in an individual cactus or yucca will help the species in colonizing new and more arid regions. It will not be useless or harmful to the species unless the competition is directed solely or mainly against other individuals like itself. . . .

All these considerations apply to war. In the first place it is obvious that war is an example of intra-specific competition—it is a physical conflict between groups within the same species. As such, it might be not merely useless but harmful to the species as a whole—a drag on the evolutionary progress of humanity. But, further, it might turn out to be harmful in some conditions and not in others. This indeed seems to be the truth. Those who say that war is always and inevitably harmful to humanity are indulging in an unjustified generalization (though not nearly so unjustified as the opposite generalization of the militarists who say that war is both necessary and beneficial to humanity). Warfare between peoples living on the tribal level of early barbarism may quite possibly have been on balance a good thing for the species —by encouraging the manly virtues, by mixing the heritage of otherwise closed communities through the capture of women, by keeping down excessive population-pressure, and in other ways. War waged by small professional armies according to a professional code was at least not a serious handicap to general progress. But long-continued war in which the civilian population is starved, oppressed, and murdered and whole countries are laid waste, as in the Thirty Years War—that is harmful to the species; and so is total war in the modern German sense in which entire populations may be enslaved and brutalized, as with Poland or Greece today, whole cities smashed, like Rotterdam, the resources of large regions deliberately destroyed, as in the Ukraine. The more total war becomes, both intensively, as diverting more of the energies of the population from construction to destruction, and extensively, as involving more and more of the countries of the globe, the more of a threat does it become to the progress of the human species. As H. G. Wells and many others have urged, it might even turn back the clock of civilization and force the world into another Dark Age. War of this type is an intra-specific struggle from which nobody, neither humanity at large nor any of the groups engaged in the conflict, can really reap any balance of advantage, though of course we may snatch particular advantages out of the results of war.

But it is one thing to demonstrate that modern war is harmful to the species, another thing to do something about abolishing it. What has the biologist to say to those who assert that war is inevitable, since, they say, it is a natural outcome of human nature and human nature cannot possibly be changed?

To this the biologist can give a reassuring answer. War is not an inevitable phenomenon of human life; and when objectors of this type talk of human nature they really mean the expression of human nature, and this can be most thoroughly changed.

As a matter of observable fact, war occurs in certain conditions, not in others. There is no evidence of prehistoric man's having made war, for all his flint implements seem to have been designed for hunting, for digging, or for scraping hides; and we can be pretty sure that even if he did, any wars between groups in the hunting stage of human life would have been both rare and mild. Organized warfare is most unlikely to have begun before the stage of settled civilization. In man, as in ants, war in any serious sense is bound up with the existence of accumulations of property to fight about.

However, even after man had learned to live in cities and amass property, war does not seem to have been inevitable. The early Indus civilization, dating from about 3000 B.C., reveals no traces of war. There seem to have been periods in early Chinese history, as well as in the Inca civilization in Peru, in which war was quite or almost absent.

As for human nature, it contains no specific war instinct, as does the nature of harvester ants. There is in man's make-up a general aggressive tendency, but this, like all other human urges, is not a specific and unvarying instinct; it can be moulded into the most varied forms. It can be canalized into competitive sport, as in our own society, or as when certain Filipino tribes were induced to substitute football for head-hunting. It can be sublimated into non-competitive sport, like mountain-climbing, or into higher types of activity altogether, like exploration or research or social crusades.

Thus in the perspective of biology war first dwindles to the status of a rare curiosity. Further probing, however, makes it loom larger again. For one thing, it is a form of intra-specific struggle, and as such may be useless or even harmful to the species as a whole. Then we find that one of the very few animal species which make war is man; and man is today not merely the highest product of evolution, but the only type still capable of real evolutionary progress. And, war, though it need not always be harmful to the human species and its progress, indubitably is so when conducted in the total fashion which is necessary in this technological age. Thus war is not merely a human problem; it is a biological problem of the broadest scope, for on its abolition may depend life's ability to continue the progress which it has slowly but steadily achieved through more than a thousand million years.

But the biologist can end on a note of tempered hope. War is not inevitable for man. His aggressive impulses can be canalized into other outlets; his political machinery can be designed to make war less likely. These things can be done. . . .

3. Causes of War Are To Be Found in Society, Not in Human Nature

(The following is an extract from *Social Psychology*, by Otto Klineberg,[54] a psychologist at Columbia University. Dr. Klineberg has done extensive research in the sociological and psychological aspects of international affairs, including UNESCO's project, "Tensions Affecting International Understanding," of which he was director.)

The problem of the innateness or universality of aggressive behavior is one of obvious practical significance. It would probably be agreed that the occurrence of war and the threat of war in our society represent its worst feature— one which may even contain the germs of the destruction of our whole civilization. The assertion is sometimes made that war will never be abolished because it is rooted in an instinct of pugnacity which is natural to man. Psychology and ethnology have an important contribution to make in connection with this problem.

Aggressive behavior is of course found widely in the animal kingdom. It must be borne in mind, however, that it is by no means an invariable rule of

[54] Otto Klineberg, *Social Psychology*, rev. ed. By permission of Henry Holt and Company, Inc., copyright 1940, 1954, pp. 89–94, 96.

behavior. Cases of mutual help and cooperation also occur in abundance, even between members of different species. When aggressiveness is found it is frequently in association with other drives, such as self-preservation, sex, and maternal love, and probably is not to be regarded as an end in itself.

On the physiological side no basis has been discovered for the existence of aggressiveness as such. It has been amply demonstrated by Cannon that in anger there is a whole series of biochemical and physiological changes under the influence of the sympathetic nervous system and the adrenal glands. . . . The general result of these changes is that in the presence of an enemy the organism may respond with an unusual output of energy over an unusually long period of time. These changes do occur in anger, but they occur also in fear and in excitement; they constitute an organic basis for violent emotional behavior in general, rather than for aggressiveness itself.

There are some human groups among whom aggressive behavior was apparently indulged in for its own sake. An Iroquois chief is reported to have proposed to a neighboring ruler that their young men be allowed to have a little war. On the second chief's refusal, he was asked, "With whom then can my children play?" However, this may not be an example of aggressiveness as such, since the Iroquois chief was concerned with the need of his young warriors for practice. Of the Lango it is said—"They are brave and venturesome warriors, who have won the fear and respect of their neighbors, delighting in war not only for the plunder which it brings, but also for its own sake!"

These examples do not necessarily prove that aggressive behavior is innately determined. It may become an end in itself even though it originated as a means to an end. In all cases we have a long previous history of warfare and the possibility therefore that warlike habits have been developed. . . . Much of the warfare of primitive peoples is to be understood as similar to athletic contests or trials of strength, and that may be the primary motivation responsible.

On the other hand, it has been noted that warfare is by no means universal and that there are many societies to which it is foreign. In their survey of the cultural characteristics of a large number of groups, Hobhouse and his associates report that there were at least ten tribes which had no war.

There are many writers who feel that aggressive warfare, far from being native to man, develops only when culture has reached a certain degree of complexity. Letourneau states that at the beginning of society, when men were few in number and did not trouble each other, war was as strange to them as until recently it was among the Eskimo of the far north. Van der Bij also believes that the simplest and most primitive peoples were not warlike; they had no offensive war and were even unwilling to engage in defensive wars. He cites cases from a number of very simple societies in support of this point of view, and believes that war comes only with greater cultural development and an increase in the size of the groups. Elliot Smith is substantially of the same opinion. It may be that these writers tend unduly to glorify the "noble savage" and to attribute all the ills of mankind to an interference with the state of nature, and we must certainly be careful not to exaggerate the purity and nobility of primitive man. There is no doubt, however, that there were many groups who were not at all warlike, and that therefore aggressiveness, at least to the extent that it expresses itself in war, does not satisfy our criterion of universality.

Wars do of course occur with great frequency, but they may usually be understood in terms of certain very definite motives. Obviously, most peoples will defend themselves when attacked. Clearly too, they will fight for food and in many cases for plunder. Examples of this type of warfare are numerous. As Bunzel indicates, war raids for profit are characteristic of many primitive societies; even the peaceable Zuni formerly conducted raids on the sheep of their Navajo neighbors. The Crow raided for horses, as this was their favorite form of wealth, and a stolen horse was the only acceptable bride gift. Among the Kiowa, the whole economic system hinged upon warfare, the objective of which was the acquisition of horses; the enemy was killed only when it was absolutely necessary. In parts of West Africa slave-raiding was one of the main causes of war. Hobhouse and his associates found also that in forty or more peoples, where marriage by capture occurred, the possession of women was the direct object of a warlike raid.

War has often been due to religious causes. Eating a dead man was interpreted by many peoples as giving the conqueror his virtues. Among the Yoruba, hearts were regularly sold in order to give courage, and the procuring of them often led to battle. In Aztec Mexico religious factors were responsible for the major part of the warlike behavior. One of the important beliefs was that the gods, particularly the Sun, would die if deprived of food, and the only satisfying nourishment consisted of human hearts. The victim of the sacrifice was identified with the god, and his killing and eating meant a resurrection of the god and the renewal of his strength. There was a Mexican legend to the effect that the gods themselves had formerly been sacrificed to the Sun in order to endow him with strength to do his work, and they bequeathed the duty to the human representatives, directing them to fight and kill each other to provide the necessary food. There was almost perpetual warfare with the neighboring Tlaxcalans for the sole purpose of obtaining captives to serve as sacrificial victims. . . .

Among the Wyandot Indians it was believed that an increase in the size of the clan would please the animal god from which it was descended. Every effort was made to keep the clan full, that is, to keep in use the complete list of names belonging to it. For this purpose war was carried on in order to secure women and children, and occasionally men, for adoption.

The glory motive, or the quest for prestige, is one of the most frequent causes of aggressive behavior. Head-hunting, for example, although sometimes the result of religious practices, may also be due to the intense desire for a trophy which will elevate its possessor to a higher position in the community. Among the Asaba on the Niger River a man receives the honorary title of Obu if he has done a brave deed, and he most clearly earns this title if he has killed another man. In parts of New Guinea a youth must have "fetched a head" before he may be counted an adult, and the badges of distinction for warriors depend on the number of lives taken. Distinguished Masai warriors had the right to wear bracelets and bells. Among the Bagobo of the Philippines a man's clothing indicated his status, which was determined by the number of deaths for which he was responsible.

It should be pointed out further that when primitive peoples do fight they seem not to be giving expression to a spontaneous and uncontrolled pugnacious drive, but rather to a form of behavior which is regulated and modified by social conventions. In general, primitive warfare was not very destructive of human life, and the casualties were frequently insignificant. When two groups of Australian aborigines fought, the battle was over as soon as one warrior on either side had been killed. Sometimes the first wound ended the combat. Sumner and Keller state that conflicts among primitive people were generally brief and relatively bloodless. "A savage would stand aghast before the whole-sale slaughter of civilized warfare, and beside some of its methods his own are those of a gentleman."

As a matter of fact, war was really in many cases a sort of duel or game, and the attitude toward it was frequently sportsmanlike. It is said that the Arkansas Indians once gave a share of their powder to the Chickasaw with whom they were at war; an Algonquin tribe refrained from pressing an attack upon the Iroquois when it was pointed out that night had fallen. Australian tribes have been known to provide unarmed Europeans with a set of weapons before attacking. The Maori are reported to have filled canoes with food for their hungry enemies so that they might fight on more equal terms. On the other hand, sudden raids without any warning are by no means unknown in primitive warfare.

William James once spoke of a "moral equivalent for war." There are many primitive communities which have worked out some such equivalent, particularly in the case of quarrels between individuals. The Indians of the Northwest Coast settle disputes by means of the institution of the potlach. If two men have a quarrel one of them may give a potlach or feast, at which the aim is to give away or destroy as large an amount of property as possible. His rival is humbled as a consequence and regarded as having lost status in the community until he can do likewise. A Kwakiutl chief once said, "The White man fights with his hands, but we fight with property." This fighting with property may also take place under much more informal conditions. There is a story to this effect told of the Tlingit of Alaska. "Two women were quarreling. In a rage one of them said to the other, 'I'll shut you up!' At that she rushed into her house, came out with both hands full of silver money and scattered it to the crowd that was watching the proceedings. This did shut the mouth of her opponent as she could not do likewise." Goldman reports a case among the Alkatcho Carrier Indians in which a man had been insulted by being placed in a position of inferiority at a feast. He went out with his relatives and returned with a number of articles which he presented to his host, thereby humbling him and wiping out the insult.

A particularly interesting method of settling a quarrel is reported for various groups of Eskimos, from the Aleuts at one geographical extreme to the Greenland tribes at the other. An Eskimo who has suffered some injury may compose a satirical song in mockery of his enemy and challenge him to a public singing contest. The village group assembles, and the two contestants take turns mocking each other to the best of their ability. The spectators decide the victor. Sometimes this is not possible until the contestants have been recalled many times.

These examples indicate that aggressiveness, whether or not it has an innate basis, may be modified by the culture in many ways. It may be stimulated in one society and relatively lacking in another. It may arise as the result of any one of a number of different causes. It may express itself in violent physical combat or in a socially regulated contest in which no one is harmed. There is no justification, therefore, for the attempt to explain any specific type of aggressive behavior on the ground that it has a biological basis. To the question as to whether war is inevitable because of the existence of such an aggressive instinct, the ethnologist and the social psychologist have reason to give a categorical negative. War is an institution, and must be explained in relation to the whole social structure in which it occurs. After a somewhat similar survey of the pertinent material, Sumner and Keller came to the conclusion that "There is no 'instinct of pugnacity'." What there is is a set of life conditions demanding adjustment.

QUESTIONS

1. Define and illustrate each of the following: society, culture, cultural universal, race, human nature, stereotype, in-group.

2. Cite the three abilities unique to man, and describe how they give man an advantage over nonhuman animals.

3. Do you agree or disagree with Elgin Hunt that "defense and aggression" represent cultural universals? Why?

4. Is culture related to power? Is the culture of the United States superior to that of Mexico because the United States wields greater power in world affairs?

5. Critically appraise Allport's diagram of concentric circles, which demonstrate the decline in membership potency associated with an increase in size of in-group. Is it conceivable that love of mankind might accompany hate of individuals?

6. Distinguish between: (1) an attitude and an opinion, and (2) an opinion and a stereotype.

7. According to the UNESCO study discussed in the chapter, one-half the people interviewed in the United States believed that human nature could be changed. In reply to a question concerning world peace, slightly less than half indicated that they believed world peace was possible. What would be your replies to these queries?

8. Does war tend to assure the survival of the fittest or eliminate the strong and healthy? Do you think a nuclear war would have the same effect?

9. Do you feel that mankind generally is moving toward the ideal of the reasonable, rational man?

10. List several points of view, other than those presented in "Positions on the Problem," that might be held with respect to the relationship between human nature and war.

SELECT BIBLIOGRAPHY

ALLPORT, Gordon W., *The Nature of Prejudice* (Reading, Mass., Addison-Wesley, 1954). A keenly critical analysis of the origins and effects of prejudices. Attention is focused primarily upon minority-group problems in our country; numerous examples of international prejudices are also cited.

BRYSON, Lyman, FINKELSTEIN, Louis, and MACIVER, R. M., eds., *Conflicts of Power in Modern Culture* (New York, Conference on Science, Philosophy and Religion in Their Relation to the Democratic Way of Life, Inc., 1947). A series of scholarly essays on the preservation and advancement of peace, mutual understanding, and co-operation among men.

BUCHANAN, William, and CANTRIL, Hadley, *How Nations See Each Other* (Urbana, University of Illinois Press, 1953). A report on an inquiry, conducted under UNESCO's project, "Tensions Affecting International Understanding," whose objective was to discover "the conceptions which the people of one nation entertain of their own and of other nations." Provides an interesting inventory of beliefs in western nations.

HERSKOVITS, Melville J., *Man and His Works* (New York, Knopf, 1952). A cultural anthropological classic, by one of the leading anthropologists of our times, "moves from a discussion of the nature of culture, its materials, and structure, to a consideration of the processes of change that characterize it, and the general principles that govern cultural change."

HUNT, Elgin F., *Social Science* (New York, Macmillan, 1955). A textbook on social science "written in a language which students can understand." Unique in its approach to society as a whole, yet retaining unity within and between chapters.

KLINEBERG, Otto, *Social Psychology* (New York, Holt, 1954). An excellent appraisal of recent developments in the field of social psychology. One of the few psychology textbooks that considers the implications of psychology in international relations.

LINTON, Ralph, *The Study of Man* (New York, Appleton-Century-Crofts, 1936). Excellent for students beginning a study of anthropology. Points out the more important anthropological questions remaining unanswered.

LOOS, A. William, ed., *The Nature of Man* (New York, The Church Peace Union and the World Alliance for International Friendship through Religion, 1950). A brief text, with a religious orientation, outlining man's world, his spiritual resources, and his destiny.

MONTAGU, M. F. Ashley, *The Direction of Human Development* (New York, Harper, 1955). Addresses itself to the compound question: "What is man's original nature and how is that nature influenced and conditioned to assume a socially functional form?" The central theme is best summarized by a direct quotation: ". . . this evidence indicates that human beings are born good . . . that at birth they are wholly prepared, equipped, to function as creatures who not only want and need to be loved by others, but who also want and need to love others."

PEARL, Raymond, *Man the Animal* (Bloomington, Ind., Principia Press, 1946). A biologist's interpretation of man: his likenesses and differences, his numbers, and a suggested pattern for living together.

4

Nationalism:
Curse or Blessing?

THE PROBLEM
AND ITS BACKGROUND

NATIONALISM AND TODAY'S HEADLINES

Carlos P. Romulo, the well-known Philippine statesman, once cautioned his friends in the United States: [1]

The American tendency to brand any nationalistic movement whatever in Asia and Africa as communistic rests on another of those assumptions which urgently need to be examined. There are unquestionably nationalist movements in Asia which are Communist-led or which are abetted by the Communists. But this fact does not necessarily invalidate the intrinsic quality of genuine nationalist movements in this region.

In other words, according to Romulo, Americans ought to see more clearly that, although it is active in parts of the Afro-Asian world, communism is not the sole or even in many places the most important force at work in Afro-Asia. Indeed, he pointed to the "irreversible march of nationalism in Asia and Africa" as the most important movement, one to be recognized in any attempt at formulation of an effective foreign policy by the United States or any country concerned with these regions. Certainly even a cursory glance at the facts behind recently headlined upheavals in Africa and Asia substantiates Romulo's assertion.

[1] *New York Times,* June 19, 1955, p. 60.

North Africa

Perhaps the most graphic example of what Romulo meant in the preceding quotation is the course of events in North Africa since 1950. Here, in less than a decade, a vast tier of communities inhabited mainly by Arabs and Arabized Berbers broke loose from European domination at various stages and asserted their national desires for independence. In this process, communists have played a very minor role. Both leadership and mass support have come from people professing the Islamic faith and dedication to the termination of colonialism rather than affirmation of Marxist objectives.

At the extreme eastern end of North Africa, Egyptians first raised the banner of nationalism when they refused to be transferred from Turkish to British control at the end of World War I. In 1922, Egyptian independence was declared, but Britain retained control over the Suez Canal, in which its government had a controlling interest. The continued presence of a garrison of British troops in the Canal Zone became the focal point of agitation by Egyptian nationalists who saw in this arrangement violation of Egypt's complete national freedom. The agitation had reached violent proportions by 1950. No Egyptian government could hope to command popular support without taking vigorous action against Britain's hold on the Canal. In 1951, the treaty governing the Suez Zone was abrogated by Cairo, and attacks upon British soldiers multiplied. Finally, in 1953, London agreed to the evacuation of all her armed forces. In 1956, when the United States and Britain withdrew an offer of economic aid to Premier Nasser's government, Nasser nationalized the company operating the Suez Canal and declared that the proceeds from the Canal tolls would be used for Egyptian economic development.

A contributing factor in the Anglo-American decision to withdraw their offer of assistance in the construction of a giant dam on the Nile at Aswan had been Nasser's bartering of cotton for military equipment with communist-dominated Czechoslovakia earlier in 1956. The flow of Czech arms into Egypt, coupled with nationalization of the Suez Canal Co., goaded France, Israel, and Britain into armed invasion of Egypt in late 1956, in an effort to unseat Nasser and regain control of the Canal lifeline to Arabian oil sources. When the United States not only refused tacitly to support the invasion but, along with an overwhelming majority of the other members of the United Nations, insisted on a ceasefire, the three invaders complied and withdrew their forces. Despite the woefully weak showing of the Egyptian armed forces, the Nasser regime hailed the withdrawal as a "victory" and was wildly cheered by Egyptian nationalists.

Adjoining Egypt is the newly independent state of Libya. An Italian colony before World War II, and occupied by the British after the war,

Libya was the scene of nationalist demands for independence. In 1951 this independence was granted. That the transition was accomplished without violence, in contrast with much of the rest of North Africa, is attributable to Italy's defeat and the reluctance of any other European state to defy the obviously rising nationalism in Libya by attempting to impress a new colonial regime upon it. Here, as in Egypt, there has been little or no evidence of communist direction or leadership of the native nationalist movements.

To the west of Libya is the great expanse of territory known, until 1956, as French North Africa. Here in Tunisia, Algeria, and Morocco, since 1951, a very serious situation has been produced by nationalism. In these three territories, totaling over 1 million square miles, live nearly 20 million Arabs and Berbers with over 2 million non-Moslems, mostly Frenchmen. Algeria was brought under French domination a century ago; Tunisia became a French protectorate in 1881, and Morocco in 1912. Resentment of French control mounted sharply first among Paris-educated Arabs, then among the masses. Local Arab chieftains found it expedient to place themselves at the head of the nationalist movements. The more moderate Arab leaders, fearing the repercussions of violence, attempted negotiation with Paris; others encouraged coercion, especially after the success of the Egyptians and the forcible expulsion of the French from Indochina.

Unlike the Egyptian and Libyan situations, however, this one was complicated by the presence of many French settlers in the area. Reluctant to abandon them to Arab domination, and highly sensitive to any further lowering of French national prestige, especially after her military, diplomatic, and political defeat in Indochina, Paris resorted to limited concessions, combined with armed suppression of civil disturbances. The outcome was greater violence, including ferocious Arab attacks upon French settlements as well as upon French military personnel. The dispatch of over 300,000 troops, including most of France's NATO contingents, failed to stem the nationalist tide.

In March, 1956, France formally agreed to the termination of the protectorate status of Tunisia and Morocco and recognized their independence. (Spain followed suit with her Moroccan protectorate.) Although this put an end to the violence in the two states, Algerian unrest intensified. Both Tunisians and Moroccans expressed sympathy with their fellow Arabs in Algeria, the new Tunisian president, Habib Bourgiba, stating that his people could not "be truly happy until their sister nation Algeria regains her sovereignty." [2]

The sympathy was expressed in a material way as well, the two new nation-states tolerating the smuggling of arms across their frontiers to the Algerian nationalists. This flow of aid and French efforts to halt it made even more acute the critical state of affairs in North Africa. In

[2] *New York Times,* March 23, 1956, p. 10.

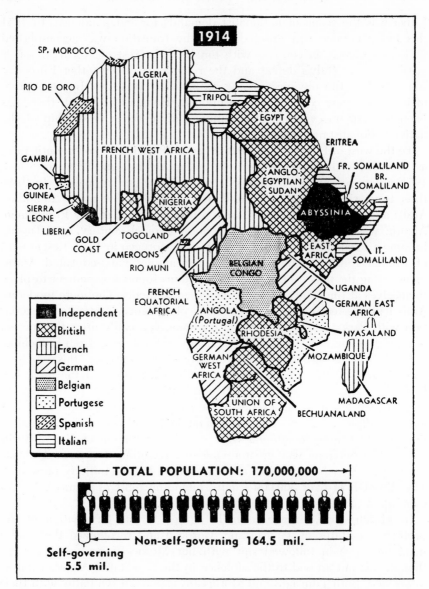

Fig. 7a. Africa in 1914. At this time only Abyssinia (officially known as Ethiopia) and Liberia were independent. (*Source: New York Times*, April 27, 1958, Section IV, p. 6E.)

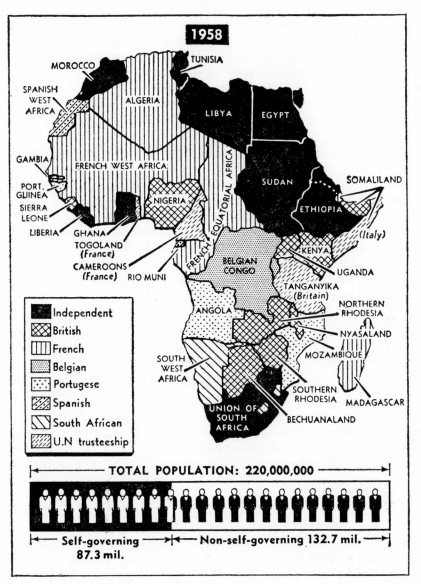

Fig. 7*b*. Africa in 1958. Nine states had acquired independence by June, 1958. (*Source: New York Times*, April 27, 1958, Section IV, p. 6E.)

1958, the world was shocked by the French aircraft-bombing of a border village inside Tunisia. Allegedly seeking Algerian gunrunners, the raiders caused the death of 68 Tunisians, including many women and children. New fires of Francophobia were ignited: Anti-French riots broke out, appeals for a general United Nations review of French North African policy were sent to the Security Council, and Tunis demanded evacuation by France of all its military bases, including the giant naval-air base at Bizerte.

Thus France, condemned throughout the world, alienated from her western allies, appeared to be waging a losing battle against Arab nationalists from one end of North Africa to the other. A growing number of Frenchmen were coming to perceive the hopelessness of France's situation, but others clung to the hope that a solution could be worked out whereby Algeria would not have to be completely detached from France. Official France in early 1958 still held to this position, strove for a solution outside of the United Nations, and bitterly castigated her western friends for not supporting her in the Algerian war. A French general had earlier been quoted as having said: [3]

If we leave, North Africa will be lost to the occidental world. Control of North Africa made the liberation of Europe possible in the last war. But the strategic loss is not the worst. The French economy will go to pieces; France will go Communist; Paris will receive its directives from Moscow.

Whether this prediction will be borne out by events is not yet clear, but even if it should, and if the Soviet bloc reaped benefits from it, it still would not contradict Romulo's insistence that nationalist movements are not necessarily engineered by communists. To date their manipulations have not been an important factor in the North African upheaval, where nationalism dominates the headlines. This holds true for other areas, as well.

The Middle East

Evidence of national consciousness and a desire for independence were apparent among the peoples to the east of Egypt before World War I. To the Arabs of Lebanon, Syria, Palestine, Iraq, Jordan, and Saudi Arabia, World War I was a struggle for freedom from Turkish rule. Hence, when French, British, and Zionist interests became active in these areas in the period after Turkey's defeat in 1918, Arab nationalists turned upon them. Saudi Arabia succeeded in establishing itself as an independent state during the 1920's, and Iraq became fully independent in 1932, but the other four Arab states did not achieve their national freedom until World War II and afterward.

Syria and Lebanon, which had been French mandates under the League

[3] *New York Times,* March 5, 1956, p. 7.

of Nations since 1920, proclaimed their independence during World War II in the wake of France's occupation by Germany. In Palestine, the British had had a League mandate but had been continually troubled by more and more turbulent Arab-Jewish rivalry. In 1947, when they were trying to reduce their heavy overseas economic expenditures, they relinquished the mandate and turned the problem over to the United Nations. Since then, Palestine has been the scene of some of the most violent nationalistic outbursts of recent times.

Unable to satisfy completely both Jews and Arabs, the United Nations in December, 1947, finally recommended the partition of Palestine. Reluctantly the Jews accepted the United Nations partition plan and announced that an independent Israeli state would be set up within the boundaries recommended by the United Nations. The Arabs, who had constituted the preponderant population of Palestine for over 1,000 years, regarded the creation of a Jewish state there as a violation of their own nationalist aspirations and rights.[4] They declared they would fight to prevent the establishment of an independent Jewish state on land that they believed belonged rightfully to them. Hence, when British forces finally withdrew in May, 1948, and Israeli independence was formally proclaimed, the Arab forces launched a full-scale invasion in an effort to wipe out the new state. By 1949, the Israelis had repulsed the Arab forces and even occupied some 2,200 square miles of land that the United Nations had originally allocated to the Arabs. An armistice was signed in 1949, based on the existing battle lines.

The constant state of tension along the armistice line flared into open warfare again when Israel joined France and Britain in the previously mentioned 1956 invasion of Egypt. Only the most persistent pressure by the United States and the United Nations forced Israel to evacuate the areas seized and occupied by her armed forces during the Suez incident. An international military patrol under the United Nations (UNEF) policed some of the disputed strips lying between the Israelis and the Arabs, but the latter left no doubt of their hopes that Israel would eventually be liquidated. The formation in 1958 by the Arab states, Egypt and Syria, of the United Arab Republic (later joined by Yemen) appeared to have two major purposes: to lead the way to unification of all Arab states, and to bring greater pressure to bear on the Republic of Israel which lay between Egypt and Syria.

In Iraq and Jordan it was Britain whose position slowly crumpled under

[4] The population of Palestine in 1922, 1931, and 1946 was distributed as follows:

	Arabs	Jews	Christians	Others	Total
1922	486,177	83,790	71,464	7,617	649,048
1931	693,147	174,606	88,907	10,101	966,761
1946	1,076,783	608,225	145,063	15,488	1,845,559

Source: United Nations Special Committee on Palestine, *Report to the General Assembly*, Vol. I, p. 11 (United Nations General Assembly, 2nd sess., 1947, Suppl. 11).

nationalist pressure. Concerned with Mesopotamian oil, London had established League of Nations mandates over these two states in 1920. The mandate terminated for Iraq in 1932, although Britain retained the right to keep troops there. During World War II restless Iraqis staged an unsuccessful pro-Axis revolt against pro-British colleagues. A decade after the war, the British position in Iraq was threatened by the collapse of all British influence in Jordan. The latter had secured complete independence in 1946, the British retaining the use of air bases and supplying of military officers to the Jordan army. In 1948, Jordan plunged into the war with Israel, sharing the major military burden with Egypt and chafing under the restraints imposed by the British. In 1956, Jordanian nationalists forced the removal of all British officers from the British-trained Arab Legion, the crack, 15,000-man corps of Jordan's army. Clearly the end of the line for traditional British Middle Eastern policy seemed to be approaching.

At this point it should be noted that the rapidly shifting relationships between the Arab states, between Arabs and Israelis, and between the Arabs and the Anglo-French opened the door to an extension of the cold war to the Middle East. The United States attempted to curry favor with the Arab nationalists by insisting upon the evacuation of Suez in 1956 by the invading forces, and in 1957 by announcing the Eisenhower Doctrine to strengthen the Middle East against communist threats. The Soviet Union also became more active in the area. A strongly antiwestern regime in Syria in 1957 was approved and supported by Moscow. An abortive attempt the same year to bring about revolution against Jordan's King Hussein produced charges by the king of Soviet assistance, and in turn prompted the extension of United States aid to Hussein's government. During this period, the Soviet bloc, too, concluded a number of aid and trade agreements with many Arab states.

In the face of Arab nationalism, of course, both the U.S.A. and the U.S.S.R. felt it necessary to disclaim all intent of interfering with the independence of the Arab states. Hussein made it clear that he had accepted American aid without commitments to Washington, and he sought greater stability and strength through federation with the Arab Kingdom of Iraq in early 1958. The Arab countries that had signed agreements with the Soviet Union boasted that no "strings" were attached. The presence of Soviet and American agents in the Middle East and the obvious Russo-American competition for influence there should not obscure the fact that nationalism has been, and is, the dominant force at work in the Middle East, as it is in North Africa. The almost universal claims by the Arab states that they are neutral in the cold war underline this fact.

Iran, though culturally distinct from the Arab states, is still another case in point. Having maintained a precarious political independence ever since westerners evinced interest in its oil resources at the turn of the century, Iran became increasingly sensitive to nationalism. In 1935 the country's name was changed from Persia to Iran to emphasize a cultural and national unity among the people of the Iranian plateau. Resentment against foreign concessionaires, especially the British Anglo-Iranian Oil Co., deepened. Inevitably, ambitious politicians attempted to capitalize on this feeling. Most successful was Mohammed Mossadegh, who organized a mass following and verbally attacked the Anglo-Iranian Oil Co. Mossadegh's movement included the Communist Party but was by no means communist-dominated. In 1951, Mossadegh was swept into office; in the name of the Iranian nation he seized the Anglo-Iranian refineries at Abadan. Saner leaders, who recognized the impossibility of operating the refineries without British technical assistance, dared not oppose this popular move. Only after two years of complete stoppage of oil production, with consequent unemployment in Iran and halting of royalties to the Iranian government, were Mossadegh's opponents able to oust him in a palace revolution and compromise with Britain. Significantly, the settlement of 1954 provided for nationalization of the oil company's properties, though with compensation to British investors and retention of British technical personnel. Thus, in Iran, nationalism became a roaring stream upon whose surface local politicians and foreign capitalists, Teheranian emotions and London pocketbooks were unceremoniously tossed about. Although communism played some role here, in contrast to the preceding examples, it was overshadowed by the far broader nationalist movement.

India

Certainly, in terms of numbers of people involved, the Indian nationalist revolution is the most significant manifestation of this phenomenon since World War II. Awakened to national consciousness only after several decades of agitation by such leaders as Mahatma Gandhi, the 400 million inhabitants of British-dominated India finally began to stir in the 1920's.

British efforts to allay Indian restlessness had resulted in a Constitutional Act (1919), providing for the election of provincial assemblies with very limited powers. The elections in 1920 were boycotted by the Indian nationalists, and from then on the national movement gained in momentum. Its distinctive Indian character was reflected in its emphasis upon nonviolent civil disobedience. Indeed, Indian nationalism is almost alone in its remarkable rejection of violent measures to achieve national goals. In 1930, this was dramatized by Gandhi's famous march to the sea, where he and his followers boiled buckets of salt water from which was derived just enough salt to violate the British government's salt monopoly. Soon other forms of civil disobedience ensued, and Indian nationalists willingly crowded the jails, until the authorities had 40,000 prisoners to care for and no room for new violators of the civil laws. Faced with this impasse, Britain opened new negotiations with Gandhi which dragged on through World War II and were concluded finally by the action of Britain's new Labor Government in 1947. That year Parliament passed the Indian Independence Act, after an agreement had been reached among Indian leaders on the separation of the predominantly Moslem areas from the rest of India and their constitution as the separate state of Pakistan.

With British rule ended, Indian nationalism evidenced itself in new ways. Friction with Pakistan over the disputed border territory of Kashmir brought India and Pakistan to the verge of war several times. Tragically, Gandhi was assassinated in 1948 by a Hindu extremist who disapproved of Gandhi's acceptance of India's partition into two states. Thus, the Mahatma became a victim of the nationalism he had helped to stimulate. India's foreign policy of nonalignment with either bloc in the cold war further emphasized the conscious national independence of this new country. Having escaped the coils of colonialism, Indians would take no chances that alliances, technical assistance, or economic aid might become the opening wedge for domination of their country by foreigners. Though many Americans were disturbed by the cordial reception in India of Premier Bulganin and Secretary Khrushchev in 1956, they might have found a plausible explanation in Indian nationalism. This was the first occasion on which the titular head of a great power had visited India, and the Indian people regarded the visit as tribute to their nation. Other factors would enter, in a more fully rounded examination, but Romulo's observation quoted at the opening of this chapter is still pertinent. Indian nationalism, more than Indian communism, is the major leavening element.

The Far East

The Far East, too, in recent times has responded emphatically to nationalism. Here, because of the imposing influence of Communist China, communism has sometimes marched with nationalism and has exploited nationalism for its own purposes. Yet, there are notable exceptions.

The Philippines. Here is the foremost example of a national movement largely free of communist connection. Many American citizens were shocked by the discovery that, when Spain ceded the Philippines to the United States in 1898 for 16 million dollars, a first-class insurrection was included as part of the deal. Restless under Spain, Filipinos in growing numbers had become sufficiently nationally conscious to endorse the idea that Spain's defeat should mean the Islands' freedom, not transfer to another colonial power. Thus, Emilio Aguinaldo and his band fought the Americans for years in jungle guerilla warfare, while Manuel Quezon and others attempted to persuade Washington by other means that the Filipinos needed national independence. "Better a government run like hell by Filipinos than one run like heaven by foreigners" was the nationalist reply to the American argument that the Islanders were not ready for self-government. In 1916, President Wilson promised future independence; in 1934, Congress initiated a transitional period, to be concluded in ten years with complete independence. World War II somewhat upset this timetable but afforded an opportunity for the growing, mutual good will between Filipinos and Americans to express itself during the bleak days of Bataan and Corregidor. On July 4, 1946, the Philippine Republic was recognized, with American approval and support. Thus Filipino nationalists won, and Americans took pride in the achievements, under their guidance, in education, communications, public health, and in the minimum of anti-Americanism remaining among their former colonial subjects.

Indonesia. The end of Dutch rule in Indonesia parallels the Philippine story so far as the absence of communist domination of a nationalist movement is concerned. After over three centuries of colonial rule, the Indonesians took advantage of the withdrawal of the Japanese invaders in 1945 and resisted forcibly efforts to re-establish Netherlands' control. With the help of United Nations mediation, the Republic of Indonesia was finally recognized by the Dutch in 1949. Demonstrating its newly won nationhood, Indonesia in 1952 rejected the continuation of American economic aid, not because Indonesia was in the Soviet bloc (which it was not), but because it desired to be as free as possible from any foreign political or military commitments. In particular, it objected to the United States' requirement that recipients of American aid contribute to the defensive strength of the free world. A year later, after much negotiation, an agreement was reached whereby Indonesia might receive American nonmilitary technical assistance without the conditions to which it had earlier objected. Indonesia since 1954 has also received some technical assistance from various members of the communist bloc.

Indonesian nationalism more recently manifested itself in the pride exhibited by Indonesians when their country played host to twenty-nine independent African and Asian states meeting to discuss their common problems in Bandung in April, 1955. It has also been evident in the persistent agitation for annexation of Dutch New Guinea (called West Irian by the Indonesians), a large area lying immediately east of Indonesia. In late 1957 seizures of Dutch property in Indonesia and the consequent departure of thousands of Dutch settlers from Indonesia was viewed partly as pressure on the Dutch for relinquishment of New Guinea, and partly as an effort to rally popular support, midst grave domestic difficulties, to the regime of President Sukarno.

Ironically, Sukarno, the leader of the Indonesian nationalist revolt

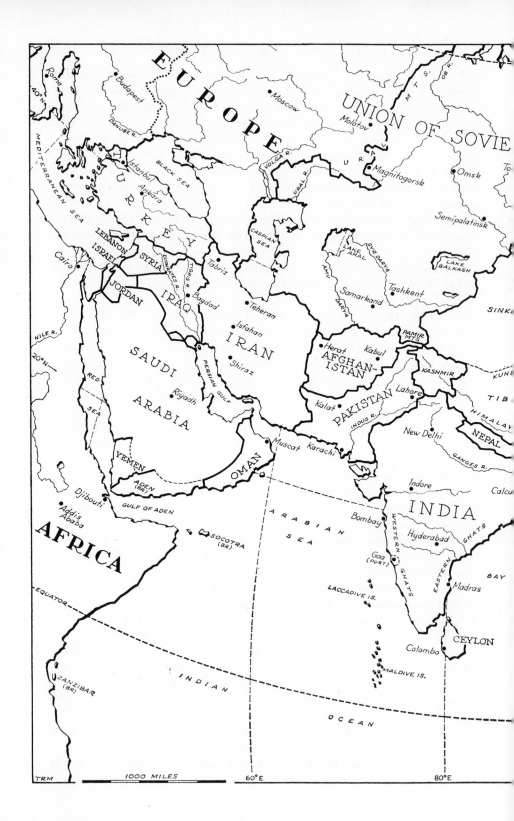

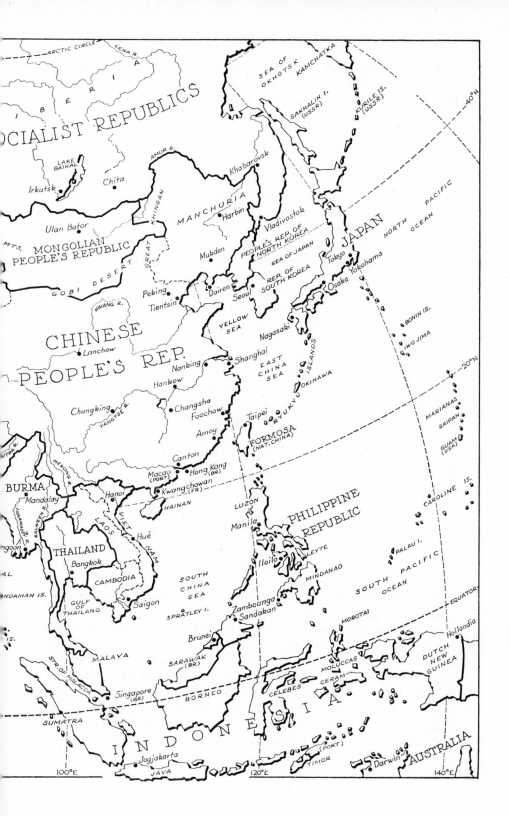

against the Netherlands, in 1958 faced a separatist movement, which had nationalist overtones of its own, among the 30 million inhabitants of the Republic's outer islands (Sumatra, Borneo, and Celebes). The armed revolt appeared to be inspired by opposition to the growing influence of Indonesian Communists in Sukarno's "guided democracy," as well as by dissatisfaction with Sukarno's economic policies and the preponderant role played in the Republic by the Javanese. In any event, the presence of the communist issue does not disprove the contention that the dominant role in recent Indonesian history has been that of nationalism.

Vietnam. This wealthier, more populous, coastal part of French Indochina resisted French reoccupation after Japan's defeat in 1945. Here, however, significant differences from the Philippines and Indonesia are to be noted. First, the Vietnamese leaders, headed by Ho Chi Minh, were Communists who fused the nationalist and communist movements. Second, the French were successful in reoccupying part of Vietnam and holding it for some years after 1945. Ho Chi Minh's forces surged dramatically toward victory only in 1953 when Communist China, free from its Korean War commitments, made aid available to the nationalists-communists. In 1954, at Dienbienphu, a remote village in northern Vietnam, a significant part of the French army stationed in Vietnam was besieged and finally destroyed. Armistice negotiations at Geneva in July, 1954, led to establishment of two provisional governments: one, under noncommunists, in South Vietnam; another, under Ho Chi Minh, in North Vietnam. It was further agreed that a plebiscite to determine the nature of a government for all Vietnam would be held in 1956. With North Vietnam tied to the Soviet bloc, the United States made strenuous efforts to encourage a native noncommunist government in South Vietnam that would satisfy overwhelming nationalist desires to be free of French rule, yet keep South Vietnam from joining the communist orbit. This South Vietnam government subsequently severed all ties with France and proceeded to conclude agreements with the United States for military and economic assistance. The plebiscite, scheduled for 1956, was not held.

Korea. In the three preceding cases, only in North Vietnam did the Communists gain control of the nationalist movement and succeed in establishing a government of their own. North Korea is the other leading example, except for China, where the Communists were able to dominate the nationalist movement. Unlike Vietnam, however, where native Communists won broad popular support in their opposition to the French, in North Korea the Communists owed their opportunity and power almost entirely to the Soviet armies which occupied North Korea from 1945 to 1949. When the Soviet forces withdrew from North Korea, they left a well-organized communist government in power which was armed with

Soviet equipment and which subsequently attempted unsuccessfully to conquer the noncommunist government of South Korea.

China. The single, most outstanding example of the manipulation of a nationalist movement by communists is, of course, China. No attempt will be made here to describe the long, involved story of the Chinese Revolution from its nationalist beginnings, during the latter part of the nineteenth and early part of the twentieth century, to its national-communist climax of 1949. Unquestionably, Chinese Communists now dominate Chinese nationalism and direct it to their own ends. Nevertheless, it was not always so.

When Sun Yat-sen first led the Chinese in their fight to break the imperialist hold of the West on their country, nationalism prevailed as the dominant force. A number of factors, however, enabled China's Communists, over a twenty-year period, to get control of the nationalist movement. Inability or unwillingness of Sun's successor, Chiang Kai-shek, to carry out far-reaching economic and political reforms made many Chinese turn to the Chinese Communists, who promised both national independence and internal reforms. Antipathy toward the western, race-conscious nations also encouraged many young Chinese intellectuals to study and visit the Soviet Union, another country of peasant masses and retarded technology. Thus, Soviet influence grew in China. The Russians encouraged the Chinese Communist Party with aid and advice. When the long struggle with Japan created additional problems for Chiang Kai-shek, the Communists capitalized on the unrest and frustration to capture the nationalist movement and ride it into power in the civil war with Chiang from 1945 to 1949.

The Chinese experience, however, does not disprove Romulo's argument. It merely demonstrates that nationalist movements can be captured by communists. Only ill-informed observers of the critical areas in Asia and Africa jump to the unfounded, and therefore very dangerous, conclusion that, wherever nationalism makes headlines, the crisis should be treated as a communist-noncommunist conflict.

Europe

Nationalism was originally a European phenomenon. Only in recent decades has it manifested itself in Africa and Asia. The nineteenth century, in particular, was for Europe an age of nationalism. It would be quite inaccurate, however, to conclude that the national movements of Europe are dead. Although most of the dramatic national uprisings since World War II have occurred elsewhere, nationalism remains a major factor in Europe, too. Indeed, the Hungarian revolt in the fall of 1956 was perhaps the most dramatic of all in the postwar world. Its character was clearly indicated, as a "spontaneous national uprising, due to long-

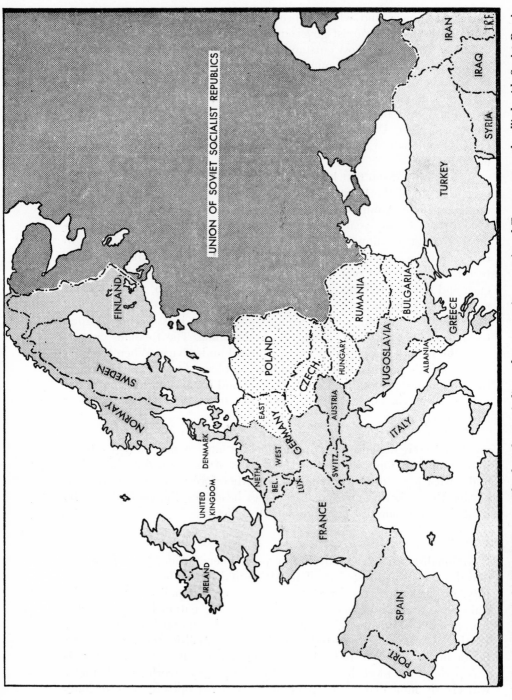

Fig. 9. Post World War II Europe. The dotted areas indicate the communist countries of Europe presently allied with Soviet Russia.

standing grievances," by a United Nations committee of inquiry in its report on Hungary in June, 1957. Less dramatic events in two other European countries, Germany and Yugoslavia, also illustrate the importance of nationalism in Europe.

Germany. The single, all-pervading issue in post-1945 Germany has been a nationalistic one. Immediately after the war, food, housing, law, and order demanded attention. Soon afterward, the great preoccupation of the German people became reunification of their nation. The Russian-supported republic in the East and the Anglo-French-American-sponsored government in West Germany were viewed by most Germans as stopgap arrangements, as an intermediate step between foreign occupation and national reunification. Germans made no attempt to conceal this feeling.

At the end of the war, the Western Allies had given serious consideration to the so-called Morgenthau Plan for the reduction of Germany to a divided, agricultural, and defenseless area in north central Europe. Within three years, the proposals had been forgotten. The advent of the cold war made the potential power and resources of a united Germany extremely attractive to both communist and noncommunist blocs. Since 1948, both the Soviet Union and the western powers have appealed to German nationalist sentiments, offering rival proposals for German re-unification. The Soviet proposals were calculated to advance the prospects of a united communist Germany, whereas the western proposals were naturally designed to assure the establishment of a united democratic Germany. The Soviet-western stalemate has thus far prevented the solution of this problem, and German nationalism has been left frustrated and unsatisfied. Further discussion of this question will be found in Chapter 11.

Yugoslavia. Another example of European nationalism will conclude this summary. The sensational expulsion of Yugoslavia from the Cominform in 1948 and the severance of ties with the U.S.S.R. and other communist-dominated states stem from nationalist factors. Spurred by a traditionally strong national feeling, the Yugoslavs for several generations had successively fought Turkish, Austro-Hungarian, and finally Nazi German invasion and domination. When membership in the Soviet bloc increasingly denoted Russian domination, Marshall Tito's government, which never disavowed communism, broke away from it. Its own brand of communism and a foreign policy dictated by Yugoslavia's own national interests were dominant after the 1948 split. It was the opinion of many experts on Eastern Europe, moreover, that, afforded the same freedom from Russian garrisons and a free avenue of communication with the West, Poland, Czechoslovakia, Hungary, Rumania, and Bulgaria would produce their versions of Titoism and assert their national independence even if they did not abandon communism. The revolutions in Poland and

Hungary in late 1956 tended to bear this out. A fuller discussion of Yugo-slav communism will be found in Chapter 9.

Thus, in Yugoslavia, there is evidence of nationalism counteracting the international aspects of communism. This is quite the reverse of the Chinese and Vietnamese situations and points up again the importance of recognizing nationalism as a distinctive and highly significant force behind today's headlines.

THE NATURE OF NATIONALISM

Like most controversial topics, nationalism is extensively discussed by people from all walks of life. Actually, although it is almost universally acknowledged, it is not a subject about which conclusive, definitive knowl-edge exists.

Not until the nineteenth century did nationalism become the object of more than passing comment by students of European civilization. However, with the intensification and extension of the movement to more and more peoples of Europe and then of the other continents, the litera-ture on the subject increased. To be sure, it revealed no very clear or generally accepted concept of what nationalism was. For example, Jules Michelet, a French writer of the middle of that century, called upon Frenchmen of all classes to unite so that they might, by their special na-tional attributes, exercise leadership of the world. These attributes, he believed, included French distinction in literature, arms, and revolutionary tradition. The world, he insisted, needed leadership in an age when the common man was rising to share power with the older upper classes, and the bond that would serve to unite these antipathetic classes was nationalism, as best exemplified in France. "France, glorious mother," wrote Michelet, "you who not only are our mother but who must bring forth every nation to liberty, make us love each other in you." [5]

In a different vein Giuseppe Mazzini called upon Italians to join in one political unit so that the Italian nation might assume its mission on behalf of humanity. The goals were, in Mazzini's mind, liberty, equality, and fraternity for all mankind. Heinrich von Treitschke extolled Bis-marck's work in creating a German state which would nurture and pro-tect the characteristics that made the German nation pre-eminent. Had not the Germans, he asked, distinguished themselves among mankind in science, economics, and war? Feodor Dostoevsky, the great Russian novelist, asserted that his people possessed a unique capacity for under-standing the conflicts and contradictions of other societies and for extend-ing the love and sympathy necessary for their harmony and peace. Ac-cording to Dostoevsky, "To a true Russian, Europe and the fate of the

---

[5] Quoted in Hans Kohn, *Prophets and Peoples* (New York, Macmillan, 1946, re-printed with publisher's permission), pp. 63–64.

whole great Aryan race are as dear as Russia herself, because our mission is the embodiment of the universal idea on earth." [6]

Such philosophizing, of which the foregoing are only a few examples, reveals the growing interest in nationalism, but it merely casts a shadowy light on its nature. It identifies groups of humans who are labeled French, Italians, Germans, or Russians. It suggests that each labeled group has special characteristics that qualify it for some kind of world mission. However, the precise character of nationalism remains obscure. Fortunately, in recent years, as nationalism has assumed increased significance in the modern world—as a contributing cause of two world wars, as a vital ingredient of totalitarianism, and as the most dynamic force in Afro-Asia—it has attracted the attention of many students of human behavior. As the preceding chapter indicates, social psychologists identify nationality as one kind of in-group consciousness. Keeping in mind this concept, an attempt will be made here to define nationalism and explore its nature more fully.

Nationalism Defined

Two leading authorities on the subject are Carlton J. H. Hayes and Hans Kohn. Hayes has described nationalism as: [7]

. . . A condition of mind among members of a nationality . . . in which loyalty to the ideal or to the fact of one's national state is superior to all other loyalties and of which pride in one's nationality and belief in its intrinsic excellence and in its "mission" are integral parts.

Kohn offers this definition: [8]

Nationalism is a state of mind, permeating the large majority of a people and claiming to permeate all its members; it recognizes the nation-state as the ideal form of political organization and the nationality as the source of all creative cultural energy and of economic well-being.

Both definitions refer to nationalism as a state of mind, involving a feeling of loyalty to the nationality group or nation-state that takes precedence over all other loyalties. Thus nationalism assumes the character of a religion, in the complete and unqualified loyalty it demands on the part of its adherents. In an extreme emergency such as war, loyalty to the nation-state may even conflict with normal moral, religious, or ethical loyalties, which are usually expected to yield to the loyalty of nationalism.

In the preceding definitions, the terms *nationality* and *nation-state* were also used, and it would be well at this point to indicate their meaning more precisely.

---

[6] *Ibid.*, p. 157.

[7] The selection from Carlton J. H. Hayes, *Essays on Nationalism*, New York, copyright 1926 by The Macmillan Company and used with publisher's permission, p. 6.

[8] The selection from Hans Kohn, *The Idea of Nationalism*, New York, copyright 1944 by The Macmillan Company and used with publisher's permission, p. 16.

Nationality

Nationality usually refers to a group of people who share a common historical background, geographical territory, customs and traditions, who usually have a common language and often a common religion, and who therefore are conscious of belonging together, regarding themselves as a distinct cultural group. Thus we speak of the French or Germans or Italians or Chinese as nationality groups.[9] In this sense, the term *ethnic group* is sometimes used interchangeably with *nationality group*.

Nation-State

As Europe emerged from feudalism and the Middle Ages, the new states which came into being in England, France, Spain, Portugal, and Russia were based essentially on nationality groups. The term *nation-state* came into being, meaning an independent, politically sovereign unit in which a majority of the people comprised a particular nationality group. There might, of course, be other nationality groups in the state, but since they do not comprise the majority of the population, they are referred to as minority nationality groups. Some nation-states, like France, Germany, or Italy, are made up almost entirely of their respective nationality groups, whereas others like the Soviet Union and the states of Eastern Europe include many minority nationality groups.

States resembling modern sovereign states, of course, are of ancient origin, as witness the Greek city-states which existed several hundred years before the birth of Christ. Only during the last four or five centuries, however, have states been based on the principle of nationality.[10]

Factors Conducive to the Rise of Nationality Groups

What are the factors that have led to the rise of nationality groups, that have caused them to feel distinctive, and have spurred them on to achieve political independence in the form of nation-states? Although

[9] In modern times, the term *nationality* is also applied in a more legal sense to designate citizenship in a specific nation-state. Thus an individual's identification papers may list his "nationality" as U.S.A. or British, meaning that he is a citizen of the United States or of Great Britain. In this sense, it is conceivable that a German-speaking person, residing in Czechoslovakia, might regard himself as a German in the ethnic or cultural sense yet legally be a citizen of Czechoslovakia.

[10] The modern sovereign state could not really be understood before the sixteenth century, since the modern concept of sovereignty was not clearly formulated until Jean Bodin wrote the famous *Six Books Concerning the State,* in 1576.

The term *nation* is often encountered in discussions of nationalism, but it is a very imprecise expression, sometimes serving to designate a nationality group and sometimes to designate a nation-state. Occasionally reference is loosely made to members of the French nation when actually what is meant is the members of the French nationality group. Or states and governments of the world are spoken of as nations of the world. For this reason, the term *nation* will be generally avoided in this chapter.

complete agreement has not been reached, certain factors have been generally accepted as important by most students of the subject.

The authorities do not, for example, accept as valid the assertion advanced from time to time, most recently by Nazi Germans, that nationality has its sole or primary basis in race. Although races, as defined in the preceding chapter, may be identified, it is a foregone conclusion for the most casual observer that such a group would not be found in a single, physically homogeneous nation-state. There are swarthy and blond Italians, tall and short Germans, brown-eyed and blue-eyed Englishmen, large-headed and small-headed Chinese. Nor does there seem to be evidence that blood relations separated by distance desire or believe they share a common nationality. Every American has blood ties with remote cousins in Europe, Asia, Africa, or in the islands in the Caribbean, but within a few generations the ties come to have little or no bearing on the American's nationality. He belongs to a group of people with diverse blood ties, bound together by a common culture and political organization.

On the other hand, the factors that are now recognized as most influential in the emergence of nationality consciousness include common physical environment and territorial unity, common language, customs, history and tradition, and common religion.

Physical environment. Probably geography was responsible for several prehistoric families, confined to the same valley or secluded on the same highland, slowly acquiring a community spirit and gradually evolving into larger associations or tribes. Certain it is that the tribes inhabiting the British and Japanese islands developed a larger sense of unity because of detachment from their continental neighbors whom they knew but did not live with. Similarly, the high, wind-swept plateau of central Iberia afforded the inland tribes of that region a physical unity not shared with coastal Iberian folk. Thus it was much more than coincidental that among the first tribal amalgamations were the British, Japanese, Spanish, and the latter's seaboard neighbors, the Portuguese, Basques, and Catalonians. These amalgamations were vital initial steps in the emergence of nationality groups.

The geographic influence notable in these classic examples cannot, however, be as plainly identified in the growth of other nationalities. For this reason, the physical environment, as some authorities suggest, must be cautiously evaluated.

Language. Generally accepted as more important are the factors of man-made environment such as language, customs, history, tradition, and religion. A common language, for example, is one of the factors most conducive to nationality consciousness. Anyone who travels in other countries, where his own language is not readily understood, quickly senses the unifying influence of a common tongue. Americans in Paris,

British in Berlin, or Frenchmen in Rome feel what might almost be described as a kinship with other members of their nationality groups because they can speak the same language.

Historically, the development of national vernacular languages and their increased substitution for Latin toward the end of the Middle Ages contributed considerably to an awareness of nationality differences. The subsequent invention of printing made the unifying influence of a common language even greater, and the stage was now set for the appearance of truly national literatures. English literature of the Elizabethan Age reflected a distinct national consciousness. Perhaps no better example of early English nationalism may be found than the following passage from Shakespeare's *King Richard II:*

> This royal throne of kings, this scept'red isle,
> This earth of majesty, this seat of Mars,
> This other Eden, demi-paradise,
> This fortress built by Nature for herself
> Against infection and the hand of war,
> This happy breed of men, this little world,
> This precious stone set in the silver sea. . . .
> This blessed plot, this earth, this realm, this England.

French and Spanish literature of this period likewise contributed to a growing nationality consciousness, and examples could be added from the literatures of other peoples.

Customs. Similarly, customs and mores furnish cultural distinctions which have contributed to nationality consciousness. Geographic factors have sometimes played an initial role here. Climate and soil, for example, dictated originally the wine-drinking habit of the Frenchman. In time, regardless of his proximity to a vineyard, the Frenchman included wine as a staple in his daily diet—in Dakar as well as in Paris, on the Mississippi as well as on the Loire, in Vietnam as well as in Burgundy. Thus wine-drinking became a distinctive characteristic of French culture. Climate no doubt encouraged the adoption by Indian women of the sari as a comfortable garment, but today Indians may be seen wearing saris in London, at the United Nations headquarters, and in Moscow. The sari has become the Indian woman's national costume.

It is interesting to note that many Russian customs and mores such as adherence to the Eastern Orthodox Church, its architectural distinctions, and until recently the seclusion of women, drew original inspiration from nearby Byzantium and Asia but in time became typically Russian and as such were fundamental to Russia's cultural uniqueness.

Thus, as with language, customs often have roots in the physical environment, but with the passage of time they proliferate, mutate, and make their own contributions to a people's distinctive development.

History. History and heroes are still another influence. Anthropologist have established the fact that most societies evince a longing for immortality that is partly satisfied by consciousness of a past, either historic or legendary. When the historic awareness is shared by a community it has the effect of binding it more closely together. The Saga of the Vikings has done this for the Danes and Norwegians. Germans have derived a common satisfaction from their ancestral tie with the ancient Teutonic tribes who resisted successfully the advance of Roman power across the Rhine. The very fact that China possesses a written history dating not centuries, but millenniums, before the Occident's, affords the Chinese a unique source of national pride and consciousness. Visible remains on the Acropolis of ancient Athens remind Greeks, as those of the Roman Forum remind Italians, of an historic era of which people in the very same place partook. It might be (erroneously) believed that they were even of the same blood. This the Greeks, and only the Greeks, can collectively sense under the shadow of the Parthenon's Doric columns. And what American of six or more years of age can remain ignorant of America's frontier epoch? Have any people in so brief a time amassed more heroes, legends, and profits than the Americans from their fantastic cult of the "wild west"?

Religion. A common religion may also be a force welding a people together and reinforcing the other factors which have led them to feel unified. The Roman Catholic faith in France and Italy, the Anglican faith in England, Lutheranism in the Scandinavian countries, and the Orthodox Church in Russia have all played an important part in strengthening the nationalism of the respective countries. The Reformation itself, by challenging the universal authority of the Pope in Rome, provided a strong incentive to the rise of national churches in many countries.

The foregoing are the principal factors which tend to make a people feel distinctive as a nationality group. All of them may not be present with every nationality group. The Swiss, for example, have a strong nationality consciousness despite their use of three major languages, and the people of the United States do not feel that the strength of their nationality is in any way diminished by lack of a common religion. Most of them are present, however, in every nationality group, and their combined effect makes a nationality think of itself as a distinctive cultural group.

The nationality consciousness may and often has come into being long before the nationality group achieves independent statehood. Likewise, the feeling of nationalism, with its emphasis on supreme loyalty to the nationality group, may become a dynamic force in the mind of a people even though they have not yet achieved their political independence. This is abundantly evident in the anticolonial revolutions of Asia and Africa today. An examination of the historical evolution of nationalism will make the point even clearer.

THE HISTORICAL EVOLUTION OF NATIONALISM

The undeniable pre-eminence of nationalism in contemporary society—in the United States as elsewhere—cultivates the popular notion that nationalism and national loyalty are a permanent feature of civilization, a "natural" part of human society. This legend, for such it is, is vigorously encouraged by national-minded leaders, educators, publicists, and historians. Americans, of course, trace their history only as far back as the seventeenth century and so cannot distort their own national development as much as can others. Modern Greek nationalists would believe that nationalism among the Greeks was a strong force in the Age of Pericles (fifth century B.C.); German Wagnerian nationalism traces its origin to the dim mythological age of Wodin and Thor. Italians include Julius Caesar in their national history; the English, Queen Boetia; and the Russians, Cyrillus—figures dating back a thousand and more years. Actually, nationalism is not nearly so traditional or "natural." It is of recent origin and it is* man-made. Moreover, most great currents that have shaped human history—the great religions, Chinese and Roman imperialism, feudalism, the Renaissance, the Reformation, scientific advances—were not national and did not teach nationalism, though inadvertently some did foster it. What, then, have been the major steps in the evolution of nationalism?

The Rise of Nation-States

Nationalism has been defined as a state of mind in which the individual's supreme loyalty is to the nation-state; consequently, its first manifestations may be seen in the emergence of the first nation-states in the fifteenth and sixteenth centuries. It was during the disintegration of western European medieval society that this new form of political organization first appeared. The unfixing of the medieval economy by increased trade and capitalistic enterprise, the inadequacy of decentralized feudal institutions as a proper environment for this growing commerce, the intellectual revolution initiated by the Renaissance, the geographic discoveries of the fifteenth century—all these contributed to a growing fluidity in Europe's Atlantic seaboard communities.

The greatest impetus and fervor for the changes came from the new class which arose with them, the town folk or bourgeoisie. This was the element that turned to certain feudal nobles who possessed the power necessary to erect new, much larger political units, within which the bourgeoisie would find the law and order conducive to their economic activities. Thus emerged the unified monarchies of Portugal, Spain, France, and England. On a smaller scale Denmark, Sweden, and the Netherlands also followed this pattern. In each of the enlarged monarchies the bourgeoisie paid taxes and gave personal service to a king whose obligations were to provide internal peace, a court system, protection against outside invasion, and, in some cases, a unified coinage, tariff protection against outside competition, and naval support for overseas commercial undertakings.

It is not surprising that within these nation-states, in all classes, there developed a sense of belonging to the new community. Much of this loyalty had originally found expression in devotion to the person of the king or to heroic figures who had aided the king in the exercise of his power—Joan of Arc of France, the Black Prince in England, and the Cid in Spain. The unity attendant upon centralization of political power in strong monarchs was further reinforced by the factors that had contributed to the rise of nationality consciousness such as national languages, national literatures, and national churches. People were now more conscious of belonging to English, French, or Spanish states than of belonging to the more universal Christian or European society of the Middle Ages.

By the seventeenth century, the nation-state and its sense of national consciousness characterized the political organization of most of western Europe. Yet, it was not until the French Revolution of the eighteenth century that modern nationalism really came into its own.

The French Revolution and Nationalism

It might seem paradoxical that the French Revolution, which included an attack upon the French monarchy, could have fostered nationalism, since the monarchy was one of the forces originally instrumental in creating the nation-state. As a matter of fact, one school of thought maintains that the monarchy was attacked just because it was not sufficiently national. Too many vestiges of feudalism had survived in France, and it was the need to eliminate these, along with the inefficiency and financial mismanagement of the monarchy, which precipitated revolution in 1789. Further lack of sensitivity by French royalty to this emphasis on national politics was evidenced in the royal family's secret negotiations with the Austrian government for aid against the revolutionaries. Revelation of that "unnational" activity brought about the fall of the monarchy in 1792 and the execution of the king.

The most important reason for the impact of the French Revolution on the new, modern nationalism lay in the character of the new political philosophy with which the French challenged the world. With its emphasis on "liberty, equality, and fraternity," it stressed the right of all citizens to have a voice in the control of their government. Popularly controlled government, in theory, was to replace the personal, irresponsible government of absolute monarchs. In the past, the people as a whole had not had an opportunity to influence government in any regular way, and few, if any, had evinced much interest in doing so. Government was the affair of kings and their ministers.

With the philosophy of the French Revolution, however, government was no longer to be the "property" of kings alone. It was to have a broader base in the masses of citizens, and something was now needed to make the latter feel more closely identified with the state than in the past. Something was necessary to win the allegiance of the masses of people, on whose consent government was theoretically to rest. Nationalism, together with popular sovereignty, came to fill this need. Consciously or unconsciously, the leaders of the new French Republic sought to inculcate a loyalty to the new France on the part of all Frenchmen. A comprehensive system of national education, the first of its kind, was launched with the intent of developing in future Frenchmen a loyalty not to any king of France but to the nation-state of France. National military conscription, the first in modern history, was also introduced, and the Marseillaise became the French national anthem.

In the next few years, revolutionary France rigorously reorganized many of its institutions along national lines. Provincial tariffs, laws, and boundaries were wiped out. The Roman Catholic Church with its ties to the Papacy was officially disestablished. Even the traditional western calendar was no longer deemed sufficiently French, and a new one was introduced for a few years, dating not from the birth of the non-French Christ but from that of the French Republic in 1792. Perhaps most significant was the substitution of the single title "Citizen" for all members of the French nation-state in place of the old differentiating titles of the French nobility. Thus the development of French nationalism provided one of the first bases for the subsequent development of French democracy; the latter, on its part, further stimulated nationalism.

The involvement of France in war with her monarchical neighbors in 1792 imparted an even greater impetus to the intensification of nationalism. Now many internal cleavages tended to be dissolved in the new fervor to defend the French nation-state. A nationality was aroused to an unprecedented pitch of emotional devotion and national unity. Members of the French community who did not support the Republic in its war effort were sent to the guillotine. Expressing this emphasis upon national unity are the words of Georges Jacques Danton in 1792: [11]

France must be an indivisible whole: she must have unity of representation. The citizens of Marseilles wish to clasp hands with the citizens of Dunkerque. I, therefore, ask the death penalty against whomsoever wishes to destroy the unity of France.

[11] From *Nationalism, Its Meaning and History*, Hans Kohn. Copyright 1955, D. Van Nostrand Co., Inc., Princeton, N.J., p. 27.

Before the wars of the French Revolution were concluded, Napoleon had harnessed French nationalism to his personal ambitions to re-create the empire of Charlemagne or Caesar. This extravagant imperialistic surge not only gave rise to a legend of military prowess that further fed the fires of French nationalism; it also cultivated an anti-French nationalism among Napoleon's victims.

Thus today, while French nationalists recall the era of the French Revolution and Napoleon in terms of the glories of Austerlitz, Jena, and Wagram, Spanish nationalists are inspired by Goya's depictions of Spanish resistance to French occupation; Russian nationalists thrill to Tchaikovsky's portrayal of Napoleon's retreat from Moscow in the *Overture of 1812;* and German nationalists cherish the poetic summons of Ernst Moritz Arndt to liberation from Napoleon. Quite clearly the French Revolution marks the intensification and spread of European nationalism.

The Growth of Nationalism in the Nineteenth Century

New impetus. Of great importance to nationalism was the growing industrialization of Europe. Expanding means of production and improved transport facilities enlarged the ranks of the bourgeoisie and confronted it with the need for extending its areas of business activity. Where petty principalities survived, as in Italy and Germany, the bourgeoisie soon were endorsing the creation of larger political units, based on economic grounds. Such units would be of invaluable service to businessmen in the establishment of uniform law codes; standardization of coinage, weights, and measures; elimination of local trade barriers; and raising of national tariffs to reserve the national market for the producers of that nation-state. Powerful economic pressures reinforced the momentum of emergent nationalism.

Another new source of encouragement was the Romantic Movement, with its reaction to the preceding century's rationalism and its emphasis upon imagination, intuitive response, and emotionalism. A sentimental review of the past by romanticists uncovered a plethora of folklore, heroes, and exploits which did much to fill the pages of each nationality's history.

More accurate research by historians further aroused interest in events which thus became the ingredients for the picture of a great past for each nationality. As a people's history emerged, so did its consciousness of cultural homogeneity. This, as has been pointed out, is a vital part of nationalism.

New nation-states. The national movement did not always operate centripetally. Although it pushed Italian- and German-speaking peoples toward unification, it tended to disrupt the great multinational empires of eastern Europe. In the Austrian Empire, Czechs resented German being the official language in their Bohemia. In the Russian Empire, Poles bitterly complained against limitations placed upon their own, national tongue. Croats burned with indignation when the Hungarian government attempted to force translation of family and street names from Croatian into Magyar equivalents. The only solution for these culturally oppressed folk seemed to be disruption of the empires and establishment of independent national states.

Greeks and Belgians set off the first tremors after the French Revolution by revolting against their Turkish and Dutch rulers, respectively. When the Turks forcibly endeavored to block Greek secession from the Ottoman Empire, war broke out. Ten years and ten thousand atrocities later, in 1830, a Kingdom of Greece was recognized. The same year, the Belgians behind Brussels barricades, and with the benediction of France and Britain, secured independence from the Netherlands. The year 1848 saw revolutions from Berlin to Rome and Budapest to Frankfort. Nationalist agitators led Italians, Germans, Czechs, Hungarians, Croats, Serbs, and Rumanians to demonstrate against princes and governments which kept Italians and Germans divided and held the others "prisoners" of vast multinational empires. Although not successful, the 1848 revolutionaries revealed the strength of the rising nationalist tide.

Within a century of Waterloo the map of Europe was redesigned largely in the pattern of this growing nationalistic diversity. Italy in 1861, Hungary in 1867, Germany in 1871, Serbia and Rumania in 1878, Norway in 1905, Bulgaria in 1908, and Albania in 1913 gained sovereignty. Significantly, only the Norwegian detachment from Sweden occurred without violence. Of note, also, is the fact that, except for Norway and Hungary, not a single one of the new states was satisfied with its 1914 borders. Thanks to the mixture of Europe's population, these states could and did point to members of their cultural group still under foreign rule. Italians were governed by Austria in the Tyrol, Rumanians by Hungary in Transylvania, Serbs by Austria in Bosnia, Bulgars by Rumanians in the Dobruja. The possibility of "redeeming" these brethren dominated foreign policies and choice of sides in World War I. Indeed, it was the problem of nationally restless Serbs living in the Austro-Hungarian Empire which was the immediate cause of the war's outbreak in 1914. Their brother Serbs had successfully expelled their Turkish rulers and created an independent Serbia, with which they wished to be joined. Austro-Serbian tension over this problem reached the breaking point when Serb nationalists assassinated the heir to the Austrian throne in June, 1914.

World War I, rooted partly in nationalism, concluded with a peace conference which was much concerned with this problem. Now the map of Europe was further altered in accord with the distribution of nationalities. This action, referred to as "national self-determination," was vigorously championed by President Woodrow Wilson who visualized a peaceful Europe emerging from the separation into individual nation-states of each of Europe's nationalities. Undoubtedly this was a rational approach, but in areas where for centuries two or more cultural groups had intermingled, as in many parts of eastern Europe, there could be no national self-determination for all members of every nationality. Nevertheless, Finland, Estonia, Latvia, Lithuania, Poland, Czechoslovakia, and Yugoslavia were recognized as new nation-states. Elsewhere borders were shifted, as between Rumania and Hungary and Austria and Italy, to minimize the number of "unredeemed" members of each nationality. Often other considerations, economic and strategic, interfered, but on the whole trouble spots were reduced and Europe was organized largely on a nation-state basis.

Western imperialism. Another manifestation of nationalism requires attention to complete this survey of the century after Waterloo: Europe's imperialism in Africa and Asia during this period. Overseas expansion of this sort had, of course, been a factor in the creation of nation-states in western Europe in the sixteenth century. Now with industrialization revolutionizing the economy of all Europe, new pressures for overseas expansion appeared.

Economic factors were very important in the renewal of European expansion, this time into Asia and Africa mainly, but they were not the only ones. In addition there were religious, strategic, and nationalistic considerations. Many an English, American, or German man-in-the-street was inclined to endorse imperialism, not because he foresaw any economic profit to himself, but because a colonial empire enhanced his nation-state's prestige. Profits aside, some Englishmen took pride in the fact that the sun never set on their empire. *Rule Britannia, Rule the Waves* is a typical poetic expression of this sentiment. Many Americans in 1898 endorsed annexation of the Philippines because, were the United States not to take them, another nation would, and this, in the public mind, would somehow be humiliating to the United States. Only a sense of pride in the nation-state adequately explains this American reaction. France sought a certain compensation for her defeat by the Germans in 1871 in an expanded colonial empire. According to French textbooks, "It is the overseas territories which confer on France her rank as a great power." This subtle identification of the nation-state's prestige with a large colonial empire leads to the conclusion that nationalism is a very real force behind imperialism, and particularly behind the nineteenth century imperialism of the European nation-states.

Thus, in the hundred years after the French Revolution, nationalism became a very much more prominent and prevalent aspect of western civilization. The period terminated with a great war fought, at least in part, over nationality issues. The subsequent political reorganization of Europe followed strictly sovereign nation-state lines. It was marked also by the nationalistic endorsement and support of an economic imperialism that reduced much of Asia and all of Africa to the status of colonialism.

CONTEMPORARY NATIONALISM

Two developments in the history of nationalism are notable in the present century. One is the distortion of nationalism among the peoples of the West where this phenomenon first appeared four centuries ago. The other is the spread of nationalism to the four corners of the world, so that there hardly exists a human community which now has not reacted to it.

Totalitarian Nationalism in the West

Western nationalism in recent years has frequently assumed totalitarian forms. Nationalism has come to demand supreme loyalty from the individual to his nation-state and has come to claim priority over all other human considerations and institutions. In its earlier phases nationalism had been tolerant of or co-operated with other movements which demanded loyalty of the individual. The twentieth century has seen a marked trend in the opposite direction.

The mass media. Important in this totalitarian trend was the mushroom growth of mass media of communication. The printed newspaper, rotogravure photography, motion pictures, and radio have proved to be powerful influences in the growth of nationalism among the European masses. Starting with the efforts at mass propaganda by the warring governments of World War I, intellectuals, theatrical artists, and journalists, along with political leaders of nation-states, have employed these media to secure popular endorsement of nationalism. Many educators concerned with instruction in other matters now regret that they did not as quickly grasp the tremendous potentialities of these mass media. While they clung to more traditional methods of communicating with students, nationalist proselytizers proved the enormous effectiveness of the newer methods. Unquestionably, the greatest intensification of nationalism as a result of the application of these techniques was to be observed in Nazi Germany. Here, the Hitler forces crudely but successfully manipulated the nationalistic mood to permit the establishment of a dictatorship in the name of national needs. Fascism and Nazism are discussed elsewhere, but it is pertinent to note here that both capitalized in no small measure upon emotional nationalism, aroused through mass-media communication with large segments of the populations in Germany and Italy.

It would be wrong to give the impression that only the fascists cultivated nationalism by means of the press, movies, and radio; other nation-states in the western world have carried out similar, if perhaps less intense, programs. During World War II, particularly, when war needs demanded co-operation of all citizens, the anti-Axis governments made every effort to remind their peoples of their nation's danger and of their obligation to make sacrifices for their nation's survival. "There'll always be a Britain," "Remember Pearl Harbor," "Fight for the Soviet Fatherland," are examples of the nonfascist nation-states' appeal to nationalism.

The spiritual void. Communication devices may be overemphasized, however. Nationalism became more intense also because the nationalistic appeals fell upon fertile soil. It has been the fate of the twentieth century European to see the forces transforming his medieval world into a modern one reach a feverish and frightening crescendo. Scientific advances, industrialization, urbanization, shrinkage of distances, ideological innovations, total war—these and other powerful impacts upon human society have heightened to a maximum in this century. The result has been such a pervading sense of flux, insecurity, and loss of confidence in traditional beliefs that a great many people in the western world have found solace and emotional release in nationality. Here, if nowhere else, was something to which the bewildered citizen, whose family, village, and provincial loyalties had disintegrated, could turn. The nationality group furnished a means of satisfying man's deep-seated yearning for membership in some kind of society and for belief in some kind of immortality. Thus, the time was ripe for nationalism's appeal on a broader, deeper basis than ever before. Nationalism came to fill the spiritual void in their civilization for a growing number of westerners.

Aldous Huxley recently insisted that "nationalism is the religion of the Twentieth Century." [12] At first a shocking thought, this interpretation becomes more creditable in the light of Carlton J. H. Hayes's description of nationalism.[13]

Nationalism has its parades, processions, and pilgrimages. It has, moreover, its distinctive holy days. . . . In the United States, for example, the Fourth of July is substituted for Corpus Christi, and Decoration Day for the commemoration of All Souls of the faithful departed, whilst in place of the saints' days of the Christian calendar appear the birthdays of national saints and heroes, such as Washington and Lincoln. Nationalism has its temples, and he who would find the places and the buildings that are held most dear and most sacred by the vast majority of Americans, should seek not Christian cathedrals but Independence Hall in Philadelphia, Faneuil Hall in Boston, the shrine to General Lee in Lexington . . . and the city of Washington with . . . its great monuments to Lincoln and Washington.

Moderns, especially Americans, are inclined to regard the medieval veneration of images, icons, and relics as savouring of "superstition," but let them replace a statue of St. George by a graven image of General George Washington, an icon of the Blessed Virgin Mary by a lithograph of the brave Molly Pitcher, and a relic of the Holy Cross by a tattered battle flag, and they display a reverence which they deem beautiful and ennobling.

[12] Aldous Huxley, *Newsweek*, April 30, 1956, p. 52.
[13] The selection from Carlton J. H. Hayes, *Essays on Nationalism*, New York, copyright 1926 by The Macmillan Company and used with publisher's permission, pp. 108–109.

Walter Sulzbach's sociological analysis leads to the same conclusion.[14]

All religions prescribe certain duties toward the deity and toward other men, and impose restrictions on normal impulses. In this respect, all of them, primitive or highly developed, place restrictions upon natural egoism. The pursuit of one's own interest at the expense of others is considered sinful. Because religion commands men to live socially, some philosophers and sociologists hold that the chief characteristic of religion is its anti-egoistic social attitude. . . . It may be said that national consciousness is similar to religion in that it also exalts the social group above the individual. The commands of both the nation and religion seem to be considered by their followers as morally justified. But where religion promises some kind of individual reward, the supreme sacrifice which the nation demands of its members may deprive them of life. They die without hope of personal reward in order that the nation may live.

Too much emphasis cannot be placed on this religious aspect of nationalism. The movement did not originate with such demands upon its followers, but they have become very real in the twentieth century and now embrace, as has been indicated, the supreme loyalty of all men. If nationalism becomes the single most important element in the individual's life, it is quite understandable that the nation-state may become an object of worship, with its insistence on prior consideration over all other institutions widely accepted. Impetus has been given to this development by the decline of another bulwark against totalitarianism, liberalism.

The decline of liberalism. Liberalism (the body of thought which venerates the individual and advocates that society be organized to assure maximum individual freedom) became an important force in western civilization about the same time as nationalism. Drawing inspiration from the Renaissance, the Reformation, the birth of modern science, the rise of modern capitalism, and the Enlightenment, liberalism was the ideology of the nationality-oriented bourgeoisie. Because early nationalists also tended to be liberals, the national and democratic movements entered the nineteenth century along complementary lines.

The great Italian nationalist of the last century, Giuseppe Mazzini, was no less an ardent democrat. To him nationalism and liberalism were both aspects of freedom. Nationalism encouraged the creation of free nation-states, and liberalism, freedom for individuals within these nation-states. In this process, Mazzini felt, nationalism would aid and abet liberalism: ". . . The idea of nationality arose at the opportune moment, to multiply the forces of the individual and make known the means by which the labor and sacrifice of each man may be rendered efficacious and beneficial to humanity." [15]

Much the same line of thought influenced Woodrow Wilson and his supporters for national self-determination at the Paris Peace Conference

---

[14] Walter Sulzbach, *National Consciousness* (Washington, D.C., American Council on Public Affairs, Public Affairs Press, 1943), p. 119.

[15] Hans Kohn, *Prophets and Peoples, loc. cit.,* p. 93.

at the end of World War I. Wilson had earlier identified himself with efforts to augment individual freedom in his own free nation-state. Now he led a movement to establish other free nation-states, like Czechoslovakia, Poland, and Finland, inside of which individual freedom could flourish.

Both men, Mazzini and Wilson, and the others who endorsed the concept, believed that this was a logical, liberal organization of society toward which to strive. Mazzini gave his whole life to its realization, Wilson his last years; neither lived long enough to perceive the growing antagonism between nationalism and liberalism, and the retreat of the latter before the former.

The difficulty of maintaining individual freedom in an urban, industrial society had challenged Woodrow Wilson's America and Mazzini's Europe even before World War I. How could individual freedom be reconciled with the growing pressures of big factory, big farm, big government, and big school? Bigness demands co-operation, which in turn involves some surrender of individualism. The general dislocations within the western world after World War I accentuated the need for co-operative attacks upon unemployment, depression, juvenile delinquency, care of the aged. As a result, whether democratic, communist, or fascist in ideology, all western communities permitted or encouraged the enormous expansion of government functions. Whereas the nation-state had refrained from government regulation of economic and social life in the mid-nineteenth century, the twentieth century state moved in the opposite direction. It became the regulator of the economy, monitor of the distribution of wealth, and architect of a new social order. Russian Five-Year Plans, Nazi Four-Year Plans, Britain's National Coalition Government (1931–39), America's New Deal (1930–39), Mussolini's Corporate State, all were aspects of the reaction to the troubles of the time. Liberalism's precious individual surrendered varying portions of his freedom for greater economic and social security, and liberalism was placed on the defensive and forced to fight a strategic retreat.

Conversely, nationalism was less out of step with the urban-industrial pressures for regimentation and collectivization. It emphasized collective co-operation of millions of citizens of the same nationality. Even in the Soviet Union, where theoretically the initial steps had been taken toward an international community run by the proletariat, nationalism made itself felt. No wonder then that nationalism came to overshadow, and in some places even to crush, liberalism. The nation-state in the name of national welfare, health, conservation, population growth, and defense undertook projects, proposed by national leaders and approved by national majorities, that linked the citizen ever more closely to his nation-state. Since the citizen's economic security, social well-being, and political identity emanated from the nation-state, he quite naturally regarded it as essential to him and therefore entitled to his support and obedience. Only one step remains to total support and obedience, already increasingly evident in western civilization.

Today the Englishman and American, as well as the German and Russian, run less risk of persecution or prosecution for being a bigamist, adulterer, libeler, lyncher, or racketeer than for being disloyal to his nation-state. The hunt for Communists in the United States and the American public's deep fear of Communists clearly reflect this state of mind. The American Communist is not regarded as a completely loyal citizen of the United States, and for this reason he is the object of deep suspicion in the eyes of many who regard themselves as loyal Americans.

International repercussions of twentieth century nationalism. The impact of this most recent phase of nationalism upon international relations is readily seen. Where fascists capitalized upon the trend to seize control of nation-states, the repercussions were very disturbing internationally. First Japan in China, then Italy in Ethiopia and Albania, and Germany in central Europe with violence and brutality expanded their territories in the name of national interests. The list of small nation-states swallowed up by their more powerful neighbors was a long one, the Nazis alone between 1938 and 1941 reducing to complete subservience to the German nation-state fourteen previously independent countries. In this process, of course, World War II was ignited.

Expansion of the fascist nation-states was not, however, the only result. Less powerful nationalities confined their expression of nationalism to the persecution of alien elements within their boundaries. As noted previously, the Paris Peace Conference efforts to apply national self-determination to the whole of Europe proved impossible because of the mixed nationalities. Accordingly, many small European nation-states contained national minorities. With the intensification of nationalism, the ruling elements discriminated against those who, because of different language or religion, were suspected of less than 100 per cent loyalty to the nation-state. Jews especially were persecuted in Poland, Rumania, and Hungary. Discrimination was also practiced against Ruthenes in Czechoslovakia, Magyars in Rumania, Macedonians in Yugoslavia, and Lithuanians in Poland. Although the harassment did not lead to war, as did the aggressions of the major fascist powers, it generated much unrest and was, incidentally, an invitation to Germany and Russia to "rescue" their ethnic cousins suffering at the hands of non-German and non-Russian nation-states. For example, Soviet Russia's annexations at the end of World War II of eastern Poland, Bessarabia, and Ruthenia were justified on the grounds, over and above Nazi Germany's aggression, that these areas contained persecuted White Russian and Ukrainian minorities.

Another outcome was the trend in practically every nation-state to seek solution of its economic problems through unilateral action without regard to the effects upon other nation-states. Economic nationalism will be treated at length in Chapter 5, but it should be mentioned at this point, too. United States' tariffs, British investment policy, French currency devaluation, Belgian quotas, and German "dumping" are examples of economic actions taken by nation-states in their own alleged interest without regard for their impact upon the world economy. The unsettling effects were very great and contributed much to international tensions.

Finally, all efforts at international organization such as the League of Nations or the United Nations were affected by twentieth century nationalism. With supreme loyalty directed to the nation-state, any attempt to subordinate it to some supranational authority was intolerable to the nationalist. Accordingly, members of both the League of Nations and the United Nations carefully preserved their sovereignty. When Japan invaded China in 1931 and Italy bombed Ethiopia in 1935, League attempts to stop them by rebuke or economic sanctions ended with the withdrawal of Japan and Italy from the League in accordance with their sovereign rights. Moreover, the remaining members of the League also asserted their sovereignty by refusing to take further, more effective steps against the aggressors. Although a somewhat different situation ensued in the United Nations when South Korea was invaded in 1950, the outcome of collective action which repelled the invaders probably would not have materialized, had not the United States and South Korea been inclined to defend the latter in their own national interests. Despite the presence of international organization, the nation-states, with the fervid endorsement of most of their citizens, have pursued their own local interests. Collective security and the nationalist philosophy of supreme loyalty to the nation-state appear in many respects irreconcilable.

In summary, nationalism became greatly intensified in the environment of the twentieth century. The mass media of communication, a growing spiritual malaise, and the weakening of liberalism were among the factors conducive to nationalism's increasing hold after World War I and to its assumption of various totalitarian overtones. Its extreme character in the twentieth century has made it a formidable force militating against all international tendencies, economic, scientific, and organizational. Western civilization has found it impossible to achieve the large measure of international co-operation dictated by the world's growing interdependence, because nationalism has so emphatically buttressed the nation-state system. A similar trend has become evident in the rest of the world since the 1930's.

Anticolonial Nationalism in Africa and Asia

Somewhat different circumstances have given rise to a no less intensive nationalism in Afro-Asia during recent years. The references at the beginning of this chapter to North Africa, the Middle East, India, and other regions pointed to an extremely dynamic nationalism in those parts of the world. The efforts to erect nation-states in former colonial territories from Marrakech to Manila serve as concrete illustrations, but some examination of the elements contributing to those efforts is in order.

Alien culture of the colonial powers. At first glance the rise of nationalism in Afro-Asia, with its emphasis on free, wholly independent nation-states, appears to parallel the western world's nineteenth century experience. However, the parallelism is partly illusory. One major difference is the much wider cultural chasm between the ruling powers and the subject peoples in the colonial empires of Asia or Africa, on the one hand, and that between the ruling powers and the subject peoples of the German, Russian, or Austro-Hungarian empires of pre-1914 days, on the other. Frenchmen and Moroccans, British and Indians, Americans and Filipinos differ far more, culturally, than did Poles and Russians, Czechs and Austrians, or Irish and British. This condition has no doubt heightened the antagonism toward alien rulers and stimulated the ethnocentric tendency at the core of nationalism.

Recency of nationalism's birth. Nationalism in Afro-Asia has also had a briefer period of development; it has reached the stage of the formation of nation-states like Libya, Jordan, and India in a shorter time. An obvious complication arising from this time factor is that independence has been achieved often before experience in government could be gained. As a result, the task of operating and co-operating with a newly formed nation-state has frequently been very difficult. The Philippines and perhaps India are exceptions, but the Arab states and Vietnam illustrate the point. The new nation-states in Africa and Asia are, generally speaking, without experience of self-government. This fact, added to others, helps to account for the problems of instability which frequently arise.

Poverty of Afro-Asia. The poverty of many of the Afro-Asian peoples has also had a unique impact upon their nationalism. Although it is partly attributable to exploitation by colonial rulers, it is also due to lack of natural resources and the absence of technological knowledge for best exploiting the resources that do exist. Inevitably, however, the Afro-Asian became aware of his relative poverty by comparing himself with the westerners who came to Africa and Asia. This generated envy. Then, as he perceived the all-too-frequent exploitive activities of the western imperialist, his envy was reinforced with resentment. Thus, economic hostility reinforced nationalism.

Racism. By far the most significant and unique factor in Afro-Asian nationalism is its racial overtone. European peoples striving for national independence came into conflict most often with other Europeans, with whom they had much in common and between whom antagonisms were not aggravated by color consciousness. The opposite is true of Africa and

Asia. Although not all European empire builders were color-minded, many were. With the practice of racial discrimination and segregation, deep resentments were kindled and cultivated among natives of the colonial areas.

Rigid segregation of the Indian from the British sahib, and even more so from the sahib's wife, was only one example. The American "colony" in Manila maintained its own exclusive clubs. In south, central, and east Africa segregation was enforced by law—and still is. Curfews, signs reading "Off Limits to Nonwhites," residential zoning, and hotel and transportation segregation constantly reminded the African or the Asian that the westerner not only exercised political power over him without his consent, usually lived better than he did, but also considered him a creature somewhere between the human and animal categories. To Indians, Chinese, Japanese, and other peoples who in all aspects of their civilization except technology believed themselves to be equal or superior to the westerner, this was an intolerable situation. It was most deeply resented, of course, by the better educated, more well-to-do peoples of Africa and Asia.

Even where the dominating elements do not come as interlopers from another part of the world with an alien culture, as in the United States, racial discrimination breeds the most profound tensions in a society. When such racism fuses with nationalism, as it has in much of Africa and Asia, the results are highly explosive. This combination goes far to explain the ferocity of the Mau Mau insurrection against the white population of Kenya, and the Asian respect accorded Japan for her victory over Russia in 1905 and over the United States in 1941–42. It also accounts for the headlining in the Afro-Asian press of every episode reflecting racial prejudice in the United States, and the sense of satisfaction derived from the exclusively African and Asian attendance at the Bandung Conference in 1955.

Nationalism, then, in the nonwestern parts of the world, though basically not different from American and European manifestations, has come later and has been linked with economic and racial grievances. Indeed, Afro-Asian nationalism has emerged as a panacea for all problems, and as a violently impatient attack upon all vestiges of colonialism. Furthermore, the now almost complete liquidation of western imperialism in Asia and its rapid termination in Africa have transferred the tensions and bitterness from internal struggle against the imperialists to the international stage. Disputes over Kashmir, Goa, Dutch New Guinea, Formosa, and Tangier illustrate this point. Nationalism today has become, undeniably, the determining political and cultural force in Africa and Asia, no less than in Europe and the Americas originally. To objectively evaluate its impact on Africa, Asia, and the world is most difficult in view of its recency. Yet the Afro-Asian brand of nationalism may prove to be just as violent, divisive, and totalitarian as its western counterpart "if it is not tempered by the liberal spirit of tolerance and compromise or the humanitarian universalism of a non-political religion." [16]

CONCLUSION

Although a recent development in human society, nationalism has become a predominant force in today's world. Taking root in western Europe, nationalism accompanied the emergence of the first nation-states in the fifteenth and sixteenth centuries. In the course of the next four hundred years, all of western civilization came to be organized politically along national lines. By 1919 Europe alone contained more than twenty-five sovereign nation-states, each commanding the loyalty of its members and zealously guarding its right to independent action.

Since then, African and Asian peoples have learned nationalism from their western colonial overlords. Reinforced by factors unique to Africa and Asia, the Afro-Asians rose in a great wave of revolutions directed at creation of their own nation-states. Two world wars by weakening the colonial powers accelerated this process. By 1958, as the chart on page 161 indicates, Asia contained twenty-four independent political units. Africa, reduced by colonialism to only two nation-states in 1914 (Ethiopia and Liberia), had thrown off colonial rule in seven more by 1958 (Egypt, the Union of South Africa, Libya, Sudan, Morocco, Tunisia, and Ghana), and rumblings in other parts of the Dark Continent promised additions to this list.

Nationalism has also inculcated among individuals in all parts of the world an allegiance to their nation-states which assumes priority over most, and sometimes all, other loyalties. "My country, may it always be right, but my country, right or wrong" implies a changing set of values and a new morality basically opposed to that taught by the religions of the world, as well as to the principles enunciated in such different documents as the *Declaration of Independence* and *The Communist Manifesto*. Indeed, nationalism has proved a powerful force in opposition to democracy and even to Marxism, and has been a useful weapon in the hands of totalitarian dictators.

The influence of nationalism on economic, educational, and political policies in every country of the world has been, in varying degrees, considerable.

Do such varied ramifications of the rise of nationalism lead to the conclusion that nationalism is internationally a curse, or a blessing? Does it

[16] Hans Kohn, *Nationalism, Its Meaning and History, loc. cit.*, p. 90.

intensify tension between nations, or does it satisfy certain human needs and thereby contribute to the peaceful contentment of the human race? Considerable difference of opinion on the possible answers to this query may be found in the contemporary world. Several views on possible answers are presented in the following section.

The Nation-States of the World

Asia (24)

Afghanistan	Korea †
Burma	Laos
Cambodia	Lebanon
Ceylon	Malaya
China	Nepal
India	Pakistan
Indonesia	Philippines
Iran	Saudi Arabia
Iraq *	Thailand
Israel	Turkey
Japan	Vietnam †
Jordan *	Yemen ‡

Americas (22)

Argentina	Guatemala
Bolivia	Haiti
Brazil	Honduras
Canada	Mexico
Chile	Nicaragua
Colombia	Panama
Costa Rica	Paraguay
Cuba	Peru
Dominican Republic	United States
Ecuador	Uruguay
El Salvador	Venezuela

Africa (9)

Ethiopia	Sudan
Ghana	Tunisia
Liberia	Union of South Africa
Libya	United Arab Republic §
Morocco	

Australasia (2)

Australia
New Zealand

Europe (26)

Albania	Luxembourg
Austria	Netherlands
Belgium	Norway
Bulgaria	Poland
Czechoslovakia	Portugal
Denmark	Rumania
Finland	Spain
France	Sweden
Germany †	Switzerland
Greece	Union of Soviet Socialist Republics
Hungary	
Iceland	
Ireland	United Kingdom
Italy	Yugoslavia

* In 1958, Iraq and Jordan formed the Arab Federation. However, each state retained its sovereign identity.
† Divided into two separate sovereign regimes.
‡ Associated with the United Arab Republic but maintains its separate identity.
§ Formed in 1958 by Egypt and Syria.

POSITIONS
ON THE PROBLEM

1. NATIONALISM CAUSES MISUNDERSTANDING, TENSION, AND WAR

(The following passages have been taken from Kirby Page's widely read book, *National Defense*.[17] The author was a strong supporter of the peace movement following World War I and wrote this book to point out the origins and results of the 1914–18 war and to suggest means of preventing future war. Nationalism is singled out as one of the principal causes of international conflict.)

The emotions and dogmas of nationalism constituted the major cause of the World War. To these feelings and ideas must be attributed chief responsibility because they created or accentuated other dangerous factors. Imperialism and militarism in their modern forms are products of nationalism, as are a host of other causes of war. Nationalism is a sentiment, an emotion, a psychological experience. Out of it emerges patriotic loyalty to country. It is not dependent upon race, language, culture or religion, although all these are important ingredients. Nationalism is an artificial creation and binds together extremely divergent groups with common feelings and ideas. It is one of the most dynamic forces in the modern world.

Nationalism is both unifying and divisive: it binds together the citizens of one country with the bonds of patriotic devotion and then separates them from other peoples by walls of suspicions, fears and animosities. Through the class room, the lecture platform, the pulpit, the press and a hundred other devices, distorted images are created in the minds of children and adults alike. The cult of superiority is fostered by exaggerating the virtues and minimizing the vices of one's own country, while underestimating the good qualities and overstating the evil practices of other peoples. The inevitable consequence of this procedure is the releasing of suspicions, fears and hatreds. Thus highly explosive emotions separate the citizens of various lands from each other.

Ten thousand illustrations of these distorted mental pictures could easily be assembled from pre-war literature. Some countries seem to have been worse afflicted than others, but none escaped the perils of defective vision. "The German people," said the Kaiser in 1907, "will be the granite blocks on which the good God may build and complete His work of Kultur in the world. Then will be fulfilled the word of the poet who said that the world will one day be healed by the German character." On another occasion the Emperor said: "We are the salt of the earth . . . God has created us to civilize the world." Lord Curzon dedicated his book, *Problems of the Far East*, to "those who believe

---

[17] Kirby Page, *National Defense, A Study of the Origins, Results and Prevention of War* (copyright, 1931, by Kirby Page, reprinted by permission of Rinehart & Company, Inc., New York, publishers), pp. 4–5, 189–190, 191, 24).

that the British Empire is, under Providence, the greatest instrument for good that the world has ever seen."

"What in the first place is French mentality?" inquired Jean Finot. "It is the quintessence of civilization and of universal progress enriched by the fruit of French genius, which is at the same time both comprehensive and creative."

Pre-war nationalism proved to be a world scourge because its egotism and vituperation aroused blinding suspicions, fears, and enmities while its dogmas and policies transformed economic quarrels between individuals into cataclysmic conflicts between groups of powers. The discovery of parallel tendencies in the world today should cause us to put forth strenuous efforts to prevent a similar calamity in the future.

Illustrations of national boasting abound. Distorted images of the superiority of one's own country prevent clear thinking on international questions. Excessive national pride dulls appreciation of other peoples and blocks the way to sympathetic understanding of those persons who live across the border. Arrogance is one of the most irritating of characteristics. Walter Hines Page once said: "God has yet made nothing or nobody equal to the American people; I don't think he ever will or can." The concluding words of Poincaré's book on the origins of the war are: "In contrast with Austro-German Imperialism, France became, in the eyes of the nations, the living representative of Right and of Liberty."

The venerable British Association for the Advancement of Science solemnly asserts that "the British Empire is the greatest human institution under heaven, the greatest secular organization for good." The pupils of French schools are assured that "France represents to the world the land of liberty and justice. She has always protected the small nations against the oppression of the great. By her heroic role during the war she saved the liberty of the world." The President of the United States, in an address at Muskingum College in 1922, asserted that we "have contributed more to human advancement in a century and a half than all the people of the world in all the history of the world." A Latin American thus describes the mother country: "Spain, to the grief of her detractors, has always displayed in her colonial policy a consistent greatness, a strong idealism, a legendary heroism."

"For nearly two generations," writes Henry Emerson Wildes, "the idea that Japanese are different from other peoples has been drilled into the minds of schoolboys . . . the impression is sedulously fostered that the ideals of Japan should be regarded as a special thing apart, unique and perfect. . . . Marquis Okuma expounded this idea: "From the idea that Japan is the land of the kami (gods), her people have been led to believe that she is under special protection of these heavenly beings."

The two million readers of the *Ladies' Home Journal* were once informed that "there is only one first-class civilization in the world today. It's right here in the United States of America and the Dominion of Canada. It may be a cocky thing to say . . . that relatively it (our civilization) is first-class, while Europe's is hardly second-class and Asia's is about fourth to sixth-class."

By way of summary, let us now bring together the dangerous aspects of nationalism which have been outlined. Nationalism has been at the same time highly unifying and deeply divisive; it has been both constructive and destructive. It has separated men of different countries by its emphasis upon superiority and inferiority, by its caricatures and distorted images. The resultant emotions of suspicion and fear and hatred have led to intoxication and deeds of savagery. This menace was greatly intensified by the fixed ideas implanted by nationalism in the minds of its citizens. Rights must always be upheld, interests must be safeguarded under all circumstances, insults to national honor must be avenged, citizens must loyally support their government in all controversies with other nations and must engage in war when commanded to do so by the constituted authorities; these ideas became so deeply embedded in the public mind that in order to maintain them no cost was considered too great and no sacrifice too heavy.

2. NATIONALISM DEFENDED

(The following excerpts are from Carlton J. H. Hayes's *Essays on Nationalism*.[18] Annotations on the author may be found in the chapter bibliography. Although Hayes's work presents both pro and con arguments, only those in defense of nationalism are quoted here.)

According to most contemporary students of the subject, national consciousness is not only natural and instinctive but valuable and useful, and should be fostered rather than repressed. We shouldn't wish to get rid of it, even if we could. In the words of Mr. John Oakesmith, national patriotism "is not only explicable as a national sentiment, but justifiable as a reasonable faith." The numerous champions of nationality and national consciousness advance two major arguments in support of their position; first, that nationality possesses great spiritual value in that it is a safeguard against materialistic cosmopolitanism; and, second, that nationality possesses high cultural value. The most eloquent and convincing exponent of the first point is undoubtedly Mr. Alfred Zimmern, and we may properly set forth this argument in his own words:

"Nationality, in fact, rightly regarded, is not a political but an educational conception. It is a safeguard of self-respect against the insidious onslaughts of materialistic cosmopolitanism. It is the sling in the hands of the weak underdeveloped peoples against the Goliath of material progress. . . . The vice of nationalism is jingoism, and there are always good Liberals amongst us ready to point a warning finger against its manifestations. The vice of internationalism is decadence and the complete eclipse of personality, ending in a type of character and social life which good Conservatives instinctively detest, but have seldom sufficient patience to describe. . . . English readers can find . . . examples . . . of the spiritual degradation which befalls men who have pursued 'Progress' and cosmopolitanism and lost contact with their own national spiritual heritage. . . . No task is more urgent among backward and weaker peoples than the wise fostering of nationality and the maintenance of national traditions and corporate life as a school of character and self-respect."

"It is for this problem of the man without roots that nationality provides a solution. Nationality is the one social force capable of maintaining, for these people, their links with the past and keeping alive in them that spark of the higher life and that irreplaceable sentiment of self-respect. . . . Nationality is more than a creed or a doctrine or a code of conduct, it is an instinctive attachment; it recalls an atmosphere of precious memories, of vanished parents and friends, of old customs, of reverence, of home, and a sense of the brief span of human life as a link between immemorial generations, spreading backwards

[18] The selections from Carlton J. H. Hayes, *Essays on Nationalism*, New York, copyright 1926 by The Macmillan Company and used with publisher's permission, pp. 248–252.

and forwards. 'Men may change their clothes, their politics, their wives, their religions, their philosophies,' says a Jewish-American writer, 'they cannot change their grandfathers. Jews or Poles or Anglo-Saxons, in order to cease being Jews or Poles or Anglo-Saxons, would have to cease to be.'"

. . . We have reason to distrust the person who loves man in general and despises individual men, who prates so much about his duties to humanity that he has no time to serve his next-door neighbor. Nationality may well be a sufficiently definite, limited field in which the individual can school himself in the exercise of those virtues which are directly serviceable to his immediate fellows, but which in the long run inure to the advantages of the race. Likewise it may well be . . . that nationality is a spiritual protection against material aggression, that more and more as time goes on it will inspire and enable so-called "backward" peoples to put an end to the economic exploitation from which they suffer, and will eventually save the whole world from being turned into a cockpit for capital and labour.

. . . We must . . . acknowledge that nationality has [also] been through-out the ages a great conserver of human differences in architecture, in litera-ture, in the plastic and pictorial arts, in music, in dancing, in all aesthetic mani-festations of man's civilisation, and also in modes of thought which enrich his being and in customs and manners which embellish his life. . . .

. . . I, for one, sympathise cordially with those who rebel at the prospect of a drab uniformity of manners, customs, and arts from New York to Singa-pore, and from Helsingfors to Valparaiso. I do not look forward with pleasure to seeing each mark of civilisation to which I am accustomed at home photo-graphically reproduced in every town in France, Holland, Russia, Turkey . . . and Japan. . . . More than ever today, when the Industrial Revolution is dev-astating localism everywhere, and piling up the same sort of brick and steel girder in Asia and Africa as in Europe and America, when hotels the world over serve in the same way from *hors d'oeuvres* to coffee the same kind of dinner, when men universally array themselves in like ugly habiliments, at this very time it is a comfort that nationality still endures and still performs its delightful and wholesome function of encouraging at least minor differences in civilisation and culture.

In the light of the cultural and spiritual worth of nationality as well as in the light of its instinctive and universal character, it would seem not only utopian and idle but downright wrong-headed and mistaken to advocate a supersession of nationality by cosmopolitanism or imperialism. Some type of internationalism may be desirable and obtainable, but we shall be reasonable and practical if we accept the dictum of the friends of nationality and construct our internationalism of the future from the building blocks of existing nation-alities and even of existing nationalisms.

3. The Communist View of Good and Bad Nationalism

(The following excerpts, taken from the writings of Joseph Stalin,[19] as-sert that nationalism when used to foster capitalist imperialism is an evil force, but when used to encourage the proletarian revolution is a force for good.)

[19] Joseph Stalin, *Foundations of Leninism* (New York, International Publishers, 1939), pp. 76–80, 82–85.

During the last twenty years the national problem has undergone a number of very important changes. . . .

Formerly, the national problem was usually confined to a narrow circle of questions, concerning primarily "cultured" nationalities . . . European nationalities—that was the circle. . . . The scores and hundreds of millions of Asiatic and African peoples who are suffering national oppression in its most savage and cruel form usually remained outside of . . . [the] field of vision. . . . Leninism laid bare this crying incongruity, broke down the wall between whites and blacks, between Europeans and Asiatics . . . and thus linked the national problem with the problem of colonies. The national problem was thereby transformed from a particular and internal state problem into a general and international problem, into a world problem of emancipating the oppressed peoples in the dependent countries and colonies from the yoke of imperialism.

Formerly, the principle of self-determination of nations was usually misinterpreted, and not infrequently it was narrowed down to the idea of the right of nations to autonomy. . . . Leninism broadened the conception of self-determination and interpreted it as the right of the oppressed peoples of the dependent countries and colonies to complete secession. . . . Thus the principle of self-determination itself was transformed from an instrument of deceiving the masses, which it undoubtedly was in the . . . imperialist war [1914–18], into an instrument for exposing all and sundry imperialist aspirations and chauvinist machinations, into an instrument for the political education of the masses in the spirit of internationalism. . . .

Formerly, the national problem was regarded . . . as an independent problem having no connection with the general problems of the rule of capital, of the overthrow of imperialism, of the proletarian revolution. It was tacitly assumed that the victory of the proletariat in Europe was possible without a direct alliance with the liberation movement in the colonies, that the national-colonial problem could be solved on the quiet, "of its own accord," off the high road of the proletarian revolution, without a revolutionary struggle against imperialism. Now we can say that this anti-revolutionary point of view has been exposed. Leninism has proved, and the imperialist war and the revolution in Russia have confirmed, that the national problem can be solved only in connection with and on the basis of the proletarian revolution. . . . The national problem is part of the general problem of the proletarian revolution, a part of the problem of the dictatorship of the proletariat. . . .

The question presents itself as follows: Are the revolutionary possibilities latent in the revolutionary liberation movement of the oppressed countries already exhausted or not; and if not, is there any hope, any ground to expect that these possibilities can be utilized for the proletarian revolution, that the dependent and colonial countries can be transformed from a reserve of the imperialist bourgeoisie into a reserve of the revolutionary proletariat, into an ally of the latter?

Leninism replies to this question in the affirmative. . . .

Hence the necessity for the proletariat to support . . . the national liberation movement of the oppressed and dependent peoples.

This does not mean . . . that the proletariat must support *every* national movement. . . . It means that support must be given to such national movements as tend to weaken, to overthrow imperialism and not to strengthen and preserve it. . . . The question of the rights of nations is not an isolated, self-sufficient question; it is part of the general problem of the proletarian revolution, subordinate to the whole. . . .

The interest of the proletarian movement in the developed countries and of the national liberation movement in the colonies calls for the amalgamation of these two forms of revolutionary movement into a common front against the common enemy, against imperialism.

"Developing capitalism," says Lenin, "knows of two historical tendencies in the national problem. First: the awakening of national life and of national movements, the struggle against all national oppression, the creation of national states. Second: the development and growing frequency of all sorts of intercourse among nations; the breaking down of national barriers; the creation of the international unity of capital, of economic life in general, of politics, of science. . . . Both tendencies are the universal law of capitalism. The first predominates at the beginning of the development of capitalism, the second characterises mature capitalism. . . ."

For imperialism these two tendencies represent irreconcilable contradictions. . . .

For communism, on the contrary, these tendencies are but two sides of a single cause—the cause of the emancipation of the oppressed peoples from the yoke of imperialism; because communism knows that the union of the nations in a single world economic system is possible only on the basis of mutual confidence and voluntary agreement, and that the road to the formation of a voluntary union of nations lies through the separation of the colonies from the "integral" imperialist "whole," through the transformation of the colonies into independent states.

Hence the necessity of a stubborn, continuous and determined struggle against the imperialist chauvinism. . . .

Without such a struggle the education of the working class of the ruling nations in the spirit of true internationalism, in the spirit of rapprochement with the toiling masses of the dependent countries and colonies, in the spirit of real preparation for the proletarian revolution, is inconceivable. . . . Without this it would have been impossible to consolidate the Soviet power, to implant true internationalism and to create that remarkable organization for the collaboration of nations which is called the Union of Soviet Socialist Republics —the living prototype of the future union of nations in a single world economic system.

QUESTIONS

1. Why does nationalism in Asia and Africa capture more headlines today than nationalism in Europe?

2. How do you define nationalism? What are its basic elements? Which do you consider most important?

3. How can we best go about attempting to understand a nationally inspired tension in order to deal with it as a threat to international peace?

4. Is American nationalism essentially the same or different from the nationalism of (1) Germans, (2) Chinese, (3) the British, (4) the Arabs? Explain.

5. Do democratic communities tend to be more or less nationalistic than nondemocratic ones? Explain.

6. On the basis of your acquaintance with nationalism, do you believe there is or can be any connection between nationalism and anti-Semitism? Explain.

7. Does the contemporary nation-state meet the needs of its citizens within its own limits? Explain.

8. Do you agree or disagree with the statement: "Nationalism is a state of mind with few tangible roots and therefore must be accepted as part of the human's instinctive, non-rational personality"? Why?

9. Do you agree or disagree with the statement: "Nationalism as a state of mind can be altered or eradicated by understanding, persuasion and education." Why?

10. With which one of the three points of view presented in the last section are you most nearly in agreement? Defend your choice.

SELECT BIBLIOGRAPHY

CARR, Edward H., *Nationalism and After* (New York, Macmillan, 1945). A British political scientist, professor at the University College of Wales, and an authority on international affairs with a world-wide reputation, maintains that the importance of nationalism is declining and yielding to conflict over variant forms of supernationalism.

HAYES, Carlton J. H., *Essays on Nationalism* (New York, Macmillan, 1926). An American historian, formerly professor at Columbia University, more recently U.S. Ambassador to Spain, examines militant nationalism, its nature, rise, and inherent dangers for the mid-twentieth century.

————, *The Historical Evolution of Modern Nationalism* (New York, Richard R. Smith, 1931). Nationalism is here developed as a body of doctrines, a political philosophy, an "ism," with special emphasis upon the leaders of nationalist thought in the past 150 years.

KOHN, Hans, *The Idea of Nationalism* (New York, Macmillan, 1944). Chapter I is recommended for its definition and description of the character of nationalism. The author, Czech-born, grew up in the midst of one of Europe's most acute nationalistic dilemmas, the Austro-Hungarian Empire. He is now a professor of history at the College of the City of New York and a well-known writer on nationalism.

————, *Nationalism, Its Meaning and History* (Princeton, Van Nostrand, 1955). In addition to an analysis of nationalism and its relation to other movements in the modern world, the book contains readings from over twenty writers, from Machiavelli to Nehru, on nationalism. Anvil Original ed., pocket size.

————, *The Twentieth Century* (New York, Macmillan, 1949). A bold attempt to comprehensively view the critical state of western civilization particularly. Chapter II, "Nationalism and the Open Society," explores the unique problem of nationalism intensifying in a world with shrinking distances between peoples. Author concludes that unrepressed, rampant nationalism can only lead to tragedy.

SHAFER, Boyd C., *Nationalism: Myth and Reality* (New York, Harcourt Brace, 1955). Portrayal of nationalism as an historical process, concluding that there is no basis, historical, biological, or psychological, for believing that nationalism will or must be permanent. Author, an historian, endorses internationalism as antidote to dangers of nationalism.

SULZBACH, Walter, *National Consciousness* (Washington, D.C., American Council on Public Affairs, 1943). A social economist sets out to disprove thesis that rational economic considerations are the major impetus behind modern nationalism. A hopeful note is struck regarding the ultimate passing of nationalism as a problem in human society.

WRIGHT, Quincy, *A Study of War* (Chicago, University of Chicago Press, 1942), 2 vols. An imposing treatment of war by a professor of international law at the University of Chicago. Chapter XXVIII, Vol. II, "Nationalism and War," emphasizes that nationalism weakens rational action, cultivates mass docility, and venerates militarism, thereby contributing to war.

5

Economic Resources:
Seedbed for Conflict?

THE PROBLEM
AND ITS BACKGROUND

INTRODUCTION: THE SOURCE OF THE PROBLEM

One of the most frequent explanations of war attributes the cause to the uneven distribution of resources among the people of the world. According to this argument, wars represent one method by which a nation, or group of nations, seeks to increase its share of the world's resources.

Hitler cited the pressure of population on resources as the force behind German aggression when he replied to President Roosevelt's peace telegram in April, 1939, in these words: [1]

It ought not then to happen that one people needs so much living space that it cannot get along with fifteen inhabitants to the square kilometer, while others are forced to nourish 140, 150 or even 200 on the same area.

But in no case should these fortunate peoples curtail the existing living space of those who are, as it is, suffering, by robbing them of their colonies.

Economic problems have been cited as the principal source of aggression by Far Eastern nations also. As early as 1929, Warren S. Thompson warned the world of the population-resource pressure that was building up in Japan. Thompson saw little relief for Japan's demographic problems in birth control, acceptance of a lower standard of living, or more intensive exploitation of existing resources. He argued that ". . . the grant-

[1] *New York Times,* April 29, 1939, p. 11.
170

ing to Japan of new lands with larger resources, seems to furnish the only reasonable way out of its inevitable difficulties, and thus to present the only real alternative to a war for Japanese expansion." [2] Japan was not granted additional land, and in the early 1930's launched her unsuccessful attempt to enlarge Japanese territory and to open up new markets in the Far East.

The primacy of economic resources in explaining war is questioned by those who assert that wars are not fought between the "have" and the "have-not" nations (as implied in the economic explanation of conflict) but rather between the "have" and the "have-a-little-less" nations. Those who challenge the economic explanation of war argue that both Germany and Japan had relatively well-developed economies, with the German and Japanese people enjoying high standards of living, in relation to surrounding nation-states, during the period when both nations set out to enlarge their economic possessions. When all the facts are known, it is argued, the noneconomic forces (the nature of man, nationalism, scientific progress, and ideological loyalty) loom much larger than economic resources as the principal sources of international tension.

WORLD POPULATION: NUMBERS, DISTRIBUTION, AND GROWTH

Although man's efforts to count his numbers are as old as written history, estimates of growth of world population before the beginning of the nineteenth century are based upon unreliable data. The modern census of population was initiated in several Western Hemisphere areas between 1665 and 1703, but only a few other regions of the world compiled reliable demographic statistics before 1800. Even now, world population estimates are subject to considerable error, owing to incomplete registration of births and deaths in many underdeveloped areas. The Statistical Office of the United Nations, for example, classified as "poor" the demographic statistics for Africa, the Near East, and the Far East (excluding Japan). Population statistics for Latin America, south-central Asia, the U.S.S.R., and eastern Europe are considered "fair." Information on populations for the rest of Europe, the United States, Canada, Japan, and Oceania are deemed "good." The Office admits that, in its estimates of world population, a margin of error of 3 per cent in either direction is possible.

How Many of Us Are There and Where Do We Live?

The estimated human population of the earth totaled slightly over 2.7 billion at midyear, 1957. With the exclusion of the Asian portions of Russia, more than one-half the people of the world live in Asia (Table 1). Europe has the next largest population, comprising about one-sixth of the

[2] Warren S. Thompson, *Danger Spots in World Population* (New York, Knopf, 1929), pp. 13–14.

total. No other single continental area accounts for more than 10 per cent of the world's population.

Table 1. World Population, by Continent and Selected Countries, Midyear, 1954 and 1956

Area	Population, millions		Proportion of World Total in 1954, %
	1956	1954	
World	2,696.0	2,638.1	100.0
Europe		405.0	15.4
France	43.6	43.0	1.6
Germany, East	17.9	18.1	0.7
Germany, West	51.4	50.5	1.9
Italy	48.2	47.8	1.8
Poland	27.7	26.8	1.0
Spain	29.2	28.8	1.1
United Kingdom	51.2	50.8	1.9
U.S.S.R.	200.2	194.3	7.4
North and Central America		234.3	8.9
Canada	16.1	15.2	0.6
Mexico	30.5	28.9	1.1
United States	168.1	162.4	6.2
South America		121.1	4.6
Argentina	19.5	18.7	0.7
Brazil	59.8	57.1	2.2
Colombia	12.9	12.4	0.5
Asia		1,454.6	55.1
China	—	582.6 *	22.1
India	381.7 †	376.2	14.3
Indonesia	81.9 †	80.7	3.1
Japan	90.0	88.0	3.3
Pakistan	83.6	81.2	3.1
Philippines	22.3	21.4	0.8
Turkey	24.8	23.4	0.9
Africa		214.5	8.1
Egypt	22.9 †	22.5	0.8
Nigeria	—	30.3	1.1
Union of South Africa	13.9	13.4	0.5
Oceania		14.3	0.5
Australia	9.4	9.0	0.3

* 1953.   † 1955.

Source: Statistical Office of the United Nations, *Monthly Bulletin of Statistics* (New York, United Nations, April, 1957).

The largest populations are in China and India, their combined total representing a third of all mankind. More than 1 out of every 5 persons walking the earth is Chinese, and 1 out of 7 is a native of India. The masses of humans in these two countries dwarf the population numbers of western countries. For example, China's population is more than $3\frac{1}{2}$ times as large as that of the United States and 10 times the population of the United Kingdom or France. The population of India is only a few million less than the total European populace. The U.S.S.R. population, which is approximately 20 per cent larger than that of the United States, accounts for 7 per cent of the world's total.

In broad design, four major aggregations of humans may be outlined over the face of the earth. Eastern China represents the core of the largest concentration, although this densely populated region extends north to Korea and south to Indonesia. The Ganges Valley, southern India, Pakistan, and Ceylon make up the second largest concentration. The third and fourth largest population centers face each other across the North Atlantic Ocean: Europe, including the heavily settled portion of western Russia, has the larger of the two; the population in the eastern portion of the United States comprises the smaller aggregation.

Population Growth

Despite the absence of reliable statistical data, most demographers estimate that the world population was between 500 and 600 million in 1650. With this estimate as a benchmark, world population has experienced more than a fourfold increase in the last three centuries, 1650 to 1950. The significance of present rates of population growth is demonstrated in the following comparison: the first doubling of population, from 500 million to 1 billion, took nearly 200 years, from 1650 to approximately 1850; the second doubling, from 1 to 2 billion persons, required about 80 years, from 1850 to 1930; the present rate of growth, 1.3 to 1.5 per cent annually, would double the population in only 47 years.

Analyzing the historical growth of population, Julian Huxley has asserted that each major increase in numbers of humans has been due to some significant discovery or invention, such as agriculture, the emergence of urban life and trade, the development of mechanical (nonhuman) power, or the technological revolution. Huxley identifies scientific medicine as the major causal factor behind the rapid population growth during the twentieth century. He states: [3]

During the present century the most decisive factor in increasing population has been of a different sort—the application of scientific medicine, or what we may call death control. In advanced countries death rates have been reduced from traditional 35 or 40 per thousand to less than 10 per thousand. The average life span (life expectancy at birth) has been more than doubled in the Western world since the mid-19th century. It now stands at about 70 years in Europe and North America, and the process of lengthening life has begun to

[3] Julian Huxley, "World Population," *Scientific American*, Vol. 194, No. 3 (March, 1956), p. 65.

get under way in Asian countries: in India, for example, the life expectancy at birth has risen within three decades from 20 to 32 years.

During the twentieth century, the largest numerical increases in population have occurred in Asia and Europe. The Asian populace gained by more than 350 million persons over this period, and European numbers were expanded by nearly 175 million. Latin and North American populations, however, have experienced the largest percentage growth during this 50-year interval. The size of the Latin American population increased more than 150 per cent between 1900 and 1950; the North American population rose by slightly more than 100 per cent. In comparison, the Asian and European areas both experienced population growths of approximately 40 per cent over the same years.

Demographic projections. Although the present annual rate of growth would double world population in less than 50 years, few demographers predict that this high rate of growth will continue indefinitely. Most population specialists believe that various forms of birth control will be initiated, especially in underdeveloped countries, so as to lessen the rate of growth. Consequently, in recent years, demographers have been predicting a world population ranging between 3.0 and 3.6 billion for the latter years of this century.

Forecasting long-run changes in population, demographers generally distinguish three phases of demographic evolution. F. W. Notestein was the first to make the classifications, labeling the phases: high growth potential, transitional growth, and incipient decline.[4]

High growth potential. This least mature stage of the demographic cycle contains the majority of the world's peoples. Included are most of the countries of Asia, Africa, and Latin America. Mortality and fertility rates are still high. Population growth in these areas is determined primarily by mortality rates which vary widely. Sharp increases in numbers can be expected as mortality declines with improved sanitary and health measures. The potential for population expansion in underdeveloped areas during the initial phases of their industrialization is greater than among western countries because of the increased rate at which mortality is declining, owing to the application of knowledge from industrialized countries. The future trend of world population will depend greatly upon demographic developments in these underdeveloped countries.

Transitional growth. Included in this median stage of demographic evolution are the Soviet Union, the semi-industrialized countries of Europe, Latin America, Japan, Turkey, and Israel. This phase is characterized by rapid population growth as a result of past reductions in mortality. Fertility rates have also declined slightly, but the number of births far exceeds the number of deaths. Further decreases in mortality

[4] Frank W. Notestein, "Population—The Long View," *Food for the World*, T. W. Schultz, ed. (Chicago, University of Chicago Press, 1945), pp. 42–52.

rates are probable, so that the death rates in these areas will approximate those in the more highly industrialized regions of the world. Turkey and Israel are probably just entering this stage, whereas the Soviet Union, Japan, and several Latin American countries are in the middle of the phase. Ultimately, the incipient decline stage of demographic evolution is reached.

Incipient decline. This represents the most advanced phase of demographic evolution and includes such areas as North America, most of northwestern and central Europe, Australia, and New Zealand. Net reproduction rates are increasing moderately, and there appears to be little prospect of rapid population expansion over the long run. If fertility rates decline in the future to the levels prevalent before World War II, the populaces in many of these countries may stabilize or even begin to decline within a few decades. Notestein postulates that population growth continues here only because of favorable age distributions of the populations, which will be changed in time, thereby accelerating the decline in growth.

Population Growth and Food Supply: The Malthusian Doctrine

The relationship between population growth and food-producing resources was first postulated in 1798 by the anonymous author of *An Essay on the Principle of Population as It Affects the Future Improvement of Society*. The book aroused much discussion and controversy, and in 1803 Thomas Robert Malthus, the book's author, dropped the anonymity and published a second, more elaborate edition of his *Essay*. The source of the controversy was the pessimistic future forecast for man by Malthus. This dire prediction stemmed from Malthus' fear that population tends to outrun the means of subsistence.

Developing his argument, Malthus wrote: [5]

I think I may fairly make two postulata. First, that food is necessary to the existence of man. Secondly, that the passion between the sexes is necessary, and will remain in its present state.

Assuming then, my postulata as granted, I say, that the power of population is indefinitely greater than the power in the earth to produce subsistence for man.

Population, when unchecked, increases in a geometrical ratio. Subsistence increases only in an arithmetical ratio. A slight acquaintance with numbers will show the immensity of the first power in comparison of the second.

In the second edition of the *Essay* in 1803, Malthus summarized his doctrine in three propositions: (1) population is necessarily limited by the means of subsistence; (2) population will expand when the means of

---

[5] Thomas R. Malthus, "An Essay on the Principle of Population as It Affects the Future Improvement of Society, with Remarks on the Speculations of Mr. Goodwin, M. Condorcet, and Other Writers," a facsimile reprint in *First Essay on Population,* 1798 (printed for the Royal Economic Society, London, Macmillan, 1926), p. 11.

subsistence increase, unless prevented by positive or preventive checks; and (3) these checks, which restrain population growth, are all resolvable into moral restraint, vice, and misery. Positive checks were those which increased the death rate, such as famines and war. Preventive checks, those which diminished the birth rate, were vice and moral restraint. Malthus thought of moral restraint as operating through late marriage and abstinence within marriage.

In other words, Malthus saw man's reproductive capacity eventually triumphing over his productive capacity. It was from this gloomy prediction of man's future that economics became known as the "dismal science." Malthus' ominous predictions did not materialize, however, during the nineteenth and twentieth centuries. Population did expand rapidly during this period, as has been previously indicated, but man's capacity to produce increased even more sharply than population. Over most of the civilized world, standards of living were generally rising despite the growth in population. The failure of the Malthusian hypothesis to accurately appraise the future impact of scientific and technological developments on agricultural and industrial production led to its refutation. Within the past several decades, however, neo-Malthusians have asserted that population-resource pressures in selected areas of the world indicate that the Malthusian doctrine may yet prove to be an accurate forecast of man's future. China, India, Japan, Latin American countries, to mention only a few, are currently experiencing extreme difficulty in maintaining food production at levels above, or even equal to, rates of increase in population. For the Far Eastern and Latin American areas, for instance, per capita food production was lower in the 1955–56 period than in the prewar 1935–39 years.[6] Commenting upon the relationship of low level of economic well-being and international tension, George W. Beadle, former president of the American Association for the Advancement of Science, stated: [7]

For a world with half its nations industrialized and half not, and with its natural resources very unequally distributed, the present population of more than 2500 million is far too large. More than half the people of the world are underfed, are poorly housed, receive little modern medical care, and are inadequately educated. It is small wonder that populations who see so little hope in other directions can be so easily stirred to rebellion and led to war by power-hungry demogogs, charlatans and other persuasive men of little wisdom.

Overcrowding of hungry people who see little hope for a brighter future is by no means the only cause of war, but it is surely an important one. And without the slightest doubt, war is the most serious of civilization's immediate problems.

[6] Food and Agriculture Organization, *The State of Food and Agriculture, 1956* (Rome, FAO, 1956), p. 10.
[7] George W. Beadle, "A Geneticist's View on Population versus Resources," *Population Bulletin*, Vol. XIII, No. 1 (Washington, D.C., Population Reference Bureau, February, 1957), pp. 10–11.

NATURAL RESOURCES: DISTRIBUTION IN RELATION TO POPULATION

An examination of the distribution and use of natural resources is relevant to a consideration of international relations, since the ownership and management of natural resources rest ultimately in man. The question first assumed economic importance when the products of nature useful to man became scarce relative to human wants. Thus, natural resources or the products of natural resources have economic value because they do not exist in sufficient quantities to freely satisfy all human wants.

Land Resources

Land is the basic natural resource of the earth. In addition to serving agricultural purposes, land supports or is primarily responsible for the formation of the other stores of natural wealth such as forests, fuels or energy resources, and minerals. Although man employs land for fulfilling a variety of needs, his principal relationship with it is in the production of food. Land for agriculture, however, accounts for only slightly more than one-fourth the earth's surface. The agricultural area, consisting of 3.3 billion acres of arable land and 5.8 billion acres of pasture, comprises 28 per cent of the total land surface of the earth. Waste, urban, and unused lands make up 43 per cent of the earth's surface. Forest lands cover 29 per cent of the globe.

Distribution of arable land. Some populations of the world are more favorably endowed than others with respect to arable land. An index of the relationship between population and arable land is called the manland ratio, which states the acres of arable land available per person.[8] For the world as a whole, there is approximately 1¼ acres of arable land per person (Table 2). This world average obscures much variation, however. Asia has approximately two-thirds of an acre of cultivable land per person, whereas in Africa and Oceania 3 or more acres are available per person.

Japan, with a sixth of an acre per inhabitant, has the least favorable relationship between population and cultivable land of any major nationality group. Other Asian countries are only slightly better off. The Indonesian index is about a third acre per person; China, slightly less than a half acre per capita; India, a little less than 1 acre per person.

Low man-land ratios are not unique to Asia, however. Europe, Latin America, and Africa also contain population groups that are pressing upon arable land resources. In Europe, for example, the United Kingdom, West and East Germany, and Italy have considerably less arable land per person than the world average. In the Latin America region, Puerto Rico and Colombia have severely restricted cultivable acreages relative

[8] The relationship expressed is land to man but is popularly known as the man-land ratio.

to their populations. Among African countries, the scarcity of arable land is particularly acute in Egypt, with approximately a fourth acre per person.

Table 2. Population Densities and Man-Land Ratios, Selected Regions of the World

Region	Population Density, persons per square mile	Man-Land Ratio, acres of arable land per person
World	47	1.23
Europe *	208	0.94
France	198	1.24
Germany, East	499	0.61
Germany, West	510	0.44
Italy	401	0.88
Spain	145	1.68
United Kingdom	537	0.35
Yugoslavia	164	1.18
U.S.S.R.	24	2.71
North and Central America	24	2.77
Canada	4	6.92
Mexico	35	1.41
Puerto Rico	672	0.41
United States	51	2.95
South America	16	1.45
Argentina	16	4.21
Brazil	16	0.87
Colombia	26	0.53
Asia *	122	0.66
China	124	0.48
India	284	0.90
Indonesia	104	0.36
Iran	30	2.17
Japan	593	0.15
Philippines	175	0.82
Turkey	70	1.80
Africa	17	2.97
Belgian Congo	13	10.53
Egypt	54	0.29
Ethiopia	37	1.81
Oceania	4	4.46
Australia	3	5.38

* Excluding the U.S.S.R.

Source: FAO, *Yearbook of Food and Agricultural Statistics, 1955* (Rome, FAO, 1956), pp. 3–15.

Countries that have comparatively large areas of cultivable land relative to their populations are: the United States, the Soviet Union, Argentina, Canada, and Australia. Here, the quantity of arable land per inhabitant is at least twice as large as the average man-land ratio for the world.

The relationship between cultivable land and population is summarized in Table 3. In this context also, the Asian portion of the earth emerges as the most severely disadvantaged in terms of population pressure upon food-producing resources. Asia, with over half the world's people, contains slightly more than a fourth of the world's cultivable land. The European area is in only a slightly better position, containing nearly a sixth of the total population but slightly in excess of a tenth of the cultivable land. Thus, these two continents, containing 70 per cent of the world's people but only 38 per cent of the cultivable land, represent the two major areas in which food-producing resources are insufficient to

Table 3. Relationship Between Arable Land and Population
By Continents

Continent or Area	Proportion of World Total, %		Ratio of Col. 1 to Col. 2
	Arable Land	Population	
Europe *	11.4	15.4	0.7
U.S.S.R.	17.2	7.4	2.3
North and Central America	19.5	8.9	2.2
South America	5.1	4.6	1.1
Asia *	26.6	55.1	0.5
Africa	18.6	8.1	2.3
Oceania	1.6	0.5	3.2
World	100.0	100.0	1.0

* Excluding the U.S.S.R.

Source: Same as Table 2.

provide their populaces with adequate food supplies. Two alternatives face these areas: hunger or importation of food. The first alternative is forced on underdeveloped Asia; the second alternative is chosen by Europe.

Does this uneven distribution of arable land among the nations of the world tend to support or refute the economic-resources explanation of war? The data offer ammunition for both sides of the argument. Germany and Italy are cited as recent illustrations of European nations that resorted to force in an attempt to improve their disadvantaged population and food-producing resource balances. In the Far East, Japan resorted to force allegedly in order to alter her population-resource situation, whereas India has relied primarily upon nonviolent methods to improve her severe population pressure.

It is hazardous, however, to relate an effect (war) to a single cause (low man-land ratio). Thus, the distribution of resources other than arable land must be considered.

Energy Resources

Resources utilized for commercial sources of energy may be broadly classified into four groups: coal, petroleum, natural gas, and hydroelectric power. This is not to underestimate nuclear fission as a potential source of energy. At present, however, atomic power cannot be considered comparable to any of the aforementioned sources of energy in commercial production.

Coal continues to be the principal source of energy, although its importance has declined moderately since the late 1920's (Table 4). Whereas coal had served as the source of three-fourths of the world's output of energy in 1929, by 1956 only half was derived from it. Petroleum, on the other hand, has become an increasingly important energy resource, supplying slightly less than a third of the world's total energy production. Natural gas and hydroelectric power together furnish about a fifth.

Table 4. World Output of Energy, by Source, 1929 and 1956

Source	Proportion of Total Output of Energy, %	
	1929	1956
Coal *	77.2	50.9
Petroleum	15.0	30.0
Natural gas	4.1	11.0
Hydroelectric	3.7	8.1
Total output	100.0	100.0

* Includes lignite.

Source: Statistical Office of the United Nations, *Monthly Bulletin of Statistics* (New York, United Nations, May, 1957), p. xi.

The world's output of energy is centered primarily in North America and Europe, the two continents producing slightly more than 70 per cent of the total output in 1950 (Table 5). Most of the remainder that is developed in the world originates in the Soviet Union and Asia.

Since the 1930's, the Soviet Union has achieved a more rapid expansion of energy output than any major area. Energy supplies there were increased from 60 million equivalent units in 1929 to 327 million units in 1950, or more than a fivefold expansion. Latin America, Asia, and Africa also made proportionately large increases in output during these years. Development of petroleum sources of energy, as compared to other sources, was primarily responsible for the expansions in energy output experienced by the separate regions of the globe.

Coal. It is only in the last few centuries that coal has been regarded as more than a curiosity. Not until the latter part of the eighteenth century did coal become an important factor in world industry. Among the more important industrial developments that stimulated the opening of the "coal age" were: (1) invention of the steam engine by James Watt in 1769, along with its successful application to industrial processes after 1775; (2) inadequate supplies of fuel, wood, and charcoal as a result of localized scarcities of timber; and (3) development of the coke-making process and its application to smelting and manufacturing of iron and steel in the eighteenth century.

Table 5. World Output of Energy, by Continents, 1929 and 1950

Continent or Area	1929		1950	
	Volume, million metric tons of coal equivalent	Proportion of Total, %	Volume, million metric tons of coal equivalent	Proportion of Total, %
North America	873	46.8	1,220	44.1
Europe	729	39.1	735	26.6
U.S.S.R.	60	3.2	327	11.8
Asia	123	6.6	275	10.0
Latin America	50	2.7	151	5.5
Africa	15	0.8	34	1.2
Oceania	14	0.8	23	0.8
Total output	1,864	100.0	2,765	100.0

Source: Same as Table 4, p. 34.

Since then, however, coal deposits have played a decisive role in the development of industrial power. Britain's industrial and maritime supremacy during the nineteenth century was possible because of relatively large coal reserves. The industrial and commercial power of the United States is founded in large measure upon an abundant supply of coal. Since coal serves as a foundation for industrial development, it is important to see how the nations of the world compare in terms of coal reserves.

In 1948, the World Power Conference estimated the earth's deposits of coal at 6.3 trillion metric tons (Table 6). This estimate placed slightly less than a half of the world's coal reserves in North and Central America. The Soviet Union, according to this appraisal, has about a fifth of the deposits, Asia slightly less than a fifth, and Europe approximately a tenth. Other continents—South America, Africa, and Oceania—have less than 5 per cent of the world's reserves of coal.

The coal fields of North America and Europe have been the most important in the economic development of the world. Before World War II, coal mined from these fields made up more than three-fourths the world's annual output. In North America, the United States has the major share of the deposits, with total reserves estimated to be 20 to 25 times as large as Canadian deposits. In the European area, Germany, Great Britain, France, and Poland are the leading producers.

Petroleum. Petroleum has been utilized by man in many ways over the centuries. It is reported that bricks for the Tower of Babel were mortared with asphalt made with residue from petroleum seepages in Mesopotamia. Egyptians utilized petroleum in embalming, and the Phoenicians caulked wooden vessels with petroleum compounds. Oil was applied externally by American Indians to relieve minor ailments such as headaches and toothaches.

Table 6. Distribution of Coal Reserves, by Continents and Selected Countries, 1948

Continent or Country	Coal Reserves, billions of metric tons			
	Total or Probable °		Proven †	
North and Central America	3,066		62	
United States		2,485 ‡		—
South America	3		2	
Europe	638		289	
Germany		337		109
United Kingdom		172		130
U.S.S.R.	1,200		309	
Asia	1,101		11	
China		1,012		—
India		65		5
Africa	206		9	
Oceania	54		9	
World total	6,268 §		691 °°	

° Includes proven reserves.
† Consists of deposits for which reliable data on the actual thickness and extent of seams are available.
‡ U. S. Geological Survey estimate of 1950. Proven reserves of the United States are unknown.
§ Includes an estimate by World Power Conference of 2,880 billion tons for the United States.
°° Does not include the United States.

Source: W. S. and E. S. Woytinsky, World Population and Production (New York, Twentieth Century Fund, 1953), pp. 855, 857.

Only since the middle and second half of the nineteenth century, however, has oil become a significant element in industrial and commercial development. Within recent decades, it has not only become a potent competitor of coal as a source of energy, but it also serves as the principal lubricant for our mechanized civilization. In fact, some authorities assert that, without petroleum, machinery—the basis of modern western civilization—could not have achieved its high level of development.

The world contains two main areas of oil concentration: one in the Eastern Hemisphere, the other in the Western Hemisphere. In the eastern portion of the globe, the principal deposits are located in the area of the Black Sea, the Caspian Sea, and the Persian Gulf. The western area of concentration is centered around the Gulf Coast, the Caribbean Sea, and the central United States.

Proven oil reserves in the world total approximately 230 billion barrels, of which more than 60 per cent are in the Middle East (Table 7). Since the 1930's, proven reserves have been increased sharply with the discovery of new fields and the higher evaluation of known oil resources. In 1939, for instance, proven reserves were estimated at 34 billion barrels; by 1949, the estimate had risen to 78 billion barrels. In the 1950's, more than 150 billion barrels were added to the reserve, principally as a result of higher estimates for Middle East oil fields.

Table 7. Distribution of Oil Reserves, by Areas and
Selected Countries, 1956

Area or Country	Proven Reserves, billions of barrels		Proportion of World Total Reserve, %	
Western Hemisphere	53.8		23.3	
Canada		3.5		1.5
Colombia		0.6		0.3
Mexico		2.5		1.1
United States		32.9		14.2
Venezuela		13.2		5.7
Europe and Africa	1.7		0.7	
Austria		0.4		0.2
Egypt		0.3		0.1
West Germany		0.5		0.2
Middle East	144.4		62.5	
Iran		30.0		13.0
Iraq		22.0		9.5
Kuwait		50.0		21.6
Saudi Arabia		40.0		17.3
Asia, Pacific	6.8		3.0	
China		0.7		0.3
Indonesia		5.0		2.2
U.S.S.R. and satellites	24.3		10.5	
U.S.S.R.		23.5		10.2
World total	231.0		100.0	

Source: *The Oil and Gas Journal* (Tulsa, Petroleum Publishing Co., December 31, 1956), pp. 105–106.

Kuwait, on the northwestern shore of the Persian Gulf, contains the largest oil reservoir, with over a fifth of the world supply of oil. Other major producers in the Middle East include Saudi Arabia, Iran, and Iraq.

In the Western Hemisphere, the largest supply of oil is located in the United States. Only one other western country, Venezuela, has significant quantities of petroleum.

The Soviet Union is relatively well endowed with oil reserves, containing approximately a tenth of the world's reserve. The U.S.S.R. supply is about 70 per cent that of the U.S. reserve.

Commercial control of production shows a considerably different pat-tern than that of the distribution of oil reserves. The reasons for this are foreign ownership of petroleum resources and variations in the extent to which countries with reserves have developed their oil resources. According to C. F. Jones and G. G. Darkenwald, commercial control of the world's oil fields is dominated by the United States, the United Kingdom, and the Soviet Union.[9] Oil companies in the United States, together with United States companies operating overseas, give the United States commercial control of nearly half the world's oil output. The United Kingdom, at least until 1950, had control of more than a fifth of the world's production. The Soviet Union has commercial control of approximately a tenth of the world's supply.

The importance of petroleum to the world economy was dramatized in late 1956 by the Anglo-French-Israeli invasion of Egypt. Among the more important factors prompting this attack, as has been indicated previously, was the desire by England and France to safeguard their oil supplies, which had been threatened by nationalization of the Suez Canal Co. The crucial significance of Middle East oil to the industries of Western Europe was pointed out by T. P. Ronan: [10]

Once again turmoil in the Middle East has dramatized for the world the vital importance of that far-off region.

Strategically, and in a sense economically, the Middle East is possibly the most important area in the world. It links three continents—Asia, Africa and Europe. The nation that could control it in a world conflict would have a tremendous advantage over its opponents in land and naval operations.

It would have control of the shortest sea and an air traffic link between Europe and Africa and Asia. It would have domination, too, over the second-largest oil producing area in the world. Only the United States produces more oil. And the Middle East is far ahead in proven reserves, for it holds three-quarters of the total known to exist in the world. . . .

Economically, the Middle East has grown in importance largely because of its richness in oil. With the depletion of stocks of coal in Britain and other European countries, oil has become increasingly the source of power to keep industries expanding.

From the Middle East, West Europe now gets about three-quarters of its oil supplies. More than half of it moves through the Suez Canal in tankers, while the rest moves by pipelines—at least one of which was cut this week—to East Mediterranean ports. . . .

In attacking Egypt, Britain and France have emphasized the key importance of keeping the Suez Canal open as an international waterway. Prime Minister Eden has said repeatedly that this is vital for Britain.

[9] Clarence F. Jones and Gordon G. Darkenwald, *Economic Geography* (New York, Macmillan, 1954), p. 411.
[10] *New York Times,* November 4, 1956, News of the Week section, p. 5.

Thus in this particular incident, economic resources did constitute a "seedbed for conflict."

Hydroelectric power. The relative dearth of energy resources in Europe has led to a higher development of potential hydroelectric energy in Europe than in any other major area. Among the continents, Europe makes best use of its water power, having developed over 60 per cent of the continent's potential hydroelectric energy. North America has developed slightly more than 50 per cent of its potential. None of the other continents are utilizing more than a sixth of theirs. The world's energy potential from hydroelectric sources is estimated at nearly 665 million horsepower. Of the potential, less than 90 million horsepower, or about 14 per cent, have been developed. Failure to make greater use of hydroelectric sources of power is due largely to the distribution of water-power resources. The tropical areas, for example, contain 60 per cent of the world's potential water power; yet that developed there accounts for only 5 per cent of the total produced throughout the world. The hydroelectric potential of Asia is about twice as great as that of North America; yet Asia's developed power is only 12 per cent of the world total, whereas the developed power in North America comprises about 40 per cent of the total.

Natural gas. As a source of commercial energy, natural gas is of considerably less importance than are coal and oil. As indicated in Table 4, gas serves as the source of about 10 per cent of the world's energy output.

The world's proven reserve of natural gas has never been estimated. Data on annual output, however, provide a basis for appraising the relative importance of natural gas among the countries of the world. The United States leads all countries in natural-gas output, producing around 90 per cent of the world's total. The next largest producer is Venezuela, accounting for about 5 per cent of the total. The rest of the natural-gas output originates primarily in Russia, Canada, Mexico, Rumania, and Hungary.

Mineral Resources

With the exclusion of the mineral fuels, minerals of the earth's crust may be classified into two groups: (1) metallic ores and metals, and (2) nonmetallic minerals. Our consideration includes only the more important ores and metals.

Metallic ores and metals. Of greatest significance among this group of minerals are iron ore, ferroalloying metals, and nonferrous metals.

Although some 50 nations mine iron ore, the output from deposits in North America and northwestern Europe dominate world production. The North American deposit is centered around the Lake Superior region, with the Mesabi Range accounting for nearly four-fifths of the ore mined in that area. Relatively large quantities of ore are produced also from the ranges in the Birmingham, Alabama, region. In northwest Europe, the more important iron-mining regions are concentrated in the Lorraine district of France, Luxembourg and Belgium, and the ore fields of northern Sweden and the United Kingdom.

A meaningful analysis of the geographic distribution of iron-ore reserves requires consideration of the iron content of the deposits. On this basis, the United Nations has estimated the world's potential reserve of iron ore at 128.8 billion tons (Table 8). Africa, with over 40 per cent of the total, and North America with slightly more than 20 per cent, have the largest potential reserves. The remainder of the world's potential is distributed rather evenly among the other continents, except that Oceania has only limited deposits.

Table 8. Distribution of Iron-Ore Reserves, by Selected Countries, 1950

Continent or Country	Potential or Total Reserves *		Probable Reserves *	
	Iron Content, millions of metric tons	Proportion of Total, %	Iron Content, millions of metric tons	Proportion of Total, %
United States	25,488	19.8	1,710	6.4
Canada	2,221	1.7	930	3.5
Cuba	5,400	4.2	1,200	4.5
Brazil	10,807	8.4	4,095	15.3
France	3,876	3.0	2,546	9.5
Sweden	1,600	1.2	1,408	5.3
United Kingdom	918	0.7	672	2.5
Germany	840	0.6	256	1.0
U.S.S.R.	4,345	3.4	2,027	7.6
India	10,272	8.0	5,608	21.0
China	1,215	0.9	810	3.0
Southern Rhodesia	50,671	39.4	1,142	4.3
Union of South Africa	5,089	4.0	1,275	4.7
Other countries	6,101	4.7	3,040	11.4
World	128,843	100.0	26,719	100.0

* Potential or total reserves represent the sum of: (1) probable reserves, for which a reliable calculation of the extent of the deposits, based on actual investigation, has been carried out, and (2) other deposits, for which only an approximation could be made.

Source: World Iron Resources and Their Utilization (New York, United Nations, 1950), pp. 66–68.

Of the ferroalloying ores, the principal ores for imparting various characteristics to steel are manganese, chromium, tungsten, nickel, molybdenum, and vanadium. Generally, the higher-grade deposits of alloy minerals are found in areas that produce only limited quantities of steel.

Commercial control of these alloys is concentrated, however, among the "big three" steel producers—the United States, the Soviet Union, and the United Kingdom.

Nonferrous metals include copper, lead and zinc, tin, aluminum, and uranium. The United States is the leading supplier of smelter copper, furnishing about a third of the world's annual output. Other relatively important producers are Chile, Northern Rhodesia, Canada, and the Belgian Congo. Three countries, the United States, Britain, and Belgium, have control over approximately 80 per cent of the world's copper production.

Lead and zinc are commonly found in the same ore. Thus most companies in the lead and zinc industries process both metals. The United States contains the world's largest deposits of lead and zinc, although Canada, Mexico, Poland, the Soviet Union, and Australia have relatively large ore fields.

About three-fourths of the world's supply of tin comes from the Federation of Malaya, Indonesia, and Bolivia. Of these, Malaya is the most important producer, supplying nearly as much tin as Indonesia and Bolivia, combined. Unlike Indonesia and Bolivia, which smelter little or no tin, Malaya leads the world in smelter output. British interests control the Malayan tin industry. The relative importance of Malaya's smelter facilities has declined since the prewar period, however. When Malayan supplies of tin were cut off during World War II, the United States government erected a smelting plant at Texas City, Texas. This plant, the "Longhorn," processing nearly all the tin smelted in the United States, ranks our country as second in smelter output. A smaller smelting plant was built in New Jersey during World War II, but this operation was discontinued at the end of the war.

Aluminum is one of the most abundant metals in the earth's crust. The world's reserve of bauxite, the best of the aluminum ores, is placed at approximately 400 million tons, excluding the Soviet Union's deposits. The Western Hemisphere has about one-third of this total reserve, with Jamaica, British Guiana, Surinam, Brazil, and the United States containing the largest deposits. In the Eastern Hemisphere, significant quantities of bauxite are found in Ghana, India, Indonesia, Yugoslavia, France, and Greece. The United States smelters about one-half the world's output of bauxite ore; it produces about the same proportion of the world's aluminum, with Canada the second largest producer, the output there approximating half that of the United States.

The relative importance of uranium has increased tremendously with the development of atomic energy in recent years, and for security reasons most countries guard closely their data on uranium production. Nevertheless, four major areas of uranium production are known: (1) the Shinkolobwe mine in the Belgian Congo, (2) northwest Canada, (3) the Erz Mountain area in East Germany and Czechoslovakia, and (4) the Colorado plateau in the United States. As the search intensifies, geologists are confident that additional uranium resources will be identified, as was indicated by the discovery of uranium ores in Australia and east China.

Summary

This survey of the distribution of natural resources has demonstrated that not all nation-states share equally in land, forest, or mineral resources. Yet, the differences in levels of living among nations are far greater than those stemming from resource distribution. One of the principal reasons for the disparity is to be found in the uneven development of resources of the various countries.

PATTERNS OF ECONOMIC DEVELOPMENT

Although man does not live by bread alone, the patterns of resource use and human effort demonstrate that food production occupies the highest ranking in resource utilization. Only after his minimum food needs have been met does man turn human and natural resources toward production of lower-order items such as roads, radios, and refrigerators. An inventory of resource use, thus, can be divided into two broad classifications: (1) agricultural, including food- and fiber-producing resources, and (2) industrial and commercial utilization of resources.

Agricultural Resources and the Food Supply: Production and Consumption

Approximately 60 per cent of the world's population is engaged in working the soil. In view of this proportionately large application of human resources to natural resources, questions arise: What are the chief products of all this human effort? How well does each nation fare in feeding its population?

Production. Around the globe, man's principal food is grain. Of all the grains produced, three—wheat, rice, and corn—dominate the world's food situation.

Wheat, the staff of life of the West, is the chief food grain in North America, Europe, and Oceania. Wheat is also the primary bread grain of the Soviet Union. These areas represent the more industrialized and urbanized regions of the globe, and wheat has been called the food grain of the "plutocrats of the world's dinner table."

Rice, on the other hand, is the primary food grain of the Orient; in fact, rice is the dominant grain among the majority of the world's people. Asia annually produces about 90 per cent of the world's output, with China, India, and Pakistan the leading producers. The choice of rice as the food mainstay in the densely populated regions of the earth is not accidental. Acre for acre, rice can provide two to three times as many calories as could be produced with other cereal grains.

Corn, the third major grain, is man's principal feed grain. Although some populations, as in Mexico and Brazil, consume corn directly as grain, the bulk of the crop is consumed indirectly in the form of livestock and livestock products. Of the world's output, about 60 per cent is grown in the United States, and approximately 10 to 12 per cent each in Latin America, Europe, and Asia.

Among crops other than grain, the potato is comparatively important in several regions of the globe. Europe and the Soviet Union are the largest potato producers, with production concentrated on the northern European plain to almost the same extent as rice cultivation in monsoon Asia. In addition to being an important item in human diets, a substantial part of the European potato crop is fed to livestock.

The world's supply of animal foodstuffs is derived largely from cattle (dairy and beef), hogs, and sheep. Beef and veal account for about 50 per cent of the world's meat production, pork nearly 40 per cent, and mutton and lamb about 10 per cent.

Asia has the world's largest herd of cattle. India alone possesses about one-fifth of the world's cattle. Throughout Southeast Asia, cattle—despite their vast numbers—make only a slight contribution to the food supply. Religious customs here prevail over economic considerations,[11] so that man competes with domestic animals for plant foods and feeds. Aside from Asia, large concentrations of cattle are found in Latin America (Brazil and Argentina), Europe (France, Germany, and Britain), the Soviet Union, Australia, and the Union of South Africa.

Consumption. This brief résumé of the major food products man obtains from agricultural resources suggests that some people eat better than others. The amount of disparity in the level of food consumption is indicated in data collected in the second world food survey conducted by the Food and Agriculture Organization of the United Nations during 1950 and 1951. Per capita food consumption, as measured by caloric intake, was below nutritional requirements in all regions except Europe, North America, Oceania, and the Soviet Union (Table 9). For many countries in Latin America, Asia, and Africa recent levels of food consumption were 10 to 20 per cent below estimated physiological requirements, and these areas of malnutrition contain from a half to two-thirds of mankind. In short, well over 50 per cent of the people of the world live in the "shadow of perpetual hunger." There is no mass starvation, except when crops fail as a result of droughts, locusts, and the like, but there is a continuous erosion of physical well-being.

[11] This is especially true among Hindus and Jains, who regard the cow as sacred and inviolable.

Table 9. Per Capita Food Consumption Measured Against Estimated Requirements, in Calories, Selected Countries, Recent Year

Region or Country	Recent Level, calories	Estimated Requirements,* calories	Difference of Requirements, %
Europe			
Belgium-Luxembourg	2770	2620	+5.7
Denmark	3160	2750	+14.9
France	2770	2550	+8.6
Greece	2510	2390	+5.0
Italy	2340	2440	−4.1
Netherlands	2960	2630	+12.5
Norway	3140	2850	+10.2
Sweden	3120	2840	+9.8
Switzerland	3150	2720	+15.8
United Kingdom	3100	2650	+16.9
U.S.S.R.	3020	2710	+11.4
North America			
Canada	3060	2710	+12.9
United States	3130	2640	+18.5
Latin America			
Argentina	3190	2600	+22.7
Brazil	2340	2450	−4.5
Chile	2360	2640	−10.6
Colombia	2280	2550	−10.6
Cuba	2740	2460	+11.4
Mexico	2050	2490	−17.6
Peru	1920	2540	−24.4
Uruguay	2580	2570	+0.4
Venezuela	2160	2440	−11.5
Near East			
Cyprus	2470	2510	−1.6
Egypt	2290	2390	−4.2
Turkey	2480	2440	+1.6
Far East			
Ceylon	1970	2270	−13.2
India	1700	2250	−24.4
Japan	2100	2330	−9.9
Pakistan	2020	2300	−12.2
Philippines	1960	2230	−12.1
Africa			
French North Africa	1920	2430	−20.9
Mauritius	2230	2410	−7.5
Tanganyika	1980	2420	−18.2
Union of South Africa	2520	2400	+5.0
Oceania			
Australia	3160	2620	+20.6
New Zealand	3250	2670	+27.7

* Physiological requirements for residents of each country were based on environmental temperatures, average body weights, and age and sex distributions of the population. Allowance was also made for loss of food nutrients in marketing food products.

Source: FAO, Second World Food Survey (Rome, FAO, 1952), p. 13.

Even this somber description of the world's food situation does not tell the whole story of the differences. Measuring dietary levels by caloric intake shows only the quantitative features of the food situation. Caloric measurements indicate whether the stomach is full, or half full. Of equal or greater importance is the qualitative aspect of the diet, that is, the source of the calories.

Unfortunately, there is no relatively simple unit like the calorie for measuring the quality of diets. Quality depends on the presence in satisfactory proportions of many food nutrients, including vitamins and minerals. Animal protein content is the best available index of the quality of dietary levels because most foods of animal origin are high in protein and are good sources of other essential nutrients. Information collected in the survey indicated also that nearly three-fifths of the world's people had diets that lacked the higher-quality foods essential for nutritional balance. These qualitative deficiencies represent the "hidden hunger" to which nutritionists refer.

Levels of food consumption reflect primarily man's use of agricultural resources. The output produced as a result of man's efforts to exploit natural resources for other purposes yields further indexes of material well-being.

Natural Resources: Development and Use in Industry and Commerce

Growth and distribution of world industrial output. Only within the last few years have attempts been made to measure, with any degree of accuracy, the long-term growth of the world's industrial production. The studies indicate that industrial output of the world, excluding the communist bloc, is now about twice as high as during the years immediately preceding World War II.

Long-term changes in the geographical distribution of industrial output are indicated in a study completed by the United Nations in 1951. The survey indicated that approximately a third of the world's industrial production during 1937 originated in the United States. European industry contributed 37 per cent, the Soviet Union approximately 10 per cent, Asia slightly less than 6 per cent, and the rest of the world the remaining 14 per cent.[12] In 1953, Woytinsky and Woytinsky, adopting the same weighting procedure as that of the United Nations, estimated the distribution of industrial production for 1950.[13] According to their figures, the United States was still the world's industrial giant, producing nearly 40 per cent of the total industrial output. The reconstruction of industrial facilities in northwestern Europe was very near completion, and this region was turning out slightly more than 20 per cent of the world's industrial goods.

[12] Statistical Office of the United Nations, *Monthly Bulletin of Statistics* (New York, United Nations, April, 1951), p. 2.

[13] W. S. and E. S. Woytinsky, *World Population and Production* (New York, Twentieth Century Fund, 1953), pp. 1004–1006.

The Soviet Union's contribution comprised about 16 per cent of the total.

The iron and steel industry. One of the best barometers of the industrial capacity of a nation is steel output, for steel represents the backbone of modern industry. The industrial supremacy of the western nations is shown in Table 10, which indicates that more than 60 per cent of the total steel output originates in western bloc countries. The United States is the leading producer, with an output of about 40 per cent of the total steel produced. By contrast, the steel-producing capacity of the Soviet Union is roughly half as large as that of the United States. Steel production in the Soviet Union has been expanding, however, at a faster rate than in any other major steel-producing nation. Soviet output increased nearly threefold between 1936 and 1955, whereas production in the United States slightly more than doubled during the same interval.

Table 10. World Production of Crude Steel, for Selected Countries, 1936–55
(million metric tons)

				Countries		
Year	World Total	U.S.	U.K.	W. Germany	France °	U.S.S.R.
1936	124.1	48.5	12.0	19.2	6.7	16.4
1937	135.3	51.4	13.2	19.8	7.9	17.7
1945	113.3	72.3	12.0	—	1.7	12.3
1946	111.4	60.4	12.9	2.6	4.7	13.3
1950	188.6	87.8	16.5	12.1	10.4	27.3
1951	209.8	95.4	15.9	13.5	12.4	31.4
1954	221.4	80.1	18.8	17.4	13.4	41.4
1955	266.3	106.2	20.1	21.3	15.7	45.3

° Includes steel production in Saar beginning 1945.

Source: Statistical Office of the United Nations, *Statistical Yearbook* (New York, United Nations, 1956), pp. 261–262.

Japan is the leading steel producer in Asia, with an output of 7 or 8 million metric tons annually. China and India each produce about a third as much steel as Japan.

In most other manufacturing industries, such as machine tools, industrial and agricultural machinery, motor vehicles, and shipbuilding, the industrial supremacy of the western nations is as strikingly evident as in steel production.

The "Underdeveloped" World and the "Revolution of Rising Expectation"

The description of the distribution of resources and of their level of development clearly reveals how few other nation-states have achieved the stage of economic development characteristic of the western world.

In these underdeveloped areas, shown in Fig. 9, agriculture is still the major occupation. Industrial growth is only beginning, and the level of economic well-being is far below that of the "developed" world. The relationship between the level of economic development and the contemporary crisis in international affairs was cited in a report, in the following words: [14]

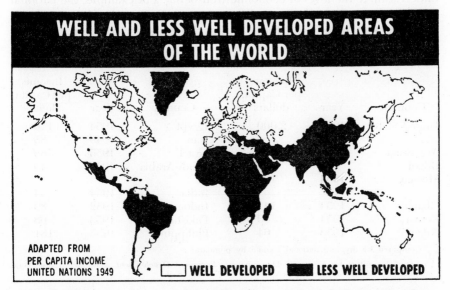

Fig. 9. Underdeveloped areas of the world. (*Source: Twentieth Century Newsletter,* No. 29, Spring, 1957, New York, Twentieth Century Fund, p. 4.)

Behind much of the discontent in the world's troubled areas of Africa, Asia, the Middle East and South America is an ever-quickening revolution, the revolution of rising expectations. It is the demand of people living in feudal conditions of poverty and deprivation to become a part of the twentieth century, to share as individuals in the plenty and dignity of much of the rest of the world.

The extremely low standards of living in most of the underdeveloped or economically disadvantaged world are reflected in Table 11, which presents the income per capita for some representative nations. Differences in per capita national income are subject to several interpretative qualifications. First, relatively few countries collect data from which accurate estimates of national incomes may be computed. The incomes of many nations are therefore subject to considerable error.

The terms in which per capita income is expressed are of even greater significance. The national-income concept is most valuable as a yardstick

[14] Twentieth Century Fund, *Newsletter,* No. 29 (New York, Twentieth Century Fund, 1957), p. 4.

of economic activity for countries in which the bulk of the goods and services produced enter the market system and thus acquire a price. For underdeveloped countries in which the economy is not organized around a complex marketing structure, and in which many goods are produced for personal consumption or for simple bartering, goods and services are either ignored or assigned computed values that undoubtedly underestimate the level of economic well-being. For example, the national income per capita in the United States in recent years has been approximately $2,000, whereas in India during the same period the national in-

Table 11. Per Capita Income, Selected Nations °

Country	Year	Income per Capita, dollars	Country	Year	Income per Capita, dollars
United States	1955	2,000	Egypt	1954	110
			Iran	1949	85
Argentina	1954	228	Israel	1955	569
Brazil	—	273	Saudi-Arabia	1949	40
Mexico	1954	159			
			India	1954	54
Ghana	1954	141	Indonesia	1952	89
Kenya	1954	60	Pakistan	1953	68
Nigeria	1953	64	Philippines	1955	181

° Computed by dividing national income by population.

Source: Committee for Economic Development, *Economic Development Assistance* (New York, Committee for Economic Development, April, 1957), pp. 8–9.

come was estimated at about $50 per capita. Does this mean the average Indian has the same level of existence as he would have living in the United States on an income of $4 a month? Obviously not. The Indian produces most of his own food. His clothing and housing needs are much less extensive than is the American's and may be self-made from animal or vegetable resources of the region. In brief, as low as the Indian subsistence level may be, it clearly does not approach the equivalent of 15 cents a day in our economy. The different ways of life and methods of economic organization of the United States and India account for a substantial portion of the variation in per capita national incomes. Despite these limitations, national-income statistics are useful in demonstrating major differences in standards of living and in comparing national incomes among countries of comparable economic development. Thus, incomes of $200 or less, common among underdeveloped countries, are approximations of the low levels of economic well-being in these areas.

A major element affecting the economic development of these disadvantaged areas is the system of trade relationships that exist among nations. This topic and its potential effect on international affairs are discussed in the following section.

INTERNATIONAL TRADE AND ECONOMIC NATIONALISM

The importance of an enlightened trade policy in reducing international tension was pointed out in President Eisenhower's recommendation to the 83rd Congress in 1954 on foreign economic policy. The President said: [15]

We and other free nations are still severely limited by the persistence of uneconomic, man-made barriers to mutual trade and the flow of funds among us . . . the solution is a higher level of two-way trade. Thus we can sell and receive payments for our exports and have an increasing volume of investment abroad to assist economic development overseas and yield returns to us.

. . . Our domestic employment, our standard of living, our security, and the solidarity of the free world—all are involved.

Another President at an earlier session of Congress also directed attention to the crucial effect of trade relations on international affairs. President Woodrow Wilson, outlining his program of peace to Congress in 1918, made the third of his famous Fourteen Points: "The removal, so far as possible, of all economic barriers and the establishment of an equality of trade conditions among all the nations consenting to the peace and associating themselves for its maintenance." [16] Wilson was convinced that equality of economic opportunity was the principal requisite of a lasting peace among nations. According to a historian, William Diamond,[17] Wilson believed that:

No peace could be permanent which did not provide guarantees against economic boycott or to exclude from markets or from sources of raw materials or to make any other kind of effort to throttle the industrial life of a nation. . . .

He believed the struggle of rival imperialism could be ended for all times by such actions as the administration of colonies as a trust, by allowing free access to the world's goods, by eliminating economic discriminations and trade barriers and by guaranteeing the freedom of the seas.

The Advantages of Trade

Foreign trade, like internal trade, permits a more economical use of resources by allowing the increased productivity from specialization of labor and resources to be fully expressed. Advantages of foreign trade are clear when a country buys abroad goods that are not produced within the country. To provide home-made substitutes for these imports would make for a most inefficient use of resources.

Despite the advantages of exchanging goods, countries around the

[15] U. S. House of Representatives, Doc. 360 (Washington, D.C., Government Printing Office, March 30, 1954).

[16] Message to Congress, January 8, 1918.

[17] William Diamond, *The Economic Thought of Woodrow Wilson* (Baltimore, Johns Hopkins Press, 1943), p. 166.

world erect barriers, principally in the form of tariffs, to restrict international trade. These barriers tend to lower the potential output that could be derived from the world's resources, and thus contribute indirectly to economic tension.

International trade is a two-way exchange, and for a nation to continue to export goods it must in the long run be willing to accept an approximately equal value of goods and services from the nations with which it trades. By erecting a high tariff wall, a nation impedes the exchange of products, for foreign goods coming in over the wall are priced out of the domestic market. A more drastic way of curtailing imports is to set a low import quota, so that not more than a specified quantity of certain goods can enter the country.

Stability of tariff rates is frequently more important than the level of the tariff. Countries specializing in one or two products for export are often placed at a severe disadvantage by the fluctuations in tariff rates in countries to which they sell.

The role of freer trade in the relaxation of economic tension may be summarized by the following statement by the National Foreign Trade Council: [18]

Increased production, freer interchange, and wider consumption are basic to the creation of a better world. To the extent that the people of any land lack adequate resources and techniques, they will achieve their maximum strength and well-being only by drawing upon the resources and techniques of others. Advantageous interchange of goods and services is the basis and justification of all international trade and investment. . . .

Production and more production, trade and more trade; these are, today, more than ever essential to the security and well-being of the peoples of the free world.

Economic Nationalism

In matters of economic policy, nationalism plays a very influential role in the actions of nation-states. Despite economic interdependence, and the natural tendency of private commerce to extend beyond national boundaries wherever profitable trade opportunities can be found, nationalism exerts sufficient appeal to lead governments to impose many restrictions on the movement of international trade.

Economic self-sufficiency in the face of war. Fear of war and the resultant desire for greater economic self-sufficiency have been substantial factors in persuading governments to reduce their reliance on foreign trade. Countries which had normally depended on the United States or Western Europe for manufactured goods found, during World War II, that because of blockade or other wartime regulations they could not obtain their normal supply of imports. Likewise, countries which had

[18] "Final Declaration of the Thirty-Ninth National Foreign Trade Convention" (New York, National Foreign Trade Council, November, 1952), pp. 7, 10.

relied on overseas supplies of foodstuffs or raw materials, such as meat from Argentina or rubber from Indonesia, found that these areas could be easily cut off in wartime. Their bitter experiences convinced many governments that, so long as there was danger of war, it was not safe to rely entirely on foreign sources for needed materials. They concluded that it would be wiser, from the standpoint of the security and welfare of their respective nation-states, to adopt programs of greater economic self-sufficiency, despite the increased cost involved. Switzerland, for example, began more intensive cultivation of wheat and other foodstuffs on its mountain slopes. The United States developed a synthetic rubber industry and began to exploit the more costly low-grade mineral reserves within its borders. Germany and other continental countries developed synthetic oil production and other "ersatz" or substitute products. In all such programs, the questions of national security and welfare overrode the purely economic considerations and advantages of interdependence and foreign trade.

Programs of national economic planning. In the light of economic crises, depression, unemployment, and shortage of critical materials, governments all over the world since the 1930's have increasingly undertaken measures of economic planning, social-welfare legislation, government subsidies to vital industries, allocation of strategic raw materials, and nationalization of certain enterprises.

Some controls have extended to foreign trade, since it was feared that a freely operating foreign trade would interfere with and jeopardize the program of domestic economic controls. Countries like Great Britain, for example, which have had serious shortages of foreign-currency holdings, have had to impose quotas on imports to be sure that their limited supplies of foreign currency would be spent only for imports regarded as essential to the national welfare. Luxuries and less vital imports were restricted.

The program of supporting farm prices in the United States has led also to restrictions on the imports of foreign agricultural commodities, which might sell at lower prices than domestically supported American farm products and thereby undermine the price-support program.

Thus, measures of national economic planning, by establishing various controls over a nation's domestic and foreign trade, may conflict with the facts of economic interdependence. Instead of the spectacle of a world becoming more economically united, we are evidencing more exclusive and independent efforts to strengthen the separate national economies.

Industrialization of underdeveloped areas. Many young nations, which have acquired their independence since World War II, are acutely aware of the comparatively low level of their economic development. As the world has shrunk in a geographical sense under the impact of modern transportation and communication, the underdeveloped nations have also become more determined to do something about their economic needs.

Most of these nation-states feel that they must become industrialized, not only to increase their productivity and general living standards, but also to free themselves from complete dependence on Europe and the United States for manufactured goods. In order to stimulate and develop their infant industries, they have to impose restrictions on the import of competing manufactured goods from the outside world. Here then is another obstacle to the operation of normal international trade. The fact that many of the younger nations are adopting broad programs of economic planning in connection with their industrial development also means that extensive controls over foreign trade are likely to be introduced.

Protective tariffs. Economic nationalism is evident also in the pressure from domestic enterprises to obtain tariffs that will protect their industries against competing foreign imports. The bicycle and watch industries in the United States, for example, feeling the competition from British bicycles and Swiss watches, seek government aid in the form of tariffs on such imports to prevent the foreign from underselling the American products. Without such tariffs, it is argued, the American industries would be disadvantaged, and this would cause unemployment and serious disruption in various segments of our economy.

Tariff levels vary, of course, from country to country, and the United States at present is actually a relatively low-tariff country. Where they do exist, however, tariffs and especially fluctuations in tariff rates operate as barriers to international trade and contradict the implications of economic interdependence.

Summary

Since World War I, then, for the reasons stated, nations have resorted more and more frequently to measures of economic nationalism. International trade has never recovered the relative place it occupied in the world economy up to 1914. It is true that the total volume of world trade has increased considerably since that time, but the total level of world income has increased even more during the same period. The actual ratio of world trade to world income, therefore, is lower at present than before World War I. It seems ironic that this trend should have occurred during a period when modern transportation and communication have shrunk the distances in the world so much and when organized international co-operation has grown so extensively. This course of economic events suggests that the appeals of economic nationalism to the peoples and politicians of the world are stronger than those of economic internationalism, and that economic considerations have yielded to the paramount demands for political and military security.

Attention is directed again to the central question posed in this chapter: Are economic resources the seedbed for international conflict? Three alternative responses are presented in the next section. The first holds that the uneven distribution of economic resources is the primary force behind international conflict. Next is presented an argument which states that economic resources, per se, are not the causes of conflict; rather, tension and war stem from the imperialist nature of capitalist economies. The final position argues that the economic explanation of war is overrated and too inclusive.

POSITIONS
ON THE PROBLEM

1. War Ultimately Stems from Underlying Economic Causes

(The following passages are taken from *War and Its Causes*, written during the latter part of World War II, by L. L. Bernard.[19] The author was an eminent sociologist whose examination of the causes of war emphasized the economic forces.)

In recent years there has been somewhat of a reaction against attributing wars to economic causes. There are several reasons for this. The conservative historians have always preferred to emphasize political causes. Palyi explains the reaction as a protest against the oversimplification of the Marxian interpretation of history in economic terms. There are still a few educated people who think of the causes of war in terms of God's anger at the sins of men and profess to believe that he uses this method to confound and punish them. . . .

. . . It is a curious fact that nearly all of those who reject the theory of the predominance of economic factors in the causation of war fall back mainly upon a theory of psychological causation.

. . . Modern economic causes of war do not usually operate to produce war directly. Therefore they are made effective through abstract channels and are not easily perceptible. Instead of making direct physical impact upon other countries through the medium of physical force, they condition psychic responses in the individuals of a country and thus result in such collective representation or attitudes as public opinion, economic and political theory, governmental policies and plans. It is these collective psychological attitudes and beliefs—particularly public opinion, carefully nurtured by interested propaganda, and governmental theory and policy, often equally actively influenced by interested economic groups—that finally push a country over the brink into

---

[19] L. L. Bernard, *War and Its Causes*, pp. 325–350. By permission of Henry Holt and Company, Inc., copyright 1944.

war. To the superficial observer, or to one who for any reason wishes to avoid "materialistic" theories of the causation of war, the psychological causes seem to be the important ones. These causes may be called public opinion, patriotism, nationalistic spirit, race or cultural prejudices, religious intolerance, or any other set of opinions, beliefs or ideologies. But back of them almost invariably lie those economic causes which have conditioned them. Even the ideologies, which are bodies of social and political, religious, or other complexes of beliefs and loyalties, and are consequently collective psychological factors, have been clearly shown to rest in nearly all instances ultimately upon economic interests and processes.

We may conclude, therefore, that it is not absolutely erroneous to attribute war to psychological causes in many instances. Such are real causes, but they are usually merely the immediate and nearly always incidental rather than fundamental causes. The fundamental causes of war must usually be looked for behind these relatively superficial and contributing causes. Some of the fundamental causes are so deeply hidden that it requires a detailed sociological analysis to uncover them.

. . . In modern times migration, the search for new lands, and the "treasure hunt" have played a markedly declining role in the causation of wars, but for a number of reasons they have not been absent as motives. Whole peoples can no longer migrate. There is not enough free land and modern populations are too large for mass movements. With all the modern developments in transportation it would be impossible to move even a small section of any national population. The economic loss to migrating peoples in the form of personal property and the disruption of their business interests and financial security would be prohibitive for all but the most impoverished and insecure. Room in foreign countries could not be found for such migrating hordes without exterminating the populations already there, and such extermination would scarcely be tolerated by modern humanitarian sentiment, as the Second World War has demonstrated.

It has been pointed out that very few of the nationals of countries, such as Japan and Italy, desperately in need of economic opportunities for their populations, migrate as individuals and families to underpopulated territories and conquered lands, while they migrate as freely as they are permitted to unconquered progressive lands. The reason for this is clear enough. There is no economic gain, but an actual loss, to people emigrating and settling among peoples of lower industrial development and economic standards of living. If they could exterminate and replace such peoples they might prosper, but where they must compete with lower standards the lower drive out the higher as effectively as cheap (bad) money drives dear (good) money out of circulation. When they go to countries with higher standards of living than their own the advantage is the other way around and they dispossess the native populations through wage competition and higher birth rates. The United States and other countries have learned this fact to their sorrow and have been forced to erect barriers against such immigrants in order to protect their own people and avoid having them eliminated. Such restrictions may themselves constitute indirect economic causes of war, since they force upon overpopulated countries the necessity of resorting to conquest in order to provide for their surplus populations.

Yet, in spite of the fact that migration to regions with lower economic opportunities is no longer a feasible outlet for overpopulation, at least under ordinary circumstances, limited migrations of this sort still do occur. Examples of this sort in connection with the Second World War have been especially noticeable. Nazi Germany moved considerable blocks of Germans into conquered territory. This occurred in the Sudeten area of Czechoslovakia, in the Rhineland provinces taken from France, in the Ukraine, and in Poland. In the Sudeten and Rhineland provinces the former residents were uprooted and German families took over their property without serious economic loss to themselves and without lowering their living standards. In the Ukraine and Poland the resident populations were either driven out or destroyed in order that Germans might take over. . . .

. . . Although migration and treasure hunting have perforce been considerably on the decline or have undergone marked transformations in the modern era, the search for land and resources to be appropriated to national uses is still very active. William Henry Chamberlin, in attempting to explain Hitler's attack upon Russia in 1941—the least expected of all his moves at that time— accounts for it in terms of a search for land and raw materials within easy reach of Germany itself. The Ukraine and the Caucasus contained not only the oil badly needed for the further prosecution of the war, but the Ukraine offered those rich agricultural lands which were so necessary to provide an abundant food supply for an ever increasingly industrialized Germany. Some years before, Hitler had declared in no uncertain terms that the Ukraine was necessary to Germany and that Germany would expand in that direction. The Ukraine also possesses valuable supplies of coal, iron and nickel. The Caucasus contains other metals. Agriculturally the Ukraine is one of the richest regions in the world. It is the granary of Russia and is capable of producing vast supplies of live stock, sugar beets and other vegetable products. Chamberlin has expressed the opinion that the primary objective of Nazi foreign policy all along was the conquest of the Ukraine and the Caucasus while the war with England and France was an unwelcome interruption of that policy brought on by Hitler's overreaching himself in his attempt to secure territorial concessions through bluff and intimidation rather than by force of arms. Hitler had intimated this line of policy when he had declared in *Mein Kampf*, "We terminate the endless German drive to the South and West of Europe and direct our gaze toward the lands of the East. We finally terminate the colonial and trade policy of the pre-war period and proceed to the territorial policy of the future. But if we talk about new soil and territory in Europe today, we can think primarily only of Russia and its vassal border states. . . ."

. . . The drive for commercial advantage in modern international relations is an even more powerful cause of war than it was in ancient and medieval times.

. . . The revolt of the Netherlands, by means of which Philip II's Spain was expelled from the Lowlands, was essentially a struggle on the part of the Dutch and the Flemmings for commercial independence. Later, England and Holland went to war to determine which should be supreme in dominating the commerce of the new world and in the northwest of Europe. One of the results was the transfer of the Dutch colonies on the Hudson, Connecticut and Mohawk rivers to England. The great three-cornered struggle of two centuries carried on by France, England and Spain for the domination of North America was a series of wars for commercial advantage. England used much of the profits from her overseas trade to build the greatest military fleet of the world with which to protect the greatest commercial navy in the world, which she had come to own.

Thus England came to dominate the seven seas both militarily and commercially. She also built up the greatest colonial empire as a support to her world dominance of commerce. This empire was constructed in the last analysis through force of arms. Her three great enterprises here mentioned were partly the consequence but mainly the cause of her early industrialization and consequent vast overpopulation. . . . When in the nineteenth and twentieth centuries other European and Asiatic countries became industrialized and over-populated they sought for a larger share of world trade in order to feed and support their growing industrial interests. This led some of them—notably Germany and Japan—to challenge British commercial, naval and colonial supremacy. These challenges were among the chief causes of the First and Second World Wars. Indeed, these two wars have constituted the most acute phase of these several challenges of British commercial world supremacy.

However, Great Britain cannot afford to relinquish this supremacy, since the very existence of fully half her population and her great wealth depends upon the profits of her commercial and industrial supremacy. Her navy has meaning almost exclusively as an instrument for the maintenance of these supremacies. She has protested bitterly against the growth of the United States and Japanese navies and has taken steps in the past to limit that of the German navy. She now has the problem of establishing and maintaining air supremacy after the end of the Second World War in the service of her commercial and industrial supremacies. Thus war and preparation for war became the chief instrument and adjunct of commerce and industry. . . .

We have presented representative historical data in support of the thesis that economic causes of war are dominant. A few concrete illustrations in support of the same principle will be in point here. Many outstanding writers on war and international relations have borne testimony in favor of this thesis. For example, David Jane Hill, of wide experience in diplomatic affairs, declared that "if there were no economic questions involved, the conflict of nationalities could soon be ended. Modern wars are trade wars." The prosecution of international trade produces a large number of complications which might easily lead to war. If trade were perfectly free and unrestricted throughout the world and if no attempt were made to direct and control it in the interest of specific groups and peoples it would probably be one of the strongest supports to international good will and cultural unity. But this is expecting too much of human beings with the interests and attitudes which dominate them. International trade is not free; it has many of the characteristics of a racket. Those activities which enrich a people also enrich a state, which subsists on taxes. They also support governments, which in modern times are elected to office by the aid of campaign contributions and the suffrages of workers in industry and commerce.

As a consequence we see governments intervening everywhere in international commerce on behalf of their nationals. They protect their interests abroad, even with threats of war and sometimes with actual war. . . . They use their navies to collect private debts, unless they are prevented by a more powerful rival or by a Monroe Doctrine. They seize customs duties and pay off debts to their nationals out of the public treasuries of the helpless states. They sometimes seize whole territories under some pretext or other in order to promote the trade interests of their own nationals, as did Japan in Manchuria in order to monopolize that country's markets. They insist on having their own courts of justice in less powerful countries in order to give favor to their own people, especially in commercial disputes. The United States and Great Britain abrogated this type of privilege in China in 1943 only after the seaports of China were in the hands of Japan. By customs rules, shipping devices, and otherwise, a country may use its concessions or conquests to exclude other countries from equal commercial privileges, as did the Japanese in driving British and American commerce from Chinese waters preceding the initiation of war by Japan against those countries in 1941. . . .

. . . A review of the material presented in this chapter should afford a better perspective from which to estimate the value of the opinions of many pacifistic and other students of war that economic causes are not important. The fallacy of this view has already been indicated. . . . It grows partly out of a prejudice and partly out of a misconception of the nature of modern commerce. Trade began originally partly in friendly gift exchange as an accompaniment to hospitality among primitive peoples. But it also had another origin in piracy, robbery and war. The friendly cooperative aspect of trade has survived and has had perhaps its greatest development in the free-trade movement of the nineteenth century which tended to divide the world into peoples producing raw materials and those making finished products. If this type of trade were dominant there would be fewer wars arising out of economic relations between countries. But the other aspect of trade, although softened in its nature, has also persisted. Subtler methods of exploitation have been substituted for the old piracy, robbery and war. But it still has many of the characteristics of a racket. It often leads to war. There are also, as we have shown, many other economic relations besides trade which eventuate in war.

2. Imperialism of Capitalistic Economies Is the Major Cause of International Struggles

(This position has been taken from *The Theory of Capitalist Development,* by Paul M. Sweezy,[20] an American Marxist. Professor Sweezy, an economist, in this work made an analysis of "capitalism and its ills." He argues that "in the absence of corrective treatment, these infirmities must become progressively debilitating and must lead to the decline and eventual fall of capitalism.")

Imperialism may be defined as a stage in the development of world economy in which (a) several advanced capitalist countries stand on a competitive footing with respect to the world market for industrial products; (b) monopoly capital is the dominant form of capital; and (c) the contradictions of the accumulation process have reached such maturity that capital export is an outstanding feature of world economic relations. As a consequence of these basic economic conditions, we have two further characteristics: (d) severe rivalry in the world market leading alternately to cutthroat competition and international monopoly combines; and (e) the territorial division of "unoccupied" parts of the world among the major capitalist powers (and their satellites). . . .

In the formative period of capitalist society, nationalism and militarism together played an indispensable role. Nationalism was the expression of the aspiration of the rising middle class for economic unity and cultural freedom as against the separatism and obscurantism of feudal society; militarism was the inevitable means to the end. There are those who do not like to admit that militarism ever played a constructive historical role, but, as Rosa Luxemburg put it, "if we consider history as it was—not as it could have been or should

[20] Paul M. Sweezy, *The Theory of Capitalist Development* (Monthly Review Press, 66 Barrow St., New York 14, N.Y., 1956, 4th printing), pp. 307–310, 319–324.

have been—we must agree that war has been an indispensable feature of capitalist development."

. . . The rise of militarism to a position of permanent and steadily growing importance in all the imperialist nations has far-reaching economic consequences. In the first place, it fosters the development of a group of specially favored monopolists in those industries, like steel and shipbuilding, which are most important to the production of armaments. The munitions magnates have a direct interest in the maximum expansion of military production; not only do they benefit in the form of state orders but also they are afforded safe and lucrative outlets for their accumulated profits. Hence it is these elements of the capitalist class which take the lead in calling for an aggressive foreign policy. In the second place, since military expenditures perform the same economic function as consumption expenditures, the expansion of armies and navies constitutes an increasingly important offsetting force to the tendency to underconsumption. From the point of view of the functioning of the economy as a whole, therefore, it becomes ever more dangerous to restrict the magnitude of military outlays. Finally, to the extent that production of armaments utilizes labor power and means of production for which there would otherwise be no demand, militarism actually provides the capitalist class as a whole with increased opportunities for profitable investment of capital. . . .

It should be clear . . . that the annexationist urge of imperialist nations is by no means confined to backward, non-industrialized regions. To include new markets and new sources of raw materials within the protective tariff walls of one's own nation is a desideratum of imperialist policy whether the areas concerned are pre-capitalist or capitalist, backward or highly industrialized. This is important to keep in mind in examining the course of events of the last three decades, for any theory which denies it is clearly inadequate to account for what has actually taken place. It may be remarked in passing that we here touch upon one of the glaring weaknesses of the theory of imperialism put forward by Rosa Luxemburg and her followers. It must also be emphasized that a picture of world economy which displays only a handful of advanced imperialist nations surrounded by backward colonial areas is an oversimplification. In reality there are other elements to be taken into account: on the one hand small and relatively advanced industrial nations, some with and some without empires of their own; on the other hand formally independent backward countries which in fact occupy a semi-colonial position relative to the great powers. In both cases such independence as these areas enjoy is essentially the outcome of rivalry among the major imperialist nations. In peace time these countries constitute, so to speak, the focal points of imperialist conflict; when the balance of forces shifts and the weapons of diplomacy give way to the weapons of force, they form the major battle grounds of wars of redivision.

Let us now attempt a very brief summary of the international conflicts of the twentieth century on the basis of our theory of imperialism. Such a summary should enable us to get a clearer view of the limits of imperialism than would otherwise be possible.

The first war for redivision of the world began in 1914 and came to an end with the peace treaties of 1918 and 1919. . . .

From the outset all the European imperialist nations except Italy were involved, and Italy joined as soon as her statesmen believed they could tell which side would emerge victorious. The two major non-European imperialist powers, the United States and Japan, were also drawn in. In 1917 the breakdown of the Tsarist regime in Russia was followed by the Bolshevik revolution, the establishment of the world's first socialist society, and Russia's withdrawal from the imperialist arena. The following year the war came to an end with the collapse of German and Austro-Hungarian resistance. The Treaty of Versailles, the major imperialist peace treaty, was dominated by England and France which took for themselves the lion's share of Germany's colonial empire. Important raw-material-producing areas on the east and west of Germany were awarded to a reconstructed Poland and to France and Belgium respectively; Germany was stripped of her navy and merchant marine, and her army was reduced to a size which it was thought would be sufficient to maintain the system of capitalist property relations within her new frontiers. Austria-Hungary broke up into pieces, and a ring of new states was established in Southeastern and Eastern Europe to isolate the Soviet Union and to act as a counterweight against a possible German risorgimento. The United States, while not profiting from the war in a territorial sense, emerged as economically the most powerful nation in the world, a creditor on a vast scale where a few years before she had still been a heavy debtor to the European capital-exporting nations. It was already clear that the United States would play a key role in future imperialist conflicts. Italy was too weak at the end of the war to collect what had been promised her for her entrance on the Allied side. Finally Japan, which was involved in the hostilities only peripherally, took advantage of the preoccupation of the Western powers to extend her territory and sphere of influence in the Far East; she was, however, as yet too weak to hold all of her gains and was forced to disgorge by the United States and England after peace was re-established in Europe.

From the point of view of the structure of world imperialism, the results of the first major war of redivision may be summed up as follows: (1) German power was temporarily smashed, and her colonial empire was taken over by the victorious nations (chiefly England and France); (2) Austria-Hungary was eliminated from the imperialist scene; (3) the United States emerged as the economically strongest nation in the world; (4) Italy and Japan, though on the winning side, were frustrated in their imperial ambitions; and, finally, (5) Russia withdrew entirely from the arena of imperialist rivalry and commenced the task of building the world's first socialist society. The basic pattern of the second war of redivision was already discernible in the results of the first.

. . . Those nations which were left out in the first partition of the world, and lost or failed to benefit from the first war of redivision, the nations in which capital had the least opportunity for internal expansion, soon set about preparing for a second redivision. The actual campaign began with the Japanese invasion of Manchuria in 1931 and continued through the Italian absorption of Ethiopia (1935), the Spanish Civil War (1936), the renewed push of Japan into China (1937), and finally the series of direct German aggressions on the European continent, beginning with the occupation of Austria in 1938 and continuing in an unbroken succession to the present time. The Second World War as a whole, however, is not, like the first, a simple inter-imperialist struggle for redivision of the world. It is in reality three distinct wars which are merged together only in a military sense and even in this respect incompletely. The first of these three wars is a war of redivision on the 1914–18 pattern with Germany, Italy, and Japan on one side and Great Britain and the United States on the other side; the second is a war between capitalism and socialism with Germany on one side and the Soviet Union on the other; the third is an anti-imperialist war of national independence waged by China against Japan. . . .

. . . If we consider the system of imperialism as a whole, rather than single imperialist nations, it is apparent that it raises up against itself two types of opponent and that its expansion enhances their potential power of opposition.

It is here that we must seek for the factors which will ultimately set the limits of imperialism and prepare the way for its downfall as a system of world economy.

The first opposition force arises, as we have already seen, from the internal development of the imperialist countries. . . . The special features of imperialist policy, which make for increased internal exploitation and international war, serve to enhance the opposition of workers, though the roots of this working-class attitude are to be found in the structure of capitalist society in general. We may speak in this connection of socialist opposition to imperialism. Such opposition is in itself not capable of preventing the expansion of imperialism. Its real significance emerges only in the closing stages of a war of redivision when the economic and social structure of the imperialist powers is seriously weakened and revolutionary situations mature in the most severely affected areas. Successful socialist revolutions then become possible; the chain of world imperialism tends to break in its weakest links. This is what took place in Russia in 1917. The Bolshevik revolution established new socialist relations of production in Russia with the result that a large part of the earth's surface was withdrawn at one stroke from the world system of imperialism and formed the nucleus for a future world economy on a socialist basis. It seems safe to predict that this process will be repeated, perhaps on an even larger scale, before the present international conflict has exhausted itself. Thus we see that the first limit to imperialism is the result of the interaction of its national and international aspects. . . .

. . . The second fundamental limit to imperialism arises from the relations between metropolis and colony. . . . Under the domination of imperialism, industrialization advances very slowly, too slowly to absorb the steady flow of handicraft producers who are ruined by the competition of machine-made products from the factories of the advanced regions. The consequence is a swelling of the ranks of the peasantry, increased pressure on the land, and a deterioration of the productivity and living standards of the agricultural masses who constitute by far the largest section of the colonial populations. Imperialism thus creates economic problems in the colonies which it is unable to solve. The essential conditions for improvement are fundamental changes in the land system, reduction of the numbers dependent upon agriculture, and increase in the productivity of agriculture, all objectives which can be attained only in conjunction with a relatively high rate of industrialization. Imperialism is unwilling to reform the land system because its rule typically depends upon the support of the colonial landlord class, both native and foreign; the interests of producers, and especially monopolistically organized producers, in the metropolis prevent the erection of colonial protective-tariff barriers and in other ways inhibit the growth of industrialism in the backward areas. The inevitable consequence is that colonial economy stagnates, and living conditions for the great majority of the people tend to become worse rather than better.

. . . it falls to the lot of the working class to lead the nationalist opposition to imperialism in the colonial countries just as it stands at the head of the socialist opposition to imperialism in the advanced countries. When this stage has been reached the two great opposition forces are united not only in their immediate objectives but also in their ultimate resolve to work for a socialist world economy as a way out of the growing contradictions of imperialist world economy. In the long run the colonial bourgeoisie is unable to play an independent historical role and must split up into two opposing factions, one of which attempts to save its own precarious privileges by means of an open alliance with imperialism, while the other remains true to the cause of national independence even though the price is the acceptance of socialism.

Hence we see, finally, that what started as two independent forces opposed to imperialism tend to merge into one great movement. Just as in the advanced capitalist countries themselves, so also on a world scale the issue becomes ever more clearly defined as Imperialism versus Socialism, with the mounting contradictions of imperialism ensuring its own decline and the concomitant spread of socialism.

3. THE "ECONOMIC THEORY" OF WAR IS OVERRATED AND TOO INCLUSIVE

(The following extract is from an essay by Willard Waller.[21] Professor Waller, a sociologist, has had a lifelong interest in the causes of war.)

. . . [One] theory of war is that it results from the pressure of population upon the food supply. A group of people with an unrestricted birth rate remains for some generations within the same territory, which in time becomes crowded. The population then flows over into surrounding regions under the impulsion of hunger. There is a measure of truth in this theory. There have been wars for which the pressure of population furnished a principal cause. The great tribal migrations and far-flung conquests at the dawn of history seem to have been conditioned in large part by population pressure. There have been a great many wars in which the pressure of population was a contributing factor. More often than not the pressure of starvation is the ostensible reason for a war, while other and more decisive reasons lie hidden in the background.

. . . Before we regard population pressure as a principal factor in war, we must explain a number of facts which seem, to say the least, peculiar. In the first place the nations which have the greatest amount of population pressure are often singularly pacific. China and India are densely populated, and, by common report, overpopulated, but, at least in recent times, they have bred no swashbucklers to demand *Lebensraum* with a rattle of the sword. Again, the nations which give population pressure as a reason for aggression frequently proceed to relieve the pressure by annexing or subjugating some even poorer and more populous region. How does this remedy the pressure of population upon food supply? Further, those very nations which profess to need room for their existing population are most anxious to keep up the birth rate. It is also quite possible for such nations to relieve the pressure of population by encouraging permanent emigration to other less populous nations, with, of course, loss of nationality, but in fact every attempt is made to combat permanent settlement of nationals abroad. How does this make sense?

The fact is that population pressure alone does not make a people warlike. When a nation experiences some pressure of population on the food supply, and has also the peculiar economic and social structure of militarism, imperialism, and nationalism, the pressure of population becomes an important factor in the causation of war.

. . . The so-called economic interpretation of war is widely accepted, and in fact has considerable merit. It is more nearly able to stand on its own feet

[21] Reprinted from *War in the Twentieth Century*, pp. 6–12. Edited by Willard Waller by special arrangements with The Dryden Press, Inc., copyright 1940 by The Dryden Press, Inc.

than any of the interpretations examined so far. Unfortunately, a great many people believe that the economic interpretation of war is a complete explanation which stands in no need of supplementation from other sources, that it contains all that need be known about the causation of war, that it is, in short, the one and only valid theory of war.

The proponents of the economic interpretation of war usually begin their argument by demonstrating the necessary connection between capitalism and imperialism. Capitalism, the system of production for private profit, developed in the highly industrialized nations, necessarily leads to the production in every nation of more goods than can be sold there. Under the spur of competition and production for profit, capitalism expands the productive plant almost infinitely, so that it becomes necessary to find foreign markets. . . . But foreign trade with other highly industrialized nations results in a mere exchange of goods; it does not dispose of the surplus of manufactured goods. The search for markets therefore turns to the less developed regions of the world, to predominantly agricultural countries. . . .

The economic interpretation of war then goes on to show that where business interest leads, the state must follow, for the state is only the "executive organ of the ruling class." And the ruling class, of course, is composed of the nation's leading businessmen. It happens inevitably that the business interests of leading nations must often clash in the attempt to control particular areas. When two imperialistic powers come into serious competition, war frequently results. And when the less developed nations resist the rule of the great powers, war may also result from that.

There is certainly a great deal of truth in this interpretation of war. There have been many imperialistic wars in the past few centuries. A principal cause, certainly, of the World War of 1914 was the clash of British imperialism and German imperial aspirations. The European nations have also fought countless big and little wars in order to reduce other peoples to colonial status, for the task of ruling all races was thought to be "the white man's burden."

Some wars fit this classic picture of imperialism perfectly; others show fragments of it. In other words, the economic interpretation of war fits many of the facts of some wars, and it fits some of the facts of nearly all wars. The American Revolution was a way by means of which colonies which had developed some economic independence finally put an end to their colonial status. The Civil War involved, among other things, a conflict between rival economic systems; the industrialism of the North, whose leaders wanted a tariff, and the plantation economy of the South, whose leaders demanded free trade. . . . The War of 1812 and the Mexican War were motivated in part by imperialism, but in each case it was largely an agrarian imperialism; industrial leaders and merchants had little part in either conflict. In yet other wars, we can find only traces of the generally accepted picture of imperialistic war. We may find one class controlling national policy in terms of its own self-interest, either by precipitating or avoiding war. An economic analysis of the political process is often revealing in the extreme, showing as it so often does that men vote as they believe their interest indicates. This is true not only of issues of war and peace but of other issues as well.

In recent years we have heard much of a sort of primitivized economic interpretation of war. Wars, it is said, are promoted by munitions makers in order to create a market for their wares; these merchants of death gladly sell arms to the enemies of their country and even stir up national rivalries in order to promote business. For other writers, international bankers play the same Satanic role. Enough unsavory facts are known about members of each group to lend some credibility to this view, but it may be doubted that their influence has ever been sufficient to start a major war. We must remember that both the munitions makers and the international bankers of the United States were recently investigated by the Senate, and that this investigation, in the judgment of most observers, disclosed little evidence that either group had very much to do with involving the United States in the first World War.

We must concede that the clash of rival economic systems frequently initiates the friction between nations which later leads to war and that it also sustains this conflict by affording a fresh supply of incidents. Economic interest also supplies influential groups with a powerful motive to promote war. While admitting all this, we must insist that economic factors are not the only factors involved in war. A multitude of things not covered by this theory must necessarily enter into any war. There are always moral and sentimental elements, for men must love their country before they are willing to die for it; most soldiers are not very brave unless they feel that their cause is just. We shall shortly call attention to a number of these non-economic factors in war.

While admitting the presence of these moral, or "ideological," factors in war, the orthodox economic determinist insists that economic factors are always dominant, and that morals and ideology assume the form which economic interest dictates. Here again we are faced with a proposition which contains some truth, but not the whole truth. Morality is influenced by economics, but it also has an independent existence of its own. Standards of right and wrong are not altogether dependent upon self-interest, and sometimes morality runs contrary to economic interest. It seems to the economic determinist that economics is the prime mover in society; it *makes* things happen, and other than economic phenomena merely change to conform to economic interest. This notion is simply an optical illusion. The economic determinist starts with the economic factor, and tries to discover changes in other social phenomena conforming to changes in the economic sphere. The changes actually occur, but it is erroneous to believe that the economic factor *makes* them happen, or that the economic factor is not itself determined. . . . If one starts with scientific knowledge, he may see the entire course of human history as a function of the growth and development of the various branches of science. Such interpretations are all equally valid and are all equally false. The truth is that all phases of society are closely interwoven; they hang together in nature and can only be separated in the mind of the scientist, and there imperfectly. It is therefore false to say that one of these aspects of society dominates over all the others. A person who is accustomed to studying one factor in social change naturally comes to overestimate its importance, whether the factor he studies be economics, geography, morality, the family, science, education, or technology. The economist's one-sided view of society can be matched with unilateralisms from all the fields mentioned and from many others; taken together these views furnish an admirable corrective for one another. If specialists could realize how easily they fall into error merely because they know so much about one of the aspects of society, there would be a great gain in our understanding of society.

There are yet other reasons for believing that the economic interpretation of war does not account for it in its entirety. The majority of the men who fight the battles of any war have little or no economic interest in their outcome; frequently they are fighting against their own best interests, but there is no record that they are any less valiant because of that. The economic interpretation may sometimes explain why great men make wars, but it does not tell us why humble men fight in them. Again, it is probably true that in any war a great number of business men have little stake, and in some wars the majority of business men stand to lose more than they gain. Why does the economic interest of one group predominate over the interest of other groups? If we explain why one economic interest triumphs over another and greater interest, are we not already outside the field of economics? Further, there are many wars for which the clearest economic reasons exist, and yet these wars do not take place. One must explain why certain wars, such as an imperialistic war against Mexico by the United States, never come off. In order to answer these questions, one would be forced to consider so-called "ideological" factors in some detail, and perhaps to grant them equal importance with the economic factor.

It is sometimes argued that the economic interpretation of war is the one correct interpretation because some economic interest can always be found in every war. Since the economic factor is always present, therefore it must be the one true cause of war. This is utterly fallacious. The fact that there are always economic elements in any modern war proves nothing at all; certainly it does not prove that the economic elements in the war make it happen. Our economic life is now so complex and ramifying that many citizens are bound to profit by any conceivable rearrangement of our life and many others to lose by it. When the economic consequences, with profit to some and loss to others, of changing the date of the Thanksgiving holiday by one week are so considerable as to start a nation-wide controversy, we can see how great the effect of war may be. When the matter of war with some nation comes up for discussion, those who would profit by it naturally attempt to promote it, and it thus seems that they have brought the war about. But these people did not make the war; at most they merely helped it along.

Although the economic interpretation of war affords some illumination, its popularity is greater than its merits seem to warrant. It is popular, no doubt, partly because of its simplicity and because its proponents are kind enough to advance it in a way which does not invite doubt or inflict upon the listener the pain of a divided mind or the torture of suspended judgment. Again, it is a theory which supplies for some persons the need for a personal devil; the men who make wars, the merchants of death, the grasping traders and the international bankers, are obviously very wicked men, and it is a pleasure to hate them. Perhaps the greatest advantage of the economic interpretation is its essentially hopeful character. If wars are the product of capitalistic imperialism, then we may hope to do away with them in a society in which capitalism has been replaced by another form of economic organization. The economic interpretation is thus justified in part by its relation to a program of action rather than on purely intellectual grounds.

QUESTIONS

1. Are there any countries which currently illustrate the Malthusian thesis? If so, identify and describe.

2. Josue de Castro claims that overpopulation does not cause starvation; rather, starvation is the cause of overpopulation. This reversal of the Malthusian doctrine is based upon de Castro's allegation that hunger increases fertility. Thus, claims the author, it is impossible to eradicate hunger by controlling the growth of population, but it is perfectly possible to reverse the process and control the growth of population by doing away with starvation. Appraise de Castro's argument.

3. Sir Charles G. Darwin, in a highly controversial book entitled *The Next Million Years* (New York, Doubleday, 1953), argues: (1) Any nation that limits its population becomes less numerous than nations which do not, and the former will then sooner or later be crowded out of existence; (2) a nation which limits its population forfeits the selection effects of natural biological competition and as a result must gradually degenerate. Do you agree? Why?

4. Should the major portion of United States' technical assistance be applied through United Nations agencies or through our own Point Four type of programs? Explain.

5. Would you require a nation receiving technical assistance from the United States to pledge its support to the free world? State your reasons.

6. It is generally conceded that a high level of employment and income in the United States is the greatest contribution that our country can make to the political stability and economic well-being of free-world nations. What reasoning lies behind this assertion?

7. Tariffs are essential for the protection of the high wages paid by American industries; without such protection, our country would "import" the low wage rates of many countries with which we trade. Evaluate.

8. Are there circumstances under which tariffs and other forms of trade barriers are justifiable? If so, identify and explain.

9. Do you agree or disagree with Sweezy's observation that: "In the formative period of capitalist society, nationalism and militarism together played an indispensable role"? Why?

10. Can you state points of view, other than those discussed in this chapter, regarding the effect of the distribution of economic resources on international conflict?

SELECT BIBLIOGRAPHY

BERNARD, L. L., *War and Its Causes* (New York, Holt, 1944). A sociological analysis of war as a social institution. The causes are classified under eight broad categories: biological, psychological, economic, political, social or cultural, religious, moral, and metaphysical.

BROWN, Harrison, *The Challenge of Man's Future* (New York, Viking, 1954). A popular yet pointed analysis of relationships between man, his natural environment, and his technology. Authored by a physical scientist.

CHANDRASEKHAR, S., *Hungry People and Empty Lands* (Baroda, India, Indian Institute for Population Studies, 1952). The author, head of the Department of Economics at the University of Baroda, was in charge of demographic research for UNESCO in 1948–49. Demographic knowledge, economic principles, and clarity in writing blended into one of best books focusing on population problems and international tension.

ESPY, Willard R., *Bold New Program* (New York, Harper, 1950). Unbiased account of successes and failures of Point Four projects. Emphasizes sociological and economic difficulties encountered in rendering technical assistance.

HOSELITZ, Bert F., ed., *The Progress of Underdeveloped Areas* (Chicago, University of Chicago Press, 1952). A collection of essays on the political and cultural factors affecting economic development in nonindustrialized countries.

JONES, Clarence F., and DARKENWALD, Gordon G., *Economic Geography* (New York, Macmillan, 1954). Fundamentally, a geography text. Organized on basis of mankind's principal occupations. Only a limited attempt is made to compare distribution of population with distribution of natural resources.

PEARSON, Frank A., and HARPER, Floyd A., *The World's Hunger* (Ithaca, Cornell University Press, 1945). A brief study (90 pp.) of world's food problem. Primary emphasis is given to physiographic aspects of food production. However, Chap. 7 discusses food production in terms of its relationship to international affairs.

Population Division, Department of Social Affairs, "The Determinants and Consequences of Population Trends" (New York, United Nations, 1953). Most recent summary of world-wide studies of relationships between population changes and economic and social conditions.

WOYTINSKY, W. S., and WOYTINSKY, E. S., *World Population and Production* (New York, Twentieth Century Fund, 1953). Unequaled single source of statistical and descriptive data concerning earth's inhabitants, resources, and industries.

ZIMMERMAN, Erich W., *World Resources and Industries* (New York, Harper, 1951). Although text has a geographical orientation, the author has woven the raw threads of geography into the world's social, political, and economic fabric.

6

THE PROBLEM
AND ITS BACKGROUND

THE PARADOX OF THE SCIENTIFIC AGE

You men and women venture forth into a world where human nature differs little, if at all, from human nature . . . in the age of Pericles. Human relations—the art of getting along with the people who work beside you and with those who live thousands of miles away—does not change in its essence with the centuries. But the age of nuclear energy . . . will likely bear no more resemblance to the age of steam than a jet-powered plane to an old-fashioned box kite. . . . Out of the use of a new and great energy source, along with boundless opportunities, come new and great human problems that require new and great solutions.[1]

In these words the President of the United States in June, 1955, delineated one of the major problems of this age. Human relations may not change, as Dwight D. Eisenhower stated, but the environment in which human relations function, both locally and internationally, most certainly has changed. Moreover, he attributed the most recent changes in human environment to nuclear energy, modern science's latest development. Since this view of the impact of science upon the twentieth century is widely held, it is appropriate for students of world affairs to seek an answer to the frequent query: Has science made war obsolete?

That there exists no quick and easy answer to this question becomes apparent with even the hastiest survey of a few of the paradoxical results

[1] *New York Times,* June 12, 1955, p. 34.

of scientific advance. Medical science, for example, has mounted such an offensive upon man's germ enemies that numerous diseases have been cheated of their prey. Literally millions of lives have been saved and deaths postponed by the miracles of a scientifically oriented medical profession. Yet, with improved transportation, the mobility of humanity has so increased that germs and bacilli, formerly restricted to certain parts of the globe, are now carried by human migrants into areas not before exposed to them. Thus, in Africa, where measles germs had been unknown previously and consequently no natural immunity had developed, serious outbreaks of the disease caused large numbers of fatalities very recently, most notably in French West Africa. Likewise, in ultrahealth-conscious America, certain heretofore unknown diseases have appeared. It would seem that what science has given with its medical right hand it has partly taken away with its transportational left hand.

Other examples of this paradox come readily to mind. At Hiroshima and Nagasaki atomic energy, as mentioned in Chapter 1, snuffed out the lives of many thousands. Yet atomic reactions also yield radioactive materials called isotopes, which may save other thousands of lives from death by cancer or hypothyroid. The precision instruments developed by modern technological science have made possible greater destruction in a shorter period of time of both human beings and the facilities that keep human beings alive. Witness the utter devastation by air attack of Rotterdam during World War II, or Coventry in the course of a few hours, or Cologne in just 120 minutes. Quite possibly the destruction of life and property was as great or even greater in wars of the prescientific age, but the job was not done with the unmatched rapidity and dispatch of the flame-throwing, TNT-belching, bomb-dropping military machine of today. On the other hand, the rapidity with which war devastation has been obliterated reveals a similar differential in time. It has been claimed that it took a century for Germany to recover from the wreckage of the Thirty Years' War in the seventeenth century. Within a decade, with the most modern equipment and methods devised by modern technologists, Germany rebuilt and improved an industrial plant which had been as badly mauled during World War II as any community sacked by seventeenth century soldiery.

The impacts of the technical age upon individual freedom have also been conflicting. Machines have freed man of heavy labor and led to increased leisure in the most technologically advanced areas of the world. Machines also have deprived many workers of their sense of accomplishment and pride in manual creation. In addition, as was suggested in Chapter 4, technical refinement of the mass media of communication has enabled dictators to enslave minds and mobilize emotions in support of attacks upon democracy and individual freedom.

Even in the scientific assault on the frontiers of knowledge apparent contradictions occur. That man's knowledge of the world and universe has greatly expanded is a truism. So, too, is the expansion of the realm of the unknown. According to a reflective authority on science: [2]

Science . . . for all its impregnable basis and the stability of its super-structure . . . is always essentially unfinished. The most pressing problems of experience are the personal ones, and their solution lies at the end of the scientific pilgrimage.

The further the scientist advances, the further he has to go, it would seem.

What then of the fate of international relations in the age of science? Technology has brought the peoples of the world closer together. Hong Kong is now nearer New York than Omaha was seventy-five years ago. Communications advances enable Bostonians to understand more clearly the problems of Nehru's India today than they understood the problems of the American Indian in General Custer's generation. It has been suggested that science promises possible solutions to unfortunate resources-population ratios. Do not such changes relieve, or promise to relieve, many tensions accompanying international misunderstanding and thereby contribute to improved world harmony? Or is the paradox apparent here, too? Has the swelling parade of American tourists, students, and soldiers through other parts of the world reduced old, or aroused new, prejudices of Americans and other peoples of the globe? Have improved communications dulled or sharpened differences between Orient and Occident? Have technological developments been conducive to improving the lot or exploiting the underdeveloped regions of the world? These are some questions and answers with which this chapter is concerned.

THE NATURE OF MODERN SCIENCE

Reference was made in Chapter 3 to the presence in all human societies of certain cultural common denominators, called "cultural universals" by the anthropologist. To focus upon the cultural universal loosely defined as "religion" is a helpful beginning in the study of the nature of science. Science, like religion, may be thought of as an effort to arrive at some meaningful explanation of human existence and experience. Man, whether living in a simple or a complex culture, has tended to reject the concept that his existence is the result of a series of fortuitous, unrelated, haphazard events. Sometimes he has sought an explanation in the whims or commands of demons and goblins, sometimes in the ordination of one or many gods and the development of religious faith, but persistently he has sought explanation of human experience. This is not to suggest that science constitutes a new religion. For some humans it does; for others it is an aid in their efforts to create a rational picture

[2] Herbert Dingle, *The Scientific Adventure* (London, Pitman, 1952), p. 2.

of human existence. For the unscientific, it has no appeal at all. As a definition of science is now attempted, however, this placing of science in the broad behavioral picture of man may be helpful.

Definitions

Science. According to Noah Webster, science is concerned with systematized knowledge. But science is considerably more than that. It is, first of all, concerned with identification and classification of phenomena. Second, it deals with statements of fact the validity of which, no matter how often tested and retested, remains unchanged and is accepted by all properly trained scientists. Beyond this, however, is the more sparsely populated realm of higher scientific thought and theory. At this level science undertakes to discover the interrelationships, often extremely complex and obscure, of masses of seemingly unrelated data. Max Planck's quantum theory and Albert Einstein's theory of relativity are outstanding examples of this kind of scientific inquiry about the unity of the universe. Thus, science is concerned with the fact that under certain circumstances water boils; it is also concerned with the kinetic dynamics involved, the fact that other materials also will become gaseous under given conditions, with the many ramifications that the principle of boiling water has in such generalizations as the universal law of the conservation of energy.

This is not to imply, however, that science is concerned with everything. For example, science relates to sunsets, but to determine whether or not a particular sunset is beautiful is not science's task. That the sunset exists and that prismatic action produces the color stimuli is verifiable knowledge; its beauty is not verifiable. The bereft lover may be moved to tears of sorrow because the sunset conjures up painful memories; the night-shift worker who does not like his job may regard it as an unwelcome signal to go to work; the Eskimo may be depressed because it marks the last appearance of the sun for six months. To none of these is the sunset beautiful. Thus, the variable, emotional response to a sunset is not scientific knowledge, though the fact that human beings react, differently it is true, to sunsets may well be of scientific interest. The definition, therefore, requires elaboration and refinement.

Physical and social science. Science is popularly understood to denote the body of generally accepted, systematized knowledge about the physical environment of mankind. This limitation flows from scientists' greater success in gaining knowledge about phenomena in the fields of astronomy, physics, chemistry, and biology than from scientific inquiry into the apparently infinite complexities of human behavior. This usage of the term *science* should not, however, obscure the fact that there is a social area of scientific research, and that social science faces a task no less important than that of physical science.

"Pure" and "applied" science. Another important qualification of terms is the distinction between "pure" and "applied" science. Even when restricted to the physical sciences, as in this volume, it is necessary to understand the designations. "Pure" science designates knowledge about the universe for knowledge's own sake. In other words, as suggested at the beginning of this section, "pure" science seeks meaningful knowledge to satisfy man's curiosity and his desire to interpret his existence as part of a rational pattern. "Applied" science undertakes to secure knowledge about how the properties of matter and the sources of power in nature may be made useful to man. Scientists themselves often prefer to refer to "pure" science as just science and to "applied" science as technology or engineering. The close relationship of the two cannot be overlooked, and their interaction is of special significance in examining the total impact of science on international affairs.

Advances in "pure" science, as in nuclear physics, lead to developments in the "applied," or technological, field. Sometimes the process is reversed, as when the harnessing of steam power led to establishment of the principles of thermodynamics. To put it another way, "pure" science enables man *to know;* "applied" science enables man *to do.*

The scientific method. Any attempt to explain what science is must also include reference to its methodology, the way in which the scientist goes about his work. Acquisition of systematized knowledge includes, first, precise, objective measurements of phenomena and determination of the conditions under which they occur. Incidentally, since these measuring techniques have become increasingly variable and numerous, one man seldom masters most of them, hence the great specialization among scientists. Second, and more important, the scientific method involves reasoning about the phenomena investigated and drawing inferences of a general character from the conditions under which the specific phenomena occur. These processes, in turn, require mental activities such as analysis and synthesis of measurements; formulation of tentative general suppositions (called *hypotheses*); testing and retesting of hypotheses to determine their validity or invalidity; comparison, description, and classification of measured phenomena. The second phase obviously calls for extensive training, a well-developed mentality, imagination, and originality. It is not difficult to understand why great masters of the scientific method are relatively rare. Even one Copernicus, Galileo, Darwin, or Einstein in a generation is an impressive average. Their limited numbers make more remarkable the impact of science upon modern society, internationally and otherwise.

In view of these qualifications and distinctions, it is necessary to arrive at a definition of science for use here. By science, it will be understood that reference is limited to physical science, but in both its "pure" and its "applied" forms. *Science, then, may be defined as man's accumulation,*

*systematic arrangement, interpretation, and application to his environ-
ment of knowledge acquired through the scientific method about the
physical world.*

Before examining the impact of this kind of science upon international
affairs, however, we should note the recent advent of science into human
experience. Like nationalism, but unlike the nature of man and his struggle to utilize resources, science is a comparative "newcomer" as a dominant factor in human society and as a factor influencing relations between
different communities. Indeed, the scientific impact of just the past hundred years has been so heavy, sudden, powerful, and shattering that a
very significant correlation might seem to exist between scientific advances
and present-day world tensions. Any such judgment must await further
examination.

Science in Historical Perspective

Five to seven thousand years ago some cultures acquired the technique
of writing, a device of tremendous importance for man. Not only did
writing mean communication between remote contemporaries; it also
meant communication between remote generations. Thus, more effectively
than by word of mouth, the heritage of the past could be passed to succeeding generations. Writing also meant recording of laws, agreements,
and understandings among men, thereby contributing to community living and orderly conduct of relations between men. It has clearly had a
revolutionary impact upon humanity.

Likewise, the development of agriculture, somewhat before the invention of writing, was of revolutionary significance for man. Freed from
the nomad's unending search for pasture, agricultural man was the first
to settle down and develop a civilization markedly different from that
which had existed before. The rise of farming communities in the great
river valleys of the world, thanks to acquisition of rudimentary knowledge about plant cultivation, constituted a fundamental alteration in
human life and institutions.

Science as a dominant factor in human existence would appear to
constitute a similar revolution. But whereas man has been adjusting to
the shift from pastoral to agricultural civilization during the past 7,000
years, and from a nonliterate to a literate society during the past 5,000
years, he has been obliged, in not more than 400 years, to adjust from
a prescientific to a scientific age, with all that that entails.

Six centuries ago humanity stood only on the threshold of the age of
modern science. Even Chinese civilization had never been a stronghold
of science. As an outstanding authority on China's history maintains: [3]

[3] Kenneth S. Latourette, *A Short History of the Far East* (New York, Macmillan,
1946, reprinted with publisher's permission), p. 176.

. . . the Chinese . . . had little or no science. Medicine called forth voluminous works. Agriculture was well represented. However, the Chinese were backward in mathematics and in most branches of what we call natural science. With all their worldliness and practical-mindedness, they did not develop the scientific method. Why this should have been we do not know. Various hypotheses have been offered. Whatever the explanation, the fact remains. For the scientific outlook and for the knowledge accumulated by science, the Chinese were to wait until their contact with the modern Occident.

What obtained for China was true of the whole of the Far East, whose center of culture was Cathay. Hindu civilization also revealed little affinity for science, most of what it contained of a scientific nature being derived from lands further west. Yet, even the civilizations to the west, notably Islam and Christendom, did not possess dynamic scientific outlooks in the early fourteenth century.

This does not mean that the world had been devoid of science up to this time. Both ancient Egypt and medieval Arabia were distinguished for their mathematics and astronomy. And, of course, Aristotelian and Ptolemaic natural-science concepts were accepted and commanded respect in European intellectual circles long after the Grecian Golden Age had been laid to rest. However, the inheritors of Egyptian, Greek, and Arabic science did little to add to their bequests.

The various cultures, then, were relatively unscientific in their orientation. Chinese civilization, the oldest and most experienced, emphasized accommodation to nature, not its mastery. Hindu, Islamic, and Christian cultures, all with deeply mystical elements, emphasized both accommodation to and withdrawal from the world in which man lived. The concept of the human being armed with scientific knowledge, setting out methodically and deliberately to harness natural forces to his will, was alien to them.

However, with the gradual alteration of the economic, political, and social life of Europe commencing in Italy, spreading slowly to northern Europe, and then rapidly accelerating with the geographic discoveries of the late fifteenth century, a more scientifically receptive atmosphere emerged. Such technological developments as the compass and gunpowder gave impetus to commercial expansion, aided by improved navigation and the rise of national governments whose cannon rendered feudal castles defenseless. The intensified search for economic profit and national political power, as well as the accompanying focus of interest on man's, rather than God's, world fostered a new interest in science.

The demolition of the Ptolemaic theory of the universe by Copernicus, Kepler, Brahe, and other observers of the motion of heavenly bodies inaugurated the new age. Full emergence of the scientific method in the sixteenth century followed Galileo's precise measurements of falling bodies and the general principles of motion which he inferred from his observations. Since then, the advances on the "pure" scientific front have been rapid, from the ages of Sir Isaac Newton and Charles Darwin to that of Albert Einstein. Equally breath-taking has been the progress achieved in "applied" science, where western man moved through the steam and electrical ages into the nuclear.

From this cursory review of the history of modern science it can be seen that science has become an imposing feature of western civilization only recently and is becoming a dominant part of other civilizations only today. This is important to keep in mind when analyzing the scientific impact upon human life in general and upon international relations in particular. The impact of science would have been enormous in any event, but having it telescoped into four brief centuries has intensified it greatly.

THE PHYSICAL IMPACT OF MODERN SCIENCE UPON INTERNATIONAL RELATIONS

The impact of science upon human activity is so extensive that cause-and-effect relations between modern scientific advances and international affairs, if not limited to the more obvious direct relationships, might well fill more than all the pages of this book. Accordingly, only some selected areas of human life will be mentioned, beginning with the physical repercussions.

Reduction of Distance

Invariably, first to come to mind of the changes wrought in man's physical world by science, especially "applied" science, is the shrinkage of distance. From the European conquest of the Atlantic by such navigating technicians as Da Gama and Columbus to today's earth-circling jets, the reaches of the globe have been brought steadily, and ever more rapidly, together.

With the aid of the compass, known earlier in the Orient, and the astrolabe, westerners succeeded in crossing vast areas of ocean in the fifteenth century. This constituted the first step. It should be borne in mind that the use of such instruments required rudimentary engineering skills and some familiarity with Copernican astronomy. In this connection Prince Henry of Portugal's navigation school at Sagres, which conducted navigational research and training, was to European technology in the fifteenth century what the Massachusetts Institute of Technology has been to American in the twentieth. The scientific and technical attack upon distance had begun.

From these beginnings emerged the revolution in transportation and communication. The steam and gasoline combustion engines, electrical and electronic communications, and jet propulsion have brought the world to the state in which, within a few minutes, one human being sitting in New York can speak with another in any city of his choosing—Bangkok, Damascus, or Calcutta. If he desired, this New Yorker could personally visit those cities, plus half a dozen more requiring his circling the globe, and still be back in New York within four days. If he wanted to be a bit more leisurely, he could take approximately one week for the journey and include enough time for one-day stopovers in London, Calcutta, and Tokyo, plus an overnight stay in Hong Kong.

Leaving New York, for example, on a Monday afternoon, he would arrive in London in time for breakfast Tuesday. He could spend the rest of the day in London, leaving late Tuesday afternoon for Calcutta, India. The flight of approximately thirty hours includes short stops at such points as Damascus, Syria, and Karachi, Pakistan, and he arrives in Calcutta in the wee small hours of Thursday morning. He has all day and evening to visit this famous metropolis of India. Late Thursday night, he boards his plane for Hong Kong. He might breakfast in Bangkok, Thailand, and arrive in Hong Kong shortly before dinner Friday evening.

After an overnight stay in this most cosmopolitan of cities, he would leave Saturday morning for Tokyo. His plane would probably fly fairly close to the island of Formosa, and he would reach Tokyo in time for dinner, Saturday evening. More than twenty-four hours is now available for his visit in Tokyo, since it won't be necessary to leave for the United States until Sunday night. The long flight across the Pacific gives him that unique opportunity to cheat Father Time out of a whole day, for although the flying time consumes approximately a day and a half, he gets credit for a day when he crosses the International Date Line. According to the calendar, he leaves Tokyo at 9 P.M. Sunday and arrives in Los Angeles at 10:30 Monday morning, even though he has been traveling for more than thirty hours. Continuing on his return trip to New York, he would be back where he started Monday night, one week after his departure.

Having circled the globe in a week or less, he might well conclude that this is one world. There is scarcely any place which cannot be reached by modern air transportation in less than two or three days' time. His conclusion might seem to be confirmed by the knowledge that, when he gets back from his trip, he can pick up the telephone in his home and after only a short delay speak with the friends he has so recently seen in London, Karachi, or Tokyo.

Yet, as a study conducted before World War II by a group of social scientists seems to demonstrate, the reduction of physical distances between the world's peoples does not correlate with improved relations between them. Sometimes the relations are improved. More often, according to this study, shrinkage of technological distance accentuates other "distances": psychic, ideologic, social, intellectual, and political. The report cites the geographic proximity in 1939 of the U.S.S.R. to Germany and Japan and the concomitant likelihood of friction between the U.S.S.R. and these two nation-states because of the enormous "distances" between them in other matters. Similarly, Germany's poor relations with the Soviet Union and the United States, and her good relations with geographically more remote Japan, are cited to illustrate that mere shrinkage of physical distance is no guarantee of improved international relations.[4]

Thus, science's assault upon geographic distance may sometimes serve to illustrate the old adage: familiarity breeds contempt. Whether or not it does, the inescapable reality is the growing obligation of the earth's peoples to communicate more with each other, to be more aware of each other's actions, and to become more responsible in dealing with each other. Bengalese famine, Vietnamese elections, Polish riots, and Siberian atomic explosions produce economic, political, psychological, and military reactions from Canton and Capetown to Cardiff and Chicago. Science has liquidated isolation. A few Saharan nomads, Congoese pygmies, and Paraguayan peons reside in small surviving pockets of remoteness that were once common to most men and are now common to almost none.

Increase in Economic Interdependence

This factor is discussed elsewhere in this study, but it must be briefly mentioned here because in large measure the world's economic interdependence is linked with technology's growth. Improved means of transport provided the key. Once man could move commodities he could specialize in his own economic activity. Instead of producing *all* his own necessities, he could concentrate on making more than he needed of the goods he could most easily produce. His surplus he transported and sold to others, who in turn produced surpluses of things he needed. This is, of course, all very obvious, but until ox cart and sailboat were replaced by truck, train, and steamship, only a limited economic interdependence was generated between neighboring communities. In the past hundred years interdependence has become global.

The average European middle-class person has a wardrobe containing Japanese silk, Australian wool, Egyptian cotton, and French lace. For breakfast he drinks Brazilian coffee and spreads his bread with marmalade made of West Indian sugar and Sicilian oranges. If he owns an automobile it runs on Indonesian rubber and contains Russian manganese, Canadian nickel, and Malayan tin. The paper he reads was originally Norwegian wood and contains items on China, Czechoslovakia, and Chile. His literature and art may come from France, Italy, Germany, or Japan.

[4] Quincy Wright, *A Study of War* (Chicago, University of Chicago Press, 1942), Vol. II, p. 1466.

He has personal friends in New York, Jerusalem, and London. A less cosmopolitan pattern would have to be drawn for an Iranian, Ethiopian, or Burman, but the trend toward ever greater material interdependence of humans all over the globe is clear. This is attributable to the technology which spawned steam and electrical communication and transport, which encouraged regional economic specialization, and which demanded supplies of raw materials from every part of the planet.

International repercussions of the growth of a world economy are not difficult to find. Economic pressures for the free international flow of the means of production—capital, labor, resources, and entrepreneurism—ran counter to political pressures for national economic organization and prosperity. Accordingly, national economic drives backed by national political power developed for control of foreign markets, sources of raw materials, and investment opportunities. Since the mid-nineteenth century this economic competition between nation-states has become acute, most evidently in certain areas not inappropriately described as bones of contention.

Colonial bones of contention. Until recently, the race between the western nation-states for spheres of economic influence and colonies overseas was marked by friction. Although imperialism was stimulated by a variety of factors, as noted in Chapter 4, its late nineteenth and early twentieth century manifestations were largely economic in origin. Sometimes the friction was restricted to nonviolent clashes such as the disputes between Russians and English in Persia, French and British in the Sudan, and British and Germans in China. On other occasions war was the result. For example, the Crimean (1854–56), Spanish-American (1898), Boer (1899–1901), and Russo-Japanese (1904–1905) were essentially conflicts between imperialist powers over areas coveted, in large measure, for economic reasons.

European bones of contention. Overseas areas were not the only economic bones of contention between the western nation-states. The contemporary economy's insatiable appetite for steel dictated the economic wedding of Ruhr and Saar coal in Germany with Lorraine iron in France. Much of the Franco-German antagonism of the past century stems from the historical and political factors that have worked against this economic wedding. Thus, Alsace-Lorraine was annexed by Germany in 1871, recovered by France in 1919, taken again by Germany in 1940, and returned to France in 1945. Each transfer was endorsed and supported by the respective national industrial interest concerned, a fact which supports the contention that growing economic interdependence, the product of technology's advance, sharpened Franco-German differences. More recently, Italo-Yugoslav controversy over the port of Trieste, international bickering over free use of the Danube, and Russo-Czech altercations on whether Czechoslovakia should accept Marshall Plan aid point up the maladjustments created by the growing economic interdependence of a world politically divided into sovereign nation-states.

Afro-Asian bones of contention. Just as technological advances and resultant industrialization accentuate western imperialism, so can they also be held partly responsible for the great contemporary uprisings of Afro-Asia against colonialism. As was indicated in Chapter 4, this revolt has many and complex facets, not least among which are the economic developments resultant upon modern technology.

Finally, the newly independent nation-states of Africa and Asia have come into conflict with each other over control of economically important areas. One of the knottiest problems in the Israeli-Arab crisis concerns the use of the Jordan River waters. Similarly, Egypt and Sudan have clashed over control of the Nile waters. The question of the resources and revenues of Kashmir contributed to the Pakistan-India dispute over that province. Furthermore, as the Afro-Asian world develops technologically and economically, its economic dependence on the rest of the world may well bring its nation-states more and more into conflict with each other.

Population Growth

Another physical impact of modern science has been demographic. The enormous increase in the world's population was discussed in the preceding chapter. Notice must be taken of the role of science in that increase. Whatever other factors may have played a role, medical science's drastic reduction of death rates is a major one.

In 1750 the average life expectancy of an Englishman, living in the medically most advanced area of the globe, was only a little over thirty. Today the Englishman (or Western European, or North American) can expect to live somewhat over sixty-six years on the average. In other regions, similar declines in death rates are indicated as the Albert Schweitzers, World Health Organization (WHO) teams, United Nations International Children's Fund (UNICEF) agents, and growing numbers of Afro-Asian doctors reduce the incidence of malaria, yaws, tuberculosis, diphtheria, and other diseases.

Instinctively, we applaud and praise the great strides made by medical science. Governments and private citizens willingly allocate large sums of money to further research in the germ theory of disease, aseptic surgery, vaccines and serums, diet, drugs, and body chemistry. In the United States a drive for donations to medical research occurs monthly. In the midst of this humanitarian and natural concern for preserving human life, the point is often missed that the resultant population growth poses serious problems, some of which are international.

Because the ramifications of great population increases have been examined in Chapter 5, further discussion is not necessary at this point. The emphasis here is that science has had much to do with the growth.

Conduct of War

Perhaps most obvious among the physical impacts of scientific advances is the effect on the waging of war. In weapons, for example, since the middle of the fifteenth century, science has made one refinement after another.

Weapons. Firearms were rapidly adopted between 1450 and the Cromwellian period (1642–58) in all parts of Europe. Next, artillery improvements, owing much to mathematicians and metal workers, were significant. By the end of the eighteenth century, technology had improved greatly the accuracy of gunfire, the weight of the metal fired, and the mobility of arms. The musket of the American Revolution was hardly a handy side arm, but it was a vastly more manageable weapon than its ancestor, the harquebus. The mobility of Napoleon's field artillery in contrast to the ponderous siege guns of the Louis XI era testified to the great advances made in cannon-casting and design. Yet the limited range and slowness of fire as late as the Crimean War (1854–56) did not make the infantryman or artillerist a much more deadly killer than the English longbowman or even the Roman legionnaire. Witness the continued employment of cavalry armed with swords and lances right through the nineteenth century.

Since the early twentieth century, science has presented the soldier with submarine, airplane, explosive projectile, breach-loading and rapid-firing small arms, bomb, tank, poison gas, rocket, proximity fuse, and a host of agents of destruction. The battlefields of France in the First World War were proof that conflict had become a contest in the maximum use of high explosives. During World War II technology steadily improved the means whereby ever larger loads of explosives could be delivered more quickly and more accurately. In the spring of 1945 the Anglo-American bombers were dropping considerably more than 100,000 tons of TNT upon targets in Germany in a single month. Simultaneously, German rocket technicians had made it possible to launch jet-propelled projectiles carrying explosive warheads from the continent upon Great Britain. Finally, at the very end, the dropping of what are now considered "baby" atomic bombs on Japan by the United States revealed a new explosive power which dwarfed the more traditional TNT bomb by a ratio of 2,000 to 1.

Since World War II the rapid development by science of new weapons has become even more incredible. Atomic-bomb research in the United States, the Soviet Union, and the British Commonwealth has been concerned with ever more powerful nuclear reactions. In 1956, a United States bomber dropped into the Pacific a bomb whose blast was the equivalent not of 20,000 tons of TNT, as a Hiroshima in 1945, but of 15 million tons of TNT, more blast in one bomb than that in all the bombs dropped during the six years of World War II. Adding to the ever more rapidly changing military picture has been the extension in ranges of bombers, so that air force personnel now calculate in terms of intercontinental missions. Mention should also be made of the descendant of the 1945 German V-2 rocket, the much publicized ICBM (Intercontinental Ballistic Missile). This weapon, with its hydrogen-bomb head, is claimed to have the capacity for crossing the Atlantic in thirty minutes

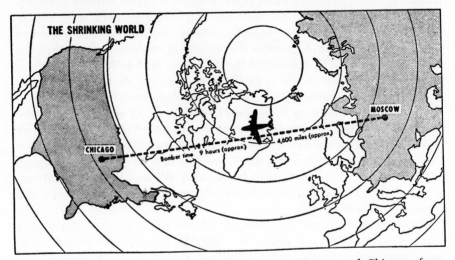

Fig. 10. The shrinking world. The distance between Moscow and Chicago of approximately 4,600 miles can now be spanned in about 9 hours by a bomber. (*Source: Background for Mutual Security, Fiscal Year 1959, A Summary Presentation*, p. 5, issued February, 1958, by the Dept. of State, Dept. of Defense, and International Cooperation Administration.)

and delivering a bomb with considerable accuracy upon a target 5,000 miles away. Certainly the success, first by the Soviet Union in 1957 and then by the United States a short time later, in firing satellites so far out into stellar space that they orbited about the earth, supports the claims by these two states that they possess the rocket-propulsion techniques necessary to launch a missile attack from great distances upon an enemy. Moreover, atomic-powered submarines capable of crossing the Atlantic or passing under the polar ice-cap can now approach an enemy's shores unseen and fire atomic missiles from relatively very close range.

No wonder President Eisenhower, commenting upon the debate between the chiefs of the various armed services about respective responsibilities in the new kind of war, said: [5]

[5] *New York Times*, May 27, 1956, p. E1.

We are going through a period of change, of fluidity, where we are deserting doctrines that have long been held sacrosanct . . . and we are going into another kind of world with respect to all military formation, policy and organization, and equipment. . . .

Technological development since World War II has outpaced military thinking mainly by making available ever greater explosives, capable of being delivered ever more quickly and accurately to ever more remote targets.

Strategy. Up to this point the discussion has revolved around the actual weapons afforded soldiers by technology. It can be said that science has made conflict more destructive in another way. The character of scientific warfare, with its complex organization of armed and civil personnel and the intricate mobilization of all human and material resources, also dictates a strategy that is highly destructive. Reference is made to the war of attrition, the kind of war that was fought 1914–18 and again 1939–45. Logic pointed the way to victory in both these conflicts through destruction of the enemy's economic, social, and psychological order, rather than through exclusive concentration on defeat of his military forces. Of course, in the latter stages, the military enemy had to be smashed, but not until attrition tactics had reduced the effectiveness of the enemy war machine entirely and thus softened up the military for the knockout. The gutting of economies as well as cities, the ripping apart of the social order as well as human bodies, which is part of contemporary conflict, represents destruction to the utmost. This is made possible by the scientific "progress" that created the weapons just mentioned.

Impersonality. To destructive weapons and warfare of attrition may be added the impersonality of conflict, as another impact of science on the conduct of war. From both an humanitarian and a rational point of view war is a repulsive form of activity for most human beings. Under certain conditions most people excuse war, but relatively few enjoy it. Accordingly, if the waging of war is made less repulsive from the personal point of view, it can be argued that the possibility of war has been increased. Such a charge has been leveled at modern science by John Nef, who has made a comprehensive study of war and human progress.[6]

There is a great difference, maintains Nef, between facing another human being and plunging a knife into his spongy flesh as he screams in protest and pain, and lighting the match to a cannon whose ball or shell may rip open many more bodies and cause many more screams, but none of which likely will be seen or heard by the cannoneer. The latter is easier to do. It becomes even easier if one is asked merely to press a button in some remote, underground, quietly efficient, missile-launching post, thus sending an ICBM off to the other side of the world

[6] John U. Nef, *War and Human Progress* (Cambridge, Harvard University Press, 1950), p. 114.

where the atomic havoc wrought may never be known to the button-pusher. Increased impersonality may make killing less shocking and therefore more frequent.

Thus, the scientific age has brought new weapons, new strategy, and a new impersonality to the conduct of modern war. All three innovations have made war more destructive.

Postwar Reconstruction

Like Mother Nature, science both gives and takes. It has furnished the weapons and altered the techniques of destruction; it also has provided the means by which the ravages of war may be more quickly washed away.

In the past, war was only the first of the "Four Horsemen of the Apocalypse," and was followed by famine, pestilence, and death. This has become ever less true. As the Allies in World War II pushed eastward from the Channel coast into bombed-out France, the Low Countries, and Germany, they brought machines and technically trained engineers who rapidly reopened canals, rebuilt bridges across rivers, resurfaced roads, and re-established railway lines. This immediate reconstruction of the means of transportation made possible the movement of food and medical supplies, as well as more machines and engineers, into the war-torn areas. This period was unquestionably a nightmare for the civilians who lived through it, but compared to the fate of earlier populations through whose front yard war had passed, theirs was a much less painful and prolonged period of recovery. Chemicals checked contamination of water, fertilizers restored farms, bulldozers pushed aside debris, innoculations checked epidemics, dried milk saved infants, and "prefabs" restored housing. Ten years after World War II, the physical rehabilitation effected by "applied" science of the war-devastated areas was truly amazing.

Similar patterns marked postwar reconstruction in eastern Europe, especially in the Soviet Union, and in Italy after World War II and in Korea after the 1950–53 war.

The international concomitants of this kind of reconstruction are not without irony. On the one hand, there is the spectacle of the enemy invader sometimes being welcomed as a savior by war-weary populations; of occupation authorities stabilizing the currency of a former enemy, as the Western Allies did in Germany in 1948; of American citizens pouring relief parcels not only into the war-ruined areas of their allies, but into Germany and Italy as well. It is difficult to assess how much such postwar activity reduced the resentments generated by the conflict, but it would seem not to have been negligible. On the other hand, there is the spectacle of defeated nations, given technological aid in rehabilitation, so quickly recovering that they evinced willingness and ability at least to prepare for another conflict by entering into alliances and rearming. The question arises: Have the advances of science, like so many aspects of life, only accelerated the cycle of preparation for war, waging of war, postwar convalescence, and preparation for war again?

The Psychological Impact of Modern Science upon International Relations

Attempts to determine modern science's psychological repercussions, especially with reference to international understanding, encounter a somewhat tenuous cause-and-effect relationship. Indeed, students of social behavior are not in complete agreement on what follows. Accordingly, the discussion of psychological tensions generated by the new technoscientific era is presented as an hypothesis for which there is considerable supporting evidence, but about which there does not exist sufficient knowledge to command the support of all social behaviorists.

Through Urbanization

Unquestionably, concentration of growing numbers of human beings in urban areas is one of the major sociological accompaniments of industrialization, which in turn is a product of modern science, "pure" and "applied." To date this movement has encompassed a relatively small part of the world's population, but the pattern is spreading. In the Atlantic Basin urbanization has already claimed more than half the population (64 per cent in the United States, 73 per cent in Italy, 81 per cent in England). The Soviet Union, more recently industrialized, is now 40 per cent urban, and industrialization in China and India reveals a similar trend. The question here is, what psychological reactions of significance for international affairs have occurred?

It is to be recalled that, for all but the past century or so of human history, man has been a ruralite, a "country boy." Whether Paleolithic cave dweller, herdsman following Abraham into Canaan, Yangtze Valley farmer, or Kansan homesteader of less than a century ago, most men in all ages have lived close to the soil. Then came the factory system requiring the concentration of workers. Scientific means of providing housing, food, water, sewage, and transport quickly made it feasible. In less than two centuries, millions of people, temperamentally, physically, and culturally conditioned to rural living, have exchanged farm for city. What has happened to such uprooted human beings?

The answer can only be tentative. There can be no doubt that the drastic shift in environment had repercussions. What happens to a person who exchanges farm isolation for close proximity to vast numbers of human beings? Or to a person whose new industrial job is often more monotonous and nearly always more exacting than his farm job? Or to the human being who has more leisure time and less steady employment than he had as a farmer? Or to the nervous system called upon to adjust to the noise stimuli of the city? Or to the digestive system which once met the demands of a wheat thresher but now must sustain a loom tender?

Although some authorities disagree, a physician writes: [7]

In candid truth, the city is not a healthful place in which to live. Its inhabitants do not live as long or as happily as dwellers elsewhere. More of them go insane. They are sick more often. Finally, and perhaps most disastrously, they fail to reproduce themselves.

Lewis Mumford, philosopher-architect, observes: [8]

. . . The cities of the Western World began to grow at an inordinate rate. . . . The result was not a temporary confusion. . . . What followed was the crystallization of chaos: disorder hardened uncouthly in metropolitan slum and industrial factory districts; and the exodus into the dormitory suburbs and factory spores that surrounded the growing cities merely widened the area of social derangement. The mechanized physical shell took precedence in every growing town over the civic nucleus; men became disassociated as citizens in the very process of coming together in imposing economic organizations. . . . As for the growing urban populations, they lacked the most elementary facilities for urban living, even sunlight and fresh air, to say nothing of the means to a more vivid social life.

Further reinforcing this picture of the reorientation of the urbanite are the observations of certain sociologists. J. J. Rhyne emphasizes a kind of natural selection by the city of human beings who are emotionally less stable and the aggravation of that instability by urbanization.[9]

The city has become the focus of a vast number of persons who crave excitement. These individuals find in their life of the large city a chance to satisfy various types of unsatisfied wishes. . . . It is perhaps primarily for this reason that the city has tended to draw a certain type of restless, maladjusted, and neurotic person . . . the American countryside would naturally fail to offer sufficient attraction to individuals of the type described. As a result, they tend to migrate to the large centers of population, where in turn they largely take up residence in rooming-house districts. . . . It is in these areas, also, that the bulk of the major problems of city life tend to concentrate. Perhaps the relatively high rate of mental disorder commonly prevalent in such areas is one reason for their being centers of delinquency, vice, and crime.

Another sociologist, identifying urbanism with neurosis, explains it as follows: [10]

[7] Jonathan Forman, "Biological Truths and Public Health," reprinted from Elmer T. Peterson, ed., Cities Are Abnormal (copyright 1946, by University of Oklahoma Press, used by permission), p. 96.

[8] Lewis Mumford, The Culture of the Cities (New York, Harcourt Brace, 1938), p. 8.

[9] J. J. Rhyne, "Social Man and His Community," in Cities Are Abnormal, op. cit., pp. 155–156.

[10] E. Gordon Ericksen, Urban Behavior (New York, Macmillan, 1954, reprinted with publisher's permission), pp. 305–306,

While no two urbanites react exactly alike to stimulation, they do have one thing in common: outwardly they appear to react to their social surroundings with their heads instead of their hearts. That is, they are inclined to exhibit a mask of indifference if not boredom while underneath often suffering from a neurotic agitation of their sentimental, role-playing world. . . . We are confronted first by the continually increasing tension between the inner personality of the individual and the social roles he is expected to play in the city. City people tend to neglect, even ignore, in one another their individual, personal, intimate characteristics. . . . Consequently the city man is submerged in an atmosphere of estrangement within which all those personal and intimate factors are excluded which constitute in reality the core of his emotional life.

Urban receptivity to radicalism. If the preceding observations emphasize any one aspect of urbanization, it is the instability and rootlessness of many human beings caught in the city environment which, it is to be remembered, is a product of industrialization. This is reflected in an urban crime rate in the United States four times greater than that in communities of less than 10,000. It may also account for the paradox of greater urban material wealth coupled with louder urban protests about its insufficiency. In other words, it is asserted that insecurity, instability, and maladjustment are accentuated among urbanites. Since psychologists agree that insecure, fearful humans are more inclined to irrational, violent activity, the hypothesis is advanced that the urban population is more inclined than the rural to aggression, organized violence, irrational attack upon established institutions, and xenophobia (fear or dislike of strangers). Such an element would obviously contribute to international tension. What is the evidence of its existence?

First, high priests of the new "isms," which offer short cuts to utopias and exciting escape from grim reality, elicited the most enthusiastic responses from the urban populations. The first "Fasci" appeared in Milan, the first "Soviet" in Petrograd, the first "Storm Troopers" in Munich, the first "Tangpu" (Chinese Communist Party cell) in Canton. Both fascism and communism, with their glorification of war and revolution, respectively, have been largely urban movements.

Second, urban populations generally, in the democracies as well as in the dictatorships, have evinced more intense nationalism. Opportunities for mass demonstrations and mob hysteria are of course greater in the city and may account for this in part. Nevertheless, the historical record is impressive. Nineteenth century nationalist movements were born and nurtured in the cities: Budapest, Genoa, Zagreb, Prague, Warsaw, Belgrade, and Rome. Nationalist endorsements of war were also given in cities. London, Paris, Belgrade, Vienna, and Berlin were the scenes, in 1914, of massive demonstrations demanding declarations of war before the government leaders themselves had made the final decision. More recently, if the nationalist trouble spots are to be accurately pinpointed, they must be Nicosia, not Cyprus; Constantine, not Algeria; Singapore, not Malaya; Athens, not Greece; Colombo, not Ceylon.

Third, it is urban society which has at once dictated and responded to "yellow journalism." In 1946 a privately financed commission investigating the mass media in the United States concluded: [11]

> . . . The news is twisted by the emphasis on firstness, on the novel and sensational; by the personal interests of owners; and by pressure groups. Too much of the regular output of the press consists of a miscellaneous succession of stories and images which have no relation to the typical lives of real people anywhere. Too often the result is meaningless, flatness, distortion, and the perpetuation of misunderstanding among widely scattered groups.

Moreover, such twisting and distortion are partly dictated by people more often urban than rural who "seldom want to read or hear what does not please them; . . . seldom want others to read or hear what disagrees with their convictions." [12]

Thus, many believe with Plato that "we have found the origin of war in those passions which are most responsible for all the evils that come upon cities and the men that dwell in them." [13]

To characterize all urbanites as xenophobic, however, is to ignore the existence of urban cosmopolites, who may have a very different outlook upon human affairs. Urbanism, product of industrialism, must also be viewed as conducive to cosmopolitanism.

Urban cosmopolitanism. If urbanites are agitated, restless, and receptive to new movements and new loyalties, are they not, by virtue of those characteristics, potentially more amenable to the new physical world and more adjustable to the new relationships ensuing between the peoples of the world? Indeed, does not American interest in the United Nations, in foreign affairs generally, center in the urban East?

Furthermore, are not American urbanites, especially in co..stal cities, the people most aware of the rest of the world, most frequently in contact with it, and most inclined to heed the need for adjusting to the presence of other peoples and other nation-states? This is certainly true in the rest of the world. The Bombay merchant, the Delhi civil servant, and the Calcutta stevedore are all more aware than is the inland Indian farmer of the non-Indian world.

Although urban response to the mass media often has been detrimental to international understanding, does not the urban population of all countries offer a potentially more reachable and educable audience for these media? As the Commission on Freedom of the Press insists, although "the

---

[11] The Commission on Freedom of the Press, *A Free and Responsible Press* (Chicago, University of Chicago Press, copyright 1947 by the University of Chicago), p. 68.

[12] *Ibid.*, p. 57.

[13] Plato, *The Republic*, A. D. Lindsay, transl. (New York, Everyman's Library volume, Dutton, 1942), Book II, p. 53.

full use of the new instruments to build a world community will require a clear national policy and a great joint effort on the part of the government and private agencies," [14] the possibility is nonetheless present.

Thus, it would seem that the new urban environment may stimulate both xenophobia and cosmopolitanism. That the psychological impact of science through urbanization has been significant is quite clear. Less clear, at least in the long run, are the repercussions of urbanization upon international affairs.

Through Colonialism

Considerable discussion of western imperialism has already taken place, and there is no need here to review the technological and industrial pressures that have stimulated western imperialism in Africa and Asia during the past hundred years. Some reference to the psychological overtones of this movement, however, are pertinent at this point.

The Occidental psychology. Among westerners, possessing technical superiority over the rest of the world, there developed an attitude commonly called a "superiority complex." The advantage of more advanced techniques, especially of a military nature which enabled the European white man to overcome and reduce to subservience red, yellow, brown, and black men in all parts of the world, led to a broader sense of superiority. Not only were his plumbing and sewage disposal superior, but the white man increasingly viewed himself as uniquely endowed with many faculties and capacities denied others. That the former was a valid claim, at least temporarily, is irrefutable. When, however, he adopted the attitude that in all respects his culture was of a higher order, he was making a subjective judgment with significant psychological impact.

The white man came to view humans of different coloration and culture as "little brown brothers," "the white man's burden," and as "poor benighted heathens." Asians, Africans, American aborigines, and Polynesians were lumped together in western terminology as less "advanced" or less "civilized" people. The cultural anthropologist emphasizes the invalidity of evaluating a people's culture by comparing it only with one's own (that is, without reference to the harmony that a culture affords a people in relation to its environment). Just such an invalid evaluation was made by the Western European and his white American cousin. The results were an arrogance toward "backward" civilizations and an unusually intense zeal to restructure these civilizations along western lines. Combined with technical power, the zeal gave western civilization a unique psychological impetus to its imperialistic relations with the rest of the world. The reactions prompted by this outlook have been highly disturbing internationally.

The Oriental psychology. It is true that there was much good will and

[14] *Op. cit.*, p. 67.

humanitarianism in the white man's assumption of his "burden." Yet, as anthropologists have pointed out, conversion of Ugandans to Anglicanism often meant destruction of their indigenous African religion and only partial replacement of it with an allegedly half-baked, shallowly rooted Protestantism. Similarly, introduction of western hygiene to the Kikuyus of Kenya meant such a drop in their death rate that the growing population found it impossible to exist longer on the lands assigned them by their colonial governors. When the white authorities, who had permitted the hygienic education in the first place, refused to consider land redistribution, the groundwork for the Mau Mau insurrection was laid. Thus, even when motivated by good will and humanitarianism, western innovators often produced deep resentments among the "backward peoples." Today, socially conscious people in Afro-Asia harbor acute sensitivity to westerners' condescension toward them. Bitter antagonism is manifested in violent aggression like the Mau Mau troubles and Chinese indignities to captured Americans.

In the realm of mental phenomena, therefore, important indications of science's impact are to be observed. The psychological products of both urbanism and colonialism, though not yet fully explored, deserve the attention of those concerned with the influence of science upon contemporary life.

The Intellectual and Spiritual Impact of Modern Science upon International Relations

Revolutionary alterations in the physical and psychological world as a result of modern science have been matched by equally revolutionary changes in humanity's intellectual and spiritual life. The religious and ideological tranquility of late medieval Europe was shattered by an unintentional but formidable attack upon long-established, deeply imbedded attitudes and beliefs. Reluctantly in the forefront of this attack were the first modern scientists.

For example, the new astronomy claimed that the earth is a minor satellite of a modest-sized star in one of the less important galaxies. It is to be remembered that Christian, Islamic, and Judaic teachings held that man was God's special creation. Accordingly, the scientifically demonstrable thesis that, in fact, man is an infinitesimally small organism clinging to a dust speck in the solar universe was bound to have profound and painful repercussions. Likewise, science's growing capacity for explaining the existence of forces responsible for natural phenomena that had formerly been attributed to divine wrath or whim also produced mental shock. Not only did conflict between science and religion ensue; throughout the world all kinds of formerly satisfying beliefs and rituals no longer satisfied an ever growing part of humanity. In the confusion and search for new concepts more compatible with the discoveries of science, the world's various cultures entered an era of intellectual flux, instability, and spiritual crisis. In this crisis, some individuals despair, others find hope for the future of humanity.

Crisis of Despair

One point of view holds that this crisis is deepening. Little relief has been afforded it by the recent insistence of many scientists that they have merely described what their observations have revealed and that their science does not offer, nor does it attempt to offer, explanations of why these phenomena exist or whether there is divine purpose behind their existence. Contemporary laymen, however, have not fully grasped the philosophical significance of the qualification. This is understandable, since from the beginning of the modern scientific age, scientific concepts have been accepted by the general populace a considerable time after the scientists have postulated them. For example, Copernicus advanced the heliocentric theory in printed form in 1543; John Milton, a representative of the literate, nonscientific public, still had not accepted it over a century later. Charles Darwin published *Origin of Species* in 1859, but biological evolution is not an accepted concept among a number of religious sects and its teaching in certain public schools in the United States is still illegal. The point is that the layman's scientific outlook lags behind that of the scientist. Therefore, although many scientists in this century have come to recognize the limits of scientific probing into the unknown, many laymen still cling to the belief that science will some day unravel all the mysteries of life and the universe. Yet the multiplication of contemporary difficulties arouses doubts. This has accentuated the layman's intellectual and spiritual crisis.

In the crisis the layman has often encountered disturbing problems. Must he carefully and somewhat uncomfortably separate his religious and spiritual beliefs from his vague understanding that science holds the ultimate answer to the meaning of life; or must he emphatically choose religion and reject science; or must he choose science and atheism; or should he permit himself to think about this seeming dilemma without resolving it in any way, thus risking possibly serious neurotic repercussions? In a word, a considerable amount of spiritual and intellectual despair has come to characterize the modern, scientific age.

How does this affect the realm of international affairs? Some argue that the average western man, cut adrift from his spiritual anchor and no longer viewing himself as the instrument of divine will, becomes a much less disciplined and self-controlled individual. Without deep religious convictions, his ethics atrophy and his values degenerate. His cupidity and materialism grow, his lust for power intensifies. This state of mind provokes aggression against strangers, nonmembers of the in-group. Thus, the growth of amorality has contributed not only to the rise of Gestapo and MVD criminality but also and more generally to the nationalistic justification of the crimes of two world wars. Arnold Toynbee believes that the irreligious attitudes of the contemporary West have not produced a more acute "time of troubles" only because the West has not yet exhausted all the spiritual capital it had accumulated in its Christian past. Unless this slide down the slope of spiritual bankruptcy is arrested, Toynbee despairs of saving western civilization.

As for eastern man, with much less time to absorb the intellectual overtones of the scientific impact, he may well find himself in an even more tragic situation. Long accustomed to tolerate physical discomfort and privation, and strengthened in his tolerance by the great Oriental religions, what will be the outcome if the Oriental, too, has his religious anchor lines cut? Will not the natural and understandable, but internationally disturbing seizure by Afro-Asians of their own resources and wealth from the hands of colonial powers constitute only the first stage of a vast shift in Oriental values, ambitions, and actions? The rapidity with which this intellectual flux has appeared in the nonwestern world may give cause for greater despair than the West's own "time of troubles."

Crisis of Hope

Of course, a different emphasis can be placed upon the undeniable intellectual and spiritual flux produced by science in the modern world. Science is something more than the accumulation of knowledge; it is a methodology, a special kind of approach to a problem. In its empiricism, its respect for facts, its logical and rational procedures, it affords mankind an instrument of great constructive potentiality.

As an American scientist warns, too much can be expected of science, but there is ground for placing hope in it: [15]

. . . The relation of science to men's hope is not a problem to be solved by a happy choice of definitions. . . . The philosophical disciplines—particularly ethics, logic, aesthetics—are not sciences of fact but address themselves to problems of critical evaluation. Sciences of fact have nothing unambiguous to say about these matters. They cannot tell us what danger is most to be feared or what shape our true hope wears. They furnish the mind with a growing repertory of practical alternatives. . . . Because it is factual, science can say only: *If* you desire this, try doing that. This is a service not to be despised, which nothing else performs so competently. Science is an almost divine ally in an undertaking with clear and limited objectives. . . . It . . . cannot work miracles. . . . It can describe and account for what happens; it can predict what will probably happen under specified conditions, it cannot prove to us what we *ought* to do.

Or to be even more hopeful about the potentiality of the new scientific intellectual climate: [16]

[15] James Street Fulton, *Science and Man's Hope* (New York, Bookman Associates, 1954), p. 16.
[16] *Ibid.*, p. 28.

Science will not save us, but we can learn from it much that would help. As a body of accurate knowledge, it furnishes abundant means for accomplishing various purposes; as conscientious knowing, it affords a suggestive clue to a defensible conception of man's hope. Science is an essential part of the effort to become fully alive by becoming alert to the full reach of the processes which sustain our existence. This sharpened sensitiveness, far from being passive or receptive only, depends upon intensely active, creative effort, such an effort as characterizes the highest works of man—scientific discovery, artistic expression, moral achievement. It may be that the fruit of these human tokens of creation is religious humility and piety.

It would appear that this new intellectual era contains positive influences for constructive, as well as for destructive, action. If international peace and understanding are desired, science may be of assistance in seeking correctives to some of the obstacles in the way of achieving them. At the very least, science makes available the proof necessary for demolishing such vicious and envenoming concepts as racism, and the means necessary for reducing physical privation.

Finally, in the scientist's allegiance to the search for knowledge, he has developed a community of interest with other scientists. It began before the era of nationalism and to a considerable degree has survived in it. Denis Papin, a French engineer of the eighteenth century, could work with the Dutch Huygens in Paris, with the English chemist Boyle in London, join the British Royal Society, study in Venice, and teach in Germany. Indeed, the eighteenth century scientist, free of passport restrictions and security regulations, traveling widely throughout the world as did Benjamin Franklin, sharing all knowledge with brother scientists regardless of nationality, epitomized internationalism. Moreover, this rational, objective intellectualism openly condemned war and predicted that it must eventually disappear, since improved techniques of destruction would make it increasingly incompatible with man's growing rationalism. Even in the twentieth century much of this sense of international brotherhood of scientists survives. International scientific meetings regularly take place and, although both the Soviet Union and the United States have been restrictive, upon occasion, considerable exchange of ideas and information takes place at such gatherings. Significantly, American scientists have been among the foremost critics of the Immigration Act of 1952 (the McCarran Act) which, in the name of national security, limits the international movement of various individuals, including American scientists who wish to go abroad and foreign scientists who wish to enter the United States.[17] There have also been indications, though understandably not publicized, of pressure on the Soviet government by Soviet scientists to relax restrictions on their international travels and affiliations. Those who see reason to hope for better things from the present intel-

[17] "Scientific Freedom and Security," in Nature, August 9, 1952, pp. 215–218.

lectual flux are impressed with the virility of this international scientific outlook in the face of great nationalistic pressures. Scientists constitute one of the most promising nuclei, to which may adhere an ever growing number of humans with an outlook that transcends local boundaries and possesses a heightened sense of humanity's common, rather than conflicting, interests.

Thus, modern science can be said to have had considerable impact upon the spiritual and intellectual life of contemporary man, as upon his physical and psychological life. It must be admitted, however, that although all these impacts are observable, only the physical is readily measureable. Until the social sciences have acquired more knowledge about human behavior, caution is in order in drawing conclusions about the other impacts.

THE POLITICAL IMPACT OF MODERN SCIENCE
UPON INTERNATIONAL RELATIONS

The concomitant growth of the roles of science and the state in modern society made their interaction inevitable. The scientist has met the politician more and more frequently in such areas of mutual concern as education, public health, conservation of natural resources, economics, national security, and foreign policy. Of particular interest here are the last two.

For example, in the formulation of a program of national defense the political and military leaders of the United States, as elsewhere, must consult with scientific leaders. Any defense program, now dependent upon and including long-range research and experimentation, is tied to the scientific laboratory. At once problems arise: the employment of scientists who are good security risks; the construction with public funds of facilities designed by scientists; and the appropriations for projects the costs of which only scientists can estimate. Inevitably, the scientists, however reluctantly, have intruded into the making of public policy. The popular image of Pentagon officers making decisions about the United States' future military establishment by drawing upon their experience in World War II and their training at West Point or Annapolis is not quite accurate. The Pentagon acts, or should act, only after briefing by its scientific advisers, who, it should be noted, are subject to correction only by other scientists, not by the generals, admirals, the Cabinet, or even the National Security Council. National defense policy can no longer be formulated without consultation with, and the active participation of, the scientist.

Nor can any disarmament policy be drawn up without him. Who, other than atomic scientists, could define what inspection steps would assure an adequate check upon another country's activity in respect to nuclear weapons? The Kremlin, should it finally accept in principle President Eisenhower's aerial inspection proposal, would have to rely upon what Soviet atomic scientists advised in the final selection of an inspection program. Washington would be equally dependent upon the advice of American atomic experts.

Similarly, in the adoption of a foreign-aid program, whether channeled through the United Nations or unilaterally administered, the scientists occupy a key position. Without medical authorities, soil experts, geologists, construction and mining engineers, a foreign-aid program would be reduced to something as senseless as dropping baskets of dollar bills from the air upon the Sahara sands, the Congo jungles, and the Indian plateau.

Logic would seem to dictate that, since many important decisions at the government level can be made only with the benefit of the scientist's judgment, he should be placed in an official position to make such decisions. Does this mean that scientists would have to run for election? Are they the kind of people who would take time away from what they deem their vital work for the time-consuming and often unpleasant task of electioneering? Could they make themselves understood to the electorate? Would the public select the best scientific candidate or the best-talking candidate? In a democracy, particularly, the growing role of the scientist in the formulation of public policy presents a serious problem.

Let us assume the election or appointment of scientifically trained personnel to important posts of public leadership accomplished, as, indeed, it has been to a limited extent, so far as appointment is concerned. Does this solve the problem for a democracy? The foregoing situations where scientific advice is essential to formulation of sound policy emphasize only one consideration. National defense, disarmament, and foreign-aid policies call for technical knowledge, but they also call for knowledge of human relations. The success of any such policy requires an analysis of the human reaction to them of the American public, the allies of the United States, the neutralists, and the cold war antagonists. Is the scientist, defined as he is here as a physical scientist, equipped to pass judgment on a policy in the light of these nonphysical considerations? Are they not more properly a task for the politicians and diplomats, or conceivably for experts on human behavior? Well then, what of the scientific considerations?

Just as appropriate would be the question whether scientists or nonscientists have more common sense, more breadth of vision, more sense of responsibility. Even if the answers were forthcoming would the course of action, especially in a democracy, be clear? As a former Under Secretary of State asks: [18] "Can the democratic process of decision-making as

[18] Adolf A. Berle, "The Democratic Future," *Saturday Review*, January 22, 1955, p. 16.

we know it survive this mighty intrusion of chemistry, physics, and mathematics into decision-making thus far reserved to popular government?"

That science is involved in the contemporary crisis of mankind is not generally disputed, but its place and the scientist's responsibility in the crisis are not a matter of general agreement, as the selections in the next section indicate. Although the opinions of a soldier, philosopher, chemist, and sociologist are cited, no inference is intended, nor should one be drawn, that they are necessarily typical of the opinion held by all, or even most, members of their professions.

POSITIONS
ON THE PROBLEM

1. SCIENCE HAS MADE WAR OBSOLETE

(The following excerpts are from a speech delivered by General of the Army Douglas MacArthur on January 26, 1955, to the Los Angeles County Council of the American Legion.[19])

. . . At the turn of the century, when I entered the Army, the target was one enemy casualty at the end of a rifle or bayonet or sword. Then came the machine gun designed to kill by the dozens. After that, [came] the heavy artillery raining death upon hundreds. Then [came] the aerial bomb to strike by the thousands—followed by the atom explosion to reach the hundreds of thousands. Now electronics and other processes of science have raised the destructive potential to encompass millions. And with restless hands we work feverishly in dark laboratories to find the means to destroy all at one blow.

But, this very triumph of scientific annihilation—this very success of invention—has destroyed the possibility of war being a medium of practical settlement of international differences. The enormous destruction to both sides of closely matched opponents makes it impossible for the winner to translate it into anything but his own disaster.

The second World War, even with the now antiquated armaments, clearly demonstrated that the victor had to bear in large part the very injuries inflicted on the foe. . . . War has become a Frankenstein to destroy both sides. . . . If you lose, you are annihilated; if you win, you stand only to lose. . . . Science has clearly outmoded it as a feasible arbiter. The great question is—does this mean that war can now be outlawed from the world?

[19] Douglas MacArthur, "The Abolition of War," in *Vital Speeches*, Vol. XXI, No. 9 (February 15, 1955), pp. 1041–1042.

. . . You will say at once that although the abolition of war has been the dream of man for centuries every proposition to that end has been promptly discarded as impossible and fantastic. . . . But that was before the science of the past decade made mass destruction a reality. The argument then was that human character has never reached a theological development which would permit the application of pure idealism. In the last two thousand years its rate of change has been deplorably slow, compared to that of the arts and sciences. But now the tremendous and present evolution of nuclear and other potentials of destruction has suddenly taken the problem away from its primary consideration as a moral and spiritual question and brought it abreast of scientific realism. It is no longer an ethical equation to be pondered solely by learned philosophers and ecclesiastics but a hard core one for the decision of the masses whose survival is the issue. This is as true of the Soviet side of the world as of the free side—as true behind the Iron Curtain as in front of it. The ordinary people of the world, whether free or slave, are all in agreement on this solution; and this perhaps is the only thing in the world they do agree upon. . . . It is the one issue upon which both sides can agree, for it is the one issue upon which both sides will profit equally. It is the one issue—and the only decisive one—in which the interests of both are completely parallel. It is the one issue which, if settled, might settle all others.

2. SCIENCE MAKES POSSIBLE THE ANNIHILATION OF CIVILIZATION

(The following excerpts are taken from Bertrand Russell, the controversial and well-known contemporary philosopher and mathematician.[20])

. . . Men sometimes speak as though the progress of science must necessarily be a boon to mankind, but that, I fear, is one of the comfortable nineteenth-century delusions which our more disillusioned age must discard. Science enables the holders of power to realize their purposes more fully than they could otherwise do. If their purposes are good, this is a gain; if they are evil, it is a loss. In the present age, it seems that the purposes of the holders of power are in the main evil, in the sense that they involve a diminution, in the world at large, of the things men are agreed in thinking good. Therefore, at present, science does harm by increasing the power of rulers. Science is no substitute for virtue; the heart is as necessary for a good life as the head.

If men are rational in their conduct, that is to say, if they acted in the way most likely to bring about the ends that they deliberately desire, intelligence would be enough to make the world almost a paradise. In the main, what is in the long run advantageous to one man is also advantageous to another. But men are actuated by passions which distort their view; feeling an impulse to injure others, they persuade themselves that it is to their interest to do so. They will not, therefore, act in the way which is in fact to their own interests unless they are actuated by generous impulses which make them indifferent to their own interest. That is why the heart is as important as the head. By the "heart" I mean, for the moment, the sum-total of kindly impulses. Where they exist, science helps them to be effective; where they are absent, science only makes men more cleverly diabolic.

. . . For this reason, it is of the greatest importance to inquire whether any method of strengthening kindly impulses exists. I have no doubt that their strength or weakness depends upon discoverable physiological causes; let us

[20] Bertrand Russell, *Icarus* (New York, Dutton, 1924), pp. 57–63.

assume that it depends upon the glands. If so, an international secret society of physiologists could bring about the millennium by kidnapping, on a given day, all the rulers of the world, and injecting into their blood some substance which would fill them with benevolence toward their fellow-creatures. . . . But alas, the physiologists would first have to administer the love-philtre to themselves before they could undertake such a task. Otherwise, they would prefer to win titles and fortunes by injecting military ferocity into recruits. And so we come back to the old dilemma: only kindliness can save the world, and even if we knew how to produce kindliness we should not do so unless we were already kindly. . . .

We sum up this discussion in a few words. Science has not given men more self-control, more kindliness, or more power of discounting their passions in deciding upon a course of action. It has given communities more power to indulge their collective passions, but, by making society more organic, it has diminished the part played by private passions. Men's collective passions are mainly evil; for the strongest of them are hatred and rivalry directed towards other groups. Therefore at present all that gives men power to indulge their collective passions is bad. That is why science threatens to cause the destruction of our civilization.

3. Science Is a Potential Aid in Rendering War Obsolete

(The following excerpts are from the work of an English chemist written since World War II.[21] He is addressing himself to more than just war, because he views war as one of the symptoms of a deeper human crisis.)

Our fundamental problem . . . is to recover a full view of the nature, situation, and destiny of man; to rebuild the half-ruined ideals of our civilisation. This is the great current problem, reflected in almost any discussion on any serious subject. We must consider now the relevance of science to it. . . .

The contribution of science to recovery from our crisis is to be sought . . . in its support of rational life and rational values. Scientific life is rational life in the little; it could be used to show forth to a wide public the principles of rational life in general. This is the source of its relevance to the rediffusion of the principles implicit in our civilisation. Properly taught, science could make clear the primacy of truth to many who might otherwise not realize it; it could bring home the necessity of collecting and analysing data, of respecting the facts, of interpreting them synthetically; it could exemplify the interplay of thought and action, the primacy of ends and the choice of means to them. . . . The practice of science could be used also to introduce the principles of respect for other people and tolerance for their opinions, and the need for personal detachment. Natural science, then, could become a stiff bulwark in favour of respect for truth and for the human person. And it seems that it is in this role, as an influential representative of reason and as a type of rational method, that science is most relevant to the recovery of our society. It is not a particular conclusion of science, nor application of science, that can help us out of the mire, but a new realization of the general outlook and principles that lie behind the spirit of science; a new approach that grasps through science the principles of rational life in general. . . .

The view . . . is briefly this. The major crisis of our time is the decline in

[21] E. F. Caldin, *The Power and Limits of Science* (London, Chapman and Hall, 1949), pp. 168–170.

our conception of man, in respect for truth and justice and the other values of Western culture. Science is concerned in the decline as an unwitting cause, for misinterpretations of science have been used to support facile materialisms, and misapplication of science has sharpened the crisis. It is concerned in solving the problem, not as a material panacea nor as the only valid method of gaining knowledge, but in so far as it is one version of rational method, and so favours respect for truth and for the human person and represents rational standards. By itself it cannot help us, but in association with other forms of knowledge it could play a useful part.

4. SCIENTISTS CAN PROMOTE PEACE BY REFUSING TO LEND THEIR TALENTS TO DESTRUCTION

(Pitirim Sorokin, author of the following excerpts,[22] is a well-known sociologist who has noted the essential amorality of science and has pointed to the need for scientists to halt the employment of science by those who wage war.)

Due to a misuse and abuse of scientific discoveries and technological inventions, their total effects upon international tensions and solidarity have been mixed, in no way uniformly beneficial. In spite of an enormous increase in scientific discoveries and technological inventions after the thirteenth century on up to the present time, neither wars, nor civil wars and internal disturbances, nor other forms of intergroup and interindividual conflicts (crime, etc.) have shown a tendency to decrease.

. . . This suggests that the widely accepted opinion that science, technology, and education invariably exert only moral, pacific, and socially ennobling effects is sheer myth. Atomic bombs, means of bacteriological warfare, and other products of a misapplied science do not show any pacifying, tension decreasing effects. A biblical myth pregnantly tells that to the dawn of history misused science ("the tree of knowledge") cost humanity its Garden of Eden. A similar misuse now threatens to destroy the very tree of human life.

The actual effects of science, technology, and education as they have existed up to the present time, are complex and work partly in favor of decrease, and partly in favor of increase of tensions. Only science and technology that are socially and ethically responsible, that refuse to serve the Mammon of Destruction, that are free from their misuse for anti-social and tension provoking purposes, can serve the cause of intergroup cooperation and solidarity. Unfortunately, this ethico-social duty is not realized, as yet, by many scientists and inventors. They eagerly participate in the discovery and invention of most destructive means of warfare. Therefore, the actual effects of science and technology remain mixed. . . .

In order for all sciences and ideologies to perform the functions of tension decreasing factors, they must undergo several changes. Science and technology must stop serving destructive purposes; they must abandon their position of being ethically and socially irresponsible. Concretely this means, among other things, that the responsible scientist and inventor is under duty to refuse to work on any discovery or invention of a destructive kind. If he does not discharge the duty, then he is socially and morally, even legally, responsible for the

[22] Pitirim A. Sorokin, "Theses on the Effects of Science upon International Tensions and Solidarity," in Learning and World Peace, Lyman Bryson, Louis Finkelstein, and R. M. MacIver, eds. (New York, Harper, 1948), pp. 106, 107–108, 113–115.

murderous consequences. If we hold a careless driver responsible for running over a child, though the driver did not have any intention to kill the child, still more responsible is a scientist-inventor intentionally working on the means of destruction of human life and civilization. If his discovery-invention kills thousands of innocent persons, he is responsible for their death and mutilation, for the destruction of cities, crops, libraries, museums, universities and laboratories. Such a mass murder and mass destruction can and should be laid down at the door of his laboratory. If there are many discoveries-inventions whose nature is not destructive *per se*, though they can eventually be used for destructive purposes, there are many explicitly destructive inventions-discoveries. These must be eliminated from the activities of the socially responsible scientist-inventor, from science and technology.

Further, socially responsible science-technology must become aware of the fact that all the great values of human culture are not exhausted by the value of truth-knowledge and cognition; there are the values of Goodness and Beauty, as great as Truth, and as necessary for the creative existence of humanity. Even more, so far as science represents the truth of the senses, . . . scientific truth is competent only in the field of the sensory, empirical aspect of the infinitely manifolded reality. In regard to the non-empirical aspects of this infinite manifold, scientific methods and scientific truth are inadequate. Its fuller and more adequate cognition demands as organic cooperation of the truth of senses, of reason, and of supersensory and superlogical intuition, mutually supplementing and checking one another. This means that science must abandon its claim for a monopolistic possession of the whole truth and nothing but the truth, and must wholeheartedly enter the great team of three dimensional truth (of the senses, reason, and intuition) as an equal partner. . . .

Such a shift of the position of science "automatically" makes it socially and morally responsible; stops its conflict with the truth of reason and intuition; unites science with philosophy and religion, ethics and the fine arts, so far as they seek indeed to discover, to unfold, and to realize the infinite manifold in all its main aspects and dimensions. The unification of these values and cognitions into one system stops the raging struggle between many "onesided truths" of science, philosophy, and religion, the fine arts and ethics. The contemporary incertitude gives place to a new age of certitude, and peace of mind and humanity.

QUESTIONS

1. Why has the age of science been described as paradoxical?

2. Distinguish between physical, social, "pure," and "applied" science. Define science.

3. How recent a phenomenon is modern science in western civilization? In the Orient? Of what significance is that recency?

4. In what ways has science had a physical impact upon the world? Which of these impacts has had most significance for international affairs? Why?

5. Do you endorse the use of science in reducing the death rate in communities where there is already a shortage of resources? Will such action lead to increased international friction?

6. How is science related to modern western imperialism? What are the Occidental and Oriental psychologies which have accompanied recent western imperialism, and how have these attitudes affected international relations?

7. What is meant by the "crisis of despair"? What is its connection with scientific advance on the one hand, and international friction on the other?

8. How, on the intellectual plane, does modern science offer promise of improved world understanding?

9. What dilemma for makers of foreign policies in the democracies has arisen from the increasingly important role of science?

10. Which of the four points of view cited in Positions on the Problem seems most defensible to you? Why? What other views might be advanced?

SELECT BIBLIOGRAPHY

BUTTERFIELD, Herbert, *The Origins of Modern Science, 1300–1800* (London, G. Bell, 1950). A British historian, now at Cambridge, points up pivotal moments in the development of modern science, with emphasis upon intellectual knots that had to be untied at various junctures in the evolution of science. Informative rather than interpretive.

DUBARLE, Daniel, "Observations in the Relations between Science and the State," *Bulletin of the Atomic Scientists,* Vol. II (April, 1955), pp. 141–144. Emphasizes growing complexity and attendant problems of the state's assuming more and more responsibility for scientific research.

FULTON, James Street, *Science and Man's Hope* (New York, Bookman, 1954). An American scholar deals with the concepts of modern science and their relationship to human philosophy. Science helps us to get the things we want, but do we want the "right" things? Conclusion is that science and technology are potential aids in man's striving for a better world because they are essentially creative and productively imaginative.

"International Scientific Relations and National Security," *Nature,* Vol. 170 (December 20, 1952), pp. 1033–1036. Article expresses concern lest the pattern of state control now exercised over nuclear energy will lead to extension of state control over other scientific fields. Trend, it maintains, would tend to reduce influence science now exerts for an international community of interest.

JEANS, Sir James, *The New Background of Science* (New York, Macmillan, 1933). A distinguished British physicist's philosophical approach to theoretical physics. Author holds view that a de-emphasis of nineteenth century materialism, partly inspired by science, is future trend. Not highly technical.

MUMFORD, Lewis, *The Culture of the Cities* (New York, Harcourt Brace, 1938). Author, an architect-philosopher, sees in dehumanizing urbanization a stimulus to contemporary man's destructive inclinations. Urges a restructuring of urban civilization as a major contribution to stability and peace in the world.

NEF, John U., *War and Human Progress* (Cambridge, Harvard University Press, 1950). An essay by an economic historian on the rise of industrial civilization. Pertinent are the sections concerned with the philosophical and technical assistance science has afforded those who wage war. Final responsibility for a resolution of the contemporary crisis is placed upon man's intellectual and spiritual capacities.

RUSSELL, Bertrand, *The Impact of Science on Society* (New York, Columbia University Press, 1951). A British philosopher emphasizes that intellectually science is conducive to sanity and objectivity; physically it is dangerous because it has placed suicidal weapons in the hands of humans who in the majority are neither sane nor objective.

SULLIVAN, J. W. N., *The Limitations of Science* (New York, Viking, 1933). A mathematician, musician, and philosopher, the author is an outstanding interpreter of physics. Underlines belief that science affords a partial, but only partial, knowledge of reality. Religious aspirations and perceptions of beauty are suggested as more than illusions.

VEALE, F. J. P., *Advance to Barbarism* (Appleton, Wisc., C. C. Nelson, 1953). Condemnation of and warning against reversion to barbarism exemplified in techniques employed in waging World War II and in "legalized" liquidation by victors of vanquished leaders in postwar trials. Both science and human nature are held responsible for this retrogression.

Part III

IDEOLOGICAL CONFLICT
and ACCOMMODATION

7

Democracy:
Merits and Prospects?

THE PROBLEM
AND ITS BACKGROUND

THE IDEOLOGICAL BATTLE FOR THE MINDS OF MEN

Ideas Are Weapons

Ideas, wrote the famous and influential economist, John Maynard Keynes, are most "dangerous for good and evil." Ideas, he asserted, "both when they are right and when they are wrong, are more powerful than is commonly supposed. Indeed the world is ruled by little else." [1]

Today, as the force of ideas sometimes overshadows the force of arms in the cold war, the significance of ideology becomes ever more marked. After our somewhat brief examination of the part that various biological, psychological, political, economic, and scientific factors play in world affairs, it is essential to consider the role of ideological factors. The importance of ideology is now recognized by the foremost American leaders as they work for the success of American foreign policy. Admiral Radford, when Chairman of the U.S. Joint Chiefs of Staff, in a speech in the fall of 1955, put America's growing concern about the ideological battle for the minds of men as follows: [2]

It is obvious that the Communists have made amazing gains, largely because they know what they believe, why they believe it, and can explain it.

[1] John Maynard Keynes, *The General Theory of Employment, Interest and Money* (New York, Harcourt Brace, 1936), pp. 383–384.
[2] Quoted in an article by James Reston, *New York Times*, October 26, 1955, p. 16.

On the other hand, we who are free have many times been incoherent or have lacked the verbal ability to explain or defend completely what our way of life really is. We must know what we mean by it. We must be convinced that it presents the best way of life in today's world—and I think we are. But we must be able to explain this conviction to others.

It should be noted that the increased postwar interest of our national leaders in ideology is occasioned first and foremost by their concern for the success of American foreign policy. World affairs, then, would seem to be inextricably linked with the ideological battle for the minds of men. What are the major ideologies in this battle? In other words, what are the patterns of ideas and ideals by which men and nations believe they ought to live?

This is the first of four chapters dealing with the major ideologies of the world, their strengths and weaknesses, their rivalry for men's minds, their effect upon domestic and foreign policies, and the possibility of peaceful accommodation between them. We shall start with democracy, for it is logical to appraise one's own ideology first. Surely, if we are to understand other ideologies, we must first know our own and have a conscious and articulate basis for comparison. Heeding the ancient adage, "Know Thyself," the American student must start with a probe of democracy, the dominant ideology of the western world.

Democracy: Battle for a Word and a World

The very word *democracy* has been the object of bitter international quarreling between ideological and political rivals. This battle for a word really symbolizes the battle for a world, but it also highlights the tremendous prestige value of the word itself in today's world.

That agreement is not universal on the meaning of the word, even within the western world, is not of primary importance here. Instead of barring the way to effective communication, semantic disagreement may actually be of assistance in drawing vital distinctions between those who follow in the western democratic tradition and those who have repudiated it.

Distinctions Within Democracy

This chapter, then, will be primarily concerned with what is generally called "western democracy," in contrast to the "proletarian democracy" of the communist world. Of major interest here are the *basic political* features of all democracies of the western variety, regardless of the specific form of government or economic system that may prevail in the country concerned. Democracy, it must be noted, may be present in different forms of government; witness the parliamentary and unitary system of Great Britain, on the one hand, and the presidential and federal sys-

tem of the United States, on the other. It may also be present within
different economic systems, such as the democratic socialism espoused
by the British Labor Party (or that of India, to be discussed in Chapter
9), and the democratic capitalism favored by the Republican and Democratic parties in the United States. The relative merits and weaknesses of
the various forms are not of immediate moment at this point; rather, attention is focused on the body of ideological principles that underlie all
democratic governments and justify their being described thus.

The discussion is therefore centered on the traits common to that constitutional democracy which first emerged in the West and has since
spread to other geographical areas of the world. A brief sketch of the
origin and development of western democracy sets the framework for a
working definition of democracy and its central ideal; then a discussion
of the cardinal elements of democratic theory becomes more meaningful.
This treatment, it should be noted, would probably be endorsed in general outline by most western democrats, although some might take exception to specific points. Within the analysis, in any event, may be found
the sense of values, appreciation of goals, awareness of relation of means
to ends, and cognizance of a pattern of living that have constituted the
underlying and motivating forces in the lives of many men and the conduct of many nations in the western world.

After this discussion, consideration of the twentieth century debate
over democracy becomes more fruitful, particularly as it relates to the
ideological battle for the minds of men throughout the world. The debate
is continued in greater detail in "Positions on the Problem" at the end
of this chapter.

BRIEF HISTORY: ORIGIN AND DEVELOPMENT

Modern Development, Older Roots

Democracy is a relatively modern development. Taking the establishment in 1789 of the American republic as a rough historical marker, we
may better appreciate how young democracy is. Even in 1789, actually,
the United States was not fully democratic, in a political sense as well as
in other ways, since suffrage was restricted on grounds of race, sex, and
property. A significant extension of suffrage, so as to permit more truly
popular rule, did not occur in either the United States or Britain until
the middle of the nineteenth century, and in both countries women did
not obtain the right to vote and hold office until the twentieth century.
Indeed, not until this century was the word *democracy* commonly applied
to describe the United States, although the term had become more and
more popular. It was Woodrow Wilson, during his two terms as President

(1913–21), who was responsible for its great popularity and prestige both at home and abroad.

Yet, democracy has very old roots. These roots go as far back as Judaic-Christian religious tradition, Greek philosophic and political thought, Roman jurisprudence, and medieval political theory.

The Ancient Heritage [3]

The word *democracy* comes from the Greek. *Demos* is the Greek word for people. The word-root *ocracy* means government or rule. Hence, *democracy:* people's rule. The Greeks, then, were the first to state and treat the concept of democracy. For them democracy involved a *means* of governing and not the *content* of law. However, because the Greek *polis* (*state*) was not strictly a political community but also embraced the religious and social aspects of life, democracy was truly a whole way of life. Still, it was not the only possibility. The alternatives were monarchy (rule by one "good" man), aristocracy (rule by the best few), plutocracy (rule by the rich), tyranny (rule by one strong man), and oligarchy (rule by a few).

For most Greek thinkers, democracy meant the rule of the less wealthy and less educated citizen-masses in contrast to that of the plutocratic and aristocratic classes. The Athenian Greek ideal of democracy has been best expressed, perhaps, in the famous "Funeral Oration" of the renowned Athenian leader Pericles, as given in Thucydides' *History of the Peloponnesian War.* A few passages serve to illuminate the Greek concept of democracy, which has had a lasting influence upon western civilization. [4]

It is true [Pericles declared] that we are called a democracy, for the administration is in the hands of the many and not of the few. But while the law secures equal justice to all alike in their private disputes, the claim of excellence is also recognized; and when a citizen is in any way distinguished, he is preferred to the public service, not as a matter of privilege, but as the reward of merit. Neither is poverty a bar, but a man may benefit his country whatever be the obscurity of his condition. There is no exclusiveness in our public life, and in our private intercourse we are not suspicious of one another, nor angry with our neighbour if he does what he likes; we do not put on sour looks at him which, though harmless, are not pleasant. While we are thus unconstrained in our private intercourse, a spirit of reverence pervades our public acts; we are prevented from doing wrong by respect for the authorities and for the laws which bring upon the transgressor of them the reprobation of the general sentiment.

An Athenian citizen does not neglect the state because he takes care of his own household; and even those of us who are engaged in business have a very fair idea of politics. We alone regard a man who takes no interest in public

[3] For the best brief discussion, see "The Heritage of Western Civilization," in A. D. Lindsay, *The Modern Democratic State* (New York, Oxford University Press, 1947), Chap. II.

[4] Thucydides, *History of the Peloponnesian War,* Book ii, Richard Crawley, transl. (New York, Dutton, Everyman's Library volume, 1936), Chaps. 37 and 40.

affairs, not as a harmless, but as a useless character; and if few of us are originators, we are all sound judges of a policy. The great impediment to action is, in our opinion, not discussion, but the want of that knowledge which is gained by discussion preparatory to action. For we have a peculiar power of thinking before we act and of acting, too, whereas other men are courageous from ignorance but hesitate upon reflection.

It would be a mistake, of course, to romanticize Greek democracy. From our modern democratic point of view, Greek democracy was incomplete. Most important here is the fact that Greek civilization was based on slavery. Furthermore, the democracy was short-lived even in the Athens that Pericles eulogized.

It remained for Christian theology and Stoic philosophy to introduce the concept of equality, which is such an integral part of modern democratic ideology, but which took centuries to become manifest in political equality, liberty, and fraternity. For example, slavery continued in the Roman period and, of course, was not abolished in the United States until 1865.

Historically, the advance of democracy has been accompanied by extension of the number of people who might share in the political process and enjoy the rights of citizenship. In this respect the Romans made a twofold contribution: They helped to keep alive, at least in theory, the concept of popular sovereignty, and they broadened the Greek concept of citizenship. For the Greeks, all foreigners were barbarians. With the Romans, however, citizenship—which brought with it the protection of Roman law—might be extended to all who came within the jurisdiction of the Roman Empire, whether they were Roman, Greek, or Jew.

Medieval Europe

Most ideas central to modern, liberal democratic theory were current in medieval political theory. For example, almost all theorists of that time contended that political rule must be just and in the interest of the people. Religiously, all men were free and equal under God, brothers under a common Father. No ruler was absolute. Medieval theorists would have nothing of political absolutism, which is a modern phenomenon. They insisted, over and over again, that princes (rulers) function under the governance of a higher law: God's law or natural (moral) law, which could be known by men possessed of "right reason." Nevertheless, political practice in the medieval world fell considerably short of modern canons of democratic government.

The Modern World

Throughout early western history, despite ancient heritage and medieval theory, there had been no successful democratic experiment of significant duration. Indeed, as has been suggested, before the establishment of the American republic in 1789, no major democratic, or republican, state had existed. It is true that the cantons of Switzerland were among the few governments where republican institutions had taken hold prior to this time, but among the major powers, with the exception of Great Britain, political absolutism predominated.

Great Britain had led the way in the development of modern concepts of constitutional and representative government, and the protection of certain basic rights—two of the earmarks of modern democracy. It was no accident, therefore, that the American colonies, nurtured in the British tradition, should have joined together to form (what was soon to become) the first major state in the modern world with a republican form of government. However, it took the French Revolution of 1789 to shatter the stereotypes of political absolutism in a largely feudal Europe and to popularize and implement democratic ideas in the western world.

The inspiring motto of the French Revolution, "liberty, equality, fraternity," became the political watchword of liberal democracy in the nineteenth century. Nationalism and liberalism were joined together in a powerful movement against absolutist governments in many quarters of the European continent. In a number of countries this led to national independence, greater political freedom, and more popular rule. Increasingly, more liberal laws and constitutions (guaranteeing basic rights, enfranchising more groups, providing for a greater measure of popular control of government) were passed or adopted. To some observers, the achievement of democracy throughout the world was the prerequisite for world peace. To many, the democratic tide seemed irresistible. This may account for the world-wide popularity of President Wilson's World War I slogan about making the world safe for democracy.

The emergence of communist and fascist dictatorships after World War I in countries like Russia, Italy, and Germany came as a surprise, consequently, to those who considered the democratic advance to be irresistible and inevitable. It was far less startling to more thoughtful observers who had earlier noted how superficial and incomplete was the new democracy in the countries of central Europe, without the historical experience of the United States or Great Britain. These more discerning critics even noted the "democratic" elements in the ideologies of communism, Nazism, and fascism, especially the mass (or popular) bases of the movements.

In spite of the communist, Nazi, and fascist challenges, democracy did endure in the twentieth century. In such democratic nations as the United States and Britain, increasing attention began to be given to the "democratic" *content* of legislation, and to the democratization of other aspects of life. In other words, democracies became more and more concerned with achieving social and economic legislation that would advance the fuller life of the many.

At this point it is relevant to note that democracy emerged and grew up alongside the economic system of capitalism. Although the exact connection between capitalism and democracy is still a highly controversial question, it is clear that early capitalism, with its emphasis on private ownership and direction of the means of production and exchange, was interested in as much freedom as possible from state interference and regulation. Adam Smith, for example, one of the principal economic theorists of the period of early capitalism, argued that the well-being of individuals in society would be best advanced by an economic system free of the government's oppressive hand.

This desire for economic freedom on the part of the emerging capitalist class harmonized closely with the principles of political and social freedom stressed by the French Revolution. Historically speaking, there can be little doubt that liberal democracy—a democracy that would advance the political, social, and economic freedom of the individual—forged ahead with the progress of capitalism and the growth of the essentially capitalistic middle class. Certainly in Europe, the new middle class resorted to democratic principles to gain greater economic, political, and social powers at the expense of absolutist governments and feudal aristocracies. Some observers have gone so far as to describe this process as "the marriage of democracy and capitalism."

Regardless of how this historic connection is understood, it helps to explain some of the confusion often encountered today in the struggle of various ideological systems. The communists have perhaps carried the tie between liberal democracy and capitalism to an extreme with their assertion that western democracy is merely the political shell of capitalism. Conversely, many in the United States have maintained that democracy cannot exist unless the system of private-enterprise capitalism also prevails. They become very apprehensive about the efforts of the democratic socialists of Europe and Asia to combine democracy with socialism, and find it difficult to believe that people may desire democracy but at the same time feel that private-enterprise capitalism is not best suited to their particular needs.

This illustrates again the confusion over the meaning of democracy and indicates the importance of attempting to set forth a definition of its central principles and ideals.

DEMOCRACY: DEFINITION AND IDEAL

A Working Definition

In brief, political democracy means that the mass of the citizenry, regardless of wealth, education, and lineage, may share and participate in determining public policy by means of a representative system. They and their representatives normally shape public policy, indirectly or directly, through the technique of majority rule. In other words, in the absence of unanimity among the electorate or in the legislative assembly, the decision reached by a majority will, until overcome, stand for that of the whole citizenry.

However, most democratic theorists today do not limit democracy either to majority rule or to broad participation in the political process. The definition of democracy is incomplete unless it also includes the establishment and preservation of basic individual and group rights. These are commonly identified with freedom of speech, press, assembly, and the rule of law, among others. Often they are summarized in the famous triad, "life, liberty, and property" of the English political philosopher, John Locke.

The argument for including such rights in the definition of democracy is quite simple. Their protection, it is held, is essential in a government based upon popular rule, because citizens and legislators cannot do their part in determining public policy if they cannot freely exercise most of these rights. In other words, the individual citizen cannot shape public policy unless he has the right to speak, read, and write about public issues, to assemble and organize in political parties, and vote for or against political candidates and measures. Without these freedoms, he cannot rule indirectly and control the government under which he lives. Consequently, these freedoms are an integral part of popular rule, that is, rule by the many which normally means rule by the majority.

Other basic rights, however, must also be protected and included in a definition of democracy. There is a realm of activity which, according to this democratic view, is or should be beyond governmental reach. Democratic government is limited government. It is not totalitarian. Popular rule is limited to a prescribed and circumscribed area. Outside this area, individuals and groups must be free from governmental power if man is to be able to worship according to the dictates of his own conscience; if man is to have the maximum opportunity to think and create intellectually, artistically, and scientifically; and if man is to be permitted to associate freely with others of like mind for these and other lawful purposes.

The Central Democratic Ideal

Democracy, unlike communism, has no authoritative "book" or books where the democratic gospel is set forth. No manifesto like the *Communist Manifesto* and no major work such as *Das Kapital* provides it with a firm creed and an inspired bible. However, there are a number of documents in the democratic tradition with certain common elements: Pericles' "Funeral Oration" (Athens, around 431 B.C.); John

Locke, *Second Treatise on Civil Government* (1690); the American Declaration of Independence (1776); the French Declaration of the Rights of Man and Citizen (1789); John Stuart Mill, *On Liberty* (1859); and Abraham Lincoln, "Gettysburg Address" (1863), to mention a few of the more famous. General agreement on the central democratic ideal will be found in all.

Simply put, *the central democratic ideal is the freest and fullest possible flowering of the individual personality.* It is the individual's opportunity, within the justifiable limitations of society, to develop the best in himself to the best of his ability.

The flowering or realization of the individual human being's best qualities is the central premise which explains why advocates of democracy believe so strongly in the cardinal elements of democratic theory—liberty, equality, fraternity, justice—which will be considered in more detail in the next section. Without them neither popular rule nor basic rights can prevail, and without these the opportunity for the individual to develop his uniquely human, good, and creative potentialities is nil.

Individual fulfillment is either restricted, curtailed, or impossible under conditions of slavery, inequality, enmity, and injustice. It is no accident, therefore, that liberty, equality, fraternity, and justice have become the touchstone of the democratic faith.

At this point it will be profitable to examine these cardinal elements and to see if it is possible—amidst the conflict as to the meaning of these words—to arrive at an understanding of them.

THE CARDINAL ELEMENTS OF DEMOCRATIC THEORY

The preamble to the Constitution of one of the most recent members of our community of nations, India, is of interest here.

We, *the People of India,* having solemnly resolved to constitute India into a *Sovereign Democratic Republic,* and to secure to all its citizens:

Justice, social, economic, and political;
Liberty of thought, expression, belief, faith and worship;
Equality of status and of opportunity;

and to promote them all

Fraternity assuring the dignity of the individual and the unity of the Nation;

In Our Constituent Assembly this twenty-sixth day of November 1949 do *Hereby Adopt, Enact and Give to Our Selves This Constitution.*

Here, the cardinal elements of democratic theory have been briefly set forth in one of the world's most recent constitutions.

Liberty

Historically, liberty has meant freedom, and actually stems from the Latin root *liber, free*. Thus liberty has signified a free man as opposed to a slave. A man was free if he could call his body (and, of course, his soul and mind, too) his own, if he could, under law, enjoy life, liberty, property, and the pursuit of happiness.

The most influential democratic school of thought has held that man's liberty or freedom is God-given or natural to man as man. Such liberty and those rights which secure it are therefore unalienable in the sense that a man cannot be a man if he loses this liberty. Government, according to this view, exists to secure liberty and rights. Perhaps the best-known expression of it is to be found in the American Declaration of Independence. In the following passage the inextricable connection between liberty and equality and also the rationale of democratic government are made clear:

We hold these truths to be self-evident, that all men are created equal, that they are endowed by their Creator with certain unalienable Rights, that among these are Life, Liberty and the pursuit of Happiness. That to secure these rights, Governments are instituted among Men, deriving their just powers from the consent of the governed. That whenever any Form of Government becomes destructive of these ends, it is the Right of the People to alter or to abolish it, and to institute new Government, laying its foundation on such principles and organizing its powers in such form, as to them shall seem most likely to effect their Safety and Happiness.

The French Declaration of the Rights of Man and Citizen spells out another aspect of this classic natural-rights view of liberty:

Liberty consists in the power to do anything that does not injure others; accordingly, the exercise of the natural rights of each man has for its only limits those that secure to the other members of society the enjoyment of these same rights. These limits can only be determined by law.

The law has the right to forbid only such actions as are injurious to society. Nothing can be forbidden that is not interdicted by the law and no one can be constrained to do that which it does not order.

Historically, in the crystallization of the concept of liberty in modern times, government has been the primary enemy of liberty. Liberty has had to be secured against government. This accounts for the historic democratic emphasis on Bills of Rights and other constitutional protections of our liberty.

A man must be *free* to worship God as his own conscience dictates. He must be *free* to speak, write, and assemble. He must be *free* to ask his government to remedy wrongs. The United States Constitution clearly illustrates these points. The First Amendment declares:

Congress [read Government] shall make no law respecting an establishment of religion, or prohibiting the free exercise thereof; or abridging the freedom of speech, or of the press; or the right of the people peaceably to assemble, and to petition the government for a redress of grievances.

Similarly, a man's body and possessions must be respected, and his house considered his castle:

The right [the Fourth Amendment declares] of the people to be secure in their persons, houses, papers, and effects against unreasonable searches and seizures, shall not be violated, and no warrants shall issue, but upon probable cause, supported by oath or affirmation, and particularly describing the place to be searched, and the persons or things to be seized.

Lawful, orderly, fair processes, not arbitrary, capricious, inhumane ones, must be followed by the government in the exercise of its legitimate duties:

No person [states the Fifth Amendment] . . . subject for the same offense [shall] . . . be twice put in jeopardy of life or limb; nor shall [he] be compelled in any criminal case to be a witness against himself, nor be deprived of life, liberty, or property, without due process of law; nor shall private property be taken for public use without just compensation.

In all criminal prosecutions [according to the Sixth Amendment], the accused shall enjoy the right to a speedy and public trial, by an impartial jury . . . and to be informed of the nature and cause of the accusation; to be confronted with the witnesses against him; to have compulsory process for obtaining witnesses in his favor, and to have the assistance of counsel for his defense.

Other rights against government are to be found in the main body of the Constitution and in amendments other than those called the Bill of Rights.

The privilege of the writ of *habeas corpus* shall not be suspended, unless when in cases of rebellion or invasion the public safety may require it [Art. 1, Sec. 9 (2)].

Here the right of an individual to know the cause of his imprisonment and the right to release in the absence of lawful cause have been safeguarded.

The right to vote, already secured for most white and male adults under state constitutions, was negatively secured for Negroes and for women by the Fifteenth and Nineteenth Amendments:

The right of citizens of the United States to vote shall not be denied or abridged by the United States or by any State on account of race, color, or previous condition of servitude.

The right of citizens of the United States to vote shall not be denied or abridged by the United States or by any State on account of sex.

This partial catalogue of rights against government (as found in the Constitution of the United States) may serve to give more concrete meaning to the concept of liberty.

Liberty, thus understood, is logically linked to the concept of *limited government* which we have already touched upon in our definition of democracy. Liberty requires government to operate in a limited or circumscribed sphere. When government bursts these limits, liberty is at an end. Totalitarianism (that is, a political philosophy wherein the government embraces *all* aspects of life—political, religious, economic, social, and cultural) appears.

It would be completely misleading, however, not to indicate the positive role that democratic government, especially in the modern world, may play in securing and advancing liberty.

First, as John Locke put it, government provides us with an "established, settled, known law, received and allowed by common consent to be the standard of right and wrong, and the common measure to decide all controversies between" men.[5] Second, government provides men with a "known and indifferent judge with authority to determine all differences according to the established law." Third, government provides the "power to back and support the sentence when right and to give it due execution." Government, then, provides men with law and order of their own making, in the form of a common legislature, executive, and judiciary. Men are enabled to enjoy life, liberty, property, and happiness by means of the law and order without which, as Thomas Hobbes, another English political philosopher, indicated, life would be a fearful, uncivilized state of war, "where every man is enemy to every man . . . wherein men live without other security than what their own strength . . . shall furnish them. . . ."[6]

In such condition [wrote Hobbes] there is no place for industry, because the fruit thereof is uncertain, and consequently no culture of the earth; no navigation, nor uses of the commodities that may be imported by sea; no commodious buildings . . . no knowledge of the face of the earth; no account of time; no arts; no letters; no society, and, which is worst of all, continual fear and danger of violent death; and the life of man [is] solitary, poor, nasty, brutish, and short.

Government, then, can both safeguard liberty under law and create the conditions that make possible civilization, the fruit of liberty and free human development.

Equality

The Declaration of Independence declares it to be a "self-evident" truth that "all men are created equal." The equality referred to is equality before God or moral equality, which leads in turn to equality before the law or political equality. It does not imply biological, intellectual, economic, or cultural equality. In other words, men may not have equal

---

[5] See John Locke, *Second Treatise on Civil Government*, many editions, Chap. IX.
[6] See Thomas Hobbes, *Leviathan*, many editions, Part I, Chap. XIII.

physical strength, mental endowment, material wealth, or aesthetic and literary tastes, but they are all equally children of the same God and citizens before the law.

As has been suggested before, the concept of equality in the western world has ancient roots in the Judaic-Christian tradition and in Stoic philosophy. St. Paul wrote to the Galatians: "There is neither Jew nor Gentile, there is neither bond nor free, there is neither male nor female; for ye are all one in Christ Jesus."

Christianity deepened and reinforced the doctrine of the natural equality of mankind first taught by Stoic philosophers: There was in all men equally, despite differences of race, culture, and station, a spark of divine reason which made moral life possible for all.

The concept of equality, first expressed in antiquity, was to echo and re-echo throughout the intellectual history of the western civilization. Although not fuel for political revolt in its strictly religious sense, the idea of equality has, nevertheless, been a highly inflammable revolutionary tinderbox for all those who have endeavored to implement equality in other aspects of life.

For example, in the peasant revolts in fourteenth century France and England, the contrast between religious equality and social and economic inequality led spokesmen for the oppressed peasants to ask in their literature: [7]

> When Adam delved and Eve span,
> Who was then the gentleman?

And even earlier:

> Naked and impotent are all,
> High-born or peasant, great and small:
> That human nature is throughout
> The whole world equal, none can doubt.

Similar thinking accompanied the peasant revolts of the sixteenth century, when the Anabaptists took too seriously and literally Luther's Christian equalitarian teaching.

Amidst the upheaval of the Puritan Revolution in seventeenth century England, the extreme left wing of the movement (a group known as the Diggers) declared: "None ought to be lords or landlords over another, but the earth is free for every son and daughter of mankind to live free upon." [8]

The more moderate left wing of Cromwell's revolutionary army sought only equality before the law and equality of political rights. The argument of these political "levellers," which was more political than eco-

[7] This quotation, and the one immediately following, may be found in G. H. Sabine, A History of Political Theory (New York, Holt, rev. ed., 1950), p. 315.
[8] Ibid., p. 491.

nomic, is powerfully conveyed in a single sentence uttered by one of their spokesmen in a debate with the more conservative Cromwell and his lieutenants: [9]

Really I think that the poorest he that is in England hath a life to live as the greatest he; and therefore truly, Sir, I think it's clear, that every man that is to live under a government ought first by his own consent to put himself under that government; and I do think that the poorest man in England is not at all bound in a strict sense to that government that he hath not had a voice to put himself under.

Eventually, the concept of political equality, already enshrined in the American Declaration of Independence, was to become embodied in the written or unwritten constitution of all democratic countries.

The first two points of the French Declaration of the Rights of Man and Citizen announced to France and to all of Europe:

1. Men are born and remain free and equal in rights. Social distinctions can be based only upon public utility.
2. The aim of every political association is the preservation of the natural and imprescriptible rights of man. These rights are liberty, property, security, and resistance to oppression.

Traditionally, equality had meant legal and political equality: equality of citizens before the law; one man, one vote. A close reading of the first point in the French Declaration of Rights reveals that the move toward greater social equality follows hard and fast upon the heels of political equality. Greater economic equality for one group is closely followed by comparable demands by other groups. Hence political democracy which may, in part, reflect newly emerging economic powers also serves to advance greater social and economic equality. Although not absent in the United States, the battle for greater social and economic equality has been more to the fore in Europe than in the United States, because most European countries had to fight a social and economic, as well as a political, revolution against feudalism. By way of contrast, in the United States this was not so true, because of the absence of a full-fledged feudal system to be overthrown and because of the invitation to social and economic mobility offered by an almost virgin continent.

This fuller social and economic revolution against a privileged *ancien régime* has also been more evident in the former colonial areas of the world, like India, than in the United States because of: (1) the race-color-caste barrier between Europeans and Indians; (2) the ancient caste system of India itself; (3) the economic exploitation of native Indians by the colonial power; and (4) the feudal structure of such areas. Social and economic equality is, therefore, bound to be of great importance in colonial or once colonial areas of the world.

[9] *Ibid.,* p. 483.

Earlier, in the West, the target had been elimination of artificial social distinctions and special social and economic privileges, under law. Now, increasingly, in democratic countries the targets have become the artificial and societal distinctions and arbitrary economic discrimination, with or without the benefit of law. Such fields as education, housing, recreation, and employment have been foremost. In the United States, for example, social and cultural inequality in some of our forty-eight states has come into conflict with the Supreme Court's interpretation of the equal-protection clause of the Constitution. This clause holds that "No State . . . shall deny to any person within its jurisdiction the equal protection of the laws." In the Supreme Court's 1954 decision against segregation in the public schools, equality before the law was deemed broad enough to cover certain aspects of social equality. This has also been true of other decisions in which the Supreme Court refused to uphold segregated bus or train travel or to enforce decisions of state courts that validated restrictive housing covenants.

Similarly, greater economic equality has made its bid for recognition, particularly in the twentieth century. Frequently, greater economic equality has been obtained in democratic countries by means of a progressive income tax and the redistribution of wealth through varying welfare programs. In this way glaring economic disparities have been alleviated. In addition, wage-hour legislation has narrowed the gap between the underpaid and the fairly paid; collective-bargaining legislation (the Wagner Act, the Taft-Hartley Act) has served to put labor and capital, union and employer, on a more equal footing in labor-management relations; farm price-support legislation has operated to achieve greater economic equality for the farmer in relation to the city worker and the rest of the country.

The same process has been going on in other democratic countries. In Britain it has been expressed in terms of "fair shares," and has manifested itself in programs providing for national educational scholarships, socialized medicine, and the like. The fuller story of the relationship of democracy to socialism will be related in Chapter 9.

In all these ways, primarily political but also social and economic, equality is given a concrete meaning in modern democratic societies. The equality involved is that of consideration for every human being. Each individual equally possesses a soul or personality with a capacity to worship the Divine or to develop his unique potentiality. Human beings, then, are entitled to develop the best in themselves, and such development is impossible if the law or other human beings treat people as nonhuman or subhuman, or deny them the legal respect, political opportunity, and social and economic consideration to which all men are entitled under law or in society.

Fraternity

Fraternity is yet another touchstone of democratic theory. It comes from the Latin word *frater*, meaning brother, and has often been used synonymously with brotherhood, fellowship, fellow-feeling, benevolence, common humanity, love, co-operation.

As a modern political theorist describes it: [10] "It is the spirit of brotherhood, of treating others not simply as though they had rights equal to ours but with loving concern for their welfare."

Fraternity is a concept that unites men in a common bond: men are human brothers possessing a common Father in God; they are jointly members of the same human race. Fraternity emphasizes man's sameness, his mutual welfare, his common humanity.

It counteracts individualistic or group selfishness, hatred, enmity, intolerance. It enables man to rise above his selfish interests and work for his common interests. By making him aware of the rights of others like himself, it highlights his duties to others. The mutual recognition of rights and duties, needs and services, operates to make compromise, concession, adjustment, and accommodation possible. In a word, fraternity enables men in the broader community to live as a family of neighbors, to work together on the same team or teams.

Justice

To keep liberty, equality, and fraternity in proper balance or harmony is the function of justice, which may be defined here as the concept that harmonizes, joins, balances, and thus reconciles liberty, equality, and fraternity. It is with good reason, then, that justice has been visually represented as a blindfolded woman holding a scale in her hand. The blindfold stands for impartiality; the scale, for proper balance. Justice measures the respective claims of liberty, equality, and fraternity and strikes the right balance among them according to the standard of the central democratic ideal, which the political theorist, Sir Ernest Barker, defines as the "maximum development of the capacities of personality in the maximum number of persons." [11]

It is a commonplace that liberty, equality, and fraternity often are in conflict with each other. Liberty, pushed to an extreme, may cause an irresponsible individualism which makes fraternity impossible. Equality, urged too far, may come into conflict with liberty when equality leads to a leveled society that takes no account of vital and inevitable economic, social, and cultural disparities. Fraternity, pressed too radically, may

---

[10] J. Roland Pennock, *Liberal Democracy* (New York, Rinehart, 1950), p. 94.
[11] *Principles of Social and Political Theory* (New York, Oxford University Press, 1951), p. 171. The treatment of justice here owes a great deal to this book.

violate liberty when a communal way of life ensues that runs contrary
to the need for privacy and individual effort.

Similarly, liberty (let us say, of the employer to hire whomever he
desires) may conflict with equality (let us say, of the union member or
member of a minority group in obtaining and keeping a job). Fraternity
can be destructive of equality when it ceases to be the brotherhood that
unites all men (regardless of nation, race, religion, economic and social
status) and becomes the perverted fraternity of the U.S.S.R. vs. the U.S.,
of white vs. colored, of Christian vs. non-Christian, or of labor vs. capital.
Equality may also come into conflict with fraternity, as well as liberty,
when it is no longer taken seriously. For example, in George Orwell's
biting satire *Animal Farm*, the leaders of the "revolution" start by preaching "All animals are created equal" but end, after they have consolidated
their revolutionary power, by interpreting equality as: "All animals are
created equal, but some are more equal than others."

There is also the problem of balancing liberty against itself, equality
against itself, fraternity against itself. The liberty of employers, for instance, may interfere with that of employees; of non-Christians with that
of Christians; of colored people with that of white people; of the U.S.
with that of the U.S.S.R. Since arguments may be advanced for the con-
verse, who decides, and according to what principle—in the event of a
conflict?

The same dilemma arises with one concept of fraternity (say, of a college social fraternity) vs. another (say, of a person opposed to discriminatory, exclusive college social fraternities); or one concept of
equality (held, let us say, by those who believe in separate but equal
education in the school system of the South) and another (held by those
who agree with the Supreme Court that separate education by its very
nature is unequal)! Who decides, and according to what principle?

The answer of liberal democratic theory has been that justice is the
deciding principle. To repeat, the final and ultimate value on the basis
of which such a decision is made (reverting to Barker's criterion) is "the
highest possible development of the capacities of personality in the
greatest possible number of persons."

Actually, of course, specific political decisions are generally made in a
democracy by an electoral or legislative majority. A critic might argue
that justice gets lost in the helter-skelter of democratic politics and
amidst the competing and conflicting claims of frequently selfish groups.
He might further argue that majority rule itself is not concerned with
justice but with power or, at best, ends up with a crude compromise that
is more expedient than just.

Three points might be made in reply to this argument. First, democratic theory does not maintain that every single decision is necessarily

just. Democratic theory does hold that the concept of justice must be the guiding and animating ideal of a democratic society. Second, there is in a democracy, operating on the basis of popular rule and basic rights, considerably more justice (more balancing, reconciling, harmonizing of conflicting claims consonant with maximum individual development) than first is apparent. Third, a democracy is an "open society" in which justice, in manifold instances, may be challenged, debated, and freely pursued, and not a "closed" totalitarian society in which *the just ordering of society* is known and all must conform to this single, rigid pattern or pay a drastic penalty for dissent.

Consequently, justice in democratic theory is a concept requiring a harmonizing of the divergent expressions of potentiality on the part of individuals, groups, nations. It must be in accord with the central democratic ideal of the freest and fullest possible flowering of the individual personality. Democratic theorists maintain that justice, along with liberty, equality, and fraternity, can best be achieved and advanced in a political community based on popular rule and basic individual rights.

DEMOCRACY: THE TWENTIETH CENTURY DEBATE

When Is a Country a Democracy?

At this point, some further questions may serve as a gauge in ascertaining whether or not a country is a democracy in the sense in which it has been treated in this chapter. They may be more helpful than a lengthy exposition of the meaning of constitutional government.

1. Do most of the people really have an opportunity, by means of genuinely free elections, to select the men and policies that will govern the nation? In other words, is the government truly based on the consent of the governed?

2. Do the people enjoy the right freely to speak, write, publish, and assemble in order to criticize the government and leaders in power? Have they the right to turn them out peacefully at the ballot box?

3. Is there in existence at least one free, independent, strong, and functioning opposition political party or coalition ready, willing, and able to supplant the governing political party, if the people in a free election turn the government in power out of office?

4. Do the people enjoy the right to worship God as their consciences dictate, to participate in religious life through a free church of their own choice, and to pay allegiance to a higher power than that of the secular state?

5. Are they protected against arbitrary and unreasonable action by government which would deprive them of their life, liberty, and property without due process of law? (Due process is here understood to forbid

two kinds of governmental action: first, action such as the systematic destruction of a religious group, race, or class; second, "legal" action such as a trial based on false evidence or coerced confession. The first action should be beyond the power of government. The second action is within the power of government but, so far as it is an improper trial, it is contrary to proper legal conduct.)

6. Is the role of the state limited to certain legitimate and necessary public functions such as maintenance of internal peace and order, protection from foreign invasion, taxation, providing a stable and uniform currency? Or does the state invade, dominate, and absorb the private, voluntary cultural and social life of the community—our books, plays, radio and television programs, the clubs and organizations to which we belong?

7. Is the state so powerful in the economic field that it not only regulates, controls, and directs the economic modes of production and exchange (and the economic livelihood of all citizens) but also uses its economic power to nullify political freedom and dominate other aspects of society such as church, press, radio, education?

These questions are relevant to both the definition and feasibility of democracy. The questions pose others about the prerequisites for the successful functioning of liberal democracy: government based on the consent of the governed, the existence of basic political rights, the functioning of two or more effective political parties, the enjoyment of religious freedom, the maintenance of due process of law, and the prevalence of limited government. Here it is appropriate to set forth these prerequisities. This may shed some light on the appeal and applicability of western democracy throughout the world.

Democratic Prerequisites for the Citizenry [12]

Desire for self-government. This is basic for the citizenry. Without it, democracy can have no beginning, and should it exist without such a desire, democracy will inevitably have an untimely and inglorious end. This does not mean, of course, that every citizen must actively govern or control government. It does mean that there must be sufficient desire among enough people, operating in the political and social system as a whole, to prevent outside rule as in colonialism. The desire must also be great enough to forestall inside domination by a dictator, "boss," oligarchy, or single party—as in many parts of the world, not excluding the United States.

Accepting and fulfilling the duties of citizenship. Willingness to carry out this responsibility is closely related to the first requirement. Here again, it should be clear, 100 per cent participation is not essential; if it

[12] With some modifications, the treatment here follows that of Pennock, *op. cit.*, pp. 211–216. The quotations are from Pennock.

were, democracy would be nonexistent. It may seem unfortunate, but it is probably true that the average citizen does not have a great deal of political motivation and interest. By ideal-citizenship standards, he is neither particularly rational, politically speaking, nor willing and able to discuss, debate, decide, and act upon political issues. Relatively few are willing to serve in a public capacity, but it is enough if a democratically oriented minority are willing and able to assume the duties of more active citizenship, to provide leadership from their ranks, and to encourage the majority to assume at least a modest citizenship role.

"At least a minimum of information and intelligence." No country "is ready for democracy until the great bulk of its citizens are able to read and write." This point is valid as long as the requisite minimum is not set too high. Even in the United States, knowledge of governmental matters is not a strong point of the average citizen, nor is he too well-informed about public affairs. Nevertheless, although he may not be an A or B or even a C student in public affairs, he may have sufficient judgment to know which party and leaders to trust and sufficient sense to defend his own interests, particularly when things are not going too well. It should be clear that the individual does not operate in the political and social system as an isolated citizen upon whom total responsibility devolves. He normally lives in a pluralistic community and functions through many groups: family, church, trade union, political party, civic and fraternal organizations. Such groups may increase his information and sharpen his intelligence. Even a relatively uninformed and politically ignorant individual may contribute his little stock of information and intelligence, via his group, to the formation of public policy.

Civic or public spirit. This means "a certain amount of group feeling, of loyalty to the whole and its ideals." It implies concern for the public welfare or interest, as distinct from selfish individual or group interest. It also denotes tolerance, moderation, and a willingness to reach reasonable compromises. Here too, it is most important that this spirit prevail in the electorate as a whole, and in the entire social and political system, rather than in each isolated individual. With the system taken as a whole, selfishness may be balanced by altruism. Either carried to an extreme might prove fatal. The democratic political and social system has room for both extremists and moderates. Individualism thus may balance collectivism; civic involvement—civic indifference; stability—flexibility; the spirit of progress—that of the status quo; and consensus may balance cleavage.

Agreement on fundamentals. This is the minimal consensus necessary to assure cohesion in the body politic. What are these fundamentals? Perhaps the most important is agreement on constitutional government, that is, government according to certain orderly and fair rules of the game, government effectively restrained in the exercise of its power, and limited in its scope. Included in this concept is the agreement to use ballots instead of bullets to resolve disputes. Constitutional government embraces agreement on peaceful, orderly change. Also involved is respect for basic rights, which permit today's minority to become tomorrow's majority.

There need not be agreement, it should be emphasized, on *all* fundamentals. People may still differ on such matters as religion, politics, economics, education, art, prohibition, monogamy, birth control, to mention a few areas of disagreement. It is only necessary that there be enough agreement on enough (minimal) fundamentals so that state and society have sufficient consensus and strength to perform their functions. Protestant may disagree fundamentally with Catholic, Democrat with Republican, capitalist with socialist, advocates of progressive education with adherents of traditional education, admirers of Beethoven with devotees of jazz, segregationists with integrationists. Yet, as long as there is sufficient consensus on the fundamentals of popular government —majority rule, the agreement to disagree peacefully, freedom of speech, press, assembly, and religion—a democratic society can be held together to accomplish its purposes.

"The successful operation of democracy depends upon a reasonable degree of international order and security." Democracy and total war are not fundamentally compatible. Democracy requires sufficient stability to permit its processes to operate and its principles to be maintained. It is extremely difficult, for example, to maintain civil liberties and democratically limited government, unimpaired, in a period of war or crisis. This is true for functioning democracies, but it is even truer for governments that lack the experience of the more mature democratic nations like the United States or Britain.

A minimum level of economic and social well-being. Without this, man—let alone democratic man—cannot rise above the level of brute existence and sheer animal survival. Although a high standard of living (along with a high literacy rate) may not automatically establish and maintain democracy, a depressed standard of living makes democracy impossible. As with literacy, the precise level cannot be ascertained, and will undoubtedly vary from country to country. The determination of that level and the ways to accomplish it will certainly help, although it cannot assure, the achievement of democracy.

The prerequisites for democracy are, then, to be viewed not solely in terms of the individual alone, but also in terms of the individual as a member of a pluralistic society and as one component within a complex and balanced social, economic, and political system.

Knowledge of the basic prerequisites for successful democracy also makes clear that its feasibility in many areas of the world, inside and outside the western world, cannot be taken for granted. Brought into focus, as well, is the importance for many countries (lacking democratic prerequisites but desiring to move in the direction of liberal democracy) of a transition period from their present status to more mature democracy. This is of special significance for the undeveloped areas of the world in Asia and Africa.

If the universal feasibility of western democracy is not readily apparent, what of its desirability and attractiveness for modern men and nations? Relating this to the preoccupation of leaders in the western world with a successful foreign policy, to what extent will its positive qualities win friends for the democratic nations of the world?

Western Democracy and the Ideological Battle for the Minds of Men

"Positions on the Problem" may now be discussed to better advantage. The twentieth century debate over the merits and prospects of western democracy in the modern world, treated in the next section too, will center on the extent to which the promise and performance of western democracy enhance the understanding and conditions making for a more genuinely free, peaceful, and creative world. The issues are set forth in the following questions: Is western democracy desirable and feasible everywhere in the modern world? Or is it a false front for an oppressive and dying capitalism and imperialism? Can only a western democracy that practices what it preaches win the ideological battle for the minds of modern men?

POSITIONS
ON THE PROBLEM

1. WESTERN DEMOCRACY IS DESIRABLE AND FEASIBLE

(In the major portion of this position, the present authors have paraphrased the arguments, relating to the desirability of democracy, presented by such democratic theorists as Barker, Lindsay, MacIver, Pennock, and Spitz. The position reflects the rationale of advocates of democracy as defended and practiced in the United States, Great Britain, in most nations of Western Europe, and in most other members of the British Commonwealth.[13] There is considerably less agreement among democratic theorists on the question of the feasibility of democracy.)

[13] Quotations from these sources will be identified in subsequent footnotes. See the Select Bibliography for more information about the democratic theorists just mentioned.

Democracy Is Desirable: Positive Arguments

Belief in the dignity and value of man. Democracy is desirable because it is firmly rooted in a belief in the dignity and sacredness of the individual soul, personality, or being. According to one religious interpretation, man is precious because he is God's creation, a manifestation of His love. Hence, man must be treated with God-like love and consideration.

Immanuel Kant, the great German philosopher, worked out a rule which expresses this point in the form of a moral imperative: "So act as to treat humanity, both in your own person and in that of others, as an end in itself, and never as a means only." Man, in other words, is not to be "used" as a slave, tool, or machine; nor is he to be viewed as a mechanistic means to an end; rather, he is to be seen as an end in himself, a moral being with the right and capacity to worship God or develop his personality.

Fullest possible flowering of the individual person. Democracy is also desirable because it is committed to the fullest and freest possible development of each man's unique, good, and creative potentialities. From one religious point of view, it might be argued, this is the meaning of the worship of God: the effort to live a godly life and to develop God-given talents.

It is interesting to note the agreement here, as with the dignity and value of man, of the varying democratic schools of thought. John Stuart Mill, who did not belong to the Lockian-Jeffersonian natural-law school, stated the central principle underlying his magnificent defense of liberty, in his essay *On Liberty,* as follows: "The grand leading principle toward which every argument unfolded in these pages directly converges is the absolute and essential importance of human development in its richest diversity."

Liberty, equality, fraternity. Democracy is desirable because it recognizes that the flowering of the individual personality requires liberty, equality, and fraternity. The liberty that includes protection and enjoyment of basic human rights, and the greatest intellectual, religious, political, social, and economic "elbow room" for human development constitutes a basis for democracy.

Personality development also demands equality: before God and the law; equality of consideration and opportunity in society. That keen, early observer of *Democracy in America,* the French writer Alexis de Tocqueville, perceived the equalitarian strain in democratic theory and was frankly fearful that it might be carried too far. Democratic theory does not postulate its being carried to an extreme; nor need it lead, as de Tocqueville thought, to either anarchy or servitude, or to an impossible quest for perfection.

Also called for is fraternity: a sense of fellowship, mutual respect, and co-operative unity. Democracy rests upon the spirit of fraternity.

Justice. Democracy is desirable because it is based firmly on the concept of justice: a harmonizing of the sometimes conflicting claims of liberty, equality, and fraternity in accord with the central democratic ideal of maximum human development. Hence, de Tocqueville's legitimate fears might have been eased had he more fully appreciated the relationship of democracy and justice, which has been neatly summed up in the following adage: "Man's capacity for justice makes democracy possible, but man's inclination to injustice makes democracy necessary."

Government, state, and society. Democracy is desirable because it is founded on a realistic view of the nature of the state and government. The state is necessary for executing certain functions of a public and compulsory character, for example, the maintenance of law and order. Need for the latter arises out of the public's requirements for protection of life, liberty, and property. The content of the law and order is determined by the government operating the state, but it is a government deriving its powers from the people's consent and it is dedicated to the principles of individual dignity and development, liberty, equality, fraternity, and justice just discussed.

Governments may come and go according to our will, expressed in free elections and through our representative institutions. The state remains, but it is not the whole of life. It is only a part, though an important part, of society, along with other vital parts (like the church, most economic enterprises, trade unions, and social organizations) which, however, are private and voluntary in nature. The democratic state is desirable because it recognizes the essential distinction between state and society and does not dominate or "take over" the other aspects of social life.

Democratic theory, unlike communist theory, does not view the state as a vicious instrument for the oppression of the working class, or a necessary tool with which the working masses will destroy the bourgeois capitalists, or a coercive organ which will wither away when the classless communist society has been achieved. Rather, democratic theory holds that the state can serve to channel class and interest struggle peacefully, compromise differences, reconcile competing claims, and harmonize conflicting forces. As James Madison expressed it in No. 10 *Federalist:* "The regulation of these various and interfering interests forms the principal task of modern legislation, and involves the spirit of party and faction in the necessary and ordinary operations of the government."

Thus, democracy is desirable because it is pledged to peaceful, orderly, rational, humane methods for putting governments in power, obtaining a change of governments, and reconciling conflicts of public policy within and outside government.

A societal way of life. Democracy is desirable because it creates a general societal environment, not only in government but in industry, education, and other fields, which facilitates each person's development according to the best of his abilities. It cannot and perhaps should not prevail in all aspects of life. Yet, its total environmental effect may serve everywhere to dull the edge of brutal, arbitrary, and authoritarian power and to encourage respect for personality.

International harmony. Finally, democracy is desirable because it is a tolerant and peaceful ideology which respects individual, group, and national differences and repudiates the idea of imposing its own values or will upon other peoples and nations. The impact of democratic ideology upon the foreign-policy principles of the democratic nations of the free world is unmistakable. In a speech on April 16, 1953, President Eisenhower enunciated the principles that guide the United States and its "valued friends, the other free nations": [14]

First: No people on earth can be held, as a people, to be an enemy, for all humanity shares the common hunger for peace and fellowship and justice.

Second: No nation's security and well-being can be lastingly achieved in isolation but only in effective cooperation with fellow-nations.

Third: Any nation's right to form a government and an economic system of its own choosing is *inalienable*.

Fourth: Any nation's attempt to dictate to other nations their form of government is *indefensible*.

And fifth: A nation's hope of lasting peace cannot be firmly based upon any race in armaments but rather upon just relations and honest understanding with all other nations.

Democracy Is Desirable: Some Negative Arguments

Democracy is preferable as a theory not only on its own merits but also because other ideologies have proved to be much worse in theory and practice. For example, all antidemocratic theories are to be distrusted. We must reject the argument of those who contend that all will be well, if only we give power to the right man, the right class, or the right principle.

Believers in democracy (who may themselves seek the truth) are highly suspicious of those who claim that they have *the truth* and, therefore, the right to impose it, by brute force or calculated deceit if necessary, upon people unwilling to accept this alleged version. Democrats rightfully distrust authoritarian power. They are heedful of Lord Acton's famous aphorism: Power corrupts; and absolute power corrupts absolutely. Proponents of democratic theory want power to be exercised within wise limits. Even then, they feel, government should be conducted according to known and fair rules of the game, with ample opportunity for power to check and balance power.

[14] *New York Times*, April 17, 1953, p. 4.

The "right" men, all too often, have proved to be the wrong men: cruel, ruthless, inhuman! Sometimes they have been mad—for how else explain Adolf Hitler's systematic dissemination of false propaganda to poison his own people, his barbaric extermination of the Jews, his deliberate unleashing of World War II? Hitler was emphatically not the right man, backed by the right class (the Nazis), acting according to the right principle (Nazism).

Other examples abound. Was Stalin the right man, backed by the right class (the communists), acting according to the right principle (communism)? Here was another carefully planned effort to destroy all opponents of the principle, the class, and the man. First, the industrial capitalists were "liquidated." Next came Stalin's own communist opponents on the left, men like Trotsky and others! Then the *kulaks* (relatively well-to-do farmers or peasants) were "collectivized"; in actuality, they were physically maltreated, starved to death, sent to Siberia, or forced into collective farms. Still later, in the 1930's, Comrade Stalin's communist opponents on the right—men like Zinoviev and Kamenev— were "purged." Today, even Stalin has been repudiated, in part, at least, by the present rulers of Russia. So, the communist authoritarian doctrine runs its course!

Mussolini was another "right man." Was Italian fascism "right" because it was more efficient than democracy, stronger, able to achieve a greater unity? The factual record does not support these claims. Yet, even if the facts did back them up, the advocate of democracy would have to reject such an authoritarian political doctrine. The price that has to be paid is too high: loss of liberty, equality, fraternity, justice; corrosion of the soul; corruption of civic virtue; and, in the end (as in Italy and Germany), death and destruction.

The same story could be told for other strong "right" men, "right" classes, and "right" principles.

Democracy Is Desirable: Qualifications and Rebuttal

Supporters of certain aristocratic doctrines attack democracy because it is so far from their ideal of rule by biological, racial, or natural aristocrats. Advocates of authoritarian doctrines reject it, as we have already seen, because democracy repudiates the rule of the right man, class, or principle. Other critics of democracy contend that it is impossible because might and not right must prevail, or because the few rather than the many must rule. Communists denounce it as an ideological smoke screen for an evil capitalism. Defenders of democracy make the following points in reply.

1. Democracy does not claim to be perfect. It is a type of government or way of life for this world, not for heaven, capable of achieving a reasonably decent ordering of life, not Utopia. It holds forth no images of

paradise because its view of man, groups, state, and society is more realistic than the antidemocratic views of certain alleged aristocrats or authoritarians. Democracy does not pretend that all men are angels (certainly not rulers), or that men can become angels if the right doctrines prevail. Perfection is not to be found in this world. Humans are an amalgam of good and evil, intelligence and ignorance, will and apathy. They do, however, have sufficient virtue, sense, and drive to be able to operate a democratic system. Democracy, then, does not claim to be immune to error or sin, but it points to self-correcting mechanisms which permit it to redress grievances, correct mistakes, and repair evils.

2. Democracy does not assume that the people rule directly, or that every citizen must be interested, intelligent, and informed enough to be able to make public policy. Democracy accepts the concept of representative government. Democrats recognize that many decision-making centers exist in a democracy in addition to the individual: the trade union, corporation, political party, not to mention the government itself. Democracy does not rule out democratic leadership, permitting an able minority to shape policies for public approval. Nor does it exclude a party system, which may select and advance issues to be decided in popular elections. This also holds for prescriptive constitutional features, such as opportunity for full debate and due process of law, which enable a democracy to use time-tested techniques to reach reasonably fair decisions.

3. Democracy does not contend that all majority decisions are wholly just, wise, and sound. It does hold that they will be reasonably so, and certainly that they will be more just, wiser, and more sound, on the whole and in the long run, than the decisions reached by biological, racial, natural, or authoritarian elites.

4. Democracy does not maintain that government without leaders is possible; on the contrary, the state needs leaders and experts, it needs a ruling class. The leaders, however, are not necessarily undemocratic, irresponsible, power-hungry conspirators. Nor does democracy believe that the experts or insiders will inevitably dominate the scene. It is pointed out that experts should and can be *on tap*, but *not on top*. By the same token, democracy asserts, the ruling class does not remain the same, immobile, permanent, and antidemocratic. The ruling class in a democracy is dynamic, fluid, constantly changing, and has proved responsible and responsive to popular control.

5. Democracy is not, as the communists claim, an ideological smoke screen to conceal the alleged evil consequences of capitalism. Workers may have been exploited in the past, but increasingly they have been able to lessen or end their exploitation in the liberal democracies of the western world by means of the collective-bargaining strength of their trade union movement and their political strength within the framework of the democratic state. The worker's lot, certainly in the most advanced

capitalistic countries (like the democratic United States), has been getting not worse but better. His real wages have increased; his standard of living has gone up. Over and above the right to organize and bargain collectively, he has obtained the protection of wage-hour laws, unemployment compensation, old-age and survivors insurance, among others. Some economists attribute the undeniable improvement in the condition of the laboring man primarily to the higher industrial productivity of a capitalistic economy functioning within the framework of a democratic state. Capitalism in democratic countries like the United States has more and more proved to be a servant, not the master, of a democratic people and nation. Democratic nations have frequently been able to minimize the effects of depression by way of government measures. Capitalism itself has shown an adaptability and creativity which is perhaps one of the most significant facts of the twentieth century. In countries like the United States, for example, it has accepted, sometimes reluctantly it is true, governmental reforms protecting the workingman, dividing national wealth more equitably (the progressive income tax), promoting the general welfare (expenditures in the fields of housing, health, and education), and safeguarding the capitalistic and competitive system itself (the Sherman Anti-Trust Act, Interstate Commerce Commission Act, Securities and Exchange Act, Federal Reserve Act). Though on a limited scale, it has also advanced its own measures to provide security and stability for its working force by way of pension, health, recreational, and unemployment compensation programs.

Thus, most arguments of antidemocratic thought cannot be maintained in theory or fact against the concept of democracy, realistically understood.

Democracy Is Feasible: Eventual Universal Triumph

So far it has been argued that democracy is desirable because it maximizes man's opportunity to develop the best in himself and minimizes the danger of the ever present forces that would destroy, enslave, curtail, or blunt this development. But is democracy feasible? Where and when?

In his study of the merits and prospects of liberal democracy, J. Roland Pennock stated his view, in connection with the two key nations in the democratic West: [15]

Our conclusion is that the essential elements of liberal democracy are still sound—sound as the human nature on which they are based; that its specific political institutions are practicable today and can be kept so with no more than the kind of continual modification that has been taking place to date, without departure from the fundamentals; and that there is a good prospect, at least as far as concerns Great Britain and the United States, that evolution will in fact continue in the liberal mold.

[15] *Op. cit.*, p. 367.

Believers in democracy must, of course, have the courage of their convictions. They must also affirm the feasibility of democracy through the world; in doing so they are not, as some argue, ignoring the realities of the world picture which presumably give the impression that too many countries lack the prerequisites for making democracy operable. That democracy may not triumph tomorrow or the day after does not refute the conclusion that its irresistible appeal makes its victory inevitable, sooner or later.

The appeal, vitality, and success of the basic principles of democracy in such countries as India, the Philippines, and Israel hold good promise for the democratic future of formerly colonial areas of the world. The remarkable democratic regeneration of both West Germany and Japan arouses similar hopes for the once totalitarian and militaristic nations. The overthrow of Perón in Argentina and the steady, if slow, progress of many Latin American countries toward a mature democracy are further proof of the feasibility of democracy. Nor should the appeal of democracy to the oppressed peoples within the communist orbit be overlooked.

Mature, stable democracy may not emerge overnight all over the world, but progress toward this goal is unmistakable.

The inevitable triumph of democracy is quite clearly connected with its ability to promote the understanding and conditions making for a genuinely free, peaceful, and creative world. This explains its desirability and attractiveness for modern men and nations, in general, and the great appeal of the United States, in particular.

In the eyes of most peoples of the world, democratic America stands for freedom and a high level of well-being, the goals toward which people everywhere strive. Democratic theory has a fundamental appeal and, sooner or later, must be universally successful, for it has reconciled the demands of the world's people and nations for individual liberty and national strength, for national freedom and international order and peace, for a generous measure of local self-government and necessary central planning and power. Democracy has been able to adhere to the cause of freedom while still championing the people's legitimate demands for an end to hunger, unemployment, depressed living standards, illiteracy, disease, and other human wrongs—in a word, for a decent standard of living as a material basis for the good ethical and cultural life.

There are, of course, barriers to the triumph of western democracy. Successful communication is still blocked by Iron and Bamboo Curtains, false Soviet propaganda, the heritage of antiwesternism and anticolonialism, suspicion of western motives in maintaining military strength against the threat of aggression, envy of western wealth and power. These should not be underestimated.

Nevertheless, liberal democracy will win the ideological battle for the minds of men because it is firmly committed to the right of people to rule themselves, and to achieve the dignity and free development that are due all men under God.

2. WESTERN DEMOCRACY IS A FALSE FRONT FOR AN OPPRESSIVE AND DYING CAPITALISM AND IMPERIALISM

(The following position, prepared by the authors of this book, draws upon the arguments of such Communist leaders as Lenin, Stalin, and Khrushchev.[16])

Introduction

No one should be fooled by liberal democratic talk of liberty, equality, fraternity, and justice, or deceived by western democratic talk of the full flowering of the individual. "Liberal democracy" or "western democracy" is still bourgeois or capitalist democracy, and consequently is a false front for capitalist exploitation of the masses at home and imperialist exploitation of "backward" peoples abroad. Democracy in the noncommunist world should be viewed, then, as a slave of capitalism. At its best it can provide freedom only for the bourgeoisie: the exploiters, the rich, the few. Real freedom is still denied the bulk of the people: the proletariat, the working masses.

Because the consciousness of the bourgeois democrat is molded by the oppressive system of capitalism, he cannot understand the lot of the working masses, their exploitation and their misery. He cannot sympathize with their revolutionary demand for freedom and therefore cannot comprehend the colonial revolt of oppressed peoples or the coming victory of communism in the western world. He simply cannot perceive that the liberal democratic ideology rationalizes wage slavery at home and imperialistic slavery abroad, foments revolution and war, and threatens the whole world with fear and destruction. Such an ideology can never appeal to the peoples of the world. It will inevitably lose the battle for the minds of men to communism, which represents the goal of historical development.

Attack on Western Liberal Democracy at Home: Oppression of the Many by the Few

Liberal or western democracy (another name for bourgeois or capitalist democracy), then, is an ideology that justifies an infamous capitalist system. It must never be forgotten that the democratic state is still the oppressive capitalist state. As Lenin put it: "Democracy is but one form of *state*, whereas we Marxists are opposed to *all and every kind of*

---

[16] Quotations from communist sources will be identified in subsequent footnotes.

state." [17] Why? Because the state "represents the organized systematic application of force against persons." [18] Democracy is no exception: "Democracy is a *state* which recognizes the subordination of the minority to the majority, i.e., an organization for the systematic use of *violence* by one class against the other, by one section of the population against another." [19]

In this connection, there should be no illusions about the seemingly greater freedom in a bourgeois democracy.

The most democratic bourgeois republic was never, nor could it be anything else than a machine with which capital suppressed the toilers, an instrument of the political rule of capital, of the dictatorship of the bourgeoisie. The democratic bourgeois republic promised the rule of the majority, it proclaimed the rule of the majority, but it could never put this into effect as long as the private ownership of the land and other means of production existed.[20]

In capitalist society, under conditions most favorable to its development, we have more or less complete democracy in the democratic republic. But this democracy is always restricted by the narrow framework of capitalist exploitation and consequently remains, in reality, a democracy for the minority, only for the possessing classes, only for the rich. Freedom in capitalist society always remains about the same as it was in the ancient Greek republics: freedom for the slave-owners. Owing to the conditions of capitalist exploitation, the modern wage-slaves are also so crushed by want and poverty that "they cannot be bothered with democracy," "they cannot be bothered with politics"; in the ordinary peaceful course of events the majority of the population is debarred from participating in social and political life.[21]

Similarly, one should never for a moment be deceived by the "formal equality" which seemingly prevails in the bourgeois democracy: "the formal recognition of the equality of all citizens, the equal right of all to determine the structure and administration of the state." [22] The equality is a sham. As Lenin pointed out: [23]

---

[17] V. I. Lenin, "The Tasks of the Proletariat in Our Revolution" (1917), *Selected Works* (New York, International Publishers, 1938), Vol. VI, p. 73. A slightly different translation appears in Emile Burns, *A Handbook of Marxism* (London, Victor Gollancz, 1935), p. 788. This handbook is a ready reference for Marxist literature in the communist tradition, although its emphasis on the economic aspects is rather heavy. The quotation cited may also be found in Dept. of State, *Soviet World Outlook,* 1954, p. 103. This work, a handy collection of pertinent extracts analytically arranged, was prepared by the Division of Research for U.S.S.R. and Eastern Europe, Office of Intelligence Research, Department of State, for the Coordinator of Psychological Intelligence, U.S. Information Agency. Reference to quotations from this volume will simply be cited as *Soviet World Outlook.*

[18] "The State and Revolution" (1917), *Selected Works,* Vol. VII, p. 91.

[19] *Ibid.,* p. 75.

[20] V. I. Lenin, "The Third International and Its Place in History," *Selected Works,* Vol. X, pp. 35–36. See also *Soviet World Outlook,* p. 108.

[21] V. I. Lenin, "The State and Revolution," *Selected Works, op. cit.,* p. 79.

[22] *Ibid.,* p. 91.

[23] *Ibid.,* p. 80.

Democracy for an insignificant minority, democracy for the rich—that is the democracy of capitalist society. If we look more closely into the mechanism of capitalist democracy, everywhere . . . on all sides we see restriction after restriction upon democracy. These restrictions, exceptions, exclusions, obstacles for the poor, seem slight . . . but in their sum total these restrictions exclude and squeeze out the poor from politics and from an active share in democracy.

Lenin castigated as false the claim by liberal or western democracy of being based on the consent of the governed. He said: [24]

To decide once every few years which members of the ruling class is to misrepresent the people in parliament is the real essence of bourgeois parliamentarism, not only in parliamentary-constitutional monarchies, but also in the most democratic republics.

"The Programme of the Communist Internationale," in 1928, also unmasked the hypocritical nature of bourgeois equality and freedom, as follows: [25]

Bourgeois-democracy, with its formal equality of all citizens before the law, is in reality based on a glaring material and economic inequality of classes. By leaving inviolable, defending and strengthening the monopoly of the capitalist and land-lord classes in the vital means of production, bourgeois-democracy, as far as the exploited classes (especially the proletariat) is concerned, converts this formal equality before the law and these democratic rights and liberties— which in practice are curtailed systematically, into a juridical fiction and, consequently, into a means for deceiving and enslaving the masses. Being the expression of the political domination of the bourgeoisie, so-called democracy is therefore capitalist-democracy.

In an appraisal of western democracy, therefore, Lenin's words must constantly be kept in mind: [26] "We are in favor of a democratic republic as the best form of the State for the proletariat under capitalism; but we have no right to forget that wage slavery is the lot of the people even in the most democratic bourgeois republic." One must never forget, Lenin argued, that in capitalist society we have a democracy that is curtailed, wretched, false; a democracy for the rich, for the minority.

Hence, it can be clearly seen that democracy's claim to merits at home are false. Its falseness has been demonstrated not only in theory but also in its loss of strength in the western world which it once dominated. It has been yielding ground to the more truthful and attractive appeal of socialism and communism. The old confidence in it has diminished even in such liberal democratic countries as the United States, and even more clearly in Britain and France. Its losing battle for the minds of men in the western world is strikingly revealed, for example, in the large communist following in such countries as France and Italy, where one out of every three or four persons votes the Communist ticket. The success of

[24] *Ibid.*, p. 45.
[25] Burns, *op. cit.*, p. 993.
[26] "The State and Revolution," *Selected Works, op. cit.*, p. 19.

the peoples' democracies in central or southeastern European countries like Czechoslovakia is further proof of the superior appeal of communist ideology.

Attack on Liberal Democracy Abroad: Imperialism

Liberal (or bourgeois or capitalist) democracy is not only false in theory and dying in practice at home. It has also enslaved peoples in other lands, in the colonial or once colonial areas of the world. It has, furthermore, produced both slavery and war throughout the world.

Lenin pointed this out vigorously in his *Imperialism: The Highest Stage of Capitalism,* which was published in 1916. He declared: [27]

Capitalism has grown into a world system of colonial oppression and of the financial strangulation of the overwhelming majority of the people of the world by a handful of "advanced" countries. [This meant, Lenin indicated, the oppression of] a *thousand million* people (in the colonies and semi-colonies), that is, more than half the population of the globe. . . .

Here, then, in the imperialist manifestation of capitalism and the bourgeois democratic state, the hypocrisy and viciousness of the bourgeois democracy of the West are revealed with unmistakable clarity.

As former Premier Bulganin said, in a report in 1955 to the Supreme Soviet of the U.S.S.R., western imperialism has meant, and still means in some countries, "severe colonial oppression," "domination," "a system of government based on violence, robbery and ruthless exploitation of the population. This system brings fabulous wealth to the colonizers but for the oppressed peoples of Asia and Africa it spells poverty and great suffering." [28]

By its colonial and imperialist fruits of exploitation, oppression, and enslavement can one best judge the merits of liberal or bourgeois democracy.

The "new" forms of colonial rule should also delude no one. Nikita S. Khrushchev declared, in this connection: [29]

Today the colonialists have decided to change the forms of their colonial rule. They use less and less crude forms of violence as the sending of their troops to colonial countries and other acts of rude intervention in the affairs of enslaved peoples.

They do all this more delicately now: they bribe people who are in power, implant "good governments" and build up aggressive blocks like the Baghdad pact.

They allot money for so-called "economic aid," give arms "free of charge" to some countries. But to pay for these arms the states getting them must provide cannon fodder to the colonialists and set up big armies, thereby wasting away their own peoples.

[27] *Imperialism* (1916) (New York, International Publishers, 1939), pp. 10–11.
[28] *Report to the Supreme Soviet on the Visit to India, Burma, and Afghanistan* (New York, New Century Publishers, 1956), p. 6.
[29] *Ibid.,* pp. 40–41.

The colonialists give a dollar as "aid" in order to get subsequently ten dollars for it by exploiting the peoples who accepted such "aid." Having achieved this end they enslave the peoples politically as well. Such are the "new" forms of colonialists' rule.

And this is the case not only in the countries of Asia, Africa or other so-called underdeveloped countries. The United States' monopolists are zealously introducing such forms of "aid" in European countries. Why, even NATO reeks strongly of the same smell.

Rightful revulsion against western colonialism and imperialism has already led many countries in Asia and Africa to burst the bonds of colonial slavery and imperialistic oppression. India, Burma, Vietnam, Indonesia, China, Korea, Egypt—these are some countries that have repudiated colonialism. Still other peoples in Asia and Africa continue the struggle for freedom against "democratic" Britain and "democratic" France.

The liberal or bourgeois democracy of the capitalist and imperialist West cannot succeed in winning the ideological battle for the minds of the peoples of Europe and Asia. These people look not to the West but to the Soviet Union. Did not the universally esteemed Prime Minister of India, Jawaharlal Nehru, declare: [30] ". . . The Soviet revolution has advanced human society by a great leap and lighted a bright flame which could not be smothered. It laid the foundations for that new civilization toward which the world would advance."

Unlike the bourgeois democracies of the West, the new Soviet civilization is devoted to peace. The so-called democratic nations of the West make a great to-do about their peaceful intentions, but their actions in World War I, World War II, and today belie their peaceful professions. Lenin long ago pointed out the connection between capitalism and imperialism, and imperialism and war. Yet the capitalist democracies become terribly irritated when the truth about such matters is told. Khrushchev said, in a speech at Rangoon, on December 1, 1955: [31]

The history of the prewar years explicitly shows that the Western Powers were making one concession after another to Hitler, nudging him on toward the East, against our country. But it so happened that the very one whom Britain, France and the United States reared as their watchdog [Nazi Germany] to be set against the USSR broke loose and attacked those who fed him.

In this connection the question arises whether there is not a certain analogy with the prewar period if we examine the measures taken with regard to present day Western Germany. Are not the same methods being used now by the very same countries in an attempt to push Western Germany on the road of aggression and new adventures?

These considerations make clear why the peoples of the world distrust the West and are skeptical of the peaceful professions of the western de-

[30] Quoted in *ibid.,* p. 34.
[31] *Ibid.,* p. 21.

mocracies, which have demonstrated their reliance on the ways of war, not on the ways of peace. Their refusal to disarm, to ban the use of the atomic bomb, and to abandon world-wide military bases and alliances indicate the shallowness of their peaceful pretensions.

Conclusion

In view of the falsity of western democracy in its own home, and in light of the evil imperialistic record of these bourgeois-democratic nations in the underdeveloped areas of the world, the merits of liberal democracy must be denied. Therefore, the world-wide prospects of western liberal democracy are hopeless.

3. Only a Western Democracy Practicing What It Preaches Can Win the Battle for the Minds of Men

(The following critique of western democracy has been written by the present authors. The position incorporates the frequently expressed views of Jawaharlal Nehru, Prime Minister of India, as well as others like Mr. Nehru who are friendly to the ideals of liberal democracy but critical of the colonial and foreign policies of the western democracies.[32])

Introduction

Sometimes, certain advocates of western democracy forget that the keenest critics may be democracy's best friends. The following criticism admittedly embodies a nonwestern orientation. It will condemn the past failures and many present policies of the western democratic nations in the underdeveloped areas of the world. Yet its anticolonial bent derives fundamentally from a prodemocratic ideology. The criticism is adverse because, both at home and abroad, the western democracies fail to live up to their own democratic ideals. The failures call into question the genuine merits of western democracy in the minds of people favorably disposed to its theory, and they also raise grave doubts among all thinking people as to the immediate and long-range prospects of western democracy.

The failure of western democratic nations to live up to their own ideas, at home and particularly abroad, is one major adverse criticism. Another is the narrowness of outlook of many western democrats, particularly those who tend to identify democracy with capitalism or with the American way of life. They are the ones who frequently condemn deviation from capitalism or the American way of life as undemocratic. Such people do western democracy a disservice; the very effectiveness of democracy is lessened in the minds of those who, for example, refuse to believe that the American political, economic, and social system can be transposed—

[32] Identification of specific quotations will be found in subsequent footnotes.

lock, stock, and barrel—to all areas of the globe. In part, this narrowness is responsible for the failure of traditional democratic ideology to provide a theory of transition which might serve the underdeveloped areas of the world. The absence of this theory and the great gulf between the under-developed lands and such mature democracies as the United States lead many former colonial peoples to view, more favorably, certain aspects of communist theory and certain achievements of the Soviet Union. In communist ideology, at least there is a theory of transition by stages from a rather primitive, agricultural, oppressed society to an advanced, industrial, free society. The Soviet Union, to many in the underdeveloped areas of the world, is a living illustration of the speed with which such a transition can be made.

Western democratic theory, therefore, needs re-examination; to win the ideological battle, the liberal democratic nations must review their policies in the light of their own principles. The review may indicate that they must live up to their own professed ideals everywhere in the world, if they are to win friends and influence people everywhere. It is especially important that they abandon practices of colonialism and domination, of racial superiority and selfish national interest, of military armament and alliances, if they are successfully to convince the peoples of the world of their dedication to a truly free, peaceful, and creative world.

The Anticolonial Attack in the Name of Democracy

Initially, it might be helpful to examine the view of democracy held by some leadership groups in Asia and Africa. To a certain extent, Nehru again may be considered representative of these groups.

Mr. Nehru's position is remarkably similar to the western democratic view, and so is his justification of it. Thus, Mr. Nehru has declared: [33]

We have placed in the forefront of our constitution those fundamental human rights to which all men who love liberty aspire—the freedom of the individual, the equality of men, and the rule of law. We enter, therefore, the community of free nations with the roots of democracy deeply embedded in our institutions as well as in the thoughts of our people.

And again: "A democratic government, in the ultimate analysis, functions largely, of course, with the good will of the people and with their co-operation." [34]

At another time he put it this way: [35]

[33] Jawaharlal Nehru, *Visit to America* (New York, copyright, 1950, by The John Day Company), pp. 6–7.
[34] *Ibid.*, p. 95.
[35] *Talks with Nehru*, by Jawaharlal Nehru and Norman Cousins (published by The John Day Company, New York; copyright, 1951, by Saturday Review Associates, Inc.), p. 19.

It [democracy] involves equality of opportunity to all people, as far as possible, in the political and economic domain. It involves the freedom of the individual to grow and to make the best of his capacities and ability. It involves a certain tolerance of others and even of others' opinions when they differ from yours.

Space does not permit a fuller development of Nehru's own view of democracy. Recognition of his commitment to the principles and central ideal of western democracy is necessary, however, to appreciate the fact that he is criticizing western democracy from "within," not from "without"; not as an enemy, not as a communist, but as a democrat in the western democratic tradition.

To understand Mr. Nehru's criticism, however, one must also appreciate that his view of democracy strongly emphasizes *economic* freedom and equality. Again and again Nehru has emphasized this point: [36] "We believe passionately in the democratic method and we seek to enlarge the bounds of democracy both on the political and the economic plane, for no democracy can exist for long in the midst of want and poverty and inequality."

This ties in with the opposition to anticolonialism precisely because the colonial powers were largely indifferent to the wants, poverty, and inequality of the colonial peoples. As recently as World War II, a colonial government—unlike a government responsible to the Indian people—might afford to see a people starving and dying of famine. Of this, Nehru has written: [37]

Three million people died in the province of Bengal [during the 1944 famine in India] through sheer starvation. That famine took place because of many underlying reasons and causes, but it was directly related to the war in the sense that India's resources were thrown into the war, without thought of how that would affect the masses generally. They were deprived of their necessaries, deprived of their food; and suddenly they had nothing. There was a bad harvest, and there were no resources left, and they died like flies.

Such maltreatment of a people, Mr. Nehru argues, could not have taken place if the government of India had then been a democratic government, responsive to the people and their needs.

Thus, political freedom and equality are inextricably woven together with economic freedom and equality. When this democratic pattern is violated, it reflects poorly on the colonial powers involved, especially when the colonial powers profess to adhere to a democratic ideology!

Nehru wrote of this as follows: [38] "We were fighting for political freedom. That was a primary urge—the nationalist urge for political freedom. But always, right from the beginning, this political freedom was asso-

[36] *Visit to America, loc. cit.,* p. 31.
[37] *Ibid.,* p. 103.
[38] *Ibid.,* pp. 96–97.

ciated in our minds with economic and social progress and freedom."

This concept of democracy had earlier been taught by Gandhi, who had written: [39] "Independence has no meaning unless you raise the masses of India, unless you raise the underprivileged, unless you give them the necessaries of life—food, clothing, shelter, education."

Nehru himself has put the idea this way: [40]

Mahatma Gandhi taught us to view our national struggle always in terms of the underprivileged and those to whom opportunity had been denied. Therefore there was always an economic facet to our political struggle for freedom. We realized that there was no real freedom for those who suffered continually from want, and because in India there were millions who lacked the barest necessaries of existence, we thought of freedom in terms of raising and bettering the lot of these peoples. Having achieved political freedom, it is our passionate desire to serve our people in this way and to remove the many burdens they have carried from generations past.

In the light of this perspective of democracy, it is easier to see why the democracies of Western Europe have been bitterly denounced for their colonial policies. Colonialism is doubly condemned: first, because it denies political and economic freedom and equality to the colonial peoples; second, because it repudiates the professed democratic ideals of countries, like Britain and France, which have been the great colonial powers.

Critics of western colonialism in Asia and Africa are not the only ones to make this point. It is also recognized in a special article written for the popular American magazine *Newsweek:* [41]

If Communism is an evil symbol to an internationally minded American, the West is a traditionally evil symbol to a nationally minded Indian. In Nehru's India, as in Sukarno's Indonesia or U Nu's Burma, the West means a colonialism which exploited Asia before it conferred benefits on it, which taught the theoretical ideas of political liberty while keeping millions of Asians practically subject. And Americans—whatever their protests—are lumped in the minds of most Asians with European colonial powers as "The West"!

The same article emphasizes that the colonial revolt is to a large extent based on western democratic principles and designed to advance those objectives: [42]

Nehru and the other Asian leaders have not rejected Western democratic thinking. On the contrary, they have accepted it. In hundreds of political prisons, the young intellectual leaders of the new Asia long studied Europe's ideas and took them to their logical conclusion. The struggle of the French Revolution became a sanction for driving the French out of Indo-China. The free inquiry of the University of Leiden nurtured the spirit that drove the Dutch out of In-

---

[39] Quoted in *ibid.,* p. 158.
[40] *Ibid.,* p. 121.
[41] *Newsweek,* March 12, 1956, p. 55.
[42] *Ibid.,* pp. 55–56.

donesia. The British theory of constitutional liberty became the club with which Indians beat their embarrassed tutors, and no one so vigorously or so long as the profoundly Western-minded Indian named Jawaharlal Nehru.

Importance of Speed; Distrust of Western Foreign Policy

India, like many underdeveloped countries—both those which have gained their independence and those which are still struggling for it—is in a hurry. And justifiably so! Kept behind by colonial domination, the underdeveloped countries must make gigantic progress before they can catch up with the rest of the world. Unfortunately, the nations of the western world, the once dominant colonial nations, are unwilling or unable to move with the speed required. They are not always willing to grant independence rapidly enough to lands still struggling for political freedom in the name of western democratic ideals. They seem unable to appreciate that the peoples of Asia and Africa are trying to accomplish in a few years what it took nations in the western world over a century to achieve. The underdeveloped countries seek results, and naturally they are impressed by the successes of the Soviet Union, even though they may oppose the coercive means of communism.

On this subject, Nehru has written: ". . . It is important for the whole world that our country should succeed in the democratic way;" "but we must hurry." [43] A development officer in a continent-wide program for agricultural reform in India also emphasized the need for speed, and stated the reason thus: [44] "My immediate fight is with poverty and apathy. My rivals are the Chinese—not the rich. We shall have failed, if we do not prove that we can accomplish more by democratic persuasion than the Communists by coercion."

One difficulty is that western advocates of democracy may not appreciate sufficiently the greater need for government intervention to accomplish the economic reforms called for in the underdeveloped countries of the world. Rigid adherence to capitalist principles, which may have been relevant to nineteenth century western Europe and America, may not suit the countries of Asia and Africa. And to identify democracy with capitalism, or to lump democratic socialism (the announced policy of India, for example) with Soviet communism, is to compound the confusion. Capitalistic economics may have worked earlier for Britain and America, as "welfare capitalism" or "planned capitalism" may work well for both countries today. They may be entirely unfitted, for example, to India's state of economic development, her lack of private capital, her history and customs, her greater need for economic reform and social justice. Compared with, say, the United States, the "public sector" in India may necessarily comprise a larger part of the economy than the

---

[43] Quoted in *Visit to America, loc. cit.,* p. 53.
[44] Quoted in *ibid.,* p. 53.

"private sector." Mr. Nehru's frank dedication to a "socialist pattern of society" must be interpreted in the light of India's special problems. India is dedicated to socialist planning, but it is democratic planning, designed to advance the cardinal principles and central ideal of liberal democracy. This point must be thoroughly appreciated by the liberal democracies of the West—by all those who help shape policy in such countries—if they are to understand and win the support of the rising countries of Asia and Africa.

An additional and related point must also be understood. The appeal of the liberal democracies of the West will not be greatly advanced if economic aid from the West, however generous, is tied to the strings of military alliances and the continuation of the cold war. India, for example, welcomed former President Truman's Point Four Plan and all other generous American aid, as it has the comparable, British-sponsored Colombo Plan. Such programs indicate that the West is not completely unaware of the modern implications of the western democratic ideology. But India is wary of aid that would draw peaceful countries, like itself, into the voracious vortex of the cold war.

It is disturbing that many commentators on Indian criticism of the western democracies have not heeded what John Foster Dulles, U.S. Secretary of State, said in a broadcast on March 10, 1956, from New Delhi: [45]

Our two peoples both believe in the democratic principles of government, we both believe in the dignity of man and in his individual worth. And we both recognize that one of our great tasks today is to give each and every human being a better opportunity to grow in body, mind and spirit. We both recognize that war is a scourge and are dedicated to achieving peace in the world.

This is a fine statement of ideals which India and the United States share. Why cannot the United States and other western powers live up to these democratic ideals, particularly in their foreign policy? Why do the western powers not support, unequivocally, all colonial peoples who are struggling for freedom?

Conclusion

Most spokesmen for leading countries in the underdeveloped areas of the world do not repudiate the theory of western democracy. They accept its fundamentals, but they define it in terms of national independence for the colonial or former colonial areas of the world. They also think of democracy as serving their objective of ending economic bondage for their people, and as an opportunity to raise their standards of living. They resent and condemn the colonial practices of many western democratic nations. In their opinion, democracy must practice what it preaches.

[45] Information Service of India, Washington, D.C., *Indiagram*, No. 5, March 14, 1956, p. 1.

This may also mean that democracy must be brought up to date, to face the problems of a world moving toward democratic socialism. Only when this is done will democracy achieve a new and convincing appeal to the peoples of the world.

QUESTIONS

1. Explain and illustrate the character of the present ideological battle for the minds of men and the control of nations. How significant is it?

2. Briefly sketch the genesis and development of democracy. Historically, what has been the relationship between democracy and capitalism? Between democracy and democratic socialism?

3. How would you define democracy and defend your definition against those who disagree with you?

4. Do you agree that the four cardinal elements of democratic theory are liberty, equality, fraternity, and justice? Why? Why not?

5. When is a country a democracy? How do you appraise the key questions used in this chapter to identify a democracy?

6. What are the prerequisites for democracy? State why you agree or disagree with the democratic prerequisites treated in this chapter.

7. Is democracy a tolerant or intolerant, peaceful or militant, unifying or divisive ideology? Do you believe that democracy is both desirable and feasible everywhere in the modern world? Why? Why not?

8. What is the distinction between democracy in the western world and the communist concept of democracy? Do you believe that democracy is a false front for an oppressive and dying capitalism? Why? Why not?

9. Have democratic nations practiced the ideology they preach, both at home and abroad? Explain and illustrate your answer. Do you believe that democracy cannot win the ideological battle for the minds of modern men until it practices what it preaches? Explain.

10. Comment critically on the following statement: "If all nations in the world today were as genuinely democratic as the United States, true international understanding could be achieved and war among nations abolished forever."

SELECT BIBLIOGRAPHY

BARKER, Ernest, *Principles of Social and Political Theory* (New York, Oxford University Press, 1951). Outstanding modern work on democratic theory by a keen British political theorist. Maintains that liberty, equality, fraternity, and justice are the cardinal elements of democratic theory. A closely reasoned study, in the classic Aristotelian tradition, deserving of diligent study.

FRIEDRICH, Carl J., *The New Belief in the Common Man* (Brattleboro, Vt., Vermont Printing Co., 1942). Restatement and defense of democratic theory by a German-born political scientist, now an American citizen.

HARTZ, Louis, *The Liberal Tradition in America* (New York, Harcourt Brace, 1955). Underscores unique conditions that made possible the triumph of liberal democracy in America. Skeptical of the feasibility and triumph of American democracy in lands where same conditions do not prevail.

LINDSAY, A. D., *The Modern Democratic State* (New York, Oxford University Press, 1947). Concerned with the modern democratic state as an operative ideal in today's world. Succinct history of contributions to the modern democratic state.

MACIVER, R. M., *The Web of Government* (New York, Macmillan, 1947). Broad-gauged defense of democracy by a sociologist. Chapter VIII, "The Ways of Democracy," is a good summary.

MCKEON, Richard, ed., *Democracy in a World of Tensions* (Paris, UNESCO, 1951). A symposium prepared by UNESCO.

MAYO, H. B., *Democracy and Marxism* (New York, Oxford University Press, 1955). Author is a Canadian political scientist. Chapters 8 and 9: "Theory of Democracy" and "Democracy and Marxism" are most pertinent.

NIEBUHR, Reinhold, *The Children of Light and the Children of Darkness* (New York, Scribner, 1954). A vindication of democracy and a critique of its traditional defenders. Stimulating for naïve liberal democrats.

PENNOCK, J. Roland, *Liberal Democracy* (New York, Rinehart, 1950). Appraises merits and prospects of liberal democracy. Examines challenges to the ideal, democracy's altered foundations, and its practicability in light of challenges and changes.

SCHUMPETER, J. A., *Capitalism, Socialism, and Democracy*, 2nd ed. (New York, Harper, 1947). Reflections of an Austrian-born economist on the prospects of capitalism. Concludes, unhappily, that socialism will come about, but not for Marx's reasons.

SPITZ, David, *Patterns of Anti-Democratic Thought* (New York, Macmillan, 1949). Analysis and criticism of antidemocratic thought, with special references to recent American thought. Contains detailed refutation of arguments of antidemocratic schools of thought.

TOCQUEVILLE, Alexis DE, *Democracy in America,* 1840 (New York, Knopf, Bradley ed., 2 vols., 1945). Probably the most perceptive commentary on American democracy ever written. This now classic study by a young critical Frenchman is still remarkably illuminating.

WELDON, T. D., *The Vocabulary of Politics* (London, Penguin, 1953). Argues that all attempts to demonstrate superiority of democracy's foundations to those of communism and totalitarianism are pointless and futile. Maintains that no alarming consequences (cynicism, skepticism, or rejection of moral or political evaluations) follow from discrediting of all political ideologies.

8

Communism: Doctrine and Challenge?

THE PROBLEM
AND ITS BACKGROUND

Introduction

"A Spectre Is Haunting Europe"

"A spectre [wrote Karl Marx and Friedrich Engels in *The Communist Manifesto* in 1848] is haunting Europe—the spectre of Communism." [1]

Today, over a hundred years later, communism is haunting not only Europe but the entire world.

Unlike 1848, today communism is more than a spectre, a ghost or apparition, an unreal, if terrifying, embodiment. Today it is a powerful reality, which has assumed the blood and bones, sinew and muscles, heart and brain of Soviet power, its satellites, allies, and friends.

In *The Communist Manifesto*, Marx and Engels, with the bravado characteristic of the revolutionary mind, declared that "Communism is already acknowledged by all European Powers to be itself a Power." [2] This was far from true at the time it was written. No great state or little state was then communist. No organized communist party existed in any European state. The left wing of European politics was split among many different groups, which frequently argued and bickered, quarreled and feuded with

[1] See *Capital, The Communist Manifesto, and Other Writings* (1932) (Modern Library ed., New York, Random House, 1936). Hereafter, all references to *The Communist Manifesto* will be to this edition. The quotation is on p. 320.

[2] *Ibid.*

each other as much as with their right-wing opponents. No communist mass movement existed. The laboring class (the basis, according to communists, for the communist revolution) was by no stretch of the imagination united, strong, and fired with revolutionary zeal. Yet, though Marx and Engels were wrong in holding that communism was then considered a power, they were not wrong in indicating the fear, groundless or not, with which communism was held at that time.

Today, that fear is not groundless: The dimensions of communist power are formidable. As Chapters 1 and 7 have demonstrated, the communist attack on both the theory and practice of democracy in the major western nations has thrown down the gauntlet in a world-wide struggle for the minds of men and the control of nations.

Importance and Difficulties of Appraisal

From the outset it is essential to appreciate the importance of studying communist theory. In a significant sense, communist theory is one key to the communist challenge. As Lenin himself recognized: "Without a revolutionary theory there can be no revolutionary movement."[3] Fortunately for those who wish to understand it, communists have made great efforts to publicize their theory. Along with the revolutionary bravado characterizing such a document as The Communist Manifesto, there goes another quality, frankness, which is exemplified by this passage from that work:[4] "It is high time that Communists should openly, in the face of the whole world, publish their views, their aims, their tendencies, and meet this nursery tale of the spectre of Communism with a Manifesto of the party itself." This frankness can be helpful to the student seeking to understand communist theory and tactics and their relationship to world affairs.

In this connection Mein Kampf might also be recalled. Analogy may have its shortcomings as a method of reasoning, but it is at least suggestive that too many people scoffed at taking Hitler's "bible," Mein Kampf, seriously as a possible blueprint of Nazi theory and practice. For too many persons, the discovery came too late that there was a definite relationship between Mein Kampf and the actual policies of Nazi Germany.

Communism, however, is a more difficult ideology to understand than fascism or Nazism, and in a relatively brief presentation of such a complex doctrine there is always the risk of oversimplification and distortion. It is hoped that the following sketch will serve the student as a beginning for a more thorough investigation and appraisal of this powerful force and challenge in world affairs.

[3] "What Is To Be Done?" in Emile Burns, A Handbook of Marxism (London, Gollancz, 1935), p. 585.
[4] The Communist Manifesto, op. cit., p. 320.

The Several Meanings of the Communist Challenge

It might be helpful first to clarify the several meanings of "challenge" in the question: Communism: Doctrine and Challenge? First is the challenge of ideology: the free appeal of communist ideas to the minds of men and the rulers of nations. Communism's promise of a more ideal society based on greater economic and social equality constitutes an ideological appeal of considerable strength in many areas of the world. The appeal may be quite distinct from the efforts of a communist party to gain power in a specific state, and it may have little or nothing to do with the role of the Soviet Union as a powerful nation-state in world affairs.

A second challenge is that of communist parties throughout the world: their political, economic, social, and cultural activities within the various nations. The activities may be lawful or unlawful, constitutional or revolutionary; they may involve trouble-making, espionage, and subversion, or they may, overtly at least, add up to no more than dissent, protest, and demands for radical change. The fact that the Communist Parties of France and Italy, for example, poll 25 to 30 per cent of the popular votes in these countries means that the governments in power cannot completely ignore these parties in making policies. It also means that the United States must keep this in mind when formulating its own policies in regard to France and Italy.

Third is the challenge of the Soviet Union, a powerful nation-state whose official ideology is communism. Since World War II, Soviet control has been established over several Eastern European countries, and in Asia the victory of the Chinese Communists has given the Soviet Union an ally of considerable potential influence. Currently, Soviet economic penetration of Asia and the Middle East poses a new and perhaps even more formidable challenge.

If communism in world affairs is to be understood, it is frequently necessary to distinguish among these three challenges. Although interrelated, they are not always identical.

For example, in the countries outside the present communist bloc, neither communist ideology nor the native communist parties may be able by themselves to gain sway over the people or the government. When the power of the Soviet state is added to the struggle, however, the threat to free institutions in those countries may become formidable. In the present struggle for Germany, as an illustration, it is the awesome threat of Soviet power in Central Europe which is far more to be feared than either the appeal of communist ideology or the activity of the German Communist Party. It should also be remembered that, except for Yugoslavia and China (and possibly North Vietnam), no communist regime has gained power in an entire country without the direct or indirect support of the Soviet armies.

Then, too, what increases the effectiveness of one communist challenge sometimes blunts the edge of another. The Nazi-Soviet nonaggression pact of 1939, for example, with its secret partition of Poland and other parts of Eastern Europe, was regarded by the Soviet leaders as necessary for the security of their state, but the momentary strategic advantage for the U.S.S.R. was achieved at the expense of the prestige of communist parties and ideology outside the Soviet Union. The Nazi-Soviet agreement disillusioned many ideological communists, party members, and Soviet sympathizers. The loss of face and influence was not regained until Germany invaded the Soviet Union in 1941 and native communist parties could turn their full energies against Nazi aggression.

The Doctrinal Appeal of Communism

Popular orators often sway audiences today by emphasizing the idea that communism is a conspiracy against free men. This may be true, but it is not the whole truth. The appeal of communism to various segments of the world's population cannot be fathomed without keen appreciation that there is more to it than its conspiratorial character.

Communism is a prophecy of a better world. With messianic fervor, communist doctrine holds out to all men and women a vision of an earthly Utopia, that of freedom, happiness, peace, and material well-being for all, regardless of race, color, or sex. It appeals to all, but most pointedly to the oppressed. To the maltreated, the exploited, the enslaved, the abused, the lowly, it promises triumph on this earth.

Communism is a philosophy of history. Communism purports to explain rationally the evolution and structure of human society. It describes historical development in terms of clashing material forces related to how man earns a living. The present period of history, it asserts, is characterized by the clash between the capitalists and the working class, which will end in the overthrow of capitalism and the eventual establishment of communism and a higher state of freedom. The philosophy emphasizes a theory which maintains that human ideas and behavior are primarily a reflection of the material environment in which men live.

Communism is a comprehensive, systematic critique of capitalism and imperialism. Communism condemns the exploitation of man which is allegedly inherent in a system of private ownership of the means of production and exchange. It views capitalism and imperialism as inseparable phenomena in the modern world, and it castigates what it contends are the consequences of these movements: the misery of the worker, war, and colonialism.

Communism is a strategy of revolutionary action. Communism has developed a strategy for overthrowing capitalist society and enabling the workers of the world to establish the bases for the inevitable communist society.

In communist theory, all these facets are combined to form a mighty doctrine which the communist considers impregnable to assault and bound to triumph eventually.

This chapter will be concerned with all four aspects of communist theory, particularly as they provide background for an understanding of the world-wide communist challenge. However, before our fuller treatment of these four aspects, we shall introduce the master communists of the modern world.

THE MASTER COMMUNISTS

Karl Marx: Master Theoretician

From Lenin's essay "The Three Sources and Three Constituents of Marxism," many commentators have noted that Germany made Marx a philosopher, France made him a revolutionary, and England made him a political economist. Frequently forgotten is the fact that the Western European Enlightenment made Marx a prophet of a better world.

The Enlightenment was a complex and influential movement that dominated the mind of the western world in the eighteenth century, the century, significantly, of the American and French Revolutions. Many at that time condemned the follies and barbarities of an oppressive and ignorant past and looked forward to the earthly emancipation of man. Believing in reason, freedom, and progress, they appealed to reasonable men, extolled liberty, and hailed man's march toward a better world. In a very significant sense, then, Marx carried the Enlightenment, in the name of freedom, to one of its logical conclusions: real freedom for all in the Utopia of a classless, communist society.

He derived most of his major philosophical ideas from two German philosophers, Georg Hegel and Ludwig Feuerbach. Their contributions (Hegel's concept of the dialectic and Feuerbach's theory of materialism) will be examined later, in the discussion of one of Marx's key concepts, that of dialectical materialism, which constituted the basis for his interpretation of historical evolution.

Marx drew heavily upon French socialist literature, and revolutionary theory and experience, which he interpreted in the light of his philosophy. He was influenced by French socialist leaders like Proudhon and theorists of the French Revolution like Augustin Thierry, whom he regarded as "the father of the class struggle in French historical writing." The French Revolutions of 1789, 1848, and 1871 greatly influenced Marx's thinking and facilitated his development of basic strategy, which Lenin, freely adapting Marx, was to sharpen and then apply in the Russian Revolution of 1917.

It was England which made Marx a political economist. Engels' first-hand study of British labor conditions, published in 1845 as *Conditions of the Working Class in England,* interested him enormously. Here was specific information on the actual working of industrialism in the most advanced capitalistic country in the world. Later, Marx himself spent long years grubbing through reports in the reading room of the British Museum, in order to document (in the three volumes of *Capital*) the central thesis about capitalism that he had already drawn up.

Despite changes made by Lenin and Stalin in Marx's theory, the basic theoretical outlook of communist doctrine remains that of Karl Marx. A nineteenth century figure, he did not, of course, live to see communism triumph in any country of Europe. Actually, the first victory achieved by communism took place in a country that lay partly in Europe and partly in Asia.

V. I. Lenin: Master Revolutionary Tactician

In the wake of Marx, the master communist theoretician, came Lenin, the master revolutionary tactician. His modifications of Marxist doctrine were intimately related to practical communist strategy and tactics in his home country, Russia, a land whose history made it strangely receptive to many communist ideas. His contributions must, therefore, be viewed in the context of that politically autocratic and economically backward state. The conditions there apparently convinced Lenin that peaceful evolution toward socialism was a delusion and that only revolutionary Marxism could succeed. Lenin, then, applied Marxist doctrines to the new conditions of the twentieth century, in general, and to the Russian Revolution of 1917, in particular.

As the next chapter will make clearer, Marx is the fountainhead of modern socialism, which has two main branches: one, evolutionary or democratic socialism (as it exists in the Labor, Socialist, and Social-Democratic Party of Britain, France, and Germany, respectively); the other, revolutionary socialism or communism (as in the U.S.S.R., China, and the satellite countries of Europe). Before the Russian Revolution of 1917, the democratic socialists were the larger and more influential of the two groups in Europe, and it is within the framework of his opposition to them that Lenin's contributions to communist theory must be viewed in large part. The evolutionary socialists were sometimes called revisionists because they wanted to revise or bring Marx up to date, acknowledging his mistakes, the changing circumstances, and the feasibility of the peaceful, parliamentary achievement of socialism in countries like Britain, France, and Germany. These socialists did not accept Lenin's revolutionary interpretation of Marx. As already indicated, it may well be that Lenin's fight with the more moderate socialists is to be explained in terms of the autocratic and repressive Russian environment. These conditions seemingly doomed the peaceful achievement of socialism by parliamentary means and made the only alternative a more sharply revolutionary, conspiratorial, dictatorial theory. In any event, it is clear that Lenin proceeded to commit "true" Marxism to a violent revolutionary program and to the ultimate inevitability of war with the capitalist world.

The First World War gave Lenin a unique opportunity to apply his revolutionary program. As a result of terrible losses on the battlefield and widespread discontent in the factory and on the farm, Russia was ripe for revolution. The German General Staff contributed more than a mite by sending the radical agitator, Lenin (then in political exile in Switzerland), back to Russia in a sealed boxcar, enabling him to add his voice to the mounting dissatisfaction within Russia. They hoped that this might help knock Russia out of the war and thus free the German armies for a final push against the Allies in France. Lenin shrewdly addressed himself to the disaffected elements in Russia. To all, but particularly to the soldiers, he promised peace; to the city workers—jobs and bread; and to the millions of land-hungry Russian peasants—land. When convenient, his slogan was: "All power to the Soviets" (councils of workers). Such revolutionary councils were set up in the principal cities and factories, and within the army. It is important to note that at the time Russia was still at war, even though the Czar had abdicated and been replaced by a provisional government interested in establishing liberal, democratic institutions. When the time seemed ripe, the Leninist-led communists overthrew the provisional government and seized power.

In the treatment of Lenin's contribution to communist theory later in this chapter, attention is focused on Lenin's theory of state and revolution. That theory illuminates the Bolshevik Revolution in 1917, and became the doctrine of the Soviet state under Lenin and Stalin. A better understanding is obtained, as well, of Lenin's concept of the role of the communist party, a role which became more prominent as a result of the opportunities created for the seizure of power by communists in capitalistic countries weakened by imperialistic war.

Joseph Stalin: Master Builder of Soviet Power

If "Leninism is Marxism in the epoch of imperialism and of the proletarian revolution" (as Stalin remarked), Stalinism is Leninism in the epoch of the building of Soviet power. Lenin, of course, had appreciated the importance of consolidating the Bolshevik Revolution in Russia. He took Russia out of the war against Germany, even though it meant signing a very harsh peace treaty (Brest-Litovsk) with the Kaiser's Germany. When the communist experiment was jeopardized by too speedy an effort to advance the revolution, Lenin called a halt in 1921 and established the New Economic Policy (NEP), which temporarily reestablished the legitimacy of a number of capitalist undertakings in agriculture and retail trade, and put a brake on other socialist measures.

Lenin justified both Brest-Litovsk and NEP on the basis of preserving the Bolshevik Revolution in Russia.

Stalin thus could cite Lenin's action to justify his own emphasis on "socialism in one country" when he was accused of surrendering "internationalism." For the sake of "socialism in one country," he took over from Marx and Lenin those ideas which fitted his own program and abandoned any which interfered. The most important single clue to understanding the Stalinist contribution to, and influence on, communist theory and strategy is the priority that was given to the consolidation of communist power in the Soviet Union.

A related clue is, of course, the consolidation of Stalin's personal power which began with Lenin's untimely death in 1924 and with Stalin's emergence as the First Secretary of the Communist Party, and therefore the key man in control of the party apparatus. The struggle for power led to the elimination or exile in the late 1920's of Stalin's principal rivals: Trotsky, Kamenev, Bukharin, and others. The ruthless purges of the mid 1930's broadened and intensified the systematic elimination of all whose loyalty to Stalin was questionable. Even the Red Army was included in these purges. Stalin's dictatorship, which continued to rely on the purge apparently right up to his death, had an important effect on communist theory and strategy.

Testimony to support the indictment and implications of Stalin's ruthless regime has come from no less a figure than Nikita S. Khrushchev, First Secretary of the Soviet Communist Party and, as of March, 1958, Premier of the Soviet Union. In 1956, three years after Stalin's death, Khrushchev, then only First Secretary, denounced Stalin's use of terror. He also denounced Stalin's fostering of "the cult of the individual," a doctrine which makes a "particular leader a hero and miracle worker." These evils, Khrushchev stated, were "alien to the spirit of Marxism and Leninism." [5]

Aside from price considerations, it is perfectly clear that the Soviet Union, under Stalin's rule, was transformed from a backward, illiterate, primarily agricultural land into a powerful, literate, industrialized state, which is without a doubt one of the two mammoth powers of the modern world. That this tremendous transformation, wrought under Stalin's dictatorship, would be reflected in communist theory was to be expected: by totalitarian methods, state power was applied to socialize the nation's farms and factories, to create and expand the heavy industries, to organize a mighty Soviet army, and to brook no opposition in achieving these aims. With a communist government in power in the Soviet Union only, the cause of world revolution must remain subservient to the interest of Russian security. Almost inevitable, also, was Stalin's insistence upon a single Soviet path to socialism, a pattern to guide the course of the

[5] *New York Times*, February 15, 1956, and June 5, 1956.

communist revolution in other lands, wherever Soviet armies were in a position to translate Stalin's views into practice. So, indeed, it proved to be, in the adjacent countries of Central and Southeastern Europe, Poland, Hungary, Bulgaria, among others, which came under Red Army control with the defeat of Germany in World War II.

Against this background of the master communists, it is pertinent to pose the following questions, directed toward a central problem in this chapter, the communist challenge: Is the communist challenge that of the free appeal of communist ideology, divorced from Russian (or Chinese) national power? Is it the challenge of revolutionary communist parties throughout the world? Or is it the challenge of Soviet, and perhaps also Chinese Communist, power? Is Soviet strength communist or Russian strength? In the light of communist doctrine, how are the sincerity and significance of apparent shifts in the Kremlin party line since Stalin's death to be appraised? How are the challenge or the several challenges of communism to be met?

To prepare the student to answer these questions, it may be profitable to examine in more detail communism as a prophecy of a better world, as a philosophy of history, as a critique of capitalism and imperialism, and as a strategy of revolutionary action.

Communism as a Prophecy of a Better World

It may seem arbitrary to single out for separate treatment the communist prophecy of a better world, since communists themselves do not treat it as a distinct principle of communist doctrine. Yet there is considerable justification for doing this. Communists might or might not admit it, but the belief in a better world is a major factor in explaining the religious-like dedication, revolutionary ardor, and dogged loyalty of indoctrinated communists throughout the world. Certainly it is this championship of a better world which constitutes communism's greatest ideological appeal to men all over the earth: among the untutored masses, as well as among the well-educated intellectuals.

Throughout the writings of Marx and Engels (who was, to a large extent, Marx's *alter ego*), the prophecy of the good life is announced and reiterated, until it almost becomes a ritualistic invocation by which all communist action is blessed. Almost always, in this messianic prophecy, the contrast is made between the children of light and the children of darkness. The communist claims to stand for freedom as opposed to slavery: human bondage or wage servitude, political serfdom or social subjection. His is the side of plenty as opposed to want; happiness as against misery; peace vs. war. His is an altruistic concept of community struggling against a selfish individualistic doctrine of profit-making; real equality and fraternity as contrasted with inequality, sham equality, racial and religious hostility. Ultimately, his alleged goal is the free and voluntary acceptance of society's necessary rules and regulations as against coercion and brutal oppression by the government, law, police, and army of the capitalistic state.

The Communist Manifesto declares that in the communist society "the free development of each is the condition for the free development of all." [6] As a result of the communist revolution, the working masses, who have nothing to lose but their chains, will have won a world. According to Engels, the communist revolution will be an act of "universal emancipation." "It is the ascent of man from the kingdom of necessity to the kingdom of freedom." "Man, at last the master of his own form of social organization, becomes at the same time the lord over Nature, his own master—free." [7]

Life in the communist society, according to Marx and Engels, will be abundant and happy. In the "higher phase of communist society," Marx asserts, "the springs of collective wealth will flow with abundance." Such a communist society will be able to realize the motto: From each according to his ability; to each according to his needs. Then, too, the all-round development of the individual will be possible. [8]

Always, this better world is contrasted to the oppressive, miserable, unhappy present lot of the working classes in the capitalist world. Of course, in his day Marx could abundantly document the picture he drew of the wretched situation of the working classes: long, grinding hours; low pay; poor working conditions; miserable living conditions. Even today, in countries such as the United States—where the level of well-being of workers has been greatly elevated, and improvements made as a result of the work of free trade unions, a progressive capitalism, and government programs like wage-hour laws, old age and survivors insurance, unemployment compensation, and other comparable protective measures—conditions persist (especially racial mistreatment) that give communists a basis for invoking the Marxist prophecy of a better world.

Today, the litany is also sung in the colonial and former colonial areas of the world. In many of these underdeveloped lands the communists draw an even more dramatic contrast between a colonial past of political subjugation, economic exploitation, and racial inequality and the communist promise of political freedom and independence, economic well-being and progress, and genuine equality.

The fact remains, however, that the largest communist parties outside the communist bloc are in France and Italy. In both countries communist

---

[6] *The Communist Manifesto, op. cit.,* p. 343.

[7] *Socialism: Utopian and Scientific* (1880) (Chicago, Kerr, 1908), p. 139.

[8] From "The Criticism of the Gotha Program," in *Capital, The Communist Manifesto, and Other Writings, op. cit.,* p. 7.

promises of a better life for the working class have led many noncommunist workers to vote communist as a protest against the failure of their governments to achieve significant political, economic, and social reforms.

At this point the question may arise: Is the communist prophecy of a better world the mere picturing of the world as it ought to be? Or is it, as the communists claim, based on a philosophy of history which demonstrates that this is actually the direction in which the world is moving?

COMMUNISM AS A PHILOSOPHY OF HISTORY

The Communist Outlook

Communism aims at establishing a classless society in which all the means of production, distribution, and exchange will be owned by the community. In this community, the state (seen as an instrument of coercion and oppression) will have disappeared. Between the revolution which abolishes the capitalist order and this communist society lies a transitional period, known as the dictatorship of the proletariat. This is the period of socialism, or the first stage of communism. (This is, of course, revolutionary socialism, not the evolutionary socialism that is discussed in the next chapter.) It is the period through which Russia claims to be passing now. Communism, which is the highest state of social development, comes after this transitional period. When communism arrives, the ideal political life becomes possible, the oppressive state will disappear, and complete freedom will obtain.

What philosophical and historical outlook lies back of this perspective? To answer this question, it is necessary to examine Marx's materialism, his views on historical materialism and class struggle, and his theory of dialectical materialism. It was from Hegel that Marx borrowed the concept of the dialectic as a means of interpreting historical evolution. According to Hegel, the principal clue to historical development lay in the clash of opposing ideas. Marx was impressed with Hegel's concept of the dialectic, but he disagreed with him on the nature of the opposing forces whose clash resulted in historical development. Hegel had argued that *ideas* were the opposing forces, but Marx concluded that material forces, *economic classes,* rather than ideas, explained evolution in history. Marx's materialist philosophy was adapted from that of Feuerbach. Marx thus combined Hegel's dialectic method with Feuerbach's theory of materialism to formulate his key philosophical concept, dialectical materialism. It is based on the struggle in history of opposing material forces and their dynamic development (through class struggle) toward a higher state of human freedom. Since Marx's philosophy of history is not easily grasped, it may be helpful to examine the components of this philosophy separately.

Materialism. For Marx, the material world is the ultimate reality, and in history econcmic causes are fundamental. The materialist, economic "productive forces" in society constitute the "substructure," or ground floor of society. These forces are the instruments of production, like labor and capital, and they are primary. The "productive relations" in society constitute the "superstructure," or upper floors of society. They create law, political organizations, religion, art, and so forth, and they are secondary.

Engels explained the materialist basis of Marxism thus: [9]

Marx . . . discovered the simple fact, hitherto concealed . . . *that mankind must first of all eat and drink, have shelter and clothing,* before it can pursue politics, religion, science, art, etc.; and that therefore *the production of the immediate material means of subsistence, and consequently the degree of economic development attained by a given people or during a given epoch, form the foundation* upon which State institutions, the legal institutions, the art and even the religious ideas of the people concerned must have been evolved, and in the light of which these things must be explained instead of vice versa as had hitherto been the case. [Italics added.]

This materialist outlook has a direct bearing on the communist view of human nature. Human nature is not basically evil, say the communists, but simply reflects a basically evil environment. Change man's environment, and it is possible to change man's behavior. The ideal material environment of a classless communist society, according to communist theory, will produce ideal, socially adjusted human beings.

In summary, the following points in Marx's materialistic outlook may be distinguished:

1. The ultimate reality in the world is man's material environment. Man's ideas do not originate independently; they merely reflect his material environment.

2. Economic factors are the most important material factors influencing life and the organization and development of society; bluntly, food and work come before politics and art.

3. The economic factor most decisive in a society is the prevailing method or mode of production of that society. Changes in the modes of production during successive periods of history are responsible for the rise and fall of the various societies under which man has lived.

4. The economic structure of society constitutes its real foundation, upon which is built the "superstructure" of law, politics, religion, art, morality, thought. This economic and material foundation determines the character of the legal, political, religious superstructure.

Historical materialism and the class struggle. Marx saw history in terms of class struggles. This idea is perhaps the most important in understanding communist doctrine. As has already been indicated, these struggles were grounded in economics.

[9] Quoted in R. N. Carew Hunt, *The Theory and Practice of Communism* (London, Geoffrey Bles, 1950), pp. 37–38 (5th rev. American ed., Macmillan, 1957).

Marx wrote in *The Communist Manifesto:* "The history of all hitherto existing society is the history of class struggles." And again: [10]

Freeman and slave, patrician and plebeian, lord and serf, guildmaster and journeyman, in a word, oppressor and oppressed, stood in constant opposition to one another, carried on uninterrupted, now hidden, now open fight, a fight that each time ended either in a revolutionary reconstitution of society at large, or in the common ruin of the contending classes.

Throughout history, then, there has been an oppressing class which owned and controlled the means of production and exchange in its own interest. The same class dominated the social, political, and religious scene. Representing this class have been the Greek freeman, the Roman patrician, and the feudal lord, respectively. Correspondingly, there has always been an oppressed and exploited class, represented by the slave, plebeian, and serf, respectively.

In the modern period the oppressing class is the bourgeoisie; the oppressed class, the proletariat. Marx defines the two terms in *The Communist Manifesto* as follows: [11]

By bourgeoisie is meant the class of modern Capitalists, owners of the means of social production and employers of wage-labor. By proletariat, the class of modern wage laborers who, having no means of production of their own, are reduced to selling their labor-power in order to live.

Up to the modern period, Marx argued, the arrangement of society into various orders was complicated. The distinctive feature of the "epoch of the bourgeoisie" is that "it has simplified class antagonisms. Society as a whole is more and more splitting up into two great hostile camps, into two great classes directly facing each other: Bourgeoisie and Proletariat." [12]

What is most significant about any society is that its economic organization is not static but dynamic. It is constantly undergoing change, and this change, argued Marx, is traceable to the economic contradictions or conflicts inherent in a given economic organization.

Marx made this point neatly in a famous passage in the Preface to his *Critique of Political Economy.* The excerpt, not always easy for the beginning student, is as follows: [13]

At a certain stage of their development [e.g., late feudal] the material forces of society [e.g., incipient capitalistic] come into contradiction with the existing production-relations [e.g., feudal]. . . . From being forms of development of the productive forces, these [feudal] relations turn into fetters upon their [economic] development. Then comes an epoch of social revolution. With the change in the economic foundation the whole immense feudal superstructure is slowly or rapidly transformed [into a capitalistic one].

[10] *The Communist Manifesto, op. cit.,* p. 321.
[11] *Ibid.,* note 1.
[12] *Ibid.,* pp. 321–322.
[13] The passage will also be found in the Modern Library ed., *op. cit.,* p. 11.

Thus, bourgeois capitalism emerged out of feudalism because of certain inherent contradictions in the feudal economy. The contradictions were the result of development of the industrial and commercial mode of production and exchange within the feudal economy. As industrialism grew within the feudal economy, the latter was bound to disintegrate and ultimately to be replaced by a capitalist economy.

Just as capitalism emerged, and had to emerge, from feudalism (because of the contradictions within the feudal economic system), so communism must emerge from capitalism, because of the contradictions within the capitalist system.

What are these contradictions in capitalism which, for Marxists, operate in history according to an "inexorable law" of society? The major ones are:

1. The creation by the capitalist system of a large class of workers who are exploited by that system, become conscious of their exploitation, band together to defend themselves, and eventually overthrow their capitalist masters and exploiters.

2. The faulty, uneven operation of the capitalist system itself, which produces more goods than can be profitably absorbed by the market, progressively exploits the worker, and causes not only overpopulation but also periodic catastrophic depressions.

Marx concludes: [14]

The development of Modern Industry, therefore, cuts from under its feet the very foundation on which the bourgeoisie produces and appropriates products. What the bourgeoisie therefore produces, above all, are its own grave diggers. Its fall and the victory of the proletariat are equally inevitable.

Consequently, not only is the fundamental reality in the world materialist, but the materialist forces in society are actively at work in history, developing, as they shape up in the economic mode of production and exchange, according to dialectical laws that are the laws of historical reality.

It was this historical process that Engels had in mind when he said: [15] "Just as Darwin discovered the law of evolution in organic nature, so Marx discovered the law of evolution in human history. . . ."

Dialectical materialism. What, more exactly, do Marxists mean by *dialectics,* the term that they allege explains the operation of the dynamic materialistic forces of history? Here again, Engels provides us with a definition: [16] "Dialectics is nothing more than the science of the general laws of motion and development of Nature, human society and thought."

[14] *The Communist Manifesto, op. cit.,* p. 334.
[15] Quoted in Carew Hunt, *op. cit.,* p. 38.
[16] "Anti-Dühring," in Burns, *op. cit.,* p. 266.

In other words, evolution in human history operates dialectically. The general dialectical law of development in history is summed up in the dialectical formula "thesis, antithesis, and synthesis," which Marx borrowed from Hegel.

The "thesis" represents the dominant force of any epoch of history. According to Marxist materialism, this is the prevailing economic mode of production. Thus, capitalism is the dominant force or "thesis" of the present period of western civilization, just as feudalism was of the pre-capitalist epoch.

The "thesis" or dominant force of each period of history is, in time, confronted with an opposing or conflicting force, called an "antithesis," which arises from the introduction of new inventions or discoveries that begin to challenge and alter the existing means of production. Thus, according to the Marxists, the introduction of commercial and industrial techniques in seventeenth and eighteenth century society became the "antithesis" opposing feudalism.

A struggle between "thesis" and "antithesis" ensues, resulting eventually in a new system or "synthesis," based on the best or correct elements inherent in the former "thesis" and "antithesis." Capitalism is an example of the "synthesis" produced by the struggle between feudal and industrial modes of production. This "synthesis," capitalism, in turn becomes the new "thesis" or dominant force of a new period of history. Following the dialectical pattern, the capitalist "thesis" in time is faced with a new "antithesis," reflecting the contradictions or conflicts that Marxists claim are inherent in capitalism. These conflicts are intensified by the development of monopoly capitalism and imperialism. The organization of the working class (proletariat) and the development of worker class consciousness lead to a new social revolution in which capitalism will be overthrown and replaced, first by dictatorial socialism (dictatorship of the proletariat), and eventually by the more utopian pattern of communism.

The "thesis," then, affirms or describes a given state of affairs, for example, the economic state of affairs called capitalism. The "antithesis," referring to the contradictions in capitalism, denies, "negates," or contradicts what is going on in the capitalistic state of affairs. The "synthesis"—here, communism—joins together or harmoniously embodies what is true or correct in both the original "thesis" and the "antithesis." Thus, the "synthesis" brings the state of affairs closer to harmonious reality.

Since this is not an easy formula to grasp, it may be helpful to explain it in another way. As already seen, the dynamic factors in the evolution of a given economic system (say, capitalism as the "thesis") are the contradictions ("antithesis") in that system. Since the contradictions cannot be resolved within that system's framework, the system changes. The "false" elements in the old and decaying system are sloughed off. The "true" elements, combined with "new" elements that have developed in opposition to the old system, are now joined together in a new system (the "synthesis" of communism), which is now free of the old system's contradictions.

The "false," "true," and "new" elements in this explanation can be illustrated in the following way. The "false" contradictory elements (in the old, decaying capitalistic system) that are sloughed off are the exploitation of the worker, periodic depression, and, as Lenin was to point out later, imperialist rivalry and colonial exploitation. The "true" elements in capitalism that are retained are the co-operative, rational, efficient productive methods of capitalism. The "new" elements that are combined with the "true" elements are unionization of workers, worker class consciousness, and worker conversion to socialism. This combination eventually produces a new system, the "synthesis" of communism, based upon the socialized ownership of the means of production.

When communism is reached, presumably the dialectic process as it has hitherto operated throughout history will cease, since the motor fuel of the dialectical machine (the contradictions inherent in a given economic system) will have disappeared. There will be no more contradictions because class struggles will have terminated with the socialization of the means of production and exchange. Communism, by establishing social ownership of the means of production and exchange, gives all workers a share in this ownership, thereby establishing the basis for a single economic class including all workers and producers. This is what is meant by a "classless society." No classes—therefore, no class struggle! With no class struggle and no exploitation, an ideal society will have been created.

Because Marxists believe that their analysis is based on observable and predictable laws of historical development, they maintain that their outlook is "scientific." So viewed, the dialectic can be better understood as the general law of historical development which provides the basis for the "scientific" communist prophecy of a better world.

In this light, it can be seen why the Marxist philosophy of history, whose general outline and key principles have remained fundamentally unchanged since Marx wrote, bolsters the conviction of communists of the inevitability of the communist triumph.

An intimate part of the communist philosophy of history is the communist critique of the evils of capitalism and imperialism. Since it is so crucial to Marxist theory, and since parts of it, divorced from the Marxist philosophy of history, have been or could be accepted by noncommunists, the critique merits separate treatment.

COMMUNISM AS A CRITIQUE OF CAPITALISM AND IMPERIALISM

According to Marx's philosophy of history, economic forces are fundamental and operate according to the dialectical principle. Why, however, do these economic factors produce exploitation and oppression of workers? The answer demands a more detailed examination of Marx's economics, particularly his theory of surplus value.

Theory of Surplus Value: Keystone of the Marxist Economic System

Influenced by certain economic theorists, like Ricardo, who had preceded him, Marx contended that labor alone creates value. As he put it in *Capital:* [17]

A use-value, or useful article, therefore, has value only because human labour in the abstract has been embodied or materialized in it. How, then, is the magnitude of this value to be measured? Plainly, by the quantity of the value-creating substance, the labor contained in the article.

If, Marx asked, the value of a commodity is wholly due to the labor that has gone into it, why should it not be paid to the laborers who produced the commodity? Manifestly, they are not being paid their rightful share, according to the labor theory of value. Instead, as Marx and Engels had already noted in *The Communist Manifesto:* [18] "The average price of wage labor is the minimum wage, i.e., that quantum of the means of subsistence which is absolutely requisite to keep the labourer in bare existence as a labourer."

The worker, by his labor, produces commodities of greater value than the worker's means of subsistence. Actually, Marx pointed out, the value the worker has created by his labor is divided into two parts: wages for the worker (determined by the amount necessary to enable the worker to subsist), and profits (for the capitalist or employer). The profits, Marx contended, constitute "surplus value," really belonging to the worker but wrongly taken by the capitalist.[19]

According to Engels, this is the secret of capitalist production and capitalist exploitation. Together with the materialist conception of history, this discovery, Engels wrote, revealed the existence of economic laws in historical development and enabled socialism to be transformed from the status of a dream into that of a science.

Thus, Marx could conclude that the exploitation of the worker under capitalism is inherent, not accidental, in the nature of the capitalist

[17] In Burns, *op. cit.,* p. 408.
[18] *The Communist Manifesto, op. cit.,* p. 336.
[19] See also Carew Hunt, *op. cit.,* p. 56.

economic system. Therefore, only a different economic system, that of communism, would end this exploitation.

Three economic laws of capitalism. Marx deduced three laws from his theory of surplus value.[20] The first is "the law of capitalist accumulation." Marx maintained that capitalists are driven by competition to accumulate capital, that is, to install more and more labor-saving machinery in order to produce more goods. This, however, adversely affects his profits since, Marx held, he can make greater profits by means of exploited human labor than by machinery.

The second law is "the law of the concentration of capital." Marx argued that competition will drive the weaker capitalists out of business, that smaller businesses will disappear. Inevitably, capitalism leads to monopolies, trusts, and cartels, for they alone are strong enough to withstand the recurrent capitalist economic crises. This law also sees the gulf widening between proletariat and capitalists (many of whom, as a result of this law's workings, have been pushed back into the ranks of the proletariat).

The third is called "the law of increasing misery." The capitalist, whose profits have already declined with competition and the introduction of labor-saving machinery, can recoup his losses only by intensifying the exploitation of the worker. This is facilitated because labor-saving machinery has caused an increase in unemployment. Consequently, from the desperate worker, threatened by unemployment, the capitalist employer can exact more and more hours of unpaid labor. The great mass of unemployed workers serve as further pressure to depress already depressed wages. The misery of the workers, the bulk of the population, will become more and more unendurable. It will lead them to combine for their own protection, and so create a force that will eventually destroy the capitalist system.

Marx portrayed this misery in these words: [21]

In proportion as the bourgeoisie, i.e., capital, is developed, in the same proportion is the proletariat, the modern working-class, developed, a class of labourers who live only so long as they find work, and who find work only so long as their labour increases capital.
Masses of labourers, crowded into factories, are organized like soldiers. . . . Not only are they the slaves of the bourgeois class and of the bourgeois state, they are daily and hourly enslaved by the machine, by the overlooker, and above all, by the individual bourgeois manufacturer himself. The more openly this despotism proclaims gain to be its end and aim, the more petty, the more hateful and the more embittering it is.

The operation of the three laws of capitalism, Marx maintained, jeopardizes the existence of capitalistic society. Marx had noted this in

[20] *Ibid.*, pp. 58–60.
[21] *The Communist Manifesto, op. cit.*, pp. 328–330.

The Communist Manifesto [22] before developing (in *Capital*) an economic theory to support it.

It is enough to mention the commercial crises that by their periodical return put on its trial, each time more threateningly, the existence of the entire bourgeois society. . . . In these crises there breaks out an epidemic that, in all earlier epochs, would have seemed an absurdity—the epidemic of overproduction.

According to Engels, capitalism clearly demonstrates the fundamental "contradiction between socialized production and capitalistic appropriation." Indeed, "the contradiction between socialized production and capitalistic appropriation . . . presents itself as *an antagonism between the organization of production in the individual workshop and the anarchy of production in society generally.*" [23] On the one hand, capitalist production is, if heartless, technologically efficient, rational, well-organized: The factory has been socialized. On the other hand, "production in society," the sale, exchange, distribution, and consumption of products, is both heartless and anarchical: It operates according to no satisfactory over-all plan in the interest of all in society. The result is disastrous both to capitalists and to proletarians: [24]

It is the compelling force of anarchy in the production of society at large that more and more completely turns the great majority of men into proletarians; and it is the masses of the proletariat again who will finally put an end to anarchy in production.

This "contradiction in capitalism" (known in modern parlance as "boom and bust"), industrial prosperity followed by industrial depression, is stressed here because Marxists consider it one of the central contradictions in capitalism that will bring about its downfall.

It was in this way that Marx's analysis of capitalism served to buttress his philosophy of history and his revolutionary theory.

The historical role of the capitalist system. The preceding discussion shows how difficult it is to completely separate Marx's philosophy of history from his economic analysis, and how closely knit both are with his theory of revolution. For Marx argued that capitalism was necessary: It was necessary for the destruction of feudalism and as preparation for communism. Capitalism had produced the proletariat, socialized the means of production, and reduced society, increasingly, to two classes. It had set the stage for the proletariat to appropriate the appropriators (the capitalists), that is, for the communist revolution by means of which the proletariat seizes public power and transforms the socialized means of production (hitherto used for private gain) into public property to be

[22] *Ibid.*, p. 327.
[23] *Socialism: Utopian and Scientific, op. cit.*, pp. 105 and 110.
[24] *Ibid.*, p. 111.

used, according to Marxists, to advance the well-being and freedom of all.

Marx's gloomy critique of capitalism was to be matched by Lenin's slashing attack on capitalist imperialism, a criticism which not only explained capitalism's extended lease on life in the twentieth century but reinforced the prediction of its ultimate demise.

Lenin's Theory of Capitalist Imperialism

Lenin's theory, although not highly original, is very important for an understanding of the communist mind and communist propaganda today. His thesis is made clear in the major work he wrote on the subject, *Imperialism: The Highest Stage of Capitalism*. Written in 1916, it was designed to show that World War I was an imperialist war on both sides. Lenin's main contention was that imperialism is a natural outgrowth of capitalism within the nation-state. Imperialism is the monopoly stage of capitalism, Lenin argued.[25]

> Imperialism is capitalism in that stage of development in which the domination of monopolies and finance capital has established itself; in which the export of capital has acquired pronounced importance; in which the division of the world among the international trusts has begun; in which the partition of all the territories of the globe among the great capitalist powers has been completed.

He held that the evolution of capitalism into the higher stage of imperialism brings into being another set of contradictions within the world-wide system of capitalism that will further contribute to its inevitable collapse on an international scale. Those antagonisms involve, first, the conflict between rival imperialist states, and, second, the struggle between the colonial powers and the natives of the colonial areas they dominate. Capitalist states, Lenin maintained, are inevitably driven to a point where they must seek cheap raw materials and markets for their excess production outside their national territory. The rivalry between various capitalist states for the materials and markets available leads sooner or later to imperialist wars. Capitalism cannot survive except by resorting to imperialism and war, but these wars will in the long run so weaken capitalism that it will not be able to survive.

Lenin's views on imperialism helped Marxists to explain the staying power of capitalism. Thus, imperialism, by creating new markets abroad, gave crisis-ridden capitalism a new lease on life. By the same token, the lot of the proletariat in the advanced capitalist countries might seem to be improved.

The price of this apparent relief and improvement was intensified exploitation of the toiling masses of the colonial countries, a world-wide division of peoples into exploiting and exploited, and the possibility of

[25] V. I. Lenin, *Selected Works* (New York, International Publishers, 1938), Vol. V, p. 81.

what might today be called colonial revolutions: The exploitation of the colonial natives by the colonial powers created the basis for a revolution by the natives against their foreign masters. The groundwork for the revolution against capitalism was thus extended from the domestic realm to the world-wide arena of colonial possessions.

The fight against imperialism and colonialism therefore assumed a major place in communist doctrine and tactics. Just as Marx had sought to arouse the political and revolutionary consciousness of the workers in the countries of western Europe, transformed by the impact of the Industrial Revolution, so Lenin undertook to awaken the revolutionary consciousness of toilers in the colonial areas of the world. The class-conscious revolutionary efforts of a world-wide proletariat would now be directed at overthrowing an oppressive capitalism, at home and abroad!

This Leninist view of imperialism and colonialism casts considerable light on communism in many underdeveloped areas of Asia, Africa, and Latin America. It also helps to explain why communist leaders today have made the underdeveloped areas of the world a major target for penetration. Many thoughtful observers believe that the fate of a free and peaceful world may well hinge on the success of the communist challenge in those parts of the earth.

After having prophesied a better world, enunciated a philosophy of history that allegedly demonstrated the inevitable emergence of communism from capitalism, and criticized in detail the contradictions in the capitalist system that would lead to its replacement by a communist system, leaders of communist thought still had the task of arousing the revolutionary consciousness of the working class and of leading the proletariat to the anticipated communist victory.

COMMUNISM AS A STRATEGY OF REVOLUTIONARY ACTION

Here again Marx provides communists with their general orientation.[26]

The communists disdain to conceal their views and aims. They openly declare their ends can be attained only by the forcible overthrow of all existing social conditions. Let the ruling classes tremble at a Communist revolution. The proletarians have nothing to lose but their chains. They have a world to win.

Working men of all countries, unite!

Politically and economically, Marx argued, the revolution would proceed according to the logic of the dialectic. Politically, there would be two phases. In the bourgeois revolution feudalism would be destroyed by capitalism. The proletariat would support the bourgeoisie in this revolution since success would advance the inevitable proletarian revolution.

Under a bourgeois-democratic government, the gains achieved by the workers (extension of suffrage, the right to form unions) would help

[26] *The Communist Manifesto, op. cit.,* p. 355.

them gain the experience needed to fulfill their destined goal. When the situation was ripe politically, the workers would bid for power in their own right, overthrow the bourgeois state, and complete the second phase.

There is evidence to support the view that Marx in his later years felt that, in certain advanced bourgeois-democratic countries (like the United States and Great Britain), Marxists might be able to achieve their aim by peaceful means. This idea, substantially repudiated by Lenin and Stalin, seemed to come to the fore again in pronouncements by Soviet leaders after the death of Stalin, but it may be some time before the true meaning of those statements can be ascertained.

The logic of dialectical development would also apply economically, Marx contended, in what might be called the principle of "economic maturity." Capitalism could give birth to the proletarian revolution only after it had fully, within its own womb, developed the material conditions that would sustain this revolution. A jump could not be made from a feudal to a communist economy without first passing through the stage of capitalist economic development.

Marx's argument that the achievement of bourgeois political democracy and a fully developed capitalist economy must precede the proletarian revolution could have had enormous practical significance. For instance, if his point here were valid, the proletarian revolution in industrially backward and nondemocratic countries (like Russia in 1917 or China in 1949) could not have occurred, or would have had to await fuller capitalist and democratic development in those countries. Whereas the Russian Mensheviks and other European social-democrats accepted this view, Lenin refused to be bound by such theoretical restrictions.

Whatever may have been Marx's modification of his views in relation to Russia in later life, it is clear that Lenin interpreted Marx as allowing for the possibility of proletarian revolution in industrially backward and relatively undemocratic Czarist Russia. Even before the unsettling effects of World War I created a unique opportunity for the proletarian revolution in Russia, Lenin had advocated a creative and active role for the communist party in shaping the revolution. He had also urged an alliance of a revolutionary proletariat and a revolutionary peasantry, under the leadership of a revolutionary communist party, as essential to socialist triumph. Under the circumstances—with a revolutionary party leading a revolutionary proletariat and peasantry, the weakening of capitalism in Russia in what Lenin called the "imperialist" war, and a weak bourgeois class—given these conditions, the communist revolution in industrially backward and undemocratic Russia could take place.

Lenin of course claimed to be the orthodox interpreter of Marx's views on state and revolution; the claim was reinforced by Lenin's successful leadership of the Bolshevik Revolution of 1917. Consequently, for a more detailed exposition of the communist theory of revolution, which prevailed under Lenin and Stalin, it is appropriate to examine the former's views.

State and Revolution [27]

Lenin wrote his famous pamphlet *State and Revolution*, on the eve of the Bolshevik Revolution of 1917, for the purpose of justifying his theory of violent revolution and dictatorial use of state power. He sought to defend his views against the attacks of two other revolutionary groups: the moderate socialists, who thought that socialism could be established by democratic and parliamentary methods; and the anarchists, who imagined that the oppressive state would wither away immediately upon the overthrow of the bourgeoisie by the proletariat.

The state: agent of class exploitation. According to Lenin, the state is an organ of class rule, for the oppression of one class by another, and for the exploitation of the oppressed class. In a bourgeois society, obviously, the state is the organ of the capitalist class for the oppression of the working class. A standing army and a police force serve to assure the exploitation and oppression. The state also creates a legal order, which enables the dominant class to perpetuate its rule.

Although the legal order moderates the collision, it is not an organ for the conciliation of classes or of class conflict. Consequently communists must oppose the false idea of class harmony in the bourgeois state, as they must oppose the peaceful submission of the majority to the minority.

This view of the state helps to explain the communist hostility to it.

The proletarian revolution: violent overthrow of the bourgeois capitalist state. Lenin argued that there could be no liberation of the oppressed proletarian class without a violent revolution. The workers could not be free until they destroyed the apparatus of state power as built and operated by the ruling, oppressing class. He insisted that bourgeois state power must be smashed, not merely taken over; destroyed, not perfected. He clearly rejected the possibility of evolution to communism or of peaceful communist revolution, and attacked advocates of gradual reform, who contended that it was possible to evolve peacefully toward socialism.

The smashing of the bourgeois state would be accomplished, of course, by the armed working class, but the destruction, Lenin emphasized, of the bourgeois apparatus, did not mean the abolition of the state, for this repressive agency must be used temporarily (now by the proletariat) to wipe out all vestiges of capitalism. Here, it should be observed, Lenin was attacking the anarchists who maintained that, with the overthrow of the bourgeois state, this coercive power would cease to exist. Lenin concluded that the "withering away of the state" did not refer to this stage of the revolution.

[27] The summary given is based on Lenin's work "State and Revolution" (1917), *Selected Works, op. cit.,* Vol. VII.

The dictatorship of the proletariat: socialism. What is to supersede the smashed bourgeois state machine? This question confronted Lenin in a practical sense in the very midst of the Russian Revolution of 1917, and he was obliged to give a more concrete reply than had Marx. Lenin's answer was, superficially, Marx's answer: the dictatorship of the proletariat, but the interpretation and emphasis were different.

Lenin asserted that the dictatorship of the proletariat is the special repressive force for the suppression of the bourgeoisie. It must be noted that Marx's dictatorship of the proletariat was opposed to the dictatorship of the bourgeoisie, not to democracy. Marx had not said that the proletarian revolution (even though it might use the state against the bourgeoisie) would necessarily abolish all vital features of the bourgeois state, including parliamentary government. Lenin, however, proceeded to repudiate bourgeois democracy, and to raise the banner of "proletarian democracy" and Soviet organization and government. The "Soviets," Lenin declared, are the direct organization of the toiling and exploited masses, enabling them to organize and administer the state themselves in every possible way. Bourgeois democracy, he maintained, is false and hypocritical, a paradise for the rich and a snare and deception for the poor. Proletarian democracy is a million times more democratic than any bourgeois democracy, and the Soviet government a million times more democratic than the most democratic bourgeois republic. "Democracy for the vast majority of the people and suppression by force, i.e., exclusion from democracy of the exploiters and oppressors of the people —this is the change democracy undergoes during the *transition* from capitalism to communism." [28]

The armed people, Lenin continued, would replace the standing army and the police of the bourgeois state. The old administrative machine would also be destroyed and replaced by a new one, drawn from the people. There would be a reversion to a simple and easy form of government, to enable everyone to discharge the functions of the state.

During the period of the dictatorship of the proletariat (which is the period of socialism), the liquidation of the bourgeois state and society would continue. Private ownership of the means of production would be abolished, and with state ownership of these means, the old exploitation of the worker would come to an end.

During this period, the proletariat would exercise its power to restructure society along communist lines. It was, however, not to be expected that, in the period of socialism, all vestiges of bourgeois society could be sloughed off speedily. Since socialism would not be able to create an economy of abundance immediately, the distribution of goods would have to continue to be made according to the amount of work each person did. The socialist motto is, "From each according to his ability; to

[28] "State and Revolution," *ibid.,* p. 81.

each according to his work." Workers would thus be paid equal wages for equal work, as under capitalism, but this would not be communist equality, since it does not take the workers' needs into account.

Communism and the withering away of the state. The communist motto is, "From each according to his ability; to each according to his needs." This is true communist equality. Some workers might get more than others for the same amount of work. Yet, since they might need more (to provide for their wives and children, for example, in contrast to a bachelor and/or childless worker), they would receive more. This genuine communist equality would now be possible since communist production would be great enough to assure an economy of abundance.

At this time, too, society would have been transformed completely, from the economic substructure through the political, legal, and cultural superstructure. All capitalist elements would have been purged, and class oppression eliminated. Since everyone would now have all he needed, there would be no cause for antisocial behavior. The need for violence, coercion, and subjugation would have disappeared, for the "people will have *become accustomed* to observing the elementary conditions of social life *without force* and *without subordination*." [29] This would be the result of a new generation, brought up under the new and free conditions of socialism. At this point, the state as a coercive power would "wither away."

The Role of the Communist Party

As early as 1902, in *What Is To Be Done?* Lenin had grasped the supreme importance of a revolutionary party imbued with the right revolutionary theory. Only a revolutionary party, equipped with "an advanced theory," could indoctrinate the masses and lead a successful revolution.

Not only must this revolutionary party be equipped with the right theory; it must also be united, ideologically homogeneous, strong, disciplined, and centralized. Lenin early fought for this kind of party: in which the minority would be subordinated to the majority; which would be directed by a central organ and a central committee; and whose central committee would have the power to purge itself of unreliable members. [30]

When the idea of a disciplined, "iron party" is linked with Lenin's concept of the dictatorship of the proletariat, the Soviet one-party system is a certainty. The dictatorship of the proletariat becomes the dictatorship of the party which, in turn, boils down to the dictatorship of the Central Committee of the Communist Party.

Marx and Engels had argued that communists are leaders in the work-

---

[29] *Ibid.*, p. 75.
[30] *One Step Forward, Two Steps Back* (1904), quoted in Carew Hunt, *op. cit.*, p. 149.

ing class struggle, but they had specifically asserted that "Communists do not form a separate party opposed to other working-class parties." [31] Lenin, however, whether forced by the revolutionary conditions of the twentieth century, by his own temperament, or by an intuitive grasp of the inner nature of the communist revolution, developed a concept of a limited, tightly disciplined party. This party, organized on the principle of "democratic centralism" (subordination of the lower organs to the higher), had very definite tendencies toward dictation from the top down, which became clearer when "centralism" received the emphasis at the expense of "democratic" in the operation of the party.

Lenin, then, saw the need for the party to lead the revolution and the working masses organized into Soviets (workers' councils). Yet, he did not wish the Soviet system to fail, nor did he envisage the party dominating the Soviets and replacing the Soviet system permanently. He looked, rather, to co-operation between the two.[32]

Under Stalin, two developments took place: The party emerged as the absolute authority in the Soviet Union, and the dictatorship of the party and its Central Committee clearly became the dictatorship of the Politbureau (the innermost committee of the party), which turned out to be the dictatorship of Joseph Stalin.

These phenomena are not unrelated to Stalin's thesis of "socialism in one country," the dominant strategic conception of the Stalinist era which shaped communist tactics in the building of Soviet power.

"Socialism in One Country"

This idea developed during the 1920's, as it became evident that communism on a world-wide scale was not imminent and that the socialist dictatorship of the proletariat would for some time be confined to Russia. Although the concept began to emerge in the closing years of Lenin's life, it was Stalin who developed the principle into a major doctrine.

He argued that a socialist society could be built in one country, the U.S.S.R., by its own efforts, despite the relative lack of industrial ripeness there and the absence of proletarian revolutions in other key countries. This did not mean, however, that world revolution was to be abandoned or even temporarily jettisoned while the Soviet Union achieved socialism. The inference was clear that a complete, final, and guaranteed socialist victory could not be secured in that country without successful revolutions in such other countries as would make a counter-revolution against the Soviet Union impossible.

However, there can be no doubt whatever that Stalin's position had deep and far-reaching effects on Soviet power and international communism. It instilled confidence in many people in industrially backward Russia

[31] *The Communist Manifesto, op. cit.,* p. 334.
[32] Carew Hunt, *op. cit.,* pp. 151–152.

that they could build socialism there without waiting for proletarian revolutions in the more industrialized countries of Western Europe. Momentarily, at least, it blunted the edge of immediate world revolution everywhere. It may have given the Soviet Union a breathing spell in the field of international relations. Above all, it made the Soviet Union the keystone of world communism beyond any doubt. The maintenance of Soviet power was to be primary; international communism, for the sake of its own advancement, was to be subject to the interest and hegemony of the Soviet Union.

Later, in 1938, Stalin could assert that the building of socialism in one country was not only possible but had been accomplished. The reservation was still made that the socialist victory in the Soviet Union could not be fully secure as long as that country was encircled by hostile capitalist countries. Permanent security for the communists could not be expected until communism had been established on a world-wide scale.

The Triumph of the Party, Politbureau, and Dictatorship

Lenin's role in making possible the transformation of the dictatorship of the proletariat into the dictatorship of the party has been mentioned previously. Stalin consolidated this trend and carried it to its logical conclusion: the dictatorship of the "indispensable" man in the party.

The Soviets were now made subordinate to the communist party organization, which, though working through the formal structure of the workers' councils, emerged as the real ruling class in the Soviet Union. The party remained a "narrow" party, a very small minority of the total voting population. Its make-up tended to be less proletarian, and its operation less democratic. Its ranks underwent purges that made the controversies in Lenin's day seem like innocent child's play. Power within the party, almost unlimited, devolved clearly and authoritatively upon the central party organs, of which the Politbureau [33] (the highest policy-making body in the party) and the Secretariat (the all-important executive group) became the most important. The key man within the Secretariat, the Secretary-General of the party, the party's chief executive, Joseph Stalin, emerged after the purges of the communist leaders in the late 1920's and mid-1930's as the real and undisputed ruler of the Soviet Union, the heart of the communist revolution.

The Totalitarian Use of State Power

If socialism was to be built in the Soviet Union and a monolithic Communist Party to lead the proletariat in the building of socialism in industrially backward Russia and in a hostile capitalist world, the party would have to use the power of the Soviet state fully, completely, and without qualms.

[33] Since 1952 this highest organ of the party has been called the "Presidium."

Consequently, in several five-year plans the industrialization of the country was pushed at an accelerated pace, a pace which placed the demands of heavy industry ahead of the demands for consumer goods. Similarly and contrary to Lenin's admonitions against coercion of the peasants, Stalin in 1929 embarked upon a ruthless policy of forced collectivization of agriculture.

The five-year plans required gigantic economic planning, which involved state or public ownership and direction of the means of production and exchange, in industry and agriculture. This, of necessity, increased the power of the state and its control over the lives of the citizens of the U.S.S.R.

The totalitarian use of state power posed two theoretical questions:

1. How did it square with the theory of Marx and Lenin?

2. Was it not reasonable to assume that there would be at least an internal relaxation of state power when socialism had been secured, when the exploiting bourgeois class had been destroyed, within the Soviet Union?

Stalin's answers, when they finally came, were as follows:

1. The mightiest and strongest form of state power must be developed "in order to prepare the conditions *for* the withering away of state power. . . ."

2. The state cannot wither away so long as the Soviet Union is "surrounded by the capitalist world [and] is subject to the menace of foreign military attack"; the state must be maintained in sufficient strength "to defend the conquests of socialism from foreign attacks." [34]

Presumably, for Stalin, the Soviet state, as a coercive and repressive organ, would not gradually wither away, even though the Soviet Union were to pass from the socialist to the communist stage of development. Rather, state power would continue to grow and become intensified, and would explode away at precisely the moment that internal and external conditions made internal coercion (within the Soviet Union) and external defense (against the foes of the Soviet Union) no longer necessary.

Communist World Revolution

As stated earlier, the commitment to the policy of "socialism in one country" had great significance for the communist world revolution. Lenin had previously maintained that communist parties could achieve a victorious revolution only if they secured mass support—the support of millions. This could not be gained if communist parties isolated themselves from the masses, from noncommunists, and thus from power. He had insisted that power could be attained only if communists worked within governments, trade unions, and other mass movements, currently

[34] *Problems of Leninism* (Moscow, Foreign Languages Publishing House, 1940), p. 659. See also Carew Hunt, *op. cit.*, pp. 182–183.

controlled by their opponents. To use a phrase more familiar to the reader, they must bore from within, but in doing so they must know how to combine complete loyalty to the ideas of communism with an ability to make all the necessary practical compromises—to tack, make agreements, zigzag, retreat, and so on. Only by beating the bourgeois politicians at their own game (of elections and parliamentary government, for example) could communists build up mass support in preparation for the seizure of power.

In brief, Lenin argued, communist parties are to seize the opportunities presented them to build mass support, never hesitating to use others for their ends, always boring from within by means of "united fronts" and "front" organizations. They must never forget that their most dangerous rivals are the anticommunist socialists who compete with communists for the good will of the workers. They must also zigzag when necessary to keep up with the latest instructions from the highest authority in the party, never losing sight of the goal of the proletarian revolution.

It was upon this foundation that Stalin proceeded to build, but in the course of it he subordinated all other communist parties to the hegemony of the Soviet Communist Party. Prompting his action was the recognition that the maintenance and success of Soviet power—the primary hope of the proletarian revolution in other countries of the world— was paramount. This helps to explain Soviet dominance of such communist world organizations as the Comintern and Cominform, the connection between the communist parties of various countries throughout the world and the Communist Party of the Soviet Union, and the zigs and zags of those parties in pursuance of the foreign policy of the Soviet Union.

Stalin's insistence upon a single Soviet path to socialism (a policy which could be maintained when the communist parties of the world were generally subservient to his direction) assumed great significance at the end of World War II. At this time, under the protection of Soviet arms, it was relatively easy to set up communist or communist-controlled regimes in Central and Southeastern Europe and in areas like North Korea. Even though these regimes called themselves peoples' democracies and at first made a pretense of coalition government, it soon became clear that they were following the Stalinist pattern of revolution. In Europe, Yugoslavia was the only communist regime whose leadership group was not specifically approved by Stalin and did not follow the Stalinist concept of revolution. The so-called peoples' democracies might constitute a form of government between western bourgeois democracy and Soviet socialism, yet it would only be a matter of time until all opponents of the regime were liquidated and the stage set for the more complete emulation of the Soviet regime.

The doctrinal pronouncements by current Soviet leaders since Stalin's death in conjunction with their veering and tacking in their relations toward the several countries of the Soviet bloc make it difficult to gauge whether a shift has really been made away from Stalin's strategy and tactics of revolution. Both pronouncements and deeds are of great importance in attempting to assess the communist challenge, but they must still be appraised against the background of communist doctrine, strategy, and tactics expounded earlier by Marx, Lenin, and Stalin.

Communism: The Continuing Debate

At this point it is appropriate to summarize the major principles of communist doctrine, strategy, and tactics, and the communist impact on the world before World War II, after which the changes since World War II and Stalin's death will be noted.

1. Communism remains a prophecy of a better world.

2. Communism remains a substantially deterministic philosophy of history which purports to explain, in terms of "laws" of historical development, the inevitable triumph of communism in the world.

3. Communism remains a full-fledged critique of the evils of capitalism and imperialism.

4. Communism remains a strategy of revolutionary action, although from Marx to the present it underwent considerable alteration at the hands of Lenin and Stalin.

Lenin, it will be recalled, committed communism to a forthright revolutionary program of action. It was based squarely on violence, and was unalterably opposed to the peaceful, parliamentary transition to socialism. Lenin was firmly convinced of the inevitability of a final war with the capitalistic, imperialistic powers. He also stressed the necessity of leadership of the proletarian revolution by a disciplined, dedicated, centralized, ruthless communist party, while underscoring the opportunities for such a revolutionary party to triumph in countries that were relatively immature economically and politically, as a result of the weakening of capitalist nations in modern imperialist wars. Finally, he emphasized the importance of expedient tactics to further the firm and unalterable goal of world-wide communist revolution.

Wherever necessary, Stalin subordinated orthodox Marxist-Leninist doctrine to his central purpose of building and consolidating the power of the Soviet Union as the key bastion of the world-wide communist revolution. He carried the principle of the dictatorship of the proletariat (which had become, with Lenin, the dictatorship of the communist party) to a logical conclusion in his personal dictatorship, based on his position as Secretary-General of the Communist Party. He set forth a theory of "capitalist encirclement" to explain the continued growth of the domestic power of the Soviet state, despite the achievement of socialism and the march toward communism, and he maintained that the state would become even more powerful before it disintegrated, upon the secure achievement of communism. Communist movements throughout the world were made subservient to the Soviet national interest and Stalin's policy of a single Soviet path to socialism.

Before World War II, however, communist power was Soviet power. The challenge of communism, although apparent, did not command forceful world-wide attention, until the clear-cut emergence after World War II of the Soviet Union as the major power in Europe and one of the two giant powers on earth. Many observers, it should be noted, believe that communist postwar successes are not to be attributed to the free ideological appeal of communist doctrine but rather to the unsettling effects of World War II, the defeat of Germany and Japan, and the dominance of Soviet power on the Eurasian continent. These factors enabled the Soviet Union to set up the so-called peoples' democracies in Central and Southeastern Europe, helped the Chinese Communists to win a civil war for the control of the Chinese mainland, stimulated the bid of the North Koreans (and later the Chinese Communists) for the military unification of Korea, and facilitated Ho Chi Minh's victory in North Vietnam. These observers point to the failure of communist efforts outside the reach of Soviet armies, or where the western powers were determined and able to support existing governments against Soviet pressure (as in Turkey) or internal revolt (as in Greece).

Communists counter by noting that the weakening of capitalist regimes in World War II is to be explained in terms of the contradictions inherent in a capitalist system which leads to disastrous imperialist wars. They argue that many more countries would today have communist governments were it not for the power of western arms, which support "reactionary" regimes and colonial governments throughout the world. They underscore the high percentage of communist voters in France and Italy.

Apparent Changes Since Stalin's Death

Against this background, it is pertinent to examine the doctrine, strategy, and tactics involved in the new Soviet diplomatic offensive launched since Stalin's death. This offensive brings into sharp focus the nature and effectiveness of the current communist challenge for the control of the minds of men and of nations in the modern world.

Doctrinally, it seems to involve a rejection or modification of hitherto accepted views of both Lenin and Stalin.[35] Although Stalin received the brunt of adverse criticism, it seems clear that the Kremlin's doctrinal pronouncements involved a denial or qualification of certain Leninist

[35] See the significant speech of the First Secretary of the Soviet Communist Party, Nikita Khrushchev, *New York Times*, February 15, 1956, p. 10.

tenets, as well as a repudiation of, or reservation about, certain Stalinist theories and harsh practices.

The superficial purpose of this new offensive, it would seem, is to make the Soviet Union appear as a confident, liberal, broad-minded friend of peace, freedom, independence, and well-being. The gist of the new position is summarized thus:

1. It seemingly denies Lenin's view that war with capitalism is inevitable. Now, Soviet leaders are saying that war is only possible if the capitalist nations insist on starting it.

2. Apparently violence is no longer inevitable as a condition of the proletarian revolution. Now, the use and extent of violence will be determined by the resistance of the capitalist class itself.

3. Soviet leaders now assert the possibility of peaceful, parliamentary progress to socialism and communism, in rather sharp contradiction to Lenin's revolutionary program in *State and Revolution*.

4. Soviet leaders seem to have rejected Stalin's view of capitalist encirclement. Apparently, now the Soviet Union and its allies have burst out of the capitalist encirclement; at least they have been successful in creating a powerful "zone of peace" in the world.[36] This may also explain the well-publicized easing of domestic conditions within the Soviet Union.

5. The present leadership seems also to have rejected the Stalinist view of a single Soviet path to socialism or communism. It is in this framework that they would have the world view the reconciliation with Tito, the belated apologies for past purges in the satellite countries, and the dissolution of the Cominform in 1956. Now, they seem to be saying, there may be several roads to socialism and communism.[37]

The new Soviet offensive in foreign policy—which appears to represent a shift from military and political force to economic inducement and diplomatic enticement—thus takes on added meaning. Key questions still arise to plague the interested student. Are the Moscow pronouncements really fundamental doctrinal changes or merely expedient tactical shifts? If we disregard this question, can we say that these changes intensify the nature of the communist challenge? If so, which communist challenge: that of Soviet diplomacy? of communist ideology? of native communist parties?

The changes, it should be noted, do not deny the belief in the ultimate inevitability of communism itself or the revolutionary reconstruction of capitalist countries in the coming communist order. They do not even

[36] The Soviet Union's enhanced military might, its sputnik "coup," and its increased nuclear-bomb and ICBM strength should be kept in mind, as well.

[37] In view of the brutal suppression by Soviet troops of the revolt in Hungary, the taut feelings between Poland and the Soviet Union, and the still troubled relations between Yugoslavia and the U.S.S.R., fundamental changes in Soviet policy must be appraised with great circumspection.

repudiate resort to violence, since it may have to be applied if others employ it first. Yet, will these changes encourage the social-democrats (or evolutionary socialists) to work with the communists in "united front" movements? Will they allay world-wide fears of Soviet intentions? Will a lessening of fear of the Soviet Union lull the nations of Western Europe into a false sense of security? Will the new Soviet offensive soften the underdeveloped areas of the world—already highly sensitized to the evils of colonialism—and make them more susceptible to economic penetration now and political penetration later?

These are the questions that confront the student as he faces the continuing debate over communism: its doctrine and challenge.

In "Positions on the Problem," three of the many questions related to this continuing debate will be examined: Will communism, sooner or later, triumph throughout the world? Or can the free world prove that communism is wrong in theory and in practice? Or can the free world rest content, as far as the underdeveloped areas of the world are concerned, convinced that a liberating, independent, and progressive nationalism is the best safeguard against the evils of communism?

POSITIONS
ON THE PROBLEM

1. Sooner or Later, Communism Will Triumph Throughout the World

(The following excerpts are from a speech by Nikita S. Khrushchev, First Secretary of the Soviet Communist Party, delivered before its Twentieth Congress. In this speech Khrushchev freely interprets the doctrine of Marxism-Leninism-Stalinism and adapts it to enhance the effectiveness of Soviet foreign policy.[38])

The World-Wide Emergence of Communism and the Fight for Peace

The principal feature of our epoch is the emergence of socialism from the confines of one country and its transformation into a world system. Capitalism has proved impotent to hinder this world-historical process.

The simultaneous existence of two opposed and world economic system[s]

[38] N. S. Khrushchev, "Speech to the Twentieth Congress of the Communist Party of the Soviet Union," *New York Times*, February 15, 1956, p. 10.

. . . capitalism and socialism, developing according to different laws in the opposite direction, has become an irrefutable fact. . . .

The forces of peace have grown considerably with the appearance in the world arena of the group of peace-loving states in Europe and Asia, which have proclaimed non-participation in blocs to be the principle of their foreign policy.

As a result, an extensive "zone of peace," including both Socialist and non-Socialist peace-loving states of Europe and Asia, has appeared on the world arena.

This zone extends over a vast area of the globe, inhabited by nearly 1,500,-000,000 people, or the majority of the population of our planet. . . .

Today many Social Democrats are for an active struggle against the war danger and militarism, for closer relations with Socialist countries, and for unity of the labor movement. We sincerely welcome the Social Democrats, and are ready to do everything possible to unite our efforts in a fight for the noble cause of the defense of peace and the interests of the working people. . . .

We believe that if the famous five principles of peaceful coexistence were made the basis of relations between the U.S.S.R. and the United States, this would be of truly outstanding significance for all mankind and would, of course, be no less beneficial to the people of the United States than to the peoples of the U.S.S.R. and all other nations. . . .[39]

We want to be friends and to cooperate with the United States in the effort for peace and security of . . . [all] peoples. . . .

If good relations are not established between the Soviet Union and the United States, and mutual distrust exists, this will lead to an arms race on a still greater scale and to a still more dangerous growth of the forces on both sides.

We intend to continue to work for the further improvement of our relations with Great Britain and France.

We welcome the desire of the people of the Arab countries to uphold their national independence. . . .

Counterposing the slogan of the North Atlantic pact: "Let us arm," we advise the slogan: "Let us trade."

The Leninist principle of peaceful coexistence of states with differing social systems was, and remains, the general line of our country's foreign policy. . . .

The Meaning of the World-Wide Triumph of Communism

When we say that in the competition between the two systems of capitalism and socialism, socialism will triumph, this by no means implies that the victory will be reached by armed intervention on the part of the Socialist countries in the internal affairs of the capitalist countries.

We believe that after seeing for themselves the advantages that communism holds out, all working men and women on earth will sooner or later take to the road of the struggle to build a socialist society.

---

[39] "These principles [the "famous five principles of peaceful coexistence"] proclaim that countries different from one another politically, socially and economically can and must cooperate on the basis of mutual respect, and non-interference in each other's home affairs, and must abide by the policy of active and peaceful coexistence in the common desire to attain the ideals of peace and the improvement of man's living conditions." From the Joint Statement of N. A. Bulganin, N. S. Khrushchev, and Jawaharlal Nehru, December 13, 1955, in Report to the Supreme Soviet on the Visit to India, Burma, and Afghanistan (New York, New Century Publishers, 1956), p. 32.

We have always asserted and continue to assert that the establishment of a new social order in any country is the internal affair of its people.

Such are our positions, based on the great teachings of Marxism-Leninism. . . .

As will be recalled, there is a Marxist-Leninist premise which says that while imperialism exists wars are inevitable.

While capitalism remains on earth the reactionary forces representing the interests of the capitalist monopolies will continue to strive for war gambles and aggression, and may try to let loose war.

There is [however] no fatal inevitability of war.

Now there are powerful social and political forces, commanding serious means capable of preventing the unleashing of war by the imperialists, and—should they try to start it—of delivering a smashing rebuff to the aggressors and thwarting their adventuristic plans. . . .

The enemies are fond of depicting us, Leninists, as supporters of violence always and in all circumstances. It is true that we recognize the necessity for the revolutionary transformation of capitalist society into Socialist society.

This is what distinguishes revolutionary Marxists from reformists and opportunists. There is not a shadow of doubt that for a number of capitalist countries the overthrow of the bourgeois dictatorship by force and the connected sharp aggravation of the class struggle is inevitable.

But there are different forms of social revolution and the allegation that we recognize force and civil war as the only way of transforming society does not correspond to reality.

Leninism teaches us that the ruling classes will not relinquish power of their own free will.

However, the greater or lesser degree of acuteness in the struggle, the use or not of force in the transition to socialism, depend not so much on the proletariat as on the extent of the resistance put up by the exploiters, and on the employment of violence by the exploiting class itself.

In this connection the question arises of the possibility of employing the parliamentary form for the transition to socialism. For the Russian Bolsheviks, who were the first to accomplish the transition to socialism, this way was excluded.

However, since then radical changes have taken place in the historical situation that allows an approach to this question from another angle.

Socialism has become a great magnetizing force for the workers, peasants and intelligentsia in all lands. The ideas of socialism are really conquering the minds of all toiling mankind.

At the same time, in a number of capitalist countries, the working class possesses in the present situation realistic opportunities of welding under its leadership the overwhelming majority of the people and of insuring . . . [the] transition of the principal means of production into the hands of the people.

The right-wing bourgeois parties and the Governments they form are becoming bankrupt more and more often.

In these conditions, by rallying around itself a toiling peasantry, the intelligentsia and all the patriotic forces, and by meting out a determined rebuff to opportunistic elements incapable of abandoning a policy of conciliation with the capitalists and landlords, the working class has the possibility of inflicting a defeat on the reactionary anti-popular forces and of gaining a firm majority in parliament, and converting it from an organ of bourgeois democracy into an instrument of genuinely popular will.

In such an event, this institution, traditional for many highly developed capitalist countries, may become an organ of genuine democracy, of democracy for the working people.

The winning of a stable parliamentary majority, based on the mass revolutionary movement of the proletariat and the working people, would bring about for the working class of a number of capitalist and former colonial countries, conditions insuring the implementation of fundamental social transformations.

Of course in countries where capitalism is still strong and where it controls an enormous military and police machine, the serious resistance of the reactionary forces is inevitable.

There the transition to socialism will proceed amid conditions of an acute class revolutionary struggle. . . .

The Tasks of the Communist Party

What are the further tasks of the party in the sphere of foreign policy?

1. Undeviatingly to follow the Leninist policy of peaceful coexistence among different states, irrespective of their social order. To fight actively for peace and the security of nations, and for confidence among states, by seeking the conversion of the relaxation achieved in international tension into lasting peace.

2. To strengthen by all means the fraternal relations with the Peoples Republic of China, Poland, Czechoslovakia, Bulgaria, Hungary, Rumania, Albania, the [East] German Democratic Republic, the Peoples Democratic Republic of [North] Korea, the Democratic Republic of [North] Vietnam, and the Mongolian Peoples Republic, remembering that the greater the unity and might of the Socialist countries the more secure is the cause of peace. To strengthen by all means friendship and cooperation with the fraternal people of the Federal Peoples Republic of Yugoslavia.

3. To reinforce indefatigably the bond of friendship and cooperation with the republic of India, Burma, Afghanistan, Egypt, Syria and other states that stand for peace. To support countries that refuse to be involved in military blocs; to cooperate with all forces seeking to preserve peace. To develop and strengthen friendly relations with Finland, Austria, and other neutral countries.

4. To conduct an active policy of further improving relations with the United States of America, Britain, France, Western Germany, Japan, Italy, Turkey, Iran and other countries, with a view to strengthening mutual confidence, extending trade, and expanding contacts and cooperation in the sphere of culture and science.

5. To follow vigilantly the intrigues of circles not interested in the relaxing of international tension, and to expose in good time the subversive activities of the enemies of peace and security of the nations; to take the necessary steps to strengthen further the defense capacity of our Socialist state; to maintain our defenses at the level demanded by modern armament and science, and to insure the security of our Socialist state.

2. THE FREE WORLD CAN PROVE THAT COMMUNISM IS WRONG

(The following extracts are taken from a publication of the House Committee on Foreign Affairs, *The Strategy and Tactics of World Communism*.[40])

[40] U.S. Congress, House Committee on Foreign Affairs, 80th Congr., 2nd sess., House Doc. 619, *The Strategy and Tactics of World Communism* (Washington, D.C., Government Printing Office, 1948), pp. 1, 4–5, 53–56, 57–61.

Communism Cannot Be Disregarded

There have been times, as at the bottom of the depression in 1932, when it was not easy to be sure that communism would fail, that we had the better case. There have been other times when the faults and weaknesses of communism, and its archaic goals, have not been apparent, and we forgot them. As a result of this we have not always been as conscious of the difference between communism and our own democracy as is necessary for clear-headed action. Today we know that 100 years have not brought the fulfillment of Communist prognostications. But they have brought a time, now, when communism cannot be disregarded. . . .

Ten Conclusions

An examination of all aspects of Soviet and Communist policy and tactics leads directly to some simple conclusions.

1. The Communists have one goal—world revolution.

2. They assume that the revolution will be violent.

3. They are incapable of accepting the idea that peace can endure from now on, and they expect one more catastrophic war.

4. The Soviet Union is regarded as the main force of the revolution.

5. They fear a coalition against the Soviet Union.

6. They therefore fear reconstruction or federation in the non-Communist world.

7. They utilize the most modern and effective means of cold warfare to strengthen their own forces and to weaken all others.

8. The Communist Parties outside the Soviet Union are junior partners or auxiliaries.

9. The tactics are based upon a definite theory, and the central propositions of that theory do not change.

10. The division of Europe and Asia between the victors of World War II is to be settled by power politics and not by negotiation. . . .

Communist Mythology and the Facts:
Russia and the United States

(a) According to the Communists we are the prime embodiment of the capitalist system. What they mean by this . . . in particular [is] the deprivation of the producing class of the fruits of production. If there is any country in the world of which this is more true than of any other today it is not, however, the United States but the Soviet Union. And at the same time there is no country in the world where labor gains the benefit of high production so much as in the United States.

(b) They charge us with being in the monopoly and imperialist phase of capitalism. Yet they maintain a foreign trade monopoly and we do not. They have monopolies in every major industry and we in none.

(c) They claim that labor is exploited in our system. But it is they, not we, who use the slave labor of millions on political grounds, plus the slave labor of war prisoners by the hundreds of thousands.

(d) They claim that our trade-unions are a false front, designed to betray the interests of labor, and covertly under capitalist control. But it is their unions that are iron-bound organs for state control, with strikes prohibited, used only as instruments to prevent labor from seeking justice.

(e) They hold that we have a vast spread between the rich and the poor. But their army has a wider range of pay than ours, and the general wage spread in the Soviet has increased while ours has decreased.

(f) They claim that our form of democracy is a sham and theirs is the true one. But in ours the party in power can lose an election, voters can shift their allegiance, new parties can be organized. What they call democracy involves a vote of more than 99 per cent for the party in power, with no criticism of policy. . . .

(g) The Communists hold that our parties mislead and deceive the voters. No party in the United States has ever deceived all the voters if it deceived any of them. The single party in the Soviet enjoys unchallenged monopoly of the art of deception.

(h) The Communists declare that the capitalist press is the corrupt instrument of capitalist controlled propaganda. . . . The simple fact that the Communist side of the case can be covered by citations to the American press should make further comment unnecessary. But it may be added that their theory of the party and of democratic centralization provides a role for agitation and propaganda, "agitprop" in their vocabulary, but no role for freedom of information.

(i) They hold that corruption is characteristic of our system, and cite our prolific scandals in evidence. But scandal as such depends upon standards of public behavior, and scandal is rarest just where corruption has become the rule instead of the exception. . . . The existence of corruption in the Soviet is not unheard of, however, and standards of public honesty in the United States have made enormous progress. The evolution of their tactics on the basis that "the end justifies the means," is really a sort of systematic universal corruption, instituted and legitimicized.

(j) They call us reactionary. Yet we are the land of maximum progress toward freedom and welfare for all, and the Soviets the land of maximum reassertion of the ancient characteristics of tyranny. Their thinking rejects the possibility of peace while ours asserts it, and theirs rejects the capacity of free men for self-direction while ours asserts it. . . .

(k) According to Marx and his followers the capitalist[s] . . . are too hidebound, and too limited in vision by their own special interests, to see the necessary way out of the contradictions of capitalism into a system where production will be unimpeded. Both production and democracy in the United States have been less hide-bound than anywhere else. And in the Soviet, while production has grown it has grown only for the power of the state, and democracy in the sense of freedom has not grown at all.

(l) The Communists hold that we are doomed to suffer another great economic crisis. It is too early to claim that we have proved the expectation false. If we can prove that it is false we will have to go on proving it for a long time to come. But we have already gone past the time when they expected it. Meanwhile they are set in a condition called permanent revolution in their theories. This is not precisely the same as an economic depression, but it is a condition requiring dictatorial controls, the sacrifice of welfare for capital formation, and maintenance of an iron curtain, agitation and propaganda instead of a free press. Permanent revolution is only another way of saying that they live permanently with the conditions that we know only as the consequences of depression.

(m) They denounce us for economic imperialism. Meanwhile we have given freedom to the Philippines, and our imperialist partner, Britain, has granted freedom to more people than any conqueror ever conquered. The United States has freely given away more than the amount of foreign investments ever held by any imperialist power. And the Soviets have grasped every economic means to exploit territories under complete or partial control.

(n) They equally denounce our political imperialism. But it is we who aid others, not to become "Yankee stooges" but to get on their feet and be themselves, and it is they who can tolerate no independent power whatever except for the time being and pending the "inevitable conflict."

(o) They call us "war mongers." But it is we who have believed that there need not be another war, and we who are disillusioned at the difficulties of preventing one, now that the difficulties are apparent. And it is they who lay down as fundamental doctrine that there must be a final ghastly struggle.

(p) They accuse the capitalist world of resorting to terrorism against the challenge of revolution. The roots of Communist terror may originate in communism or in Russian brutality. Russia never went through the historical development of humanitarianism that has reduced brutality in western countries. . . .

(q) They regard us as "hard to get along with," and attribute this naturally to our capitalist-imperialist designs. An opinion on the subject has been expressed by a source with which few will choose to differ. Mrs. F. D. Roosevelt, in her column in the *Washington Daily News* for January 3, 1948, said: "I do not think we have always been wise or tactful in our approach to the Government of the U.S.S.R., but basically we have been the ones to make the constructive offers and they have been the ones to refuse."

(r) Their general charges against any idea of hope or successful reform in our system are variations on the old charge that all such hopes offer the workers "pie in the sky." But if conditions for labor in the United States today are "pie in the sky" or if recovery in other countries by immediate American aid is so described, what figure of speech can be devised to cover the withering away of the state only after a world proletarian dictatorship, which will not begin until after one more great holocaust of war, which may itself not occur until after three or four more 5-year plans have armed the Soviet [Union]. . . .

Such a catalogue of Communist charges and answers may not be conclusive on each single point, but its general weight suggests an irrelevance between the Communist mythology and the facts. A direct approach to the questions that this raises may be made through an examination of Stalin's list of the three great "contradictions" of capitalism. . . . These contradictions are the one between the capitalist class and the working class within a capitalist country, the one between the competing imperialist nations, and the one between the imperialist nations and the subject peoples. . . . So far as the first contradiction goes, the working class in the United States, while not finally and forever satisfied, now enjoys life in a system that gives the average worker a larger share of the benefits of production than is true in the Soviet. Marx included in his original theory of capitalism the conclusion that the rich must get richer and the poor poorer until the revolution. Under rising wage standards, and with graduated income and inheritance taxes, just the opposite has occurred.

As for the second contradiction, and the third one, both have been succeeded by the present tendency toward the granting of freedom to former colonial areas. The United States has played a small part in this for the simple reason that it has had but few colonies to turn loose. But Britain has spent a century in freeing her dominions from colonial status, and has now extended the process to India and Burma. . . .

The case of the United States expressed in Marxist terms would be somewhat as follows: The United States has passed through and beyond the capitalist system as described by Marxism. The contradictions of capitalism have been eliminated, or are on the way to elimination through genuine and adequate remedies. . . .

Meeting the Communist Challenge:
Negative Countermeasures

The first conclusion to be drawn from the strategy and tactics of world communism is that we have to do something about them. Whether the revolution is inevitable or not, their ability to disturb and disrupt is such that they might make a revolutionary smashup unavoidable. To prevent this, to make sure that there will not be another world war and a violent world revolution if it is humanly avoidable, requires that the non-Communist world have the chance to prove itself. In order to do so it must be insulated against Communist tactics. Communist action will increase the economic and social strains in non-Communist countries, and if they have free opportunity to do so there may be catastrophe that would not have occurred without them.

In order to take protective measures we must be clear about what part of the world must be protected. A positive goal of economic stabilization, international collaboration, and peace cannot be worked out by each nation for itself. All are dependent in large degree upon the iron necessities of material requirements. Modern industry and modern civilization cannot exist without materials that are found in no one country. The abolition of the causes of war cannot go on in each country by itself. . . .

This means that the area within which an experiment, to prove that war and revolution are obsolete, can be conducted with hope of success is approximately the same as the present non-Communist world.

Within this non-Communist area, the all-important measures will be the positive ones. But the positive ones cannot be carried on unless Communist sabotage and interference is fended off. In order to fend them off, the following measures are needed.

First. We must analyze communism more thoroughly than in the past, and this study of communism must not be only by specialists on the subject, but must be clearly expressed in terms that can reach the democratic peoples of the world. The fact that Communists do not believe in peace, nor in economic recovery, and that their hopes are only for chaos and dictatorship must be clearly seen by all. The fact that sincere cooperation for our goals is impossible must be put beyond dispute.

Second. We must deny the Communists any favors or special opportunities to practice their infiltration tactics. . . .

Third. Certain measures of political defense must be taken in many non-Communist countries. . . .

Fourth. Measures of economic defense are needed, by the United States and by all other non-Communist countries. . . .

Fifth. Our propaganda to the Communist-controlled countries should not be conducted on the defensive. We should tell them that we are more advanced than they are, that we are already post-revolutionary, that we promise peace, not war, while they can only promise war, not peace. We should emphasize every success as a success toward the fulfillment of this promise.

Sixth. We must avoid a drift into recrimination and abuse. . . .

Seventh. If we succeed in the only kind of project that can make positive sense, one of the accompaniments will be a new turn of Communist policy from a radical offensive drive to a moderate defensive drive. . . .

Meeting the Communist Challenge: Positive Countermeasures

The . . . most indispensable thing we have to do is to keep our economy on an even keel, and go forward without a depression. . . . If we have one more real smash it may shift the scales of power beyond repair. . . .

. . . We must clarify our own argument. One factor in the weakness of morale in the non-Communist world, and in the strength of morale in the Communist world, is the clarity of their ideas and the vagueness of ours. . . . Actually our government has said much of what ought to be said. . . .

We have a policy toward the United Nations, a policy of hope that it can serve greatly in the mastery of the causes of war. We have a military establishment of our own, designed to guarantee that no power will find an opportunity to start a great, aggressive war with hope of victory. We have a policy on the international control of atomic energy, designed to place this control above the sovereignty of nations, and to make atomic energy a great factor in civilization instead of in war. We have a policy on world trade, designed to make increasing trade a factor in economic stability and economic progress. We have, with our near neighbors, the policy of the good neighbor designed to introduce a common means of mastering common problems. . . . We have a policy of extending loans and free gifts to countries needing aid. . . . We have been extending the good neighbor policy in many ways to all areas of Europe and Asia that show any readiness to cooperate. There is little quarrel with most of these principles of our policy taken singly. But the fact that they add up to make a program is almost unknown. . . .

In a nutshell, our objective is to prove that Lenin was wrong.

3. A Liberating Nationalism Is the Best Safeguard Against Communism

(The following extracts are taken from two sources: a discussion between Jawaharlal Nehru and Norman Cousins, in *Talks with Nehru,* and Nehru's remarks at the Bandung (Asian-African) Conference in Indonesia, April, 1955.[41])

Asia's Resistance to Imposed Solutions

[Nehru] Now the world as we find it today is unbelievably varied, and various parts face different problems. In Asia the primary problem is, let us say, food or raising terribly low living standards. The people lack the necessities

[41] The question-and-answer extract may be found in *Talks with Nehru,* by Jawaharlal Nehru and Norman Cousins (published by The John Day Company, New York; copyright, 1951, by Saturday Review Associates, Inc.), pp. 41–45. Nehru's Bandung remarks may be found in George McTurnan Kahin, *The Asian-African Conference* (Ithaca, Cornell University Press, 1956), pp. 65, 67, 74.

of life. They think primarily in those terms. They have just come out of the colonial stage and they have a certain vitality. They have a certain resistance to any attempt to reimpose that colonialism, and, while they may not be strong enough positively, they are strong enough to resist any imposition of any form of foreign domination. One cannot think in terms of imposing anything on Asia today against the will of the people. No solution that is not accepted by large masses of people can have any possible enduring quality.

[Q] In that connection isn't it possible, Mr. Prime Minister, that the spread of Communism may actually result in another form of foreign domination? Instead of the danger of colonial expansion may there not now be the danger of ideological expansion? Would this not in effect represent another form of foreign domination?

[Nehru] Undoubtedly. If, as has often happened recently, Communism comes not only as an economic doctrine but rather as an extension of [anti-] imperialism, then for a moment it might appeal to people because it comes as something that appears to them to be a liberating force. But there is bound to be resistance to it, which resistance will grow. The difficulty today in Asia is that the country or the group or the idea that represents any kind of liberating force appeals to the people. That liberating force when applied to the political domain might be called nationalism. It may be applied to the economic domain when it deals with, let us say, land problems or others that appeal to people. And so the right appeal to the people should be connected with their idea of liberation—either political or economic.

[Q] How, then, do we go about checking the spread of Communism on those two levels on which it is presently operating. First, the nationalist level, on which Russia apparently is attempting to carry out a design that was fashioned long before the Communist leaders came to power. For example, we know that Communist expansion, or rather Russian expansion in the Far East—in China, in Japan—is something that goes back to 1896, 1900, and 1904. Then there is the second level—the ideological level. Each level is used as the means of advancing the other. It is entirely possible, is it not, that Russia today is using its ideology as a means of advancing expansionist aims that go far beyond any ideology?

[Nehru] You mentioned Russia's activities long ago in the nineties, etc. They were purely imperialistic. There was no ideology behind them except the expansion of a powerful country. And other countries that are dominated by Russia reacted more or less in the ways that colonial countries react. Then came the Communist phase of Russia, which apparently broke away from the imperialist tradition and spoke to many countries in Asia on anti-imperialist lines and appeared to be a kind of liberating force. It appealed to them a quarter of a century ago. They didn't know much about it, but this appealed to them; and there is no doubt that the measure of sympathy—a large measure of sympathy —that Russia a quarter of a century ago obtained in Asia was because of that. That is, it allied itself to the nationalism of various peoples.

In recent years there has been a very marked difference in approach, and the Communist tendency has come into conflict with the nationalist tendency in . . . India, Indonesia, Burma, and some other countries. Where this has happened thus far the nationalist tendency has proved the stronger—provided always that the nationalist tendency does not support reactionary social tendencies, because reactionary social tendencies come in the way of the economic change that is so urgently desired—more especially in regard to land but in other matters, too.

[Q] In connection with your statement that whenever the Communist tendency comes into conflict with the nationalist tendency, the nationalist tendency triumphs, would you care to enlarge on this as it concerns India?

[Nehru] Yes. Communism in India right up to the beginning of the Second World War has very little importance except as a vague idea that appealed to some people in support of the national movement. Therefore it was a very small fringe of the national movement that didn't count for much otherwise. It did count for a little among the industrial workers then. But in the larger scheme of things it was not important. It was really in the later days of the war that Communism became more important, partly because of the opportunities given to it in wartime to build itself up, because it was supporting the war. (That is, after the Soviet Union came into it.) It built itself up at the cost of breaking away from nationalism. It did gain something in the organization, but it lost a good deal in its break with the nationalist movement and therefore in the hostility it aroused among the members of the nationalist movement.

Today in India Communism is definitely opposed to nationalism. It can create, it can give a lot of trouble in local areas—either industrial or agricultural —but even that is very limited. Now the question is: how far can the nationalist movement go forward in solving some of the urgent economic problems? If it fails, naturally that is an encouragement to Communist ideas. If it succeeds, then Communism or Communist ideas in India shrink.

[Q] You are confident, then, Mr. Prime Minister, that the national development of India will move at a pace that will make it possible for this country to resist Communism and, indeed, to set up the antibodies within it, over the long range, which can protect it against Communism?

[Nehru] When you talk about Communism you must distinguish between certain ideological, economic bases of Communism that we vaguely call Socialism in its various aspects and the particular tactics employed by the Communist Party, say in India. By mixing the two together certain confusion is created in the mind because there are certain things about Socialism rather than Communism that attract large numbers of people in India. But there is very great resentment and opposition to the tactics of the Communists in India, who really have become purely terroristic and who challenge not only the Government but most things in India. Therefore, I think that unless any government in India completely fails to satisfy the economic urges and wants of the people, Communism will not gain very much hold here.

[Q] If Communism, as you define it, through terrorism or otherwise does not take hold in India ideologically, is it at all possible there may be an attempt to take hold more directly—by overt action or aggression? How do you interpret the invasion of Tibet [by Communist China]? Would you say that this constitutes a direct threat to India, apart from whatever ideological progress or lack of progress the Communists may make on the home front?

[Nehru] No. I am not afraid of any external threat to India of that kind. . . . The real reason and the basic reason is that I do not think that India and China are going to function in that way toward each other.

[Q] Do you think it possible that China, because of her connections with Russia, might be persuaded that her interests lie more in the direction of fulfillment of Russia's ideological and national aims than in the direction of the type of United Asia you described?

[Nehru] I don't think so. China thinks for itself. . . . I do not see how it can possibly profit China or even, for that matter, Soviet Russia to think in terms of taking India.

Nehru's Remarks at the Bandung Conference

We [in India] do not agree with the communist teachings, we do not agree with the anti-communist teachings, because they are both based on wrong principles. I never challenged the right of any country to defend itself; it has to. We will defend ourselves with whatever arms and strength we have, and if we have no arms we will defend ourselves without arms. I am dead certain that no country can conquer India. Even the two great power blocs together cannot conquer India; not even [with] the atom or the hydrogen bomb. I know what my people are. But I know also that if we rely upon others, whatever great powers they might be if we look to them for sustenance, then we are weak indeed. . . .

So I submit, let us consider these matters practically, leaving out ideologies. Many . . . do not obviously accept the communist ideology, while some . . . do. For my part, I do not. I am a positive person, not an "anti-" person. I want positive good for my country and the world. Therefore, are we, the countries of Asia and Africa, devoid of any positive position except being pro-communist or anti-communist? Has it come to this, that the leaders of thought who have given religions and all kinds of things to the world have to tag on to this kind of group or that and be hangers-on of this party or the other, carrying out their wishes and occasionally giving an idea? It is most degrading and humiliating to any self-respecting people or nation. It is an intolerable thought to me that the great countries of Asia and Africa should come out of bondage into freedom only to degrade themselves or humiliate themselves in this way. Well, I do not criticize these powers. They are probably capable of looking after themselves and know what is best for themselves. But I will not tie myself to this degradation. Am I to lose my freedom and individuality and become a camp follower of others? I have absolutely no intention of doing that. . . .

Are we copies of Europeans or Americans or Russians? What are we? We are Asians or Africans. We are none else. If we are camp followers of Russia or America or any other country of Europe, it is, if I may say so, not very creditable to our dignity, our new independence, our new freedom, our new spirit and our new self-reliance.

QUESTIONS

1. Identify the several meanings of the communist challenge. Which of these challenges do you think is most formidable? Explain.

2. The text focuses on four aspects of communist doctrine. Which is most appealing to those who might be tempted by communist ideology? Defend your answer in the light of communist strength over the globe.

3. Historically, what factors helped to shape the thought of Karl Marx, the revolutionary strategy of V. I. Lenin, and the political tactics of Joseph Stalin?

4. In what sense is communism a prophecy of a better world?

5. What role do the following play in the communist philosophy of history: materialism? class struggle? dialectical materialism?

6. In *The Communist Manifesto* Marx and Engels distinguish their brand of socialism (what others call communism) from other brands by calling theirs "scientific socialism." Why did they conclude that communism was "scientific"? Appraise their argument.

7. Appraise the communist critique of capitalism and imperialism.

8. Identify the most important points in the communist strategy of revolutionary action.

9. To what extent do recent doctrinal pronouncements by Nikita Khrushchev represent a departure from or adherence to the ideology of Marx, Lenin, and Stalin? Explain.

10. Explain which of the three positions in the last section presents the most cogent argument in connection with the doctrine and challenge of communism.

SELECT BIBLIOGRAPHY

ASPATURIAN, Vernon V., "Soviet Foreign Policy," in Roy C. Macridis, ed., *Foreign Policy in World Politics* (Englewood Cliffs, N.J., Prentice-Hall, 1958). A brilliant analysis of the role of cultural, geographical, ideological, social, and political forces in the formulation of Soviet foreign policy.

FAINSOD, Merle, *How Russia Is Ruled* (Cambridge, Harvard University Press, 1953). Analyzes the physiology and anatomy of Soviet totalitarianism. Seeks to communicate a sense of the living political process in which Soviet rulers and subjects are enmeshed.

HUNT, R. N. Carew, *The Theory and Practice of Communism* (London, Geoffrey Bles, 1950; 5th rev. American ed., Macmillan, 1957). Probably the best single introduction to communism. An accurate summary and a reliable criticism. Contains a short annotated bibliography.

KOESTLER, Arthur, *The Yogi and the Commissar* (New York, Macmillan, 1945) and *Darkness at Noon* (New York, Macmillan, 1941). These imaginative works by a popular novelist and ex-communist cast much light on the nature of communism under Stalin. Psychologically more revealing than standard historical works.

LEITES, Nathan, *A Study of Bolshevism* (Glencoe, Ill., Free Press, 1953). Attempts to portray the spirit of Bolshevism by analysis of its doctrine, its operational code or conceptions of political strategy. Concerned primarily with Lenin and Stalin. Seeks to contribute to our knowledge of the varieties of man and to enhance the skill of western policy-makers in dealing with the Politburos of the Soviet and other communist parties.

MAYO, H. B., *Democracy and Marxism* (New York, Oxford University Press, 1955). A keenly critical account, designed to enable the democrat to reject communism soberly and on the right grounds.

MOORE, Barrington, *Soviet Politics: The Dilemma of Power* (Cambridge, Harvard University Press, 1950). Concerned with the role of ideas in social change and political action. On communist ideas and world affairs, see Chap. 9, "Revolution and World Politics," Chap. 16, "The Pattern of Soviet Foreign Policy," Chap. 17, "The Relations of Ideology and Foreign Policy," and Chap. 18, "Conclusions and Implications." See also his *Terror and Progress* (1954), an attempt, with an eye to the future, to weigh sources of stability and potentialities for change in the Bolshevik regime.

ORWELL, George, *Animal Farm* (New York, Harcourt Brace, 1946) and *Nineteen Eighty Four* (New York, Harcourt Brace, 1949). Two anti-Utopian fables which point up the antitotalitarian moral in simple, yet frightening, fashion. Available in pocket book editions.

PARES, Bernard, *A History of Russia* (New York, Knopf, definitive ed., 1953). Also available in a pocket book (Mentor) edition, 1949. A brief, fairly popular history which serves as a good general introduction to the background of communist thought. Contains brief accounts of Lenin, Stalin, and the communist revolution of 1917.

SABINE, George H., *A History of Political Theory* (New York, Holt, rev. ed., 1950). The best single history; mature and critical. Chapter 23 deals with Marx and dialectical materialism, Chap. 24, with communism.

SETON-WATSON, Hugh, *From Lenin to Malenkov: The History of World Communism* (New York, Praeger, 1954). Concerned primarily with the comparative historical analysis of communist movements on a world scale. Emphasizes the relationship of communist movements to social classes and to the internal balance of political power. Deals with the efforts of communists to win recruits and to seize and wield power in their respective lands.

9

Other Ideologies:
Reality and Role?

THE PROBLEM
AND ITS BACKGROUND

THE "EITHER-OR" POINT OF VIEW

The preceding chapters have examined the nature and challenge of the two ideological systems, democracy and communism, which seem today to be the principal contenders for the allegiance of men's minds. The question is now raised: Are these the only alternatives from which the peoples of the world may choose?

There is much confusing discussion along America's "Main Street" about the ideological allegiance of various countries and governments. Greatest speculation centers around the Indian government of Premier Nehru. Here is a country and leader that have been outspokenly critical of certain aspects of American life and policies and seemingly sympathetic toward certain features of Soviet society. If the United States—one of the oldest and foremost defenders of democracy—is so regarded by Nehru's India, what is the Indian ideological preference? Is it communism? Then why has Nehru waged political war on the Indian Communist Party? Why did A.J.B. Kriplani in 1946 say to the Indian Congress:

We watch with equal interest the Russian adventure with Communism, the British experiment in Democratic Socialism, and the American faith in private enterprise. We must not be duped by ideological claptrap into taking sides. . . .[1]

[1] Quoted in Werner Levi, *Free India in Asia* (Minneapolis, University of Minnesota Press, 1952), p. 133.

India does not fit neatly into one category or the other, American democracy or Soviet communism. Accordingly, the conclusion must be that, like much of South and Southeast Asia, it has adopted a third, alternative ideology. Most observers who concur in this view label India a socialist democracy, an ideology to be examined more fully in this chapter.

Similar frustration is encountered upon reading in the American press that Britain, land of the Magna Carta and parliaments, has taken the "ruinous" road of the "welfare state." If hospitals have been "socialized" and coal mines "nationalized," can Britain really be called a democracy any longer? Both Conservatives and Laborites would emphatically insist that their country is a democracy. Prime Minister Clement Attlee was hardly a dictator, and fiery Aneurin Bevan, leader of the radical wing of the Labor Party, has been implicated in no plots to liquidate his political enemies in the Kremlin tradition. Yet, the confusion persists because Britain quite obviously does not practice democracy as it is understood in the United States. Here, too, there appears to be an ideological variation worth examination.

No less confounding, to those who strive to delineate all countries as either democratic in the American form or communist in the Russian, is Yugoslavia. Here is a country in which collective farms and communized industry exist and where the controlling party is called communist. Nevertheless, in 1948, the Cominform denounced Yugoslav leaders for thinking: [2]

That by a series of concessions to imperialistic states they can gain the favor of these states to make an agreement with them about the independence of Yugoslavia and gradually implant in the Yugoslav people the orientation of capitalism. . . .

Yugoslav leaders presumably do not understand, or at least pretend not to understand, that a similar nationalistic conception can lead to a lowering of Yugoslavia to the usual bourgeois republic, to a loss of independence to the imperialistic countries.

In other words, the Cominform Communists charged the Yugoslav Communists with gravitating toward the "bourgeois-capitalist-imperialist" West, or toward what the West calls democracy. Is "Titoism," then, to be equated with western democracy, if not with Russian communism? Here is another ideological variation, perhaps most accurately termed national communism.

Still another ideology, almost overlooked today but disturbing to advocates of the "either-or" view, is fascist Spain. This is a dictatorship which was closely associated with Hitler and Mussolini. Simply because it has leased air bases to the United States, it cannot now be defined as a democracy. Alignment in the cold war with the West can no more provide the key to a country's ideology than can nonalignment. Fascism

[2] *New York Times*, June 29, 1948, p. 10.

is a distinct and well-defined ideological alternative to democracy and communism.

When time is taken to survey the governments of Saudi Arabia, Egypt, Syria, Burma, Indonesia, and a number of others, the conclusion appears to be inescapable that highly significant variations of democracy and communism, as well as other ideologies, have reality and a role in the contemporary world. The remainder of this chapter is devoted to a study of three of these ideologies—democratic socialism, national communism, and fascism.

DEMOCRATIC SOCIALISM

The word *socialist* has served to designate so many different movements, programs, and parties that a definition of its meaning here must be undertaken. Karl Marx referred to certain pre-Marxist collectivists as Utopian socialists. He called his own followers (now popularly known as communists) scientific socialists. As the preceding chapter indicated, contemporary communists apply the term *socialism* to a transitional period before the final stage of communism is reached. None of these designations expresses the meaning of democratic socialism as discussed here, and other uses of "socialist" must also be excluded. For example, Hitler styled himself a National Socialist, a French political party for years called itself Radical Socialist, and certain opponents of Franklin D. Roosevelt labeled him and his New Deal supporters as socialists. These, too, are not "socialists" in the context of this discussion, although they reflect certain aspects of socialism.

Definition of Democratic Socialism

Perhaps the shortest route to the heart of this matter of definition is to discard at once the premise that socialism and capitalism are the basic distinctions to be made in the world's economic institutions and, inferentially, in the world's ideologies. To be sure, there is an important difference between a society in which the means of production are in private hands and one where they are owned by the state. Of crucial significance, however, is that between a society in which the freedom, welfare, and happiness of individuals come first and one where the power and interest of the state claim highest priority. The former can be characterized as democratic, the latter, totalitarian. It is in the democratic category, as its name indicates, that democratic socialism falls.

Democracy, as mentioned previously, was closely connected with capitalism in its early development. The freedom from government interference desired by capitalists led to a fusion of *laissez-faire* economics and democratic politics. Although *laissez-faire* in the industrial environment caused the exploitation of woman and child labor, sweated industries, periodic unemployment, insecurity, and squalor, it was defended by many democrats on the ground that the automatic laws of supply and demand would ultimately work out for the best interest of all. Socialism rejected this line of reasoning, however, and became one of the major forces challenging *laissez-faire* democracy.

The challenge was directed not so much at democracy as at its ties with *laissez-faire* capitalism. Socialists condemned the growing separation of ownership from productive activity in the increasingly larger units of production. That ownership and profit-taking were concentrated in a few hands while production became a collective operation, involving large numbers of wage-earning humans contributing labor, management, and technology, was deemed unjust. They proposed to correct this condition by establishing collective ownership of the collectively operated production units. Such collectivization, they reasoned, would eliminate absentee, irresponsible, monopolistic capitalists and permit collective enjoyment of the fruits of labor.

Democratic socialism did not, however, endorse abolition of private property where it could be used for production by the owner without sacrifice of efficiency or technology. In agriculture, retailing, personal services, the professions, even in some manufacturing, large areas existed in which the small economic unit, owned and operated by the same individual, was to be protected and preserved.

Moreover, the advance toward political democracy in the latter half of the nineteenth century had a profound effect upon socialism. The possibility of achieving socialist reform through peaceful, democratic means loomed more and more as a possibility. When socialists reached the point of supporting use of the democrat's ballot box instead of the communist's cartridge box, democratic socialism may be said to have finally crystallized. It was a distinct ideology in its own right. It was divorced from communism by its commitment to democratic means and to only partial liquidation of private property accompanied by compensation of the former owners. It parted from traditional nineteenth century democracy on the issues of inviolability of private property and *laissez-faire* capitalism.

It should now be clear that a definition of democratic socialism, as of democracy or communism, cannot be encompassed within one sentence. The basic essentials in its creed have, however, just been outlined. The ideology accepts the democratic view of, and concern for, the individual. His freedom of self-expression and self-government is of primary importance. Any and all limitations upon individual freedom, moreover, must be established in the democratic manner—peacefully, popularly, and constitutionally.

This ideology would go considerably further than traditional liberal democracy in the limitations it would impose in the realm of economics. Freedom to maximize profits by the impoverishment of labor, to monopolize supply at the expense of the consumer, and to amass private wealth to the detriment of the commonwealth was rejected by democratic socialism. Nonsocialist democrats, too, in time became less tolerant of such economic freedom. But democratic socialism from its very inception advocated collective ownership of wealth wherever these "antisocial" circumstances existed, whereas liberal democracy has been more inclined to impose regulation without disturbing ownership.

The Historical Evolution of Socialist Democracy

Since the democratic element in democratic socialism has already been surveyed in Chapter 7, there would appear to be no need for retracing its origins. It is, however, necessary to examine the roots of the socialist element, because, although links between socialism and communism exist, it would be quite inaccurate to characterize socialism as simply domesticated or tamed Marxism-Leninism.

Essentially, socialism is a nineteenth century phenomenon which accompanied the rise of modern industry. It is admitted that the concept of social equality can be traced far into the dim past. Old Testament prophets, Christ, Mohammed, Confucius, St. Dominic, and a host of others may be cited as early socialist thinkers and practitioners so far as they rejected undue emphasis upon "what I have is mine and what you have is yours." The words themselves, *socialism* and *socialist*, first appeared in print in Italian in 1803, in English in 1827, and in French in 1832.[3] Even then, they described a wide variety of movements dedicated to the social reorganization of society. (Today, too, as was pointed out previously, diverse figures, such as Hitler, Stalin, and Franklin Roosevelt have been called socialists.) Nevertheless, the stream of socialism referred to in socialist democracy does have tributaries which are identifiable. Five are noteworthy: the Utopian, Christian, Marxist, revisionist, and Fabian.

Utopian socialism. Because it was influenced by the concept of a perfect society, conforming to an ideal plan as presented in Sir Thomas More's *Utopia* (1517), one group of nineteenth century socialists was known as Utopian. Best known were the British manufacturer, Robert Owen (1771–1858), the French noble-businessman-philosopher, Claude-Henri Saint-Simon (1760–1825), and the French traveling salesman, François-Marie-Charles Fourier (1772–1837). Although differing in their socialist thinking in many ways, they shared certain thoughts and theories that comprise the Utopian socialist doctrine.

[3] George D. H. Cole, *A History of Socialist Thought* (London, Macmillan, 1953), Vol. I, p. 1.

All were deeply disturbed by the impact of industrialization upon the laboring classes. All, as rationalists, had questions about this impact: Were its results unavoidable? Could not man apply reason, and reorder society along more just, happier lines? Their answers were positive, although their solutions varied.

Owen placed major emphasis upon environment. If productive facilities could be arranged so that workers lived and labored in surroundings conducive to work and happiness, the worst aspects of industrial capitalism would be eliminated. Education was his key! A corrected environment, his solution! Saint-Simon called for scientific planning of industrial development by experts, who could build a peaceful, orderly, highly productive society free of poverty and exploitation. Fourier recommended collective ownship and operation of production units in which all would be workers and capitalists.

The significance of the Utopians rests largely with their role as the first group to be concerned with the lot of the modern industrial worker and with their desire to ameliorate it through some kind of social restructuring. They are noteworthy, too, for placing great hope in the reasonableness of man and the possibility of achieving reform through voluntary, peaceful co-operation outside the realm of the established state. In this they had much in common with the Christian socialists.

Christian socialism. As the name signifies, Christian socialism represented a religious approach to the problems of industrial development. As Charles Kingsley (1819–75), founder of this movement in England, insisted, Christianity was a failure if it did not direct attention to the economic and social conditions that accompanied industrialization. How could any advocate of the teachings of Christ remain indifferent to the inequities, inhumanity, and callous wretchedness of certain aspects of industrialization?

Germany, Austria, France, Italy, and Britain were all areas in which this theocratic social consciousness manifested itself. It was given great impetus in 1891 by Pope Leo XIII, the "workingman's Pope." After a conference of Christian socialists at Freiburg, Leo XIII issued his encyclic *Rerum Novarum*, in which he reminded Roman Catholics, especially, to keep in mind that each Christian was his brother's keeper, that owners of wealth had a social obligation before God to use that wealth in a Christian manner, and that workers who resorted to industrial strife and endorsed class warfare were forgetting that they were Christians.

The belief in the religious obligation of all Christians to be socially conscious, especially in the new industrial era, was and still is a powerful influence: in British socialist thinking, expressed today largely through the Labor Party; in contemporary Christian Socialist and Christian Democratic parties in Italy, Austria, Belgium, and Germany; and in the Catholic labor unions of France, Belgium, the Netherlands, and other countries.

Perhaps best expressing the Christian socialist outlook is the British Labor Party's George Lansbury, writing in 1934,[4]

Socialism, which means love, cooperation, and brotherhood in every department of human affairs, is the only outward expression of a Christian's faith. I am firmly convinced that whether they know it or not, all who approve and accept competition and struggle against each other as the means whereby we gain our daily bread, do indeed betray and make of no effect the "will of God."

Thus, to Utopian socialism was added a Christian endorsement of socialism. Ridiculing the former and rejecting the latter was still another socialist response, Marxist socialism.

Marxist socialism. This aspect has been extensively dealt with in Chapter 8, but any review of the various sources of democratic socialism must include Marxism, though not Leninism and Stalinism.

The writings of Karl Marx, somewhat like the Bible, have been interpreted to support various ideological positions, including Leninism-Stalinism, Titoism, and democratic socialism. For the latter, the dictum of Marx, as repeated by Engels—in England "the inevitable social revolution might be effected entirely by peaceful and legal means" [5]—became more and more important as other countries, in addition to England, adopted democratic institutions. The way appeared to be opening for a nonviolent introduction of socialism, and Marx himself endorsed it. This, at least, was the belief of an increasing number of socialists who opposed Leninism but still claimed adherence to Marxism. Democratic socialism is indebted to Marxism for other concepts, although considerable revision was made. This revisionism eventually divorced its followers from orthodox Marxists sufficiently to give birth to another distinct socialist current, called revisionist socialism.

Revisionist socialism. Of all the founders of this brand of socialism, perhaps the most famous is the German, Eduard Bernstein (1850–1932). The following ideas were expressed most explicitly by him, although essentially they are representative of all revisionist socialists.

Just as the Leninists, when faced with the concrete situation of having to implement the theories of Marxism, altered and elaborated the original communist ideology, so Bernstein and his colleagues found the challenge of an actual situation disturbing to their theoretical principles. The Leninists, of course, were influenced by the retarded industrialization and despotism of Russia, whereas revisionists like Bernstein were impressed by the more industrial, more politically liberal western Europe of the 1890's. Revisionists discovered that their empirical experience in this environment contradicted their Marxist indoctrination, and many Marxists, including

---

[4] Quoted in William Ebenstein, *Today's Isms* (copyright, 1954, by Prentice-Hall, Inc., Englewood Cliffs, N.J.), pp. 164–165.

[5] Frederick Engels' Preface to the first English translation of Karl Marx, *Capital*, transl. from 3rd German ed. (Chicago, Kerr, 1912), Vol. I, p. 32.

Bernstein, entered "an era of doubt which usually follows on the heels of a time of dogmatic creativity." [6]

The neatness, completeness, compelling logic, and awe-inspiring predictions of Marxism did not, in the opinion of these revisionists, stand the test of examination in the light of a quarter century of industrialization. "The law of capitalist accumulation" was undoubtedly operating as Marx had predicted, along with the gap increasing between the material wealth of upper and lower segments of society. But statistics did not demonstrate the validity of either "the law of the concentration of capital" or "the law of increasing misery," both defined by Marx as immutable laws of capitalism. Not only were bourgeois property owners surviving; their numbers were increasing! Not only were workers surviving; they were achieving an increasingly higher standard of living. Under these circumstances, could the collapse of capitalism and the proletarian revolution be considered imminent possibilities? The realistic answer seemed to be no! This was disquieting to men whose lives were dedicated to preparing themselves and the masses for the Marxist revolution. To Bernstein, some rethinking appeared to be in order. The result was revisionist socialism with its modification of several Marxist philosophic, economic, and political concepts.

Philosophically, the Marxist dialectic was partly discarded. Instead of emphasizing the doctrine of class struggle, Bernstein pointed out that, owing to various economic and social reforms, the lot of the worker was steadily improving. These improvements, obtained as a result of the pressure of trade unions and socialist parties, had modified the dire picture of the class struggle drawn by Marx. The bourgeoisie were not becoming proletarians; instead, the proletariat was tending to become more like the middle class. Bernstein also maintained that the class struggle was becoming less and less bitter instead of more intense, as Marx had asserted. Thus, to Bernstein, it seemed more practical to stress an evolutionary type of reform than a revolutionary pattern of class war.

In economic theory, too, the revisionists questioned Marxist doctrine. The theories of labor and surplus value were not discarded, but they were considered of limited validity. Did labor alone, as Marx claimed, create value? Was not value also dependent upon the demand and utility of a product, so that those requiring the same amount of labor might, because of demand and utility, have very different values to society? A pair of shoes and a mechanical toy might require the same amount of labor, but to a shoeless person the shoes might be far more valuable than the toy. Could it be claimed that the value of shoes and toy were equal here? This oversimplifies revisionist thinking, but it illustrates their reevaluation.

[6] Peter Gay, *The Dilemma of Democratic Socialism* (New York, Columbia University Press, 1952), p. 153.

The contradictions in capitalism, which Marx predicted would lead to its inevitable collapse, were also subjected to qualifications. Although the gap between wealthiest and least wealthy was growing, as the revisionists agreed, it could not be said that the least wealthy were becoming poorer. The standard of living of the whole of society was rising, although the rise was much more rapid for the upper than for the lower segments. If it continued, this trend would seem to postpone the climactic day, foreseen by Marx, when the vast bulk of society would reach so poverty-stricken a point as to be provoked to revolution against the few fat capitalists possessing everything.

It was this type of observation which led Bernstein to emphasize the continuation of economic reforms rather than the conduct of class war. Capitalist crises had not borne out the Marxist position that they would become increasingly severe. On the contrary, there were indications that capitalism was dynamic and that new forces were at work which might well change its basic nature. For example, the market appeared to be less anarchic, credit was more flexible, cartelization cushioned the blows of depression, overproduction was limited, and possibilities for adjustment within the capitalist economy generally were greater. The revisionists agreed that inequality and underconsumption had persisted, but a "contradictory" and "collapsing" capitalism was not following the rules of Marx's and Engels' book, and therefore did not provide the opportunity for a solution such as they had anticipated. Marxist economics, like Marxist philosophy, simply did not furnish completely satisfying and all-inclusive answers to the industrial situation of the end of the nineteenth century in Europe. Inevitably, with the necessary revision of Marxist theory would have to come revision of Marxist practice.

Here, the Bernstein school again revealed its empiricism. Since the stage was not being set for a cataclysmic collapse of capitalism (at least not in the foreseeable future), the preparation for seizure of the state and inauguration of revolution was discarded. With the evidence, also, of a strong trend toward increased parliamentary, democratic government in the Europe of the 1890's, the revisionists adopted tactics aimed at accelerating this trend. The expectation was that when the proletariat peacefully secured political power, a gradual, evolutionary reform of the economic and social order could follow. Thus, political democracy and then socialization of all large-scale enterprise became the action program of revisionist socialism.

On the basis of the earlier definition of democratic socialism, it is now clear that its taproot is revisionism (possibly excepting British democratic socialism, to which reference will be made shortly). Thus, at the end of the nineteenth century there emerged, throughout continental Europe, the revisionist-oriented social-democratic and socialist parties. By 1914, in Germany and Italy, these parties commanded more votes and parliamentary seats than any other single party. Only in the Russian Social-Democratic Party did the revisionists remain a less significant element. The Second International, founded in 1889, was largely dominated by the revisionist viewpoint and provided the various social-democratic parties with an international organization to foster and co-ordinate their activities. Although the International collapsed in 1914, when most socialists, yielding to nationalism, supported their nation-states in World War I, the parties survived. After the Russian Revolution and in the postwar disorganization of European society, left-wing minorities broke away from many revisionist socialist parties and formed outright communist parties. As a result, social-democrats and socialists now became wholly revisionist and, in bourgeois eyes, more "respectable." Indeed, after 1918, revisionist socialists played leading roles in coalition with bourgeois parties in every European state except Soviet Russia, and in Germany, Austria, France, and elsewhere, even premiers came from the ranks of the revisionists.

With its abandonment of revolutionary tactics and its emphasis upon economic reforms achieved through democratic means, revisionism, then, became the foremost European form of socialism outside Russia. Its program was a more popular one than that of Utopian and Christian socialism, and less radical than the Marxist, although its concepts bore the imprint of all three.

Fabian socialism. In Britain still another socialist current is to be observed contributing to democratic socialism. This is Fabian socialism, so called because its first proponents belonged to the Fabian Society.

Founded in 1884, this society was named after the Roman general Fabius, whose tactics in defeating Hannibal entailed avoidance of pitched battle in favor of attrition and harassment. The Fabian Society's members, interested in eliminating what they regarded as the unjust social and economic consequences of industrialization, adopted the motto: "For the right moment you must wait, as Fabius did; but when the right moment comes you must strike hard, or your waiting will have been vain and fruitless." [7] Obviously, this group of reformers would eschew shock treatments and sudden revolutionary actions. Such a point of view was more natural to citizens of a country that had not known political violence since the mid-seventeenth century; it was more easily arrived at by members of the upper classes, and the Fabians were writers, intellectuals, and artists like George Bernard Shaw, H. G. Wells, Sidney and Beatrice Webb, and Graham Wallas—not the sort of people who incite crowds to raise barricades and violently defy the law. Thus, Fabian socialism is associated with a gradualist approach to the correction of ills precipitated by industrialization.

[7] Ebenstein, *op. cit.,* p. 168.

The gradualism constituted one of the similarities to revisionist social-ism. Both movements also were flexible in the analysis of action to be taken, and both placed great stress on democratic institutions as the means of bringing about reforms. Yet, they were sufficiently different to merit the distinction made here. First, the Fabians predated the revision-ists. Second, they did not begin as Marxists and become dissatisfied with the doctrine of a high priest. Third, they were never a large group and made no attempt to enlist large membership, as did the revisionist social-democrats. Finally, most of them devoted their efforts to "permeating" the upper and middle classes (not the working class) and arousing their in-terest in social and economic reform. Thus, Fabians and revisionists are not identical.

Like the Utopians, the Fabians became more distrustful and more criti-cal of industrial capitalism as they observed its effects on late nineteenth century Britain. Their response was typically English and typically ra-tional. Changes were in order, so that the new industrial economy would be more sensitive to all the people's needs. The best way to achieve change was within the British parliamentary framework, and since the upper and middle classes dominated the parliamentary machinery, they would have to be induced to make the reforms. As rational humans, these upper segments of British society would undertake social reform if they were convinced of its need and efficacy. Thus, the Fabians became edu-cators, not demagogues; pamphleteers, not organizers; research sociolo-gists, not metaphysicians.

The initial impact was felt in such specific issues as public control over municipal transport, labor conditions in laundries, health regulations for the milk industry, and liquor licensing. With each, they attempted to demonstrate the need for collective action by society, buttressing their case with irrefutable statistics and facts, clearly and succinctly presented. They made no pretense of seeking answers to the meaning of history or the future of western civilization. Social reform was reduced to the level of mundane common sense and rational action in a very limited area.

In time, the approach did "permeate" Britain's upper and middle classes, arousing their social consciousness and inclination to attack spe-cific problems collectively. The Fabians also gave their support to the Labor Party, founded in 1901, and became a kind of intellectual board of directors of this party of trade unionists and middle class socialist re-formers of the Clement Attlee type. As Hugh Gaitskell, a leader of Brit-ain's Labor Party, put it: [8]

. . . While the trade unions provided the solid and well-organized movement, the most important intellectual contribution [to the Labor Party] came from

[8] Hugh Gaitskell, "Socialism's Way," in the *New York Times,* magazine section, April 8, 1956, pp. 14, 74.

the members of the [Fabian] society. They were a group of middle-class men and women who, though especially interested in ideas, did not hold themselves aloof from political action. Their influence upon Labor policy in Britain in the last fifty years has been substantial.

. . . The special contribution of the Fabians to Labor policy and practice lay in this acceptance of democratic gradualism.

When it is recalled that the Labor Party has been the dominant vehicle for socialist action in Britain in the twentieth century, Fabian socialism, as a vital stimulant to that party, assumes an important place alongside Utopian, Christian, Marxist, and revisionist socialism in giving rise to democratic socialism.

If these have been the roots of the social-democratic tree, what are its fruits? How widespread is its appeal? Where does it command support? What are its outstanding manifestations? These questions will be the concern of the next section.

Socialist Democracy Today

Geographic centers of strength. A check of the 1954 voting strength of the social-democratic, socialist, social credit, and labor parties, whose platforms reflect social-democratic principles, indicates that the foremost centers of the social-democrats are Australia, Austria, Denmark, Great Britain, New Zealand, Norway, and Sweden. In each, more than 40 per cent of all votes cast were for social-democrats.[9] If the list were expanded to include countries where over 25 per cent of the votes were captured by social-democrats, the following would be added: Belgium, Finland, Israel, the Netherlands, Switzerland, and West Germany.[10] In Canada and France, social-democrats have polled between 10 and 20 per cent of the total vote cast,[11] and the social-democratically oriented Congress Party is the majority party in India.

This analysis indicates very substantial support for social-democratic movements, particularly in northern and western Europe but also in Australasia, India, and Israel. Moreover, it does not represent a sudden or episodic surge, for social-democratic strength has stayed at this level consistently since 1946. If we added the unmeasurable but considerable social-democratic sentiment in the dictatorships where it cannot openly express itself, the total would constitute an even more impressive part of the world's political opinion. Any global view of today's ideological patterns which places every people in either the communist or the traditional democratic camp is patently unrealistic. Democratic socialism does, of course, reveal an affinity for traditional democracy, which it does not for communism. In fact, democratic socialism has generally elicited re-

[9] Ebenstein, *op. cit.*, p. 159.
[10] *Ibid.*
[11] *Ibid.*

sponse only in communities where democracy is already established. This relationship bears further examination.

Democratic centers of strength. By tradition and by nature, democratic socialism could only grow where political institutions of democracy existed. Both in means and in ends social-democrats have emphasized democratic concepts. Furthermore, only in a political democracy would socialist democracy face an opposition that would not resort to totalitarian methods to destroy it. Opponents of social-democrats in Britain, Scandinavia, or Switzerland might bitterly combat the socialism of social-democrats, but for the sake of preserving the basic conditions of democracy they would limit their opposition to constitutional means. If the socialists were elected to office, their democratic opponents would turn over the machinery of state to them, planning and hoping to unseat them at the next election, and confident that, if defeated, the social-democrats would surrender their power and not resort to revolution. It is the mutual confidence of socialist and nonsocialist democrats, their willingness to abide by the democratic rules of the political game, that explains the coincidence of democratic socialism's growth in lands where earlier democrats had pioneered.

Concrete evidence of social-democrats' respect for the democratic operation of government is the British Labor Party's advent to, and then surrender of, political power to the opposition upon three occasions (1924, 1931, and 1951). Similar resignations of power have occurred in all the other states. In addition, social-democrats have evinced maximum respect for civil liberty. In any listing of the nation-states "primarily in the light of their respect for civil liberty, Great Britain, Norway, Denmark, Sweden, Holland, Belgium, Australia, New Zealand, and Israel would be at the top of the list; and all these countries are, or recently have been, governed by socialist administrations." [12]

Conversely, democratic socialism has been least effective in winning a following in areas where democratic traditions are weakest. How could enthusiasm be created for a social-democratic program where democratic means for its implementation did not exist? Russian social-democrats saw little hope of ever bringing about more economic and social equality in the Czarist era. Accordingly, democratic socialism fought a losing battle with communism (though doubts occur as to whether there were more communists than social-democrats in Lenin's day despite the communist victory in the revolution).

The weakness of democratic traditions in Germany, under the Imperial Government's semiautocracy before 1914 and under the Weimar Republic after 1918, explains the inability of the German Social-Democrats to launch a full-fledged socialist program. Most of their efforts were diverted into the battle to establish and then preserve political democracy against

[12] Ebenstein, *op. cit.*, p. 157.

Kaisers, Junkers, Army, and Nazis. Such battling, however necessary, was not conducive to enlisting those who impatiently awaited socialist modification of German capitalism.

In Italy, too, social-democrats have had difficult times. The difficulties had begun even before Mussolini's advent to power in 1922. Under his fascist dictatorship (1925–43), democratic opposition, too, disappeared. Since underground organization, sabotage, and revolutionary preparation were the strong point of communists, anarchists, and syndicalists, these movements gained at the expense of democratic socialism. Post-Mussolini politics have been carried on in a more democratic atmosphere, and the social-democrats have played an important, if not a dominant, role. National elections in May, 1958, revealed that the socialists (though divided between right and left wings) were maintaining their postwar position as a political force of consequence. There is considerable evidence, then, of the correlation between a healthy social-democratic movement and the existence of a strong democratic tradition. Where the latter is weak or nonexistent, the former has not flourished.

One further observation should be made on the question of correlation. In the traditionally democratic United States, democratic socialism has attracted a very small following. Although many factors are involved in an explanation of this phenomenon, it may be briefly noted that the relatively high standard of living of the working population has led to labor's support of direct negotiations by trade unions with capital, rather than of a political movement like democratic socialism. Actually, although the word *socialism* has never been popular in the United States, under a different label considerable collective action by the state has been authorized by the electorate. There is little or no realization of the fact that such actions frequently are in the social-democratic pattern. Government construction of highways and canals; municipal ownership of water and gas works, and electric-generating plants; public schools; social security; flood control; and progressive income and inheritance taxes—all bring to the American scene the very kind of development advocated by European social-democrats. Recently, the emergence of this "mixed" American economy, which contains both socialistic and private enterprise elements, has caused some questioning of the extent to which society, acting collectively through the state, can directly or indirectly limit individual freedom without jeopardizing democracy.

A clearer understanding of democratic socialism may be obtained at this point by a review of its specific application. Accordingly, a survey of several contemporary social-democratic regimes follows.

In Great Britain. During the Labor Party's most important ministry (1945–51), the outlines of British democratic socialism became apparent. First, through expansion of the welfare services of the state, social equality was markedly increased. This expansion increased opportunities for free education even at the university level for students who lacked the means to pay for it. It provided for extension of sickness, unemployment, and old age insurance to every British subject. Most striking was its organization of all medical facilities into a state-supported national health service to which all citizens had access. Certain modifications were effected by the Conservatives after 1951, but the system remained essentially intact and popular with the majority of the electorate. A corollary to the establishment of a "cradle-to-grave" welfare state was Fabian taxation. High income and inheritance taxes, instituted as a war measure, were retained as a means of eliminating extremes in economic wealth and of supporting the welfare services. This does not imply that complete equality is a goal. It is not. It does mean, however, that the millionaire has been virtually eliminated from British society, and no British subject need exist any longer below a subsistence income.

The second outstanding innovation of Labor was the nationalization of certain basic industries, aggregating about 20 per cent of the entire economy. Autonomous government corporations replaced the older, privately owned companies, shareholders in the latter receiving shares of roughly the same value in the new corporations. This policy, reflecting revisionist socialist theory, was indifferently received by the British public, including the working classes, and did not prove economically sensational. The coal industry, which had been deteriorating for several decades in private hands, was still only convalescent under the National Coal Board. Railway workers were still striking for higher wages despite the change in railway ownership. Consumers found that rising costs in the manufacture of electricity kept rates rising under government as under earlier private operation. Generally, the matter of public ownership of industry has caused questioning of its advisability among Laborites themselves. A minority wing under Aneurin Bevan stands for further nationalization as a matter of principle. The Gaitskell majority, in 1956, however, resolved to postpone further nationalization until additional experience made clear the advisability of expanding the program when a Labor government came to power.

In Sweden. The pattern of Swedish democratic socialism has been somewhat different. As in Britain, extended social services and an equalizing structure are evident. Nationalization, conversely, is not a major plank in the Swedish program. Instead, following Utopian ideas, privately owned co-operatives are a major feature of the economy. Over 30 per cent of all retail and 10 per cent of all wholesale business in Sweden are in the hands of these expanding co-operatives. Everything, from groceries to galoshes and matches to margarine, is manufactured and distributed co-operatively. State-owned monopolies comparable to those in Britain exist only in the tobacco and liquor trade and in radio broadcasting.

Another feature of the Swedish experiment is the competition between private and state industry in the same fields. In housing, lumbering, mining, power, and transport, the Swedes accept this kind of competition as healthy. The state industries are a check on excessive profiteering by private concerns, which in turn, retaining the profit motive and seeking new efficiencies, serve as a brake upon bureaucratic inefficiency penetrating the state enterprises.

In India. The most recent and potentially perhaps the most significant experiment in democratic socialism is under way in India. As has been observed above, European democratic socialism has thus far implemented its principles of public ownership only in certain major sectors of industry, transportation, and utilities. It has not attempted in any broad way to apply socialist principles to agriculture. Communists, on the other hand, have applied their doctrine to both industry and agriculture. They have carried out forced collectivization of the land, a policy which has consistently aroused bitter opposition among all farmers except tenants and landless agricultural workers. Indian social-democracy is unique in its efforts to apply its principles to the problems of agriculture.

In India, as in most of Asia, land ownership constitutes one of the outstanding problems of the economy, and land reform is one of the most pressing needs. Inasmuch as land reform is a promise frequently made by communists to gain support among the peasant masses of Asia, any democratic program of land reform assumes special importance as an alternative appeal. Nehru's program in India represents that alternative, and its beginning was favorable and popular. Outside observers often compare the democratic economic reforms of India with the dictatorial economic reforms of Communist China and suggest that the future development of Asia may depend largely on which proves more successful.

The essentials of the Indian agricultural reforms involve improvement of techniques without drastic alteration of the ownership of private property. There is interest in breaking up large estates, but the major concern is with education of the mass of poor farmers in the direction of improved agricultural methods. They have been given better seed, aided in undertaking co-operative irrigation projects, and instructed in the advantages of crop diversification. Although this does involve extensive activity by the Indian state, it has encouraged Indians to improve their lot as individual entrepreneurs, not as members of giant collective farms.

Indian social-democrats, led by Nehru, also have an industrial program. Here, as with European democratic socialism, the role of the state looms larger, but the similarity ends at this point. In Europe, social-democrats faced the problem of establishing collective ownership over industries already established. In India, they face the very different problem of collectively creating industries. Although some foreign private capital may be used, India's sensitivity to imperialism is a barrier. Therefore, much of the capital for Indian industrialization must come from India itself, and such capital can be secured only by the government. Thus, whether the social-democrats can build an industrial plant sufficiently quickly to alleviate Indian poverty stands alongside the question concerning agricultural reform.

It is not yet clear whether this slow, democratically innovated, evolutionary program will succeed, or whether communist promises of quick relief will draw the Indian masses into a rapid, totalitarian, collectivistic revolution. What is obvious is that in India the fate of democracy in large measure depends upon the success of this social-democratic program. And as goes India, so may go much of the rest of Asia that has not adopted the communist pattern of economic reorganization. In the opinion of some, then, democratic socialism comes closer than capitalist democracy to offering a democratic solution for the peculiar and pressing problems of Asia.

Summary

Democratic socialism, despite its lack of adherents in the Soviet Union and the United States, is a very real and dynamic ideological movement in the contemporary world. Under its banner lives a very sizable part of humanity, imbued, along with the United States, with a dedication to democracy. Social-democrats however, endorse extensive experimentation in collective ownership (through the state or through co-operatives) of the means of production as an antidote to the economic and social inequalities generated by the industrial revolution in the West. In Asia, the movement now represents a potential means of creating an industrial economy and reorganizing an underdeveloped agricultural system without recourse to totalitarian policies.

"Titoist" Communism

Brief reference was made at the beginning of this chapter to Yugoslavia's break with the Kremlin and the ejection of the Yugoslav Communist League from the Cominform in 1948. Optimistic anticommunists hailed this development as the first step in the collapse of the Soviet satellite system and a reversal of the tide of communism, presumably in democracy's favor. However, in 1956, the assiduous cultivation of Marshal Tito by Soviet post-Stalin leaders brought about a re-establishment of Soviet-Yugoslav good relations. Since then, these relations have fluctuated. In 1958, on the eve of a Yugoslav Communist League party congress, the Soviet Communist Party criticized as "non-Marxist, non-Leninist" the Yugoslav draft program. When the Yugoslav League's party congress unanimously adopted its program, it emphasized differences between Russian and Yugoslav communists that are pertinent to this study of alternative ideologies.

Evidence suggests that communism as practiced in Yugoslavia, regardless of that country's flirtations with both East and West, has deviated sufficiently from Soviet communism to justify its serious consideration as a distinct ideologic variation. The recency of this development is a caution against drawing too many or final conclusions, but it does appear to have great potential significance. Yugoslav communism (and certain hesitant Polish steps in that direction) may constitute proof that there are paths to communism other than the Russian. If the Kremlin continues to concede this fact, the possibility of national variations may make communism's appeal more effective in other countries.

Nationalism and Communism

A number of factors help to explain the Titoist break with Moscow and the subsequent alterations in Yugoslavia's communist experiment, but the fundamental element is nationalism. Stalinist Russia's attempts in 1945–48 to reduce Yugoslavia to economic and political subservience aroused national resentment among the Yugoslavs. This, no doubt, was true of the other satellite peoples, but Yugoslavia's geographic detachment from Russia and the absence of Soviet troops (the Yugoslavs in effecting their liberation from the Axis had afforded no opportunity for occupation by Soviet troops) enabled this country, alone among the smaller communist states of Eastern Europe, to defy Moscow. Marshal Tito, moreover, was a man who dared to take advantage of the situation. In 1948, to the national satisfaction of the Yugoslavs, Soviet agents were expelled and economic subordination to the Soviet Union was terminated. Moscow's application of the heaviest pressure short of invasion to overthrow Tito intensified Yugoslav nationalism. The breach between Belgrade and the other communist regimes widened and was accentuated by the extension of United States' economic and military aid to Yugoslavia, beleaguered as it was by neighboring, pro-Russian Bulgaria, Rumania, Hungary, and Albania.

It was in this atmosphere of national defiance that Yugoslav communism, popularly referred to as "Titoism," began to undergo the variations from Leninism-Stalinism receiving attention here.

"The Return to True Marxism"

In pointing out the differences that have come to distinguish "Titoism," it is important to note that the movement claims to be truly Marxist. By inference it was Stalinism which had deviated from the teachings of the founding fathers. Innovations are portrayed as bringing the Yugoslav experiment into closer conformity with Marxist teaching. Actually, they reflect an attempt to adjust policy to the realities of the Yugoslav environment, as the following illustrations indicate.

Variations in agriculture. As in other communist countries, Yugoslav collectivization of agriculture had encountered serious peasant resistance. Whereas Stalinist policy, however, ruthlessly forced collectivization in the face of the resistance, Titoist policy took a new tack in 1952. Most significant was the abandonment of forced collectivization. Where collective farms were proving either economically inefficient or unpopular (usually the two conditions coincided) dissolution was permitted. Between 1950 and 1953, the number of collectives declined from 7,000 to 1,300, owing to peasant withdrawals.[13] The dissolution did not signify a complete shift to agricultural capitalism. In 1953 a ceiling of 25 acres was established for all individual farms, and peasants were persuaded, but not coerced, to continue co-operatives in such enterprises as agricultural machinery, livestock breeding, and plant nurseries.

Quota payments in farm produce to the state were replaced by conventional taxation, altering the agricultural picture so drastically that its character came to resemble that of Scandinavian agriculture more than it did the Soviet system.

Variations in industry. In 1950, contrary to the prevailing Soviet system of centralized state management of industrial enterprises (which was not modified until 1957), Yugoslav industry was decentralized and in considerable measure turned over to workers' management. Workers' participation in management took place through workers' councils and management boards. The former are elected by all the employees in an enterprise, the latter, from the councils. That these organs have not been a sham is shown by the role they have played in the disposition of profits, some of which has been dispensed as bonuses and wage increases. When this experience is contrasted with Lenin's expulsion from the Russian Communist Party of a group who attempted to establish a similar system in Soviet Russia, the difference between Yugoslav and Russian practice is quite evident. Indeed, the Yugoslav trend closely resembles Daniel De Leon's (1852–1914) earlier Marxist plea, emphatically rejected by Leninism, for replacement of rule by a political bureaucracy with government by representatives of the workers.

Another industrial modification took the form of according enterprises the right and responsibility of operating at a profit. Profits, as previously stated, might be retained by the local enterprise, but bankruptcy is also tolerated. When enterprises have not maintained solvency, they have been obliged to dissolve, and their workers join the ranks of the unemployed. In 1953, the Tito government officially announced that unemployment stood at 8 per cent,[14] an unheard-of step in other communist countries. Competition between enterprises in the same business is also permitted, a further variation of Yugoslav industry from that of the rest

[13] Thomas T. Hammond, *Yugoslavia—Between East and West* (New York, Foreign Policy Association, 1954), pp. 29, 31.
[14] *Ibid.*, p. 24.

of the communist world. Generally, worker energy and morale seem to have been heightened in this atmosphere.

Variations in government. Several changing aspects of political life suggest the same flexibility and inclination to experiment as has been revealed in agriculture and industry. Outstanding has been the transfer of authority to local governments. All but two federal ministries concerned with economic affairs, for example, have been abolished and their responsibilities transferred to state (in the American sense) governments. People's committees in planning, budgeting, and tax-collecting at the local level exercise the authority that was visualized by communist idealists as vested in the Russian Soviets but was never permitted in practice. The flexibility and reduced bureaucracy attending these changes are in sharp contrast to the traditional Soviet bureaucratic pyramid, with Moscow at its apex. It is noteworthy, however, that the U.S.S.R., in 1957, also initiated decentralization of its own industry.

Since 1952, two candidates must be offered for every elective office on the election ballot. Of course, only one party exists; however, the law not only permits but insists that the voter make a choice between candidates, quite the opposite from the single slate presented to the Soviet population.

In contrast to the Supreme Soviet of the U.S.S.R. which meets only once or twice a year for about ten days, the Yugoslav legislature has been in session almost continuously, and its deputies have been paid. Considerable debate and amendment of proposed bills, legislative committee meetings and hearings, and presentation by deputies of local constituencies' interests further distinguish legislative practice.

Finally, the Communist League, the only legal party in Yugoslavia, has been confronted with a problem the attack upon which is also at variance with communist practice elsewhere. The problem was that of declining Communist League influence and dynamism in the more relaxed atmosphere of "Titoism." At times, orders from League headquarters had been disregarded; in other places, party activity had ceased altogether. At the Communist League's Central Committee meeting in early 1956, Tito, asserting that it was imperative to restore party discipline and vitality, laid down the significant precept that the Yugoslav Communists "must educate, not dictate." The continued circulation of western newspapers, magazines, books, and movies has suggested that Iron Curtain tactics have been dropped in certain respects. The reestablishment of youth labor brigades pointed to limited avoidance of coercion. In the work brigades young people are housed and fed by the state for an average of one month while working on public projects like highway and canal construction. Not always economically efficient, the concentration of the youth for indoctrination lectures and ideological entertainment in their free hours is deemed highly important in the efforts to prevent the withering away of the communist party in Yugoslavia. Should such persuasive, in contrast to dictatorial, tactics be continued, this, too, would constitute another distinction of "Titoist" communism.

Reservations and Conclusions

It would be quite inaccurate to conclude, from this discussion, that a communist dictatorship does not exist in Yugoslavia. The single party system, secret police, arbitrary imprisonment of prominent figures critical of the regime like Milovan Djilas (former Vice President of Yugoslavia), limited sources of public information, the absence of multiparty elections, and the existence of religious disabilities make the dictatorship very real, and the variations noted do not divorce Yugoslavia from communism. Indeed, Djilas was imprisoned because he wrote: "National Communism has been unable, despite ever increasing possibilities for liberation from Moscow, to alter its internal nature, which consists of total control and monopoly of ideas, and ownership by the party bureaucracy." [15] But the survival of its totalitarian character should not obscure the fact that communism, especially when planted in a national environment free from Soviet control, displays a capacity for development along new lines.

Conceivably, "Titoism" may prove to be patterned after Lenin's strategic retreat under NEP (1921–28), a breathing space for a regime faced with great problems and internal dissatisfaction. "Titoism" may, however, turn out to be a permanent departure from communism as practiced in the Soviet Union. To quote Djilas again: [16] "Where a Communist revolution has won victory independently, a separate, distinct path of development is inevitable." With this, Moscow reluctantly concurred in the 1956 Soviet-Yugoslav communiqué, which reads:[17]

Abiding by the view that the roads and conditions of Socialist development are different in different countries . . . and starting with the fact that any tendency of imposing one's own views in determining the roads and forms of Socialist development are alien to both sides, the two sides have agreed that the foregoing cooperation should be based on complete freedom of will and equality, on friendly criticism and on . . . the exchange of views on disputes between the two parties.

Thus, with communists themselves confirming a divergence in Yugoslav communism, several questions are important here: First, what are the possibilities for variations in other communist countries? The Gomulka regime in Poland and the 1956 Hungarian uprising appear to be symptomatic of national communism. China and other Asian communist states inevitably come to mind in this connection. Their cultural and geographic remoteness from Moscow is a factor conducive to national communism

---

[15] Milovan Djilas, *The New Class* (New York, Praeger, 1957), p. 183.
[16] *Ibid.*, p. 175.
[17] *New York Times*, June 21, 1956, p. 10.

that bears watching. Second, what would be the influence on the world ideological struggle of such possible splintering of the communist bloc? Finally, what effect may "Titoism" have upon communist movements in noncommunist lands? Will communism, if it demonstrates a capacity for escaping Russian domination, increase its appeal? Or is Djilas closer to the truth when he says,[18] "In reality, National Communism is Communism in decline," the beginning of disintegration of the power monopoly (which he believes to be the essence of communism), whether it be Russian or national? Although categorical answers to these questions cannot now be made, they emphasize the potential significance of "Titoist" communism for the current ideological struggle.

FASCISM

In the preceding pages evidence was presented to explode the "either-or" thesis that there are only two clear-cut ideological alternatives in the world. Variations in both democracy and communism are not the only testimony. In fascism there exists still another ideology, which is by no means defunct despite the disappearance of Mussolini and Hitler.

Today, Spain and Portugal are the homes of regimes most accurately described as fascist, and Argentina in 1955 came to the end of a decade of fascist rule under Juan Perón. Fascist parties today survive under new names in postwar Italy and Germany, and movements with pronounced fascist inclinations can be identified in many countries. Fascism cannot be consigned to the category of a dead philosophy. Overshadowed as it has been in recent years by the East-West ideological cleavage, fascism continues to attract adherents, and, should the conditions recur that gave birth to it in the 1920's and 1930's, it might again become one of the world's foremost ideologies.

Origins

Fascism's debut took place in Italy where, by 1922, the first fascist leader, Benito Mussolini, had become Prime Minister after his fascist squads had marched on Rome. Eleven years later the "Bavarian Mussolini," Adolph Hitler, headed a fascist regime in Germany. Portugal, Spain, Japan, and Argentina must be added to the list of countries that have manifested fascist characteristics in varying degrees. It is on the basis of the experience of these half dozen countries that the following analysis of the rise of fascism is made.

Sympathizers with democracy have upon occasion denounced fascism as simply communism under another name. It is true that certain characteristics have been common to both: a totalitarian ideology, dictator-

---

[18] *Op. cit.*, p. 190.

ship by a single party usually dominated by one man, a police state, and a centrally directed economy.[19]

Both communism and fascism, then, are committed in practice to fostering the power of the state rather than the freedom of the individual. In the pursuit of statism, certain common policies have led to a drastic invasion of the life of the individual citizen by an undemocratic authority.

Communism and fascism, however, are not identical in their more precise ideology, appeal, or environmental history. For example, communism generally has been identified with societies that have known neither democracy nor extensive industrialization—Russia, China, Vietnam, Eastern Europe. Fascism, on the other hand, has been identified most often with technologically advanced, industrial-urban societies which, in addition, have had some experience with parliamentary democracy—Germany, Italy, Japan.

The identification suggests that the origins of fascism should be sought in a type of response to problems associated with industrialization and/or democratic government. Moreover, fascism's attraction has proved much greater for some elements in society than for others.

The circumstances leading to fascism have invariably included serious national economic maladjustments, with attendant personal insecurity

[19] C. J. Friedrich and Z. K. Brzezinski, *Totalitarian Dictatorship and Autocracy* (Cambridge, Harvard University Press, 1956), pp. 9–10. Note the identification of both fascism and communism with the six characteristics of totalitarianism as defined by Friedrich and Brzezinski:

1. an official ideology, consisting of an official body of doctrine covering all vital aspects of man's existence to which everyone living in that society is supposed to adhere, at least passively; this ideology is characteristically focused and projected toward a perfect final state of mankind, that is to say, it contains a chiliastic claim, based upon a radical rejection of the existing society and conquest of the world for the new one;

2. a single mass party led typically by one man, the "dictator," and consisting of a relatively small percentage of the total population (up to 10 per cent) of men and women, a hard core of them passionately and unquestioningly dedicated to the ideology and prepared to assist in every way in promoting its general acceptance, such a party being hierarchically, oligarchically organized, and typically either superior to, or completely intertwined with, the bureaucratic government organization;

3. a system of terroristic police control, supporting but also supervising the party for its leaders, and characteristically directed not only against demonstrable "enemies" of the regime, but against arbitrarily selected classes of the population; the terror of the secret police systematically exploiting modern science, and more especially scientific psychology;

4. a technologically conditioned near-complete monopoly of control, in the hands of the party and its subservient cadres, of all means of effective mass communication, such as the press, radio, motion pictures;

5. a similarly technologically conditioned near-complete monopoly of control (in the same hands) of all means of effective armed combat;

6. a central control and direction of the entire economy through the bureaucratic co-ordination of its formerly independent corporate entities, typically including most other associations and group activities.

for large numbers of people, combined with a growing lack of confidence in the ability of parliamentary government leadership to find a satisfactory solution to the economic crisis. Fascism was spawned in the post-1918 economic derangements, in the form of foreign trade difficulties, inflation, and unemployment. Conditions in Italy were acute immediately after World War I. In Portugal, Germany, Spain, and Japan the great depression of the 1930's brought severe distress. In Argentina post-World War II inflation and foreign-trade contraction were factors. In each of these countries, democratic regimes of recent origin bore the brunt of the unrest. Italy's parliamentary government was the oldest, dating back to the nineteenth century, but it had not yet gained wide support and endorsement. Portugal had had a shaky parliamentary regime since 1910, Germany's Weimar Republic was established in 1919, Japan's twentieth century democratic facade hid a feudal oligarchy, and Spain had escaped royal dictatorship in 1931. Like most Latin American states, Argentina had had only spasmodic experiments with democracy. Thus, experience with democratic institutions had been too brief for democratic roots to penetrate deeply, but long enough for democracy to be held responsible for economic distress and the ominous rumblings accompanying it. In these circumstances political upheaval could be anticipated, but the reason why the unrest acquired a fascist complexion must be sought in the reactions of the peoples and their leaders. After all, communism, too, showed increased strength in the same countries in these critical times and failed to achieve power.

Sociological analysis of the groups of people who supported fascism in these countries throws considerable light on the movements' origins. Although there were some people from all classes, the predominant social group represented was the middle class—businessmen, property owners, white-collar workers. A notable exception to this is Perón's enlistment of support among the urban proletariat, the *descamidos*. Generally speaking, however, fascism has been a middle-class movement. Large landowners and professional military officers also were profascist, whereas intellectuals and the laboring classes were not conspicuous in their support. As communists, socialists, and democrats, the workers were more often found in opposition to fascism, although there were important exceptions. Thus, in addition to economic distress, fascism depended upon the reaction of certain social strata to the situation.

Fascism, however, cannot be explained only in deterministic terms, for it also has had a very wide appeal on psychological grounds. Claiming to produce the leaders who would lead the nation out of its troubles, fascism appeared as a panacea to distraught people. Not only did it promise to free the nation of its trials, but the only demand it made was obedience from most people in finding the escape. Those who craved leadership and reform found it a welcome relief.

If these were the circumstances in which fascism originated, what were the doctrines accompanying it and providing grounds for describing it as an ideology? The reply requires an approach to fascism from two points of view: as a defensive ideology, and as a dynamic, revolutionary ideology.

Fascism as a Defensive Ideology

Since fascism appeals primarily to social elements with something to lose rather than to gain, and therefore fundamentally conservative in orientation, it is not surprising to discover much in fascism that is defensive and negative.

Against communism. The Russian Revolution of 1917, the open schism between communists and social-democrats at the end of World War I, and abortive communist revolutions in Germany and Hungary in 1919 suddenly brought into clear relief the actuality and imminence of communism. Though a welcome development to many, it was terribly frightening to the middle and upper classes of European society. Democratic governments, which because of their nature permitted communist activity, appeared to many anticommunists to be too weak for successful resistance to communism. Some stronger anticommunist force was sought. Fascism provided an answer, for it took the stand that the bolshevist evil could be dealt with only as a malignant cancer is treated—with radical surgery.

Mussolini and the original *fasci* of Milan in 1919 battled in the streets with communist demonstrators, and every fascist movement since has taken a vigorous anticommunist stand. Indeed, fascism adopted the position that only two ideologic choices face today's world: communism and fascism. When evidence was not sufficiently convincing, fascists were not above dramatizing the communist threat by any means available. Hitler's Nazis set fire to the Reichstag building in Berlin and then pointed to the episode as an example of communist arson. Francisco Franco, leader of the Spanish fascists, denounced the Republic of Spain as a communist regime which was preparing to liquidate private property and Christianity. That communists later played an important role in the Republic does not validate Franco's charges, but the accusations served their purpose, of alerting propertied and clerical interests to support Franco. Anticommunism is not, of course, unique to fascism, although communists apply the word *fascist* to all their opponents. Nevertheless, opposition to communism is a cardinal precept of fascism.

Against equality. Since all humans are not equal in strength, stamina, imagination, intelligence, and in other ways, in some cultures it has been held that equality in the political, social, and economic realms is an unsound ideal. Fascism strongly endorses this position. On the one hand, it designates as followers all those who are not capable of leadership. Although fascist doctrine readily admits that this element will be the majority, it takes the view that most humans are more content and satisfied when freed of the responsibility of making important decisions. Therefore, the majority should and will take orders. On the other hand, it proposes vesting authority over all matters in an "elite," those who will give the orders.

The crucial task is that of finding this authority-wielding elite. The initial elite, in both theory and practice, were those who exhibited the courage, leadership, and will to power in establishing fascist regimes. Thus, Nazi Germany's elite were those who captured control of the German government in 1933 and proceeded to establish and operate the Nazi dictatorship. In Spain it was Franco and his civil war supporters, organized in the Falange Española Tradicionalista (Spanish Traditional Phalanx), a group of army officers and political adventurers. The National Union Party of Antonio de Oliveira Salazar became Portugal's elite, and in Japan the Young Officers Association so viewed itself. It was the duty of the elite, in addition to its exercise of authority over all national matters, to train a second generation of leaders. For this purpose, fascist regimes organized youth indoctrination corps—the Hitler Jugend being perhaps the best known—from which would come recruits for the nation's future leadership. Such ideological training of youth is, of course, also a feature of communist practice.

Against democracy. Not surprising, in view of fascism's rejection of the principle that all individuals have a right to share in the great decisions of a government, is its rejection of democracy. A system of government which, like democracy, accords equality to the ignorant and weak, as well as to the intelligent and strong, in fascist eyes is certain to lead to disastrous confusion and negativism. Italian fascists emphasized Italy's deplorable economic situation; the Nazis attacked the Weimar Republic as responsible for unemployment; Japanese parliamentarians were charged with failing to seek escape from Japan's economic dilemma in a dynamic East Asia "Co-Prosperity Sphere"; Salazar, Franco, Perón, all could point to the undeniable shortcomings of democracies, though they failed to point out that nondemocracies had equally serious problems.

In place of the democratic regimes which, in both concept and practice, were unacceptable to them, the fascists proposed to establish what they openly called totalitarianism. As Mussolini first explained,[20]

Anti-individualistic, the Fascist conception of life stresses the importance of the State and accepts the individual only in so far as his interests coincide with those of the State, which stands for the conscience and the universal will of man as a historic entity. . . . And if liberty is to be the attribute of living men and not of abstract dummies invented by individualistic liberalism, then Fascism

[20] *Enciclopedia Italiana* (Milano, Treves-Treccani-Tumminelli, 1932), Vol. XIV, pp. 847–848.

stands for liberty, and for the only liberty worth having, the liberty of the State. The Fascist conception of the State is all-embracing; outside of it no human or spiritual values can exist, much less have value. Thus understood, Fascism is totalitarian.

The implementation of a policy to liquidate democratic institutions has varied considerably in actual fascist experience. Within fifteen years Italian fascism had abolished parties, parliament, free press, and the right of association. In a much briefer time Nazism had "accomplished" more —most notably in its denial of citizenship and frequently the right to property and life to German Jews. In Spain today the absence of political parties, elections, a free press, public meetings, and safeguards against arbitrary imprisonment, exile, and execution testify to Falangist Spain's extirpation of democracy. On the other hand, opposition parties continued to campaign, though under severe restrictions, for seats in still surviving parliaments in Argentina and Portugal. Yet, suppression by Perón of such papers as Buenos Aires' world-famous *La Prensa;* the arrest of antifascist politicians; and attacks upon democracy's "fatal encouragement of irresponsible, anti-social individualism, and ennervating materialism" revealed a kinship with the more ruthless and thorough destruction of democratic institutions in Hitler's Germany.

Against internationalism. In this attitude will be recognized a corollary of totalitarianism. If the state is the focal point of civilization, allegiance to anything above or outside the nation-state is rejected. Not only was membership in the League of Nations scorned (fascist Germany, Italy, and Japan left it demonstratively), but fascists also stood for a more vigorous defense of their nations' interests.

The fascist appeal to nationalism was particularly effective in Germany saddled with the Treaty of Versailles, in Italy denied some of its claims at the Paris Peace Conference (1919), and in Japan, the victim of racial discrimination in the immigration policies of the United States and the British Commonwealth. Spain, Portugal, and Argentina have not been nearly as truculent in their international relations, but Spain's pretensions to leadership of the Hispanic world and Argentina's bid for leadership of a Latin American bloc hostile to the United States are milder manifestations of the fascist national outlook.

Fascist emphasis upon the national group as removed from, and even antagonistic to, the rest of the international community has fitted into the ideologic mosaic in other ways. It has appealed to the natural prejudices and in-group feelings of its adherents. It has afforded an outlet for external resentment generated by internal repression. Above all, it has encouraged the growth of a doctrine of national superiority. In Germany, the Nazis went beyond Mussolini's reminder to the Italians that they were descended from the Romans. Germans were told that their superior capacity for great ventures and conquests was biologically ordained.

More recently, fascists in the Union of South Africa professed to find biblical endorsement for domination of the black majority by a white Afrikaner elite.

Nationalism is, of course, no monopoly of the fascists, but they have, perhaps more effectively than supporters of other ideologies, incorporated it in their doctrinal appeal.

Against pacifism. In view of the doctrines already discussed, it is understandable that strong antipacifism would characterize the movement. Fascism was born in a turbulent, critical, disjointed atmosphere. Concentrating on the emotional side of man, it has deliberately encouraged the perpetuation of the restless, agitated mood in which it had its origin.

The vocabulary of fascism early acquired words and slogans suggesting this antipacifism. *Struggle, conflict, war, battle,* and *survival* remind men that life is not a tea party and that preparation for violence is conducive to survival. Hitler called his autobiography not "My Life" but "My Battle." Mussolini called upon Italians to recognize that it was "Better to live an hour as a lion, than one hundred years as a lamb." The fascist ideal has been the warrior, the man of action, the Nietzschean superman. Certainly, the violent means employed by fascists to seize and maintain power has not contradicted in deed what it has taught as a theory—the pacific are trampled underfoot.

The foregoing attitudes do not afford a total picture of the fascist ideology. They do serve to emphasize its response to the fears and insecurity of the middle and upper classes, of people who had something to lose—wealth, social status, political power—and dreaded the loss amid the confusion and unrest of the times. Fascism has not, however, been exclusively negative or defensive. It has also proclaimed itself the pioneer of a new era, a great revolution.

Fascism as a Permanent Revolution

It has been said that, in its emotional and conflicting appeals, fascism is peculiarly suited to the frustrations encountered by modern man as he gropes for adjustment to the present dynamic age. It can even be asserted that fascism has had its greatest popularity where it has been most irrational and emotionally disturbing. Salazar and Franco, compelled to compromise with older, vested interests (Church, landowners, army, big business), have fallen considerably short of the fascist totalitarian ideal approximated by the fanatic Hitler in Germany. Nonetheless, fascist regimes everywhere have been characterized by a much heralded revolutionary program.

Italian "corporativism" and German four-year plans, along with their smaller editions elsewhere, set out to solve economic problems in the interest of the whole nation by state planning and elimination of industrial strife. Yet, whereas both socialists and communists have endorsed state ownership of private property in their programs of economic reorganization, fascism did not officially reject the institution of private property. Through extensive government control, however, it has effectively subordinated the entire economy to the interests of the state. Extension of social services has also marked fascist practice, its distinguishing feature being their denial to those the state designated as "unworthy": Jews in Germany, liberals in Argentina, anarchists in Spain.

Having found mass emotionalism conducive to its rise, fascism has tended to continue stoking the fires of antagonism and aggression. Franco's assaults upon communists, republicans, and anarchists, and Perón's attack upon the Roman Catholic Church were feeble echoes of the Nazi and Japanese militarists' efforts to deepen religious and racial antagonisms. The brutalities of the Nazis and the fanaticism of the Japanese suicide pilots in World War II reveal the extremes to which fascism's constant emotional stimulation has sometimes led. But such emotional engineering has served to harness much of the restless energy of the masses to the purposes of the elite.

Finally, fascists have proclaimed the great future of their specific nation-state. Italy could anticipate, according to her elite, domination of the Mediterranean. Germany was encouraged to prepare for the acquisition of *Lebensraum*. A great empire in Asia was the expectancy cultivated among the Japanese. Even Franco hoped that from the murky waters of international tensions Spain might gain Gibraltar and French Morocco. Perón was obliged to confine his goals to the more nebulous "high destiny which God has seen fit to assign our country." He added, "the day cannot be far off when all humanity . . . will fix its eyes on the flag of the Argentines." [21] In a word, fascism has been dynamic and aggressive in the kind of foreign policy it has preferred. Circumstances have not always permitted pursuit of such a policy, as in Spain and Portugal, but fascism has manifested an affinity for the hungry "have-not" nation-states.

The Core of Fascism

Recognizing man as irrational and emotional, fascism has made little pretense of being a rational, logical ideology. It has openly reveled in expediency and opportunism, and has focused more on means than on ends. Accordingly, a summary of its concepts is difficult.

If one ideal stands out, it has been the frank glorification of the state as the undying representative of a nation. It has even gone so far as to endow that state with mystical biological characteristics. Human beings are cells of very limited life which of themselves are unimportant, but, co-ordinated in the body politic of the fascist society, they become part

---

[21] Quoted in George I. Blanksten, *Perón's Argentina* (Chicago, The University of Chicago Press, copyright 1953 by the University of Chicago), p. 293.

of something meaningful and immortal. Here, then, is a new meaning to life and an escape from the crass, shallow, frustrating materialism that both communism and democracy foster. These are the pronouncements made by fascists when they have had time to interrupt their careers of action and pontificate upon philosophy.

Fascism's critics have charged that it is a patchwork of double talk serving as a cloak for political gangsterism. Reduced to its bare essentials, say its enemies, it seeks only augmentation of the power of the state. But power for power's sake represents no scale of values, no goals, no awareness of ends, no meaningful pattern of human existence. Man does not live by bread alone, but he also does not live by power alone. Fascism, therefore, has been described by both communists and democrats as essentially nihilistic, an ideology without a core.

Whether or not there is a central matrix of ideas in fascism, and their delineation if they do exist, becomes an academic question when it is realized that some of the world's largest nation-states have had fascist regimes, and an appreciable number of people have lived under, and profess to believe in, fascist doctrine in the years since the defeat of the Axis in World War II. In this sense fascism constitutes another ideology in the struggle for the minds of men.

In the next part of this chapter are presented evaluations and justifications for the existence of the three ideologies just reviewed. After the plea for democratic socialism by a Swedish Social-Democrat come explanations of "Titoist" communism by Marshal Tito and of fascism by one of its most eloquent founders, Benito Mussolini.

POSITIONS
ON THE PROBLEM

1. A Defense of Democratic Socialism in Sweden

(The author of the following remarks, Kaj Bjork, is Secretary for International Affairs of the Social-Democratic Workers' Party of Sweden. In these remarks he points out the basic principles of democratic socialism as endorsed by his party, and the flexible approach Social-Democrats believe necessary because of ever changing conditions in society.[22])

[22] Kaj Bjork, "Socialism and Democracy," in Review of International Affairs, November 16, 1952, pp. 12–13.

. . . Sweden has lived in peace for almost 140 years, and social developments during this period have not been disturbed by revolutionary or counter-revolutionary clashes. Our people is unusually homogeneous with respect to language, race and creed, and conflicts in these fields have been of little importance for political developments. Industrialization began relatively late in Sweden but has brought a rapid economic expansion during this century, which has given our people the highest standard of living in Europe. Parallel with industrialization an industrial working-class emerged, which followed the banner of Social Democracy. Under the impression of the revolutions in other countries at the end of the First World War, the old governing classes accepted a total political democratization, which made it possible for [the] Social Democratic Party to take over the government at the beginning of the 1930's. Although the Social Democrats have had an absolute majority only during part of the 20 years since 1932, it has been possible to introduce reforms and changes, which have brought a considerable shifting in power and influence to the advantage of the working classes. It has been possible to maintain full employment for a number of years, part of the national income has been redistributed by taxation and social policy, and the power of private capitalists has been limited on many points. Efforts have been made to lead and plan economic developments as a whole, and in agriculture and housing policy it is possible to speak of systematic planning. Although the Social Democrats have not brought about large-scale nationalization, an important role is played by State, municipal and cooperative enterprise. A strong trade union movement has influenced economic developments, and other groups have followed the example of the industrial workers and formed their own professional or economic organizations. In recent years interest in workers' participation in the management of industry has increased, and experience gained from consultation in industry has been rather positive. This whole development has helped to convince the Swedish workers that they have good chances to defend their interests within a democracy with several Parties, while developments in the Soviet Union have made them turn with growing determination against Stalinist propaganda. They have come to regard political democracy with several parties as a value in itself and are prepared to defend it against any attack. . . .

. . . It may be said that we only talk about minor concessions by the capitalists, which do not really change their position of power, which is based on their ownership of the means of production. But the fact that Capitalist groups within the Democratic states fight such changes seems to show that they do not themselves regard them as only minor concessions. Today, it is exactly those Capitalist groups which try to arouse suspicion against the State in the more progressive democracies. It seems to us that the nature of the State is changing with the changes in power-relationships between classes within the modern democracies. The modern Welfare State is replacing the old police state. . . . This is not exactly to say that the State is lifted above classes, but it reflects a changed power-relationship between classes. It may also be added that the nature of classes is changing by the emergence of new social groups and the improvement of the workers' position, so that one cannot simply speak of a bourgeoisie standing against a large proletariat.

The role of ownership of the means of production is also changing. State, municipal and cooperative enterprises create a picture different from undiluted private capitalism. But even though most industries have remained in private hands in Western democracies such as Sweden, the content of ownership is not the same as before. If a private capitalist cannot fix wages and prices, hire and fire workers, start or stop production without interference from the State or the trade unions, he is in rather a different position from that of his classical predecessor, even though the legal forms of ownership remain. We do not claim to have solved the problem of too much power in the hands of private capitalists, but we believe a further gradual change is possible without violent upheavals. It may be said that private capitalists will react more strongly when their basic privileges are threatened and that the democratic system will then be unworkable. This belief was widely held by Left-wing Socialists in the early 30's, especially after Hitler's conquest of power in Germany, but recent experience from Britain, Scandinavia and other countries seems to show that even far-reaching changes in the power of Capitalist groups need not destroy the functioning of Democracy. Since this road means much smaller sacrifice for the working-class and can be combined with increasing production during the period of transition, there is certainly a strong case for reformist tactics in a well-established Democracy.

2. MARSHAL TITO'S COMMENTS
ON YUGOSLAVIA'S OWN BRAND OF COMMUNISM

(In July, 1955, Marshal Tito was interviewed by a group of visiting Americans in Belgrade. In the course of this interview, questions pertinent to communism's distinctive features in Yugoslavia elicited the following remarks from Tito.[23])

I . . . speak of the different systems between the Soviet Union and Yugoslavia—how they are building their countries internally compared to how we are doing it. If we start from this point of view, we shall see that there are a number of substantial differences. But it does not mean that our differences are of such a nature that a conflict between Yugoslavia and [the] Soviet Union would arise. After Stalin's death the new leaders of the Soviet Union have reached the conclusion that one type of social system, regardless of what it is, cannot reign in the world—that there are many nations in the world with different historical developments; that it is necessary for all nations to determine their own course, and that it is impossible to subject them to any single standard pattern. . . . In substance, they agreed that Yugoslavia should build a social system in her own way, and they would build theirs in their own way. . . .

We did proceed with [agricultural] collectivization, but the administrative formation of cooperatives was not the correct course to follow in our country. Production did not increase but, on the contrary, resulted in the loss of interest on the part of the peasant to increase his productivity of work. This way of proceeding was not satisfactory. But neither is the method of small farm enterprises which we have today. . . . The average small sized farm consists at the utmost of 5 hectares [about twelve acres]. These small farm enterprises, which are self-consuming, cannot provide sufficient wheat or other agricultural produce to feed our population in the cities and working centers, because they can neither cultivate their land as it should be cultivated nor attain the required productivity of work.

Our policy is to promote and secure in the largest possible degree, the cooperatives and State farm enterprises which we already have, to mechanize

[23] *Yugoslav Review,* Vol. 5, No. 7 (September, 1955), pp. 5, 15, 16, 25.

them to the largest possible extent, and increase the productive capacity of the land.

This does not mean to say that we leave unaided the small farm enterprise whose produce is small or even nil, sometimes even becoming a burden. We have not abandoned the idea that Yugoslavia will succeed some day in uniting her small farms and that a *modus vivendi* in this respect will be found. . . . We do not wish to use forcible methods. However, we are trying to convince our peasants that this method of individual cultivation is not advantageous either to them or the country. . . .

With this one exception, we have not changed our policy, but we have been improving and perfecting our administrative and economic system in general. We have been carrying out decentralization both in administration and economy. . . .

. . . When I speak of decentralization in our country I can say that in this respect we have made an enormous step forward, not only through the decentralization of State power, but also through one of the most democratic acts of all—the participation of the workers in the form of self-management in economy. This is a new thing which has not heretofore existed. It would be erroneous to compare what existed in the Soviet Union around 1920 with what we have in our country. This is an innovation which has so far given ample proof of its value. In this way we have given free outlet to the initiative of the workers themselves, so that they are now not the object but the subject capable of fully directing and managing their own enterprises. Of course, they have their obligations to the community and this has to be borne in mind, but they are fully aware of these obligations. This is a major achievement which is significant for our further development. Herein lies the withering away of the State with regard to management and to the political, economic, and various other functions which are being transferred to the lower organs.

3. FASCISM DEFENDED AS A LIVING FAITH

(Most vigorous and clear in stating the doctrines of fascism was Benito Mussolini (1883–1945). The following are selections from his contributions on fascism to the *Enciclopedia Italiana* in 1932.[24])

Fascism is now a completely individual thing, not only as a regime but as a doctrine. And this means that to-day Fascism exercising its critical sense upon itself and upon others, has formed its own distinct and peculiar point of view, to which it can refer and upon which, therefore, it can act in the face of all problems. . . .

And above all, Fascism, the more it considers and observes the future and the development of humanity quite apart from political considerations of the moment, believes neither in the possibility nor the utility of perpetual peace. It thus repudiates the doctrine of Pacifism—born of a renunciation of the struggle and an act of cowardice in the face of sacrifice. War alone brings up to its highest tension all human energy and puts the stamp of nobility upon the peoples who have the courage to meet it. All other trials are substitutes, which never really put men into the position where they have to make the great de-

[24] Quoted in Albert R. Chandler, *The Clash of Political Ideals*, 3rd ed. (New York, Appleton-Century-Crofts, 1957), pp. 172–175, 177–178.

cision—the alternative of life or death. Thus a doctrine which is founded upon this harmful postulate of peace is hostile to Fascism. And thus hostile to the spirit of Fascism . . . are all the international leagues and societies which, as history will show, can be scattered to the winds when once strong national feeling is aroused. . . . Thus the Fascist accepts life and loves it, knowing nothing of and despising suicide: he rather conceives of life as duty and struggle and conquest, life which should be high and full, lived for oneself, but above all for others—those who are at hand and those who are far distant, contemporaries, and those who will come after.

Such a conception of life makes Fascism the complete opposite of that doctrine, the base of so-called scientific and Marxian socialism, the materialist conception of history; according to which the history of human civilization can be explained simply through the conflict of interests among the various social groups and by the change and development in the means and instruments of production. . . .

After Socialism, Fascism combats the whole complex system of democratic ideology, and repudiates it, whether in its theoretical premises or in its practical application. Fascism denies that the majority, by the simple fact that it is a majority, can direct human society; it denies that numbers alone can govern by means of a periodical consultation, and it affirms the immutable, beneficial, and fruitful inequality of mankind. . . .

But the Fascist negation of Socialism, Democracy, and Liberalism must not be taken to mean that Fascism desires to lead the world back to the state of affairs before 1789 . . . we do not desire to turn back. . . .

. . . Given that the nineteenth century was the century of Socialism, of Liberalism, and of Democracy, it does not necessarily follow that the twentieth century must also be a century of Socialism, Liberalism, and Democracy: political doctrines pass, but humanity remains; and it may rather be expected that this will be a century of authority, a century of the Left, a century of Fascism. For if the nineteenth century was a century of individualism . . . it may be expected that this will be the century of collectivism, and hence the century of the State. . . .

The foundation of Fascism is the conception of the State, its character, its duty, and its aim. Fascism conceives of the State as an absolute, in comparison with which all individuals or groups are relative, only to be conceived of in their relation to the State. The conception of the Liberal State is not that of a directing force, guiding the play and development, both material and spiritual, of a collective body, but merely a force limited to the function of recording results: on the other hand, the Fascist State is itself conscious, and has itself a will and a personality—thus it may be called the "ethical" State. . . .

. . . For Fascism, the growth of empire, that is to say the expansion of the nation, is an essential manifestation of vitality, and its opposite a sign of decadence. Peoples which are rising, or rising again after a period of decadence, are always imperialist; any renunciation is a sign of decay and of death. Fascism is the doctrine best adapted to represent the tendencies and the aspirations of a people . . . who are rising again after many centuries of abasement and foreign servitude. But empire demands discipline, the coordination of all forces and a deeply felt sense of duty and sacrifice: this fact explains many aspects of the practical working of the regime, the character of many forces in the State, and the necessarily severe measures which must be taken against those who would oppose this spontaneous and inevitable movement. . . . If every age has its own characteristic doctrine, there are a thousand signs which point to Fascism as the characteristic doctrine of our time. [That Fascism is a "living thing"] is proved by the fact that Fascism has created a living faith; and that this faith is very powerful in the minds of men, is demonstrated by those who have suffered and died for it.

QUESTIONS

1. On what grounds have advocates of democratic socialism rejected (a) nineteenth century democracy, and (b) communism?

2. Has democratic socialism, since World War I, moved closer in its doctrine and practice to communism or nonsocialist democracy? Explain.

3. What significant differences have appeared between social-democratic policies in Great Britain, Sweden, and India? What is the basis for saying that India at present is undertaking the potentially most important social-democratic experiment?

4. Comment on the validity of the communists' assertion that fascism is the last stand of capitalism in its struggle for survival.

5. Compare the relationship of citizen to state under nonsocialist democracy, communism, democratic socialism, national communism, and fascism.

6. What do you understand by the term *national communism* as applied to contemporary Yugoslavia? Does this development weaken or strengthen the appeal of communism to the world? Why?

7. Of the various ideologies discussed in this chapter, namely, democratic socialism, national communism, and fascism, which would be the one most likely to appeal to Americans? Why?

8. How does Kaj Bjork in the first position (pp. 366–368) explain and defend a Swedish democratic socialist program which does not encompass large-scale nationalization?

9. In what ways, according to Marshal Tito (pp. 368–369), have Yugoslav communists pursued policies different from Russian communists? How significant do you believe these differences are?

10. In the third position (pp. 369–370), what arguments are offered in support of the contention that fascism and international peace are incompatible? What exceptions to this argument may be cited and how may they be explained?

SELECT BIBLIOGRAPHY

ASHTON, E. B., *The Fascist: His State and His Mind* (New York, Morrow, 1937). A popularly written but systematic appraisal of fascism, delineating its political, economic, administrative, and diplomatic aspects. One of the earliest efforts to objectively analyze fascism in Italy and Germany. Tends to overemphasize the formalization of fascist doctrine.

COLE, George D. H., *A History of Socialist Thought* (London, Macmillan, 1953–54), 2 vols. A prolific writer on the history of Britain's working classes and the socialist movement, the author, a British socialist, covers the history of socialist thought, not action, from 1789 to 1890. Particularly helpful in tracing the evolution of Utopian, Christian, and revisionist socialism. Other volumes, bringing the survey down to the present, are planned.

DAVIS, Jerome, *Contemporary Social Movements* (New York, Appleton-Century, 1930). This work remains a standard text on modern social movements. Its chapters on socialism, fascism, and the British Labor movement are detailed. Liberal selections from documents add to its value.

DJILAS, Milovan, *The New Class* (New York, Praeger, 1957). The author, long-time Yugoslav communist leader, is disillusioned with communism, not as a theory, but as a practice. Chapter on national communism emphasizes "inevitable" splintering of communism into deviating national movements, each becoming prisoner of its own tyrannical bureaucracy.

DRAGNICH, Alex N., *Tito's Promised Land* (New Brunswick, N.J., Rutgers University Press, 1954). An accurate description of the Tito regime during its first ten years. The author, cultural attaché in Belgrade 1947–50, observed at first hand Tito's break with Moscow and the initiation of his brand of communism. Concludes that dictatorship and decentralization program are incompatible and that, therefore, the latter is not likely to continue.

EBENSTEIN, William, *Today's Isms* (Englewood Cliffs, N.J., Prentice-Hall, 1954). A brief but useful summary of communism, fascism, capitalism, and socialism by an American political scientist. Contemporary ideologies are divided into two general categories, the aggressively totalitarian, and the free democratic. Special emphasis is placed upon their psychological aspects.

GAY, PETER, *The Dilemma of Democratic Socialism* (New York, Columbia University Press, 1952). A critical, well-documented history of revisionist socialism. Eduard Bernstein's intellectual biography as a theme adds color and readability. Gay poses the question: How can social revolution be accomplished without political revolution? He analyzes the revisionists' response.

HAMMOND, Thomas Taylor, *Yugoslavia Between East and West* (New York, Foreign Policy Association, 1954). A concise, informative pamphlet in the Headline Series, containing an interpretive survey of Yugoslavia since the 1948 break with the Cominform. Although cautious in his appraisal, the author sees evidence of considerable deviation of Yugoslav communism from the Russian pattern.

LEVI, Werner, *Free India in Asia* (Minneapolis, University of Minnesota Press, 1952). A dispassionate effort, based on personal observation, to present India's role among the nations of Asia since 1947. Chapter on communism and democracy in India emphasizes the eclectic intellectual climate in India and the Indian refusal to endorse or commit itself to a western ideology *in toto*.

U.S. Library of Congress, Legislative Reference Service, *Fascism in Action* (Washington, D.C., Government Printing Office, 1947). A description of fascist activities in Italy, Germany, Spain, and Japan, indicating what the general fascist pattern of behavior has been in specific realms such as education, religion, economics, and foreign policy.

10

Is Peaceful Coexistence Possible?

THE PROBLEM
AND ITS BACKGROUND

INTRODUCTION

Of course, the bourgeois governments have no sympathy for us, for the socialist countries. But the socialist and capitalist countries live on one planet, and in the interest of peace among nations it is necessary to pursue a policy of peaceful coexistence and to subordinate emotions to common sense.

Thus spoke Nikita S. Khrushchev, at a reception at the Bulgarian Peoples' Republic Embassy, February 18, 1957.[1] Soviet leaders in recent years have repeatedly spoken of the possibility of peaceful coexistence between different economic and political systems, thereby confronting the noncommunist world with a most puzzling question. How can an ideology that preaches the inevitable collapse of capitalism and the ultimate triumph of communism speak at the same time of peaceful coexistence? Are the Soviet professions of peaceful coexistence a reliable guide to their policies, or are they merely a tactical device to lull the rest of the world into relaxing their defenses?

These questions are more easily asked than answered. Unfortunately the statements and writings of communist leaders over the years have been so contradictory that it is difficult to deduce what they actually believe or intend to do. For example, Joseph Stalin, replying to the questions of a group of American newspaper editors, said: [2]

[1] *Pravda,* February 20, 1957, pp. 3–4. (English translation is in the *Current Digest of the Soviet Press,* April 3, 1957, p. 34.)
[2] *New York Times,* April 2, 1952, p. 11.

The peaceful coexistence of capitalism and communism is fully possible, given the mutual desire to cooperate, readiness to perform obligations which have been assumed, observance of the principle of equality, and non-interference in the internal affairs of other states.

At the Bandung Conference of African and Asian states in April, 1955, Chou En-lai, the Premier of Communist China, declared: [3]

By following the principles of mutual respect for sovereignty and territorial integrity, non-aggression, non-interference in each other's internal affairs, equality and mutual benefit, the peaceful coexistence of countries with different social systems can be realized. When these principles are insured implementation, there is no reason why international disputes cannot be settled through negotiation.

Yet alongside such statements, a regular reader of the Soviet press would frequently encounter a viewpoint like the following, which appeared in *Komsomolskaya Pravda* on February 6, 1952: [4]

A new attempt by the American imperialists to establish their world domination will present to the peoples of the world in still more acute form the question of the injuriousness of the capitalist system, which cannot live without war, and the question of the necessity of changing this bloody system, of replacing it with another, the socialist system. A new war can only hasten the fall of world capitalism.

On the occasion of the one hundredth anniversary of *The Communist Manifesto* in 1948, the Soviet periodical, *New Times,* declared in an editorial: [5]

The age of capitalism is coming to an end. Communism is invincible because social development is ripe for it. It brings to the people salvation from war and bloody gambles, from poverty and want, from atomic vandalism, and cultural degradation. The future belongs to the glowing ideas proclaimed 100 years ago in the Communist Manifesto. . . . [In] our age, all roads lead to Communism.

In more recent years, particularly since the Twentieth Congress of the Communist Party of the Soviet Union in February, 1956, the new Soviet leaders have frequently reiterated their confidence in the ultimate triumph of revolutionary socialism and communism. As was pointed out in Chapter 8, these leaders seem to have modified Leninist-Stalinist theory by stating that wars between capitalist and communist states are not necessarily inevitable, and that it is possible for the transition from capitalism to communism to take place in a peaceful, parliamentary manner. Apparently apprehensive over the potential destruction of another major war, they seem to have chosen a path of peaceful competition with the capitalist world, but they remain supremely confident of an ultimate communist

[3] *Ibid.,* April 20, 1955, p. 8.
[4] *Current Digest of the Soviet Press,* March 22, 1952, p. 21.
[5] *New Times,* February 25, 1948.

victory in such competition. Thus Mr. Khrushchev, in his principal report to the Twentieth Party Congress, after emphasizing that peaceful coexistence remained the basis of Soviet foreign policy, went on to say: [6] "We believe that after seeing for themselves the advantages that communism holds out, all working men and women on earth will sooner or later take to the road of the struggle to build a socialist society."

A year later, in a television interview with three American news correspondents in Moscow, he declared: [7]

And I can prophesy that your grandchildren in America will live under socialism. And please do not be afraid of that. Your grandchildren . . . will not understand how their grandparents did not understand the progressive nature of a socialist society.

He went on to explain the kind of peaceful competition he envisaged between capitalism and Soviet socialism:

Now, as far as competition between capitalist and socialist ideologies are concerned, we have never made a secret of the fact that there will be an ideological struggle going on between these two ideologies, but we never believe that that is the same thing as a war, because this would be an ideological struggle in which the system which will have the support of the people . . . will come out on top.

At the present time your American people do not support the Marxist-Leninist theories. They are following the bourgeois political leaders, but is that a reason for war? Is that a reason for any enmity between us and the United States? No. Let us live in peace. Let us develop our economy. Let us compete. Let us trade with each other. Let us exchange experience in agriculture, in industry, in the field of culture, and as far as the question of which system will come out on top, let history, let our peoples decide that. I think this is a good way.

We believe that our socialist system will be victorious, but that does not mean under any conditions that we want to impose that system on anyone. We simply believe that the people of each country themselves will come to realize that that system is best for them. That is up to the people concerned to decide. We have no intention of imposing our ideas on anybody.

The Communist Concept of Peaceful Coexistence [8]

According to the foregoing statement, Soviet leaders envisage a considerable period in which capitalism and communism will exist simultaneously, side by side, during which time there will be intense ideolog-

[6] *New York Times,* February 15, 1956, p. 10. Excerpts from this address appear in Chap. 8. Soviet leaders, it will be noted, often refer to their system as "socialism" rather than "communism." They mean by this "revolutionary socialism," characterized by the dictatorship of the proletariat, as distinct from the "democratic socialism" of Western Europe described in Chap. 9. The reader should be careful to make this distinction in his own mind when the Soviet leaders speak of "socialism."

[7] *New York Times,* June 3, 1957, p. 6.

[8] For a concise analysis of the communist concept of coexistence, see Vernon Aspaturian, "What Do the Communists Mean by Peaceful Coexistence?" *The Reporter,* March 10, 1955, p. 35.

ical, economic, and political competition. Finally, they assert, communism will win out and capitalism will lose, because the communists believe their system is stronger and superior. Peaceful coexistence, in present communist usage, does not therefore mean the indefinite perpetuation of capitalism but only a temporary period of intense competition between the two systems, at the end of which communism will be triumphant. The duration of this temporary period is somewhat vague, but on a few occasions Soviet leaders have suggested that it might run until approximately the end of the twentieth century. For example, Khrushchev, inadvertently or intentionally, was fairly specific when he predicted that the grandchildren of the present American generation would live under socialism.

Western Concepts of Peaceful Coexistence

It is not very comforting or reassuring to the western world to contemplate peaceful coexistence as simply a forty-year respite before communism is triumphant throughout the world. To the average western mind, the term *peaceful coexistence* suggests a peaceful "live-and-let-live" relationship, in which countries with different political and economic systems do not attempt to interfere in one another's affairs and can settle their differences through normal channels of discussion and negotiation.

This concept of coexistence, which corresponds to the natural, peaceful aspirations of peoples everywhere, would, if put into practice, remove many causes of tension between the Soviet Union and other countries of the world. It would presumably do away with communist expansion at the expense of independent peoples and with communist interference in the internal affairs of other countries. Since it envisages a "live-and-let-live" relationship, it also would not assume (although it might conceivably hope) that any one system would inevitably triumph over all the others.[9]

At times, communist leaders have tried to convince the rest of the world that they, too, hope for a period of "live-and-let-live" relationships. The statements of Stalin and Chou En-lai, quoted at the beginning of this chapter, are examples of this, and many others could be cited.[10] By emphasizing principles of mutual respect, nonaggression, and noninterference in the internal affairs of other states, communist leaders have seemed to endorse a "live-and-let-live" concept of peaceful coexistence.

Many people in the noncommunist world would welcome evidence that the communists were prepared to accept a "live-and-let-live" relationship with other countries. Yet, since communism frequently portrays itself as a

[9] Supporters of democracy sometimes assume that it will inevitably triumph throughout the world, and that the collapse of communism is inevitable.

[10] See, for example, Joseph Stalin, *For Peaceful Coexistence, Postwar Interviews* (New York, International Publishers, 1951).

world revolutionary movement which will inevitably replace capitalism and western democracy, it is exceedingly difficult for the man in the street to know what to believe. Reports of espionage and disloyal activities by native communist sympathizers make it doubly difficult to believe that communists sincerely accept coexistence on a "live-and-let-live" basis.

Most people in the western world have therefore come to regard coexistence as a kind of armed truce between two antagonistic systems. No overt military conflict exists, save for sporadic outbreaks in certain localized areas, and there is some limited mutual toleration, based primarily on a realistic recognition of the strength of each side. The struggle between the two systems is not abandoned, but it assumes such forms as infiltration, subversion, psychological warfare, propaganda, and the encouragement of "liberation" movements among the peoples of the rival regimes. Apart from the periods of World War II and the Korean War, coexistence in this sense has characterized the relations between communist and noncommunist powers since 1920, and reflects the actual state of affairs in recent years (the word *peaceful* is not the most accurate description of these relationships).

The "armed truce" concept of coexistence seems similar in some respects to the current communist concept of "peaceful competition" between the communist and democratic systems. As applied by communist leaders today, however, the concept of "peaceful competition" seems to contemplate a dynamic and imaginative communist effort to appeal to the peoples of Asia, the Middle East, and Africa in terms of anticolonialism, economic development and higher living standards. The "armed truce" concept, on the other hand, has been primarily a byproduct of the political stalemate between the communist and noncommunist worlds. As such, it seems more negative in its approach and less challenging in its appeal than the present communist "invitation" to a period of "peaceful competition."

PEACEFUL COEXISTENCE AND THE COMMUNIST THEORY OF WORLD REVOLUTION

It is very difficult, if not impossible, to reconcile the idea of peaceful coexistence, except as a temporary stratagem, with certain principles of communist theory which are summed up under the broad heading of world revolution. These were discussed in Chapter 8 as part of the basic ideology of communism, but they must be re-examined here in relation to the problem of peaceful coexistence.

The Communist Theory of World Revolution

By world revolution, communists mean that the communist revolution will not be confined to a single country, but will spread, as fast as local conditions ripen, to all countries of the world. According to dialectical materialism, capitalism will inevitably be overcome by its internal contradictions, and will be replaced first by socialism (dictatorship of the proletariat) and later by communism. Since capitalism is an international institution, its collapse will also be international in character. The final establishment of communism on a world scale represents the communist idea of the millennium.[11]

The communist theory of world revolution is based on three main beliefs: the international solidarity of the working classes of all countries; the inevitable collapse of capitalism on a world scale; and the need for communism to triumph in all or at least several major countries of the world to assure the security of communism in one country.

The international solidarity of the working classes. One of the central beliefs of Marxism holds that the interests of the working class in any one country extend beyond its national boundaries. The class struggle between the bourgeoisie and the proletariat is world-wide in character, and the alleged exploitation of the workers and peasants by the capitalists and landowners occurs in every noncommunist country. Consequently, the workers and peasants of all countries have more in common with each other than they have with the bourgeois class of their respective countries. As Marx put it in *The Communist Manifesto*, "The workingmen have no country."

The Communist International, established by Lenin in 1919 to stimulate communist activity throughout the world, proclaimed in its Statutes of 1920 that previous attempts to emancipate the working classes had failed "because of the lack of solidarity between the workers in the different industries of each country, and the absence of the fraternal union between the working class of the different countries." The Statutes went on to say that "the emancipation is neither a local nor a national problem but a problem of a social character embracing every civilized country." [12]

The concept of the international solidarity of the working class movement is reiterated each year in the May Day slogans of the Communist Party. In 1957, for instance, the slogans of the Central Committee of the Communist Party of the Soviet Union began with the appeal: [13] "Long live May Day—day of the international solidarity of working people, day of brotherhood of the workers of all countries! Workers of the world, unite! Up with the banner of proletarian internationalism!" The slogans went on to appeal to the working people of all countries to strive for

---

[11] For a good discussion of the theory of world revolution, see Michael T. Florinsky, *World Revolution and the U.S.S.R.* (New York, Macmillan, 1933).

[12] William Henry Chamberlin, *Blueprint for World Conquest* (Chicago, Human Events, 1946), p. 33. For the full text of the Statutes of the Communist International, see pp. 33–40. The Constitution, adopted in 1928, appears on pp. 249–258.

[13] *Pravda*, April 21, 1957, p. 1. (English translation of complete text is in the *Current Digest of the Soviet Press*, May 22, 1957, pp. 4–5.)

reduction of armaments, relaxation of international tension, and complete banning of atomic and hydrogen weapons.

Soviet leaders use the idea of international working class solidarity to identify the interests of the "working classes" of all countries with those of the Soviet Union. This serves as an ideological justification of Soviet efforts to "assist" the working classes of other countries in "freeing themselves" from capitalist and imperialist domination. Thus, the "liberation" of Eastern Europe by the Soviet armies after World War II and the subsequent establishment of communist regimes in those countries, protected by Soviet occupation troops, become a natural expression of this idea.

The defense, as well as the prosecution, of communist world revolution is justified on this basis. An article on Soviet military ideology appearing in *Red Star*, the Soviet Defense Ministry newspaper, vindicated Soviet military intervention in Hungary, in 1956, in terms of the "international duty" of the Soviet armed forces. It said in part: [14]

The concept of the international duty of the U.S.S.R. Armed Forces is an integral part of Soviet military ideology. The idea of enslaving other nations is alien to Soviet military ideology, as it is to socialist ideology in general. Soviet military ideology, while developing in servicemen a sense of Soviet patriotism, also develops in them an appreciation of their lofty liberation mission, of their noble international duty, strengthens their feeling of profound respect for the rights and dignity of all freedom-loving peoples as well as their sense of burning hatred for the enemies of socialism and communism, for the imperialist aggressors. . . .

Trained by the Communist Party, the U.S.S.R. Armed Forces live up to their international duty. This was demonstrated by the aid they gave to the working people of Hungary in suppressing the counterrevolutionary rebellion organized by international imperialism. The U.S.S.R. Armed Forces performed their international class duty with honor.

The inevitable collapse of capitalism on a world scale. According to communist theory and the laws of dialectical materialism, capitalism will be unable to resolve the class struggle peacefully and will therefore inevitably collapse. This belief is another of the cardinal principles of Marxism-Leninism-Stalinism. Because of the international character of the class struggle and the rise of imperialism on a world scale, capitalism's collapse will not be confined to one country but will spread to the entire world. The slogan "All roads lead to communism" is frequently heard.

The communist views on imperialism were discussed in Chapter 8. According to this concept, capitalism in its highest monopolistic stages turns to imperialism, and imperialism in turn leads to war. In the course of such war, the proletariat of the belligerent countries and the peoples

[14] Col. G. Fedorov, "On the Content of Soviet Military Ideology," *Krasnaya Zvezda* (*Red Star*), March 22, 1957, pp. 2–4. (English translation appears in the *Current Digest of the Soviet Press,* June 5, 1957, pp. 27–28.)

of the colonial areas, aware of their common interests, have the opportunity to join hands and fight their capitalist overlords. Thus, an international imperialist war would be converted into an international civil war, and world revolution would quickly spread.

With these ideas, it was natural for the Bolsheviks, having achieved power in Russia in November, 1917, to expect similar communist uprisings soon in Germany and elsewhere throughout Europe. They anticipated, for example, that German soldiers, upon encountering the Bolshevik armies, would fraternize and refuse to fight with their fellow-workers. The Russian revolution would thereby serve as a spark to ignite a series of revolutions across the world.

The optimism of the early Bolshevik leaders about the imminence of world revolution was reflected in an article by Gregory Zinoviev, president of the new Communist International. He wrote, in May, 1919: [15]

. . . as we write these lines, the Third International already has as its foundation stones three Soviet republics—those in Russia, in Hungary, and in Bavaria. [A Soviet republic was in power in Hungary from March to August, 1919, and a short-lived Soviet republic was set up in Bavaria in April, 1919.] But no one will be surprised if at the moment when these lines appear in print we have not three but six or more Soviet republics. Old Europe is dashing at mad speed towards the proletarian revolution. . . . In the historical sense, the whole of the European bourgeoisie is beginning to resign. The victory of communism in Germany is inescapable. Separate defeats will still occur in the near future. Black will, perhaps, still win a victory here and there over red. But final victory will, nevertheless, be to the red; and this in the course of the next months, perhaps even weeks. The movement is proceeding at such terrific speed that we may say with full confidence, within a year we shall already begin to forget that there was a struggle for communism in Europe, because in a year the whole of Europe will be communist. And the struggle for communism will be transferred to America, perhaps to Asia, and to other parts of the world.

Zinoviev's confidence did not prove to be well founded. By 1920, the Soviet republics in Hungary and Bavaria had been crushed. The Bolshevik regime in Russia had barely survived bitter civil war with its White Russian opponents and the western powers that had been supporting the White Russians since mid-1918. The anticipated communist revolutions in Germany and elsewhere in Europe had not materialized, while in Italy the trend was to the opposite extreme with the establishment of Mussolini's fascist regime in 1922.

Although conceding that their timetable had proved incorrect, communist leaders still held that their principle of world-wide proletarian revolution was basically sound. One of their most eloquent spokesmen, Leon Trotsky, explained their position at the Third World Congress of the Communist International, in 1921, as follows: [16]

[15] Quoted in Florinsky, *op. cit.*, reprinted with publisher's permission, pp. 42–43.
[16] *Ibid.*, p. 90.

Taken as a whole, our line is still valid. We have only failed in the past to foresee its deviations and fluctuations, but now we are conscious of them. . . . Only now we begin to see and understand that we are not yet on the threshold of one realization of our ultimate aim—the seizing of power on a world scale, the world revolution. Then—in 1919—we said that it was a question of months; we say now that it is a question of years. We do not know exactly how long it will take, but we know that we are moving toward that goal and that our position today is much stronger than it used to be.

The failure of capitalism and democracy to collapse on a world scale forced the Soviet leaders to make certain adjustments in both theory and practice in the 1920's. The delay in world revolution was subsequently explained by Stalin on the basis of what Lenin had called the uneven economic and political development of capitalism. In 1915, Lenin had said: [17] "Uneven economic and political development is an absolute law of capitalism. Hence the victory of socialism is possible first in a few or even in one single capitalist country taken separately."

The ultimate collapse of capitalism was still regarded by Stalin as inevitable, but it would occur at different times in different countries. In the meantime, the Soviet leaders would have to reconcile themselves to the continued existence of capitalist states alongside their own socialist system.

These were the circumstances which first led Lenin early in the 1920's to speak of the "coexistence" of different economic and social systems. In 1922, for example, the Soviet delegation to the Genoa Economic Conference, guided by Lenin's directives, declared: [18]

. . . in the present historic era, which makes possible the parallel co-existence of the old and of the newly born social system, economic cooperation between states representing these two systems of property is an imperative necessity for universal economic restoration.

Stalin further developed the meaning of "peaceful coexistence" in reporting to the Fourteenth Communist Party Congress in December, 1925: [19]

There has been established a certain temporary balance of power; a balance which has determined the current phase of Peaceful Coexistence between the land of the Soviets and the countries of capitalism. That which we once believed to be a short respite after the war has turned out to be a whole period of respite. Hence a certain balance of power and a certain period of "Peaceful Coexistence" between the world of the bourgeoisie and the world of the proletariat. . . . We are living through a period of accumulation of strength which has great significance for future revolutionary initiatives.

[17] V. I. Lenin, *Collected Works,* Vol. XVIII, *The Imperialist War* (New York, International Publishers, 1930), p. 272. Quoted in Stalin, *Problems of Leninism* (1926), Little Lenin Library series (International Publishers, 1934), Vol. 19, p. 69.
[18] G. Zadorozhny, "Lenin and Stalin on Peaceful Co-existence of the Two Systems," *U.S.S.R. Information Bulletin,* January 26, 1951, p. 38.
[19] Quoted in C. L. Sulzberger, *The Big Thaw* (New York, Harper, 1956), p. 2.

"Peaceful coexistence," then, which seems contradictory to the original ideas and assumptions of communist world revolution, found a place in early Soviet thought as a description of the actual relations between the Soviet Union and the rest of the world in the 1920's, when world revolution had (for the time being) failed to materialize. Yet it was only a "certain temporary balance of power," and the ultimate victory of the proletarian revolution in other capitalist countries remained "a matter of vital concern to the working people of the U.S.S.R." [20]

Two years later, when Russia had more fully recovered economically and was about to embark on the first Five-Year Plan, Stalin informed the Fifteenth Communist Party Congress that the temporary period of peaceful coexistence might be drawing to a close. He said: [21]

If two years ago it was possible and necessary to speak of a period of a certain equilibrium and "Peaceful Coexistence" between the U.S.S.R. and the capitalist countries, now we have every basis for declaring that the period of "Peaceful Coexistence" is receding into the past.

Actually, coexistence was not to recede into the past, as Stalin intimated in 1927, and Soviet socialism was not established in any other country between World Wars I and II. On the contrary, with the rise of the Hitler threat in the 1930's, the Soviet Union went to great lengths to co-operate with the western democracies in an effort to check potential Nazi expansion.

After World War II, however, communist-dominated regimes backed by the Soviet Union came to power in East Germany, Poland, Czechoslovakia, Hungary, Yugoslavia, Albania, Rumania, and Bulgaria. By the end of 1949, the Chinese Communists had gained control of the mainland of China. North Korea came under communist control after 1945, and North Vietnam in 1954. In addition, World War II had seriously weakened the economies of all the major capitalist powers except the United States, which remained as the only strong representative of capitalism. To the communist leaders of Russia, all this was the unfolding of a series of chapters in the inevitable weakening of capitalism and the progressive establishment of communism on a world-wide basis.

A clear expression of their viewpoint is contained in an address by the late Andrei Zhdanov in September, 1947, to the conference which established the Cominform (Communist International Information Bureau). Zhdanov was then one of the leading members of the Soviet Politburo. He declared: [22]

[20] *History of the Communist Party of the Soviet Union* (New York, International Publishers, 1939), p. 275.

[21] Quoted in Sulzberger, *op. cit.*, pp. 2–3.

[22] The text of Zhdanov's address is given in the document *The Strategy and Tactics of World Communism* (U.S. Congress, House Committee on Foreign Affairs, 80th Congr., 2d sess., House Doc. 619, Washington, D.C., Government Printing Office, 1948), Suppl. I, pp. 211 ff., at pp. 212–214.

Whereas the principal result of World War I had been that the united imperialist front was breached and that Russia dropped out of the world capitalist system . . . World War II and the defeat of fascism . . . resulted in a number of countries in Central and Southeastern Europe dropping out of the imperialist system. . . . The impressive lesson given by the Patriotic War of the Soviet Union and the liberating role of the Soviet Army were accompanied by a mass struggle of the freedom-loving peoples for national liberation from the fascist invaders and their accomplices. . . .

The war immensely enhanced the international significance and prestige of the U.S.S.R. . . . Instead of being enfeebled, the U.S.S.R. became stronger.

The capitalist world has also undergone a substantial change. Of the six so-called great imperialist powers (Germany, Japan, Great Britain, the U.S.A., France and Italy), three have been eliminated by military defeat (Germany, Italy and Japan). France has also been weakened and has lost its significance as a great power. As a result, only two great imperialist world powers remain—the United States and Great Britain. But the position of one of them, Great Britain, has been undermined. The war revealed that militarily and politically British imperialism was not so strong as it had been. . . . After the war, Britain became increasingly dependent, financially and economically, on the United States. . . .

Of all the capitalist powers, only one—the United States—emerged from the war not only unweakened, but even considerably stronger economically and militarily.

The continued economic strength of the United States, together with the economic recovery of Western Europe and Japan, has been a challenge to the communist belief in the inevitable collapse of capitalism. Doubts have occasionally been expressed by communist writers as to the accuracy of their assumptions,[23] but the official communist position still maintains that capitalism is doomed, and Khrushchev's prophecy for the grandchildren of the present American generation is a reflection of this assumption.

A lengthy analysis of the world economic situation in 1956 by the prominent Soviet economist, Eugene Varga, offers further evidence of the communist belief that capitalism still contains the seeds of its own destruction. After noting the postwar economic improvements in the capitalist countries, Varga declared: [24]

. . . However, these economic successes of capitalism do not by any means signify that [the] deepening of the general crisis of capitalism has ceased; it continues with undiminished force.

The tempo of industrial growth in the countries of socialism is two or three times as great as in capitalist countries. As is known from Comrade Khrushchev's report at the 20th Party Congress, industrial output in the U.S.S.R. between 1946 and 1955 increased (1929 = 100) from 466 to 2049, and in the capitalist world from 107 to 193. Now one can calculate with some accuracy

[23] See pp. 391–393.
[24] E. Varga, "On the Economics of Postwar Capitalism," *Kommunist*, March, 1956. (Condensed English translation appears in the *Current Digest of the Soviet Press,* July 4, 1956, pp. 3–8.)

when the U.S.S.R. will overtake the leading capitalist countries economically. . . .

The postwar decade has been a time of irreparable political defeats for imperialism. . . . The disintegration of the colonial system of imperialism is continuing. The peoples of colonial countries are waging the national liberation struggle with unabating vigor. . . .

The improvement of the economic situation has not weakened the class struggle in capitalist countries, since the situation of the working class has not improved. Output has grown primarily through increased automation of the production process, the introduction of new technology and further speed-up to reduce the working time per unit of output. Mass unemployment, heavy taxes and rising prices are lowering the workers' living standards. The struggle between labor and capital is growing sharper, as can be seen from big, prolonged strikes in the capitalist countries.

Varga concludes with this statement: [25] "Thus, the capitalist world, in accordance with its own inner laws, is inevitably approaching a new world crisis. Of course, it cannot be predicted with accuracy when the new crisis of overproduction will break out, but the present strain cannot continue for long."

This typical analysis provides an important part of the perspective with which communist leaders at present view the question of peaceful coexistence. The "temporary" improvement of capitalism makes a continued period of "coexistence" likely for some time. During this period, intense, peaceful competition between capitalism and communism will take place, in the course of which communism, according to its leaders, will prove its superiority and will triumph. Thus, the theory of world revolution will ultimately be vindicated.

Permanent security of communism by extension on world-wide basis. The third major belief underlying the communist doctrine of world revolution is the conviction that, although Soviet socialism and communism may be established in only one major country or area of the world, the complete security of the communist system cannot be assured until communism has been established on an extensive or world-wide basis. Soviet leaders have frequently argued that there will be a constant danger of capitalist intervention so long as the so-called "capitalist encirclement" around their frontiers remains unbroken.

This belief is derived partly from the original principles of Marxism and partly from the practical problems Lenin and Stalin faced after 1920, when it became apparent that world revolution was not right around the corner. As noted previously, Lenin and the early Bolshevik leaders, adhering to Marxist principles regarding the international character of the class struggle and the inevitable collapse of capitalism on a world scale, confidently expected the rapid spread of revolution from Russia to Germany and the rest of Europe. This was not only a matter of

[25] *Ibid.*, p. 8.

ideological principle to them but also a development which they regarded as important to the survival of their new regime in Russia, dangerously exposed at the time to the superior military power of Germany. "Without a revolution in Germany, we shall perish," declared Lenin in March, 1918, as he prepared to accept the harsh and humiliating terms of the Brest-Litovsk Treaty.[26]

In 1918 and 1919, with their backs against the wall in a bloody civil war, many Bolshevik leaders regarded the extension of the revolution abroad as a matter of life and death. That fourteen Allied governments were then supporting the anti-Bolshevik White Russians with armed forces served to confirm the communist theory that conflict between capitalism and communism was inevitable. Hence, the organization of the Communist International in 1919 and the effort to stimulate communist propaganda and activity abroad were considered vital steps in a counteroffensive, designed to maintain the Bolshevik hold on Russia. Some of the most militant communist statements on world revolution and the seeming impossibility of peaceful coexistence date from this critical period of civil war and foreign intervention. Thus, Lenin on April 14, 1919, emphatically declared: "World imperialism cannot live side by side with a victorious soviet revolution." On November 27, 1920, he added: "As long as capitalism and socialism remain side by side we cannot live peacefully—the one or the other will be the victor in the end."

The regime survived, and the Bolshevik leaders in Russia gained a respite from the immediate danger of a military attack. They had managed to hold on, but they were now isolated and alone in the world because the communist revolution had not taken hold elsewhere, as had been originally expected. The very fact that they had survived, despite the failure of world revolution to materialize, also surprised them since it seemed to contradict their theory that communism was doomed to destruction unless it spread beyond the frontiers of a single state. Having won the civil war, and having gained at least the *de facto* right to exist in the family of nations, the Bolshevik regime now faced the task of adjusting its theory and practice to the problem of living in a world that was unreformed and unfriendly from the Bolshevik standpoint. As has been mentioned earlier in the chapter, this was the period when the ideas of peaceful coexistence were first enunciated by Lenin and Stalin.

During the years after 1920, Lenin and more especially Stalin undertook to rebuild the war-devastated economy of their country and to strengthen the foundations of revolutionary socialism in the Soviet Union. Under Stalin, this became known as the policy of "socialism in one country" which was discussed in Chapter 8. The concept of socialism in one country involved an apparent toning down of the emphasis on world

[26] This and the next two quotations appear in R. N. Carew Hunt, *The Theory and Practice of Communism* (New York, Macmillan, rev. ed., 1951), pp. 172–173.

revolution but not an abandonment of it as an ultimate goal. While the Soviet government turned to the more immediate tasks of domestic economic development, the Communist International, which maintained a separate legal identity from the Soviet government, continued the program of encouraging communist propaganda and activity abroad.

Although Stalin was criticized by Trotsky and others for subordinating the cause of world revolution to the interests of socialism in the U.S.S.R., Stalin consistently reiterated the idea that the permanent security of the Soviet socialist system could not be assured until the revolution had occurred in a number of other countries. He drew a distinction between the possibility of completely constructing socialism in a single country without the aid of world revolution, and the possibility of permanently guaranteeing such a socialist regime against the danger of capitalist intervention without the extension of the revolution abroad. The first of these possibilities, he argued, could be achieved in one country unaided by the development of world revolution. This was where he disagreed so sharply with Trotsky. The second possibility would still, in Stalin's judgment, require the extension of world revolution. Here there was no basic disagreement between Stalin and Trotsky.[27]

A little over a decade later, after socialism had been established in almost the entire Soviet economy by virtue of the five-year plans for industry and the forced collectivization of agriculture, the question arose as to whether the final victory of socialism had been achieved and the danger of foreign intervention removed. Stalin, in his now classic reply to a young Communist apprentice, Comrade Ivanov, in February, 1938, repeated the essence of his 1925 position: [28]

. . . in the first aspect of the question of the victory of Socialism in our country . . . we have succeeded in liquidating our bourgeoisie, in establishing brotherly co-operation with our peasantry and in building up, in the main, a Socialist society, despite the fact that there has been no victory of Socialist revolution in other countries. . . .

The second aspect of the question of the victory of Socialism in our country concerns the problem of the mutual relations of our country with other countries, with capitalist countries. . . . This is the domain of external, international relations. Can the victorious Socialism of one country, which has for its environment a number of strong capitalist countries, regard itself as absolutely secure from the danger of military aggression (intervention) and consequently, from attempts to re-establish capitalism in our country? . . .

Leninism gives a negative answer to these problems. Leninism teaches that "the final victory of Socialism, in the sense of complete security from the restoration of bourgeois conditions, is possible only on an international scale." . . . This means that the serious help of the international proletariat is that force

---

[27] One of the clearest statements of Stalin's views on this question appears in his report, in 1925, on the Fourteenth Party Conference, *Problems of Leninism, op. cit.,* p. 64.

[28] Stalin's letter is quoted in full in *The Strategy and Tactics of World Communism. op. cit.,* Suppl. I, pp. 149–152.

without which the problem of the final victory of Socialism in one country cannot be solved. This does not, of course, imply that we must sit with our arms folded and await help from outside. On the contrary, the help on the part of the international proletariat must be combined with our efforts towards reinforcing the defences of our country, reinforcing the Red Army and the Red Navy, and mobilizing the whole country in the struggle against military aggression and attempts at restoring bourgeois conditions.

The last few sentences of this quotation are especially significant, for they indicate, in the absence of world revolution, the increasingly important role to be played by the Soviet state and its armed forces in the defense of the regime. This theme was frequently emphasized by Stalin in the critical years that followed. Faced by the menace of fascism and by the extreme unlikelihood of the early spread of communist revolution, Stalin concluded that the Soviet state, instead of withering away, must become the main source of security for the socialist system of the U.S.S.R. The ultimate and perhaps distant victory of socialism and communism might still depend on the extension of world revolution, but the immediate security of the newly consolidated socialist regime would have to rest with the Soviet state.

This significant reformulation of the Marxist-Leninist theory of the state was explained more fully by Stalin, in his report to the Eighteenth Congress of the Communist Party in March, 1939, and has already been discussed in Chapter 8. Although Stalin now assigned a much more important and permanent role to the state than had been envisaged in Marxist-Leninist theory, he continued to stress the oft-repeated theme of the dangers of capitalist encirclement and implied that only when this was replaced by a "socialist encirclement" could the Soviet system feel permanently secure.

The defeat of Germany in 1945 brought the first major opportunity, since 1919, to extend communism into Eastern and Central Europe, and it was exploited very effectively by the Soviet Union. Under the shadow of Soviet occupation armies, coalition governments were set up in Poland, Czechoslovakia, Hungary, Rumania, Bulgaria, and Albania.[29] The local communist parties played an ever more dominant role in these coalition governments, and within three years all of them were completely communist-controlled. The Soviet Union meanwhile directly controlled its zone of occupation in Eastern Germany, while advancing proposals regarding a German peace treaty and the organization of a future united German government, which apparently rested on the hope that all of Germany would ultimately be won over to the communist side.

These were the most vigorous steps the Kremlin had ever taken to "liquidate" the "capitalist encirclement" of the U.S.S.R. and to replace it

[29] The communist government of Yugoslavia was established without such Soviet military influence, although Soviet forces did briefly enter Yugoslavia in the fall of 1944.

with a "socialist encirclement." [30] Yet, it should be clear that these efforts involved not simply an extension of world revolution for its own sake. Rather, Soviet national security seems to have played an equal, if not more important, part in determining upon the measures taken. In their desire to prevent a repetition of a German attack on Russia, Soviet leaders were very conscious of the absence of strategic geographic barriers on their western frontier, and of the existence during the 1920's and 1930's of strongly anti-Soviet, right-wing governments in most of eastern Europe except Czechoslovakia. In the creation of "friendly" proletarian governments in eastern Europe and Germany, they therefore saw a very effective means of reducing what had been regarded as serious handicaps to their security position before 1939.

The victory of the Chinese Communists in 1949, and the subsequent establishment of close political, economic, and military ties between Peiping and Moscow enhanced the general security position of the U.S.S.R., although the latter has undoubtedly been handicapped at times by the fact that China has to be treated as an equal rather than as a satellite. The relationship, therefore, between Soviet national-security interests and the extension of communist revolution abroad seems to have been very close both in Europe and in Asia.

DOUBTS ABOUT UNDERLYING COMMUNIST IDEAS OF WORLD REVOLUTION

Three main beliefs underlying the communist doctrine of world revolution have been noted: the international solidarity of the working classes; the inevitable collapse of capitalism on a world scale; and the need for world revolution as a means of guaranteeing the permanent security of communism. So far as these beliefs actually control the actions of communist leaders, they would seem to render impossible any permanent peaceful coexistence between communism and other systems on a live-and-let-live basis.

A gap exists, however, between the beliefs and the realization of them. Developments frequently have not corresponded to what might have been expected, according to communist theory. Moreover, the national-security interests of the Soviet state have, from time to time, dictated new interpretations regarding the desirability of world revolution. It is therefore not inconceivable that, despite continued public reiteration to the contrary, Soviet leaders may at times entertain private doubts as to the complete accuracy of their theories.

[30] Soviet leaders now no longer speak of "capitalist encirclement" of the U.S.S.R. Since revolutionary socialism has come to power in China as well as in Eastern Europe, Soviet leaders speak broadly of two "world systems," socialism and capitalism, which are competing with each other.

Nationalism and International Proletarian Unity

National loyalty and patriotism have constituted one of the strongest barriers to the international solidarity of the working classes, especially so in time of war. Although Marx and Lenin envisaged the working classes of all countries standing together, even with their respective governments at war, this idea has broken down in every war that has occurred. In the Franco-Prussian War of 1870–71, French and German workers rallied behind their respective national governments, rather than standing together and refusing to fight each other. Again, in World Wars I and II, the workers of the various belligerent countries responded to the appeals of national patriotism rather than to theoretical international proletarian solidarity. It is true that in World War II the communist parties throughout the world adhered closely to the policy lines laid down in Moscow, even when this meant opposition to the foreign policies of their own respective national governments.[31] Yet, confusion and a loss of popular following were usually the result when the native communist parties ran counter to popular national feeling and seemed to be serving Soviet interests rather than the interests of their own national governments.[32]

National Communism

The growth of "national communism" in Yugoslavia, already noted in Chapter 9, also revealed the competitive appeal of nationalism as compared with that of communist internationalism. Tito's unwillingness to allow the Soviet pattern of communism to be forced on Yugoslavia and his successful perseverance in an independent position, despite the bitter hostility of Moscow, constituted a major breach in the line of international working class solidarity. After the death of Stalin, the Soviet leaders apparently decided that the traditional doctrine could be more effectively maintained if it were not so closely identified with conformity to Soviet policies and practices. The dramatic trip of Khrushchev and Bulganin to Yugoslavia in May, 1955, and their public apology to Tito for the events of 1948 appeared to set the stage for a new pattern.[33] The

[31] During the period of the Nazi-Soviet nonaggression pact (August, 1939, to June, 1941), the communist parties in countries like France and Britain opposed their own governments' war efforts against Nazi Germany. Only after Germany attacked the Soviet Union in June, 1941, did the European communist parties support their respective national governments in the war against Hitler.

[32] For a detailed discussion of the French Communist Party and its vacillations on foreign policy, see A. Rossi, *A Communist Party in Action: An Account of the Organization and Operation in France* (New Haven, Yale University Press, 1949), especially pp. 1–2, and p. 82. See also M. Einaudi, J. Domerach, and A. Garosci, *Communism in Western Europe* (Ithaca, Cornell University Press, 1951), pp. 73 and 150.

[33] *New York Times*, May 27, 1955, p. 4.

official Soviet-Yugoslav agreements a year later [34] seemed added evidence that the Kremlin was at last prepared to acknowledge the strength of nationalism even in communist countries.

The reconciliation with Tito was undoubtedly dictated by the Soviet desire to weaken the ties between Yugoslavia and the West, and to draw Tito back into closer relations with the communist bloc, an indication that the national interests of the Soviet state may at times lead to actions apparently not entirely consistent with communist theory, in this case, the theory of international working class solidarity.

Since 1956, Khrushchev and his associates have frequently stressed the view that the roads and conditions of socialist development may vary in different countries. Indeed, when Molotov was dropped from leadership of the party in June, 1957, one of the charges against him was that he had opposed this view.[35] As a consequence of this significant modification in the Stalinist interpretation of international proletarian unity, some signs of "national communism" appeared in other countries of the communist bloc, most conspicuously in Poland, China, and in the brief, abortive Hungarian revolution of October, 1956.[36]

Soviet leaders dislike the implications of the term *national communism,* and have been apprehensive lest it get out of hand. In fact, Soviet armed intervention in Hungary in October and November, 1956, seems to have been prompted by fear that the Hungarian revolution was going to extremes and would lead to the overthrow of all forms of communism, national or otherwise. A further token of this desire to "apply the brakes" to "national communism" is to be found in numerous articles which appeared in the Soviet press in 1957, reiterating that true "national communism" did not separate the interests of one communist country from those of other communist countries. In April, 1957, for example, Madame Y. A. Furtseva, the only woman member of the Communist Party Presidium, criticized some tendencies toward extreme independence on the part of other communist states, suggesting that "national communism" represented "the newest variety of the old ideology of nationalism, which reflects the pressure of petty-bourgeois elements infected with nationalistic prejudices." [37] She went on to say:

The proponents of "national communism" think they are patriots, that they better serve their people's national interests when they separate themselves from the socialist camp. However, this is a perverse understanding of national interests. Under no circumstances can it be called patriotism, for socialist

[34] See Chap. 9, p. 357. But Soviet actions in 1958 seemed to modify this stand.

[35] Resolution of the Central Committee of the Communist Party of the Soviet Union, June 29, 1957, *New York Times,* July 4, 1957, p. 2.

[36] A selection of documents on the uprisings in Poland and Hungary appears in Paul E. Zinner, ed., *National Communism and Popular Revolt in Eastern Europe* (New York, Columbia University Press, 1956).

[37] *Pravda,* April 23, 1957, pp. 2–3. (Condensed English translation appears in the *Current Digest of the Soviet Press,* May 22, 1957, pp. 6–9, at p. 8.)

patriotism and nationalism are diametrically opposed by their very essence. The true patriot of a socialist country does not detach the interests of his fatherland from the interests of other socialist countries. He knows that his nation's true prosperity, its glory, its wealth, freedom, and independence are possible only along the path of building socialism, that the building of socialism is the common international cause of workers in every country.

Notwithstanding the attempt to reconcile the two ideas, perhaps the present Soviet leaders are beginning to harbor some reservations about the validity of the previously held concepts of international proletarian unity. For very practical reasons, they now seem disposed to be a little more tolerant of national variations within the communist world. If the toleration should increase and the communist tendency to intervene in other countries decline significantly, the long-run possibilities of a more genuine peaceful coexistence would seem to be enhanced.

Uncertainty Regarding the "Inevitable Collapse of Capitalism"

It was pointed out earlier in this chapter that Soviet leaders repeatedly assert that communism will ultimately triumph over capitalism. Peaceful coexistence, then, is at best a temporary state of affairs during the period of capitalism's survival. But should capitalism remain strong indefinitely, despite communist theory, peaceful coexistence would presumably continue indefinitely, and communist leaders would have to revise their concepts of its temporary character. The possibilities of long-run peaceful coexistence are closely related, therefore, to the strength and durability of the noncommunist economic systems.

There appears to have been some controversy among Soviet leaders and economists over how "healthy" the capitalist system is in the United States, and how long it might be before American capitalism "inevitably" collapses. Immediately after World War II, for example, Soviet publications regularly predicted a severe postwar depression in the United States and a general aggravation of the "crisis of capitalism." [38] When this depression did not materialize, Soviet leaders and economists attempted to explain its nonappearance in terms of the artificial stimulus furnished to the American economy by increased government armament expenditures and foreign-aid programs like the Truman Doctrine and the Marshall Plan. As a result of "war hysteria," it was argued, American heavy industry received several billion dollars of new war orders. Although this was "short-term and insignificant," it nevertheless "permitted some postponement of the oncoming economic crisis." [39]

[38] *New York Times,* November 14, 1948, p. 24.
[39] *Ibid.* See also Andrei Zhdanov's major address at the first Cominform conference, September, 1947, in which he referred to the Marshall Plan as an American effort to overcome its own approaching economic crisis. *The Strategy and Tactics of World Communism, op. cit.,* pp. 211–230, at p. 228.

The obvious strength of the American economic system during and after World War II led the Soviet economist, Eugene Varga, to suggest that capitalism in the United States, with its extensive regulation of monopolies and its measures of economic planning, might be able to play a more decisive role in future history than was contemplated by traditional communist theory. Varga was sharply criticized in the Soviet press for intimating, contrary to Marxist theory, that American capitalism might avoid major depressions and serious unemployment.[40] He subsequently acknowledged certain "errors" in his analysis, and modified some of his interpretations.[41] The later position, noted earlier in this chapter,[42] was that capitalism, although momentarily strong in certain countries like the United States, was still headed for inevitable collapse.

Although the doctrine of the inevitable collapse of capitalism is still officially maintained, occasional signs of doubt as to its validity appear on the part of Soviet economists. In 1955, for example, an American visitor to the Soviet Union, who had several opportunities to speak directly to Soviet officials and intellectuals, reported privately that there was still division of opinion among Soviet economists on the strength of the American economy and whether or not its collapse was inevitable. At about the same time, twelve Soviet farm experts, making a two-month tour of the United States and Canada, demonstrated deep interest in many aspects of American and Canadian farm economies. They were visibly impressed by the mechanization and electrification of the American farms, and by the household appliances and conveniences available to the farmers' wives. "How much does it cost," they asked. "What is your profit? How much taxes do you pay?"[43] It is not difficult to conclude that the Soviet visitors, including the First Deputy Minister of Agriculture and the Deputy Chairman of the State Planning Commission, could not have left the United States and Canada without some private doubts as to the accuracy of the official communist portrayals of the western economies.

Further evidence of Soviet respect for these western achievements was seen in July, 1955, when Marshal Bulganin sharply criticized Soviet industrial leaders for failing to keep abreast of foreign, especially American, technological advances. He declared: [44]

Some of our people think there is no point in studying foreign experience and indeed these peoples try to mask their ignorance by boasting. One should condemn such an attitude toward the study of achievements of science and technology abroad. We must constantly study everything.

[40] *New York Times,* January 27, 1948, p. 14.
[41] *Ibid.,* June 13, 1949, p. 4.
[42] See pp. 383–384.
[43] *New York Times,* July 19, 1955, p. 3.
[44] *Ibid.,* p. 8.

Later in 1955, the theoretical journal *Kommunist* criticized a Soviet economist for painting too dark a picture of the current capitalist economic situation. It went on to demand that capitalist economic life be presented honestly and objectively, asserting: [45] "The oversimplified stereotype of capitalism's decay that has been presented in our propaganda has led to the denial or ignoring of the capitalist countries' attainments in production, science and technology."

If Soviet economists and technicians study the systems of noncommunist countries thoroughly and honestly, as they have been urged to do, it is not inconceivable that they may eventually question the accuracy of their official theories regarding the inevitable collapse of other economic systems. Even Stalin's analysis of western capitalism was subjected to sharp criticism at the previously mentioned Twentieth Party Congress. [46]

These points cannot, of course, be taken as conclusive evidence of genuine Soviet doubts regarding the expected collapse of capitalism. Moreover, the successful launching of two Soviet satellites in 1957, several months before those of the United States, seemed to reinforce communist conviction as to the superiority of their system over all others. It must also be remembered that the official Soviet position continues to predict an inevitable capitalist collapse. Yet, insofar as their leaders occasionally doubt the correctness of their official diagnosis, a practical basis is laid for more than just a temporary period of coexistence. Further, should they some day conclude that the economic systems of the noncommunist world are likely to survive indefinitely, peaceful coexistence on a live-and-let-live basis would then become a much more realistic possibility.

World Revolution and Soviet National Interests

Although communist theory has held that world revolution was necessary to assure the permanent security of communism, Soviet leaders since 1920–21 have relied more and more on the strength of the Soviet state to guarantee their security. As the Soviet state has expanded and developed, Soviet officials have acted increasingly as might be expected of the rulers of any independent sovereign state. They repeatedly refer to the ideological principles of world revolution but have not attempted to practice them when the national security of the Soviet Union might be jeopardized. National security, in practice, seems to take precedence over the purely ideological aspects of world revolution. When revolution abroad was em-

---

[45] *Ibid.*, October 12, 1955, p. 11.

[46] See, for example, the speech of Anastas Mikoyan, stating that Stalin's *Economic Problems of Socialism in the U.S.S.R.*, published in 1952, did not explain "the complexity and the contradictory nature of events in contemporary capitalism or the fact of the growth of capitalist production in many countries since the war" (*New York Times*, February 19, 1956, p. 26).

phasized, as it was in the early period from 1918 to 1920 and again after World War II, it was associated with the security interests of the Soviet state as the leaders then regarded them. Conversely, when the security interests of the Soviet Union seemed to dictate a policy of conciliation and co-operation with various noncommunist states, as during the 1920's, the 1930's, the period of war against Nazi Germany, and apparently the period since about 1954 or 1955, Soviet leaders have taken a more moderate position on world revolution and given greater emphasis to the ideas of peaceful coexistence.

Peaceful coexistence, then, apparently occupying little place in basic communist ideology except as a temporary state of affairs until capitalism "collapses," may have some practical basis in the requirements of Soviet national security. In an era of nuclear warfare, avoidance of a major conflict may understandably become the first objective of both the communist and the noncommunist states. So far as this is true, the possibilities of coexistence on one or another basis are obviously increased. It seems appropriate, therefore, to review the historical relationship between coexistence, world revolution, and the practical requirements of Soviet national security.

Coexistence and the Security of the Soviet State

During the period of civil war and foreign intervention, 1918–20, most Bolshevik leaders, as has been noted, viewed world revolution as an important element in the achievement of security for their new regime. Although some differences existed as to when revolutions in other countries would occur, they all expected that sooner or later they would take place and reinforce the communist position in Russia. When it became evident that communism was not taking permanent hold in any other country, they were confronted with a different set of circumstances. Starting in 1921, and continuing for over two decades to the end of World War II, a "normalization" of relations with the outside world and a toning down of world revolution seemed necessary for the survival and development of the new Soviet regime. In the following discussion, for greater ease of analysis, the span of years 1921–45 will be divided into four periods, each of which has emphasized certain distinctive approaches to the problem of Soviet security.[47]

[47] See the convenient summary in U.S. Congress, Senate Committee on Foreign Relations, *Trends in Russian Foreign Policy Since World War I*, 80th Congr., 1st sess., Committee Print, 1947. A detailed discussion of Soviet foreign policy during the 1920's is given in Louis Fischer, *The Soviets in World Affairs*, 2 vols. (London, Jonathan Cape, 1930). The period of the 1930's is covered extensively in Max Beloff, *The Foreign Policy of Soviet Russia, 1929–1941*, 2 vols. (London, Oxford University Press, 1947, 1949).

1921–33: Period of Rapprochement

Needs of economic recovery. The beginning of this period found the Bolshevik government economically prostrate and politically isolated from most of the world. Diplomatic recognition of the new regime had been withheld by most governments, and economic contacts were just being established after the lifting of the Allied blockade in 1920.

The Bolshevik leaders needed a period of time in which to rebuild Russia's war-devastated economy. It was also vital that there be no renewal of foreign intervention, such as had occurred from 1918 to 1920. A resumption of intervention would jeopardize their program for building and strengthening socialism in Russia. These were the basic considerations that in the 1920's led first Lenin and later Stalin to place less emphasis on immediate world revolution, to speak of the possibilities of peaceful coexistence, and to seek more normal political and economic relations with other countries.

Diplomatic and trade relations. In 1921, the Soviet government succeeded in obtaining its first *de jure* recognitions from Persia, Afghanistan, Turkey, and the Canton government of China. That year also, trade agreements were signed with Great Britain, Germany, Italy, and Norway. A major diplomatic feat was accomplished in 1922 when a treaty was signed with Germany providing for *de jure* recognition of the Soviet government, mutual cancellation of financial claims, and nondiscriminatory treatment in foreign trade matters. During 1924, Britain, France, Italy, and a number of governments extended formal *de jure* recognition to the Soviet government. By early 1925, when diplomatic relations were established with Japan, the Soviet Union had obtained formal recognition from all the major powers of the world except the United States.

Nonaggression and antiwar pacts. From 1925–26 on, the Soviet government sought to assure itself more fully against possible foreign intervention by concluding a series of neutrality and nonaggression treaties with a number of its neighbors, notably, Turkey, Persia, Afghanistan, Lithuania, and Germany. In 1928, it quickly ratified the Kellogg-Briand Pact outlawing war as an instrument of national policy, although it expressed doubts as to the effectiveness of such an agreement. By 1932, additional treaties of nonaggression had been concluded with Finland, Latvia, Estonia, Poland, and France. Several, incidentally, included pledges to refrain from interference in one another's internal affairs and to abstain from propaganda against one another's political and economic institutions. In this manner, the Soviet government sought to disassociate itself officially from the program of world revolution, which still remained a basic principle of communist theory. Obviously, since this was the period (1928 ff.) of intensive industrialization under the five-year plans and collectivization of agriculture, Soviet leaders considered it essential to obtain security of normal relations with the outside world.

Disarmament. In what may have been a further attempt to overcome the disadvantages of its military weaknesses, the Soviet government in 1926 agreed to take part in the League of Nations discussions on disarmament. In 1927 the Soviet representative there, Maxim Litvinov, startled the world by proposing a plan for universal, immediate, and total disarmament. Whereas this was interpreted by various observers as another sign of the Soviet government's desire for peaceful relations, the communist leaders themselves apparently did not expect the other powers to take it seriously. A resolution adopted at the Sixth Congress of the Communist International in 1928 stated that the Soviet disarmament proposals were not intended to spread any "pacifist illusions," but "to propagate the fundamental Marxian postulate that disarmament and the abolition of war are possible only with the fall of capitalism." [48]

Activities of the Comintern. Throughout this period, while the Soviet government was establishing more normal relations with the outside world, the Communist International, or Comintern as it was called, was carrying on the program of communist propaganda and agitation. At times the overzealous activities of communist parties abroad became a source of acute embarrassment to the Soviet government, which had pledged a number of countries by treaty not to engage in propaganda or to interfere in their domestic affairs. Great Britain, for example, in 1927 suspended diplomatic relations with the U.S.S.R. because it regarded the propaganda activities of the British Communist Party as a violation of pledges against such activity given by the Soviet government in 1921. The Soviet government consistently maintained that the Comintern was a separate organization and that the Soviet government was in no way responsible for Comintern actions. Few close observers accepted this legal fiction as representing the true state of relations between the two. Leaders of the Soviet Union held dominant positions in the Comintern, and the policies adopted by the Comintern always reflected their views. Thus, in 1928, when the Comintern Congress adopted a vigorous program stressing world revolution as its ultimate aim,[49] many suspected that the peaceful relations the Soviet government was then cultivating with the outside world represented short-range rather than long-range objectives. Later, however, in the 1930's and during World War II, as the direct menace of fascism became greater, even the Comintern modified its emphasis on world revolution. National-security interests of the U.S.S.R. now clearly were to be given precedence over whatever importance might otherwise be given to the ideological desires of furthering world revolution.

[48] *Trends in Russian Foreign Policy Since World War I, op. cit.,* p. 6.
[49] Chamberlin, *Blueprint for World Conquest, op. cit.,* p. 179. For the full text of the 1928 program of the Comintern, see pp. 149–245.

1933–39: Period of Active Co-operation

The rise of Hitler and the fear of Japan. Hitler's advent to power in January, 1933, provided the impetus to much more intensive Soviet efforts to establish close co-operative relations with other states, especially those which were also menaced by potential Nazi expansion. Hitler's desire for territory in eastern Europe, as well as his professed hatred for communism, had been stated at length in *Mein Kampf*. Soviet leaders were fully aware of his views. At the same time, the Japanese attack on Manchuria and China in the 1930's had heightened Soviet fears of a possible clash between Russian and Japanese interests in the Far East. Averting this dual threat became the prime consideration of all Soviet foreign-policy decisions during the 1930's. The fear of imminent war also led to a moderation of Comintern strategy in 1935.

Recognition by the United States and membership in the League of Nations. In November, 1933, *de jure* recognition was finally extended to the Soviet Union by the United States. An important condition accompanied it: comprehensive Soviet pledges to abstain from interference and propaganda activities in the United States. In September, 1934, the Soviet Union joined the League of Nations, despite the fact that it had previously regarded the League as an association of capitalist, imperialist powers which, in communist eyes, could not possibly advance the cause of peace because capitalism and imperialism inevitably led to war. Despite these precepts of communist theory, Litvinov, the Soviet representative, found it possible to say, in his first address at the League: [50]

. . . the idea in itself of an association of nations contains nothing theoretically inacceptable for the Soviet state and its ideology. . . . The Soviet state has never excluded the possibility of some form or other of associating with states having a different political and social system, so long as there is no mutual hostility, and if it is for the attainment of common aims.

Soviet support for collective security. After the Soviet Union joined the League of Nations, it became one of the most ardent champions of the principle of collective security, and it tried repeatedly to make the League more effective in dealing with Japanese aggression in Asia, the Italian invasion of Ethiopia, and the threat of Nazi expansion in Europe. It is somewhat ironic that the U.S.S.R. at this time was more vigorous in its support of the League system of collective security than were the British or French.[51] These major powers, during the mid-1930's, were displaying ominous signs of either acquiescing in or not strongly challenging the expansionist policies of Japan, Italy, and Germany. In 1935, a Franco-Soviet

[50] *Trends in Russian Foreign Policy Since World War I, op. cit.,* p. 12.
[51] For a fuller discussion of Soviet foreign policy and the League of Nations and collective security, see Beloff, *op. cit.,* Vol. I, Chap. 11 and Appendix A, and Vol. II, Chaps. 4–7.

alliance and Czech-Soviet alliance were concluded, after efforts to negotiate a broader eight-power mutual security pact for eastern Europe
proved unsuccessful.

Moderation of Comintern strategy. Even the Comintern's program of
world revolution was now directly affected by the Soviet need for all the
allies possible. Up to this time, despite the growing co-operative attitude
of the Soviet government in world affairs, the Comintern had continued
to sponsor a vigorous program of communist propaganda and agitation
in many countries.[52] Communist parties throughout the world had been
called upon to rally the working classes to the support of the Soviet Union
in the event of a capitalist war against the "land of socialism." Trade-
unionist liberal parties and democratic socialists in particular had been
branded as traitors to the working classes.

In 1934 and 1935, however, Soviet security needs seemed to dictate a
shift toward more moderate Comintern policies. Consequently, at the
Seventh World Congress of the Comintern in August, 1935, a resolution
was approved instructing communist parties in all countries to join with
any socialist or liberal groups willing to form coalition governments or
united fronts against fascism. Criticism of democratic socialists and other
liberal groups was toned down in an effort to attract them into antifascist
coalitions. Soviet security considerations therefore evidently brought even
the Comintern to the position of *temporary* coexistence and co-operation
with all antifascist groups. The word *temporary* is emphasized because
Comintern leaders made it clear at the time that their ultimate objective
was to encourage Soviet-type governments throughout the world.[53] It was
against this background that Stalin, in an interview on March 4, 1936,
with Roy Howard of the Scripps-Howard newspaper chain, discoursed
on the possibilities of coexistence and declared that the Soviet government had no intention of exporting revolution to other countries. Revolutions, Stalin explained, would come only when local conditions were ripe
for them, and it was unrealistic to think that revolutions could be exported, like merchandise, across national frontiers.[54]

The Munich Pact and its aftermath. Soviet efforts to develop a stronger
collective-security system in Europe were not successful, and it became
increasingly difficult during the latter part of the 1930's to reconcile the
different security policies of Britain, France, the Soviet Union, and their
various allies. The Soviet Union was not even invited to the Munich conference in September, 1938. There the British and French agreed to the
German annexation of the Sudetenland frontier of Czechoslovakia, a step

    [52] For a fuller discussion of Comintern activities during the 1920's and 1930's, see
Martin Ebon, *World Communism Today* (New York, Whittlesey House, 1948), Chap.
2.

    [53] Beloff, *op. cit.*, Vol. I, pp. 190–196. See also the *New York Times*, August 3, 1935,
p. 5, and August 7, 1935, p. 4.

    [54] *New York Times*, March 5, 1936, p. 16.

which greatly strengthened the German strategic position in central Europe. Subsequent German occupation of all of Czechoslovakia in March, 1939, together with the inability of the British, French, and Soviet governments during early summer to agree on any security guarantees for eastern Europe, led the Soviet Union finally to abandon its efforts to co-operate with the western powers. In a determined move to keep war away from its frontiers, it concluded a neutrality and nonaggression pact with its most dangerous enemy, Germany, in August, 1939. Coexistence and co-operation with the nonfascist powers were now to be scrapped for attempted coexistence with the fascist powers.

August, 1939–June, 1941: Period of Soviet-German Truce

The abrupt shift in Soviet foreign policy toward Nazi Germany shocked the outside world, for it would be hard to think of two ideologies more hostile toward each other in 1939 than Nazism and communism. In July, 1935, the Executive Committee of the Comintern had called for the destruction of Hitler's government and its replacement by a "German Soviet Republic under Communist leadership fraternally allied to the U.S.S.R." [55] Now, in the name of security, the Soviet government had come to terms with the same government the Comintern had hoped to destroy. "Ideological differences," declared an article in *Izvestia* on August 24, 1939, "as well as differences in the political systems of both nations, cannot and must not stand in the way of the establishment and maintenance of good neighborly relations." [56]

There was a good deal more to the Nazi-Soviet pact than the reciprocal pledges of neutrality and nonaggression. Under a secret protocol signed at the same time, Germany recognized a Soviet sphere of influence in the Baltic states, eastern Poland, and a Rumanian region known as Bessarabia. The Soviet Union in turn acknowledged other areas of central and eastern Europe as within the German sphere of interest. [57] The Soviet sphere of influence in eastern Europe conceded by Germany in this agreement was far greater than the offer the British and French had felt they could make in their discussions in 1939. It is not surprising, therefore, that the Soviet Union, in spite of its sharp ideological differences with the Nazis, should have come to terms with the latter rather than with the British and French.

Soviet-Nazi collaboration was not long lived. It foundered on the question of drawing a new line in eastern Europe and the Middle East between Soviet and German areas of influence. Who should be dominant in Bulgaria seems to have been one of the crucial points leading to the

---

[55] *Trends in Russian Foreign Policy Since World War I, op. cit.,* p. 14.

[56] Beloff, *op. cit.,* Vol. II, p. 270.

[57] For this and other developments related to the Nazi-Soviet pact, see Dept. of State, *Nazi-Soviet Relations, 1939–1941* (Washington, D.C., Government Printing Office, 1948). The text of the secret protocol appears on p. 78.

breakdown of relations. Disagreement over these questions, involving conflicting concepts of national security on the part of Germany and the U.S.S.R., produced the Nazi attack on the Soviet Union in June, 1941.

With the onset of Nazi-Soviet collaboration, communist parties throughout the world, reflecting the new orientation of Soviet policy, changed their "united front" antifascist methods of the 1935–39 period and adopted a line of violent denunciation of the western powers that were at war with Germany. Then in June, 1941, another equally sudden shift occurred with the Nazi invasion of the U.S.S.R. The united-front and collaboration policies of the 1930's were now revived and extended.

June, 1941–1945: Period of Soviet-Western Wartime Unity

This period brings to mind the familiar saying, "War makes strange bedfellows." Despite the bitter denunciations of the western democracies by communist spokesmen during the period of Soviet-German collaboration, western leaders, notably Churchill and Roosevelt, quickly announced that they would assist the Soviet Union in what had suddenly become a common cause. On June 22nd, the day after the German attack on the U.S.S.R., Churchill declared that any man or state fighting against Nazism would have British aid. Ideological differences obviously had to be subordinated to the demands of a united war effort.

Wartime unity was not easy to achieve with the background of suspicion, rivalry, and ideological conflict that had characterized Soviet-western relations so often in the past. Friction was especially sharp over the establishment of a second front in Western Europe and the stationing of western military observers behind Soviet lines. Nevertheless, effective collaboration was accomplished. Comintern propaganda and agitation against the western powers were now dropped, communist-sponsored strikes in those countries were abandoned, and finally in May, 1943, the Communist International itself was officially disbanded on the grounds that it had outlived its usefulness. The western world hailed this step as signifying the intention of the Soviet government to abandon the program of world revolution and to respect the independence and integrity of all nonfascist states.

The Soviet Union co-operated in the development of the United Nations and joined in various proclamations of postwar objectives that seemed generally consistent with western democratic principles. Unity of the Big Three was at its height at the war's end in 1945, and became the underlying assumption of the main policies for the postwar period.

Soviet Security and Coexistence Since 1945

The Soviet Union had a large deposit of good will in the United States and Western Europe in the summer of 1945, according to former Secretary of State James Byrnes, and in his judgment it was tragic that Soviet actions afterward should have caused the good will to vanish.[58] Leaders of the western powers generally assumed that wartime unity would be continued and that genuine co-operation and peaceful coexistence would be possible. Unity of the major powers had been an underlying assumption of the United Nations Charter, for on no other basis could the Security Council achieve the great-power unanimity necessary to enforce the peace.

Communist domination of Eastern Europe. A major development that weakened the unity of 1945 was the progressive establishment of communist-dominated governments in Eastern Europe. As noted earlier in this chapter, this was the most vigorous effort to date to extend communism beyond the frontiers of the Soviet Union. The Yalta Agreement of 1945 had envisaged co-operative action among the Big Three to help the liberated countries set up representative democratic governments based on free elections. Now the Soviet Union in effect said that it could not permit genuinely free elections in East Europe since the results would undoubtedly be anti-Soviet regimes. In the judgment of the Kremlin leaders, Soviet security required "friendly governments," meaning proletarian dictatorships, in these strategically located countries. The presence of Soviet occupation forces in or around these countries would and did assure the desired results. For over two years, the United States and Great Britain protested to the Soviet Union, but to no avail. Finally in 1947, the United States extended military aid to Greece and Turkey (Truman Doctrine) so that those governments would be able to withstand the internal and external communist pressures against them.

Stalemate on Germany. Another major factor contributing to the breakdown of unity among the major powers was their inability to agree on a peace treaty for Germany. With the largest population and potentially strongest industry in Europe outside the Soviet Union, Germany would have been an exceedingly valuable prize either to the West or to the East. Consequently, neither the Soviet Union nor the western powers were prepared to accept any arrangements that would facilitate Germany's being drawn into the orbit of the other side. The western proposals for free elections were rejected by the Soviet Union since they would have meant the communist loss of East Germany. The Soviet plan, in turn, was spurned by the West because it envisaged a greater communist role in the proposed German government than the strength of the communist movement in Germany warranted.

The stalemate on the German peace treaty in 1947 caused the western powers to decide, in 1948, to integrate their three zones and form a democratic West German government. The Soviet Union tried to prevent this by the Berlin blockade, but it was unsuccessful and, by 1949, a West German government had come into being. Shortly thereafter, a separate

[58] James F. Byrnes, *Speaking Frankly* (New York, Harper, 1947), p. 71.

communist-controlled government was established in East Germany.

The cold war and coexistence. The unity of 1945 had disappeared by 1947 and been replaced by the cold war. The Truman Doctrine, the Marshall Plan, the North Atlantic Treaty, and more recently the plan for German rearmament constituted major efforts of the West to check communist expansion in Europe. The Soviet Union replied in September, 1947, by having the communist parties of nine European countries organize an international co-ordinating body, known as the Cominform. Its purpose was to mobilize more effective communist resistance to the Marshall Plan and later to other western policies. The initial manifesto was couched in challenging language, reminiscent of the more militant statements of its predecessor, the Comintern. One of the more striking passages, for example, declares: [59]

Two opposite political lines have crystallized: on the one extreme the U.S.S.R. and the democratic countries aim at whittling down imperialism and [at] the strengthening of democracy.[60] On the other side the United States of America and England aim at the strengthening of imperialism and choking democracy. . . .

In this way there arose two camps—the camp of imperialism and anti-democratic forces, whose chief aim is an establishment of a worldwide American imperialists' hegemony and the crushing of democracy; and an anti-imperialistic democratic camp whose chief aim is the elimination of imperialism, the strengthening of democracy and the liquidation of the remnants of fascism.

The battle of the two opposite camps—capitalistic and anti-imperialistic—is waged amid conditions of a further sharpening of the universal crisis of capitalism, a weakening of the forces of capitalism and a strengthening of the forces of socialism and democracy.

In the Far East, the communist victory in the Chinese civil war in 1949, although not primarily the result of Soviet assistance, enhanced communist influence in Asia. In Korea, the cold war became a "hot war" from 1950 to 1953, and in Formosa and Indochina, a "hot war" on several occasions seemed perilously imminent.

This tremendous communist expansion after World War II seemed to indicate that world revolution was again on the move, now frequently serving as a useful means of extending the influence and power of the Soviet Union beyond its frontiers. Many observers in the West described it as "communist imperialism." Against this background, it was difficult to believe that the communist statements of 1946–54 regarding the desirability of peaceful coexistence really evinced a belief in long-run, "live-and-let-live" relations with the noncommunist world.

Trends toward a more moderate Soviet foreign policy. The death of Stalin in March, 1953, with the subsequent shake-ups in Soviet leadership,

---

[59] The text appears in *The Strategy and Tactics of World Communism, op. cit.,* pp. 209–211.

[60] The word *democracy* here refers to the Soviet concept of "proletarian democracy."

introduced many elements of uncertainty into the analysis of Soviet foreign policy. It did become apparent, particularly after 1954 and 1955, that some sort of change had occurred in Soviet policies and methods if not in long-range objectives. The "summit meeting" of the heads of the Big Four powers in July, 1955, at Geneva was symbolic of the more cordial atmosphere that characterized international relations.[61] This had been preceded, in May, 1955, by Soviet acceptance of a peace treaty for Austria and the public apology of Soviet leaders to Tito. Both events seemed to indicate that the Soviet Union genuinely desired to see an improvement in the international situation. The "summit meeting" in July, 1955, which was characterized by much cordiality on all sides, instead of attempting to negotiate detailed settlements of outstanding issues, referred them to the Foreign Ministers of the four powers for discussion at a subsequent conference in October and November, 1955. This meeting, which tried to come to grips with the problems of European security, German reunification, and disarmament, was a great disappointment to those who had hoped for a continuation of the good spirit of the "summit conference." No agreement was reached on any major issue, and when the conference broke up, the question on many lips was whether or not the cold war would be resumed on a full scale.[62]

The developments of 1956 and 1957 intimated that, although Soviet-western relations might not again become as cordial as they had appeared to be in mid-1955, they would also not be quite as strained as they had been before 1954. The de-Stalinization campaign, launched by Khrushchev at the Twentieth Party Congress in February, 1956, was accompanied by a modification of certain Stalinist tactics and ideas. As previously mentioned, Soviet leaders now repudiated the concept that war with the capitalist states was inevitable. They also spoke of the possibility of "peaceful" transition to communism by parliamentary means, and of different paths to communism in various countries. In April, 1956, evidently as a concession to the strength of nationalism in the communist countries, the Cominform was abolished.[63] Khrushchev and his associates, moreover, were now speaking repeatedly of the possibilities of "peaceful competition" and coexistence with capitalism.[64]

In the realm of foreign policy, the more conciliatory trend was mani-

---

[61] The principal spokesmen for the Big Four were President Dwight D. Eisenhower for the United States, Prime Minister Anthony Eden for Great Britain, Premier Nikolai A. Bulganin and Communist Party First Secretary Nikita S. Khrushchev for the Soviet Union, and Premier Edgar Faure for France. For a report on the conference, see Dept. of State, *The Geneva Conference of Heads of Governments*, Dept. of State Publ. 6046 (Washington, D.C., Government Printing Office, 1955).

[62] For a report on this conference, see Dept. of State, *The Geneva Meeting of Foreign Ministers, October 27–November 16, 1955*, Dept. of State Publ. 6156 (Washington, D.C., Government Printing Office, 1955).

[63] *New York Times*, April 18, 1956, pp. 1, 14.

[64] See pp. 373 and 375.

fested in the Soviet revision of its previous attitude toward Japan and in its acceptance of some western ideas on disarmament. The Soviet Union had strongly opposed the conclusion of a separate peace treaty between Japan and the western powers in 1951, and had objected particularly to the association of Japan with the American system of defensive alliances. On these grounds Soviet leaders had refused to end the formal state of war which had existed since August, 1945. In October, 1956, however, the Soviet government adopted a more temperate position and signed an agreement with Japan, ending the state of war between the two countries and providing for resumption of normal political and economic relations.[65] Presumably, through the strategy of moderation, the Soviet Union was trying to increase its own influence in Japan and to restrict that of the United States.

The "new look," as it was sometimes described, was also apparent in the slight progress during 1957 toward some form of limited disarmament agreement. This progress was made possible by a moderation of both Soviet and western positions, and by the disposition to consider a limited, experimental agreement rather than insisting on one which was comprehensive and all-embracing. The Soviet willingness to accept a much greater amount of armament inspection than previously seemed to indicate a genuine desire for some arrangement to curb the race in nuclear weapons.

With the successful launching of two Soviet satellites in the autumn of 1957, however, the positions of both sides resumed a greater rigidity, and the disarmament negotiations again became deadlocked. But throughout the early months of 1958, the Soviet Union pressed repeatedly for a new "summit meeting," in an apparent effort to portray itself as the leading advocate of peaceful accommodation and the reduction of international tension. On March 27, 1958, Foreign Minister Andrei Gromyko announced to the Supreme Soviet and the world that the Soviet Union would suspend nuclear tests unilaterally, reserving the right to re-examine her decision if the United States and Britain continued their testing. At the time of the declaration, the Soviet Union had just completed a series of tests, and the United States was about to begin a scheduled new series.

Possible reasons for the "new look" in Soviet foreign policy. Behind these manifestations of moderation in Soviet foreign policy since 1956 lie a number of factors that may explain them. Perhaps one of the most compelling is the deeper realization by Soviet leaders of the consequences a major nuclear war would have for the Soviet system. Although they do not admit that communism would be destroyed by such a holocaust, Soviet leaders frequently acknowledge that another war would be "calamitous." In his television interview with American correspondents

[65] *New York Times,* October 20, 1956, p. 2.

in June, 1957, Khrushchev, discussing his concept of coexistence, remarked: [66]

War would bring tremendous calamities to the whole of mankind, tremendous losses in lives and material values, but still mankind would not be destroyed, and since mankind would continue to live, that means that the ideas would continue to live, and the immortal idea of mankind is that of communism. But that is a very high price, and it would be a tremendous calamity both for capitalist and socialist countries, and, therefore, we have to live on one planet. You prefer the capitalist system. We prefer the socialist system. We'll continue to have ideological differences. We will continue to compete, but we must live on this one planet. As a matter of fact, we believe that we would have friendly contacts with you. We think that is possible even though there would be ideological differences, because there are many questions which unite us, and we would readily cooperate with the people of the United States.

Here is reflected the "nuclear stalemate," now prevailing in international affairs, in which each side realizes the full magnitude of the damage that can be inflicted on the other. National survival on both sides, therefore, points to the wisdom of moderate policies that will avoid a major war and channel the competition between the two systems into nonmilitary activities. Whether or not this will lead the Soviet leaders eventually to regard peaceful coexistence as a period of indefinite rather than temporary duration is the crucial but still unanswered question of our time.

Other reasons for a more moderate Soviet foreign policy seem to be:

1. Heightened Soviet respect for the economic and military strength of the West, especially since the 1955 ratification by the western powers of the treaties providing for the Western European Union, German rearmament, and German membership in NATO.

2. A desire to recoup the political and psychological losses in world opinion caused by Soviet intervention in Hungary in the fall of 1956.

3. A desire to win Yugoslavia back to closer relations with the Soviet Union and to prevent further upheavals within the communist bloc.

4. A greater strain on the Soviet economy produced by a crisis in agricultural production, the burden of a heavy military program, and the demands of the Soviet Union's major ally, Communist China.

All these factors, combined with the difficulty of preserving harmony under a system of "collective leadership," might have led Soviet officials to conclude that an improvement in relations with the West was in their national interest.[67] One wonders, therefore, whether the paramount interests of Soviet security and national welfare may not again lead the

[66] *New York Times*, June 3, 1957, p. 6.

[67] Useful accounts of recent Soviet foreign policy may be found in *Current History*, February, 1957, which was devoted entirely to the subject "Russian Foreign Policy after Stalin." See also Philip E. Mosley, "Soviet Foreign Policy: New Goals or New Manners?" *Foreign Affairs*, April, 1956, pp. 541–553.

Soviet government to decide that the practicable limits of world revolution have been reached and that coexistence on a prolonged basis may
better serve their national interests. Although the ultimate objective of
a completely communist world has of course not been abandoned, it is
reasonable to ask whether the continued use of moderate tactics by
Soviet leaders will not ultimately induce some moderation in their more
extreme objectives. These questions will be explored more fully in the
next section of this chapter. Brief consideration is first given, however, to
some views on coexistence held by leaders of the democratic, noncommunist world.

ATTITUDES TOWARD COEXISTENCE IN THE
DEMOCRATIC, NONCOMMUNIST WORLD

Democracy, most observers would agree, is basically sympathetic
toward the idea of coexistence, provided that the term implies a permanent relationship between states based on the principles of peaceful
co-operation, mutual tolerance, and "live-and-let-live" behavior. It is because the communist concept of coexistence does not seem to include
these principles that many spokesmen in the democratic, noncommunist
world remain skeptical regarding any moderation of Soviet long-range objectives. If communism were to confine itself primarily to the domestic
affairs of a country and not attempt by propaganda or force to spread
beyond its frontiers, coexistence might become more of a genuine possibility.

These views have characterized American attitudes toward the Soviet
Union since the Bolshevik Revolution, and they were in part responsible
for the long delay in American recognition of the Soviet government.
They were clearly expressed in a note which Secretary of State Colby
wrote in 1920, in which he said: [68]

> In the view of this Government, there cannot be any common ground upon
> which it can stand with a power whose conceptions of international relations
> are so entirely alien to its own, so utterly repugnant to its moral sense. . . .
> We cannot recognize, hold official relations with, or give friendly reception to
> the agents of a Government which is determined and bound to conspire against
> our institutions; whose diplomats will be the agitators of dangerous revolt;
> whose spokesmen say that they sign agreements with no intention of keeping
> them.

Closely related to this is the opinion, held by at least some believers
in democracy, that democracy itself can never be secure until dictatorship, and especially its modern communist form, has disappeared from
the face of the world. It is sometimes expressed in the familiar words of

[68] Foster Rhea Dulles, *The Road to Teheran* (Princeton, Princeton University Press,
1945), p. 166.

Abraham Lincoln, to the effect that the world cannot remain "half-slave" and "half-free." Here, it will be observed, there is some similarity to the communist assertion that the permanent security of communism will be impossible until that system has been established on a world-wide basis.

Such views not only prompted American nonrecognition of the Bolshevik regime; they also lay behind the American decision to join with other Allied governments between 1918 and 1920 in support of the White Russians in their civil war with the Bolsheviks. Thus, it was hoped that the potential threat of communist revolution would be removed once and for all.[69]

As the Soviet government gained firmer control of Russia, western attitudes became more tempered. Many of these powers recognized the Soviet government during the 1920's, to be followed by the United States in 1933. Stalin's program of socialism in one country, and his liquidation of Trotsky who had stood for more immediate prosecution of world revolution, led the western democracies to feel that it was becoming possible to have live-and-let-live relations with the Soviet government.

However, wary of the implications of the communist concept of world revolution, the western powers, when establishing formal trade and diplomatic relations with the Soviet Union, requested written pledges from the Soviet government to abstain from all forms of intervention in the internal affairs of other states. The United States, for example, obtained one of the most comprehensive pledges when it formally recognized the Soviet government in 1933. The Soviet government agreed: [70]

1. To respect scrupulously the right of the United States to order its own internal life in its own way and to refrain from all interference in American internal affairs.

2. To restrain all persons connected with the Soviet government or with any organizations under its direct or indirect control from any action which would injure the tranquillity or security of the United States; and in particular to prevent any encouragement of armed intervention or agitation designed to bring about by force any change in the internal order of the United States or its possessions.

3. To prevent the formation or activity in Soviet territory of any organization which has as its aim the forceful overthrow of the political or social order of the United States or its possessions.

Had these pledges been scrupulously observed by the Soviet government, American officials might more readily have accepted at face value subsequent Soviet professions of a desire for peaceful coexistence, but continued Communist Party activity in the United States, apparently in

[69] See Chap. 10, *ibid.*, for a fuller discussion; also Thomas A. Bailey, *America Faces Russia* (Ithaca, Cornell University Press, 1950), Chap. 19 ff.

[70] Note of November 16, 1933, from Soviet Foreign Minister Litvinov to President Franklin Roosevelt, *Foreign Relations of the United States: The Soviet Union, 1933–1939* (Washington, Government Printing Office, 1952), pp. 28–29.

close association with Moscow, caused much alarm. Furthermore, the holding of the World Congress of the Communist International in Moscow in 1935, and the attendance at it of prominent American Communists, seemed to be a clear violation of the 1933 pledges. American protests against the violations were of no avail, inasmuch as the Soviet government refused to assume responsibility for the activities of the Comintern.[71]

The growing threat of Hitlerism during the 1930's and the common war against Germany from 1941 to 1945 intensified the practical need for co-operative relations with the Soviet regime. It was mentioned earlier that considerations of national security in the face of a common foe took precedence over ideological differences with the western powers as with the Soviet Union. At the end of World War II, General Dwight D. Eisenhower expressed his belief in the possibility of coexistence, as follows: [72]

Americans at that time [1945]—or at least we in Berlin—saw no reason why the Russian system of government and democracy as practiced by the Western allies could not live side by side in the world, provided each respected the rights, the territory, and the convictions of the other, and each system avoided overt or covert action against the integrity of the other.

The development of the cold war after 1945 and the establishment of communist control over Eastern Europe and China made General Eisenhower's estimate of Soviet policy seem unduly optimistic. Thus, a bulletin of the U.S. Department of State, released in 1951, stated: [73]

From the days of Lenin . . . the leaders of the Soviet Union have pursued their aim of dominating the world through communism. Upon occasion, they have found it expedient to "cooperate" with other groups and other movements, but their will to world domination has been constant throughout the abrupt changes in Soviet foreign policy.

By whittling down the area of the free world by aggression, subversion, and wars-by-satellite, the men of the Soviet Union are attempting to acquire, bit by bit, the control of world power. Their aim is to build up a real and potential military strength greater than any force that could be brought against them. According to their announced intentions, they would then use that strength to establish a political and economic dictatorship throughout the world.

In 1954, Senator William Knowland put his ideas this way: [74]

Coexistence and atomic stalemate will result in ultimate Communist victory. Unless one believes that the men in the Kremlin have completely changed their long-term strategy of ultimately having a Communist world. . . . We must face up to the fact that the Communist concept of "peaceful coexistence"

[71] Bailey, op. cit., pp. 275–276. For details of the American protests, see Foreign Relations of the United States: The Soviet Union, 1933–1939, pp. 218–268.

[72] Dwight D. Eisenhower, Crusade in Europe (New York, Doubleday, 1948), p. 475.

[73] Department of State, The Kremlin Speaks, Dept. of State Publ. 4264 (Washington, D.C., Government Printing Office, 1951), p. 3.

[74] New York Times, November 16, 1954, p. 18.

means that the United States or other free nations of the world will be allowed to exist only until communism is able to subvert them from within or destroy them by aggression from without.

Yet, the consequences of nuclear war would probably be as calamitous for the western world as for the Soviet Union. Various western spokesmen have placed it before the world as a question of "coexistence or no-existence." Winston Churchill stated it eloquently in the House of Commons in 1946: [75] "It is better to have a world united than a world divided; but it is also better to have a world divided than a world destroyed."

Two years later, Churchill developed this further: [76]

It is idle to reason or argue with the Communists. It is, however, possible to deal with them on a fair realistic basis, and in my experience, they will keep their bargains as long as it is in their interest to do so, which might, in this grave matter, be a long time, once things were settled.

Mr. Churchill apparently thinks that coexistence is a practical alternative, with its basis not in ideology but in the interest of survival.

In the next section, three viewpoints will be presented, to stimulate further discussion of this controversial problem. In question form, these alternatives might be put as follows: Is peaceful coexistence a moral and practical imperative? Is it simply a communist tactic to further the goal of a communist world? Or is a basic change in Soviet policy under way which may make coexistence a greater possibility?

POSITIONS
ON THE PROBLEM

1. Peaceful Coexistence Is a Moral and Practical Imperative

(The following excerpts are quoted from an article written by Dr. Harry F. Ward,[77] professor emeritus of Christian ethics at Union Theological Seminary.)

---

[75] *Parliamentary Debates* (Hansard), 5th series, Vol. 423, House of Commons, June 5, 1946 (London, Her Majesty's Stationery Office, 1946), p. 2030.
[76] *Ibid.*, Vol. 446, January 23, 1948, p. 560.
[77] The article appeared in the *New World Review*, a periodical that is frequently sympathetic toward Soviet policies and actions, November, 1954, p. 9 ff.

The H-Bomb, on top of the A-Bomb, germ weapons, and jellied gasoline, has reduced the question of the peaceful co-existence of the capitalist and communist led sections of mankind to its essence. It is now a stark choice between peaceful co-existence and unlimited mutual destruction.

This situation removes the issue from theoretical discussion to the plane of practical necessity. It was on this ground that the Soviet Union first raised the question. Their advocacy of peaceful co-existence expresses the need to protect socialist construction. Today the capitalist world has a similar need to protect the means of maintenance for its people—industrial plant and food supply.

The present situation also transposes peaceful co-existence from an ethical ideal to a moral imperative. Unless the war of the new weapons of mass destruction can be avoided it will destroy the basis of social morality—the value of human life it has taken thousands of years to build up.

The practical necessity for peaceful co-existence is absolute, and the moral imperative is categorical, because there is no other choice but unlimited destruction. The cold war, offered as a substitute, has shown itself to be the broad highway that leads to more death and desolation than the world has ever known or been able to endure. It keeps us building a stockpile of A- and H-bombs, preparing for and testing germ warfare. . . .

Beside the possibilities of annihilation opened up by the H-bomb there is another historic fact operating to produce the choice between peaceful co-existence and unlimited destruction. That fact puts co-existence into history as a reality, leaving only the question of what kind. It is the demonstration that socialist economy is workable and consequently is here to stay. The proof was provided by the amount and quality of Soviet war production in the joint war against Hitler. It is now being reinforced by the rise in Soviet living standards since the war, and also by the amount and quality of the economic aid being sent to the New Democracies of Eastern Europe and to New China.

Our cold war planners have been brought up to believe that a socialist economy cannot work. So they involve themselves in the ruinous contradiction of disbelieving and denying that it works and then planning to destroy it. The propaganda they create to deceive the public also deceives them by its continuous underestimate of the elements of strength in the socialist economy. It overestimates the amount and nature of the dissent and discontent that always follow a social-economic revolution. So ignoring the fate of Hitler, and forgetting the failure of the early capitalist counter-revolution, which had a better chance to succeed, they plot to overthrow the governments that direct a socialist economy, or the approach to one, by subsidizing and arming counter-revolutionary forces. At the same time they get ready for the preventive war, which would be Armageddon. It is not for military reasons alone that their published war plans direct the first air attack at the industrial plants of the Soviet Union.

This is the madness that leads to destruction. When has an economic order that brings a higher standard of living and more opportunities for education to more people ever been overthrown or replaced as long as it continued to move in that direction? The longer socialist economy works, and the better it works, the more impossible it becomes for the capitalist world to destroy it, or to subvert and overthrow the government that directs it. The more it succeeds the more it begets both the means of resistance and the loyalty of the people it serves. Also the more will the industrially under-developed peoples see it as the way to use their own natural resources and labor capacities for their own needs without paying tribute to vested capital interests.

It is equally true that the capitalist economy cannot be destroyed from without and is not yet ready for dissolution within. That the Soviet leaders have learned this from recent history is one of the weighty factors in the possibility of peaceful co-existence. Lenin began the building of socialism in one country when he saw that Germany did not follow Hungary into revolution and the Hungarian revolution was subverted. Since then Soviet leaders have repeatedly affirmed that revolution cannot be exported, it must await the necessary internal conditions. Their support of the world peace movement is part of their reaction to the new historic situation created by weapons for wholesale destruction. They know that if the series of wars started by World War I is allowed to continue, its weakening effect upon capitalist economy will be counterbalanced by the delay in the building of socialism it brings to the communist led countries.

A further pressure toward peaceful co-existence is the need of both Russia and China for machines and techniques the capitalist world can supply. Russian experience includes the fact that the purchase of these between World Wars I and II enabled the planned socialist economy to move forward fast enough to become a vital factor in the winning of World War II. Consequently, both Russia and China know that when they offer trade which will help prolong the capitalist economy for a period they are also shortening the coming of age of their socialist economy. Also they are providing a partial alternative for the war economy United States policy has fastened on the rest of the capitalist world, thus lessening the trends toward the war of total destruction.

To say we cannot trust the communists is both futile and dangerous. What is there in our record that would justify them in trusting us? It is self-interest, as well as the ancient religious desire to "learn war no more" which the socialists inherited, that speaks in their advocacy of peaceful co-existence. A similar self-interest and ideal would lead the people of the United States to speak in the same way if they could free themselves from the propaganda created by those whose self-interest leads in the opposite direction. It is when self-interest joins a common need that moral, spiritual and material forces are united for human progress. Such an opportunity now lies before us.

2. Peaceful Coexistence Is Merely a Soviet Tactic to Further the Goal of a Communist World

(The following position is taken from an article by Harold H. Fisher,[78] professor of international relations at San Francisco State College, professor emeritus of history at Stanford University, and visiting professor of history at the Russian Institute of Columbia University during 1957.)

The Soviet Communists are now calling their program "the world liberation movement." . . .

In the new line now being promulgated neither the old goal nor the old gospel on which it is based has been changed. The C.P.S.U. still aims at a Communist world. It still bases its long range strategy on the familiar dogma of the contradictions of capitalism. But for short range objectives the C.P.S.U. has revived and revised old tactics that were used with some success some 20 years ago. The new tactical objective on the home front is to isolate what is called the "state monopoly capitalists" by developing a united front of workers into a united front of workers, peasants, small businessmen and intellectuals. If this

[78] "New Lines and an Old Gospel," *Current History*, February, 1957, pp. 65–70.

tactic succeeds, it may lead to a peaceful conquest of power along the parliamentary path.

On the international front the tactical objective is the political, economic and cultural isolation of the United States. This is to be accomplished by creating dissension between us and our allies and by drawing the uncommitted governments into the Communist orbit—called a zone of peace—by trade, economic, military and technical aid and cultural exchange, all under the formula of peaceful coexistence and competition. This, in turn, may lead to the peaceful achievement of Communist world dominance by the steady attrition of the Free World and increasing Communist control of world organizations.

From the evidence available in the last weeks of 1956, it seems clear that the decision to modify the aggressive "hard" policies of the Cold War period had been reached as early as 1952, a few months before the nineteenth Congress of the C.P.S.U. and perhaps a year before Stalin's death in March, 1953. These changes gathered momentum slowly during the months while Malenkov, Stalin's designated heir, occupied the first place in the Communist hierarchy. The momentum of change gathered speed and was carried further after Khrushchev took Malenkov's place as the first among equals in the new collective leadership.

Two things are worth noting about the general significance of these changes with respect to Soviet-American relations. One has already been suggested, that is that the changes were not the accidental result of Stalin's death, the result of some sudden improvisation which might be just as suddenly abandoned if and when someone shoves Khrushchev out of his place at the head of the ruling circle. The second thing to note is that while the Soviet government adopts policies aimed at serving the national interests of the U.S.S.R. as a great power, the definition of those national interests is made by the ruling circle of the C.P.S.U., which pursues its aims not only by laying down the line for Soviet foreign policies but also by controlling, directing or influencing the policies of the 75 other Communist parties with their 30 million members.

Ever since 1917, the C.P.S.U. has made use of both these agencies—the Soviet government and the Communist movement—shifting the emphasis from one to the other according to circumstances, but never abandoning either altogether. Now the United States, with its containment system of military preparedness, its multilateral and bilateral collective security alliances, its military, economic and technical aid programs, is the greatest barrier to the extension of Communist power either by direct aggression or by indirect aggression through subversion and civil strife carried out by local Communist parties. The C.P.S.U. is too realistic to place any hope in the feeble American Communist party as the agency to undermine or neutralize the American barrier.

Moreover, even before Stalin's death things had reached the point where the opposition to the Communist movement was being unified and strengthened rather than weakened by policies such as the promotion of class wars, guerilla wars, civil wars, or by the negative "nyet" diplomacy that Molotov made notorious, or by cultural isolationism such as the anti-cosmopolitan movement and the outrageous exaggeration of Russia's cultural achievements.

These considerations plus the difficulties within the Soviet Union, which are not easy to assess, and the trouble in Eastern Europe, which events have shown was exceedingly serious, all undoubtedly helped to convince the big bosses of the C.P.S.U. that the time had come to shift the emphasis of policy from the Communist movement to those departments of the Soviet government concerned with the propaganda of peace, foreign trade, economic development and cultural exchange. Events in Hungary and the Middle East have shown that the C.P.S.U. has not given up entirely the use of naked force and terror or the encouragement of national hatreds and local strife.

These events have made the new course vastly more difficult. But it does not appear to me that these new difficulties are so great that the C.P.S.U. will be compelled or persuaded to revive those Stalinist foreign policies that had produced such unwanted results that Stalin himself seems to have been ready to change them.

When they seized power by force of arms in Petrograd on November 7, 1917, the Communists, who then called themselves Bolsheviks, issued a decree on peace. Ever since that time they have followed the dual policy of advocating peace while deriding pacifism and justifying all wars which Communists anywhere found it necessary or advantageous to engage in. Since World War II, they have used the much circulated Stockholm Petition and several peace congresses outside of the U.S.S.R. to convey the impression that Communists were more devoted to peace than anyone else and were doing more to make it a reality. Many non-Communists have been drawn into association with the Communist movement through peace front organizations.

But the C.P.S.U. has made its most substantial gains in this direction through the exploitation of the Five Principles of Peaceful Coexistence. These Five Principles have achieved great popularity among Asians and Africans partly because they are admirable principles for the governance of international relations; partly because they were originally sponsored by two eminent Asians, Jawaharlal Nehru and Chou En-lai, who issued them in connection with the Indo-Chinese Agreement on Tibet. The Five Principles were also included in a declaration of basic principles issued by the twenty-nine nations participating in the Afro-Asian Conference at Bandung, April 18–24, 1955. . . .

Reflecting on the speeches made at the twentieth Congress of the C.P.S.U. in February, 1956, Walter Lippmann interpreted the emphasis put on peaceful and competitive coexistence as meaning that the U.S.S.R., having first broken the Western monopoly on nuclear weapons, had "now broken also the Western monopoly of economic leadership in the development of under-developed countries." The Communist bloc had now become "fully 'competitive'" and, he went on to say, "can no longer be 'contained' at the frontiers of the Middle East, South Asia, and it may also be, Latin America."

I believe Mr. Lippmann's interpretation is the correct one. Surely the answer is not for the United States to make more and bigger nuclear weapons and do nothing else. Nor, as Mr. Lippmann points out, can the challenge be met "simply by appropriating a lot of new money for foreign aid."

The Communists are slipping through the containment frontiers by means of Soviet foreign economic policies designed to weaken or destroy the relationships between the United States and the advanced countries with which it is allied and with the underdeveloped countries which must have economic and technical assistance for the realization of their national aims. The Communists explain their economic foreign policies as merely the expansion of business relations. They say that this expansion is according to the Leninist principle of peaceful coexistence of states with different social systems. At the same time they stress the political implications of these policies by contrasting the Soviet slogan of "Let's trade" with the alleged American slogan, "Let's rearm." They contrast their unpolitical, business-like offers with American interference with trade in strategic materials, embargoes and so forth. They offer aid without the strings they say the United States attaches to such relations. . . .

The new course of Communist policy rests on the assumption that what has been officially called "the great commonwealth of socialist nations" will be able to produce and trade with steadily increasing efficiency because the members of this commonwealth have common ideals and adhere to the principles of proletarian internationalism. From this economic base they propose to "liberate" the peoples of the world from the Western imperialists who, as *Pravda* has explained, "fight among themselves for domination over other peoples" and so expose their profound and fatal contradictions.

The United States has never before faced this kind of a challenge. To meet this challenge we must be prepared for changes in our foreign policies more revolutionary than the Truman Doctrine, the Marshall Plan, the Vandenberg Resolution, and Point Four, and we must make these changes without the incentive of a threat of Communist aggression and subversion in Europe. . . .

The United States cannot, of course, control the policies of the C.P.S.U. but it may perhaps influence those policies by two types of policy of its own—a policy of defense and a policy of cooperation. Defense involves the maintenance of our military establishment at such a level of preparedness and efficiency that the C.P.S.U., regardless of its leadership, will not attack the United States nor provoke a general war by attacking our allies. This implies that we keep our allies, and we can do this and keep the friendship of other free peoples only by the establishment of a system of economic and cultural cooperation that will enable the other nations not only to maintain their present levels of living but to raise them to narrow the gap between their levels and ours.

The development of this cooperation involves the continuation of our support of and participation in the 45 or 50 organizations that make up the United Nations system. It involves the creation of new international agencies to develop and use the new sources of energy that science and technology are bringing under control. . . .

The best response to the new Soviet course would appear to be to continue to discourage aggression by being prepared to resist it, to prevent economic disintegration of the free world by creating new ways of cooperation and by looking for new areas of cooperation like the International Atomic Energy Agency in which it will be to the interest of all including the Communists to take part.

3. Peaceful Coexistence May Be Possible Since a Basic Change in Soviet Policy Seems to Be Under Way

(The following position is taken from an article written by the well-known British historian, Arnold J. Toynbee.[79])

. . . Can the present indications of a change on the Russian side signify something more than a mere political maneuver? Is it reasonable to hope that, this time, a more sincere and more durable change may be on the way? Can the Soviet Government make a genuine change in its policy without repudiating some of the fundamental tenets of Marxism? These are some of the questions that we have to ask ourselves. I will give the gist of my own answer at once, before explaining how I arrive at it.

It seems to me unlikely that any of the fundamental tenets of Marxism will be, or could be, repudiated in a country in which this ideology has been the officially established faith now for nearly forty years. At the same time, it

[79] "The Question: Can Russia Really Change?" *New York Times,* magazine section, July 24, 1955.

seems to me possible that a sincere and durable change in Russian policy may be on the way. This seems possible because there have been cases in the past in which hallowed tenets have unavowedly been put into cold storage.

Let me illustrate what I mean by taking two familiar examples.

One of the tenets of Islam is that the Islamic world is in a permanent state of war with the non-Islamic world, and that this war is a holy war because the conquest of hitherto non-Moslem countries is the Moslems' religious duty. One of the tenets of the Roman Catholic Church is that, in carrying out its mission to bring all mankind into its fold, it ought to call in the aid of the secular arm, when the secular arm is willing to put its force at the church's purpose. Today, both these tenets are, in practice, "dead letters." We no longer worry about them, as we are worrying now about the tenets of Marxism.

But, in the days before Marx was born, the waging of the Holy War and the invocation of the secular arm were as great a menace to "unbelievers" as the Marxian world revolution has been to "capitalists" in our time.

Vienna was besieged by the Turks no longer ago than 1683. The Edict of Nantes was revoked by Louis XIV no longer ago than 1685. What has happened since the Sixteen Eighties to two tenets that, as recently as the seventeenth century, were still capable of setting the world in a blaze?

So far as I know, neither tenet has ever been repudiated by the official custodians of the faith. If, in 1955, one were to ask a doctor of the Islamic law whether the jihad [Holy War] was still incumbent on Moslems, I believe he would be bound to reply that it was. If one were to ask a Roman Catholic theologian whether it was still the church's duty to invoke the secular arm, I suspect that it might be difficult for him to reply that it was not.

There have, in fact, quite recently been sporadic examples of the persecution of Protestants being supported, or at any rate being countenanced, by the Government of a Catholic country, and of the jihad being waged by a Moslem people. It was waged, for example, by the Sudanese from 1882 to 1898.

These local outbreaks show that there are still people who believe in trying to propagate a religion by force. They believe in this with sufficient conviction to act on it.

All the same, these latterday outbreaks of Christian and Moslem fanaticism do not keep us awake at night. We take them calmly, because we feel sure that, in our time, the great majority of Moslems and Christians are not going to take up arms in the cause of religion, as they have done so often in the past. . . .

So we feel ourselves safe from a peril that haunted our seventeenth-century ancestors. Our confidence is founded on guesswork. It might be difficult for us to prove that we had appreciated the position correctly. Yet our common sense would reject the suggestion that the Islamic Holy War is one of the major perils of the twentieth century. . . .

Is it not conceivable that the Marxian doctrine of the World Revolution may go the same way as the Islamic doctrine of the Holy War? It may never be repudiated. It may still be cherished by some fanatics. But it may become a "dead letter," all the same. The power and the will to apply it on the grand scale may vanish, "softly and silently," like Lewis Carroll's snark.

Let us try to assess the forces in the Soviet Union that are working for and against a genuine change in Soviet policy.

The greatest force working for a change is surely the Soviet Union's need to give first place to its own vital interests. Ever since the Bolsheviks seized power in 1917, there has been a tension in the Soviet Union between Russia's interests and communism's. Is Russia to be communism's tool, or communism to be Russia's? This was the issue between Trotsky and Stalin, and, in that round, Russia's interests won.

It is one of the ironies of the situation that the issue becomes acute when another great country, besides Russia, is converted to communism by Russian efforts.

This problem would have confronted the Kremlin in 1923 if Germany had gone Communist in that year, and it confronts the Kremlin now, since China did go Communist after 1945. What does it profit Russia to spend her resources on building up the strength of another great Communist country that might repay Russia, one day, by snatching from her the leadership of the Communist world?

Perhaps this risk might be worth running for the sake of acquiring a first-class ally. But what profit is there in an alliance if it is going to lead to an atomic war in which everybody is going to be wiped out? The Soviet Union needs all its resources for its own development. Like the United States in the nineteenth century, the Soviet Union has a subcontinent to open up.

But, unlike nineteenth-century America, twentieth-century Russia cannot borrow resources from abroad. Her fidelity to Marxism has ruled out that. The Soviet Union has to depend on herself; and this makes it all the more irksome for her to lend Russian resources for developing other underdeveloped Communist countries.

The Soviet Union's forced march to catch up with the West in technology and industrialization is arduous enough in itself. The whole enterprise is a tour de force. If important parts of it have miscarried, that would not be surprising or discreditable. But it would mean that Russia now had two urgent needs.

One of her needs would be to husband her resources for her own development. Another of her needs would be peace, to give her a chance of repairing the miscarriages and carrying the enterprise through to completion. This looks like a powerful force in favor of a genuine change in foreign policy.

There is an allied force working in the same direction. Industrialization is the Soviet Government's aim. You cannot industrialize a primitive peasant country without calling a new class of workers into existence. You must have plenty of managers, designers and engineers, and you must have trained foremen and skilled technicians in vast numbers.

You must not only have them; you must have them doing their work effectively; and you cannot get this kind of work out of human beings by the brutal methods that are effective (more or less) for making a galley slave row or a plantation slave hoe. Skilled work cannot be exacted by force; it has to be coaxed out of people by inducements.

So the Soviet Government has a choice. It can cling to the Russian governmental tradition of coercion at the cost of falling behind in the technological race; or it can go ahead with technology at the cost of giving its technicians the modicum of freedom without which they will not do what is wanted of them. This looks like a powerful force in favor of a genuine change in domestic policy. But domestic policy and foreign policy cannot be kept in separate watertight compartments nowadays.

Of course, there are also forces working the other way. Doctrinaire Marxism is, no doubt, still a living force in the Kremlin. But in a seat of government an ideology must surely be a wasting asset. Academic doctrine is a diet for political exiles. They have to live on it as a medieval chameleon lived on air. But as soon as the Bolsheviks were translated from the British Museum Reading Room to the Kremlin, they found other fare to live on and other things to think about.

The first concern of every Government in power is to keep itself going. If ideology gets in the way of *raison d'état*, so much the worse for ideology. If this diagnosis is correct, we may expect to see doctrinaire Marxism fight a stubborn rearguard action in Russia but fail, in Russia, to hold its own.

An ideology's everlasting mansions are not to be found in a converted country. . . . Doctrinaire Marxism is likely to survive in Bloomsbury and Greenwich Village longer than in Moscow or Peiping.

Another force in Russia that might work against a change of policy is the traditional Muscovite appetite for the acquisition of more territory. This is a force with a formidable momentum, for it has been at work since the fourteenth century.

For six hundred years the Muscovite grain of mustard seed has been steadily growing into the tree that now overshadows the earth. The Muscovite empire has spread from the suburbs of Moscow to the Bering Straits and the Pamirs and the Oder-Neisse Line. Can the men of the Kremlin break this inveterate habit of adding field to field?

Undoubtedly this might have been difficult if Russia had remained the peasant country that she used to be. But a government that already possesses a great estate and that has decided to go in for industrialization is perhaps likely to give priority to the development of its existing assets. Twentieth-century Russia, like nineteenth-century America, may be inclined to turn her attention inward to the exploitation of her own subcontinent.

These are, perhaps, some of the more obvious pros and cons. An analysis of them will not give us any conclusive answer to our question. We shall still be left guessing; and, in dealing with the Russians in this critical year, we shall therefore be feeling our way in the twilight, as human beings have to do in so many episodes of practical life, public and private.

At any rate, the situation today is not analogous to the situation in the Nineteen Thirties. Unlike Nazi Germany, the Soviet Union does not need *Lebensraum*. It is not faced with a choice between war and downfall. And, in the atomic age, war could no longer bring victory either to the Soviet Union or to any other belligerent. It could bring nothing but annihilation for us all.

In these circumstances, it is evidently possible that Russian policy may have changed bona fide. The West's decision to explore this possibility must surely be right.

QUESTIONS

1. What do you think the communists mean by "peaceful coexistence"?

2. Is peaceful coexistence the same as peaceful co-operation?

3. Explain the principal ideas underlying the communist theory of world revolution.

4. What reasons would you advance if you were trying to persuade a communist that his assumptions regarding world revolution were unsound?

5. What possible effects may "Titoism" and other versions of "national communism" have on the Soviet concept of world revolution?

6. Soviet leaders claim that their economic system is potentially superior to that of the West since their rate of industrial productivity is increasing far more

rapidly than is that of the capitalist world. They point out that industrial output in the U.S.S.R. between 1946 and 1955 increased (1929 = 100) from 466 to 2049, whereas the increase in the capitalist world was only from 107 to 193. How would you analyze and answer this argument?

7. Explain the major occasions on which the Soviet requirements of national security led to a toning down of the theory of world revolution.

8. Do you think that the long-run security of democracy can be assured so long as communism remains firmly established in major countries like the Soviet Union and China?

9. The de-Stalinization program and the upheavals in Hungary and Poland led John Foster Dulles, Secretary of State, to say that an "irreversible trend" had started which would lead to greater freedom for the people now living under communist control. Do you think Dulles or Khrushchev will be the better prognosticator, the former when he predicts the "irreversible trend" toward the downfall of communist dictatorship, or the latter when he predicts the inevitable collapse of capitalism?

10. What do you say to the argument that the advent of nuclear warfare leaves us with no alternatives but coexistence or no existence?

SELECT BIBLIOGRAPHY

BAILEY, Thomas A., *America Faces Russia* (Ithaca, Cornell University Press, 1950). A very readable survey of the history of American-Russian relations from American independence to the cold war. Emphasizes American public opinion on the subject.

CHAMBERLIN, William Henry, *Blueprint for World Conquest* (Chicago, Human Events, 1946). Contains the verbatim text of three basic documents of the Communist International: The Theses and Statutes, the Program, and the Constitution and Rules. An introductory essay discusses the nature and strategy of the world communist movement. Author is a former correspondent for the *Christian Science Monitor* in Moscow.

CRANKSHAW, Edward, *Russia Without Stalin* (London, M. Joseph, 1956). A stimulating interpretation and analysis of the changes in Soviet policies and practices since the death of Stalin. Author is a well-known British historian.

Current History, February, 1957, "Russian Foreign Policy after Stalin." A symposium of articles on different aspects of Soviet foreign policy after Stalin's death.

DEGRAS, Jane, ed., *The Communist International, 1919–1943* (New York, Oxford University Press, Vol. I, 1956). Volume I covers the period 1919–22; the first in a series that promises to be an excellent source of basic documents concerning the Communist International. Being prepared under the auspices of the Royal Institute of International Affairs.

EBON, Martin, *World Communism Today* (New York, Whittlesey House, 1948). Summarizes the activities of the international communist movement up to 1948, and presents the operations of the communist movement in individual countries throughout the world.

FLORINSKY, Michael T., *World Revolution and the U.S.S.R.* (New York, Macmillan, 1933). An excellent and readable discussion of the theory and practice of world revolution from 1917 to 1933, with special reference to Soviet foreign and domestic policies.

KIRKPATRICK, Evron M., ed., *Target: The World, Communist Propaganda Activities in 1955* (New York, Macmillan, 1956). A documented presentation of communist propaganda activity throughout the world in 1955. Shows how propaganda supplements the techniques of diplomacy, economic pressure, and military activity and plays a major part in communist strategy. Also points out how communist propaganda revises its tactics from time to time to reach its objective of a World Union of Soviet Socialist Republics.

SULZBERGER, C. L., *The Big Thaw* (New York, Harper, 1956). Popular treatment by a *New York Times* correspondent of the new forces at work in Russia and other communist countries since the death of Stalin.

U.S. Congress, House Committee on Foreign Affairs, *The Strategy and Tactics of World Communism*, 80th Congr., 2nd sess., House Document 619 (Washington, D.C., Government Printing Office, 1948). Analyzes the theory and practice of international communism; has a useful supplementary collection of speeches, articles, and documents.

Part IV

TECHNIQUES of ADJUSTMENT
in WORLD AFFAIRS

11

Is Diplomatic Negotiation Feasible?

THE PROBLEM
AND ITS BACKGROUND

POLICY PATTERNS

It was the intent of the preceding chapters to emphasize some major factors that generate tension and conflict today in the sphere of international relations. Attention has been given to human nature, nationalism, the uneven distribution of natural resources, scientific advances, and clashing ideologies. If the reader has been sufficiently impressed, and not overly depressed, by the variety and complexity of these factors, he should now be ready to examine the means that human beings have used or considered for the adjustment of the grave and ominous differences between their nation-states. Thus, this chapter and the several following are devoted to a study of the techniques of adjustment in world affairs.

By way of introducing these chapters, some generalizations about the policy patterns characterizing international relations should be made.

National Interests and Policies

Despite the fact that nations differ from each other in many respects, in at least one they have all behaved in the same way. All have sought primarily to promote and safeguard their respective concepts of national interest. The government of a nation-state is expected to seek security from external attack and from outside interference in its domestic affairs. It must also endeavor in a variety of ways to promote what it regards as its citizens' general welfare. These are recognized fundamentals of international relations, at least since the emergence of the nation-state system.

Whereas all nation-states are in agreement about their search for security, they are obviously not in accord about the policies that should be pursued to reach that end. Each takes into account its own geographic, demographic, economic, and strategic situation. Each is influenced by its history, national outlook, and ideology. Almost inevitably, each nation-state arrives at a definition of its national interest which is not compatible with the concepts other nations have of their national interests. The lack of compatibility may be slight and therefore not of serious international consequence, but often the area of discord is sufficiently important to create international tension and sometimes open conflict.

For example, France may consider its national interest as requiring a weak Germany, but quite clearly Germany's concept of its national interest would be otherwise. The Arab states have often given the impression that their national interests require the liquidation of the Republic of Israel. The Israeli national interest, however, is incompatible with such an outlook.

It may, therefore, be said that because nation-states have conflicting concepts of national interest, conflicting foreign policies result. A major concern of international politics is the adjustment of these foreign-policy clashes, and a number of courses of action have developed to serve this purpose.

The Conduct of International Politics

The point was made in Chapter 2 that power—the capacity to influence and control the actions of others by persuasion, threat, or forcible coercion—pervades all politics. It may be useful to distinguish between international relations and international politics, because power does not necessarily characterize both. The term *international relations* may serve to describe all intergovernmental relations, whether or not the power factor is present. The term *international politics,* however, may be applied in a more limited sense to intergovernmental relations where power is a factor. Some writers use *international relations* and *international politics* interchangeably and synonymously. The authors of this book feel it is clearer to distinguish between them. Thus, it is possible to say that all international politics are in varying degrees power politics, but not all international relations involve power politics.

A few examples will point up this important distinction. When two or more nation-states reach agreement on such matters as international health regulations, the exchange of weather data, the control of ocean and air traffic, or the operation of international postal services, the nations involved have certainly engaged in international relations. The relations have had little or no reference to power, and have been entirely free of reference to the forcible use of power. When the United States and Canada agreed upon mutual action to preserve wild life, their mutual benefits were so obvious, their sacrifices so small, and their national interests so much in harmony that only a time and place for negotiation were necessary. In this situation we speak of international relations, not of international politics. As will be noted in Chapter 13, a considerable part of United Nations activity in the social, technical, and scientific fields does not involve power considerations.

Conversely, when national interests conflict, as they usually do in the political realm, the resolution of such conflicts is very apt to reflect the relative power positions of the disputants. This does not mean that power is always overtly applied. The United States did resort to naked power to expel Spain from Cuba, but after the Spanish-American War it was economic and political pressure which the United States brought to bear to secure a naval base on the island. Since then, the mere presence and known outlook of the United States have been sufficient to deter the Republic of Cuba from pursuing a policy considered dangerous by Washington to United States' national interests. Power was present in all three phases of United States' policy toward Cuba, but its role differed in each phase. With such variations in the application of power in international politics understood, certain policy patterns may be delineated.

A policy of noninvolvement. When a nation-state is able to limit the use of its power to the defense of its own territory, and the areas immediately adjacent to it, and to avoid involvement in the conflicts of other nations, it is pursuing a policy of noninvolvement. No major European state has been able, for an appreciable length of time, to follow such a policy in modern times. As will be discussed more fully in the next chapter, even the United States in the last century found a noninvolvement policy (sometimes called a policy of isolationism) difficult and dependent upon factors beyond its control. Although Switzerland and Sweden managed to avoid involvement in both world wars, the growing interdependence of all nation-states suggests that this policy pattern will be less and less feasible.

It is true that India today heads a bloc of states that insist upon nonalignment in the cold war, and some argue that this constitutes a policy of noninvolvement, but whether they could continue to pursue such a policy in the event of another war is doubtful, to say the least. Moreover, the efforts of India, in particular, both to create this bloc of states and to induce a world climate of opinion supporting peaceful coexistence are not strictly compatible with a noninvolvement policy.

A policy of domination. This is a pattern of seeking and exercising rather complete influence, authority, and control over a region, continent, or even over the world in order to secure one's national interest. Frequently a policy of domination entails violence and war, since it leaves little or no room for accommodation of other nations' national interests. When Japan in 1931 seized Manchuria and later North China by military means, it was pursuing a policy of domination which China forcibly resisted. Similarly, in 1939 the German policy of domination, manifested in armed invasion of the Polish Corridor, precipitated not only counter military action by the Poles but World War II. On the other hand, the German destruction of Czechoslovakia (1938–39) and Soviet control of Eastern Europe since 1945 are examples of the policy of domination executed without war.

It should be noted that this kind of policy is generally adopted as a last resort, after other policies have proved unsuccessful, and even then they may be combined with other patterns.

A policy of balance of power. Another pattern, and one more widely followed in the contemporary world than either of the two just discussed, is that of balance of power. It is intended to prevent any one or group of states from undertaking a policy of domination. This objective is sought by achievement of an equilibrium of power on a regional or world basis. Since Chapter 12 is devoted in its entirety to this policy pattern, it will not be discussed here.

A policy of collective security. This policy signifies the establishment of an organization of sovereign states in which each member promises, under certain specific conditions, to aid any other member who is attacked. Originally, the policy reflected a certain disillusionment with the traditional balance-of-power policies of the era before World War I. In essence, the pattern involves the pooling of the power of all members for use against any state which attacks another. It embodies the familiar principle of "all for one and one for all."

Such a collective security system has been the aim of the League of Nations and the United Nations. Facilities for negotiation of conflicting national interests are established, and the members pledge themselves to take collective action against any state which resorts to force in violation of its obligations.

According to some, the logical end of collective security is not a league of sovereign states but a world government, which would possess the power necessary to prevent violence between the member states. The states would surrender enough of their sovereignty to the world government to make that government effective. The power exercised by the world government would correspond to the internal police powers exercised by a nation-state today. Further consideration of this policy pattern, as exemplified both in the United Nations and in the movement for world government, will also be deferred to later chapters.

These four patterns illustrate various national policies and the involvement of power in each. The next task is to determine how diplomacy is related to the pursuit of these policies.

Diplomacy and International Politics

No deep perception is necessary to understand that these policies all depend for their implementation upon some kind of negotiation between the nation-states. Even when a policy of domination leads to war as an instrument of that policy, negotiations take place between allies, between warring powers and neutrals, and sooner or later between belligerents. The generally accepted techniques, procedures, and code of conduct involved in these international negotiations are known as diplomacy.

When the traditional practices of diplomatic procedure are ignored, usually the consequences are confused, irritating, and sometimes futile negotiations. Those who have not conformed to diplomatic custom, from Thomas Jefferson to the Russian Bolsheviks, soon learned that diplomatic negotiation was more fruitful than undiplomatic negotiation. Mr. Jefferson eventually recognized that there was an established hierarchy among diplomats, and Soviet ambassadors to the Court of St. James now ride sumptuously, in royal coaches, to Buckingham Palace to present their credentials, thus yielding to the conventions which through the centuries have become part of the practice of diplomatic negotiation.

THE EVOLUTION OF DIPLOMACY

Though the word *diplomacy* was used in its modern sense for the first time by Edmund Burke in 1796,[1] its practice dates far back into the past. The word itself is derived from the ancient Greek word *diploma,* meaning written copy. But diplomacy was born even earlier—no doubt at the prehistoric moment when two humans perceived the advantage of haggling instead of fighting with each other over their disputes. By fighting, both combatants ran the risk of serious injury; in the avoidance of this risk they shared a community of interest; once this community of interest was recognized by both sides, diplomacy became possible. For, in essence, *diplomacy is a means of obtaining for oneself or one's family, tribe, or country the maximum of one's objectives from an opposing person, tribe, or country without resort to war and with the generation of a minimum of ill will and tension between oneself and the opposing negotiator.*

The recognition of the value of negotiation early in human existence meant that mutual agreement on how such negotiations could be conducted also came early. In its long history, however, diplomacy underwent considerable alteration before reaching the refined and complex

[1] Harold Nicolson, *Diplomacy* (New York, Harcourt Brace, 1939), p. 28.

form familiar today. A cursory examination of the evolution of some of the more important features of diplomacy will reveal its deep roots and illustrate its contemporary institutions.

Diplomatic Immunity

Among the earliest practices which may be designated as diplomatic was the granting of safe-conduct guarantees to the negotiators by both sides in a negotiation. In its most primitive form it involved negotiators laying aside their arms and entering a conference ring where haggling, not physical violence, was the agreed procedure. The conferees were promised a safe return to their families, tribes, or countries regardless of the success or failure of the negotiations. Sometimes, as Homeric literature reveals, diplomatic immunity was violated, but its practice was fundamental to diplomacy.

Today, even in an era of total war, diplomatic immunity has been generally observed. With the outbreak of World War II each belligerent arranged for its enemies' diplomatic personnel to return home as soon as arrangements could be made. Moreover, a diplomat residing in a foreign country is accorded freedom from arrest and search within his official diplomatic residence. Without permission, Russian police can no more enter the United States Embassy in Moscow than can Washington police enter the Soviet Embassy. From long experience the conclusion was drawn that such immunity is essential to the negotiating that is diplomacy's task.

Treaties

The necessity for recording the results of negotiations led quite naturally to treaty-making. The oldest treaty in existence (an agreement between the Kings of Lagash and Umma to submit a boundary dispute to arbitration by the King of Kish) dates from about 3000 B.C. and is now in the Louvre Museum,[2] but no doubt the treaty is an even older device. In any event, the ancient Greeks later made wide use of treaties and institutionalized treaty-making. Treaties of peace, of alliance and mutual defense, of federation, and of arbitration between the Greek city-states were numerous. It is also evident that the Greeks appointed their treaty negotiators with care and ceremony, insisted that all signatories bind themselves by oath to observe treaty provisions, and published the treaty texts so that all concerned were aware of their obligations. From this early practice has descended the treaty-making of our time.

A collection of treaties to which France became a party between 1713 and 1906 fills 23 fat tomes.[3] International treaties and agreements signed

[2] Frederick L. Schuman, *International Politics*, 4th ed. (New York, McGraw-Hill, 1948), p. 27.
[3] France, *Recueil des traités de la France* (Paris, 1864–1917).

by the United States just between the Revolution and the Civil War fill 8 volumes.[4] And the treaties and agreements between nations registered with the United Nations between 1946 and 1956 fill 246 volumes.[5] Thus, the recording and signing of contracts between sovereign states, the treaty-making process, have come to be very widely accepted by modern society.

The Language of Diplomacy

The adoption of a common and mutually acceptable language was also important in the evolution of diplomatic practice. Latin served medieval European diplomacy well but of course was limited to a small area of the world. Even this facility disappeared with the rise of national languages during the Renaissance. With the adoption of French, a language of exceptional clarity and unity, European diplomats in the seventeenth century acquired a necessary tool for their work. In time, French became the world's diplomatic language. Not only did most diplomats learn French, but the original text of every major treaty between European states from 1648 to 1939 was drawn up in French. The entry of the Americans into the diplomatic arena and France's decline as a world power contributed to the emergence of other languages of diplomacy. Today, in the United Nations, French, English, Russian, Spanish, and Chinese are the official languages in which negotiations are conducted and treaties written.

Diplomatic Officials

No less important to the practice of diplomacy are the diplomats themselves. Although chiefs of state, among their many duties, are responsible for the foreign policies of their states and therefore must be considered as at least part-time diplomatic officials, there has emerged a corps of officials who serve under the chiefs of state and are concerned exclusively with diplomatic matters. First, in order of appearance, are consuls. Renaissance Italian traders in foreign ports found it expedient to select one of their own number to deal for them collectively with the government of the port in which they traded. Subsequently, consuls were officially appointed, charged with the protection of the commercial and legal interests of their countrymen abroad, and were subordinated to ambassadors.

Known as *legati* in medieval times, then as *ambaxiatores* in Renaissance Italy, ambassadors became the government representatives sent abroad to reside in the countries to which they were appointed and facilitate continuous diplomatic contact with their host governments on all matters of interstate concern. The Venetian Republic was the first to require

---

[4] Dept. of State, *Treaties and Other International Acts of the United States of America* (Washington, D.C., Government Printing Office, 1931–48).

[5] United Nations, *Treaty Series* (New York, United Nations).

periodic ambassadorial reports, which were then kept on file in Venice (to the delight of historians who, in the 21,000 dispatches still in existence and dating from 883 to 1797, have found major sources on all subjects from the price of Flemish woolens to the boudoir activities of French kings). When representatives of full ambassadorial rank were not appointed, ministers undertook the same task. Ministers reside in legations, whereas ambassadors reside in embassies. In the past, ambassadors have usually been accredited to larger states and ministers to smaller states, but the distinction is less true today. Representatives with the rank of ambassador are more often appointed to both large and small states.

Foreign ministers (called Foreign Secretaries in Britain, and Secretaries of State in other countries), charged with the co-ordination and direction of a nation-state's diplomacy, appeared in the seventeenth century. It was Cardinal Richelieu who, in 1626, established in France the first permanent government department responsible exclusively for the conduct of foreign policy. This ministry became a prototype for similar offices in all governments during succeeding years, China being among the last to establish such a ministry, in 1861.

In recent years, as international affairs have become more complex, an increasing number of specialists have been added to the diplomatic services of various countries. Thus, there are military, cultural, economic and financial, labor, and agricultural attachés who specialize in the fields suggested by their titles. They may participate in negotiations dealing with their specialties, and they may advise the ministers and ambassadors under whom they serve. As can be readily seen, diplomacy today demands personnel competent to deal not only with traditional political issues but also with a growing myriad of technical, economic, and social problems.

Diplomatic immunity, treaties, language, and personnel, however, are not the only essentials in the evolution of diplomatic practice. In addition to these, diplomacy has acquired certain adjuncts which bear some attention at this point.

Adjuncts of Diplomacy

Mediation and conciliation. Sometimes direct, face-to-face negotiations between two disputants break down and result in stalemate. In such circumstances mediation and conciliation were found helpful in reviving negotiations and reaching a solution to disputes. Mediators have often found means of compromising two conflicting viewpoints and persuading disputants to resume broken negotiations. Conciliation commissions, composed of neutral parties, have often made objective studies of difficult disputes and suggested solutions that ultimately formed the bases for terminating disputes.

In both mediation and conciliations the disputants retain the freedom to accept or reject the suggestions of mediators and conciliators; accordingly, these two methods have frequently proved acceptable to sovereign nation-states. A major function of the United Nations has been to furnish disputing states with mediation and conciliation services. They have been used in the Kashmir dispute between India and Pakistan and in the Arab-Israeli crisis. Count Bernadotte of Sweden and later Ralph Bunche of the United States served as United Nations mediators in negotiating the Arab-Israeli armistice of 1949. Dag Hammarskjold, Secretary-General of the United Nations, later played a mediator's role in the continuing Arab-Israeli dispute.

Arbitration. In contrast to mediation and conciliation, arbitration involves prior agreement by the disputants to accept the judgment of a third, mutually acceptable party—an arbitrator. In agreeing to arbitration, therefore, the disputants were obliged to surrender their freedom to make the final decision. Interestingly, ancient Greek arbitrators were often selected from the ranks of Olympic Games champions because they were men known and respected throughout the Greek world.

Because of its limitation upon the disputants' freedom to make the final decision, however, arbitration has not often been acceptable to nation-states in their negotiation of major political issues. One of its most famous historic applications was in the settlement of the Anglo-American dispute, known as the "Alabama Claims," in 1872. This case involved claims by the United States against Great Britain for the damages wrought during the American Civil War by Confederate cruisers, including the *Alabama*, which Britain had permitted to be built in British shipyards. An Italian, a Swiss, and a Brazilian served as neutral arbitrators and awarded the United States $15\frac{1}{2}$ million dollars, which the British government paid in gold.

After World War I, a Permanent Court of International Justice was established alongside the League of Nations as an international arbitration agency. It consisted of a panel of fifteen justices and met regularly each year, from 1922 on. In the twenty-two years of its existence the court considered some 65 cases, and rendered 32 judgments and 27 advisory opinions, none of which were disregarded.[6] Although many cases were of a nonpolitical character, and not the type that have usually led to war, the use of arbitration has not been without significance. Since 1946 the International Court of Justice, a carbon copy of, and successor to, the older Permanent Court, has continued to make arbitration facilities available as an adjunct to diplomatic practice.

International law. Reference should also be made to another adjunct of diplomacy, international law. By international law is meant that set of principles and obligations which are acceptable as governing relations between nation-states. Confusion and dismay are rife among people who

[6] Daniel S. Cheever and H. Field Haviland, *Organizing for Peace* (Boston, Houghton Mifflin, 1954), p. 338.

expect international law to function similarly to domestic law. Since sovereign states are naturally reluctant to accept the binding force of law on any broad scale in their international relations, international law has operated on a different set of assumptions from domestic law. For example, at the international level there has existed no authority comparable to a national executive or legislature, there have been no courts with powers comparable to domestic courts, and there has been no police force comparable to the police power standing behind domestic law.

International law, therefore, has been limited to the principles that nation-states have found it mutually advantageous to observe in their relations with one another. Diplomatic immunities, the sanctity of treaties, regulations governing treatment of prisoners of war, and rules of commerce on the high seas are examples of the kind of questions with which international law has been concerned. The various states usually observe such law because it is generally in their interest, broadly defined, to do so. Should they violate it, the states know they may expect retaliation.

It should, of course, be clear that the nature of the sovereign state makes it difficult for international law by itself to prevent aggression and war. Nevertheless, it has been useful in establishing certain procedures in international relations, and thus has served as an adjunct to diplomacy.[7]

In an evolutionary manner, therefore, the practice of diplomacy has become formalized. Certainly by 1700, if not before, the knowledge of procedures, custom, and languages necessary to undertaking a diplomatic career had raised diplomacy to the level of a profession. Extensive education and experience were characteristics of most diplomats. Ambassadorial posts were sought as marks of distinction, and foreign ministers ranked next to prime ministers. International negotiation had been systematized, and a pattern for its conduct established under the name of diplomacy. The question now to be considered is: How effective has diplomatic negotiation been in adjusting international differences in modern times?

AN APPRAISAL OF DIPLOMACY

The most hasty survey of European history during the last three or four hundred years makes it perfectly clear that diplomatic negotiation did not always prevent clashing national policies from precipitating wars. Indeed, diplomacy has sometimes been enlisted to arrange alliances and isolate enemies in preparation for war. Bismarck's diplomacy before the Franco-Prussian War (1870–71) was of this character. Sometimes negotiations conducted in the best approved diplomatic manner may be employed to lull an opponent into a false sense of security while aggression

[7] For an excellent discussion of international law, see James L. Brierly, *The Law of Nations* (Oxford, Clarendon Press, 1949).

is being planned. Japan's dispatch of the Kurusu mission to Washington on the eve of Pearl Harbor demonstrates this use of diplomacy. Even when it is carried on legitimately, to seek a solution to an international dispute, diplomatic negotiation has by no means proved consistently successful. It must be recognized, therefore, that diplomacy has been an imperfect technique, subject to important limitations which bear examination.

The Limitations of Diplomacy

The very magnitude of the task diplomats face in the modern nation-state epoch poses a challenge which they, humans as they are, cannot always meet. The great fluidity of international relations accounts for one aspect of the diplomats' difficulties. National interests of the various nations are not static. Economic, political, social, and ideological currents are continually changing the international picture, and although the task calls for flexibility and adjustability, diplomats have not always been successful in the undertaking.

An equilibrium between states has been temporarily achieved on various occasions and has been accompanied by periods of relative peace. Europe experienced such an era in the mid-seventeenth century after the religious wars. It did so again after the Treaty of Utrecht in 1713, when the wars of Louis XIV (1667–1713) came to an end. No war involving more than three great powers was fought for a century after Waterloo in 1815. Still, the equilibrium broke down each time, and diplomats found themselves struggling to adjust new disputes. Thus France by 1667, with growing wealth and population, an increasingly centralized government, and a new, ambitious ruler, no longer defined its national interest as it had in 1648, under the Treaty of Westphalia. By 1740, British commercial and Prussian dynastic interests had sufficiently changed to lead those states to seek alteration in the 1713 peace settlement. Shifting economic, political, and national pressures in the dynamic nineteenth century led first Russia, then France, and finally Germany to embark upon new foreign policies, which smashed the equilibrium constructed at the Congress of Vienna in 1815. As for the more recent past, the peace of 1919 began to split at the seams with Germany's reoccupation of the Rhineland as early as 1935.

With such developments, the diplomatic task of maintaining peace becomes increasingly more difficult. Without diplomatic negotiation, new conflicts would probably have taken place much sooner than they did. Diplomacy has a creditable record in the settlement of certain international problems since 1815: Greek independence (1830), Belgian neutralization (1839), military neutralization of the Black Sea (1856), separation from the Ottoman Empire of Rumania and Serbia (1878), the partition of Africa (1885), and termination of war in the Balkans

(1912–13). But the fact remains that changing conditions beyond the diplomats' control have sooner or later led to an international dispute in which war, not negotiation, was the method of settlement attempted.

It may be said of diplomacy, therefore, that its history has not been one of consistent success because factors beyond its control have continually intruded and periodically defied settlement by diplomatic technique. This is one of the limitations of diplomatic negotiation.

Another limitation not always appreciated by the layman is the frequent inability of diplomacy, by its very nature, to achieve agreements wholly satisfactory to all parties to a dispute. At least, this holds for many political disputes involving national interests. Negotiation entails bargaining, haggling, threatening, cajoling, bluffing—every technique of persuasion short of violence (no wonder a seventeenth century English ambassador described a diplomat as "an honest man sent abroad to lie for his country"!).[8] Such activity aims at a compromise between the disputants, but the result is seldom completely satisfying. Perhaps a few examples will make this clearer.

The United States believes that its national interests require a united, friendly Germany playing a leading role in the western military alliance, but the Soviet Union seems to hold that her national interests will not permit this. Without resort to force, there appears to be no solution to this clash, unless a compromise through negotiation is reached. Conceivably, Moscow would permit free elections, which would probably place a pro-western government in power in Berlin, but only if the Soviet government had guarantees that Germany, like Austria, would be barred from military alignment with the West. In a word, American diplomacy in the present German situation is not likely to achieve all that it is striving for.

When the United States negotiated with Franco Spain for the use of air bases in that country, something less than a totally satisfying settlement was reached. First, the United States was obliged to pay for the privilege. Second, Washington was obliged to give succor to a regime that is ideologically antipathetic to democracy and hated by Spanish antifascists who may sometime come to power. Yet, it was the best that could be secured through negotiation by American diplomats.

Anglo-Iranian negotiations over British oil concessions in Iran finally terminated in 1954 in compromise. The British relinquished ownership of the Abadan refineries to Iran, but Iran, in order to secure British technical aid in the operation of the refineries, consented to indemnification of British investors.

Hitler's diplomacy at Munich in 1938, when Germany secured permission to dismember Czechoslovakia, would at first glance seem to be an example of complete success through negotiation. Apparently, Hitler

[8] Hans J. Morgenthau, *Politics Among Nations*, 2nd ed. (New York, Knopf, 1954), pp. 512–513.

secured his maximum demands and surrendered nothing in return. Yet even this instance might be considered a compromise. Hitler did publicly pledge Germany to seek no further gains. It was a paper pledge, it is true, which he violated shortly afterward, but then he destroyed whatever remained of his reputation for reliability and pushed into implacable opposition Great Britain and many democratic countries which later became agents of Hitler's downfall.

Summarizing this second limitation of diplomacy, it may be said that diplomatic negotiation is not an instrument capable of achieving *in toto* a nation-state's foreign policy objectives when they are in conflict with the national interests of other states. It is an instrument of compromise. Astute, well-trained diplomats may secure more favorable terms than less able negotiators, but total success in diplomacy is not to be equated with total satisfaction of national interests. Failure to recognize this limitation, as well as that mentioned first, leads to unjustified criticism of, and misplaced faith in, diplomatic negotiation as an instrument for relieving international tensions.

The Potentialities of Diplomacy

It is not valid, however, to conclude that, because of its limitations, diplomacy can serve no useful purpose. It has, in fact, constituted a familiar, long-established communication facility between sovereign communities. Permanent embassies, frequent reporting by overseas diplomats to their home governments, availability of foreign service personnel with command of foreign languages, a generally accepted form for diplomatic correspondence, an international code of courteous behavior for diplomats—these have been vital elements in the international communication medium. They have enabled governments to maintain rapport with other governments, to observe how those governments act, and generally to possess knowledge of those governments' national interests and policies. The knowledge is invaluable in the formulation of one's own policies and in the anticipation of clashes with the policies of others. When clashes occur, the facilities for discussing them rationally and tactfully (significantly, the word *diplomatic* has now assumed the meaning of "tactful") are available. The "loss of face" attendant upon a nation-state having to swallow its pride and be the first to undertake a mission to another state is precluded. The delicate matter of couching opinions, demands, and even threats in terms conveying the meaning desired, yet not unduly offending the recipient, is provided for by standard diplomatic form and vocabulary. Diplomats have been trained to say the nastiest things in the nicest way! In a word, diplomacy has been a valuable lubricant of international politics.

How this lubricant has prevented international gear-stripping and burned-out bearings can be readily demonstrated. The briefest survey of

United States diplomacy will reveal that major issues such as the annexation of Louisiana, defining the Canadian-United States border, opening
Japan to western commerce, and founding the United Nations were accomplished through diplomatic negotiation.

The United Nations, itself, is a continuing, multilateral diplomatic
conference. Unending negotiations, involving so many nation-states in
every part of the globe, represent something new in diplomacy, but
fundamentally the United Nations functions within the framework of
older diplomatic practice.

Finally, in time of war diplomatic negotiation has played an important
role. Belligerents formally break their diplomatic ties with each other,
but through neutrals they continue to maintain tenuous diplomatic contact. Before the innovation of total war aimed at unconditional surrender
by the enemy, circuitous diplomatic channels generally made peace
negotiations possible before either side collapsed militarily. Indeed,
history would record most wars being ended in this fashion, despite the
experiences of World Wars I and II. Most recent examples would be the
truces of 1953 in Korea, and 1954 in Vietnam.

Upon the foregoing evidence is based the assertion that diplomacy has
contributed very significantly to the relief of international tensions, many
times avoiding a test of armed force, frequently abbreviating such a test.
Indeed, it has been the principal and normal means of adjusting international differences since the emergence of the nation-state system.

To be impressed with the past role of diplomatic negotiation, however,
does not necessarily warrant a positive answer to the question: Is diplomacy feasible today? At least two factors in the current environment have
created difficulties that diplomacy has not faced before: popular or
democratic participation in foreign affairs, and the unique international
situation bequeathed by World War II. Examination of the impact of
these two developments, therefore, follows.

DEMOCRACY AND DIPLOMACY

It may come as a surprise to learn that until very recently diplomatic
activity was not nearly as apparent to the average citizen as it is today.
The public, even in totalitarian states, is now offered a front-row seat in
many current diplomatic negotiations. Special conferences are scheduled
in an unending stream. Preconference publicity ranges from newspaper
reporting of the agendas to televised tours of the conference city. The
meetings themselves are blanketed with newsmen, who record the words
of everyone and freely interpret what they mean. Photographs of smiling
chiefs of state and issuance of communiqués impress the public with its
proximity to diplomatic activity. In addition, legislatures investigate,
deliberate, and legislate foreign policies. Treaty provisions not imme-

diately revealed, such as the Yalta agreement, occasion criticism by press and parliaments against secret and, by implication, bad diplomacy. All this is a recent development, which considerably postdates both the arrival of democratic government and a free press.

Diplomats' Autonomy Before 1914

Up to World War I, diplomacy was carried on largely without the knowledge or control of the electorate. Several factors were responsible: First, the prolonged period without a general European war and the abbreviated course of local conflicts created an atmosphere in which foreign relations did not seem very vital to the average man. Second, of all areas of government activity democratization had least affected the foreign service corps. A diplomatic career required education, a private source of income, and not infrequently political connections. As a result, diplomatic personnel was drawn mainly from the leisure class. It maintained an exclusiveness, a dignity, a prestige that permitted it to go about its business without very much prying by legislators, journalists, or politicians. As a matter of fact, the European diplomat before 1914 was a good deal more at home in the company of foreign diplomats than in that of most of his fellow countrymen. He was distinguished by a certain loyalty to his profession, as well as to the international social set which practiced it.

The resultant atmosphere was of considerable significance to diplomatic negotiation. Men of long experience, with confidence in the personal integrity of the foreign diplomats with whom they did business, carried on negotiations in the quiet seclusion of embassies, chateaux, and manor houses. They haggled, compromised, and sometimes lied, but they did so behind closed doors. Their brilliant strokes and their mistakes remained largely unpublished. They answered only to their foreign ministers who listened attentively to their advice and accorded them considerable freedom of action. Decisions in foreign policy, therefore, were made without amateurish meddling and the pressure of public opinion. They were also made with binding effect upon millions of people, who had no opportunity to register protests over how these diplomats defined national interests or committed the public to courses of action not of its choosing.

Because "secret diplomacy" of this kind came to be associated with the factors behind World War I, considerable criticism of it developed, and the way was paved for certain innovations in the traditional conduct of diplomacy.

Democratic Diplomacy of the Post-1918 Period

The principal charge against prewar "secret diplomacy" was that it not only had failed to prevent war, but it had actually hastened war's coming. This charge was based on the evidence that, by making alliances with some states against others (Germany and Austria against Russia, France and Russia against Germany), the diplomats had divided Europe into two armed camps. When an international crisis arose, these alliances quickly involved all the major powers of Europe in a conflict which had started as a relatively localized affair. Thus, in the 1914 crisis, Germany allied with Austria supported the latter in an uncompromising policy which produced war with Serbia backed by Russia. Similarly, France, instead of exerting her influence for conciliation, gave priority to her Russian alliance and promised military support to Russia if needed. The actions led to a deepening of the crisis and eventually to general war.

This kind of diplomacy was viewed as bankrupt. Who was responsible for it? Many eyes turned to the professional diplomats and chiefs of state who had authored the alliances and then tragically given them support. Why had their fatal course of action not been arrested? Because, came the answer, the diplomats had been permitted to pursue their trade in secret, without the knowledge or approval of the citizens whose lives were at stake. Had the people known of these secret agreements, they, the ardent advocates of peace, would have insisted upon a different course of diplomatic action. The corrective cited for this dangerous, secret, undemocratic kind of diplomacy was democratic control of foreign policy. Because Woodrow Wilson was the chief exponent of this school of thought, the new twist to diplomacy is often referred to as Wilsonian diplomacy.

Wilsonian diplomacy. In his famous Fourteen Points, defining the war aims of the United States, Wilson expressed the criticism of the old diplomacy just noted. Point One called for: [9] "Open covenants of peace, openly arrived at, after which there shall be no private international understandings of any kind but diplomacy shall proceed always frankly and in the public view." Wilson visualized foreign affairs being conducted in the same manner as domestic affairs in a democracy. This implied confidence in the citizenry's interest, knowledge, and judgments of foreign policy, public debate on it, expression of majority opinion on it in the legislative branch of the government, and approval by the legislative branch of all action undertaken in foreign affairs.

With its facilities for publicly recording all treaties and its planned substitution of collective security for alliances, the League of Nations represented a major attempt to inaugurate this new diplomacy.

It is true that, contrary to his precepts, Wilson found it necessary at the Paris Peace Conference (1919) to engage in a certain amount of secret diplomacy. In his very battle to secure the agreement of other nations to his League concept, he was obliged to go into closed sessions

[9] Dept. of State, *Papers Relating to the Foreign Relations of the United States* (1918) (Washington, D.C., Government Printing Office, 1933), Suppl. I, Vol. I, p. 405.

with the leaders of Britain, France, Japan, and Italy. Behind those closed doors, certain of the Fourteen Points had to be delicately compromised— to accommodate the territorial gains secretly agreed upon by the Allies during the war. For example, Japanese claims to economic concessions in Chinese Shantung were supported reluctantly by Wilson to secure Japanese adherence to the League of Nations. This dilemma, however, and the way in which Wilson met it did not alter his fundamental endorsement of open diplomacy.

To illustrate the new diplomatic approach upon his return to the United States, Wilson made a speaking tour of the nation in order to win public support for ratification of the Treaty of Versailles. And in the election of 1920, Wilson committed the Democratic Party to a clear-cut stand in favor of United States' membership in the League.

At the Washington Naval Conference (1921–22), the Republican Secretary of State, Charles Evans Hughes, endorsed the new diplomacy in a dramatic public announcement to the delegates of what the United States sought at the conference and what the United States sought from the other nations represented. The pacts drawn up at that conference were made public, as were all treaties entered into by the United States during the interwar period.

Throughout the world generally, Wilsonian diplomacy was much in evidence during the 1920's. Secret clauses were contained in certain agreements negotiated by the European states, most notably in 1925 between disarmed Germany and ostracized Russia, in which Russia granted Germany the right to carry on military training in Russia where Allied supervisors of German disarmament could not check. Nevertheless, the League of Nations printing office did a "land office" business publishing the texts of "open covenants of peace, openly arrived at."

With the rise of dictatorships, the diplomatic crisis over Fascist Italy's attack upon Ethiopia in 1935, French efforts to build a new alliance against Nazi Germany, and the birth of the Rome-Berlin Axis in 1936, Wilsonian diplomacy went into eclipse everywhere, except perhaps in Britain and the United States. To the bitter end of his "appeasement" policy, Neville Chamberlain, British Prime Minister (1937–40), dealt with Hitler in conferences whose proceedings and agreements were made public. Both Chamberlain and Roosevelt made public addresses the occasions for appealing to Hitler to abandon aggression; both responded to public opinion in their respective electoral campaigns; and both devoted much attention to persuading public opinion to accept their foreign policies and the diplomatic means of pursuing them.

During World War II diplomacy was, of course, considerably restricted since it ceased almost entirely between the Axis states and the Allies. However, relations between allies, between belligerents and neutrals, among neutrals, and even between belligerents just before the surrender did afford much room for diplomatic activity. Much of it, in spite of military considerations, was of the Wilsonian variety. Press releases and public announcements accompanied every one of the numerous conferences between the Allies. Probably the single major exception was that of the Crimean conference (February, 1945). There, the terms for Russia's entry into the war against Japan, and an Anglo-American agreement to release to the U.S.S.R. all Soviet citizens found in Axis prison camps, or in the Axis armed forces, were not made known publicly. In contrast, the San Francisco and Potsdam conferences (1945) followed Wilsonian diplomacy.

Since 1945 democratic diplomacy has also been much in evidence. This does not mean that all diplomatic activity in the United Nations, or in the many postwar bilateral and multilateral conferences, has been carried on in full view of the public or in response to popular wishes. The layman cannot be certain how large a role secret diplomacy may have played since 1945. Certainly, corridor conversations and private "off-the-record" meetings remain a part of diplomatic activity. Nevertheless, Wilsonian diplomacy is very much alive today, as is evidenced by a few examples. The long, persistent search by the various postwar British governments for diplomatic formulas to reduce East-West tension reflects a response to the British public's intense desire for peace. Undoubtedly, one of President Dwight D. Eisenhower's most significant actions was the negotiation of a popularly demanded Korean truce in 1953. Despite the practice of limiting the Soviet public's sources of information, Moscow leaders also reveal an awareness of the Russian public's yearning for peace by their frequent preachments on how the Kremlin labors for international understanding. As Dag Hammarskjold, Secretary-General of the United Nations, commented: [10] "The diplomat who works . . . without recognition—and a proper handling—of the publicity aspect of his work, or without giving to public opinion its proper place in the picture, has little place in our world of today."

Further emphasis upon democratic formulation and implementation of foreign policy has been evinced in the United States Congress' insistence that it exercise more control over the expenditure of funds it has appropriated for foreign affairs. The delayed publication of the complete text of President Franklin D. Roosevelt's Yalta Agreement, in which certain "secret" clauses had been incorporated, added support (in the opinion of many Americans) to the argument that more popular control of diplomacy was needed. This reaction was one of the contributing factors to the movement headed by Senator John Bricker, which was directed at limiting, through constitutional amendment, the President's powers to conclude executive agreements without congressional assent.

[10] Dag Hammarskjold, "New Diplomatic Techniques," in *Vital Speeches,* December 1, 1953, pp. 107–108.

Wilsonian diplomacy has not, however, been endorsed by all demo-crats. Even some who initially believed it desirable have become critical of popular participation in diplomatic negotiation.

Criticisms of Wilsonian diplomacy. A principal objection to Wilsonian diplomacy has been the charge that publicity of the kind now surround-ing diplomatic negotiation has a very damaging effect. Such criticism can best be understood if the fundamental objective of negotiations is recalled. Negotiations are often initiated when each side discloses its maximum demands to the other side. This step is then followed by persuasion, bargaining, and pressuring until a compromise line of agree-ment is reached somewhere between the positions from which each side began. To carry this operation on successfully, in full view of the bargain-ing states' citizenry, is almost impossible, according to some observers.

When a nation's diplomats pose their maximum demands, the people of their country are inclined to assume that this is what should be ob-tained from the negotiation. How far to retreat from the maximum toward the minimum demands is a matter of shrewd judgment, based on skillful analysis of the opposition. It is not a matter for the divided and more emotional opinion often held by the public. If the public is a partner to the negotiation, its opinion will intrude into the situation with often fatal consequences. The nature of the compromise, or even the issue of whether there should be any compromise, can become hopelessly snarled in debate. Diplomats can hardly help becoming unduly sensitive to what the press is saying and to the sometimes irresponsible charge that they are sacrificing principle in their diplomatic maneuvering. They become rigid so as not to be called weak. As Dag Hammarskjold put it, "Open diplomacy may . . . easily become frozen diplomacy" [11] because it sheds its maneuverability; the maximum conditions, originally intended as a bargaining device, become the minimum terms, and no compromise is ever reached. It is a common temptation of a western diplomat to return from an international conference as a hero because he has not "yielded" to the communist bloc rather than as one who has "made a deal" with it. The public dreads war, but "Heroes, not horse-traders, are the idols of public opinion." [12]

In another way, too, public participation in diplomatic intercourse can prove disruptive. Assuming that a compromise between two opponents is reached, the parliamentary ratification of that agreement may be blocked by legislators under pressure of public opinion in their constituencies. Although this is undoubtedly in the democratic tradition, this kind of repudiation of diplomatic agreements further hinders successful negotia-tion.

Finally, and perhaps most fundamentally, to admit the citizenry to a

[11] *Ibid.*, p. 108.
[12] Morgenthau, *op. cit.*, p. 520.

share in diplomacy at the negotiating stage means opening the door to participation by people who are not only divided in opinion, but who, today at least, are frequently not qualified to deal with foreign policy. The average citizen is not qualified because he lacks accurate and complete information; he lacks information partly because he lacks sustained interest in the course of diplomacy and partly because it is a full-time job to acquire the necessary information. Further, not having a comprehensive outlook, he is more susceptible to short-range rather than to long-range considerations. For example, the public of Britain eventually saw the unwisdom of saddling Germany with the reparations it had demanded in 1919, but by the time it recognized it, the damage had already been done.

Charles B. Marshall, a former member of the Department of State's Policy Planning Staff, summarized these charges against the public speaking as a participant in diplomatic activity: [13]

> Popular opinion is not of much, if any, value in helping in the discovery of answers to the problems in this field [diplomacy]. It certainly counts, however, in setting bounds to the area of maneuver available to those charged with the responsibility.

In conclusion, criticism of Wilsonian diplomacy is directed at the limitations that experience has revealed is placed upon diplomatic negotiation by the requirement of "open covenants, openly arrived at." Critics insist that foreign policy cannot be conducted in the same manner as domestic policy. An international conference is not the same as a New England town meeting. Negotiations over international control of atomic weapons cannot be approximated to one in which two school districts negotiate a merger.

Responding to democratic ideals the conduct of diplomacy has changed since World War I, but the democracies have been confronted with a new dilemma. How can the long-established techniques and procedures of diplomats be applied effectively and at the same time subjected to appropriate popular control? Some suggested answers to this as yet unresolved problem are presented later in the chapter, in "Positions on the Problem." First, however, attention must be directed to the international situation as it has taken shape since the end of World War II.

DIPLOMACY IN THE NEW DIMENSIONS OF COLD WAR

The great changes wrought in so many areas of human activity by World War II have confronted diplomacy with conditions which, even more than the issue of democratic control, pose questions about its cur-

---

[13] Charles Burton Marshall, *The Limits of Foreign Policy* (New York, Holt, 1954), p. 13.

rent value. That international relations, after 1945, entered an era unique in many ways is indicated by the coinage and popularity of the somewhat contradictory phrase *cold war,* to describe relations between communist and noncommunist states. According to the definition offered earlier, that *diplomacy is a means of obtaining for one's country the maximum of one's foreign-policy objectives without resort to war,* it would be logical to maintain that diplomacy, not war, is more characteristic of international relations today. Yet, diplomacy of contemporary East-West relations differs so markedly from the familiar traditional diplomacy (which, incidentally, still prevails in several other areas of international relations) that there has been a reluctance to label it diplomacy—hence cold war. What are the features that make the present diplomatic environment unique?

The Threat of Atomic War

In the past, the threat of war has been invoked on occasion to achieve success in negotiations. However, with the development of atomic weapons, the use of a war threat as a means of bringing pressure to bear in negotiation has very great handicaps. First, in atomic war, where delivery of the first blow is of utmost importance, the suggestion of, or first steps in preparation for, war might easily lead the other party to abandon all negotiation in favor of a quick atomic attack of its own. Consequently, talk of war by diplomats is a much more hazardous business today. Second, no diplomat negotiates, unaware that recourse to war by either side could mean mutual destruction. This is not to say that no government would dare launch an atomic war, but it would be done only in desperate circumstances. In the practical operation of diplomacy, there is no longer room for atomically armed, major powers to threaten war. The atomic age has rendered it obsolete.

Reduction in the Number of Great Powers

Since World War II, the number of great powers has drastically declined. Germany and Japan were defeated and occupied. Italy, a former ally of Germany, was deprived of its previous modest powers and influence. France and Great Britain, greatly weakened by World War II, no longer exercise the power they previously did. Only the United States and the Soviet Union remain as the principal great powers. This reduction in the number of great powers has posed another difficulty for diplomats.

In the past, diplomats were generally successful in preventing war or negotiating its conclusion by mobilizing against an aggressor all or most remaining major powers. The key to this operation was, of course, the presence of more than two power centers, which could be enlisted on the side of the weaker to deter the stronger from resorting to a policy of domination. Today there exists no third force sufficiently strong to influence decisively the policy of one or the other superpower by threatening to join the other. Even Great Britain, the third strongest military power, has not been capable of undertaking an independent foreign policy and of performing her historical role as the balancer in the power scheme.

So long as it persists, this situation means that only an elementary, bipolar balance of power obtains, and because of its simplicity, the balance is one which can be more easily upset by one of the two centers of power, thereby making the possibility of war more likely. This confronts diplomats today with an even heavier burden than in the days before World War II.

Peculiarities of the Two Superpowers

Had the U.S.A. and the U.S.S.R. been, as they formerly were, only two of half a dozen great powers, their own peculiarities in international behavior would have been less important. However, by the nature of their predominance their peculiarities are of great significance for diplomacy.

Reference is made, on the one hand, to the sudden catapulting of the Soviet Union into a position of world leadership with very little preparation for the role, to the Soviet leaders' dialectic approach to foreign affairs, and to the Soviet concept of the ultimate establishment of a world communist society.

Long isolated and partly Asiatic, Russia has had less experience with the "give and take" of diplomacy than any other European state. The replacement of Czarist diplomats, since 1917, by men raised in the seclusion of Soviet society has not been conducive to change in this respect. Furthermore, if, as is alleged, Soviet diplomats are wedded to the idea that immutable economic processes control the major course of events, they must view diplomacy as useful only in arriving at temporary and expedient settlements. Finally, if, as has also been alleged, coexistence with noncommunist states is only a temporary and not a permanent state of affairs, diplomacy is merely a skirmish in preparation for world revolution and eventual abandonment of diplomacy.

On the other hand, the United States, in an equally important role, possesses peculiarities also troublesome to diplomacy. Like Russia, America is a relative newcomer to world diplomacy. Long secure in its oceanic isolation and dominated by the attractions of the continental interior, the United States had little occasion to act as a world power before 1898. Unfortunately, this remoteness from foreign problems was conducive to a feeling among Americans that they need not be bothered with diplomatic headaches. When the United States emerged as a world power and the headaches intruded into their lives, Americans resented them. With characteristic optimism and confidence, they anticipated their elimination, just as Indians, Mexicans, the prairie, the Rockies, and Spaniards had been "eliminated" as unwanted obstacles in the stream of American history. This inexperience and unrealistic approach to diplomacy has made the task of United States foreign policy most arduous. Easy, rapid, and permanent solutions to diplomatic problems have been publicly expected. When the solutions were not immediately forthcoming, in a world over which the United States did not have absolute control, many people became disillusioned and tried to explain it as, for instance, the machinations of munitions-makers, the allegedly belligerent predilections of leaders like Franklin Roosevelt, Winston Churchill, or Adolph Hitler, communist aggression and subversion, or the ineptitude of the American Department of State. This has not been helpful to the development of a diplomatic corps with high morale, dedication of purpose, and professional competence.

In other ways, too, America brought peculiar attitudes to the diplomatic arena. Unconscious of a balance of power through much of its history, the United States adopted a critical attitude toward this device. Idealistic in their outlook, Americans echoed President Wilson's condemnation of secret diplomacy and his insistence that all states, like all men, should be given an equal voice in the diplomatic councils of the world. Finally, as democrats locked in battle with a frightening and alien ideology, many citizens of the United States came to believe that their country could not establish the community of interest with the Soviets that diplomacy demands in order to function.

These unprecedented points of view on diplomacy and international affairs generally held by many Russians and many Americans constitute another new condition to which diplomatic practice has had to adjust.

The Expansion of the Diplomatic Arena

A factor responsible for vastly complicating foreign policy-making in the period since 1945 has been the rapid shrinkage of distance, referred to in Chapter 6. United States' national interest, Soviet Russian national interest, the national interests of every nation-state are now global, in the sense that they cannot be defined or defended without consideration of events and situations all over the world. As recently as the late 1930's, the United States Department of State regarded places like Cyprus, India, and Vietnam as beyond its area of concern and of little consequence in the formulation of American foreign policy. The Kremlin viewed Guatemala, Iceland, and South Africa similarly. The British Foreign Office, with wide imperial interests, was more global-minded, and today brings more experience and background to the task of global diplomacy. Britain, however, as has been pointed out, today is not one of the two superpowers responsible for the most important decisions.

Aside from the geographic growth of diplomacy's area of action, problems far more complicated than the narrow political questions of the past make greater demands upon diplomacy today. The economic, ideo-logical, psychological, and military factors now entering into diplomatic consideration weigh heavily upon diplomats. It is one thing to negotiate a border between the United States and Canada, and quite another to formulate a policy in Washington toward India. American national inter-ests are so much more difficult to define where India is concerned, and a policy so much more difficult to undertake. What kind of economic aid, if any, is best for India—and the United States? How should aid, if any, be extended? What should America's position be toward Indian nonalignment in the cold war? How best can the United States represent itself ideologi-cally to these Asian people? What repercussions upon United States' rela-tions with Pakistan, or SEATO, or the neutralist bloc should be anticipated from America's Indian policy? Complexities like these, which press daily upon the staffs in the State Department building and its twenty annexes in Washington, did not confront Secretaries of State Jefferson, John Quincy Adams, or even Seward or Hay.

Added to these diplomatic burdens is the emergence from a colonial status of a large number of new states in Asia and Africa. Not only must these nation-states be fitted into the diplomats' global picture, but state departments and foreign offices face the added difficulty of unfamiliar cultures, hypersensitive nationalism, and lack of tradition and experience in diplomacy as practiced by the West. In a sense Afro-Asia constitutes a new, unpredictable, fluid element in world politics with which all the older nation-states, but especially the United States and Russia, are still striving to come to grips. Indeed, Afro-Asia has become potentially the most significant arena in the cold war. Witness the tour of Premier Bul-ganin and Party Secretary Khrushchev through South Asia in 1955, Secre-tary of State Dulles' frequent trips to Asian capitals, Washington's invita-tions to leaders of Burma, Indonesia, India, and other Asian states to come to the United States, and the Soviets' efforts to launch an economic offensive in this area!

These growing responsibilities lead to another new set of problems. Even if recognized, how can such far-flung, complex, dynamic challenges to diplomats be met? What can be done to bring together the informa-tion—economic, political, military, ideological, and psychological—essen-tial to formulating a comprehensive, effective foreign policy? Who shall undertake thoughtful reflection upon this information preliminary to de-ciding upon a course of action? And once decided, how should such a policy be carried out? Policies do not implement themselves. Government agencies must be given assignments, the efforts must be co-ordinated, and all must be kept informed of alterations in plans.

A cursory glance at the United States Department of State discloses the extent of expansion of United States' diplomatic facilities and per-sonnel as a result of the growing responsibilities. In 1790, Secretary of

State Jefferson had a staff of 8 persons, a number which expanded to 5,444 in 1939, and to 29,000 in 1956. The State Department's budget in 1939 stood at 17 million dollars, in 1956 at 271 million dollars.[14] Moreover, these statistics do not include the 200,000 civilians employed overseas by 40 other agencies of the United States government, or the foreign-aid budgets which have been between 3 and 6 billion dollars annually since the end of World War II. In 1777, Benjamin Franklin and his hotel room served to represent the American government in Paris. In 1956, the United States Embassy in Paris occupied seven buildings, employed a staff of 2,485, and cost 15 million dollars annually.[15] This gigantic operation, in its administration alone, imposes a heavy responsibility upon those charged with carrying on American diplomacy. A similar responsibility devolves upon diplomats in other countries.

The factors enumerated should make clear why and how the task confronting diplomats has been altered and complicated by the new dimensions of the contemporary international scene. If diplomatic activity has increased, so have the challenges. How diplomacy has functioned in this altered environment of the cold war is the final concern of this section.

THE DIPLOMATIC RECORD SINCE 1947

As has been noted, from World War II there emerged two major centers of world power. These two centers have been the nuclei for coalitions of nation-states, now designated as western and Soviet blocs. In Central Europe and the Far East, power vacuums, created by the defeat of Germany, Italy, and Japan in World War II, brought the two blocs face to face in highly sensitive situations. In both continents the Soviet and western blocs vied with each other to fill these vacuums and defined their minimum objectives in terms at least of preventing their rivals from dominating the areas in question. Each also sought means of attaching the zones between the two power blocs to its own side ideologically, militarily, and economically. The ensuing tension and the diplomatic efforts seeking reduction of it can be understood better with a brief survey of each of the vital areas caught between West and East.

Germany

Because of its human and natural resources and its central European location, Germany even in defeat became a major and focal point of tension and negotiation in the cold war.

Symbolic of the completeness of Germany's defeat was the initial Allied decision to divide Germany into four zones of occupation, one each to the British, Americans, French, and Russians. No central German govern-

---

[14] *U.S. News and World Report,* August 10, 1956, pp. 74–75.
[15] *Ibid.,* p. 80.

ment was to be allowed, at least until after a formal peace treaty had been drawn up at some indeterminate future date. A four-power Allied Control Council, consisting of the military commanders of the four zones, was to serve for the administration of German affairs. The Council's decisions were to be unanimously approved by the four commanders. Economically, Germany was to be treated as a unit by this Council. The arrangement, placing a high premium upon diplomatic negotiations between the occupying powers, proved unworkable.

Difficulties arose almost immediately in late 1945 because of French and Russian opposition to effective economic integration of the four zones. This led the United States to halt reparations deliveries from its zone to the Russians. In this atmosphere, the prospects for agreement among the occupation powers on peace terms for Germany evaporated. Accordingly, the Anglo-Americans, and in time the French, undertook to win West German support by granting local self-government in their zones and, in 1949, recognizing a West German Federal Republic encompassing the former British, French, and American zones of occupation.

Russian response to this policy was a blockade of Berlin—still jointly occupied and inside the Russian zone—in 1948–49. The pressure, it was hoped, would force the western powers to abandon their program in West Germany. The Allies, by means of an air-lift, indicated that they would not yield. Stalin then evinced a willingness to negotiate, and the *status quo* in Berlin was re-established, but the policy of integrating the three western zones continued. The Soviets next countered with the creation of the German Democratic Republic in 1949.

While the German problem remained within the sphere of diplomacy, no permanent solution to the problem was found. The deadlock on German reunification was revealed again and again at diplomatic conferences. There was no war, but there also was no negotiated settlement. Why was diplomacy not more successful in this area?

The answer must be sought in the positions of the East and West power blocs. The United States and its allies agreed to German reunification on the condition that free elections be held throughout Germany to elect the government of the new Germany. Since such an election, it was generally believed, would result in a prowestern German regime, the Russians did not accept the western proposal. Obviously, Moscow preferred a divided Germany to a prowestern Germany. Similarly, if the West could not win Germany to its side, it, too, would accept a disunited Germany.

Austria

In many respects, Austria demonstrated all the characteristics of the East-West stalemate encountered in Germany. Jointly occupied, with all four powers maintaining troops in the capital, Vienna, inside the Russian zone, Austria was another Germany on a smaller scale. As with Germany, neither East nor West would countenance Austria's gravitation into the other's camp. Ending occupation and free elections promised to produce an anticommunist government in Vienna which Russia was unwilling to tolerate. No wonder the diplomats found Austria as frustrating an issue as Germany! As Secretary of State Dulles reported,[16] "Throughout 8 years, approximately 400 four-power meetings were held at various levels. The Western Powers made every effort to conclude a treaty, but the Soviets, time after time, found new and irrelevant excuses for refusing agreement." One of the final Soviet objections, raised after most of the others had been resolved, was insistence upon the prior completion of a German treaty.

Early in 1955, however, the Russians indicated a willingness to consider the Austrian problem separately from that of Germany. From this point on, events moved quickly. By May, 1955, a treaty of peace between the four occupation powers and Austria was signed. Under its terms, the occupation ended and Austria regained her independence and borders of 1938 (the date when Hitler annexed Austria to Germany). In return, Austria agreed neither to possess nor to work upon atomic weapons or guided missiles, nor to enter into military alliances, nor to permit establishment of foreign bases upon Austrian soil. Austrian reparations to the amount of 150 million dollars were to be paid in goods to Russia, and the latter agreed to return her oil fields and Danube steamship company to Austria. By October, 1955, all occupation troops had been withdrawn and the treaty became fully operative. What had produced this about-face? Could diplomacy take credit for this break in the East-West diplomatic log-jam?

Fundamentally, the resolution of the Austrian issue seems to be related more to changing conditions than to greater efficiency by the diplomats. The West's approval of West German rearmament and membership in NATO apparently stimulated the post-Stalin Soviet leaders to modify their foreign policy in several aspects, including their position on Austria. In order to stall German rearmament, the Russians, it is believed, hoped by their Austrian policy to induce the Germans to accept a peace settlement like that of Austria, which would similarly neutralize Germany. If the analysis is correct, diplomatic negotiation was not directly responsible for the Austrian settlement, although it would not be incorrect to credit western diplomacy with partial responsibility for this conspicuous reduction of cold war tension.

Other Vital Areas

Along the rest of the periphery that marks the border between the Eurasian-centered Soviet bloc and the more widespread western bloc are a number of other tension-ridden areas—the eastern Mediterranean,

---

[16] U.S. Senate, 84th Congr., 1st sess., *The Austrian Peace Treaty* (Washington, D.C., Government Printing Office, 1955), p. 2.

Indochina, Formosa, and Korea. Here, diplomatic negotiation has not been outstandingly successful in achieving adjustments, although it has been employed and has achieved some relaxation of tension.

In Greece, where a communist revolt (1945–48) against the prowestern government invited outside intervention, and in Turkey, upon which Soviet pressure was exerted for a share in control of the Dardanelles Straits, economic and military measures were adopted instead of diplomacy. Under the Truman Doctrine, the United States extended aid to the Greek and Turkish governments; as a result, the Greek communists were forcibly suppressed, and the Turks refused concessions to Russia.

In Indochina, negotiation was not quite as completely ignored. The general background of this issue was discussed in Chapter 4. It need only be noted here that French military weakness and Anglo-American reluctance to commit armed forces to the area persuaded the West to seek a negotiated settlement. The communists, on the other hand, apparently were willing to halt hostilities rather than risk full-scale western intervention. The outcome was diplomatic negotiation at the Geneva conference of 1954. Here, an armistice was signed, with the condition that France would immediately abandon northern Vietnam and gradually evacuate southern Vietnam. It was further agreed that elections would be held in both North and South Vietnam in 1956, as a step toward reunifying the countries. Both sides undoubtedly hoped that such elections would be in their favor. The elections were not held, owing largely to the unwillingness of the South Vietnam (noncommunist) government to risk the step without assurances that the elections would be wholly free and democratic. Thus, diplomacy was effective in enabling the warring sides to reach an armistice and divide Vietnam, but it did not produce a final settlement.

Diplomatic negotiation has not yet taken place on the Formosa issue. United States naval forces and Chiang Kai-shek's U.S.-equipped Nationalist Army on Formosa face Red Chinese military forces on the mainland of Asia. The military watchful waiting will continue until one or the other side does one of two things—seeks a military showdown with armed force, or seeks to find a settlement through negotiation. If negotiation is to be fruitful, diplomatic experience makes it clear that some bargaining points will have to be introduced. Conceivably, these points would include Red China's recognition of Formosan independence, United States' recognition of Red China, and the seating of Red China in the United Nations.

In Korea, where the war of 1950–53 came closest to precipitating a general conflagration, diplomacy again was resorted to only in the armistice negotiations. Although the armistice is not to be ignored, it should be recognized that it was preceded by a highly dangerous and bloody military probing between Red China and the United States, assisted mainly by the British Commonwealth. The armistice recognized the military situation as it was, although negotiations hinged mainly on the issue of prisoners of war. The United States and its allies insisted that prisoners be given the choice of repatriation or seeking asylum elsewhere. Well-founded fears that many prisoners in Allied hands would elect not to return to communist territory delayed communist agreement, but eventually it was reached. Neutral India supervised the prisoner exchange, and truce teams were established to assure observance of the armistice line and to check on the pledges that neither side would build up its military installations, especially airfields, during the armistice period. The failure of subsequent attempts to negotiate a final settlement of the Korean War emphasized once again the very limited part that diplomatic negotiation has played in the cold war.

Advocates of diplomatic negotiation, as a means of adjusting international differences without war, do not agree, however, that diplomacy's record since 1947 proves it is not a feasible instrument. Diplomacy has not been more effective, they say, because its nature and purpose have been largely ignored in the tenseness of the cold war. Dorothy Fosdick, a former member of the Policy Planning Staff in the Office of the Secretary of State, has emphasized in her book *Common Sense and World Affairs* the need for clearer perception of what foreign policy can and cannot accomplish—and concomitantly what negotiation can and cannot accomplish. Some of Miss Fosdick's maxims on common-sense diplomacy furnish a helpful note upon which to conclude this section. The maxims are chapter titles in her book: [17]

To make a fine choice, yet decline to pay for it, is folly.

Fashioning your methods in the light of your end is prudence.

To believe you are more generous than you really are is hazardous.

Asking only for immediate and tangible rewards is shortsighted.

Safety lies in acting on the truth of the matter rather than the imagination of it.

To talk as well as you perform makes sense.

Since there is not universal agreement on the value of traditional diplomatic negotiation as a technique of international adjustment in the twentieth century, differing views on the contemporary merits of diplomacy, in its traditional and its democratic contexts, are presented in the next section. The first view presented is that of the American Friends Service Committee, whose Quaker approach to foreign policy the reader has already encountered. A second view is that of the philosopher and publicist, James Burnham, who has maintained that the United States is already at war with the Soviet Union, and who has urged that the United

[17] Dorothy Fosdick, *Common Sense and World Affairs* (New York, Harcourt Brace, 1955), pp. xi–xii.

States turn from what he calls a policy of defense ("containment") to a policy of offense ("liberation"). A third view is that of the "realist" student of international politics, Hans Morgenthau. All three positions focus most sharply on the feasibility of diplomatic negotiation with the Soviet Union. It will be noted that the American Friends Service Committee and Professor Morgenthau agree on the importance and necessity of diplomacy, in contrast with Mr. Burnham who believes that traditional diplomacy (as far as the Soviet Union is concerned) ended with the advent to power of the Soviet regime in Russia. However, it should be clear that, although Morgenthau and the Friends agree on the value of diplomacy and implicitly attack Burnham's defeatist attitude toward diplomacy and his crusading, more militant alternative to diplomacy, they differ markedly in their own presuppositions and probably in the way in which they would employ the instruments of diplomacy. The Friends, for example, write from a candidly pacifist position, are committed to nonviolence, and are deeply hostile to a philosophy of power politics. Morgenthau calls himself a "realist" in international politics; regards the concept of national interest and the pursuit of it as the principal signposts in international politics; is critical of applying abstract and universal moral principles to the actions of states; and criticizes as "idealistic" both those who would abstain from the allegedly evil struggle for power and those who would exercise power in a crusading and imperialistic fashion.

POSITIONS
ON THE PROBLEM

1. DIPLOMACY CAN WORK IF THE UNITED STATES
CAN APPROACH NEGOTIATION IN A NEW SPIRIT

(The following position is taken from *Steps to Peace: A Quaker View of U.S. Foreign Policy*, a report prepared in 1951 for the American Friends Service Committee.[18])

In the foregoing analysis we have suggested that the attempt of the United States to limit the expansion of Soviet Communism by force has not only failed to advance our ultimate purposes, but has tended to alienate our friends and increase the risk of all-out war. Since the only alternative to attempting to reach a decision by force is to attempt to reach one by negotiation and diplo-

[18] The selections appear on pp. 31–38 and p. 63. *Steps to Peace,* American Friends Service Committee, 20 South 12th St., Philadelphia 7, Penn.

macy, we have suggested at a number of points that great reliance must be placed upon negotiation if satisfactory progress is to be made toward building the kind of world we want.

Negotiation with other governments is a permanent assignment of the American Department of State. It must not be defaulted if the people's interests are to be served, and yet, unfortunately, the word itself has acquired an unpleasant connotation when applied to the international scene. Many Americans equate it with appeasement, and appeasement has a stigma not likely to be overcome, despite the innocence of its dictionary definition. Indeed, we have reached a point in our international thinking where any suggestion that we should sit down with other parties to a dispute and discuss the basis for settlement is certain to be branded by large segments of the press and public as a scheme to sell out American interests. This confusion of terms presents a dangerous block to peace, for negotiation has always been an honorable and valid method for settling international disputes. . . .

Not only should we be prepared to negotiate, we should also be prepared to accept the compromises which are its inevitable accompaniment. There is nothing wrong with compromise, as long as it is honorable. Indeed it often materially advances a nation's long-term interests. What we need to guard against in negotiating with Russia or with any other nation is unprincipled diplomacy—the effort to make settlements at another's expense, as happened at Munich. These negotiations have been rightly stigmatized because the concessions offered were dishonorable. We must never stoop to dishonorable negotiation, but the mere fact that it is possible to negotiate dishonorably ought not to keep us from negotiating at all.

There is a substantial block of American opinion that rejects negotiation because of discouragement. This block feels that the United States has tried to negotiate with Russia for five years and has failed; it feels that we have honestly desired agreements, and that many of our offers have been generous. The representatives of the Soviet Union, on the other hand, appear to have twisted the meaning of our proposals, been evasive in their responses, and vague in their own suggestions. This block of opinion has, therefore, lost confidence in Russian good faith and is prepared to apply force as the only other means at hand. Negotiation continues to receive lip service in so far as it is said that the door is always open, but these expressions of willingness are frequently hedged with pessimism regarding the prospects. Even when conferences are arranged, American leaders express doubt of their success, which is hardly the most promising attitude with which to begin.

All of this discouragement and pessimism is understandable. There is no debate about the difficulty of negotiating with Russia or the fact that up to this point negotiation has not been very fruitful. No one, indeed, can say with assurance that it ever can be fruitful; but before we abandon it altogether, it is worth-while to see whether or not we have taken all the steps we can to make our negotiating efforts successful. Force cannot provide a satisfactory settlement and only a satisfactory settlement will make possible real progress toward our American objective of peace with liberty and plenty for all. If we as Americans are earnest in our desire to achieve these aims, there is nothing more important for us to do at this time than to re-examine our past efforts to negotiate with the Soviet Union. We must ask ourselves whether failure has been due entirely to Russian blocks or whether shortcomings in techniques and procedures of negotiation may also have contributed. The requirements for successful negotiation in domestic affairs are well known, and while it cannot be assumed that what has worked in one framework will necessarily work in another, the least we can do is to apply diligently the best we know to the most difficult problem of our day. . . .

Negotiation Requires a Flexible Attitude

Two conflicting points of view must be reconciled, and this can only happen if both sides are prepared to give up non-essentials for the sake of agreement on essentials. Basic principles must not be compromised, but give-and-take is at the very heart of the whole process, and negotiators must be free to alter their first suggestions as the exploration of conflicting points of view proceeds. It is important to avoid taking a "final" position from which there can be no retreat, for that means the failure of the negotiation effort unless this "final" position is acceptable to the other party. . . .

Negotiation Requires an Open Mind

Each side must be prepared to examine the proposals of the other on their merits. Flexibility on one's own position must be matched by a willingness to try to understand other points of view. This requires that neither side assume its opinion to be clothed in moral infallibility. . . .

Negotiation Requires Privacy

It is important to maintain an atmosphere in which either side can make concessions without embarrassment. This suggests that negotiation cannot always be carried on in a goldfish bowl, a fact industrial negotiators have long been aware of. When differences are under discussion, the representatives of labor and management closet themselves without benefit of press or public. Only the results become public property, to be either accepted or rejected as the constituencies see fit. This technique might well be called one of "open covenants secretly arrived at." It is a sound concept, for it makes possible the essential give-and-take of negotiation which would be quite impossible if the negotiators were required to speak for the record each time they entered the discussion. Positions can be shifted and concessions discussed in the privacy of the conference room in a way that would be impossible in a public forum. Indeed, without privacy, it is doubtful if any delicate negotiation can be carried forward. . . .

Negotiation Requires Persistence

There may come a time when fundamental disagreement on matters of genuine principle forces negotiations to be broken off, but no termination should ever be regarded as permanent, for new developments may serve at any time to break an apparent deadlock. If negotiators become discouraged or exhausted, they should be replaced. . . .

This analysis will indicate why the present writers believe that more could be accomplished in international diplomacy if greater attention were paid to the methods of securing agreement. What has passed for negotiation in the international field since the war has often been something quite different, and there is need for applying the best negotiating techniques of which we are capable. It is doubtful, indeed, if even much less complicated internal disputes could have been resolved by the negotiating techniques we have been using in the international field. . . .

To what extent can new negotiations with the Soviet Union succeed? No one knows. Suspicion and lack of confidence in mutual good faith have grown so great that negotiation on any basis is difficult. Moreover, even if the United States were to make a fresh start, it will still require a new approach on the part of the Russians, whose conduct at the negotiating table has contributed to the present impasse. Patience, and rigid adherence on our part to the best traditions of negotiation may yet bring an end to the Soviet habit of using conferences as a forum for ideological statements. In any event, we have the responsibility of making the record clear as regards our own conduct. A new spirit in diplomacy by this country undoubtedly would have a greater chance of eliciting more constructive responses from Soviet representatives than have past tactics.

Possibly the approach that offers best promise is to attempt negotiation first in those areas where there is a maximum degree of mutual self-interest in an agreement on both sides. . . .

Unless Americans can overcome their emotional distaste for negotiation, there is no hope for reaching the objectives that they have set for their foreign policy. . . .

2. Traditional Diplomacy Won't Work with the Soviet Union [19]

Since 1943 there has been a long series of high-level conferences in which the Soviet Union and the United States have been the principal participants. These have taken place among the heads of state or foreign ministers at Teheran, Yalta, Potsdam, London, New York, and Paris, and they are still taking place. The meetings of the United Nations, both of the Security Council and of the Assembly, are a running addition to the series which, at lower levels, has been almost continuous in one or another field of international activity from refugees to trade regulation to freedom of the press.

The labors of the diplomats in the conference delivery rooms never fail to give birth to public words—memoranda, "understandings," and even treaties like those for Italy, Hungary, Bulgaria, and Rumania. If we consider these documentary offspring singly and at face value, they do not seem at all bad from the point of view of the United States. They are always polite and often friendly. Agreement, at least up to a point, is always reached. There seems, from the documents, to have been a meeting of minds, a give and take, with points conceded and points won on both sides. Democracy, freedom, law, and justice are invariably upheld.

Nevertheless, the historical accompaniment of this succession of documents has been the steady advance of communist power, and the loss of one after another anti-communist position. It somehow works out that when a conference document assigns an asset to the communists—territory or port rights or reparations or administrative control or economic privileges—then that asset is always taken over, usually with back interest. But when the documents allot an asset to non-communists—free elections or political rights (in Berlin, say, or Dairen) or powers of intervention under peace treaties (in the Balkans, for example) or respect for a church or non-communist political parties—then somehow the asset evaporates during the months succeeding the proclamation of the document, and even turns into a liability.

[19] This extract is reprinted from James Burnham, *The Coming Defeat of Communism*, New York, published by The John Day Company, copyright, 1949, 1950, by James Burnham. The selections appear in Chap. III, "The End of Traditional Diplomacy," pp. 35–43.

Something seems to have gone wrong with these conferences and their verbal issue.

The historical function of diplomatic conferences and the agreements or treaties which such conferences produce is very generally misunderstood. In spite of the contrary conviction of most diplomats who attend them, and who need the conviction in order to sustain their own sense of self-importance, diplomatic conferences seldom have much independent causal force in history. Important historical problems are settled by wars, and by the semi- or non-military clash of economic, political, social, and ideological forces. The conferences reflect and articulate the real power equilibrium that has been reached by other means. . . .

We are periodically told that there ought to be "another meeting" . . . in order to "come to an agreement" or to "settle things." But there is really very little that a meeting or a conference can do about agreeing and settling. If basic disagreement exists on the plane of fact, of the real relations of forces, then the conference can only, in the semantically obscure way that conferences have, express that disagreement (express it, perhaps, by coming to an apparent positive agreement on secondary and irrelevant points). If real relations are confused and unsettled, then the meeting will only be symptomatic of that condition by the confusions of its own proceedings. A conference can come to a productive agreement only when the real basis of agreement exists independently of, and prior to, the conference itself.

It does not follow that international conferences are of no use whatever. Merely to record and formalize the facts of political and economic relations is itself a useful function. Then, though their casual influence on history is slight, it is not quite zero. So far as the conferees operate within a common frame of interest, even if that common frame is very spare, their deliberations can show positive results. . . .

But if I want war and you want peace, what is there for us to confer about? . . .

The diplomats of the nations of modern Western civilization have usually entered international conferences with the assumption that, whatever the disputes that divided them, there existed a fundamental basis of agreement; that, with respect to at least certain aims, they were seeking the same thing. Each knew that he was expected to press the particular interests of his own nation as skillfully as he could; but he was aware that these interests were limited on the one hand by his nation's power and on the other by the common framework. If a war had been fought to redress the broken balance of European power, each did as well as he could for his own; but all were agreed that a reasonably viable European structure was the objective. If England and the United States were in dispute over a boundary line, each argued for the most favorable parallel, but both assumed that the line was going to be drawn somewhere, and without war. No one aimed at the literal destruction of peoples. Each might want a favoring arrangement on extradition or tariffs or exchange or radio bands or marine law, but all wanted some arrangement.

The Western representatives have carried this same assumption into the conferences with the Soviet Union. They are not so naïve as some of their critics imagine them to be. They understand, and have understood from the beginning, that there are multitudinous conflicts between the interests of the Soviet Union and those of the Western powers. They have not expected the task of resolving those conflicts to be short or easy. They have also, however, assumed that they and the Soviet representatives share at least some basis of final agreement, however narrow, and seek also at least some of the same things, however few. The Kremlin, they have known, wants as much as it can possibly get—but not, they have thought, everything. The Kremlin is at least agreed that peace, however hard to assure, is desirable. It strives for the most one-sided possible agreement in its favor; but at least it aims at some agreement, on some terms.

In their assumptions, the leaders of the Western nations have been deceived. . . .

The communist objectives with respect to meetings in which non-communists also participate were defined in the early years of this century by Lenin. . . . These meetings or conferences, organized by or with the consent of non-communists, are, like congresses or parliaments in non-communist nations, "agencies of the class enemy." The communist representatives to them are not negotiators, but "agents of the Communist party within the camp of the enemy." A resolution of the Second Congress of the International threatens with immediate expulsion any communist representative who, forgetting that he was only an instrument of the party, might undertake bona fide negotiation with the non-communists.

The communist aims in the conferences (meetings, parliaments, Leagues of Nations, United Nations, whatever the form that the counterrevolutionary organizations might take) are the following:

(1) To use the conference as a "forum" from which to speak to "the masses," and to influence world public opinion in the direction of world communist policy.

(2) By these appeals to the masses, to weaken and to undermine the non-communist representatives and their governments in relation to their respective citizens. . . .

(3) To use every opportunity offered by the inside position at the conferences to divide and embitter relations among the non-communist delegates and governments. . . .

(4) To block or shunt aside, again from the advantageous inside position, attempts by the non-communist governments, particularly by the United States, to develop and pursue an independent anti-communist policy.

(5) To use the conferences as a cover, a screen, a diversion, under the protection of which world communism can proceed with a minimum of hindrance in the carrying out of its own communist policy: namely, the preparation for the open stage of the third world war and the triumph of the world communist empire. Thus a conference on Trieste can cover a coup in Czechoslovakia; or a long, futile meeting on Berlin and Germany can divert attention from China.

It is not excluded that at a particular conference the communists may actually want, for reasons of immediate expediency, agreement on some definite point, usually secondary. They will [seek agreement], if this is consistent with the tactics of the moment. . . .

In general, however, communists do not go to these international conferences —whether of foreign ministers or their deputies, or of heads of state or of United Nations—in order to get agreements. They go precisely in order to block agreements that might inconvenience their plans, and to implement those five aims which I have just summarized. The communists and the non-communists at the conferences are not, thus, in any respect "seeking the same thing."

The result is that, so long as we enter them with the point of view of traditional diplomacy, international conferences with the communists can never serve our interests. . . . The record from 1944 shows that, when judged by the objective terms of the world power balance, we have lost from every conference that has ever been held with the communists, and they have invariably gained. No matter what seemed to have gone on at the conference—Yalta or Potsdam or London or Teheran or New York or Paris, no matter what memoranda or contracts were signed and published at the conclusion, the aftermath never shows a net gain for us, and always shows at least some gain—ranging from a factory or a ship to entire nations—for the enemy.

These uniformly negative results cannot be explained by accident or by the personal ineptness of our representatives. There is no reason to suppose that our representatives are, on the average, any less intelligent or loyal or learned than the communists. The cause of our failures lies in part in the inadequacy of our general foreign policy, and partly in our lack of understanding of the meaning of these conferences with the communists.

Let us put the truth more sharply. For the communists, the international conferences are not mechanisms whereby to secure deals, bargains, adjustments, agreements, or steps toward peace. For the communists, these conferences are battlegrounds; and the performances of the communist delegates are acts of war. Against an enemy who does not fight back, they inevitably win all the victories.

They will continue to do so, until we revise our assumptions, and realize that our problem is not to debate issues but to defeat an opponent.

3. A Realistic Use of Diplomacy Is the Best Means Now Available for Preserving Peace [20]

We have seen that international peace cannot be preserved through the limitation of national sovereignty, and we found the reasons for this failure in the very nature of the relations among nations. We concluded that international peace through the transformation of the present society of sovereign nations into a world state is unattainable under the moral, social, and political conditions prevailing in the world in our time. If the world state is unattainable in our world, yet indispensable for the survival of that world, it is necessary to create the conditions under which it will not be impossible from the outset to establish a world state. As the prime requisite for the creation of such conditions we suggested the mitigation and minimization of those political conflicts which in our time pit the two superpowers against each other and evoke the specter of a cataclysmic war. This method of establishing the preconditions for permanent peace we call peace through accommodation. Its instrument is diplomacy. . . .

THE DECLINE OF DIPLOMACY

Today diplomacy no longer performs the role, often spectacular and brilliant and always important, that it performed from the end of the Thirty Years' War to the beginning of the First World War. The decline of diplomacy set in with the end of the First World War. In the twenties, a few outstanding

[20] Passages are reprinted from *Politics Among Nations*, by Hans J. Morgenthau, by permission of Alfred A. Knopf, Inc., copyright 1948, 1954, by Alfred A. Knopf, Inc., New York, 2nd ed., pp. 505, 511, 516–519, 521, 523–524, 526–529.

diplomatists were still able to make important contributions to the foreign policies of their countries. In the decade preceding the Second World War the part diplomats took in shaping foreign policy became ever smaller, and the decline of diplomacy as a technique of conducting foreign affairs became more and more patent. Since the end of the Second World War, diplomacy has lost its vitality, and its functions have withered away to such an extent as is without precedent in the history of the modern state system. . . .

. . . Imbued with the crusading spirit of the new moral force of nationalistic universalism, and both tempted and frightened by the potentialities of total war, two superpowers, the centers of two gigantic power blocs, face each other in inflexible opposition. They cannot retreat without giving up what they consider vital to them. They cannot advance without risking combat. Persuasion, then, is tantamount to trickery, compromise means treason, and the threat of force spells war.

Given the nature of the power relations between the United States and the Soviet Union, and given the states of mind these two superpowers bring to bear upon their mutual relations, diplomacy has nothing with which to operate and must of necessity become obsolete. Under such moral and political conditions, it is not the sensitive, flexible, and versatile mind of the diplomat, but the rigid, relentless, and one-track mind of the crusader that guides the destiny of nations. The crusading mind knows nothing of persuasion, of compromise, and of threats of force which are meant to make the actual use of force unnecessary. It knows only of victory and of defeat.

If war were inevitable this book might end here. If war is not inevitable, the conditions for the revival of diplomacy and for its successful operation in the service of peace remain to be considered.

The revival of diplomacy requires the elimination of the factors, or at least of some of their consequences, responsible for the decline of the traditional diplomatic practices. Priority in this respect belongs to the depreciation of diplomacy and its corollary: diplomacy by parliamentary procedures. In so far as that depreciation is only the result of the depreciation of power politics, what we have said about the latter should suffice for the former. Diplomacy, however morally unattractive its business may seem to many, is nothing but a symptom of the struggle for power among sovereign nations, which try to maintain orderly and peaceful relations among themselves. If there were a way of banning the struggle for power from the international scene, diplomacy would disappear of itself. If order and anarchy, peace and war were matters of no concern to the nations of the world, they could dispense with diplomacy, prepare for war, and hope for the best. If nations who are sovereign, who are supreme within their territories with no superior above them, want to preserve peace and order in their relations, they must try to persuade, negotiate, and exert pressure upon each other. That is to say, they must engage in, cultivate, and rely upon diplomatic procedures.

The new parliamentary diplomacy is no substitute for these procedures. On the contrary, it tends to aggravate rather than mitigate international conflicts and leaves the prospect for peace dimmed rather than brightened. Three essential qualities of the new diplomacy are responsible for these unfortunate results: its publicity, its majority votes, its fragmentation of international issues.

The Vice of Publicity

Much of the confusion attending discussion of the problem of secret diplomacy results from the failure to distinguish between two separate aspects of the problem: between "open covenants" and "covenants openly arrived at," between publicity for the results of diplomatic negotiations and publicity for the diplomatic negotiations themselves. Disclosure of the results of diplomatic negotiations is required by the principles of democracy, for without it there can be no democratic control of foreign policy. Yet publicity for the negotiations themselves is not required by democracy and runs counter to the requirements of common sense. It takes only common sense derived from daily experience to realize that it is impossible to negotiate in public on anything in which parties other than the negotiators are interested. This impossibility derives from the very nature of negotiation and from the social context in which negotiations generally operate. . . .

The Vice of Majority Decision

The evil wrought by the public conduct of diplomacy is compounded by the attempt to decide issues by majority vote. In the General Assembly of the United Nations this method has developed into the tradition of at least two thirds of the members voting down at least the Soviet bloc. That this method of conducting the business of diplomacy has strengthened the Western bloc, but has made no direct contribution to the peaceful settlement of a single issue outstanding between East and West, is obvious from the results. . . .

The Vice of Fragmentation

The decision by majority vote implies the third of the vices that stand in the way of a revival of the traditional diplomatic practices: the fragmentation of international issues. By its very nature, the majority vote is concerned with an isolated case. The facts of life to be dealt with by the majority decision are artificially separated from the facts that precede, accompany, and follow them, and are transformed into a legal "case" or a political "issue" to be disposed of as such by the majority decision. In the domestic field, this procedure is not necessarily harmful. Here the majority decision of a deliberative body operates within the context of an intricate system of devices for peaceful change, supplementing, supporting, or checking each other as the case may be, but in any case attuned to each other in a certain measure and thus giving the individual decisions coherence with each other and with the whole social system.

On the international scene, no such system of integrating factors exists. Consequently, it is particularly inadequate here to take up one "case" or "issue" after the other and to try to dispose of them by a succession of majority votes. . . .

THE PROMISE OF DIPLOMACY: ITS NINE RULES

Diplomacy could revive itself if it would part with these vices, which in recent years have well-nigh destroyed its usefulness, and if it would restore the techniques which have controlled the mutual relations of states since time immemorial. By doing so, however, diplomacy would realize only one of the preconditions for the preservation of peace. The contribution of a revived diplomacy to the cause of peace would depend upon the methods and purposes of its use. The discussion of these uses is the last task we have set ourselves in this book. . . .

Four Fundamental Rules

1. *Diplomacy must be divested of the crusading spirit. . . .*

2. *The objectives of foreign policy must be defined in terms of the national interest and must be supported with adequate power. . . .*

4. *Nations must be willing to compromise on all issues that are not vital to them. . . .*

Five Prerequisites of Compromise

1. *Give up the shadow of worthless rights for the substance of real advantage. . . .*

2. *Never put yourself in a position from which you cannot retreat without losing face and from which you cannot advance without grave risks. . . .*

3. *Never allow a weak ally to make decisions for you. . . .*

4. *The armed forces are the instrument of foreign policy, not its master. . . .*

5. *The government is the leader of public opinion, not its slave.* Those responsible for the conduct of foreign policy will not be able to comply with the foregoing principles of diplomacy if they do not keep this principle constantly in mind. As has been pointed out above in greater detail, the rational requirements of good foreign policy cannot from the outset count upon the support of a public opinion whose preferences are emotional rather than rational. This is bound to be particularly true of a foreign policy whose goal is compromise, and which, therefore, must concede some of the objectives of the other side and give up some of its own. Especially when foreign policy is conducted under conditions of democratic control and is inspired by the crusading zeal of a political religion, statesmen are always tempted to sacrifice the requirements of good foreign policy to the applause of the masses. On the other hand, the statesman who would defend the integrity of these requirements against even the slightest contamination with popular passion would seal his own doom as a political leader and, with it, the doom of his foreign policy for he would lose the popular support which puts and keeps him in power.

The statesman, then, is allowed neither to surrender to popular passions nor to disregard them. He must strike a prudent balance between adapting himself to them and marshaling them to the support of his policies. In one word, he must lead. He must perform that highest feat of statesmanship: trimming his sails to the winds of popular passion while using them to carry the ship of state to the port of good foreign policy, on however roundabout and zigzag a course. . . .

The way toward international peace which we have outlined cannot compete in inspirational qualities with the simple and fascinating formulae that for a century and a half have fired the imagination of a war-weary world. There is something spectacular in the radical simplicity of a formula that with one sweep seems to dispose of the problem of war once and for all. This has been the promise of such solutions as free trade, arbitration, disarmament, collective security, universal socialism, international government, and the world state. There is nothing spectacular, fascinating, or inspiring, at least for the people at large, in the business of diplomacy.

We have made the point, however, that these solutions, in so far as they deal with the real problem and not merely with some of its symptoms, pre-suppose the existence of an integrated international society, which actually does not exist. To bring into existence such an international society and keep it in being, the accommodating techniques of diplomacy are required. As the integration of domestic society and its peace develop from the unspectacular and almost unnoticed day-by-day operations of the techniques of accommoda-tion and change, so any ultimate ideal of international life must await its realization from the techniques of persuasion, negotiation, and pressure, which are the traditional instruments of diplomacy.

The reader who has followed us to this point may well ask: But has not diplomacy failed in preventing war in the past? To that legitimate question two answers can be given.

Diplomacy has failed many times, and it has succeeded many times, in its peace-preserving task. It has failed sometimes because nobody wanted it to succeed. We have seen how different in their objectives and methods the limited wars of the past have been from the total war of our time. When war was the normal activity of kings, the task of diplomacy was not to prevent it, but to bring it about at the most propitious moment.

On the other hand, when nations have used diplomacy for the purpose of preventing war, they have often succeeded. The outstanding example of a successful war-preventing diplomacy in modern times is the Congress of Berlin of 1878. By the peaceful means of an accommodating diplomacy, that Congress settled, or at least made susceptible of settlement, the issues that had separated Great Britain and Russia since the end of the Napoleonic Wars. During the better part of the nineteenth century, the conflict between Great Britain and Russia over the Balkans, the Dardanelles, and the Eastern Mediter-ranean hung like a suspended sword over the peace of the world. Yet, during the fifty years following the Crimean War, though hostilities between Great Britain and Russia threatened to break out time and again, they never actually did break out. The main credit for the preservation of peace must go to the techniques of an accommodating diplomacy which culminated in the Congress of Berlin. When British Prime Minister Disraeli returned from that Congress to London, he declared with pride that he was bringing home "peace . . . with honor." In fact, he had brought peace for later generations, too; for a century there has been no war between Great Britain and Russia. . . .

Diplomacy is the best means of preserving peace which a society of sovereign nations has to offer, but, especially under the conditions of modern world politics and of modern war, it is not good enough. It is only when nations have surrendered to a higher authority the means of destruction which modern technology has put in their hands—when they have given up their sovereignty—that international peace can be made as secure as domestic peace. Diplomacy can make peace more secure than it is today, and the world state can make peace more secure than it would be if nations were to abide by the rules of diplomacy. Yet, as there can be no permanent peace without a world state, there can be no world state without the peace-preserving and community-building processes of diplomacy. For the world state to be more than a dim vision, the accommodating processes of diplomacy, mitigating and minimizing conflicts, must be revived. Whatever one's conception of the ultimate state of international affairs may be, in the recognition of that need and in the demand that it be met all men of good will can join. . . .

QUESTIONS

1. What do you understand by diplomacy, and how is it related to power?

2. For how long has diplomatic negotiation been employed, and what limitations have been revealed in the course of its employment?

3. On what grounds did Woodrow Wilson criticize diplomacy as conducted before 1914, and what changes in its practice were advocated by him?

4. What complications for diplomats arose from efforts to practice Wilsonian diplomacy?

5. How has the environment in which diplomatic negotiation has taken place since World War II differed from the diplomatic environment before World War II?

6. What has been the role of diplomacy in the cold war? Cite specific roles in the critical zones of Germany, Austria, Greece and Turkey, Indochina, Formosa, and Korea.

7. What is the basis for James Burnham's conclusion that traditional diplomacy will not work with the Soviet Union?

8. Do the American Friends Service Committee and Hans Morgenthau cope with Burnham's central arguments? Explain.

9. With which of the three positions presented in the last section do you agree most fully? Why?

10. Should diplomats be held responsible for their shortcomings and failures, or should they be considered victims of forces beyond their control?

SELECT BIBLIOGRAPHY

ALMOND, Gabriel A., *The American People and Foreign Policy* (New York, Harcourt Brace, 1950). Examines the reaction of various social groupings in America to foreign affairs and points out the complications created by the varied outlooks. Although hope for national consensus on foreign-policy issues is not entertained, the author emphasizes necessity for more rational thought and meeting of minds among "elite" elements in American society with the most pronounced impact on foreign policy.

BELOFF, Max, *Foreign Policy and the Democratic Process* (Baltimore, Johns Hopkins, 1955). Author's knowledge of Soviet foreign policy helps him assess, by contrast, the advantages and limitations of foreign policy conducted by a democratic state. Emphasizes American foreign policy in its historical perspective and capacity for meeting the Soviet challenge.

BUTTERFIELD, Herbert, *Christianity, Diplomacy and War* (Nashville, Tenn., Abingdon-Cokesbury, 1954). A British historian makes a case for the greater effectiveness of diplomacy over war in adjusting differences between nations. Emphasizes the emotional chasms that develop between warring peoples and make postwar accommodations much more difficult. Diplomacy, coupled with Christian morality, is a more effective way of dealing with international friction.

FOSDICK, Dorothy, *Common Sense and World Affairs* (New York, Harcourt Brace, 1955). A primer for every American, whose business it is, according to the author, to understand the fundamentals of international politics. Principles, not recommendations for specific situations, are clearly set forth for the conduct of foreign policy by a former member of the State Department's Policy Planning Staff.

HAMMARSKJOLD, Dag, "New Diplomatic Techniques in a New World," *Vital Speeches*, December 1, 1953, pp. 107 ff. An address by the Secretary-General of the United Nations. His plea is for neo-Wilsonian diplomacy channeled through the United Nations.

KENNAN, George F., *Realities of American Foreign Policy* (Princeton, Princeton University Press, 1954). The author spent 27 years in the U.S. Foreign Service, served as director of the State Department's Policy Planning Staff and Ambassador to the U.S.S.R. Basic thesis is the inescapable tie between national life generally and foreign policy. Only when Americans accept this as fact, and realize that the forces in international life are realities to be faced as they are, will American foreign policy come of age.

LIPPMANN, Walter, "The Rivalry of Nations," *Atlantic*, February, 1948, pp. 17 ff. A typical, forthright, hard-hitting plea for realism (as Lippmann defines it) in American foreign policy by one of American press's foremost analysts of world affairs. For the present, the United Nations cannot be counted upon as an instrument that will protect the vital interests of the United States. Advocates more careful study of the power factors present today and the fashioning of a diplomatic approach based on power realities, which do not make it possible for the U.S. to have a world with which it is completely satisfied.

MARSHALL, Charles Burton, *The Limits of Foreign Policy* (New York, Holt, 1954). A former member of the State Department's Policy Planning Staff emphasizes difficulties and limitations imposed upon American diplomatic action since 1945 by public intrusion into international negotiations. Diplomacy cannot function in a mass-meeting environment.

MORGENTHAU, Hans J., *Politics Among Nations*, 2nd ed. (New York, Knopf, 1954). Already frequently cited, this text may be read with great profit in its entirety.

NICOLSON, Harold, *The Evolution of Diplomatic Method* (London, Constable, 1954). A very brief summary of the growth of diplomacy, ending on the optimistic note that diplomacy as the tool of democratic foreign policy will in time prove as effective as before 1914. Author is an historian and professional diplomat; was with the British delegation to the 1919 Paris conference and personally observed Wilson's efforts to democratize diplomacy.

12

Are Balance-of-Power Policies
Outmoded?

THE PROBLEM
AND ITS BACKGROUND

INTRODUCTION: POWER AND POLICY

Whither Diplomacy?

During and after the conclusion of World War II, one question challenged the thinking of all who were concerned with the maintenance of a free, peaceful, and creative world. On behalf of what policy should nations use their diplomacy and exercise their power? One answer, in the western world, was that of collective security, as it was intended to function through a world organization like the United Nations. Since Chapter 13 is devoted to the United Nations, it will not be discussed here. Another reply, which became more widespread with the cold war, was that of an up-to-date balance of power. The policy of the balance of power, especially as related to present American foreign policy, will be the central concern of this chapter.

For the United States, both replies to the challenging question signified a remarkable revolution in American thinking. The transformation must be more fully appreciated if the United States' leadership of a free-world coalition is to be understood. More clearly seen also will be the logic of America's commitment to a modified balance-of-power policy as one best calculated to secure adjustment of major international conflicts in the postwar world.

The Revolution in American Foreign Policy

It is one of the cardinal political facts of the mid-twentieth century that the United States has lost its innocence, immunity, and privacy with respect to its relations with the rest of the world. Gone are the days of aloof curiosity, isolation, and leisurely nonpolitical contacts which were, with a few exceptions, characteristic of American foreign affairs during the years when the nation was growing to maturity.[1]

This is the comment of a student of American foreign policy on the remarkable transformation by which the United States, once so preoccupied with its own New World problems and so hostile to entangling alliances in the Old World, had become a leader of a world-wide coalition against the expansion of Soviet and communist power. The extent of America's actions and commitments in the world after World War II has been staggering. It was the United States which shouldered a major share of responsibility for the relief and rehabilitation of the people in countries liberated by war. It joined and vigorously backed the United Nations. It took an active part in the occupation and reform of the defeated Axis powers—Germany, Japan, and Italy. It also announced, in the Truman Doctrine of economic and military aid to Greece and Turkey, that it would vigorously resist internal and external communist pressure against these two powers in the eastern Mediterranean. In the Marshall Plan it proclaimed its intent to help rebuild the war-torn economies of Europe. Recognizing the need for firmer military ties with Western Europe, the United States entered the NATO alliance, which required it to regard an armed attack against one North Atlantic Treaty country as an armed attack against all. It supplemented this with other alliances in Asia and the Pacific. It spent billions for economic and military aid to foreign countries. To give support to the principle of collective security, it fought a "police action" in Korea under the flag of the United Nations. It accepted peacetime conscription and the expenditure of almost two-thirds of its annual budget for purposes of military defense.

This summary of a few of America's actions and commitments since World War II hardly begins to tell the story of the revolution by which a nation, so fundamentally convinced of the wisdom of avoiding entanglements in the affairs of the Old World, has become involved on a tremendous scale around the entire globe.

Superficially, the involvement is all the more impressive when compared to the philosophy of noninvolvement found in classic documents in American foreign policy, such as Washington's Neutrality Proclamation (1793), his Farewell Address (1796), and the Monroe Doctrine (1823).

---

[1] Richard C. Snyder, in the Foreword to William G. Carleton, *The Revolution in American Foreign Policy, 1945–1954* (New York, Random House, 1955), p. v.

The juxtaposition of pertinent passages in Washington's Farewell Address (1796) and the NATO Treaty (1949) is startling. Washington said: [2]

The great rule of conduct for us, in regard to foreign nations is, in extending our commercial relations, to have with them as little political connection as possible. So far as we have already formed engagements, let them be fulfilled with perfect good faith. Here let us stop.

Europe has a set of primary interests, which to us have none, or a very remote relation. Hence she must be engaged in frequent controversies, the causes of which are essentially foreign to our concerns. Hence, therefore, it must be unwise in us to implicate ourselves, by artificial ties, in the ordinary vicissitudes of her politics, or the ordinary combinations and collisions of her friendships and enmities. [Italics added.]

Our detached and distant situation invites and enables us to pursue a different course. . . . [Italics added.]

. . . Why quit our own, to stand upon foreign ground? *Why,* by interweaving our destiny with that of any part of Europe, *entangle our peace and prosperity in the toils of European* ambition, rivalship, *interest,* humor, or caprice? [Italics added.]

'Tis our true policy to steer clear of permanent alliances with any portion of the world. . . .

Taking care always to keep ourselves, by suitable establishments, in a respectable defensive posture, we may safely trust to temporary alliances for extraordinary emergencies.

Compare this excerpt with the following provisions of the North Atlantic Treaty. Note how the treaty involves the United States in European affairs unmistakably and for a prolonged period (10 or 20 years, according to the text).

Here are the pertinent parts of the North Atlantic Treaty: [3]

PREAMBLE

They [the parties to this treaty in 1949: Belgium, Canada, Denmark, France, Great Britain, Italy, Luxembourg, The Netherlands, Norway, Portugal, and the United States] are determined to safeguard the freedom, *common heritage and civilization of their peoples, founded on the principles of democracy, individual liberty and the rule of law.* [Italics added.]

They seek to promote stability and well-being in the North Atlantic Area.

They are resolved to unite their efforts for collective defense and for the preservation of peace and security.

ARTICLE 2

The parties will contribute toward the further development of peaceful and friendly interrelations by strengthening their free institutions, by bringing about a better understanding of the principles upon which these institutions are

[2] The Farewell Address appears in Henry S. Commager, *Documents of American History,* 6th ed. (New York, Appleton-Century-Crofts, 1948), Vol. I, pp. 169–175. For original source, see James D. Richardson, ed., *Messages and Papers of the Presidents* (Washington, D.C., 1896), Vol. I, pp. 213 ff.

[3] For the full text, see 63 U.S. Stat. 2241.

founded, and by promoting conditions of stability and well-being. They will seek to eliminate conflict in their international economic politics and will encourage economic collaboration between any or all of them.

ARTICLE 5

The parties agree that an armed attack against one or more of them in Europe or North America shall be considered an attack against them all; and consequently they agree, that if such an armed attack occurs, each of them in exercise of the right of individual or collective self-defense recognized by Article 51 of the Charter of the United Nations, will assist the party or parties so attacked by taking forthwith, individually and in concert with the other parties, such action as it deems necessary, including the use of armed force, to restore and maintain the security of the North Atlantic area. [Italics added.]

Here may be detected an identity of ideological purpose, a recognition of the need for mutual defense, and an appreciation of the need for economic co-operation.

The contrast is even more startling when it is recalled that as late as the 1930's America had rejected even the noncompulsory jurisdiction of the World Court, made the decision to retire from the Philippines, refused to build up the fortification of Guam, abandoned its neutral rights at sea (in the neutrality legislation of 1935 and 1937), for which the United States had fought in the past.

What does this revolution mean in terms of American attitudes toward techniques of adjustment in world affairs? If, as many argue, international politics is the struggle for power, how is this power to be used? What is the role of power in adjusting the seemingly inevitable rivalries, conflicts, and tensions among sovereign nation-states? Does the revolution in American foreign policy also indicate a revolution in our approach to the use of power in seeking adjustment in world affairs? What are some possible attitudes toward power which influence diplomacy's role in adjusting major international conflicts generally, and which condition American appraisals of the balance of power specifically?

Different Attitudes Toward Power

Power is evil, unnecessary, and corrupting. "Power tends to corrupt [and] absolute power corrupts absolutely." This is the famous aphorism, cited previously, of the perceptive nineteenth century British historian, Lord Acton. Without attempting to probe the more exact meaning of the dictum or to criticize it as a facile, half-true generalization, we should note that it is a phrase frequently quoted by persons who condemn the role of power (conceived in terms of force and violence) in world affairs. Adherents of this school of thought may admit that such power *is* ubiquitous and that brutal power politics has been and is dominant in world affairs. They are, however, morally opposed to what they see about them. This is not the way things *ought* to be. They are opposed because of their conviction that primary reliance upon power does corrupt and prevent men and nations from achieving constructive adjustment in world affairs. A free, peaceful, and creative world, they frequently conclude, cannot be constructed out of the building blocks of such power. There can be no adjustment of conflicting and competing ideologies and interests so long as men and nations operate on the premise of brutal power politics.

Theoretically, those who believe that power is evil and corrupts might reach differing conclusions as to its role in world affairs. They might, for example, come to hold one of several pacifistic views. One, the Gandhian position of nonviolence, has already been touched upon in Chapter 1. Many pacifists in the United States take a similar position. They believe, too, that the basic reason for our failure lies in the nature of our present commitment to violence.[4] Some who hold this view may desire to abolish physical force in every form and to rely upon a policy of nonviolence, whereas others may conclude that power must be taken from the separate sovereign states which now wield it and be given to an international organization or world government, which will link might to right and obligation to consent. Still others may feel that nations should not participate in power politics and its frequent concomitant, balance-of-power politics, because it is a sordid way of conducting international relations— by force or threat of force without consideration of right and justice.

Anarchism, paradoxically perhaps, might be another conclusion of those who look upon power as evil. Many anarchists looked forward to the elimination of coercion in society. They looked upon the state as an evil coercive force, and maintained that the way to achieve a society based on consent was first to destroy, by means of violent revolution, the states now based on force. This attitude toward power, which advocates violent means to achieve an Utopian end, has obvious implications for adjustment in world affairs.

These are only a few of the more important attitudes toward power that flow from acceptance of the view that power is evil, unnecessary, and corrupting.

Power is good, necessary, and ennobling. Here, too, we see that those who hold that power is good, necessary, and ennobling do not necessarily reach the same conclusions on the role of power in world affairs.

One conclusion might be that of the German philosopher Nietzsche, as actually applied to world affairs by Mussolini, the late dictator of Italy: the glorification of power devoid of traditional morality.[5]

Nietzsche and Mussolini, and advocates of this view, extol the will to

[4] See, for example, American Friends Service Committee, *Speak Truth to Power* (1955), pp. 2, 25, 31.
[5] See Friedrich Nietzsche, *The AntiChrist*, in *The Complete Works of Friedrich Nietzsche* (Edinburg, T. N. Foulis, 1911), Vol. 16, p. 128; see also H. W. Schneider, *Making the Fascist State* (New York, Oxford University Press, 1928), pp. 259–260.

power, praise war, and condemn the morality that supports only the weak and cowardly. The brutal use of power seems to run counter to the traditional morality of the western world, but, they contend, they are merely being realistic about the power struggle that is politics. Success in one's endeavors, they may argue, can only be assured if one harnesses power (unmindful of the charges of immorality), with single-minded devotion to one's objectives. In this way, a policy of imperialism may be justified.

Others, however, who think that power is good, necessary, and ennobling may frame a different argument. They may contend that legitimate power is the very basis of civilization: The power of God, of law, of constitutional government, of the right nation, or of the right ideology is the very basis for a free, peaceful, and creative civilization. Such power —defined as influence or control of the minds, bodies, and actions of men and the policies of nations—is good, necessary, and ennobling. In this sense, power is good because it is the force that organizes the world according to rightful principles. Organization is necessary so that men may be free, live peacefully, and act creatively, and only a free, peaceful, and creative man can be a noble man. This view of power may frequently underlie the policy of collective security, the balance of power, or imperialism.

A variant is that of persons who maintain that only when power is harnessed to moral principles is it possible to create a better world order. This is the view of those who insist upon the realism of idealism, correctly understood. They theoretically condemn the moral utopianism of the naïve and doctrinaire idealists, who refuse to face up to the realities of power in international politics, but they also condemn the glorification of power—brutal, naked power—and international politics based on the premise that justice is the interest of the stronger. Yet they also criticize certain "political realists" for what they allege is too narrow a view of national interest and too great a devotion to an outdated balance of power. They feel that national interest rests upon universal moral principles, which are identical with the world's interest. Universal moral purpose, they argue, based on such principles, is the strongest foundation for power, rightly understood.

Other possibilities. Obviously, these two generalized attitudes do not exhaust the possibilities. They have been presented here to stimulate the reader to evaluate his own attitude toward power, as a preliminary to appraising the balance of power, with which this chapter is concerned. Innumerable attitudes, many of which are very complex, might be set forth.

For example, some people maintain that power itself is politically and morally neutral. It can be harnessed for good or evil ends, dependent upon the motives of those doing the harnessing and the actions that result.

Other observers insist that the truth about international politics is the truth about power and the struggle for power, elemental, undisguised, and all-pervading. They maintain that the study of international politics must center on the manifestations, configurations, and limitations of power.[6]

Walter Lippmann is another critic of American foreign policy who has urged Americans to awaken to what he considers the reality of power in international politics. Lippmann contends that the failure of the United States to recognize the international facts of life has prevented, and still prevents, the United States "from forming an effective foreign policy."[7]

This survey of conflicting attitudes toward power and the balance of power will better prepare the reader to understand the "Positions" in the next section of this chapter. In order more critically to appraise the policy of balance of power, it is appropriate here to examine balance of power as the central principle of power politics.

The Balance of Power as a Classic Policy of Nation-States

The Central Principle of Power Politics

The balance of power has been accurately called the "central principle in what we might call the 'mechanics' of power politics."[8] Similarly, the balance of power has been aptly described as the "way Powers group themselves in a state of international anarchy," that is, a world condition where nations are sovereign and do not mutually recognize a higher common authority above all sovereign nation-states. Historically, the policy of the balance of power has been a dominant one in European politics since the rise of the modern nation-state.

The Many Meanings of Balance of Power

Equilibrium or preponderance. Discussion of the balance of power is often confused by failure to distinguish between two meanings of the word *balance* itself. Does it mean "equilibrium," as when a scale is evenly balanced; as when the military, economic, political, social, and psychological strength of the U.S. and its allies is evenly balanced against the comparable strength of the U.S.S.R. and its allies?

Or does balance mean "preponderance," as when we have a "balance" in the bank; not a condition where our assets have been canceled or

---

[6] See Hans Morgenthau, "The State of Political Science," *The Review of Politics*, Vol. 17 (October, 1955), particularly p. 455.

[7] Walter Lippmann, "The Rivalry of Nations," in *The Atlantic Monthly*, Vol. 181 (February, 1948), particularly pp. 18–20.

[8] Martin Wight, *Power Politics* (London, Royal Institute of International Affairs, 1946), p. 42.

"balanced" out by our debits but where we have some money to our credit in the bank?

Frequently, an observer will comment that he sees a balance of power prevailing in the world; by this he means equality of power between opposing groups. Another observer will say that there is a favorable balance of power (as far as he is concerned), when he thinks that his side is stronger than the opposing side. It is important to know the sense in which balance is understood if balance of power is to be appraised as a technique of adjustment in world affairs.

Actual behavior or optional policy. The balance of power is seen by some as a "law" or principle of international politics, explaining or describing *how nation-states actually behave in fact.*

Others, however, think of the balance of power as a *policy* (among other policies) which *may or may not be adopted* by a nation-state.

Actually, of course, these two views may seem to be the same when a a given nation-state adopts the balance of power as a desirable policy, while recognizing that it is also the most realistic policy so far as it characterizes the actual policy of most nation-states.

As a "law" of international politics, the balance of power may be thought of as an application of the more fundamental law of self-preservation. In other words, nations will resort to the balance of power as a device to protect themselves from actual or potential enemies. Hence, if nations are moved by a "law" of self-preservation, they will use the balance of power to protect themselves.

In the past the balance of power has come into play when the dominance of one nation has threatened the safety of a second or third or many nations menaced by the dangerous strength of the one nation. A third nation may then join forces with a second nation attacked by a dominant nation. It does so to protect itself against the threat to its own preservation that would be posed by the victory of the dominant nation over the attacked second nation. The following example is a classic illustration.

A classic illustration of the balance of power. In a speech in 1936, Winston Churchill made clear the meaning, purpose, and moral character of the balance of power when applied by what he judged to be a liberty-loving nation.[9]

For four hundred years [declared Churchill] the foreign policy of England had been to oppose the strongest, most aggressive, most dominating Power on the Continent, and particularly to prevent the Low Countries falling into the hands of such a Power. . . . Moreover on all occasions [in those years] England took the more difficult course. Faced by Philip II of Spain, against Louis XIV under William III and Marlborough, against Napoleon, against William II

---

[9] *The Gathering Storm* (Boston, Houghton Mifflin, 1948), pp. 207–208, 209, 211. It should be pointed out that not all observers agree that Britain has consistently followed a balance-of-power policy.

of Germany, it would have been easy and must have been very tempting to join with the stronger and share the fruits of his conquest. However, we took the harder course, joined with the less strong Powers, made a combination among them, and thus defeated and frustrated the Continental military tyrant whoever he was, whatever nation he led. Thus we preserved the liberties of Europe, protected the growth of its vivacious and varied society, and emerged after four terrible struggles with an evergrowing fame and widening Empire, and with the Low Countries safely protected in their independence. Here is the wonderful unconscious tradition of British foreign policy. . . .

Observe that the policy of England takes no account of which nation it is that seeks the over-lordship of Europe. The question is not whether it is Spain, or the French Monarchy, or the French Empire, or the German Empire, or the Hitler regime. It has nothing to do with rulers or nations; it is concerned solely with whoever is the strongest or the potentially dominating tyrant. Therefore, we should not be afraid of being accused of being pro-French or anti-German. If the circumstances were reversed, we could equally be pro-German and anti-French. It is a law of public policy which we are following, and not a mere expedient dictated by accidental circumstances, or likes and dislikes, or any other sentiment.

In 1936, Churchill saw the danger of a "Germanized Europe under Nazi control," and he related the strategy of the balance of power to the self-preservation of the British Empire.

Therefore, it seems to me that all the old conditions present themselves again, and that our national salvation depends upon our gathering once again all the forces of Europe to contain, to restrain, and if necessary to frustrate German domination. For, believe me, if any of those other Powers, Spain, Louis XIV, Napoleon, Kaiser Wilhelm II, had with our aid become the absolute masters of Europe, they could have despoiled us, reduced us to insignificance and penury on the morrow of their victory. We ought to set the life and endurance of the British Empire and the greatness of this island very high in our duty, and not be led astray by illusions about an ideal world, which only means that other and worse controls will step into our place, and that the future direction will belong to them.

Commenting on this speech after World War II, Churchill brought his argument on behalf of the balance of power up to date:

If we add the United States to Britain and France; if we change the name of the potential aggressor; if we substitute the United Nations organization for the League of Nations, the Atlantic Ocean for the English Channel, and the World for Europe, the argument is not necessarily without its application today.

Not all observers, incidentally, agree with Churchill's reliance upon the balance of power.

Multiple balance (the chandelier) and simple balance (a pair of scales). The actual balance of power occurs as a multiple balance (comparable to a chandelier) or as a simple balance (comparable to a pair of scales). In the eighteenth century, Europe was largely characterized by a multiple balance. There were more than two sides, blocs, or alliances in the balance. In western Europe and in the contest for empire overseas, three major nations were involved: Britain, France, and Spain. They were not the only nations involved, for in central and eastern Europe there was a balance involving Austria and Prussia, and Russia and Turkey, as well as a number of smaller states. Furthermore, the western European balance interacted with the central and eastern European balance. Britain, for example, was not only concerned with France and Spain but also with Russia. In addition, nations shifted in the balances that were worked out. Thus, Britain, which in 1740 was allied with Austria against France and Prussia, joined forces with Prussia against France and Austria in 1746.

The multiple balance that had characterized Europe in the eighteenth century broke down with the French Revolution, with Napoleon's efforts to dominate Europe as the decisive factor. Temporarily, Napoleon succeeded in extinguishing some of the "lights" (Prussia, Austria) in the chandelier-like multiple balance of power.

In the Vienna settlement, following Napoleon's defeat, an effort was made to restore a multiple balance, to sustain the nations necessary for its maintenance, and to prevent the continental dominance of one nation, France, which had jeopardized the balance. However, Britain, Prussia, Austria, and Russia did not remain together long in the Quadruple Alliance, designed to stop France from again attempting to dominate Europe.

The situation changed significantly with the unification of Germany and Germany's defeat of France in the Franco-Prussian War. Austria's power, once so prominent in central and southeastern Europe, was now declining as a result of her expulsion from Germany and Italy, and the strong centrifugal nationalistic movements within the Austro-Hungarian Empire. Fearing Russia more than Prussian-led Germany, however, Austria joined forces with Germany and Italy in the Triple Alliance. Germany, which had under Bismarck maintained friendly relations with Russia, shifted away when Bismarck stepped down as Chancellor in 1890, and in 1893 France joined in an alliance with Russia. France and England, in the meantime, were moving toward closer relations with each other. This configuration, determined in large part by the rise of a powerful Germany in central Europe, destroyed the possibility of a multiple balance, as the rise of Napoleonic France had a hundred years earlier. The chandelier-type balance was replaced by a pair of scales. There ceased to be more than two major blocs. The great powers now tended to divide into opposite camps. International tension reached new heights, the arms race proceeded at top speed, and one crisis after another threatened to throw the two blocs into collision with each other. Finally, the collision did occur—World War I.

A similar pattern prevailed in the 1930's with the formation of the Berlin-Rome Axis in 1936. The Axis, aimed at the League powers, in time became the Berlin-Rome-Tokyo Axis. The ultimate collision here, of course, was World War II.

Today, again, a simple balance is evident in the world. Indeed, the division of the world into two camps seems sharper today than it has ever been in the past. Our world has frequently been called a bipolar world: East vs. West, or the communist bloc vs. the western democratic bloc. Moreover, one leviathan power, the Soviet Union and the United States, respectively, exercises primary leadership in each bloc.

The Balancer in the Balance of Power

If a country is said to hold the balance of power, what is generally meant is that that nation has the freedom and will to maintain an equilibrium between opposing groups. It may do this by preserving a judicious neutrality when an equilibrium between opposing powers already exists, or by joining the weaker side when any single nation threatens to obtain a preponderance of power. As Churchill's remarks indicated, holding the balance of power has been Britain's classic foreign policy. There is also the point of view that the United States played the role of balancer in connection with World Wars I and II.

Today, many critics believe that it is no longer possible to have a balancer. They argue that Britain no longer possesses the detachment and freedom of action that would permit her to serve as a balancer or balance wheel. Indeed, they contend that the same argument holds for the United States. Both are committed to one side in the bipolar struggle. Neither can maintain a judicious neutrality in the struggle, for without the participation of one or both, the Soviet Union would have a clear preponderance of power. In other words, today both Britain and the United States are integral parts of the western alliance. It seems improbable that either could now, or in the foreseeable future, withdraw from the western alliance on the grounds that the alliance now possesses, or could possess, sufficient power to match that of the Soviet Union and its bloc. It is even more improbable that the United States would act the traditional role of the balancer, by feeling free to join the Soviet bloc if the United States concluded that preponderance of power had tipped in favor of the western alliance.

Ways in Which the Balance of Power Operates

At this point it will be helpful to examine how the balance of power works a little more exactly. The motivating force in balance-of-power politics, as has been seen, is a nation's desire to preserve an equilibrium of power most compatible with its vital interests, lest they be jeopardized by a hostile, dominating nation. A nation is often compelled to arm itself or ally itself with others if it is weak or threatened. Here is pressure to rely upon *armaments* and/or *alliances* as a means of increasing or pooling power necessary to restore the threatened equilibrium. The maintenance of an equilibrium also calls for the division of territorial, economic, or political booty, which, if not shared, would disproportionately increase the power of a given nation, and thus upset the balance of power. This division is frequently called *compensations*. Similarly, a nation frequently attempts to prevent the rise of a hostile power by seeking to keep that nation divided. This is the technique of *divide and rule*. Again, more powerful nations sometimes pursue a policy of bringing smaller states, located in areas between the greater powers, within their sphere of influence, at times as outright protectorates. Sometimes they neutralize the smaller states in the contest of power. This technique establishes and/or maintains *buffer states*. Still another device in balance-of-power politics, perhaps not separable from some already mentioned, is that of *intervention* in the internal affairs of another nation. The action is generally defended as necessary to prevent a change that would upset the balance of power or adversely affect the intervening nation.

A few illustrations may clarify the "game" of international politics, as it has frequently been played in the last three hundred years. The cold war provides some excellent examples. For instance, the rearmament of the United States (and of its friends) after hasty American demobilization at the end of World War II demonstrates the attempt to increase the power of the western world against the threat of Soviet and communist expansionism in the postwar period. Similarly, America's efforts to construct a system of world-wide alliances emphasize recognition of the need to pool power in the face of threats to the balance of power all over the world. American intervention in the Greek civil war (here, with the blessing of the Greek government) indicates the need to prevent seizure of power there by Greek communist forces, aided and abetted by sympathetic communist neighbors. A communist victory, it was felt, would adversely affect the balance of power in the Mediterranean, and in this situation, the United States staked out a sphere of influence there. The techniques of divide and rule and of maintaining safe buffer states are illustrated by the examples of Germany and Austria. The Soviet Union apparently prefers to see Germany divided rather than united and allied with the West. A divided Germany is less of a threat to the Soviet Union. Austria, a buffer between East and West, was permitted to regain its sovereign independence and real unity, but at the price of neutrality in the cold war.

The principle of compensations is less dramatically evidenced in the cold war. Nevertheless, it has played a prominent part in international politics, perhaps more so in earlier generations and centuries; witness the several partitions of Poland in the eighteenth century; the division of

Africa among the great powers in the nineteenth century; the distribution of Germany's overseas possessions after World War I.

The illustrations drawn from the cold war may, of course, reflect the bias of an observer sympathetic to the United States and the West. A Russian or communist observer would undoubtedly defend Soviet armaments, alliances, intervention and influence in the satellites in Central and Southeastern Europe (and elsewhere) in terms of the aggressive intentions of hostile capitalist powers. And because nations—rival or even generally friendly nations—see and play the balance-of-power "game" in terms of their own national interests, as they define them, many observers conclude that balance-of-power politics is bound to be unstable, uncertain, and insecure.

The Instability, Uncertainty, and Insecurity of the Balance of Power

Modern nation-states are dynamic and competitive. They tend to expand or contract; to grow and decline; to struggle for advantage and advancement. These are characteristics that make the maintenance of a stable balance impossible and lend an uncertain quality to the balance of power. A nation-state cannot be absolutely sure which other nation-states are its friends and which its foes; whether friends will give it support in adversity; and whether foes will fight or compromise on disputed matters. Great insecurity ensues, which intensifies suspicion and fears, rivalry and conflict, tension and crisis. War and imperialism have been the notorious concomitants of balance of power.

Other observers have noted that the conditions which made the balance of power more workable in the past are absent from today's bipolar world. In the past, the number of powers in the "game" was sufficient to permit the flexibility indispensable to the operation of the balance of power. Today the number of great powers has been reduced to two, and the old-style flexibility is gone. Then, too, there is no place for a balancer in a bipolar world. A third vanished factor is a colonial frontier, which permitted maneuvering and allowed (by way of expansion and compensations) for the adjustment of interests so important to the successful operation of the balance of power. Fourth is agreement on certain fundamentals, which in the past served to restrain continuously brutal and ruthless power politics, thus permitting nations to adopt a balance-of-power approach without fear of annihilation. Today, in the bipolar world, the intellectual and moral consensus necessary for the successful functioning of the balance of power is not present. For these reasons, the conclusion reached by certain critics is that the old balance of power is obsolete in today's world.

American Policy in the Cold War and the Balance of Power

"Positions of Strength" as a Modified Balance-of-Power Policy

At this point it is appropriate to consider the balance of power as it is related to the policy of "positions of strength," which the United States adopted and has been pursuing in the cold war. That policy—one of maintaining strength among the western allies sufficient to make it clear to potential aggressors that aggression will be severely penalized—is, in fact, based on a modified balance of power.

Present American policy is not explicitly labeled a balance-of-power policy by American leaders. More frequently, it is called collective security. Yet, it should be clear that it is not universal collective security, based on the principle of using the overwhelming power of the entire world community to prevent or defeat aggression by a single nation or world minority. Although the United States has supported the United Nations in its efforts to apply collective security, the weaknesses of the United Nations security system have led the United States and its allies to develop regional alliance systems in Europe, Asia, and the Middle East for greater certainty of operation than the United Nations offers. So long as the communist and western blocs do not see eye to eye on the question of aggression, the overwhelming power of the peaceful world cannot be mobilized against aggression by a single nation or by a minority. This is obvious when the expansionist power is the Soviet Union itself; and when the aggressor is North Korea, backed by Red China, and indirectly supported by the Soviet Union, it is again clear that universal collective security cannot work. It would be more accurate to say that, although United States policy is based on collective as opposed to "house-to-house" defense, and although the United States would like to move toward universal collective security, it has been forced, by the division of the world into two major camps, to rely upon regional security pacts and an interlocking system of free-world alliances.

Perhaps the phrases "balance of power" and "modified balance of power" are avoided by American statesmen because the man in the street reacts unfavorably to the terms. In large part, he is still prone to think of power politics and the balance of power in terms of the immoral and un-American activities of selfish foreign nations, conducting their foreign policies without regard for considerations of right and justice.

It is also true that the government of the United States has continued to voice its confidence in the United Nations and the principle of collective security upon which the United Nations is based. When he was President, Harry S. Truman declared that a major reason for supporting the United Nations was that it provided a way of utilizing the collective strength of member nations, under the Charter, to prevent aggression. John Foster Dulles, as Secretary of State, declared that the "free world has practical means for achieving collective security . . . through the United Nations" by bypassing the Soviet veto in the Security Council and permitting the General Assembly to recommend to members "collective measures against any future aggression." [10]

The fact remains, however, that the United States has taken the leadership in building a free-world coalition against Soviet and communist expansion. This coalition seeks to balance Soviet and communist power in the world, in the interest of preventing its expansion and domination of free nations.

Reasons for Adoption of Policy of "Positions of Strength"

The United States adopted the policy of "positions of strength" for two primary reasons. The first was the failure of the United Nations to operate and on the principle of collective security cope adequately with Soviet expansion and intransigence and communist aggression. The second was the hope that a policy of "positions of strength" would remedy the uncertainty of the old balance of power, which seemed to invite aggression so frequently in the past.

The United States did not adopt this policy immediately after World War II. American hopes for co-operation were high at the end of the European war. President Eisenhower thus expressed the high hopes felt by many at the time of the defeat of Hitler in Europe: [11]

In that spring of victory [1945: V-E Day] the soldiers of the Western Allies met the soldiers of Russia in the center of Europe. They were triumphant comrades in arms. Their peoples shared the joyous prospect of building, in honor of their dead, the only fitting monument—an age of just peace. All these war-weary peoples shared too this concrete, decent purpose: to guard vigilantly against the domination ever again of any part of the world by a single, unbridled aggressive power.

The United States, President Eisenhower declared, sought to co-operate with all peace-loving nations in the spirit of the United Nations. It sought "to prohibit strife, to relieve tensions, to banish fears." He went on to say: [12]

This was to allow all nations to devote their energies and resources to the great and good tasks of healing the war's wounds, of clothing and feeding and housing the needy, of perfecting a just political life, and of enjoying the fruits of their own toil.

[10] Speech of Harry S. Truman, "Partnership of World Peace," *Bulletin of the Department of State*, Vol. 23 (October 20, 1950); John Foster Dulles, "Principles in Foreign Policy," April 11, 1955, Department of State Press Release 203.
[11] President Dwight D. Eisenhower, Speech to the American Society of Newspaper Editors, April 16, 1953.
[12] *Ibid.*

Between 1945 and 1947 the United States generally attempted to co-operate with the Soviet Union and other nations in the spirit of the principle of universal collective security upon which the United Nations was based. Said President Truman: [13]

. . . After the bloodshed and destruction of World War II, many of us hoped that all nations would work together to make sure that war could never happen again. We hoped that international cooperation, supported by the strength and moral authority of the United Nations, would be sufficient to prevent aggression.
But this was not to be the case.

This was not to be the case, President Eisenhower argued, because the "Soviet government held a vastly different vision of the future." "In the world of its design, security was to be found not in mutual trust and mutual aid but in *force:* huge armies, subversion, rule of neighbor countries." [14]

A number of events produced disappointment and disillusionment in those in the United States who believed in and sought to make effective the principle of collective security through the United Nations. One was the Russian use of the veto in the Security Council to block action by the United Nations majority. Another was the failure of the United Nations to implement Articles 43 and 45 of the Charter, which provided that member nations set aside armed forces for the use of the Security Council. Another was the failure to achieve agreement on the vital question of control of atomic weapons. Another was the failure of the Soviet Union to join some of the specialized agencies related to the United Nations. Still another was the growing friction between the big powers in such countries as Germany and Greece, as well as Russia's establishment of satellites in Central and Southeastern Europe. This meant, in effect, the division of Germany, the danger of communist victory in the Greek civil war, and the forced communization of such countries as Poland, Bulgaria, Rumania, and Hungary.

Reluctant recognition of the inability of the United Nations to cope with Soviet expansionism in Europe led the United States, in 1947, to adopt a policy of "containment," the logic of which is explained in the following passages by George Kennan: [15]

It is clear that the United States cannot expect in the foreseeable future to enjoy political intimacy with the Soviet regime. It must continue to regard the Soviet Union as a rival, not a partner, in the political arena. It must continue to expect that Soviet policies will reflect no abstract love of peace and stability, no real faith in the possibility of a permanent happy coexistence of the Socialist and capitalist worlds, but rather a cautious persistent pressure toward the disruption and weakening of all rival influence and rival power.

[13] "Partnership of World Peace," *op. cit.*
[14] *Op. cit.*
[15] George F. Kennan, "The Sources of Soviet Conduct," *Foreign Affairs,* Vol. 25 (July, 1947), pp. 580–581, 575, 576.

Therefore, Mr. Kennan concluded,

In these circumstances it is clear that the main element of any United States policy toward the Soviet Union must be that of a long-term, patient but firm and vigilant containment of Russian expansive tendencies. . . .

In the light of the above, it will be clearly seen that the Soviet pressure against the free institutions of the Western world is something that can be contained by the adroit and vigilant application of counter-force at a series of constantly shifting geographical and political points, corresponding to the shifts and manoeuvres of Soviet policy, but which cannot be charmed or talked out of existence.

Even before Mr. Kennan's article had appeared, President Truman had taken an important first step in implementing the policy by extending aid to Greece and Turkey.

The policy of containment required counterforce, and the role of counterforce led to the second primary reason for adoption of the American policy of "positions of strength": the need to replace the old uncertainty of the old balance of power with crystal-clear certainty, in advance of aggression, that the aggressor "can and will be made to suffer for his aggression more than he can possibly gain by it." [16]

Mr. Truman, when President, had declared that the United States "must oppose strength with strength." The "peace-loving nations must have the military strength available, when called upon, to act decisively to put down aggression." [17] The Korean War underscored America's determination to use its military power against aggression. At the same time, the Korean War emphasized anew the element of uncertainty in the balance of power. Aggression was checked in Korea by means of war, but it had not been forestalled.

In their speeches President Eisenhower and Secretary of State Dulles endeavored to make it very clear to the communist bloc nations that they would lose in any aggressive effort to upset the world balance of power in their favor.

Thus, in his State of the Union Message on January 6, 1955, President Eisenhower declared:

To protect our nations and our peoples from the catastrophe of a nuclear holocaust, free nations must maintain countervailing military power to persuade the Communists of the futility of seeking to advance their ends through aggression. If Communist rulers understand that America's response to aggression will be swift and decisive—that never shall we buy peace at the expense of honor or faith—they will be powerfully deterred from launching a military venture engulfing their own peoples and many others in disaster.

Mr. Dulles, too, underscored this point. For example, in a single article he repeated the point at least five times. [18]

[16] John Foster Dulles, "Policy for Security and Peace," in *Foreign Affairs,* Vol. 32 (April, 1954), p. 358.
[17] "Partnership of World Peace," *op. cit.*
[18] "Policy for Security and Peace," *op. cit.*, pp. 354–364.

It may be argued, however, that an element of uncertainty remains in the policy of "positions of strength." Should the United States, for example, have openly intervened, with its own forces, in Indochina? How are distinctions to be made between intervention to deter aggression in Korea and in Indochina, both of which involved civil wars? Where does one decide to fight only a local war, limited in character and with conventional weapons; and where to resist aggression, even if it means a world war fought with atomic weapons? How is communist expansion via internal subversion to be countered? How far does one go to the brink of war without slipping over? And most important today, what is to be done to cope with the new Soviet policy of reliance upon economic and diplomatic expansion?

At this point it will be useful to consider the world-wide system of alliances which has emerged to implement the policy of "positions of strength."

"Positions of Strength" and America's Alliances

In the Truman Doctrine the United States recognized that the eastern Mediterranean would be threatened in the event of a communist victory in the Greek civil war or successful Soviet pressure on Turkey. When the British withdrew from Greece in 1947, the United States apparently recognized that unless it replaced the British, the balance of power in the Mediterranean might be overturned, and with it perhaps the entire balance of power in Europe and the Near East. Here, the United States acted alone, although with British blessing.

It was, of course, recognized that the United States had a vital interest in a free and strong Europe, and on June 5, 1947, Secretary of State George C. Marshall urged adoption of a plan to stabilize Europe, thus permitting free institutions to continue to flourish there. Even at this date, it should be noted, the promise of aid implicit in Marshall's speech did not exclude the Soviet Union and its satellites. Marshall said: [19]

It is logical that the United States should do whatever it is able to do to assist in the return of normal economic health in the world, without which there can be no political stability and assured peace. Our policy is not directed against any country or doctrine but against hunger, poverty, desperation, and chaos. Its purpose should be the revival of a working economy in the world so as to permit the emergence of political and social conditions in which free institutions can exist.

In the Marshall Plan, as in the Truman Doctrine, the United States acted outside the United Nations. Congress again responded, and, as Secretary of State Dulles later declared, in a speech before the Council

---

[19] Dept. of State Bull., June 15, 1947; see also Francis O. Wilcox and Thorsten V. Kalijarvi, *Recent American Foreign Policy: Basic Documents, 1941–1951* (New York, Appleton-Century-Crofts, 1952), pp. 823–825.

of Foreign Relations on January 12, 1954, the "European Recovery Program [Marshall Plan] . . . helped the peoples of Western Europe to pull out of the post-war morass." In connection with the Marshall Plan, it should be noted, the Western European nations, who agreed to participate, banded together jointly to work out a plan for European recovery. They did this under OEEC, the Organization for European Economic Co-operation.

Although the Soviet Union and its Eastern European satellites refused to accept the Marshall Plan offer, the Soviet Union reacted vigorously. Russia countered with a program for economic integration in its own orbit. In the fall of 1947, the Cominform, successor to the Comintern, was established.[20] In February, 1948, Czech communists seized power in Czechoslavakia in a bloodless coup. All these steps made a deep impression on the western world.

However, President Truman did not call for American rearmament until the spring of 1948, and the United States did not decisively move toward an alliance with friendly nations in Western Europe until June, 1948, when the United States Senate (in the Vandenberg Resolution), with the Truman Administration's strong support, urged association of the United States with regional and other collective arrangements, based on continuous and effective self-help. The upshot was the North Atlantic Treaty, signed on April 4, 1949, by the United States, Canada, and ten nations of Western Europe—Belgium, Denmark, France, Iceland, Italy, Luxembourg, the Netherlands, Norway, Portugal, and the United Kingdom. Greece and Turkey became members in February, 1952, and the Federal Republic of (West) Germany, in May, 1955.

This treaty, the heart of America's system of post-World War II alliances, explains and symbolizes the United States' policy of "positions of strength." The treaty was new and revolutionary in at least three significant senses. First, never before had the United States committed itself, in peacetime, to go to the aid of a country outside the Western Hemisphere in the event of attack. Second, never before had the United States received similar guarantees from other countries. Finally, never in peace had the United States agreed to join other nations in an active effort to build their mutual defensive strength.

A few extracts from an official Department of State publication indicate clearly why the United States decided to adopt this new and revolutionary policy, and how it is related to the balance of power.[21]

Twice in the last 50 years the United States has thrown its full economic and military power into a deadly struggle to prevent the triumph of a dangerous

[20] For discussions of both the Cominform (Communist International Information Bureau) and the Comintern (Third International), see Chap. 10.

[21] *North Atlantic Treaty Organization: Its Development and Significance,* Dept. of State Publ. 4630, General Foreign Policy Series 75 (Washington, D.C., Government Printing Office, 1952), p. 2.

aggressor in Western Europe. Our action was not accidental nor solely the result of moral duty. We acted because the people of the United States have long recognized that the freedom and security of this part of the world are essential to our own freedom and security.

Why is the United States so concerned about the nations of Western Europe? And what is it that links our interests with those of the peoples across the North Atlantic?

First and most important of all is Western Europe's strategic value to the United States and the free world as a whole. While Europe remains free, the total strength of the free world is far greater than that of any potential aggressor. However if Western Europe should be absorbed within the Soviet empire, the *balance* would be radically altered and the United States and the other nations of the free world would be compelled to struggle for survival against heavy odds. [Italics added.]

The extent of the NATO alliance is shown in Fig. 11, and Fig. 12 gives a complete picture of the United States' collective defense arrangements.

In support of its program of mutual security, the United States has spent billions of dollars in military aid all over the world. However, it is important to keep in mind that the policy of "positions of strength" is not based exclusively on military power.

In a speech entitled "Peace Through Strength," delivered on June 13, 1950, Secretary of State Acheson called attention to the importance of other elements of strength.[22]

A great deal of talk about this program [for strengthening the free world] has concerned military strength. While this is an essential element, it is not by itself sufficient. The military strength of the free world must be adequate to deter Soviet leaders from any rash adventures. But, this effort must be accompanied by other elements of strength—economic, political, and moral. Only in this way will the free world be able to resist the external threat of Soviet military power and internal threat of subversion, by the international Communist movement.

Nevertheless, the policy of "positions of strength" represents a real revolution in the long-dominant, traditional foreign policy of the United States. It is appropriate now to examine in more detail the major themes in United States foreign policy, and to assess more fully the balance of power in American history. This review will set the stage for the differing appraisals that appear in "Positions on the Problem."

HISTORIC BACKGROUND OF U.S. FOREIGN POLICY

Three Major Themes in U.S. Foreign Policy

Continentalism. With important exceptions, notably in 1898, 1914, and 1941, the dominant theme of American foreign policy up to the post-

---

[22] The speech appears in *Strengthening the Forces of Freedom*, Dept. of State Publ. 3852a, General Foreign Policy Series 28 (Washington, D.C., Government Printing Office), pp. 4–5.

World War II period was that of continentalism. The term serves to denote America's efforts, relying primarily upon her own strength, to achieve freedom, prosperity, and security on the North American continent. It was a policy that combined both isolationism and imperialism: political isolation from Europe, earlier the primary center of international politics, and westward expansion and dominance on the North American continent.

With regard to Europe, the United States was isolationist. Starting with Washington's Neutrality Proclamation in 1793, crystallizing in Washington's Farewell Address in 1796 and in the Monroe Doctrine of 1823, the idea emerged that the United States could best advance its national security and well-being by not becoming involved in the political "broils" of Europe. The United States, which had a special mission to advance freedom in the world, would do best to develop its free republican institutions in the New World, removed from the corruptions, temptations, and dangers of the Old World.

Washington did not urge complete and total isolation upon his fellow Americans. He advocated "good faith and justice towards all nations," "peace and harmony with all," "harmony, and a liberal intercourse with all nations." He cautioned his fellow Americans against "permanent, inveterate antipathies against particular nations, and passionate attachments for others." Both "excessive partiality" and "excessive dislike" were to be avoided.

The policy he recommended was not one of blind isolationism. Washington, it should be noted, identified the national interest of the United States with the maintenance of national union, a free constitution, good laws, true liberty, popular happiness, national peace and prosperity. He assumed that the national interest could then (in 1796) best be preserved if the United States steered clear of European controversies not primary to its vital interests, and held aloof from irrelevant European issues, meddling in which could only jeopardize United States' peace and security. Bearing in mind the young republic's condition, and the geographical, economic, and political facts of 1796, many critics believe that Washington's Farewell Address embodied sage advice.

Political isolationism also found expression in the words of Thomas Jefferson. He wrote to Baron von Humboldt: [23]

The European nations constitute a separate division of the globe; their localities make them part of a distinct system; they have a set of interests of their own in which it is our business never to engage ourselves. America has a hemisphere to itself. It must have its separate system of interests, which must not be subordinated to those of Europe. The insulated state in which nature has placed the American Continent should so far avail it that no spark of war

[23] Thomas Jefferson to Alexander, Baron von Humboldt, December 6, 1813, *The Writings of Thomas Jefferson* (New York, Putnam, 1898), Vol. IX, p. 431.

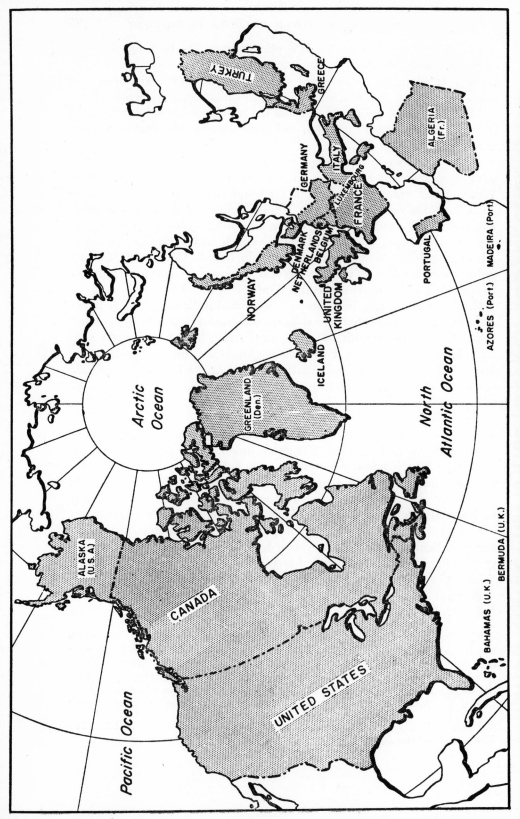

Fig. 11. The geographies of the North Atlantic Treaty Organization. (Source: NATO: Its Development and Significance, Dept. of State.

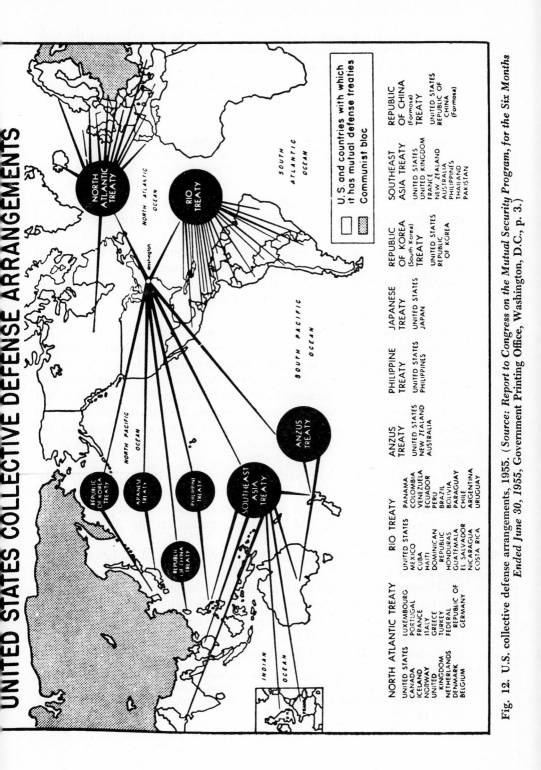

Fig. 12. U.S. collective defense arrangements, 1955. (*Source: Report to Congress on the Mutual Security Program, for the Six Months Ended June 30, 1955,* Government Printing Office, Washington, D.C., p. 3.)

kindled in the other quarters of the globe should be wafted across the wide oceans which separate us from them. And it will be so.

When the Monroe Doctrine was announced in 1823, the political isolationism that had characterized United States' relations toward Europe was extended so as to include both American continents. Monroe declared: [24]

In the wars of the European powers in matters relating to themselves we have never taken any part, nor does it comport with our policy so to do. . . .
We should consider any attempt on their part to extend their system to any portion of this hemisphere as dangerous to our peace and safety.

The dominance of a politically isolationist view with regard to Europe, then, dovetailed with the principle of the Monroe Doctrine as it related to the New World.

America was concerned with its own interests in the New World. As a result, the United States stayed out of the regular course of European politics, warned European nations not to attempt to extend their unwanted system to the New World, and was preoccupied with exploiting the American continent.

There followed the expansion of the original thirteen states on the eastern seaboard to forty-eight states spread across the North American continent from Atlantic to Pacific, from Canada to Mexico. Sometimes achieved peaceably, as in the Louisiana Purchase of 1803, sometimes as a result of war (the innumerable wars with Indian tribes, the Texas and Mexican wars), the expansion must certainly be called imperialistic in large part. From the point of view of the American Indians and the Mexicans, the United States must have seemed a nation bent on domination.

It should be noted, however, that whether American policy was isolationist with regard to Europe or imperialistic with regard to the American Indians and the Mexicans, it was always characterized by the desire to develop a free, secure, and prosperous nation on the American continent.[25]

Imperialism. Continentalism (itself a composite of isolationism and imperialism in North America), up to the post-World War II period, may have been the dominant theme of American foreign policy, but it has not held undisputed sway. Accompanying it has been imperialism as regularly understood, a policy of domination that obtained "colonies" and spheres of influence for the United States, not only in the New World but in the Pacific and in Asia as well. The event that marked the general abandon-

[24] In Commager, *op. cit.*, p. 235. See also Richardson, *op. cit.*, Vol. II, pp. 207 ff.
[25] For a brief plausible explanation of American isolationism, see Dexter Perkins, *The American Approach to Foreign Policy* (Cambridge, Harvard University Press, 1952), pp. 11–12.

ment of the policy of continentalism and the clear-cut emergence of the United States as a first-rate power in international affairs was the Spanish-American War of 1898.

There is a relation between continentalism and imperialism proper. It has been mentioned that there were imperialistic elements in the policy of continentalism, as the westward expansion rolled on. When America reached California and the Pacific Coast, the only places left to expand on the North American continent were Mexico and Canada. Mexico had already suffered substantial losses to her North American neighbor in the Texas and Mexican wars in the form of the present states of Texas, California, parts of Arizona, New Mexico, Nevada, and Utah. Americans had once dreamed of adding Canada to the United States, but Canada had not been conquered in the War of 1812, and good Anglo-American relations afterward led to peaceable settlement of border differences and disputes.

If Mexico and Canada were to be bypassed and Europe avoided, expansion—which now took on a more clearly recognizable imperialistic color—would have to take place in the Pacific and Asia, in the Caribbean or South America.[26] Hence, it is no accident that the blowing up of the battleship *Maine* in the harbor of Havana, Cuba, a Spanish colony, precipitated a war which led to the acquisition by the United States of Puerto Rico, Hawaii, Guam, and the Philippines, and the establishment of a protectorate over Cuba.

Shortly after the Spanish-American War, Secretary of State John Hay enunciated the policy of the Open Door in China, by which he tried to commit the great nations of the world to a policy of commercial opportunity in China in return for respect of her territorial integrity. The policy has been described cynically as "no special privileges for individual exploiting nations, equal opportunity for all exploiting nations."

America's interests in the Pacific (outright control in the Philippines, Hawaii, Guam, Samoa; trade, and support for the territorial integrity of China) stimulated pressure for a larger navy and a canal to link our fleet in two oceans. The Panama Canal, after vigorous action by Theodore Roosevelt to secure a site, called for protective naval bases in the Caribbean and hegemony over the countries of the Caribbean area. Now a major power, with a modest empire in the Caribbean and the Pacific, the United States lost its old continental isolation.

Even in its heyday, however, imperialism was vigorously challenged. Why keep the Philippines, seven thousand miles away from the United States, closer to the Far East than to North America? The imperialists replied that the United States must shoulder the white man's burden,

---

[26] Apparently, Africa was never seriously considered as an area for imperial expansion.

carry the blessings of Christianity and civilization to the heathen, open up opportunities for American investments and markets, acquire strategic lands before they were gobbled up by other powers. Anti-imperialists charged that imperialism was a betrayal of the principles of freedom upon which the republic had been based, that in ruling alien peoples America would be corrupted, that imperial rule would bring with it the necessity of large armies and navies and a threat to civilian principles of government, and that the United States would inevitably be swept up in the sordid storm of power politics, with its entangling alliances and pernicious "deals."

Generally speaking, the American conscience has been uneasy about imperialism. In the Philippines, after an unhappy but brief period of military rule, the country was gradually prepared for independence, which was promised in 1934 and fulfilled in 1946. Similarly, the United States has substantially abided by the principle of self-government for other American acquisitions of the Spanish-American War, such as Hawaii and Puerto Rico.

It is true that, between 1898 and 1918, the United States intervened in the affairs of Cuba for a three-year period (1906–1909), and occupied the territory of Nicaragua, Haiti, and the Dominican Republic for longer periods. Yet, invariably, the United States has not only abstained from "gobbling up" the smaller powers, but has endeavored to set them on the path of responsible self-government. It is also true that Theodore Roosevelt's corollary to the Monroe Doctrine in 1904 pre-empted the right for the United States to police certain Latin American countries, whose "chronic wrongdoing" or "impotence" tempted European powers to intervene. Yet, by the time of Franklin Roosevelt the policy of the "big brother" had been replaced by that of the "good neighbor." Direct American intervention in Latin American affairs was explicitly rejected. Subsequently, the American states moved toward closer co-operation for settlement of American problems and for mutual security against aggression.

World-wide involvement. With continentalism the dominant theme of American foreign policy, imperialism, as symbolized by the Spanish-American War, represented a break with that policy, and pushed the United States into greater involvement in world affairs. This was to become more noticeable with World War I, and later World War II, which marked the end of political isolation from Europe and the beginning of what might be called a policy of full-fledged involvement in international politics.

America entered World War I presumably because Germany refused to abandon its policy of unrestricted submarine warfare, which the United States considered harmful to America's maritime neutral rights. The

United States used its power to help defeat Germany, and it is now generally agreed that American intervention was decisive in bringing Germany to terms.

However, America's first major involvement in European affairs was brief. With the end of the war, isolationist sentiment reasserted itself. The United States turned its back on both balance of power and collective security. The Senate rejected the American-British-French pact urged by the French and designed to protect France from future German aggression; it also spurned the League of Nations, an international organization designed to maintain peace by providing means for collective action against aggression.

In the 1920's American policy was a combination of isolationism and limited international co-operation. The United States participated in some League activities, assisted in the settlement of the German reparations question, joined with other naval powers in reducing armaments, and promoted the Kellogg Peace Pact, by which signatories would renounce war as an instrument of national policy. Yet, the United States sharply curtailed immigration to this country, insisted on at least partial payment of its war debts, even making payment difficult by raising tariffs, and abstained from commitments either to maintain the balance of power or to support collective action against aggression.

In the 1930's, objection to participation in European affairs culminated in the passage of neutrality legislation. The legislation, in large part, reflected the view that the United States had been needlessly involved in World War I by poor leadership, Allied propaganda, and the pressure of financial interests and munitions makers. It was a reaction against war and its consequences. It forbade Americans to travel on belligerent ships, prohibited loans to belligerents, outlawed traffic in arms and ammunition, and required that payment be made for other purchases before shipment from the United States.

It is true that Secretary of State Stimson in 1932 sought to rally world opinion against Japanese aggression in Manchuria and that President Franklin D. Roosevelt in 1937 suggested that lawbreaking nations be placed in quarantine. Still, the dominant tide in the country was against major involvement in either Asia or Europe.

It was not really until 1939–41 that the United States came alive to the inevitability of its participation in international affairs, as a major power in a major way. By this time the reality of Japanese expansion and domination in Asia were clear for all to see. Japanese aggression mocked the policy of the Open Door in China by violating China's territorial integrity. She had moved against the defeated French in Indochina and proclaimed her ultimate intention of dominating Asia. Similarly, the fall of France and the Low Countries, and the British retreat at Dunkirk, made a vivid impression on the American mind. The United States then moved to place its power behind Britain and to adopt a "harder" attitude toward Japan. It adopted conscription, repealed much of its neutrality legislation, and began to function as the arsenal of democracy under the Lend-Lease Act. Unofficially, the United States entered the naval war against Germany in the Atlantic, occupied Greenland and Iceland in 1940, extended its naval patrols, resorted to convoys in the North Atlantic, and even ordered United States' vessels to shoot German submarines on sight.

The Japanese attack on Pearl Harbor on December 7, 1941, brought the United States into the war in both the Pacific and the Atlantic, and in Asia, Europe, and Africa, for Hitler and Mussolini, in accord with their treaty of alliance with Japan, promptly declared war on the United States.

World War II, and the memory of United States' semi-isolation in the 1920's and neutrality in the 1930's gave the *coup de grace* to isolationism in America. Isolationist sentiment might still hamper the more generous and liberal commitment of the United States to the United Nations, programs of foreign aid, and a system of world-wide alliances, but the commitment to remain involved in a major way in international politics would not be altered. Similarly, quasi-imperialistic sentiment might urge the enforcement, unilaterally, of a *Pax Americana*, a more vigorous pursuit of policy in Asia (against the Chinese Communists), a forthright policy of liberation in Europe, and even a policy of preventive war against the Soviet Union. Still, the United States officially adopted a policy of containment, not of preventive war, and eschewed the risky ventures of extending the Korean or Indochina wars or of embarking upon an outright program of liberation of the Soviet Union's satellites in Europe.

Yet, the precise nature of this full-fledged participation in international politics was not immediately clear. Should the United States rely primarily upon a policy of collective security, functioning through the United Nations or some new world organization? Or should it rely upon the balance of power, based upon alliances with friends against foes? Or should it, in view of the alleged weaknesses of a policy of containment, mount an offensive against the Soviet Union with the object of freeing captive peoples and destroying the communist will to power?

The Balance of Power in American History

The American Revolution and the French Alliance. Initially, it is important to note the decisive role of the alliance made by the infant American nation with the French monarch. Most historians agree that this alliance, and the substantial help that it brought, played an important part in America's victory against the British in the War for Independence. What is too often forgotten, however, is that this alliance was part and parcel of the European balance of power, which Americans were later to loathe. Had not Britain and France been rivals in Europe, had not the French desired to inflict harm on a traditional enemy, and had not the French hoped to recoup in the New World some of the losses they had suffered in the Seven Years' War in Europe (known as the French and Indian War in America), there would probably have been no French Alliance. In this sense, the infant American republic profited from the Old World struggle in the balance of power.

The Napoleonic wars. With Napoleon's advent to power, a train of events was set in motion that was to make France the dominant power in Europe. British policy, pursuant to the principle of the balance of power, was to resist Napoleon's domination of the continent. Three illustrations point up how vitally this struggle in Europe affected the United States. The first two involve President Jefferson and Louisiana; the third relates to the War of 1812.

In 1802 Jefferson wrote to the American Ambassador in France: [27]

There is on the globe one single spot [the mouth of the Mississippi] the possessor of which is our natural and habitual enemy. The day that France takes possession of New Orleans seals the union of two nations [the United States and Britain], who, in conjunction, can maintain exclusive possession of the sea. From that moment [that France controls the mouth of the Mississippi] we must marry ourselves to the British fleet and nation.

Here was Jefferson—formerly America's French Ambassador, a friend of the French Revolution, and an earlier critic of what he felt was the pro-British, anti-French policy of early administrations—recognizing the necessity of joining with Britain to balance French power in the New World. The letter demonstrates his concern lest a dominant European power, France under Napoleon, threaten vital American interests in the free navigation of the Mississippi. It can be inferred that self-preservation and the fear of domination would have thrust the United States into the balance-of-power struggle had Napoleon cut off the mouth of the Mississippi.

The second Jefferson illustration relates to the Louisiana Purchase, universally conceded to be a diplomatic coup. In one magnificent stroke, for the paltry sum of 15 million dollars, Jefferson acquired a huge new empire for the lusty young republic. By this action the land under the United States' flag was more than doubled. Yet few stop to realize that this rich prize, which freed the United States for the eventual march to the shores of the Pacific, fell to it as a result of Napoleon's preoccupation with the European struggle and balance of power. Because he was faced with the possibility of a new war with Britain, Napoleon had to fill the nation's coffers. Fifteen million American dollars paid for Louisiana,

[27] The letter appears in Commager, *op. cit.*, pp. 189–190.

which had been easily secured from the decadent Spanish Empire, helped to replenish Napoleon's war fund.

The third example, the War of 1812, also indicates how the United States profited from the preoccupation of Britain and France with the European struggle and balance of power. The war itself had been brought on by American insistence upon a neutral's rights at sea, and was fed by America's appetite for western expansion. Both ran counter to British national interest in the war against Napoleon and her imperial interests in the New World. Britain, however, was tied up with Napoleon in what seemed, at times, to be a life-and-death struggle in Europe, and was therefore unable to prosecute the war in America with vigor. In 1814, even before the American victory at New Orleans, Wellington, fatigued by the ordeal with Napoleon on the Continent and hearing of Perry's victory on the Great Lakes, reached the conclusion that the United States could not be defeated.

1815–1914. At this point an intriguing question occurs. Why could the United States, between 1815 and 1914, enjoy the luxury of political isolation from Europe, the cockpit of international politics? A number of answers might be given. A few of the more important and interrelated factors will be mentioned here. First, the century was, relatively speaking, one of peace; at least no major European war, which generally also meant a world war, plagued the earth. This may have been due largely (a second factor) to the fact that, after Napoleon and before the rise of the Kaiser's Germany, no nation on the Continent threatened to dominate Europe, and thus the Atlantic community. The third and fourth factors are fairly obvious: In this period the United States had nothing to fear from rival nations in the New World; nor was there any threat in the Pacific until the rise of Japan, which was only clearly indicated by the Japanese victory in the Russo-Japanese War in 1904–1905. The fifth and perhaps most important factor deserves fuller treatment: the silent alliance between Britain and the United States. The alliance permitted the United States to turn its back on Europe politically, because Britain was ready, willing, and able to maintain the European balance of power protecting not only Britain but also the United States and the New World.

The silent Anglo-American alliance. Only Britain, a major naval power dominant in the Atlantic and on the other seas, could threaten the United States, which was sheltered by two great expanses of ocean. A vital question arises: Why did Britain not seek to dominate the United States? Why did she participate willingly in the silent, unwritten, informal but highly significant Anglo-American alliance?

At the outset, it should be noted that British interests substantially coincided with those of the United States in seeking to prevent an extension to the New World, by way of further colonization or imperialistic aggrandizement, of the power of Old World nations. Canning, the British Foreign Minister, had originally proposed a doctrine comparable to that which President Monroe later announced on his own. What is not generally known is that Canning helped to make the Monroe Doctrine effective by informing the French—and thus other continental powers—that if France tried to send an army to South America for purposes of conquest, the British fleet would intercept and sink the transporting French armada! This Anglo-American community of interest (which, of course, extended beyond power politics into common heritage, language, commitment to constitutional government) is illustrated by many examples of peaceful settlement of disputes. Just as the United States could rely upon Britain to maintain a protective balance of power in the Old World, the latter could rely upon the former to uphold British interests in the New World.

A second factor was Britain's dominant foreign policy with regard to the world generally, and the New World particularly. Britain did not seek dominion in the New World; she was interested only in the opportunity for investment and trade. This conformed to Britain's general policy, which with some exceptions was a liberal one, based on the desire to see nations become self-governing and (in peace) on the principle of freedom of the seas and of trade. A third factor, which presumably assumed greater significance as the young American republic grew in strength, was the proximity of Canada and the United States. Canada, a part of the British Empire, undoubtedly figured as an American hostage in the event of an Anglo-American war; its safety, therefore, depended on peaceful Anglo-American relations.

Still another factor was Britain's increasing preoccupation with the defense of her interests elsewhere in the world, against the French, Russians, and Germans, for example. This preoccupation made harmonious Anglo-American relations a British necessity.

A final factor relates to a lesson which Britain was taught in the American Revolution, but which apparently did not sink in until the War of 1812: that Britain could not defeat the United States on the American continent and stood to gain more from a free, strong, great, united, and independent America than from the extension of Old World struggles and divisions to the New World.

World Wars I and II. With a closer approach to the modern period, it becomes more difficult to reach agreement on the role of balance of power in American history. One school of thought maintains that both world wars taught the United States that the protective role Britain had played in the old balance of power was no longer possible. Hence the United States fulfilled Canning's remark, at the time of the Monroe Doctrine, that he had called forth a New World to redress the balance of the Old.

In World War I, it is argued, the United States recognized the threat to its interest that lay in the potential domination of the Atlantic community by the Kaiser's Germany. Hence, the United States used its power to defeat Germany. Unfortunately for the American people, however, President Wilson's idealistic appeals to make the world safe for democracy obscured the fact that America was now vitally affected by the European balance of power.

A similar argument holds for World War II. Hitler's Germany now replaced the Kaiser's Germany as a threat to the Atlantic community, which could no longer be defended by Britain, struggling to maintain the balance of power on the European continent. The threat to the United States posed by a western Europe under Hitler's heel produced America's decision to redress the balance of power by intervening against Hitler. In World War II, of course, the situation was complicated by the threat of Japanese domination of Asia and the Pacific, areas made more vulnerable by Hitler's victory over the French and Dutch and by Britain's inability to adequately defend her interests in Asia and the Pacific. Here again, America's power serves to weight the balance against Japan.

Other observers have argued that our entry into one or both wars was a mistake. Here, various critics advance different arguments. Some say our vital interests were not threatened in one or both wars. Others contend that we defeated the Kaiser's Germany only to be confronted by communism and fascism a generation later. Still others believe we could best have advanced our national interest and indirectly that of the world by avoiding entanglements such as those of World Wars I and II. Some say we defeated Hitler's Germany and militaristic Japan in World War II, only to be faced by Communist Russia and China at the end of it.

It is the purpose of this chapter to stimulate this debate, not to resolve it. This debate is highly relevant to an evaluation of the modified balance-of-power policy that the United States adopted after World War II.

Must the United States rely upon a modified balance of power to achieve adjustment in world affairs—a balance of power based on the premise that the free world must have sufficient strength and be willing to apply it to deter aggression? Should the United States reject the balance of power as a way of maintaining a free and peaceful world because its disadvantages heavily outweigh its advantages? Or should the United States reject outdated balance-of-power policies in favor of a policy of liberation, in which power is exerted on behalf of moral principles?

POSITIONS
ON THE PROBLEM

1. THE UNITED STATES MUST RELY
UPON A MODIFIED BALANCE OF POWER

(The following extracts are taken from Louis J. Halle, *Civilization and Foreign Policy*.[28] Mr. Halle was associated with the State Department roughly from 1941 to 1954. In his last few years there, he served as a member of the Policy Planning Staff in the Office of the Secretary of State.)

America and the European Balance of Power

. . . When we entered World War I we did so as England had entered the wars of Europe before us, to redress the European Balance of Power. . . .

. . . By our intervention in World War I we associated ourselves with the European Balance of Power and assumed a part for ourselves in the conduct of international power politics.

For us to do this was surely not evil. We were defending ourselves and, at the same time, defending the cause of freedom in so far as we represented it. Using the jargon of those times one may say that we invoked our might to defend the right—or to defend, at least, our rights. Few of us doubt that it would have been wrong for us not to do so. But we, the American people, could not allow ourselves to take a realistic view of what we were doing because we had grown up believing that "power politics" and "the Balance of Power" were evil in themselves, representing the nefarious policies of monarchs bent only on their own imperial aggrandizement. The terms stood for a cynical game that the crowned heads of the old world played among themselves with their armies, at the expense of the masses that languished under their feudal sway. We saw power supporting evil, and it was not difficult for us to take the step from this view to the view that power was evil. . . .

To think of power as being of itself evil, however, is tantamount to thinking of life as being of itself evil. Life is dynamic by nature, it is animated by kinetic energy, it expresses itself in power. . . .

The eternal problem of politics, national or international, domestic or foreign, is not to do away with power but to tame it, to control it, to confine it within legitimate channels. . . . A close analysis might show, I think, that the balance of power tends, in fact, to be inimical to tyranny and to provide certain safeguards for freedom. If the alternative to a balance of power is a concentration of power we ought to hesitate before preferring the latter. . . .

[28] Louis J. Halle, *Civilization and Foreign Policy* (New York, Harper, copyright, 1955, by Louis Joseph Halle, Jr.), pp. 41, 44–45, 49–52, 203–204, 221, 231, 255–256, 259–260.

Having abandoned our isolationist policy in 1917 we undertook to crown our intervention by reforming the old world in our image. We sought to establish, in the League of Nations, a regime of explicit constitutional law to regulate relations among the nation-states to the end of maintaining an environment of general freedom in which our own freedoms would be safe. We thought of such a regime as supplanting the Balance of Power rather than supplementing and reinforcing it, as if law were somehow an alternative to power. Believing that power politics meant war as well as tyranny, we undertook to illegitimize rather than legalize them, to disenfranchise rather than regulate them, to denature power by solemn declarations and pledges to which it would submit, and to disarm the nations. We had recrossed the ocean, we thought, not to restore the Balance of Power but to abolish it. By refusing to accept power as a fact in international relations, we ruled out any measures shrewdly designed to regulate it. . . .

. . . When . . . the reality of power was made manifest in the peace settlement [after World War I] we withdrew across the ocean in moral indignation and resumed our isolation. And we erased from our minds, as a frightening dream, the lesson of 1917 that, if we valued our safety, we could not longer be indifferent to the maintenance of the European Balance of Power. . . .

One may speculate wistfully that if we (perhaps in cooperation with the British) had assumed the former British role of regulating and maintaining the European Balance of Power we might all have enjoyed another century of such relative peace and stability as had distinguished the period from 1815 to 1914. . . .

Then again Germany embarked on the conquest of . . . Europe. Again at the eleventh hour we saw the threat and responded to it. Again at an incalculable cost to Western civilization we and the British—allied with the Soviet Union by force of necessity like crusaders allied with the infidel—repulsed Germany's assault and overcame her.

And once again, because we had so assiduously resisted the lesson of World War I, we undertook as victors to create a world in which power would be bridled by agreements and solemn pledges so that it would not have to be balanced. In the new form which our misconception of the world took we concluded that the nation-states were divisible into two categories: the aggressor states and the peace-loving states. If the aggressor states were deprived of power and if political machinery was created for reaching and registering agreement among the peace-loving states, who would by definition use their power to preserve peace, the problem of ordered freedom in the world was solved.

It seems strange to us now, though the logic will escape no one, that Germany, Italy, and Japan were named the aggressor states while the Soviet Union was associated with China and ourselves as one of the peace-loving states. On the basis of this continuing refusal to see a balance of power as either good or necessary we cooperated with the Soviet Union in creating the German and Japanese "power vacuums" on either side of her into which, while we confidently demobilized our forces, she proceeded to expand her power. We saw our error, again at the eleventh hour, and ever since have led Western civilization in a desperate effort to restore that Balance of Power which it had been our custom to decry. . . .

American Leadership of a Free-World Coalition

(Halle poses the question "What should our policy be?" and rejects the policies of isolation and dominion in favor of a policy of American leadership in a free-world coalition. Apropos of isolation, he concludes: "The isolationist policy appears to violate the principle that security, at least in the absence of absolute dominion, depends on a balance of power. It proposes in effect a retreat from present positions that, in itself, would reduce our relative weight in the world-wide balance." Dominion, which might include preventive war, must be rejected because "it conduces to the spread rather than the retraction of barbarism." He concludes that "our survival as the kind of nation we are requires us to defend our civilization as a whole, to associate ourselves with its other representatives in a defensive coalition, and to exercise the leadership of that coalition on a basis of consent.")

. . . To retain the consent of our allies for our policy and to preserve ourselves we must maintain such a posture of force as promises either to prevent a major war altogether or, at least, to make enemy use of nuclear weapons against population centers and industries in a war unlikely. . . .

. . . In order to realize the objective of deterring a nuclear attack by our opponents and the further objectives of deterring or frustrating other kinds of military aggression we need:

(a) To maintain a nuclear offensive power of our own sufficient to make the probable cost to our opponent of starting a nuclear war unacceptable;

(b) To protect that power and the nation on which it is based by provisions for defense against nuclear attack that would discourage our opponent from undertaking to incapacitate us and destroy our nuclear capability by a surprise attack;

(c) To develop and maintain such military forces as would deter or, at least, frustrate any military attack of a more traditional nature, in the event that the nuclear power on both sides was such as to deter either side from using it against the population centers or industries of the other. . . .

Having seen what we may expect from the alternative policies of isolation and dominion, we should ask ourselves now what we may plausibly expect if we brace ourselves to follow the general course we have at last set for ourselves here.

We can expect no abrupt solutions to our problems at all. They will continue to remain with us, although undergoing those constant, slow, churning transformations that characterize the general movement of history. We cannot expect any finality, since finality is to be found only in death. We cannot expect a world without rivals and challenges to what we represent. We cannot expect a world in which our power is not balanced by other powers antagonistic to it. We cannot, in other words, expect either an American world or an external environment that does not bear more or less dangerously upon us. What we can expect is that our present barbarian challengers, unable to prey on us, will have to make adjustments in their own dispositions to our strength. We can expect the gradual restoration of a relatively stable balance of power in the world and the consequent creation of a situation in which such wars as occur may well remain limited because the antagonists have tacitly agreed to accept each other's survival as an alternative to mutual destruction. We can hope for, say, another century of troubled peace in which barbarism is frustrated and our nation finds itself gradually emerging on the high road of a more secure future. Beyond that one cannot see.

2. THE UNITED STATES CANNOT RELY UPON THE BALANCE OF POWER TO MAINTAIN A FREE AND PEACEFUL WORLD

(The following passages are taken from Edward V. Gulick, *The Balance of Power*. This pamphlet was one in a series entitled *Coercion: A Study in the Use of Force*.[29])

Introduction

Adherents of the Balance of Power must be willing to face the disadvantages of their policy. They must admit that it means continued existence for the system of sovereign, independent states and full-blown career for power politics. From this it is possible to deduce the disadvantages of the Balance of Power.

Costs; Arms Races

If the state must rely upon its own power in its struggle for survival in a hostile world, a premium is placed upon the instruments of power; more efficient weapons give a margin of superiority in their category and a neighbor nation cannot overlook such a threat to its own security. . . . The margin of superiority for one state is a margin of inferiority for its neighbor. Thus security for one means insecurity for another.

Nothing could seem more inevitable in history than the development of an armament race out of such a background, each nation seeking to accumulate more power than its potential rivals. . . .

Rivalry for Strategic Bases

If the nation-state must look to the Balance of Power for its own security, it is usually tempted to take advantage of any gain which will enhance its power. It cannot overlook the possibility of war with other states, and cannot lightly overlook what will give it superiority at that time. . . .

Once the race for geographical advantage is fairly begun, statesmen must resort, if necessary, to the most sordid "grabbing" of land and population. . . . And we can be sure that such a race will repeat itself as long as the state-system remains unmodified.

Secret Diplomacy

. . . Secret diplomacy . . . is usually used to mean *secret policy and negotiation*. The public is informed of neither, nor is the knowledge imparted freely to foreign governments. Great disadvantages attach to such conduct: the often needless fear which it gives rise to, and the ignorance in which voters must act when they know little or nothing of the real facts. . . .

[29] *The Balance of Power* (Philadelphia, The Pacifist Research Bureau, 1943), pp. 37–57 *passim*.

One of the contributing causes of World War I was the matter of "secret diplomacy." When diplomats could not be sure just what was going on between potential enemy powers, their safety lay in reporting the maximum potential danger, which in turn led to maximum preparation by their own countries for such danger. . . .

Treaty-Breaking

. . . At the height of the Balance of Power in the seventeenth and eighteenth centuries, treaties were made and broken so fast that our heads swim to read of them today. Contemporaries denounced Louis XIV for his breaking of treaties in much the same way that Hitler was cursed in the 1930's for his continual violation of German pledges. . . . The central point is not the fact that Hitler himself engineered these violations of Germany's pledged word, but the fact that sooner or later in a system of Balance of Power this will be done by someone, whether his name is Hitler or not. . . .

The Individual Must Make Difficult Decisions

The state-system and the Balance of Power place the individual in a difficult position: he may have to choose between personal ethics and his loyalty to the nation-state. Peaceful citizen that he may be in private life, in time of war he cannot follow the non-violent teachings of any of the great religious leaders without running counter to the nation-state. . . . The nation-state, in the race for power, has to spread its own influence over more and more of the private life of the individual citizen. A drug store clerk in Portland, Oregon, who was not yet born when the Treaty of Versailles was written, and who knew little and cared less about international affairs, suddenly found himself in the army because of distant convulsions in the international scene—and along with him, salesmen from New York, accountants from Cleveland, fruit pickers from California, and mechanics from Georgia. These facts are evidence of the dominance of the nation-state in crucial matters in the lives of private citizens. Other loyalties are pushed aside. Fidelity to ethics, to the labor movement, to one's own family, to art, to learning, are all secondary to the nation-state. Scientists pervert their calling by making explosives, artists work on propaganda, scholars do the same, internationally-minded members of the labor movement kill each other in battle, and doctors heal that more killing may be possible. It is futile to think of freeing the individual from the degradation of such compromises as these, unless the state-system be altered to take instruments of war away from the nation-state. Half-measures will not suffice.

The Balance of Power and Democracy Are Incompatible in the Long View

. . . Freedom of speech is not compatible with the maximum power of the state; therefore it must be shelved. Conscription for the armed services replaces voluntary enlistment. . . . As the weapons of warfare become more intricate, they mount in cost. . . . Taxes rise to a point that our ancestors would have believed fantastic. In addition, indoctrination of the populace must ultimately be exploited as a source of power. Average citizens, if not born good soldiers, can be made such by methodical teaching begun in childhood. The instruments of propaganda—press, radio, movies, poster art, and textbooks—are thus mobilized for power. The democratic process of discussing policy before its adoption must be abolished in favor of a more efficient method; democracies move too slowly. . . .

. . . Democracy is impossible in the long run in such a system. Between wars there may be lulls in which democracy can be practiced, but even these must eventually be ephemeral as power becomes further expanded. If we insist on preserving our complete sovereignty and unlimited independence of action in the post-war world, we shall do so at the sacrifice of our democracy.

The Concept of the Balance of Power Is Faulty

But can't we say that the Balance of Power has merely been poorly applied, and that we, with better information and more skill in science today, could make it into a scientific concept and apply it with success? This is impossible for several reasons: (A) the idea of Balance of Power is inexact; (B) power defies precise measurement; and (C) international relations are dynamic, not static. . . .

Warfare Is Inevitable Under the Balance of Power

It is not surprising that such complexity [the complexity of modern international politics] should defy the nimbleness of statesmen and result in war sooner or later. The history of the state-system indicates that the Balance of Power has not been and cannot be a peace policy. Its most discriminating adherents will have to admit that much. . . .

In view of the evidence, we are impelled to say the Balance of Power is no longer a practicable mechanism for adjustment in any sense of the word; it was a sixteenth and seventeenth century machinery for adjustment to conditions which demanded only small armies and navies. Twentieth century nation-states armed to the teeth are in a very different class. As an adjustment, it never was especially desirable, but it is infinitely harmful in the twentieth century because it threatens the existence of millions of people, to say nothing of much that is precious in our civilization.

Conclusion

The Balance of Power postulates an anarchic system of sovereign, independent states. This system possesses certain advantages and disadvantages, the former being to a great extent illusory, and the latter very real. . . .

The disadvantages . . . heavily outweigh the advantages: secret diplomacy is a natural outgrowth of the system; treaty-breaking and other forms of international immorality will continue to be a necessity under the Balance of Power; religion must see itself compromised and the individual pushed into the position of one who has to choose between irreconcilable loyalties; democracy is impossible in the long run under the Balance of Power; the concept of the Balance of Power is inexact, and successful practice of it is impossible without resort to war, an extremity which is continuing to exact a greater and yet greater toll in lives and money and material as weapons become more powerful.

Balance of Power in its customary form means international immorality, terrible economic costs, ultimate disappearance of democracy and perpetuation of warfare threatening the life of everyone. There is, however, another general line of approach to the security problems of the twentieth century, and that is the utilization of what is good in balanced power and elimination of what is bad. It is apparent that the armed sovereign state and the Balance of Power are great dangers to our civilization. It is equally apparent that if the Balance of

Power could be radically modified, and a strong impartial international authority set up, the main aspects of a solution to our urgent security problems would be present. . . .

It would be presumptuous to submit a blueprint for a new world order at this point . . . but the main lines of the solution can confidently be stated to lie in some kind of extensive international government. Ultimately such a government must possess practical legislative and judicial control over *all* the important friction-areas in international affairs. . . .

It will take great sacrifice to produce world government and to give up our luxuries of sovereignty and hyper-nationalism, but this century must inevitably be a period of great sacrifice, either for war or for peace. Unless we buy our world peace by establishing world government at great sacrifice, we shall be called upon to offer our fortunes and energies and lives in other wars for the nation-state. If we and our statesmen fail so to alter the state-system that the Balance of Power will be unnecessary in its present form, the uneasy future demands that we shall have to think in terms of balancing one armed continent against another with World Wars III, IV, V, and VI as our inevitable rewards.

3. THE SOUNDEST BASIS FOR FOREIGN POLICY IS THE USE OF POWER IN THE SERVICE OF MORAL PRINCIPLE

(The material reprinted here is to be found in Thomas I. Cook and Malcolm Moos, *Power Through Purpose*.[30] The authors are professors of political science at The Johns Hopkins University.)

Preface

The United States is the heir and standard-bearer of a culture begotten and bred in Europe. That culture rests on the twin foundations of Graeco-Roman politics and law and Judaeo-Christian ethics and religion. Our own tradition and history give us a unique position as modern champions of those ancient insights. Our constitutional democracy and our industrial technology provide us with unique opportunities to realize the Western promise in the daily practice of our lives and through the sure functioning of free institutions. We are equipped to achieve both citizenship as social and political participation in the shaping of our lives and destinies and the full development of the ultimate and irreducible person. Possessed of vast power and called to leadership in the world, we can, if we will, spread our ideals elsewhere and help others on the road to their realization. Our middle-class society is marked by an increasingly shared amplitude of economic means and by broad enjoyment of leisure for the cultivation of humane ends. It is the true classless society, without benefit of revolution or need for totalitarian discipline. It is the leader in the fight against these needless and soul-destroying ills, and against their spread. Its mission is to persuade those still free that they can with its help profitably and successfully follow its way, and to rescue those who are the victims of tyranny and set them, too, on the right path. To that end it must first strengthen its adherence to its own ideals and institutions at home, and purify its political practice. It must fight without compromise the internal enemies of its method of freedom. It must

[30] Thomas I. Cook and Malcolm Moos, *Power Through Purpose* (Baltimore, Johns Hopkins Press, 1954), Preface, pp. 109–110, 112–113, 203, 212 *passim*.

maintain without compromise the essential rights of those committed to those methods, and must champion the values of creative dissent and personal difference. Its foreign policy must no less clearly and forthrightly distinguish between friend and foe, and must be devised as an integral part of the total politics of a nation whose interest is international and whose ethical principles rightly claim universal validity.

Such are the theses of this book. In propounding them, the authors have sought to clarify the issues in the present "Great Debate," and to fight the extremes of utopian worldism and realistic nationalism. . . .

Criticism of a New Balance-of-Power System

Some of the more moderate among the present proponents of American policy based on realistic calculations of national interest correctly argue that the United States has taken the place as a world power once held by Britain. . . .

. . . The lesson, the balance-of-power advocates insist, is plain. America, possessed of England's sometime power, must also adopt and adapt its concept of policy. . . . The only real alternative is between a narrowly selfish and expansionist use of power, accompanied by delusions of grandeur whose outcome is apt to be defeat, and an enlightened and responsible promotion of the national interest, directed to the sustained husbanding of American leadership through moderation in objective combined with firmness in action. But the latter choice, these advocates tell us, involves the proper selfishness of minimizing risks which could dissipate power. We must speedily become aware that the United States can by deliberate action create and preserve a balance of power in the rest of the world. On the other hand, it cannot impose its will or its way on that world, or over a major part of it. Likewise, it cannot attain security by a callous or indifferent isolation, provocative of envy and resentment. . . .

. . . The policy of balance of power is today impracticable. Its initiation would immediately necessitate the organization and buttressing, if not the creation, of at least one side of the balance. The force to be counterpoised against the U.S.S.R. would have to be brought into existence. In Europe, an old world would have to be called into being by revivification ere the new world could make itself the balancing force. In the Far East, the radically different problem of organizing a modern system of independent and modernized states would present equal difficulties. From the outset, therefore, it is clear that such a program is artificial. It involves a mechanical attempt to manufacture an equivalent of what was in its day a growth of policy out of living political forces and established conditions of international relations. In the name of reliance on historical experience and use of the teachings of history, it overlooks or fails to understand the reality of history as living and changing situations. These necessitate new techniques to implement our lasting moral objectives. . . .

Those who argue that American national interest necessitates a balance-of-power policy do not seriously contemplate a possible future when we should be required to throw our weight to the Russian side. From such a line of action they would quite properly recoil in horror. Moreover, they are no doubt correct in the assumption that within a foreseeable future it is the anti-Communist powers which will need the support of a make-weight. Yet a policy whose defined conditions and enduring consequences would be unacceptable to its own proponents cannot be a proper formulation of national interest, nor a genuine realism. The nature and degree of support which ought to be given to actual or potential opponents of Communist and of Soviet ambition, East or West, are still open to debate. But bipolar opposition and conflict are lasting and fundamental as long as the Soviet Union adheres to neo-Marxist teaching and promotes it as a world program. Hence debate over policy cannot be conducted, nor American interest furthered, on the theory and practice of balance of power.

A new American balance-of-power system is not, then, a practicable way to further the nation's interests. . . .

A Preferable Strategy

Our own strategy, which may indeed lead soon or late to war being thrust upon us by an increasingly insecure Russian regime, must be directed to encouraging germs of discontent within the Soviet Union and its satellites wherever possible, and to the extent possible. We must organize and aid potential revolutionaries there, yet as far as possible restrain them from ill-calculated or premature action. We must persuade the Russian people that we are opposed to a tyranny which at once deprives them of immediately available material well-being, personal security, and freedom, and threatens the peace and prospects of ameliorative prosperity for the rest of the world. We must ourselves develop our own system, including its military power, so that at the ripe moment we may aid them first to throw off their chains with minimum cost and disruption, and then to reconstruct society on their own design and tradition, without undue suffering, and without intervention designed to impose our special dogmas or institutions or to further interests peculiar to ourselves. . . .

For our sway over others will be no imperial rule, but the respected influence of demonstrated success and primacy in devotion to a common humanity. Our arts will be wise assistance and unfailing support towards liberation, towards others sharing in and contributing to a common, yet vastly rich and varied, culture. Peace will indeed be our end, and a custom sought for the world, through international law and international institutions founded on principle, to which we ourselves are also willingly subject because their leading proponents. In search of that law, it will be our ardent mission not simply to spare the humble but to deliver the oppressed. To that end we shall indeed make war *à outrance,* with no compromise, on the proud dictators who pervert all principle and debase men whom they have first oppressed. Thus our moral empire will rest on a freely accepted appeal to the minds and hearts of peoples liberated with our assistance, enjoying our respect on grounds of a common humanity, and welcomed as partners in the human venture who by their efforts and insights enrich the stock of human culture. Only such uncompulsive empire is consonant with our heritage, our insights, our concept of mission, and the moral security of our own institutions. By reason of that heritage and inspiration, we can accept no less, and seek no more.

QUESTIONS

1. What is meant by the "revolution in American foreign policy"?

2. State and defend your own attitude toward power. How does it compare with the attitudes set forth in this chapter?

3. How would you define the balance of power?

4. What has been the role of the balancer in the balance of power?

5. Illustrate the varying ways in which the balance of power operates.

6. Do you agree that the balance of power, as it has operated in the past, has been unstable, uncertain, and insecure? Explain.

7. What is the nature of the American modification of the old balance of power? Why was a policy of "positions of strength" adopted?

8. What have been the major themes of United States' foreign policy?

9. What has been the role of the balance of power in American history?

10. With which of the three positions just presented do you agree most fully? Why?

SELECT BIBLIOGRAPHY

BEARD, Charles A., *A Foreign Policy for America* (New York, Knopf, 1940). Defends a policy of continentalism in opposition to imperialism or internationalism. Maintains that continentalism wisely represents the true American center of gravity. Recognizes America's limited power to achieve peace and democracy throughout the world. Without becoming a "hermit nation" and while adhering to a restrained diplomacy, America should concentrate on building a magnificent American civilization.

BRYSON, Lyman, and others, eds., *Conflicts of Power in Modern Culture* (New York, Harper, 1947). Interesting and stimulating collection of short articles on conflicts of power. Represents many disciplines.

CARR, Edward H., *The Twenty Years' Crisis: 1919–1939* (London, Macmillan, New York, St. Martin's, 1949). Maintains that we can neither moralize power nor expel it from politics. Criticizes the Utopian, who believes that democracy is not based on force, and the realist, who believes that, if you look after power, moral authority will look after itself. See also his *Conditions of Peace* (1944), and *Nationalism and After* (1945).

COOK, Thomas I., and Moos, Malcolm, *Power Through Purpose* (Baltimore, Johns Hopkins Press, 1954). Argue that the dynamo generating power is ethical appeal. Maintain that a great nation, endowed with power and forced into leadership, can retain its position and achieve its national interest only by making power the servant of morality. America's true national interest is moral and international, and can be secured only by its application of the universally applicable moral principles of which it is chief proponent.

KENNAN, George F., *American Diplomacy, 1900–1950* (Chicago, The University of Chicago Press, 1951). A brief historical and analytical account of recent American foreign policy by the foremost advocate of the policy of "containment." See also his *Russia, the Atom, and the West* (New York, Harper, 1958), for Kennan's modification of his earlier containment policy in the light of changing conditions.

LIPPMANN, Walter, *U.S. Foreign Policy: Shield of the Republic* (Boston, Little Brown, 1943). Defends the thesis that United States' foreign policy must be based on a clearheaded recognition that our commitments must be undertaken only in support of vital national interests, and that we must make certain of our power to fulfill them. See also his *Cold War* (1947), and *Isolation and Alliances* (1952), which are also premised on the inevitability of rivalry among nations, the desirability and necessity of balance of power, and the virtues of a sane and cool-headed diplomacy.

MACHIAVELLI, Niccolò, *The Prince* (around 1513, many editions). Believed that the Prince (the ruler or would-be ruler) in order to achieve his objective must be prepared to use power expediently, ruthlessly, regardless of traditional moral considerations. Machiavelli himself sought the establishment of a strong and united Italy, which seemed impossible of accomplishment in view of the facts of his day, except by the means he advocated.

MERRIAM, Charles E., *Political Power: Its Composition and Incidence* (New York, McGraw-Hill, 1934). Deals, respectively, with the method, symbols, conditions, and control of power. Chapter III discusses "The Balancing of Power; the Expectation of Violence." Chapter VI treats "Imperialistic Movements; the Demand for Supremacy."

MORGENTHAU, Hans J., *Politics Among Nations: The Struggle for Power and Peace*, 2nd ed. (New York, Knopf, 1954). First edition (1947) contains the more hard-hitting frontal assault upon an allegedly false conception of foreign policy based, fundamentally, on the belief that a rational and moral political order, derived from universally valid and abstract principles, can be achieved here and now. Second edition is more concerned with consolidation of political realism, the author's own position. Without condoning indifference to political ideals and moral principles, emphasizes the sharp distinction between the desirable and the feasible. Maintains that in international politics statesmen act and think in terms of interest defined as power. See also his *Scientific Man vs. Power Politics* (1946), and *In Defense of the National Interest* (1951).

NIEBUHR, Reinhold, *Christian Realism and Political Problems* (New York, Scribner, 1953). One of the latest works by the Protestant theologian who has greatly influenced the "political realist" school. See also his *Moral Man and Immoral Society: A Study in Ethics and Politics* (1932), and *Christianity and Power Politics* (1940).

WIGHT, Martin, *Power Politics* (London, Royal Institute of International Affairs, 1946). Probably the best general introduction to the subject of power politics. A 66-page pamphlet.

13

Can We Count on
the United Nations?

THE PROBLEM
AND ITS BACKGROUND

INTRODUCTION

In a statement of greeting to visitors to the United Nations, Trygve Lie, the former Secretary-General of the organization, said: [1]

. . . the United Nations . . . was created out of the suffering, the needs, the hopes and ideals of the peoples of the world.

What it achieves or fails to achieve depends on the faith of all human beings expressed through the representatives who meet in these halls.

This building is anchored forty feet deep in the solid rock of Manhattan Island. But the true foundations of the United Nations are in your faith and support.

All that the United Nations is and can become belongs to you, the peoples of the world.

Cherish it as your most precious possession.

This summarizes well the faith which many people have in the United Nations. They remember that it was born out of the anguish and suffering of World War II, and that it was based on the conviction that a supreme effort should again be made to organize the nations of the world to prevent another such catastrophe. Moreover, in its aspirations for collective security, international justice, economic and social welfare, and

[1] *Your United Nations* (New York, United Nations Dept. of Public Information, 1952), p. v.

human rights, the United Nations reflected the deep hopes and ideals of most of mankind.

A visit to the United Nations quickly reveals how even the buildings have become symbolic of the international co-operation which the organization seeks to promote. The basic construction plans were designed by an international committee of architects from twelve countries representing all regions of the world. They considered 50 basic schemes and 100 secondary designs before agreeing on the final plans. Speaking of their efforts, Warren R. Austin, former United States Ambassador to the United Nations, declared: [2] "This demonstration by these architects of many countries was a milestone on the road to accord. No less than statesmen, they had strong opinions and vital differences to harmonize. They did it unanimously."

The actual construction and furnishing of the buildings also reflected the contributions and special gifts from many countries belonging to the United Nations. The construction costs were financed largely by a 65-million dollar, noninterest-bearing loan from the United States. The land along the East River where the buildings were erected had been bought with an 8½-million dollar gift from John D. Rockefeller, Jr.

Other governments and private groups contributed special gifts of materials or furnishings for the buildings. Norway, for example, made the principal contribution to the design and furnishing of the Security Council Chamber. Denmark and Sweden did likewise for the Trusteeship Council Chamber and the Economic and Social Council Chamber, respectively. The seven huge nickel bronze doors at the public entrance to the General Assembly building were the gift of Canada. The carpeting in the lobbies and corridors was donated by the United Kingdom, France, India, and Ecuador. The drapes in the Security Council lounge came from Czechoslovakia.

In front of the Secretariat building is a large circular fountain given by the children of the United States, Alaska, Hawaii, Puerto Rico, and the Virgin Islands. The children collected $50,000 for the project. A unique feature of the fountain is the black striped design on the bottom of the pool. This was made with a large number of black pebbles, gathered and sent by the women and children of the Greek island of Rhodes. Even the casual visitor to the United Nations senses something of the faith and hope which must have lain behind such gifts.[3] Whether this faith and hope are well placed, and whether the United Nations is competent to do what is expected of it are the questions to be examined in this chapter.

Consideration of these questions is particularly significant now in view

[2] *Ibid.*, p. 5.
[3] The booklet, *Your United Nations, op. cit.,* contains many examples of the contributions from various countries to the furnishing of the United Nations buildings.

of the fact that American foreign policy, as indicated in Chapter 12, relies more upon regional alliances like NATO for assuring American security than upon the United Nations. The hopes and optimism of 1945 that the United Nations would be an effective organization for the preservation of peace have been largely replaced in Washington by the feeling that a modified balance-of-power policy is a more appropriate means of dealing with the security problems of the cold war. The United States nevertheless continues to play an active part in the United Nations, even though it does not at the moment feel that it would be realistic to rely exclusively upon the world organization for the prevention of war and aggression.

ANTECEDENTS OF THE LEAGUE OF NATIONS AND THE UNITED NATIONS

The hopes of the future usually reflect the experiences and lessons of the past. This is especially true of the United Nations and its predecessor, the League of Nations. These organizations constitute the most ambitious and comprehensive efforts in the history of mankind to deal with the age-old problems of war and peace. Neither organization had a completely new or original approach to the problem of peace. Both drew heavily on the ideas and experiences of the past, and both received their strongest impetus from the devastating consequences of the two most destructive wars in human history.

Pre-Nineteenth Century Peace Plans

Proposals for some sort of international organization to preserve peace are as old as the nation-state system itself. The poet Dante, for example, about 1310 proposed a kind of world state governed by a single ruler. He reasoned that the existence of a number of independent sovereign princes, competing with one another, was a constant invitation to warfare, and that, in order to assure peace, mankind should be ruled by a single prince and one law. In 1693, William Penn advocated a Parliament of Europe, empowered to establish laws and settle disputes among all the European states. If any state disregarded the decisions of this parliament, the combined military forces of all the other sovereigns would be brought to bear against it. A century later in 1795, the German philosopher Kant set forth a plan for perpetual peace that envisaged an international federation of free states committed to representative government, nonintervention in one another's internal affairs, and the progressive abolition of standing armies.

Many other proposals were made in the period before World War I. One careful study of the subject has summarized 75 plans promulgated between 1306 and 1914, advocating various forms of international union, programs of disarmament, and procedures for the arbitration of peaceful settlement of disputes.[4]

Nineteenth Century International Organization

The above proposals were usually viewed as Utopian by the rulers of the day and were ignored in the practice of international relations. During the nineteenth century, however, the governments of Europe turned more frequently to international conferences to resolve problems of common concern. Several international agencies were created—the Rhine River Commission (1815), the Danube River Commission (1856), and the Universal Postal Union (1874)—to deal with the increasing problems of international commerce and communication.[5] Some idea of the greater resort to international conferences during the nineteenth century may be gained from the fact that during the period 1840–70, some 106 were held, whereas 149 convened during the decade 1870–79, 284 during the decade 1880–89, and 469 during the decade 1890–99.[6]

The conferences of this period lacked many of the techniques and organization that characterize the conferences since World War I. Formal, carefully prepared agenda and regular rules of procedure were not common. The conferences were not held regularly, but only when special problems arose which the major powers wished to discuss. Despite these limitations, the conferences were not without effect during the period 1815–1914 in preserving peace between the major powers and in dealing with such questions as Russian expansion in eastern Europe, European imperial rivalry in Africa, and the establishment of various independent nations in the Balkans.

The Hague conferences of 1899 and 1907 deserve special mention. They devoted considerable attention to codifying the rules of warfare, discussing the reduction of armaments, and establishing procedures for the conciliation and arbitration of international disputes. A major result of the 1899 conference was the establishment of a Permanent Court of Arbitration, consisting of a panel of distinguished arbitrators who might be called upon by states desiring to submit their disputes to arbitration. Although there were no compulsory features in the procedure, seventeen cases had been submitted to the jurists of the Permanent Court by World War I.[7]

Despite its limited successes, the nineteenth century system of inter-

[4] Edith Wynner and Georgia Lloyd, *Searchlight on Peace Plans* (New York, Dutton, 1944), pp. 29–81.

[5] For further details concerning the development of international organization during the nineteenth century, see D. S. Cheever and H. F. Haviland, *Organizing for Peace* (Boston, Houghton Mifflin, 1954), Chap. 2, and L. L. Leonard, *International Organization* (New York, McGraw-Hill, 1951), Chap. 2.

[6] Cheever and Haviland, *op. cit.*, p. 32.

[7] Cheever and Haviland, *op. cit.*, pp. 31–40; Leonard, *op. cit.*, pp. 33–38.

national conferences did not prevent Europe from becoming divided into two rival alliances before World War I (the Triple Alliance of Germany, Austria-Hungary, and Italy; and the Triple Entente of England, France, and Russia). The alliance system, together with the balance-of-power principle, contributed to the transformation of a local Austrian-Serbian clash in 1914 into a major continental conflict which quickly assumed world-wide proportions.

The magnitude and destructiveness of World War I led many to believe that more comprehensive organized efforts would be needed to prevent future war. The normal channels of nineteenth century diplomacy and conferences, in their judgment, were not enough.

League and U.N. Efforts to Improve upon Existing Channels of International Co-operation

Broader and More Open Diplomacy

The founders of the League of Nations and those of the United Nations appreciated the importance of diplomacy, negotiation, conciliation, and arbitration in the settlement of disputes, but they felt that these familiar techniques should be broadened and used more regularly and systematically. They envisaged more diplomatic negotiation than ever being conducted through these new organizations by means of regular assemblies of all the members at least once a year. With many more nations participating in the discussions, it was believed that diplomacy could be more effective in resolving international differences.

This new diplomacy, moreover, would not be carried on secretly, but more openly, so that the peoples of the world could be better informed as to the nature of the negotiations. Woodrow Wilson, it will be remembered, had laid great stress on this idea in the first of his famous Fourteen Points: [8] "Open covenants of peace, openly arrived at, after which there shall be no private international understandings of any kind but diplomacy shall proceed always frankly and in the public view." Open diplomacy, it was believed, would be more conducive to peace than secret diplomacy.

Collective Security

Perhaps the most significant innovation by which the League of Nations and United Nations sought to improve upon the pre-1914 institutions of international organization was the formation of a comprehensive system of collective security. This is undoubtedly the principle which

---

[8] Frederick H. Hartman, *Basic Documents of International Relations* (New York, McGraw-Hill, 1951), p. 43. The full text of Wilson's Fourteen Points is quoted here.

first occurs to most people when they think of the League of Nations or the United Nations, and it was on this principle that the founders of the League and the United Nations placed their main hopes for preserving peace.

The essence of collective security is the familiar principle, "All for one and one for all." Drawing on the lessons of the history of the balance of power, the founders of the League and the United Nations attempted to provide for an overwhelming array of collective power always to be available to maintain the peace. If a member state were the victim of aggression, all other members would come to its aid. The preponderance of force thus mobilized would be so great that no state, however powerful, could undertake aggression with impunity.

More Extensive International Economic and Social Co-operation

A third development for which the League of Nations and United Nations were responsible took place in the area of economic, social, and humanitarian co-operation. It is somewhat ironic that most statesmen who drafted the League Covenant did not actually envisage a very important role for the League in handling economic and social problems. Woodrow Wilson himself showed no active interest in these matters and, like many of his colleagues at the peace conference, was more concerned with creating a system of collective security. Hence the League Covenant authorized no special economic organs except in the field of international labor problems,[9] and provided for work to be done on only a few economic and social questions such as freedom of communications and transit, control of the narcotics traffic, international control of disease, and promotion of equitable policies of world trade.

Although the Covenant provisions for economic and social action were limited, the actual conditions of economic distress, famine, and inflation in postwar Europe quickly led League officials from 1919 onward to establish various economic and financial committees to deal with these problems. The committees secured much needed loans for Austria, Hungary, and other impoverished countries in the 1920's, and met regularly to discuss means of promoting economic recovery and financial stability. The League also established a Communications and Transit Organization, a Health Organization, and an Intellectual Co-operation Organization. In addition, it worked closely with the International Labor Organization and other agencies like the International Institute of Agriculture. Between World Wars I and II, the economic and social activities of the League grew to be regarded as contributing most constructively to world peace. In retrospect, it appears that these activities, not originally

[9] The International Labor Organization was actually created not under the League Covenant but by a separate section (Part XIII) of the Versailles Peace Treaty of 1919.

considered essential by the League founders, had a far more encouraging effect throughout the world than the collective-security actions, regarded at first as the primary function of the League.[10]

The United Nations has continued and greatly expanded the economic and social functions of the League. Much more attention was given to them in the Charter than in the Covenant, and an Economic and Social Council was created specifically to supervise the myriad activities undertaken. Article 55 of the United Nations Charter recognized the importance of economic and social well-being as a necessary foundation for peaceful and friendly relations throughout the world. In the words of two authorities, "one of the most striking differences between the Covenant and the Charter is the way in which the latter brings the economic and social aspect out of the shadows into the spotlight." [11]

International Supervision of Certain Colonial Areas

Finally, the League and the United Nations went far beyond any of their predecessors in the supervision of certain colonial areas, with the aim of ultimate independence for them. This program has been conducted through the mandate system of the League of Nations and the trusteeship system of the United Nations. Their supervision has been limited to the colonies which formerly belonged to the defeated powers in World Wars I and II. Thus, the colonial possessions of Germany and Turkey were not annexed outright by the victorious powers after World War I, as had been the custom after other major wars of the past. Instead, they were placed under the supervision of the League as mandates and were administered by certain League members: Britain, France, Belgium, and Japan. These powers were not, for the most part, permitted to administer the mandated areas as freely as they might their own colonies, but were supposed to observe certain principles designed to foster the well-being of the native populations. The administering powers were also obliged to submit annual reports to the League on the territory under their charge.[12]

Only one of the mandated areas, Iraq, attained its independence during the interwar period, but four others, Syria, Lebanon, Trans-Jordan, and Palestine (Israel) were freed shortly after the end of World War II.

The United Nations trusteeship system has been granted authority over all except one of the remaining League mandated areas,[13] and has con-

---

[10] See Cheever and Haviland, *op. cit.*, Chaps. 7, 17, and 20 for details of League action in economic and social matters.

[11] Cheever and Haviland, *op. cit.*, p. 187.

[12] See Cheever and Haviland, *op. cit.*, Chaps. 10 and 22 for details of the League mandate system.

[13] The Union of South Africa has refused to place its mandated area of South-West Africa under the United Nations trusteeship system.

tinued, with somewhat broader supervisory powers, to watch over the development of these territories. It was also granted temporary authority over the former colonies of Italy, of which one, Libya, achieved full independence in 1952 after a two-year period of supervisory aid by the United Nations Trusteeship Council.

In addition to the provisions for administering the trusteeship territories, the United Nations Charter in Article 73 for the first time proclaims the principle that *all* member states possessing colonies shall recognize the paramount interests of the inhabitants of their territories, and shall take the necessary steps to promote the political, economic, social, and educational development of these peoples. In this way, the hitherto closed domain of colonial administration is being gradually opened to international supervision as another means of reducing the causes of war and tension.

THE UNITED NATIONS AS VIEWED BY DIFFERENT PEOPLES OF THE WORLD

In the remainder of this chapter, we shall be concerned primarily with an appraisal of the United Nations and its effectiveness in resolving international differences and conflicts. Although the experiences of the League of Nations provided many valuable lessons for the United Nations, they will be referred to only indirectly in considering the more immediate problems and activities of the United Nations.

In examining the United Nations, it is always necessary to remember that the organization means different things to different people. To the average resident of midtown New York, the United Nations may be nothing more than the attractive, modernistic buildings along the banks of the East River, dominated by the 38-story "skyscraper of glass" which is the Secretariat headquarters. For the casual visitor to its buildings, the United Nations may take on a more cosmopolitan meaning as he sees representatives from all over the world mingling in the corridors and meeting chambers, and as he listens through earphones to the debates, translated simultaneously into five languages.

For people in other lands, who have been direct observers or beneficiaries of various United Nations programs, the organization has a more specific meaning. In the village of Patzcuaro, Mexico, for example, which relies largely on fishing for its livelihood, the United Nations means a program of technical assistance which has helped check a decline in the quality and quantity of the fish in their lake, and has thereby laid the basis for an improvement in the economic well-being of their community.[14] At Patzcuaro, a fundamental education program has been

[14] The UNESCO film *World Without End* very effectively depicts this program.

conducted by UNESCO since 1951 to train teachers from all Latin American countries in basic principles of public health, community services, and literacy. The fourth class of sixty students was graduated from this center in November, 1955.[15]

To some 80 million children in war-devastated or underdeveloped areas, the United Nations has, since 1946, meant a daily supply of milk, a gift of clothing, or an inoculation against tuberculosis, or perhaps a "miracle shot" of penicillin to cure what had previously been regarded as an incurable tropical disease known as yaws. This program has been conducted by UNICEF, the United Nations Children's Fund.[16]

Many farmers of Europe, if queried about the United Nations, would probably think first of the development of a hybrid corn seed which increased the value of the European corn crop by 24 million dollars in 1952. This was the outcome of a program launched in 1947 by the Food and Agriculture Organization to enable corn producers to catch up rapidly with the technical progress made during World War II in the countries not devastated by fighting. FAO made an initial investment of $40,000 in this project, a sum repaid 60 times by the results in 1952 alone. Each year afterward witnessed an even greater increase in the corn production of the seventeen participating countries, with the total accumulated value of the increase amounting to 187 million dollars by the end of 1955.[17]

The people of Indonesia and Libya will undoubtedly think of the United Nations as the organization that played a very significant role in helping them achieve political independence. In South Korea, on the other hand, the United Nations in all likelihood is regarded with mixed feelings. It helped the Republic of Korea establish its independent status in 1948 but was unable to bring about the unification of the country which it had hoped to achieve. Although the United Nations repelled the initial communist aggression in 1950–53, and has held the communist forces in check in North Korea, the government of President Syngman Rhee has displayed much dissatisfaction with the unwillingness of the international organization to support him in a military campaign to drive the communists out of North Korea.

The majority of the people of the United States, according to various public-opinion polls, support the general purposes and actions of the United Nations. Many important civic and economic organizations have expressed approval of its basic principles. Among them are the U.S. Chamber of Commerce, AFL-CIO, American Legion, Veterans of Foreign Wars, American Veterans Committee, League of Women Voters, National

[15] New York Times, November 6, 1955, p. 12.

[16] The UNICEF film Assignment Children, featuring a visit by Danny Kaye to various UNICEF projects in Asia, is an excellent portrayal of this work.

[17] New York Times, January 6, 1957, p. 28.

Council of Jewish Women, and the General Federation of Women's Clubs.[18]

Some Americans, however, have had misgivings and disappointments because of the inability of the United Nations to do all they had expected it to do. They point out that it has not prevented the development of the cold war and generally has not been able to do very much with major cold war issues such as German unification, Korean unification, Formosa, and the Hungarian uprising of 1956. Some Americans also felt discouraged when the United Nations accepted a truce in Korea in 1953 rather than enlarging its military operations sufficiently to expel the communists from the northern part of the country.

Other Americans feel that we were oversold on the United Nations in 1945, since big-power unity, the basis of the Charter, has disintegrated, making it impossible for the United Nations to function as it was originally intended. Instead of being able to deal effectively with major issues, it has degenerated into a mere debating society and a forum for the propaganda blasts of East and West.

Considerable apprehension has also been expressed in Congress that treaties sponsored by the United Nations might deal with subjects that are essentially domestic in character and might therefore be inconsistent with certain provisions of the United States Constitution. Specifically, it has been feared that international treaties guaranteeing economic and social welfare and human rights might regulate matters which, under our Constitution, are largely within the jurisdiction of each of the 48 states. The proposed Bricker amendment to the Constitution was introduced with a view to prohibiting any treaties which might conflict with the Constitution, or might enlarge the jurisdiction of the national government at the expense of the states in a manner incompatible with the Constitution.[19]

This wide divergence of views not only reflects a comparable diversity of actions undertaken by the United Nations, but at times indicates confusion as to what the United Nations actually is and can do. One reason for the popular disappointment in the United States regarding certain United Nations activities may be that some people have regarded the organization as the answer to all our international problems. It is therefore pertinent to examine what the United Nations actually is, and what it is not.

[18] U.S. Senate, *Review of the United Nations Charter,* Hearings before a Subcommittee of the Committee on Foreign Relations (84th Congr., 1st sess., 1955), Part 12. Statements and testimony by representatives of the various national organizations are given here. The American Legion's approval of the United Nations was given at its national convention, October 13, 1955. *New York Times,* October 14, 1955, p. 1.

[19] A good summary of the arguments for and against the Bricker amendment may be found in the Senate report on the proposal. U.S. Senate, Senate Report 412 (83rd Congr., 1st sess., 1953).

WHAT THE UNITED NATIONS IS AND IS NOT

An Association of Sovereign States—
Not a Supranational Government

The United Nations is an association of sovereign states based on the "sovereign equality of all its Members" (Article 2 of the Charter). It is not a supranational government and has no independent power of its own to compel member states to do anything against their will. The member states retain all the fundamental elements of national sovereignty, including the right of each state to decide what its policies shall be. Although member states have assumed certain obligations under the Charter, they are free in practice to interpret these in the light of their own respective national interests. The Charter further safeguards the sovereignty of the individual member states by providing that the United Nations may not intervene in matters that are essentially within the domestic jurisdiction of any state. There is only one situation when this prohibition does not apply, and that is when the United Nations is engaged in enforcing the peace. Then, it may take any measures necessary to make its action effective.

The powers of the United Nations, as will be seen later in this chapter, are essentially those of persuasion and conciliation rather than those of coercion. If the member states appear to do the bidding of the United Nations, it is because they have decided that it is in their best interest to do so, not because it has any independent power to make them do so.

The Purposes of the United Nations

The members have agreed on four broad purposes of the organization (Article 1 of the Charter):

1. To maintain international peace and security.

2. To develop friendly relations among nations based on respect for the principle of equal rights and self-determination of peoples.

3. To solve international problems of an economic, social, cultural, or humanitarian character, and to develop respect for fundamental human rights and freedoms for all persons.

4. To be a center for harmonizing the actions of nations in the attainment of these common ends.

It is evident, then, that the preservation of peace is not regarded simply as an enforcement process. Collective security is only one of the four main functions of the United Nations. Peace is to be fostered within a broader framework of actions designed to help solve some of the sorest problems that have made for war in the past. Although listed in the Charter as the first responsibility of the United Nations, collective security actually comes into operation only as a last resort, when other constructive efforts to remove the causes of war have proved inadequate. The collective-security actions, as in Korea, make far more newspaper headlines than do the other activities of the United Nations, but the quiet, unspectacular work of conciliation, negotiation, and economic and social co-operation constitutes the largest part of the program.

The Obligations of United Nations Members

All members of the United Nations, in their capacity as sovereign equals, have assumed certain obligations under the Charter. The most important of these obligations are:

1. To settle their international disputes by peaceful means (Article 2).

2. To refrain from the use or threat of force against other states or in any manner inconsistent with the purposes of the United Nations (Article 2).

3. To assist the United Nations in carrying out any action it takes under the Charter, and to withhold assistance from any state against which the United Nations is taking preventive or enforcement action (Article 2).

4. To carry out the decisions of the Security Council regarding the maintenance or enforcement of peace in accordance with the Charter, and to make available to the Security Council any armed forces or assistance which the Security Council deems necessary (Articles 25, 43, 45).

5. To co-operate with the United Nations in promoting better economic, social, health, and educational conditions, and in developing universal respect for, and observance of, human rights and freedoms without distinction as to race, sex, language, or religion (Articles 55, 56).

In addition to these obligations, the United Nations members that possess colonial territories are pledged to promote the well-being of the inhabitants of these territories, to assure their political, economic, social, and educational advancement, and to help develop self-government. The member states are also obliged to report regularly to the United Nations on the economic, social, and educational (but not the political) conditions in their colonial territories.

The obligations are extensive, and would, if completely observed by all member governments, assure the peaceful resolution of international differences and the steady improvement of political, economic, and social conditions throughout the world. But the United Nations, as has already been observed, has no independent power of its own to enforce these obligations. Fulfillment of them, as is true of all treaties, depends on the willingness of the individual sovereign states to do so. This willingness in turn depends on how each sovereign state happens to interpret its particular interest and on the extent of its practical ability to carry out the obligation.

When a state decides that it is unable to fulfill its obligations under the Charter, or that it is contrary to its interests to do so, the United Nations is seldom able to do more than criticize or reprimand the offending party. It is not able, unless the Security Council or the General Assembly should agree to threaten war or other extreme pressure, to force the observance of all Charter obligations. There is little likelihood that the Security Council (where the veto prevails) or the General Assembly (where a two-thirds vote is needed) would agree to such steps except when there is a major violation of the Charter.

The Korean War illustrated clearly the uncertainty of how United Nations members would choose, or be able, to fulfill their Charter obligations. In response to the Security Council's request for assistance to repel the aggression in Korea, approximately 40 of the 59 United Nations members sent some form of aid. The remainder, consisting principally of the Soviet bloc, the Arab bloc, four small Latin American countries, and Yugoslavia, furnished no assistance to the United Nations forces in Korea. The members of the Soviet bloc actually aided the North Korean and Chinese Communist forces, which had been declared aggressors by the United Nations. Of the 40 states that sent some form of aid, only 16 sent military aid, and over 90 per cent of the military aid came from the United States and the Republic of Korea.[20] The British and French, for example, explained that they could not furnish more than small contingents for Korea because they already had extensive forces engaged in Malaya and Indochina, respectively.

The fact that each United Nations member decides when and how it will observe its obligations under the Charter strikingly demonstrates that the United Nations is not a supranational government, with power to coerce recalcitrant members in the same way as a national government punishes individual lawbreakers. The United Nations at best offers its members certain useful facilities for co-operative action when they feel it is in their interest to employ them. The organization, in the final analysis, is no stronger than its individual members are willing to make it.

The difficulty the United Nations has in trying to coerce a major power is also clearly seen in the case of the Soviet intervention in Hungary in the fall of 1956. Starting early in November, 1956, after the Soviet Union had vetoed a Security Council measure calling for the end of Soviet military action in Hungary, the General Assembly passed some thirteen resolutions on the Hungarian question. They called on the Russians to stop their armed attack, withdraw their troops, end the deportation of Hungarians, permit the holding of free elections under United Nations auspices, and permit the admission of United Nations observers to Hungary. Other resolutions authorized an emergency relief program for Hungarian refugees and urged all members to provide medicines and other supplies. On December 12, 1956, after the Soviet government had declined to heed any of these resolutions, the General Assembly, by a vote of 56 to 8 (the Soviet bloc), with 13 abstentions, condemned the Soviet Union

[20] Cheever and Haviland, *op. cit.*, pp. 454–456.

for violating the United Nations Charter "in depriving Hungary of its liberty and independence and the Hungarian people of . . . their fundamental right." Throughout the debate, the Soviet Union argued that the Hungarian problem was essentially a question within the domestic jurisdiction of Hungary itself, and that the United Nations had no right to interfere in such matters.[21] Inasmuch as none of the other United Nations members was prepared to apply further measures of coercion against the Soviet Union to force her out of Hungary, the United Nations action amounted only to a moral protest. The Soviet action, however, did lead some Asian powers to speak more critically of the Soviet Union than they had ever done previously. In this way, the Soviet reputation throughout the world may have been damaged by the intervention in Hungary, even though the Soviet Union was not actually obliged to withdraw from the country. The publication in the summer of 1957 of a United Nations committee report, based on the testimony of Hungarian refugees, provided a detailed, documentary foundation for further condemnation of the Soviet intervention in Hungary by many governments.[22]

A special session of the General Assembly met, September 10–14, 1957, to discuss this report. It adopted a resolution by a vote of 60 to 10, with 10 abstentions, endorsing the report, condemning the Soviet action in Hungary, and appointing Prince Wan of Thailand as a special representative to do what he could to secure compliance with the various United Nations resolutions on the Hungarian question. Prince Wan subsequently communicated with the Soviet and Hungarian authorities but was unable to persuade them to modify their position.

The United Nations Exerts Influence, Not Coercion

The United Nations may be unable to enforce its decisions, but this does not mean that it exerts no influence on the governments of the world. The influence was quite evident when the British and French decided to stop their invasion of Egypt in the fall of 1956, after several United Nations resolutions had called upon them to do so. Unlike the Soviet government, which ignored the General Assembly resolutions calling for withdrawal from Hungary, the British and French governments displayed greater sensitivity to the pressure of world opinion, which had been highly critical of their invasion of Egypt. Within a week after launching their attempt to occupy the Suez Canal area, Britain and France agreed to a cease-fire, as called for by an Assembly resolution of November 2, 1956. Seven weeks later, by December 22, the British and French had evacuated their forces from the Suez area, in compliance with further Assembly resolutions. Undoubtedly the strong American insistence upon evacua-

[21] For a concise summary of these actions, see the *New York Times*, March 10, 1957, p. 32.
[22] *New York Times*, June 21, 1957, pp. 10–11. For the full text of the report, see United Nations, General Assembly, *Report of the Special Committee on the Problem of Hungary*, Official Records, Eleventh Session, Supplement No. 18 (A/3592).

tion had much to do with the British and French decision, but the general expression of world feeling through the resolutions and debates of the United Nations cannot be discounted as another influential factor.[23]

The government of Israel, which had also invaded Egypt, was much slower to comply with the United Nations resolutions, and did not completely evacuate Egyptian territory until March, 1957, when it had become apparent that the United Nations, with American backing, might apply some form of economic pressure against her. An American promise to exert influence to secure recognition of Israel's right of passage through the Gulf of Aqaba also contributed to the final Israeli decision.

The United Nations, as just noted, was not successful in getting the Soviet Union to evacuate Hungary, but its discussions and resolutions on the Hungarian question may very well have a long-run influence on Soviet policies and actions. Ambassador James J. Wadsworth, Deputy United States Representative to the United Nations, speaking to the American Bar Association in July, 1957, declared that "the Soviet slaughter in Hungary, in complete defiance of the United Nations, was agonizing proof how little the United Nations can do, peacefully, to restrain a country which has very great power and no morals." Yet, he added, although the United Nations "has no power to compel, it has enormous power to persuade," and consequently can exert real influence on governments and world opinion. The Soviet action in Hungary, he explained, and the United Nations reaction to it, had a "profound impact on the Communist movement in countries outside the Soviet orbit." Widespread resignations from the Communist Parties in these countries, sharp declines in the circulation of communist newspapers, and defeat of Communist candidates in local elections were consequences he attributed to United Nations moves in the court of world opinion.[24]

Thus, despite the fact that the United Nations is not a supranational government with power to coerce recalcitrant members, its debates and resolutions may actually have considerable influence on the policies and actions of the many states of the world. It is quite conceivable, for example, that the British-French-Israeli invasion of Egypt, had it occurred fifty years ago, would not have met with the near-universal condemnation it received in 1956.[25] The Soviet intervention in Hungary, likewise, might

---

[23] A summary of the United Nations Assembly resolutions on the Middle East crisis is given in the *New York Times*, March 10, 1957, p. 32.

[24] *New York Times*, July 15, 1957, p. 1.

[25] On November 2, 1956, by a vote of 64 to 5 (Britain, France, Israel, Australia, and New Zealand), the General Assembly called on all parties for a cease-fire. On November 7, the General Assembly, by a vote of 65 to 1 (Israel), with 10 abstentions, called on the British, French, and Israeli forces to withdraw from Egypt. On November 24, 1956, by a vote of 63 to 5, with 10 abstentions, the General Assembly again called for the withdrawal "forthwith" of British, French, and Israeli forces. *New York Times*, March 10, 1957, p. 32.

not then have been investigated and held up before the world to the same extent as in 1956 and 1957.

Debates in the General Assembly and other organs of the United Nations provide a means by which any matter within the purview of the Charter may be discussed and any member nation can air its grievances. No single nation can prevent discussion of such matters. Even though a state may claim a subject to be within its domestic jurisdiction, it is up to the Assembly or the various United Nations organs themselves to decide whether or not they are competent to discuss the issue. Thus the Assembly has on several occasions discussed the racial problem and the treatment of the Indian minority in South Africa, despite the claim by the government of South Africa that these were questions exclusively within its domestic jurisdiction. The General Assembly has also considered a lengthy report and a proposed international treaty on the abolition of forced labor throughout the world.

The United Nations has been an especially valuable forum for the anticolonial powers to express their views. The colonial powers, notably, Britain, France, and the Netherlands, have opposed United Nations discussion of areas like Cyprus, North Africa, and West New Guinea, but the General Assembly on several occasions has voted to discuss the matters anyway. Even though a country like France may exercise its sovereign freedom of action and walk out of the General Assembly in protest over the discussion, the French government cannot but be influenced in the long run by the attitudes and criticisms of other governments.

The Universal Declaration of Human Rights, which was approved by the General Assembly in 1948 by a vote of 48–0, is another good example of how the United Nations wields influence if not power. Although not adopted in the form of a legally binding treaty, the Declaration sets forth certain standards and principles of human rights for all peoples and nations. Portions of it have been included in the constitutions of new governments, and it has been cited as a supporting authority by national courts and legislatures. Negotiations are now in progress to draft a binding covenant on human rights, but in its absence the Declaration continues to exert an informal influence on many governments of the world.

Finally, through its regular and continuing international conferences, the United Nations serves as a means of constant negotiation among all members. The delegates of the 81 member states are in constant touch with each other, and in the course of daily discussions have many opportunities to resolve differences, clarify issues, and formulate policies that more adequately reflect the views of all interested parties. In this steady process of multilateral diplomacy, all governments at one time or another find themselves making concessions in an effort to secure their objectives.

The principal organs through which the United Nations carries out its manifold activities are outlined in the following chart.

THE ORGANS OF THE UNITED NATIONS

International Court of Justice	General Assembly	Security Council
Located at the Hague, Netherlands.	Includes all U.N. members.	11 members:
15 judges, elected by General Assembly and Security Council for 9-year terms.	Meets annually. Sessions last 3 to 4 months.	5 permanent (U.S., Britain, France, U.S.S.R., China).
May arbitrate any dispute states are willing to submit to it.	May discuss any matter within scope of Charter.	6 nonpermanent, elected for 2-year term by General Assembly.
Has no compulsory jurisdiction, except over certain legal disputes which states may have voluntarily agreed to submit to compulsory arbitration.	May make recommendations on any matter within scope of Charter unless item is on Security Council agenda.	Meets any time it is necessary.
	$\frac{2}{3}$ vote required on all important matters.	Has primary responsibility for maintaining peace.
	Elects nonpermanent members of Security Council and Trusteeship Council, and all members of Economic and Social Council and International Court of Justice.	May investigate any dispute and recommend a basis for settlement.
	Elects new members to U.N. upon recommendation of Security Council.	Determines the existence of a threat to the peace, or an act of aggression, and decides what measures shall be taken to restore peace.
	Approves U.N. budget.	All nonprocedural decisions require 7 votes, including the 5 permanent members (veto provision).
	Supervises work of Economic and Social Council and Trusteeship Council. Receives annual reports from Security Council and all other U.N. organs.	Decisions are binding on all U.N. members.
	Has created many special commissions and bodies to carry on its work, such as: Disarmament Commission Peace Observation Commission Korean Reconstruction Agency Relief and Works Agency for Palestine Committee on Information from Non-Self-Governing Territories	
	International Atomic Energy Agency	

	Economic and Social Council	Trusteeship Council

Secretariat

Headed by the Secretary-General who is chief administrative officer of U.N.

Secretary-General makes annual report to General Assembly on work of U.N.

He may also bring to the attention of the Security Council any matter he thinks endangers peace and security.

Staff of Secretariat numbers between 3,000 and 4,000. They are international civil servants, not delegates from national governments. They provide services and assistance for all U.N. organs.

Main Secretariat Headquarters is in New York. Field offices in Geneva, Bangkok, Santiago, and The Hague.

Economic and Social Council

18 members, elected by General Assembly for 3-year terms.

Makes studies and reports regarding international economic, social, cultural, educational, health, and related matters, including human rights.

May make recommendations on above matters to General Assembly, to members of the U.N., and to the specialized agencies.

Meets usually twice a year for periods of 4 to 6 weeks each.

Majority vote required for its decisions.

Much of its work is done through special commissions and bodies such as:

Commission on Human Rights
Commission on Narcotics
Four Economic Commissions
    Europe
    Asia and Far East
    Latin America
    Africa
Technical Assistance Board
U.N. Children's Fund

Co-ordinates work of
U.N. Specialized Agencies:
International Labor
    Organization
Food and Agriculture
    Organization
World Health Organization
UNESCO
Universal Postal Union
International Bank
International Monetary Fund
International Civil Aviation
    Organization
International Telecommunication Union
World Meteorological
    Organization

Trusteeship Council

Variable number of members (12 at present), half of whom are administrators of trust territories, and half of whom are not. The latter half includes the U.S.S.R. and China, and 4 others elected by General Assembly for 3-year terms.

Considers the reports of states administering trust areas.

Examines petitions from inhabitants or groups in trust areas.

Sends visiting missions periodically to the various trust territories.

Submits an annual report on each trust territory to General Assembly.

Meets twice a year.

Majority vote required for its decisions.

How the United Nations Has Worked in Practice

Membership

Fifty-one nations signed the Charter of the United Nations in 1945 and became original members of the organization. As of January, 1958, an additional thirty-one states had been admitted to membership, for a total of eighty-two. Most of these new members were admitted after December, 1955, when a long-standing stalemate between the Soviet Union and the western powers on the membership question was finally broken.

A reflection of the cold war, the stalemate had grown out of the mutual unwillingness of the Soviet Union and the western powers to approve the admission of various states which had been proposed by each side respectively. Under the Charter (Article 4), membership in the United Nations is open to all "peace-loving" states, which accept the obligations of the Charter and which, in the judgment of the organization, "are able and willing to carry out these obligations." Determination of who is "able and willing" to carry out the Charter obligations is therefore a political decision, which has to be made by the United Nations members themselves. According to the Charter, this decision is to be made by the General Assembly, upon recommendation of the Security Council. The General Assembly can give its approval by a two-thirds vote, but in the Security Council any one of the five permanent members can veto a recommendation regarding membership. It was in the Security Council that the stalemate arose, for here, up to December, 1955, the Soviet Union had used the veto some 45 times to prevent the Security Council from recommending certain states which the western powers desired to have admitted to membership.[26] Only 9 states, out of a total of 31 which had applied for membership up to this time, had been successful in obtaining the necessary approval of both Security Council and General Assembly.[27]

The 22 unsuccessful applicants fell into three categories:

1. *Those sponsored by the western powers (13)*—Italy, Austria, Finland, Ireland, Portugal, Spain, Cambodia, Laos, Ceylon, Japan, Nepal, Jordan, and Libya.

2. *Those sponsored by the Soviet Union (5)*—Hungary, Bulgaria, Rumania, Albania, and the Mongolian People's Republic (Outer Mongolia).

3. *The communist and noncommunist regimes in the divided countries of Korea and Vietnam (4)*—North Korea, North Vietnam, South Korea, and South Vietnam.

[26] Up to this time, the Soviet Union had cast a total of 76 vetoes, 45 of which had involved the proposed admissions of new members. The applications of some states had been vetoed several times in successive years, which is why the total number of vetoes became so large.

[27] The nine states in the order of their admission were: Afghanistan, Iceland, Sweden, Thailand, Pakistan, Yemen, Burma, Israel, and Indonesia. Indonesia, which be-

Up to December, 1955, the western powers objected to Hungary, Rumania, Bulgaria, and Albania on the ground that they had consistently violated their postwar treaty obligations to guarantee political and civil liberties to their citizens. Moreover, Bulgaria and Albania, during the Greek civil war in 1947 and 1948, had refused to comply with United Nations resolutions calling upon them to stop intervening in that civil war by aiding the Greek communist guerilla fighters. For these reasons, the western powers had argued that the four East European communist states were unprepared to carry out fully their international obligations and their duties as United Nations members. As to the Mongolian People's Republic, the western powers questioned whether a truly independent government existed there, or whether the area was not more nearly akin to a province of the Soviet Union. The refusal of the Mongolian authorities to admit United Nations observers to verify local political conditions seemed to reinforce the doubts of the western powers; hence, they opposed the admission of the Mongolian Republic.

The Soviet Union never advanced any specific objection to most of the thirteen applicants sponsored by the western powers, but so long as the latter opposed the admission of the five Soviet-sponsored applicants, the Soviet Union used its veto in the Security Council to block all thirteen western-sponsored applicants. The stalemate lasted until December, 1955. The western powers also opposed the admission of the communist governments in North Korea and North Vietnam, while the Soviet Union opposed the noncommunist governments in South Korea and South Vietnam.

From time to time, beginning in 1946, the Soviet Union proposed various "package deals" under which the applicants desired by both sides would be approved as a block. Until the fall of 1955, however, the western powers, and especially the United States, opposed the idea of a "package deal," insisting that each applicant be considered on its own merits. In an advisory opinion in 1948, the International Court of Justice upheld this viewpoint as the proper legal procedure under the Charter. The Court declared that insistence on a "package deal" amounted to placing a condition not authorized by the Charter.[28]

In the fall of 1955, however, when international tension had relaxed somewhat, considerable support developed at the General Assembly for a "package deal," and even the United States now indicated willingness to acquiesce in this effort to break the long stalemate on membership. A compromise was eventually reached by which the Security Council agreed to recommend sixteen new members, twelve countries previously sponsored by the western powers and four by the Soviet Union. The

---

came the sixtieth member of the United Nations, was admitted in 1950. No further states were admitted until December, 1955.

[28] Cheever and Haviland, *op. cit.*, p. 105.

Mongolian People's Republic had to be omitted from the Soviet list because of a veto by Nationalist China, and Japan was thereafter dropped from the western list in order to assure Soviet acceptance of the twelve other countries on that list.[29] The compromise "package" did not include the two Koreas or the two Vietnams. Final approval of the sixteen new members was given by the Security Council and the General Assembly on December 14, 1955, thereby bringing the total United Nations membership to 76.[30]

Subsequent admission of the Sudan, Tunisia, Morocco, and Japan in 1956, and of Ghana and Malaya in 1957, brought the total membership to 82. The latest additions, except Japan, were all new states, which had just achieved full independence. The admission of Japan in December, 1956, followed Soviet withdrawal of opposition to that country, after resumption of diplomatic relations and termination of the state of war between the two countries earlier that month.[31]

A unique situation developed in February, 1958, with the merger of Egypt and Syria into the United Arab Republic. For the first time in the history of the United Nations, two members voluntarily gave up their separate identity to form a single state. In March, 1958, the Secretary-General of the United Nations formally recognized the new united state in place of Egypt and Syria, thereby reducing the total of United Nations members to 81. Yemen subsequently joined the United Arab Republic, but with the stipulation that she retain her separate seat in the United Nations. Shortly after the formation of the United Arab Republic, Iraq and Jordan joined together to form a rival union, known as the Arab Federation. They did not, however, alter their separate representation in the United Nations.

With a total membership of 81, the United Nations now counts as members nearly all the nation-states of the world. For purposes of comparison, the reader is referred to the list of nation-states of the world, on p. 161, Chapter 4. He will find that Switzerland, and the divided countries of Germany, Korea, and Vietnam are the principal nonmembers.

The admission of the 22 new members represents a victory for the advocates of universal membership in the United Nations. They feel that the objectives of the organization, though imperfectly achieved, will be facilitated if all states are included, regardless of their ideology or political behavior. Since the United Nations, as now constituted, must rely

---

[29] Before the final compromise was reached, there had been 16 Soviet vetoes and 1 veto by Nationalist China. *New York Times,* December 14, 1955, pp. 1, 10, and December 15, 1955, p. 1.

[30] *New York Times,* December 15, 1955, p. 1.

[31] *New York Times,* December 13, 1956, p. 1, and December 19, 1956, p. 1. For a summary of the events since December, 1955, relating to the admission of new members, see "Issues before the Eleventh General Assembly," *International Conciliation,* November, 1956, pp. 122–128.

on persuasion more than on coercion, the opportunities for persuasion will be greater, it is argued, if all states are members, with no exclusions. Critics of this view have contended that the Charter itself sets up a more selective basis for membership, by providing in Article 4 that new members must be "peace-loving" and "willing" to carry out the obligations of the Charter. To admit states that do not meet these criteria would, it is held, only weaken the effectiveness and authority of the United Nations.[32]

The question of "universal" vs. "selective" membership is the essence of the problem of whether or not to seat the Chinese Communist government in place of the Chinese Nationalist government on Formosa (Taiwan). The issue is not that of admitting a new member to the United Nations; it is one of deciding which government shall occupy the Chinese seat in the various United Nations organs. Nevertheless, it does point up the problem of what sort of state should occupy a seat in the United Nations.

In 1945, when the Charter was signed, the Nationalist government was the only legal government in China, and as such it became an original member of the United Nations. It has continued to hold the Chinese seat ever since, although the Chinese Communists gained control of all of mainland China late in 1949. Since early 1950, both the Chinese Communist government at Peiping and the Nationalist government on Formosa have claimed to be the "true" government of China.

The question of which government is entitled to China's seat in the United Nations has come up many times since 1950 and is one of the most controversial matters facing the organization. The Soviet Union and the other communist members of the United Nations, together with certain important noncommunist states like India, have urged that the Chinese Communist government be given China's seat, and that the Chinese Nationalist government be denied it. Apart from ideological considerations, one of the principal arguments for seating the communist government is that it is the only *de facto* government actually exercising authority on the mainland of China, and able therefore to speak for its 600 million people. The population of Formosa is less than 10 million, of which only a small fraction are actually Nationalist Chinese. Therefore, it is argued that the government on Formosa cannot adequately represent or speak for the 600 million mainland Chinese.

The United States has vigorously opposed seating the Chinese Communists in the United Nations, arguing that they stand accused by the General Assembly of aggression in Korea, and that they refused to comply with all United Nations resolutions and efforts to halt their intervention in the Korean War in 1950–51. Until the Peiping government clears itself of this charge of aggression by evacuating North Korea and permitting

[32] For a brief discussion of the different ideas on criteria for membership, see Clark M. Eichelberger, *UN: The First Ten Years* (New York, Harper, 1955), pp. 74 ff.

the unification of Korea on the basis of free, impartial elections, the United States contends that it would be undermining the prestige and authority of the United Nations to seat the Chinese Communists. Thus far, this viewpoint has been supported by a majority of the other members, and the question of seating the Communist Chinese has been postponed from year to year.[33] Here, then, the principle of selective membership has prevailed up to now, although whether or not it will continue indefinitely is less predictable.

Peaceful Settlement of Disputes [34]

One of the major purposes of the United Nations is to facilitate the peaceful settlement of international disputes. On a number of occasions, the organization has been able to assist its member states to find a peaceful solution to their differences. At other times, the United Nations has been instrumental in persuading states to cease hostilities and resort to peaceful procedures in seeking a settlement.

Iran complaint against the Soviet Union. In 1946, the government of Iran complained to the Security Council that Soviet troops had not been withdrawn from northern Iran by the time originally agreed to by the U.S.S.R. at the end of World War II. The complaint charged that the Soviet Union, by means of its troops, was attempting to force Iran into granting oil concessions in its northern territory, and also that Soviet forces on Iranian territory were fomenting an independence movement in that region.

The Soviet Union objected to discussion of the item by the Security Council, and argued that, since negotiations were then going on with the Iranian government, there was no threat to the peace. Despite Soviet objections, the Security Council proceeded to discuss the question, whereupon the Soviet delegate, Andrei Gromyko, walked out of the Security Council. That body confined its discussions to the procedural methods of settling the dispute, and called on the Soviet Union and Iran to continue their bilateral negotiations and report at a later date on whether all Soviet troops had been withdrawn from Iranian territory. The Soviet troops were withdrawn a few weeks later, and one of the reasons may well have been the informal influence of the Security Council's discussion and the focusing of world attention on an apparent breach of a wartime agreement by the Soviet Union.

The Indonesian case. In 1947, after a breakdown in negotiations between the Dutch and the Indonesians over the question of Indonesian

[33] For a short summary of the action of the General Assembly on this item, see *Everyman's United Nations*, 5th ed. (New York, United Nations Dept. of Public Information, 1956), pp. 98–101.

[34] An excellent analysis of the United Nations action in the peaceful settlement of disputes appears in U.S. Congress, Committee on Foreign Relations, *Pacific Settlement of Disputes*, Staff Study 5, Committee print (83rd Congr., 2nd sess., 1954).

independence, the Dutch forces began military operations against the Indonesians. The question was brought before the Security Council, which called on both parties to cease hostilities. After some delay both sides issued cease-fire orders, and subsequently accepted the aid of a United Nations Good Offices Committee in negotiating a truce agreement, which was signed in January, 1948.

Efforts to reach a political settlement continued throughout 1948 but made no progress, and in December, 1948, the Netherlands denounced the truce agreement and renewed its military actions. The Dutch arrested the President of the Indonesian Republic at the same time and took a number of political prisoners. The Security Council, on December 24, 1948, called for a cease-fire and for the immediate release of the Indonesian President and other political prisoners. The Dutch did not immediately comply, and the Security Council had to repeat its call twice. Also recommended was the establishment of an independent state of Indonesia as soon as possible.

Finally, on March 2, 1949, the Netherlands announced that the Indonesian President and political prisoners had been released, and that it was prepared to hold a conference to arrange for the establishment of an independent Indonesia. The conference was held in the fall of 1949, with representatives of the United Nations participating alongside the Dutch and Indonesians. This time the negotiations were successful, and in December, 1949, the formal transfer of sovereignty from the Netherlands to Indonesia took place. In September, 1950, Indonesia was admitted as the sixtieth member of the United Nations.

Here is a good example of the practical inability of the Security Council to enforce its cease-fire orders, even against a small power like the Netherlands. Yet it also illustrates that the United Nations is not without influence, even under such circumstances; that, through negotiation, discussion, and conciliation, it can help two disputing parties arrive at an agreement. Note should also be taken that the veto constituted no serious problem here. Although the Soviet Union did not approve of all the procedures followed, and desired a greater role for itself in the United Nations conciliation machinery set up, it did not resort to the veto to block Security Council actions at crucial moments. With these auspicious conditions, the Security Council was able to function with considerable flexibility and effectiveness.

Kashmir. The two preceding cases demonstrate that the Security Council may wield considerable influence in bringing about a peaceful resolution of disputes. The Kashmir question illustrates how the United Nations helped restrain open conflict, although it has not yet been successful in promoting a final solution to the problem. Kashmir is a predominantly Moslem state with a Hindu ruler, located between India and Pakistan, and claimed by both countries. Hostilities broke out in 1948, and the

Security Council called for a cease-fire, withdrawal of troops, and holding of a plebiscite to determine the wishes of the Kashmir inhabitants. Both India and Pakistan stopped hostilities, but they have been unable to agree on terms for a troop withdrawal and holding of the plebiscite. A succession of United Nations mediators have been negotiating with both countries in an effort to reach some agreement. The cease-fire has continued to be observed by both parties.

The Suez Canal. The developments here highlight both the strong and the weak points of the United Nations in attempting to promote the peaceful settlement of disputes. Open hostilities by Britain, France, and Israel were actually abandoned, following United Nations recommendations to this effect, but the inability of the world organization to secure complete compliance with its wishes even by small powers, such as Israel and Egypt, was evident on several occasions.[35]

The complications set in with Egyptian nationalization of the Suez Canal Co. in July, 1956. The latter was a private, international company which had built and operated the canal under a concession granted by the Egyptian government in 1856. Approximately 44 per cent of the company stock was held by the British government, and about the same amount by private French stockholders. The company's concession would normally have run until 1968. In nationalizing the company, the Egyptian government agreed to compensate the stockholders according to the closing prices in the stock exchanges. It also affirmed its intention of honoring an international convention of 1888 guaranteeing the free navigation of the canal.[36]

Despite the Egyptian pledge to keep the canal open, the British pressed hard for the principle of international operation of the canal, fearing apparently that, under exclusive Egyptian operation, it would not always remain free and open. After unsuccessful attempts to persuade Egypt to permit international operation, the British and French brought the question before the United Nations Security Council in September, 1956. After considerable discussion, the Council on October 13, 1956, unanimously approved a resolution, to which Egypt assented, setting forth six principles, which it felt should be incorporated into any settlement of the problem: [37]

1. Free and open transit through the Canal without discrimination.

2. Respect for the sovereignty of Egypt.

3. Insulation of canal operations from the politics of any one country.

[35] For a complete summary of United Nations action in the Suez Canal case, see United Nations, General Assembly, *Annual Report of the Secretary-General on the Work of the Organization, 16 June 1956–15 June 1957*, Official Records, Twelfth Session, Supplement No. 1 (A/3594), pp. 4–26.

[36] The full text of the convention was reprinted in the *New York Times*, September 13, 1956, p. 12.

[37] United Nations, General Assembly, *Annual Report of the Secretary-General* (1956–57), *op. cit.*, p. 7.

4. Fixing of tolls by agreement between Egypt and the users.

5. Allocation of a fair proportion of the tolls to canal development.

6. Arbitration of disputes between Egypt and the Suez Canal Co.

The achievement of unanimous agreement on these principles again demonstrated the Security Council's value as an organ for facilitating the peaceful resolution of disputes.

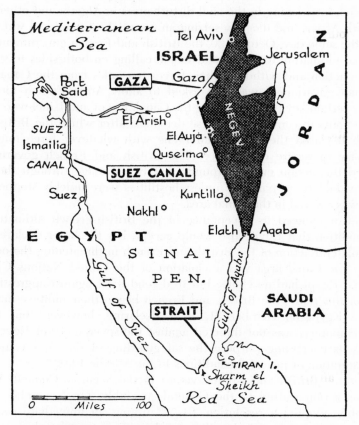

Fig. 13. Middle East area involved in Suez Canal case. (*Source: New York Times*, March 17, 1957, Section IV, p. E5.

Secretary-General Dag Hammarskjold was in the process of discussing with Egypt ways of resuming negotiations for a settlement of the canal question when the armed intervention of Israel, Britain, and France took place. The Israeli forces began their attack on October 29, 1956, and within a few days occupied most of the Sinai peninsula and the Gaza strip. The Israeli government justified its action on grounds of self-defense, arguing that Egypt had established many *fedayeen* (commando squad) armed bases in the Sinai and Gaza areas, from which systematic attacks on Israeli territory had been made, and that the *fedayeen* bases were regarded by the Arab governments as means not simply for the harassment but for the actual destruction of Israel.[38]

The Security Council met the next day to deal with the Israeli attack, but was unable to act because the British and French governments vetoed a proposed resolution calling for an immediate cease-fire by Israel and Egypt. The French delegate argued that the Council should not condemn Israel, in view of the openly affirmed Egyptian policy of annihilating Israel, intervening in the civil disturbances in Algeria and other parts of North Africa, and illegally seizing an essential international waterway.

On the same day, October 30, the British and French governments sent a virtual ultimatum to Egypt and Israel, calling on both sides to stop all warlike action and withdraw their forces ten miles from the Canal. The Egyptian government was also asked to allow Anglo-French forces to occupy certain key positions along the Canal. Egypt and Israel were given twelve hours to comply with these demands, after which the British and French declared they would intervene with whatever force might be necessary to secure compliance. The British and French governments justified this action on the grounds that free passage through the Suez Canal would be jeopardized unless hostilities were quickly stopped and order was assured in the Canal area.

Israel announced its acceptance of the British-French ultimatum on the condition that Egypt also would accept, but the latter declared that the unilateral action of the British and French in threatening the occupation of the Canal area was a violation of the United Nations Charter, and that Egypt had no choice but to defend itself against aggression. In view of this reply, the British and French began their military intervention in Egypt on October 31, 1956, declaring, however, that it was only temporary, was not directed against the sovereignty of Egypt, and had as its overriding purpose the safeguarding of the Suez Canal and the restoration of peaceful conditions in the Middle East.

After the British and French vetoes in the Security Council, United Nations action shifted to the General Assembly. On November 2, the Assembly adopted a resolution, 64–5,[39] urging an immediate cease-fire by all parties involved in hostilities and a return to strict observance of the Arab-Israeli armistice agreements. The Assembly debate was marked by almost universal condemnation of the British-French-Israeli action. This world-wide criticism may have had a moderating influence on the three governments for, by November 7, a general cease-fire had been accepted by all parties. The strong opposition of the United States undoubtedly contributed to the British and French decision to halt hostili-

---

[38] United Nations, General Assembly, *Annual Report of the Secretary-General* (1956–57), *op. cit.*, p. 8. The Israeli arguments were given in detail in the address by the Israeli Ambassador Abba Eban before the General Assembly, November 1, 1956.

[39] Negative votes were cast by Britain, France, Israel, Australia, and New Zealand.

ties although it brought Anglo-French-American relations to an all-time low and produced the strange spectacle of the United States and the Soviet Union voting together on a major issue against the British and French. The vigorous opposition of the Soviet Union made it even more difficult for the British and French to maintain their position. On November 5, after trying unsuccessfully to get the Security Council to call for military assistance to Egypt if British-French-Israeli military action were not stopped within twelve hours, the Soviet Union announced that it was prepared to use force to "crush the aggressors and restore peace" to the Middle East.[40] Some observers interpreted this as a threat by the Soviet Union to move into the Middle East with far more than just "volunteers" and munitions, as had been previously feared, and to intervene with considerable armed force of its own.

It is not easy to tell whether this Soviet threat hastened the British-French acceptance of the cease-fire, but it does indicate clearly that the British and French could not undertake a major foreign policy and military action in the face of both American and Soviet opposition. They might conceivably, with American backing, have defied the Soviet Union, or, with Soviet backing, defied the United States, but they obviously could not go it alone against both, as well as against an overwhelming majority of the United Nations.[41] This point is important to keep in mind when evaluating the capacity of the United Nations to deal effectively with cases of aggression, particularly when any major powers are involved. Although the restraining influence of an overwhelming majority of the United Nations members should never be minimized, an honest appraisal would undoubtedly attribute the British-French decision not solely, and perhaps not primarily, to United Nations action but to a combination of factors including United Nations, American, Soviet, and domestic British opposition.[42] The Suez Canal case bears out completely the observation that the United Nations exerts influence if not power, and that it is a useful organ for international action when enough countries are ready to employ it.

[40] *New York Times,* November 6, 1956, pp. 1, 10.

[41] See Harold Callender, "The Cease-Fire in Suez," *New York Times,* November 8, 1956, for an analysis of this aspect of the question.

[42] The British Labor Party vigorously criticized British intervention in Egypt in opposition to the resolution of the United Nations Assembly, and proposed a motion of censure in the House of Commons, which was defeated, 320–262, on November 8, 1956. In addition, a few members of the Conservative Party withdrew their support from the Government, and Anthony Nutting, Minister of State in the Foreign Office, and one of the best-known younger members of the Conservative Government, resigned because of disagreement with its policy in Egypt. Prominent newspapers like the *Manchester Guardian* and the Sunday *Observer* criticized the Government in their editorials, while a number of religious leaders, including the Archbishop of Canterbury, also joined in the protests. Despite the vocal strength of this opposition, the Government seems to have retained the general support of public opinion by a slight majority. *New York Times,* November 2, 4, 5, 8, 9, 12, and 15, 1956.

The Suez Canal issue was also noteworthy because it led to the establishment of a United Nations Emergency Force (UNEF), which entered Egypt with the latter's consent, to replace the forces of Britain, France, and Israel as they withdrew, and to maintain peace, order, and general compliance with United Nations resolutions. UNEF was authorized by unanimous votes of the General Assembly on November 3 and 4, 1956. The term *police force* is appropriate as a description of UNEF, since it was designed primarily to maintain peace and order, rather than to conduct military operations. Unlike the United Nations forces in Korea, UNEF did not enter Egypt to force the British, French, and Israeli forces out of the country. Rather, it entered with the consent of all parties concerned, including Egypt, and was intended among other things to make it easier for the British, French, and Israeli forces to withdraw.

Some twenty-four states offered to contribute troops, but it was finally deemed practical to accept offers from only ten, in order to assure the balanced composition and representative character required. Troops from permanent members of the Security Council (United States, Soviet Union, Britain, France, China) were expressly barred from UNEF by the General Assembly resolutions, thereby averting its direct involvement in the conflicting policies of the major powers.

Although the British, French, and Israeli governments agreed to a cease-fire early in November, 1956, they did not immediately comply with the General Assembly resolutions calling upon them to withdraw their forces from Egypt. In early December, however, when it was clear that UNEF would have some 4,000 men in Egypt, the British and French announced plans to evacuate the country later in the month, indicating at the same time that they expected the United Nations to proceed immediately to the clearance of the Suez Canal and to support the restoration of free transit through the waterway.[43] The British and French completed their withdrawal from Egypt by December 22, 1956, bringing to an end what many regarded as a very embarrassing chapter in the history of their foreign relations.[44]

As the British and French withdrew from Egypt, their place was taken

[43] *New York Times,* December 4, 1956, p. 1. Shortly after the British-French invasion of Egypt, the latter had blocked the Canal to all traffic by sinking a large number of ships at strategic points along its course. This seriously disrupted normal shipment of oil from the Middle East to Britain and West Europe, and forced the ships into the circuitous trip around the Cape of Good Hope. A serious oil shortage, accompanied in some places by gasoline rationing, struck Britain and other countries of Western Europe. According to some observers, the United States used the oil shortage as a lever with which to bring about the withdrawal of British-French forces from Egypt. According to these reports, the United States refused to help Western Europe obtain additional oil from the Western Hemisphere until the British and French agreed to withdraw their forces. *Ibid.,* p. 3.

[44] Many British Conservatives saw the withdrawal from Egypt as a "national humiliation." Some 126 Conservatives signed a motion censuring the United Nations and the United States for their attitude toward British policies in Egypt. The attitude of Labor Party leaders was summed up in the statement by John Strachey, former

by members of UNEF, who assumed the responsibilities of maintaining peace and order in the evacuated areas, and helping where necessary with the distribution of relief and other needed supplies to the local population. UNEF members also advanced into the Sinai peninsula to supervise the areas gradually being evacuated by Israeli forces. Ultimately, it was contemplated that UNEF units would be deployed along the Egyptian-Israeli armistice lines in order to restrain any hostile actions contrary to the 1949 armistice agreement.[45]

UNEF has aroused great interest as an international police force, as an example of how the United Nations could use its influence to preserve peace and order in troubled areas of the world. Secretary-General Dag Hammarskjold told the members of the Force, "You are soldiers of peace in the first international force of its kind. As members of the United Nations Emergency Force you are taking part in an experience that is new in history. You have come from distant homelands, not to fight a war but to serve peace and justice and order under the authority of the United Nations." [46]

Although British and French forces had completed their evacuation of Egypt by December 22, 1956, it was not until March, 1957, that all Israeli forces finally left the country. On January 19, and again on February 2, 1957, the General Assembly, by votes of 74 to 2, repeated its demands that the Israeli government comply with previous United Nations resolutions.[47] Not, however, until it appeared likely that the United Nations might apply economic sanctions (penalties), did Israel finally agree to the complete evacuation of Egyptian territory.

The Israeli government, by the latter part of January, 1957, had evacuated all territory except the Gaza strip and a coastal area along the Gulf of Aqaba. It refused to leave these areas until it received what it considered adequate assurances that Egypt would never again use the Gaza strip as a base for armed attacks on Israel, nor be able to blockade the Gulf of Aqaba against Israeli shipping, as it had done for some eight years in the past.[48] The Israeli government wished the United Nations

Secretary of State for War: ". . . we have marched into Egypt, marched out of Egypt, caused the canal to be blocked, stopped our oil, made every Arab in the world our enemy, opened the Middle East to Russian penetration, split the Commonwealth, quarreled with the Americans, ruined ourselves—and all for nothing." *New York Times*, December 2, 1956, p. 34.

[45] For an interesting, brief account of UNEF, see the article "The United Nations Emergency Force on Duty in Egypt," *United Nations Review*, February, 1957, pp. 25–27.

[46] *United Nations Review*, February, 1957, p. 25.

[47] United Nations, General Assembly, *Annual Report of the Secretary-General* (1956–57), *op. cit.*, pp. 18–21.

[48] The Egyptian blockade of the Gulf of Aqaba, together with its refusal to allow Israeli ships to use the Suez Canal, had been measures of economic warfare conducted by Egypt against Israel even after the conclusion of the 1949 Arab-Israeli armistice agreement. These actions had been condemned by the Security Council in September, 1951, but were not abandoned by Egypt. *Everyman's United Nations, op. cit.*, pp. 117–118.

to take appropriate action in the two strategic areas to safeguard Israeli interests and security. In an attempt to satisfy Israel on this point, the United States and other leading maritime powers stated that they would regard the Gulf of Aqaba as an international waterway, through which the right of free and innocent passage existed.[49] The statements were welcomed by Israel, and subsequently served to justify its decision to withdraw from the Aqaba area.

The decision to withdraw Israeli forces from both the Gaza and the Aqaba areas was announced on March 1, 1957, one week after a resolution had been introduced in the General Assembly by six Arab and Asian states calling on all governments to deny all military, economic, and financial assistance to Israel. The Israeli government said it was withdrawing its forces on the assumption that the United Nations would be responsible for administering Gaza, pending a final peace settlement, and that freedom of navigation in the Gulf of Aqaba would be assured.[50]

By March 8, 1957, Israeli forces had completed their evacuation of the Gaza and Aqaba areas, thus terminating a military action which had been launched a little more than four months earlier. The United Nations, although not the only factor in stopping hostilities, had shown itself to be a useful means through which the world-wide feeling against aggression could be expressed and international police action undertaken. Most United Nations members approached the subject of sanctions against Israel with slowness and reluctance. Yet, when sanctions appeared to be gaining ground, Israel announced its willingness to comply fully with the United Nations resolutions. Indeed, Israeli Premier Ben-Gurion indicated afterward that fear of sanctions had been the main reason for the final Israeli withdrawal.[51]

The termination of military action did not solve the underlying problems that had prompted the start of hostilities in October, 1956: the status of the Suez Canal and the friction between Israel and its Arab neighbors. One of the first tasks was the gigantic operation of clearing the Canal of the large number of ships and obstructions that the Egyptians had sunk into it shortly after hostilities had begun. This work was done under United Nations auspices, the first undertaking of its kind attempted by a world organization, and by the latter part of April the Canal was again open to normal traffic. It was, however, fully under Egyptian administration, as it had been previously, and the Egyptian government made it clear that it did not accept the principle of international operation, so determinedly sought by the British and French.[52]

[49] New York Times, February 12, 1957, p. 1, February 18, 1957, pp. 1, 6, and March 2, 1957, p. 1.
[50] New York Times, March 2, 1957, p. 1.
[51] New York Times, March 21, 1957, p. 2.
[52] See the Egyptian Declaration on the Suez Canal, transmitted to the United Nations, April 24, 1957, New York Times, April 25, 1957, pp. 1, 8.

Egypt reaffirmed its adherence to the 1888 Convention and to the principles of free navigation of the Canal within the limits of that convention. It also agreed, among other things, to set aside a proportion of the Canal dues to assure modern development of the Canal. It further agreed to submit to arbitration any disputes as to violation of the Canal code or interpretation of the 1888 Convention.

The Egyptian pledges only partially met the six principles approved by the Security Council in October, 1956.[53] No specific provision was made to insulate Canal operations from the politics of any one country. Egypt also, under the new arrangements, announced that it would prescribe the tolls itself, rather than in agreement with Canal users, as had been specified in the six principles.

Although the Security Council principles were not fully met, and although France and Britain were clearly apprehensive over the new arrangements, the Council at its meetings in April and May, 1957, decided to take no further action. The general feeling seemed to be that the new arrangements should be given a trial, with the hope that they would prove satisfactory.[54] Thus, after a serious six-months' crisis, the situation remained not greatly different from what it had been beforehand.

Even in the Gaza strip, the final arrangements did not satisfy the expectations of many. It will be recalled that Israel had withdrawn its forces from the area on the assumption that the United Nations would take over the exclusive responsibility for civilian and military administration. Egypt, however, strongly objected, on the grounds that the 1949 armistice agreement had provided for Egyptian administration of the Gaza strip. The Egyptian government moved quickly to name an administrative governor for the area, thereby seeming to challenge directly United Nations authority.

A compromise was ultimately worked out, under which the Egyptians performed the functions of civil administration in the Gaza area while UNEF was responsible for maintaining peace and order. No Egyptian military forces returned to the area, and UNEF units were deployed along the armistice lines to prevent any repetition of the border raids, which had formerly caused so much tension between Israel and Egypt.[55] By exercising its police functions in this way, UNEF made an important contribution to the restoration of order and quiet in the Gaza area.

Unsuccessful Efforts at Peaceful Settlement

Although the United Nations was effective in a limited sense in the Suez Canal case, it has, on other occasions, had little or no results in

[53] See pp. 532–533.
[54] United Nations, General Assembly, *Annual Report of the Secretary-General* (1956–57), *op. cit.*, p. 26.
[55] *Ibid.*, p. 25.

facilitating the peaceful resolution of international differences. This has been particularly true of disputes arising out of the cold war. If such issues came before the Security Council, the Soviet Union would veto any proposals directed against its communist allies. If the questions were taken up by the General Assembly, and if recommendations were made by the usual two-thirds vote, they would not be carried out by the communist states.

For example, in the Greek civil war in 1947, nine members of the Security Council found that Yugoslavia, Bulgaria, and Albania were giving unlawful aid to the Greek communist guerrillas and supported a resolution calling on those states to cease such assistance. The Soviet Union vetoed this resolution. In fact, it vetoed six resolutions on the Greek question during 1946 and 1947. The question was later referred to the General Assembly where the veto did not apply. Here, a resolution was adopted by an overwhelming majority calling on Yugoslavia, Bulgaria, and Albania to cease aiding the Greek communists and to settle their disputes with Greece through normal diplomatic relations. A Special Committee on the Balkans was appointed on behalf of the Assembly to watch over the Greek borders and observe whether the Assembly resolution was carried out. The Soviet Union and other communist states, however, refused to co-operate with this United Nations Committee. Yugoslavia, Bulgaria, and Albania, moreover, refused to allow Committee members to enter their territories.[56]

The United Nations Committee on the Balkans conducted what operations it could from the Greek side of the borders, and in this way collected much information on the actual amount of Yugoslav, Bulgarian, and Albanian aid going to the Greek communists. By 1950, the civil war was over, the Greek government had succeeded in defeating the communist forces, and the northern borders of Greece had become more peaceful. Responsibility for this, however, could not be assigned primarily to United Nations action, but rather to two other significant events: American military and economic aid to Greece under the Truman Doctrine, and the Yugoslav break with the Cominform and its split with the Soviet Union, which led to a cessation of Yugoslav aid to the Greek communists.

The Berlin blockade is another cold war issue which was referred to the Security Council without success. A resolution proposing the lifting of the blockade was favored by nine Security Council members but vetoed by the Soviet Union in October, 1948.

More recently, in 1956, efforts of the Security Council to stop Soviet intervention in Hungary were vetoed by the Soviet Union.[57] The General

---

[56] A summary of the Greek case may be found in *Everyman's United Nations, op. cit.,* pp. 139–143.

[57] Some 28 Soviet vetoes, up to January 1, 1958, had been cast on resolutions dealing with the peaceful settlement of disputes.

Assembly subsequently took up the matter and, as noted earlier in this chapter, passed several resolutions calling on the Soviet government to withdraw its forces from Hungary. The Soviet Union denied the competence of the Assembly to take such actions, and refused to comply with them.

Collective security: The case of Korea.[58] When the procedures of peaceful settlement are unable to stop hostilities, the machinery of collective security or enforcement action may be put to work. The Korea case is the only occasion on which the United Nations has used its collective-security system and applied sanctions against aggressor states. Although this was a situation of cold war becoming hot war, the Security Council, owing to a strange combination of circumstances, was not paralyzed by the veto in setting its machinery for collective security into motion. The Soviet Union was not attending sessions of the Security Council or other United Nations organs at this time, in protest against the refusal of these organs to accept the Communist Chinese as the legal representatives of China. Hence, when the Korean War started in June, 1950, and the Security Council was summoned into immediate emergency session, it was able within a few hours to adopt a resolution calling for a cease-fire. North Korea ignored the resolution, and the Council two days later adopted a second, calling on all United Nations members to help repel the armed attack. Even before this had been adopted, the United States government had announced that it was furnishing air and naval forces to support the South Koreans.

In July, 1950, the Security Council established a Unified Command for all forces placed at the disposal of the United Nations, and shortly thereafter General Douglas MacArthur was designated commander of these forces. The Soviet Union, perhaps surprised at the vigorous response of the United Nations, returned to the Security Council in August, 1950, but by that time all the necessary machinery of collective security had been set up. However, from then on, the Soviet Union was in a position to block any Security Council decisions of which it did not approve. In September, 1950, it vetoed a resolution calling on all countries to refrain from assisting the North Koreans. In November, 1950, after Communist China had entered the war, the Soviet Union vetoed another resolution calling for the withdrawal of Chinese forces from Korea. It also vetoed two other resolutions, calling for impartial investigation of communist charges that United Nations forces were waging bacteriological warfare in Korea.

Confronted with these vetoes, the other members of the United Nations

---

[58] The collective-security functions of the United Nations are analyzed in U.S. Congress, Committee on Foreign Relations, *Enforcement Action under the United Nations,* Staff Study 7, Committee print (83rd Congr., 2nd sess., 1955).

A summary of the Korea question appears in *Everyman's United Nations, op. cit.,* pp. 83 ff.

turned to the General Assembly. In October, 1950, it was the General Assembly which approved the extension of military action in Korea north of the 38th parallel, in order to achieve a united democratic country. Again in February, 1951, it was the Assembly which, after unsuccessful efforts to obtain a cease-fire from the Chinese Communists, declared Communist China guilty of aggression in Korea. In May, 1951, the Assembly went further and called on all United Nations members to embargo the shipment of a list of strategic war materials to that country. By June 30, 1951, 30 member states and 3 nonmember states reported that they had complied with the request.

In this way, the General Assembly took over certain of the enforcement functions that the Security Council was unable to perform because of the veto. Perhaps the most significant action of the Assembly (from the long-run standpoint), in interpreting its jurisdiction broadly, came in November, 1950, when it adopted the "Uniting for Peace" Resolution. Under this resolution, the General Assembly modified its rules of procedure to permit its being called into emergency session on 24-hour notice in the event that the Security Council was unable to discharge its responsibilities for the maintenance of peace. The Assembly, under such circumstances, might recommend whatever action was necessary to deal with a case of aggression. A Peace Observation Commission was appointed under the Assembly to observe and report on any situation where there might be a threat to the peace. The resolution also called upon United Nations members to maintain certain units of their armed forces for prompt availability as United Nations units if need arose.

Collective security in spite of the veto. Through the Uniting for Peace Resolution, the United Nations was attempting to make certain that, in the event of future aggression, the General Assembly would be able to speak for the organization, even if the Security Council could not. The Assembly could, of course, do no more than make recommendations, but it at least would provide a channel through which the majority of its members could act if they so desired.[59] The Soviet Union has contended that this is a violation of the Charter, since it permits the General Assembly to usurp the functions of the Security Council.

The supporters of the Uniting for Peace Resolution acknowledge that the procedure was not contemplated at the time the Charter was drafted in 1945, but they argue that it is not out of line with a broad interpretation of the Charter and its purposes. In defense of their position, they point specifically to Article 11 of the Charter, which authorizes the General Assembly to discuss any question regarding the maintenance of peace, and to make recommendations on the subject provided that it is

---

[59] This procedure was also followed in the Suez Canal case and the Hungarian revolution, when the Security Council could not act because of the vetoes of Britain, France, and the Soviet Union, respectively.

not at the moment on the agenda of the Security Council. Advocates contend that a broad construction of the meaning of the Charter is necessary to enable the United Nations to meet changed circumstances in world affairs not anticipated in 1945. So far as this broad interpretation is accepted by a two-thirds majority of the General Assembly, and to the extent that the procedures of the Uniting for Peace Resolution are followed, it would seem that the United Nations has found a practical method for either promoting the peaceful settlement of disputes or for organizing a system of collective security without being obstructed by the veto power of one country.

Regional alliances like the North Atlantic Treaty Organization (NATO), the Southeast Asia Organization Treaty (SEATO), and the Middle East Defense Treaty (Baghdad Pact) have also played an important role since 1949 in circumventing the veto and supplementing the United Nations system of collective security. The veto problem still remains, however, in regard to other important questions such as the admission of new members, establishment of effective control over armaments and atomic weapons, and creation of a strong, independent, international police force to enforce United Nations decisions.[60]

Economic and Social Activities of the United Nations

The political and security activities of the United Nations are usually those which make newspaper headlines, and then the disagreements are often given greater attention than the agreements. The average citizen is therefore apt to judge the United Nations primarily in terms of what it does or does not do regarding the more spectacular world events: the Suez Canal case, the Hungarian revolution, or the Korean War.

Yet, together with these political activities, the United Nations engages in a great variety of economic, social, cultural, and educational programs designed to raise living standards and provide better conditions of public health, education, and welfare in many countries of the world. A large number of the programs have been directed primarily toward the two-thirds of the world population that is grossly underfed, ill-housed, and poverty-stricken. The assumption is that genuine peace requires more than an international police force and procedures of negotiation and conciliation—that it depends also on steady progress toward the reduction of poverty, illiteracy, and disease, on the improvement of man's economic and social well-being.

Some United Nations work in these fields has been alluded to earlier

[60] See U.S. Congress, Committee on Foreign Relations, *The Problem of the Veto in the United Nations Security Council*, Staff Study 1, Committee print (83rd Congr., 2nd sess., 1954). The list of all vetoes cast up to January, 1954, is given in U.S. Congress, Senate Committee on Foreign Relations, *Review of the United Nations Charter, A Collection of Documents*, Senate Document 87 (83rd Congr., 2nd sess., 1954), pp. 577–580.

in this chapter, but a few other representative examples will be indicated here. Much of the program is carried on by the ten specialized agencies of the United Nations or by special bodies like the Technical Assistance Board or the United Nations Children's Fund.

The ten specialized agencies, with a brief indication of their responsibilities, are as follows: [61]

International Labor Organization (ILO). Organized in 1919 as an autonomous agency associated with the League of Nations. Strives for the improvement of labor conditions and labor welfare by making recommendations to the governments of the world and preparing international treaties which, when ratified, would guarantee minimum standards for various aspects of labor well-being.

Food and Agriculture Organization (FAO). Provides technical assistance and advice to governments to help them increase the quality and quantity of food and agricultural products. Engages in and encourages research in problems of aridity, forestry, and fisheries, among others.

United Nations Educational, Scientific and Cultural Organization (UNESCO). Promotes the exchange of educational, scientific, and cultural materials among nations. Aids governments in establishing programs of basic, fundamental education in underprivileged and underdeveloped areas.

International Civil Aviation Organization (ICAO). Seeks to advance international action and agreements to assure the safe, efficient, and orderly development of international civil aviation throughout the world. Helps governments in such matters as the establishment of general flight rules, standardization of communications systems, and co-operation in search and rescue operations.

International Bank for Reconstruction and Development (World Bank). Assists in economic construction and development by facilitating and guaranteeing private foreign investments of capital for productive purposes. Makes loans out of its own resources when private capital is not available on reasonable terms for these purposes.

International Monetary Fund. Encourages governments to consult and collaborate on problems such as balance-of-payments difficulties, foreign exchange restrictions, and currency revaluation. Enables member governments in financial difficulties to obtain limited quantities of foreign currency in exchange for their own currency.

World Health Organization (WHO). Assists governments in strengthening their health services, eliminating and preventing epidemics and common diseases, spurring research and training in the diagnosis as well as the treatment of disease, fostering activities in the field of mental health, and improving standards of nutrition, sanitation, housing, recreation, and general economic well-being.

[61] For further details, see *Everyman's United Nations, op. cit.,* pp. 347–405.

Universal Postal Union (UPU). Founded in 1875. Unites all member countries in a single postal territory for the reciprocal exchange of mail. Under this arrangement, the postage of the country where mail originates is recognized by all other countries through which the mail passes before reaching its destination. This avoids the necessity of paying the national postage fees in each country en route.

International Telecommunication Union (ITU). Facilitates international co-operation for the improvement and rational use of telegraph, telephone, and radio communication facilities between nations. Arranges international conferences to allocate radio frequencies and provide for their efficient distribution so as to avoid harmful interference between radio stations of different countries so far as is possible.

World Meteorological Organization (WMO). Promotes international co-operation in the exchange of weather information and the standardization of meteorological observations and records. Helps governments in the establishment of networks of stations and centers to provide meteorological observations and services. Stimulates research in such questions as hurricane warning systems and artificial rainfall.

In addition to these ten specialized agencies, a treaty has been signed providing for the creation of an *Inter-Governmental Maritime Consultative Organization.* When enough governments ratify this treaty, the organization will come into being. Among its purposes will be the promotion of international co-operation in the adoption of shipping regulations, the improvement of maritime safety and efficiency, and the reduction or elimination of discriminatory or restrictive practices by shipping concerns.

Another international organization, closely akin to the specialized agencies, which will receive more and more attention in the years ahead, is the *International Atomic Energy Agency,* established in 1957 as an outgrowth of President Eisenhower's dramatic "Atoms-for-Peace" proposal to the General Assembly in December, 1953. The agency, which will function as an autonomous international organization under the auspices of the United Nations, will be responsible for international activities associated with the study, development, and application of atomic energy for peaceful purposes.

The specialized agencies operate as independent legal entities, their relationships to the United Nations being defined in special agreements between each agency and the United Nations. Frequently, the membership is similar to, but not the same as, that of the United Nations. Switzerland and the Federal Republic of Germany, for example, do not belong to the United Nations, but they are members of most of the specialized agencies. The Soviet Union, Saudi Arabia, and Ireland, on the other hand, belong to the United Nations, but are not part of all the specialized agencies. Each agency has its own governing body and secretariat, and all except the International Bank and the International

Monetary Fund are financed by assessments on their member states, separately from the regular operating budget of the United Nations.[62] This autonomy, it is argued, enables them to carry out their economic, technical, and social-welfare activities with greater freedom from political and security entanglements than if they were directly subordinate to the General Assembly of the United Nations. The specialized agencies do, however, report annually to the Economic and Social Council, which is responsible for co-ordinating their manifold activities as much as is possible.

The Economic and Social Council, which is broadly responsible for all economic and social activities of the United Nations, has also established several commissions directly under its jurisdiction to assist in carrying out these activities. Among these bodies are the Commission on Human Rights, the Commission on Narcotic Drugs, the Commission on the Status of Women, the Social Commission, the Population Commission, and four regional economic commissions for Europe, Latin America, Africa, and Asia and the Far East. Also under the Economic and Social Council are the United Nations Children's Fund, which provides economic and medical assistance to children and mothers, and the Office of United Nations High Commissioner for Refugees, which operates programs of relief and aid in resettlement to many thousands of refugees without a homeland. Two agencies under the General Assembly—the United Nations Relief and Works Agency for Palestine Refugees, and the United Nations Korean Reconstruction Agency—have been responsible for broad programs of relief and reconstruction in Palestine and Korea.

Back of all these organs dealing with economic and social questions lies the recognition that these problems transcend the national boundaries of any single country, and that international action is needed if effective solutions are to be found. Diseases and epidemics, for example, do not automatically stop at national frontiers. In 1947, for example, when Egypt was threatened with an epidemic of cholera, the Interim Commission of the World Health Organization quickly surveyed the vaccine-production facilities in Europe and the United States, and arranged for the production of enough additional vaccine to meet the emergency. As a result, more than 32 tons of cholera vaccine, blood plasma, and other medical supplies were shipped by air to Egypt. As a safety measure, vaccine was also sent to several neighboring countries.[63]

The World Health Organization frequently sends expert consultants and teams of specialists to help governments establish programs and train native personnel in modern methods of disease control and pre-

[62] The World Bank and the Monetary Fund are financed by capital subscriptions from member governments and income from operations.
[63] United Nations, *Yearbook of the United Nations, 1947–48*, p. 916.

vention. At present, WHO, with the support of UNICEF, is conducting a long-term project aimed at the total eradication of malaria. With more intensive spraying campaigns in larger areas to cut down the transmission of the disease, it is hoped that the elimination of malaria in most parts of the world can be achieved by about 1965.[64]

In many underdeveloped areas of the world, where medical knowledge and facilities have been gravely lacking, newborn babies have an average life expectancy of only 30 to 35 years. Through agencies like UNICEF and WHO, these countries are able to obtain modern drugs and the services of medical experts to help combat chronic diseases like tuberculosis, trachoma, and leprosy. Up to mid-1957, for example, UNICEF had supplied 10 million vials of penicillin to cure the loathsome tropical skin disease known as yaws. It had also distributed 20 million tablets of isoniazid to treat tuberculosis, and 325 million sulphone tablets for leprosy.[65] It is estimated that during 1957 some 48 million children and nursing or pregnant mothers benefited from the UNICEF-aided programs.

Most of the specialized agencies participate in the United Nations Expanded Program of Technical Assistance. This program enables governments to request the services of experts to help solve the technical and economic problems involved in their development plans. They may also send their nationals abroad under special fellowships to obtain broader technical training and experience. In 1956, under this program, technical assistance was extended to 56 states and 47 dependent territories. The total cost during this period was somewhat over 30 million dollars.[66]

Typical examples of what has been accomplished might be cited at length, but only a few can be mentioned here. In Egypt, as a result of international services rendered since 1953, rice production has increased steadily, until it has become an important export commodity, second only to cotton. In Israel, United Nations experts assisted in establishing facilities for training public administrators. In Uruguay, progress was made in controlling parasitic diseases that were causing a 40 per cent loss in wool production. In Yugoslavia, new poultry techniques were introduced that increased egg production 40 per cent and reduced chick

[64] *Everyman's United Nations, op. cit.,* p. 388.
[65] *News of the World's Children* (published by the U.S. Committee for UNICEF), September, 1957, p. 2.
[66] United Nations, Technical Assistance Committee, *Annual Report of the Technical Assistance Board for 1956,* Economic and Social Council, Official Records, Twenty-Fourth Session, Supplement No. 5, pp. 1, 6. Funds for the Technical Assistance Program are secured by voluntary contributions from various governments. These are in addition to the quotas paid to the regular United Nations budget. The United States pledged about 15 million dollars to the United Nations Technical Assistance Program in 1956. For our own national program of foreign economic assistance, Congress appropriated about 400 million dollars for technical and development assistance for the fiscal year ending June 30, 1957.

mortality from 20 to 6 per cent. In Haiti, farmers' co-operatives were established, and programs of home-economics training introduced for families in rural areas.[67]

Here, then, is a minuscule sampling of how some of the United Nations agencies are helping governments to improve the economic well-being of their peoples, thus providing, it is hoped, better conditions for international peace and stability. It is impossible, of course, in the space of one chapter, to do justice to all the significant activities of the United Nations. Rather, the effort made was directed toward presenting an analysis of sufficiently representative aspects to permit a reasonable appraisal of the effectiveness of the United Nations in carrying out the broad purposes of the Charter.

The next section contains three divergent viewpoints regarding the United Nations; the ideas they provoke may spur the reader to make his own evaluation of the world organization. The three positions are summarized as follows: The United Nations is a threat to national sovereignty; collective security is based upon unsound assumptions; the United Nations is the best means we now have for fostering world peace and unity.

POSITIONS
ON THE PROBLEM

1. THE UNITED NATIONS IS A THREAT
TO NATIONAL SOVEREIGNTY

(The following position is taken from the testimony of Merwin K. Hart, President of the National Economic Council, before a Subcommittee of the Senate Foreign Relations Committee on April 20, 1955, on the question of United Nations charter revision.[68] Mr. Hart has long been a critic of American participation in international activities, which might in his judgment restrict American freedom of action in world affairs. He has also frequently criticized policies that in his opinion would lead to greater government control over economic life and might increase the general powers of the national government at the expense of the forty-eight states.)

---

[67] Annual Report of the Technical Assistance Board for 1956, op. cit., pp. 76–78.

[68] U.S. Senate, Review of the United Nations Charter, Hearings before a Subcommittee of the Committee on Foreign Relations (84th Congr., 1st sess., 1955), Part 12, pp. 1723–1729.

. . . in my opinion . . . [the Charter] is not worth the paper it is written on. . . .

Has the U.N. produced peace? Have the nations been brought closer together? Is there a more friendly feeling among the peoples of the earth? The truthful answers to all these questions is "No." I want to make several observations about the United Nations.

1. Soviet Russia has of course been, to say the least, completely noncooperative—in spite of all the $11 billion of lendlease and in spite of the tragic giveaway by the United States at Teheran, at Yalta, and at Potsdam. In fact, Soviet Russia has continued just as Lenin and other Soviet leaders have said, always, to conspire against even our existence as a nation. Our leaders have refused to believe and apparently some of them still refuse to believe Lenin's statement that the Communist system and the free-enterprise system cannot continue to live on the same planet, that one or the other must be destroyed.

2. No other nations have taken the U.N. as seriously as we have. I have traveled somewhat extensively in most European countries and elsewhere. I have talked with a great many of the leaders as well as the rank and file of people in those countries, and I find that the people simply do not pay much attention to the United Nations.

I asked one outstanding member of Parliament, whom I have known for many years, what Britain would do if the U.N. told Britain to do something that Britain did not think was in its interest. He promptly replied, "We would tell the U.N. to go to hell."

I think that is a fair attitude of any of the other large powers.

I think it is a fair statement that the United States is the only country on earth that has made serious sacrifices for the U.N.

3. In spite of the claim that the U.N. would bring peace, the U.N. General Assembly is the instrument by which, on November 29, 1947, by a vote of 33 to 13, with 10 abstentions, incidentally, Palestine was partitioned. Palestine had long been occupied by Jews and Arabs and they lived in peace side by side for centuries. It was not until the U.N. accomplished the partition of Palestine, from the outside, that war broke out—a war which is still continuing in spite of a truce. . . .

One of the results of the partition was that the good will toward America built up among 30 million Arabs and 300 million other Moslems, by American universities, missionaries and businessmen over the last century, was destroyed overnight. For all Arabs and Moslems know that the U.N., acting in New York, caused partition. . . .

4. On June 27, 1950, the Communist North Koreans having invaded the south, and President Truman having ordered American troops to resist, the U.N. Security Council called upon all 60 members of the U.N. to join in this "police action." And as we well know, only 15 countries responded, most of them with only token forces. There, I think, the countries were showing their lack of interest and lack of willingness to go along. . . .

The United States furnished at least 90 per cent of the armed forces—outside of the South Koreans—and paid nearly 100 per cent of the cost of the venture. . . .

5. What influences in or outside the U.N. instigated the steps which prevented our winning, and worse still, caused us to lose the Korean War?

MacArthur and several other commanding generals have testified that they could have won the war if they had not been restrained by the Executive at Washington who was acting in close concert with the U.N. Thirty thousand Americans died in vain.

Influences in the U.N. that prevented our winning in Korea can cause the loss of all of Southeast Asia, including Japan and the Philippines—unless American policy with respect to the U.N. is drastically changed.

6. The U.N. is heavily loaded with Communists. The McCarran Committee found even American employees of the U.N. who were Communists, or who had pleaded the Fifth Amendment under oath. When these men were fired on the insistence of the United States, they were subsequently granted high service [sic] pay, a large part of which came from the American taxpayers. Certainly, Moscow must have laughed up its sleeve.

7. Lastly, I will mention the shadowboxing of the U.N. over our imprisoned airmen. Instead of ourselves demanding directly that Red China release them, as we had been accustomed to do as a free nation, we handed the job over to the U.N. We relied on the U.N. to send the Secretary-General hat-in-hand to Peiping for a "conference." No wonder we have lost face with the Asiatics.

All these evil things happened either because of positive mischievous action by the U.N.—as in the partition of Palestine; or in spite of any attempted action by U.N.—as in the failure to secure the release of our airmen; or for sheer failure to take any action—as when Communist China walked into Tibet —and took possession, without the slightest protest from the U.N.

If the U.N. has accomplished for us any single good thing that could not have been brought about—as the International Postal Union was many years ago—by simple international action for that one purpose, and without the cumbersome U.N. organization, that accomplishment should be made a matter, not of mere assertion by U.N. idealists, but by documented proof.

Certainly the U.N. has brought no peace. It has involved the United States in war, which it has then prevented us from winning. If we continue as members of the U.N., and the U.N. Charter is not radically changed, we will be involved in other wars—which likewise we will not be allowed to win.

But there is another danger from the U.N. that apparently was little dreamed of in 1945: Namely, the growing attempts, both through the specialized agencies and through the U.N. itself, to acquire control of our domestic affairs. We now see that those back of the U.N. have as their real object the bringing about of a one-world government under which we will completely lose our sovereignty. . . .

The United Nations Charter, section 7 of article 2, says that "Nothing contained in the present charter shall authorize the United Nations to intervene in matters which are essentially within the domestic jurisdiction of any state. . . ." Had it not been for this provision, the Charter would not have been ratified by the Senate in 1945.

Yet through activities initiated by certain specialized agencies of U.N., such as ILO, the Economic and Social Council, UNESCO, as well as U.N. itself, this provision is being violated right and left. Indeed, on March 3, 1954, the Human Rights Commission voted not to include in the Covenant on Human Rights, any provision recognizing the right of an individual to own property and be secure in its enjoyment against arbitrary seizure by government. . . .[69]

[69] Authors' note: It was omitted because the socialist and nonsocialist countries could not agree on provisions defining the internal economic structure of all countries. It should be noted that the Covenant on Human Rights also contains no provision recognizing the right to socialization of property. Article I of the Draft Covenant on Economic, Social and Cultural Rights, to which Mr. Hart is referring, does guarantee all peoples and nations "the right freely to determine their political, economic, social and cultural status."

The specialized agencies of the U.N. are siphoning off, bit by bit, the sovereignty of the United States; and some of them have already made substantial headway. . . .

If we are to preserve American liberty and independence, the U.N. Charter must be drastically amended, and other important action taken by the Congress.

The following should be done at once:

1. The Charter should be amended to guarantee explicitly that neither the U.N. nor any of its specialized agencies may interfere directly or indirectly with the domestic affairs of the United States.

2. The United Nations should eject Soviet Russia and all of her satellite nations from membership.

3. The Congress of the United States should pass and refer to the States a constitutional amendment, such as the Bricker amendment, which will protect the United States and the people thereof from alien control.

If these changes cannot be accomplished, then the United States should withdraw from the U.N., and should force the U.N. to leave the United States.

2. The United Nations Program of Collective Security Is Impractical and Is Based upon Unsound Assumptions

(The following position is that of Hans J. Morgenthau.[70] Professor Morgenthau does not question the theory of collective security, but he strongly criticizes its basic assumptions.)

In a working system of collective security the problem of security is no longer the concern of the individual nation, to be taken care of by armaments and other elements of national power. Security becomes the concern of all nations, which will take care collectively of the security of each of them as though their own security were threatened. . . . One for all and all for one is the watchword of collective security.

We have already pointed out that the logic of collective security is flawless, provided it can be made to work under the conditions prevailing on the international scene. For collective security to operate as a device for the prevention of war, three assumptions must be fulfilled: (1) the collective system must be able to muster at all times such overwhelming strength against any potential aggressor or coalition of aggressors that the latter would never dare to challenge the order defended by the collective system; (2) at least those nations whose combined strength would meet the requirement under (1) must have the same conception of security which they are supposed to defend; (3) those nations must be willing to subordinate whatever conflicting political interests may still separate them to the common good defined in terms of the collective defense of all member states.

It is conceivable that all these assumptions may be realized in a particular situation. The odds, however, are strongly against such a possibility. There is nothing in past experience and in the general nature of international politics to suggest that such a situation is likely to occur. It is indeed true that, under present conditions of warfare no less than under those of the past, no single country

[70] Reprinted from *Politics Among Nations*, by Hans J. Morgenthau, by permission of Alfred A. Knopf, Inc., copyright 1948, 1954, by Alfred A. Knopf, Inc., 2nd ed., pp. 388–393.

is strong enough to defy a combination of all the other nations with any chance for success. Yet it is extremely unlikely that in an actual situation only one single country would be found in the position of the aggressor. Generally, more than one country will actively oppose the order collective security tries to defend, and other countries will be in sympathy with that opposition.

The reason for this situation lies in the character of the order defended by collective security. That order is of necessity the status quo as it exists at a particular moment. Thus the collective security of the League of Nations aimed necessarily at the preservation of the territorial status quo as it existed when the League of Nations was established in 1919. But in 1919 there were already a number of nations strongly opposed to that territorial status quo—the nations defeated in the First World War, as well as Italy, which felt itself despoiled of some of the promised fruits of victory. Other nations, such as the United States and the Soviet Union, were at best indifferent toward the status quo. For France and its allies, who were the main beneficiaries of the status quo of 1919 and most anxious to defend it by means of collective security, security meant the defense of the frontiers as they had been established by the peace treaties of 1919, and the perpetuation of their predominance on the continent of Europe. Security for the dissatisfied nations meant the exact opposite: the rectification of those frontiers and a general increase in their power relative to France and its allies.

This grouping of nations into those in favor of the status quo and those opposed to it is not at all peculiar to the period after the First World War. It is, as we know, the elemental pattern of international politics. As such it recurs in all periods of history. Through the antagonism between status quo and imperialistic nations it provides the dynamics of the historic process. This antagonism is resolved either in compromise or in war. Only under the assumption that the struggle for power as the moving force of international politics might subside or be superseded by a higher principle can collective security have a chance for success. Since, however, nothing in the reality of international affairs corresponds to that assumption, the attempt to freeze the particular status quo by means of collective security is in the long run doomed to failure. In the short run collective security may succeed in safeguarding a particular status quo because of the temporary weakness of the opponents. Its failure to succeed in the long run is due to the absence of the third assumption upon which we have predicated the success of collective security.

In the light of historic experience and the actual nature of international politics, we must assume that conflicts of interest will continue on the international scene. No nation or combination of nations, however strong and devoted to international law, can afford to oppose by means of collective security all aggression at all times, regardless of by whom and against whom it may be committed. The United States and the United Nations came to the aid of South Korea when it was attacked in 1950 because they had the strength and interest to do so. Would they make themselves again the champions of collective security if tomorrow Indonesia should be the victim of aggression, or Chile, or Egypt? What would the United States and the United Nations do if two different aggressors should start marching at the same time? Would they oppose these two aggressors indiscriminately, without regard for the interests involved and the power available, and would they refuse to violate the principles of collective security and refrain from taking on only the one who was either more dangerous or easier to handle? And if tomorrow South Korea should turn the tables and commit an act of aggression against North Korea or

Communist China, would the United States and the United Nations then turn around and fight South Korea?

The answer is bound to be either "No," as in the last-mentioned hypothetical case, or a question mark. Yet according to the principles of collective security, the answer ought to be unqualified "Yes." These principles require collective measures against all aggression, regardless of circumstances of power and interest. The principles of foreign policy require discrimination among different kinds of aggressions and aggressors, according to the circumstances of power and interest. Collective security as an ideal is directed against all aggression in the abstract; foreign policy can only operate against a particular concrete aggressor. The only question collective security is allowed to ask is "Who has committed aggression?" Foreign policy cannot help asking: "What interest do I have in opposing this particular aggressor, and what power do I have with which to oppose him?"

. . . In other words, what collective security demands of the individual nations is to forsake national egotisms and the national policies serving them. Collective security expects the policies of the individual nations to be inspired by the ideal of mutual assistance and a spirit of self-sacrifice which will not shrink even from the supreme sacrifice of war should it be required by that ideal.

This third assumption is really tantamount to the assumption of a moral revolution infinitely more fundamental than any moral change that has occurred in the history of Western civilization. . . .

Men generally do not feel and act, whether as individuals among themselves or as members of their nations with regard to other nations, as they ought to feel and act if collective security is to succeed. And there is, as we have tried to show, less chance today than there has been at any time in modern history that they would act in conformity with moral precepts of a supranational character if such action might be detrimental to the interests of their respective countries. . . .

In the light of this discussion, we must conclude that collective security cannot be made to work in the contemporary world as it must work according to its ideal assumptions. Yet it is the supreme paradox of collective security that any attempt to make it work with less than ideal perfection will have the opposite effect from what it is supposed to achieve. It is the purpose of collective security to make war impossible by marshalling in defense of the status quo such overwhelming strength that no nation will dare to resort to force in order to change the status quo. But the less ideal are the conditions for making collective security work, the less formidable will be the combined strength of the nations willing to defend the status quo. If an appreciable number of nations are opposed to the status quo and if they are unwilling to give the common good, as defined in terms of collective security, precedence over their opposition, the distribution of power between the status quo and anti-status quo nations will no longer be overwhelmingly in favor of the former. Rather the distribution of power will take on the aspects of a balance of power which may still favor the status quo nations, but no longer to such an extent as to operate as an absolute deterrent upon those opposed to the status quo.

The attempt to put collective security into effect under such conditions— which are, as we know, the only conditions under which it can be put into effect—will not preserve peace, but will make war inevitable. And not only will it make war inevitable, it will also make localized wars impossible and thus make war universal. . . .

By the very logic of its assumptions, the diplomacy of collective security must aim at transforming all local conflicts into world conflicts. If this cannot be one world of peace, it cannot help being one world of war. Since peace is supposed to be indivisible, it follows that war is indivisible, too. Under the assumptions of collective security, any war anywhere in the world, then, is potentially a world war. Thus a device intent upon making war impossible ends by making war universal. Instead of preserving peace between two nations, collective security, as it must actually operate in the contemporary world, is bound to destroy peace among all nations.

3. The United Nations Is the Best Means We Now Have for Fostering World Peace and Unity

(The following position is taken from the book *UN: The First Ten Years*, by Clark M. Eichelberger.[71] The author is Executive Director of the American Association for the United Nations. The book was written on the occasion of the tenth anniversary of the founding of the United Nations, and represents an appraisal of the world organization's work up to that time.)

The United Nations is on the eve of its tenth birthday. The framers of the Charter anticipated that the tenth year might provide an opportunity for a review of how well the organization has functioned.

They could not have anticipated how tremendous would be the stresses and strains to which the United Nations would be subjected in its first decade. Indeed, in that brief time the world has experienced scientific, political and social changes that stamp it as one of the most revolutionary decades in history.

These changes can best be described by considering four great developments which have taken place since the Charter was drafted in 1945. . . . These . . . might be described as the breakup of the five-power system, the advent of the atomic age, the rapid liquidation of the colonial system and the revolt against misery by the underprivileged half of mankind.

It is a sufficient tribute to the United Nations to say that it has survived these changes. It is an even greater tribute to say that the United Nations has helped the world to survive these changes. Indeed, without the unifying moral force of the United Nations the world might not have been able to survive them. . . .

Breakup of the Five-Power System

The five-power system has dissolved and the United Nations has survived. Russia quickly exiled herself from the circle of great power unanimity by demanding that unanimity must always be on her terms. She has used the veto some sixty times to enforce her will.[72] The Chinese Nationalist Government is in exile. France is recovering slowly. Only Britain and the United States are capable or willing to exercise the particular responsibilities imposed upon them by the Charter as great powers on the Security Council.

[71] Clark M. Eichelberger, *UN: The First Ten Years* (New York, Harper, copyright © 1955 by Clark Mell Eichelberger), pp. 1–7.

[72] Authors' note: As of January, 1958, the Soviet Union had cast some eighty-two vetoes.

It was a mistake to assume that five great powers under any circumstances could remain united for a decade. It was equally a mistake to believe that the five great powers of 1945 would necessarily be the five great powers of 1955.

The United Nations in 1950 recognized this change in the world's power situation. The Assembly adjusted the organization to the new power situation by shifting the center of gravity from the Security Council to the General Assembly where the veto does not prevail. This was accomplished through the Uniting for Peace Resolution adopted to prevent a Soviet veto from blocking further action to defeat aggression in Korea.

Advent of the Atomic Age

The closing days of the San Francisco Conference, in retrospect, present a weird picture. The statesmen did not know that soon after they were to adjourn an atomic bomb would be dropped which would profoundly change the security calculations upon which the Charter was based. Secretary Dulles, one of the drafters, has stated that had they known that an atomic bomb was shortly to be dropped, they would have made the Charter a stronger document with authority for the control of weapons of mass destruction. Be that as it may, the advent of weapons of mass destruction, first atomic and then hydrogen bombs, had a profound effect upon the world whose peace the United Nations was to safeguard.

Breakup of the Colonial System

One fourth of mankind, six hundred million people, has won its independence since the war ended. The remaining two hundred million non-self governing peoples are demanding their freedom. . . .

Important ones of these liberated nations have taken their place in the United Nations. . . . Indeed, statesmen from the major liberated areas, have provided the United Nations with some of its leadership. The United Nations has provided an opportunity for newly freed people to adjust themselves to the family of nations. It has provided a place where people could petition for their freedom. It has provided a safety valve. Without the orderly process which the United Nations provided, this revolutionary factor of six hundred million people clamoring for independence might well have upset the world with its violence and thus given communism its greatest opportunity.

Revolt Against Misery

The revolt against political colonialism has been accompanied by a revolt against economic colonialism. Miserable people over large areas of the world are aware that somewhere people are less miserable. They want to improve their lives. They are growing increasingly restless. As a response to this desire there is a program of world helpfulness to help people help themselves. It is called by the uninspiring phrase "technical assistance." It has been carried forward by the United States Point Four Program and the Colombo plan. However, the project has reached its broadest development in the United Nations where . . . [there is] a program that makes possible joint responsibility between the privileged and the underprivileged and thus even makes it possible for the underprivileged to help each other.

These four developments are basic in any measurement of the achievements of the United Nations in its first decade. Obviously other factors must be taken into consideration, such as the idealism and selfishness of governments. . . .

Moral Unity

An assessment of the value of the United Nations must take into account the fact that the organization has stood as the symbol of moral unity. This was necessary to keep the peace. This contribution is greater than any specific settlement it has made and transcends its failures.

Suppose the nations had entered the atomic age in a world of anarchy, had not under the leadership of the late President Roosevelt resolved, while fighting, to write the charter? What if they had not crystallized this intention in the formally adopted principles of good conduct with laws against war? Suppose the nations had not created a common meeting place with machinery for the peaceful settlement of disputes, or for enabling men to develop in larger freedom! It is doubtful that the world would have survived this long. The disruptive potentialities of the changes in the immediate post-war period were so great and their capacity for destruction so terrible that without the unifying moral force of the United Nations the world might have destroyed itself.

. . . [Eighty-one] nations are at least legally bound by all of the obligations of the Charter. Several more are bound by one or more of its articles. . . . The Charter provides that all nations, irrespective of membership, shall ". . . act in accordance with these Principles so far as may be necessary for the maintenance of international peace and security." An even greater number of nations belong to various specialized agencies.

A large proportion of the members of the United Nations have displayed a striking similarity of view in their votes on many of the issues before the General Assembly. Even the . . . Soviet and satellite states, who usually vote against the overwhelming majority, attempt to justify their conduct on the basis of the obligations of the Charter.

How does one describe this intangible quality of moral and spiritual unity as represented by the United Nations? Sometimes it is discernible in the political field, as when fifty-three nations supported the second Security Council resolution of June 27, 1950, on Korea. Or when the General Assembly overwhelmingly passed the Uniting for Peace Resolution, which recognized that in that body rested the strength of the organization. Sometimes this quality is displayed in the human rights field, as when the General Assembly with but eight abstentions adopted the Universal Declaration of Human Rights. One catches its spirit when some seventy nations pledge themselves to contribute amounts, some large and some small, to the United Nations Technical Assistance Fund. Sometimes it is revealed in the area dealing with dependent peoples when representatives of a large part of mankind must listen to an African native plead for self-government for his people under the provisions of the Charter.

Reflections of this spirit of unity can be found in strange places. Military men borrowed from different countries are stationed at mountain passes in Kashmir; others are supervising mixed commissions in Palestine. Modern missionaries on technical assistance missions can be found in some forty countries helping people grow better crops, check illness and establish education. All of these are practical manifestations of an intangible spirit which has held the world together so far.

The first obligation of any people and any government and any statesman is continuously to contribute to this sense of world unity for which the United Nations provides both the framework of principles and the machinery for action. Any people, any government or any statesman who unconsciously, thoughtlessly or deliberately detracts from or weakens this sense of unity is damaging the fabric of peace and contributing to a third world war.

The greatest danger that the peace of the world faces today is that the nations lose the vision of this moral unity and bypass the common meeting place of the United Nations. The greatest danger is that growing tired of the effort to think and act in world terms they may try to fragmentize their concerns in local settlements. This warning is not against regional political, economic and spiritual understanding as such; but rather against any that are not thought of as contributing to the over-all system of world order. The problems of the world are one. And if this vision is lost, the world is lost.

QUESTIONS

1. Cite the main purposes of the United Nations, and indicate which have been most successfully achieved.

2. Do you think the principles of the United Nations are better served if membership is determined on a universal or on a more selective basis? Why?

3. Would you advocate the complete elimination of the veto, the restriction of it to a narrower list of subjects, or the retention of it in its present form? Why?

4. What was the purpose of the "Uniting for Peace" Resolution? Has this resolution made the United Nations more or less effective as an organ for fostering international peace and security?

5. Do you believe that regional alliances like NATO, the Inter-American Defense Treaty, and the Warsaw Pact facilitate or hamper the operation of the United Nations?

6. How would you summarize the strong and weak points of the United Nations as revealed in the handling of the Suez Canal case?

7. Do you think it would be a wise expenditure of funds to increase the budget of the United Nations Technical Assistance Program by five or ten times?

8. Some prominent spokesmen have asserted that the defects and weaknesses of the United Nations have reduced the international organization to a mere sounding board for communist propaganda. They have consequently suggested that the United States should withdraw from the United Nations. How do you feel about this?

9. Do you agree or disagree with the argument that the United Nations is a threat to national sovereignty?

10. Do you detect any inconsistencies or weaknesses in Morgenthau's criticism of collective security? If so, what are they? If not, how do you explain the support the United States and other powers give to such a system of security?

SELECT BIBLIOGRAPHY

ASHER, Robert E., KOTSCHNIG, Walter M., and BROWN, William A., Jr., *The United Nations and Economic and Social Cooperation* (Washington, D.C., Brookings Institution, 1957). A comprehensive analysis of the varied economic and social programs of the United Nations and its specialized agencies. Devotes special attention to the problems of underdeveloped countries.

BROWN, Benjamin H., and JOHNSON, Joseph E., *The U.S. and the U.N.* (New York, Foreign Policy Association, 1954). An excellent, popular-style presentation of the operation of the United Nations and its problems, with special reference to revision of the Charter.

CHEEVER, Daniel S., and HAVILAND, H. Field, Jr., *Organizing for Peace* (Boston, Houghton Mifflin, 1954). A fine, comprehensive text dealing with the organization and operation of the League of Nations and United Nations. Excellent source for analytical summaries of all programs of the two organizations.

GOODRICH, Leland M., and SIMONS, Anne P., *The United Nations and the Maintenance of International Peace and Security* (Washington, D.C., Brookings Institution, 1955). A thorough, scholarly analysis of United Nations activities relating to the peaceful settlement of disputes, regulation of armaments, and restraint of aggression.

HOLCOMBE, Arthur N. (Chairman), *Strengthening the United Nations*, Report of the Commission to Study the Organization of Peace (New York, Harper, 1957). A fresh and stimulating analysis by a commission of experts of ways in which the United Nations might be strengthened.

KEENY, S. M., *Half the World's Children* (New York, Association Press, 1957). A popularly written, readable report, in diary form, of UNICEF work in Asia.

LIE, Trygve, *In the Cause of Peace* (New York, Macmillan, 1954). An autobiographical account by the first Secretary-General of the United Nations of his seven years' experience in this position. Provides much interesting information of behind-the-scenes activities, as well as an excellent picture of Mr. Lie's concept of his role and how he developed it into one of considerable influence.

UHL, Alexander, *The Assault on the UN* (Washington, D.C., Public Affairs Institute, 1953). A thought-provoking examination of the charges against the United Nations by various nationalist organizations, which have been very critical of many programs of international action.

United Nations, Department of Public Information, *Everyman's United Nations,* 5th ed. (New York, 1956). An official summary of the main activities of the United Nations through 1955. A much abbreviated version of the annual *Yearbook of the United Nations,* although it does not appear each year.

WILCOX, Francis O., and MARCY, Carl, *Proposals for Changes in the United Nations* (Washington, D.C., Brookings Institution, 1955). A thorough, well-organized analysis of the changes that have already taken place in the United Nations, as well as of the various proposals for changes suggested in connection with the discussion of Charter revision.

14

A New World Organization: Man's Eventual Goal?

THE PROBLEM
AND ITS BACKGROUND

THE DEMAND FOR A BOLD, NEW RESOLUTION
OF THE CONTEMPORARY CRISIS

Massive Discontent in a War-Torn, Peace-Hungry World

"No thoughtful man will fail to recognize that with the development of modern science, another war may blast the whole of mankind to perdition." [1] These are the words of General of the Army Douglas MacArthur, less than a year after the conclusion of one of the most destructive and deadly wars in man's brief tenure on the earth. Many critics ask whether MacArthur's observation will prove to be a tragic prophecy for the earthlings who inhabit one planet in a solar system which is itself one among a myriad in a marvelous universe.

MacArthur also remarked that "The idea that the world can somehow manage to survive another universal conflict is an irresponsible faith, and in that faith lies civilization's greatest peril." What, many observers wonder, is the responsible faith that may help man avoid such a peril?

The distinguished American general went on to say that "The renunciation of war is the way, and the only way to security; we must abolish it as a sovereign right." Again, the question occurs: Is the renunciation of war as a sovereign right the only way to security?

Certainly, thoughtful men are perplexed by the sea of troubles threat-

[1] Address to opening session of Allied Control Council, Tokyo, April 14, 1946.

ening to overwhelm the civilized world. High priests and lonely prophets, distinguished generals and unknown G.I.'s, great political leaders and anonymous citizens—all have expressed their distress over the troubled state of the world. The more articulate have urged men to raise their eyes, gain a clear view of mankind's past, present, and future, and chart a bold course for troubled humanity.

Sir Winston Churchill, for example, in the twilight of his great career, asked for a reappraisal in the light of the free world's recent triumph and tragedy. The subtitle of his book, *Triumph and Tragedy*, the last in his multivolume personal account of World War II, eloquently summarizes Churchill's discontent with the postwar era: "How the Great Democracies Triumphed and so were able to Resume the Follies Which had so Nearly Cost Their Life."

The historian-philosopher Arnold Toynbee, viewing man in the perspective of some twenty-six civilizations, is uncertain whether modern man can meet the challenge of two world wars within one lifetime. The Second World War, Toynbee notes, was ended by a bomb in which a newly contrived release of atomic energy is directed to the destruction of human life and works on an unprecedented scale. For Toynbee, the swift succession of catastrophic events creates dark doubts about the future of western civilization, and they, in turn, threaten to undermine our faith and hope at a time when we desperately need these saving spiritual faculties. The challenge of war is one we cannot evade. Our very destiny, Toynbee argues, depends upon our response.[2]

How can men and nations deal with the problem of war today? In previous chapters, the values of diplomacy, balance of power, and collective security have been examined. Are these methods adequate? Some say no, and argue that a much bolder and more radical approach is needed. One such approach is considered in this chapter.

The Logical Appeal of a New World Organization

A new world organization, in the eyes of its advocates, would symbolize the right and might of a world law, which all men and nations must observe if the inevitable conflicts of the modern world are to be resolved peacefully and justly. According to this view, current techniques of adjustment in international politics cannot provide mankind with an effective, permanent deterrent to war. If the present anarchy and contingent warfare of jealously sovereign nation-states is traceable to the absence of supreme global law, which all men and nations must obey, it becomes a pressing necessity for men to achieve this global law. A world-wide government must be fashioned with the right to make and the might to enforce it. Only in this way can mankind obtain a durable and

[2] In general, see Arnold Toynbee, *War and Civilization* (New York, Oxford University Press, 1950).

just peace, now impossible when each sovereign state is a law unto itself and refuses to acknowledge a common legal superior.

WORLD ORGANIZATION: CHARACTER AND COURSE

The character of this new and radically stronger world organization must now be examined, as well as the steps that might be taken to bring it into being. Surprising as it may be, there is considerable difference of opinion on these points among the various advocates of world government. They may have agreed on condemning the failure of present techniques of adjustment in world politics and on advocating a new type of world organization, but may now be in disagreement as to the more specific character of such an organization and the steps to be taken to achieve it.

To clarify the situation, it may be wise first to indicate the area of general agreement among the advocates of the new type of world organization and then to highlight the area of general disagreement.

The Area of General Agreement

The advocates of a new type of stronger world organization generally agree on the following points:

Condemnation of war. The deadly, destructive total wars of the modern world are denounced. Any international system that is unable to prevent such wars is regarded as inherently defective. If so, it must be replaced by a different system, which will satisfy the insistent human yearning for peace.

Condemnation of the present state of international anarchy. The absence of an enforceable world law is considered responsible for a state of anarchy in which disputes are resolved by brute force and war.

Condemnation of national sovereignty. It is national sovereignty, with its emphasis on the supremacy and final authority of the nation-state, which prevents the achievement of an effective law to guide and control international relations and enable nations to resolve disputes peacefully. The trouble is that nation-states retain the right to enforce their wills by means of national power without regard for a law which all nations are bound to respect on pain of punishment for lawbreakers.

Need for reign of world law and government. Such a law must be for all nations and peoples of the globe, and it must be enforceable. This will require a world governmental organization superior, within the area of its necessary and legitimate jurisdiction, to any present nation-state. The organization should be able to make and enforce world law.

Need for constitutional federal world organization. The powers of this world organization, however, must be effectively and regularly restrained in the interest of responsibility to the world's peoples. In other words, the new world organization must be based upon the consent of the governed; it must maintain the basic freedoms of free men; it must not be tyrannical; it must not absorb all the powers of today's nation-states; it must not obliterate all differences among peoples and nations—rather, it must recognize the rich and fruitful political, economic, cultural, and religious diversity of the modern world. Consequently, the organization will probably be federal in structure, with powers divided between the central world organization and its national components. The former will possess only powers related to global affairs, whereas all other powers of strictly national concern will remain with the present sovereign states.

Agreement on the need for a larger loyalty or unity. Implicit in the previous points is loyalty to all mankind. This is the universal application of the principle of brotherhood of all mankind. It is premised on the ultimate unity of all men on the great globe we call earth. Although it does not call for surrender of national patriotism, it does require a general reorientation of the citizen's allegiance and emotional attachment to his nation.

Of the six areas of general agreement, three are based on criticism of the existing international system, and three relate to certain changes felt to be necessary. Broadly speaking, there is greater agreement on the first three points than on the last three. Many who would accept the first three might object vehemently to the abandonment today or tomorrow, or for a long time to come, of their nation's external sovereignty, especially the power to resort to war to "settle" fundamental disputes with other nations.

The Area of General Disagreement

The agreements deal largely with general principles. The disagreements primarily concern the specific details involved in setting up a new world organization. These fall into two general categories: the specific powers and structure of the new organization, and the necessary steps to establish the organization.

Should the new world organization have severely limited or very generous powers? Should its powers be limited solely to the maintenance of peace and/or the prevention of aggression? Or should it also have a blanket power (under world law, of course) to form a more perfect union, establish justice, insure domestic tranquility, promote the general welfare, and secure the blessings of liberty to the peoples of the world and their posterity? Or, in addition to the power to maintain peace, should the new world organization be granted only specific powers relating to such questions as international trade or a world currency?

Each question poses others. For example, what powers are involved even in maintenance of peace and prevention of aggression? Does this require a global army, navy, air force—or a global police force? Would a global atomic energy commission be necessary to control and regulate our newest source of energy, so potent as a military weapon in the hands of global "outlaws"?

There is also the question of global citizenship. Is it a power which should be vested in the new world organization? Would it entail free global immigration? Or is free global immigration a power which the new world organization should have regardless of global citizenship? Should certain fundamental rights of men, women, and children be safeguarded by the new organization against infringement by any component political parts of the world organization? Which rights?

Should the new world organization have a "necessary or proper clause" comparable to the "elastic clause" of the American Constitution, which states that the United States Congress shall have the power "To make all laws which shall be necessary and proper for carrying into execution" such powers as, for example, those of taxation, spending money, and regulating interstate commerce? And to what extent would such an "elastic clause" enable the world organization, with originally limited powers, to "stretch" them in the course of time, in much the same way as the powers of the American national government have been "stretched," however legitimately?

These are only a few of the many questions that arise as soon as the more precise nature of the powers of the new world organization is probed. Then it is discovered that the advocates are divided. Some are "minimalists," that is, they seek only minimum powers for the new world organization. Some are "maximalists"—they want fuller powers. The specific views of selected groups will be more fully discussed subsequently.

What structure for the new world organization? Should it be bicameral or unicameral? (Should its legislative body have two chambers or one?) Should its executive branch have an American-type President or a British-type Cabinet? Should its executive head be independently elected, like the American President, or responsible to a majority of its legislative body? What should be the basis for representation? Population? Economic development? Education?

These questions highlight a few of the structural problems upon which advocates of a new world organization disagree.

What are the necessary steps to establish a new world organization? Here additional disagreements are to be found. Should one go fast or slow? Should one work through governments or through peoples? Should one start with a small nucleus of more homogeneous democratic nations and gradually persuade other nations to join? Or should one, at once, open the doors of the world organization to all who seek to enter?

There is no dearth of suggested paths to the eventual goal of a new world organization. Indeed, the road maps to the eventual goal are so abundant that the earnest seeker is likely to be somewhat bewildered. Among the various possibilities—many of which overlap on certain points—are those we might label, somewhat arbitrarily, as the "regional" approach, the "universal" approach, and the "functional" approach. These, together with some differences even within the general approaches, will be examined in greater detail later in the chapter, when specific plans of world organization are presented.

Finally, a most difficult question confronts western world-organization advocates, regardless of the specific character of the plan: What about the U.S.S.R.? Should the U.S.S.R. be excluded unless it agrees to transform itself into a democratic and constitutional nation—western style? How realistic is the possibility? Or should the door be left wide open for the U.S.S.R.? Will U.S.S.R. membership in a new world organization be meaningful, unless it too is willing to abide by global law?

For a more detailed review of the areas of agreement and disagreement, attention is now focused on three approaches advanced in the western world by advocates of a new form of world organization. Since it is manifestly impossible to treat all the variants of each approach, the discussion here will be limited primarily to a few American illustrations.

FEDERAL UNION OF THE DEMOCRACIES

In modern times, Mr. Clarence Streit is perhaps the most eloquent expounder and most vigorous popularizer of the plan for a federal union of free democracies. His now famous book *Union Now*, born of the bitterly disappointing experience of the League of Nations, was first published in 1939, even before World War II and the atom bomb caused millions of thoughtful people to cast about for a way of reorganizing a hitherto dangerously self-destructive world. The book has gone through 17 editions and has sold over 300,000 copies. It has greatly influenced the thinking of almost all subsequent advocates of a new form of world organization.

Mr. Streit's plan in 1939 called for the union of the United States, the British Commonwealth (specifically, the United Kingdom, Canada, Australia, New Zealand, and South Africa), France, Belgium, the Netherlands, Switzerland, Denmark, Norway, Sweden, and Finland. It was subsequently modified and developed in the light of World War II, the advent of the atom bomb, and more recent developments such as the North Atlantic Treaty Alliance.

The Only Hope: Federal Union of the Free

Streit argues that the only hope for freedom, peace, and prosperity in the modern world lies in a federal union of the free—a union of all the western democracies. Past historical experience indicates, Streit admonishes, that disunion produces danger, depression, and war. A free, peaceful, and prosperous world can only be secured if we now create the nucleus of an eventual free world government. This nucleus must be limited to the free democracies of the West, the democratic nations that have grown up in the North Atlantic community and those closely allied with the North Atlantic democracies.

According to Mr. Streit, the historical record points imperatively toward a regional federal union of the free. Together with the British and French in 1917–18, he argues, the United States won a military victory against German autocracy. With the relatively weak organization of the League of Nations and the division of the great Atlantic democracies, however, the fruits of victory were lost. Again, in the union born of World War II, the same nations achieved a military victory over the Axis in a war that might have been prevented by a federation of the Atlantic democracies. Yet, after the war, union was again abandoned, and the United Nations proved to be little stronger than its predecessor, the League of Nations. Unless a strong federal union can now be established among the free, democratic nations, the free world will remain in peril.

The Inadequacies of Present Techniques of Adjustment

Streit maintains that, like the League of Nations—indeed, like all leagues, alliances, or other agreements among independent governments —the United Nations cannot keep the peace or promote human liberty for long. Such attempts are the mere patching of an essentially faulty fabric, faulty because it is woven of the threads of national sovereignty. Here Streit would confirm the weaknesses of the United Nations that stem from the principle of national sovereignty: failure to resolve disputes peacefully under law and inability to enforce decisions of an association of sovereign states. Only a real government with clear powers over police, taxation, and foreign relations, can keep the peace. In other words, a new state must be set up, not just a league of old states.

Streit also asserts that policies of isolationism and balance of power are as inadequate as the system of collective security, because they leave untouched the right of the sovereign nation-state to wage war. Although he feels that peace requires the establishment of government among nations, he does not believe, as do some advocates of world government, that that government can now be set up on a world-wide basis. It is inconceivable to Streit that totalitarian dictatorships like the Soviet Union would participate in a genuinely democratic federal union.

A federal union of the free nations, on the other hand, not only would be a step forward in the direction of ultimate world government, but it would also, in Streit's judgment, immeasurably strengthen the free world in its current struggle with the communist world. A real union of the Atlantic democracies would be so strong that Russia would not dare break the peace. It would be far more effective than our present policies of containment and military alliances.

The First Step: The Exploratory Atlantic Constitutional Convention

What steps must be taken to advance the goal of Atlantic Federal Union according to Streit? The most important step would be for the United States to take the initiative in calling a "federal convention," patterned on the American federal convention of 1787, of the nations now allied in the North Atlantic Pact. To this end the Congress of the United States should pass the resolution sponsored by Senator Estes Kefauver and a bipartisan group of thirty in both houses of Congress. The enacting clause of this resolution is as follows: [3]

Resolved by the Senate (The House of Representatives concurring), That the President is requested to invite the other democracies which sponsored the North Atlantic Treaty to name delegates, including members of their principal parties, to meet in a convention with similarly appointed delegates from the United States and from such other democracies as the convention may invite, to explore and to report to what extent their peoples might further unite within the framework of the United Nations, and agree to form, federally or otherwise, a defense, economic, and political union.

This convention, it should be clear, would be an exploratory convention. It would

. . . explore the possibilities that Atlantic Union offers of preventing another war and another depression, and of advancing immeasurably peace, higher living standards and individual freedom, by applying between democratic nations the great principles of free government that were first embodied in our own United States Federal Constitution, and have advanced these goals so far since then.[4]

Advocates of Atlantic Federal Union believe, of course, that the outcome of the exploratory convention, like the outcome of the American Constitutional Convention in 1787, should be a genuine Atlantic Federal Union.

Atlantic Federal Union Within the United Nations

There must occur, Streit argues, a union of the democracies within the United Nations, centered around a nucleus of such countries as the United States, Britain, and others in the Atlantic community. The charter members of this union would be the nations that have proved most capable of assuring basic individual liberties: freedom of speech, press, religion, political opposition, and the other safeguards of liberal democratic jus-

---

[3] The entire text of the Atlantic Union resolution, and statements in connection with it, may be found in U.S. Senate, Committee on Foreign Relations, *Hearings Relating to the Calling of an Atlantic Exploratory Session* (84th Congr., 1st sess., July, 1955). The text, known as Senate Concurrent Res. 12, appears on p. 1.

[4] Excerpt from statement of Clarence Streit, in *ibid.*, p. 40.

tice. Most of these nations, it should be noted, are currently allied in the North Atlantic Treaty Organization.

The Principles, Powers, and Functions of Atlantic Union

Principles. Although the proponents of Atlantic Union feel that it would be inappropriate for them to take a firm stand on the details of structure of the proposed union, they do indicate the basic principles upon which the union would be based.[5]

Thus the constitution of the Union would include a *bill of rights*, guaranteeing the citizens in the Union all the rights they now enjoy in each and all proposed member nations. No one would lose any rights, according to the proponents of Atlantic Federal Union.

The constitution would also establish a *frame of government*, designed to secure the citizens' rights against aggression, dictatorship, and anarchy. It would embrace a legislature elected by the people, an executive capable of enforcing Union law upon the citizens, and a judiciary empowered to adjudicate disputes between citizens and between member states.

Powers. In addition, the constitution would embody the principle of *division of powers:* certain powers would be reserved to the people by the bill of rights, others would be retained by the member states, and certain specific powers would be delegated to the Union.

The powers delegated to the Union would be clearly defined in a *definition of powers,* and would provide for a Union defense force and foreign policy, a Union free market, a Union currency, a Union postal system, a Union citizenship (in addition to national citizenship), and a Union power of taxation to enable it to implement and exercise its delegated powers.

The powers of the Union, it should be noted—in comparison with other plans for a new world organization—are "maximalist," that is, they would involve not only defense and foreign policy but also fiscal and other far-reaching powers.

Membership. Certain obligations would, of course, be required of all members. All nations would be invited to join the Union, and would be eligible for membership as soon as they could qualify in two essential respects: First, they would be required to invest their supreme legislative power (in areas within Union jurisdiction) in a freely elected Union parliament. Second, they would be required to maintain certain basic liberties, including freedom of the press, freedom to organize, habeas corpus, trial by jury, and other constitutional safeguards.

Eventual development into world government. Finally, it is envisaged

[5] See Clarence Streit, *Freedom Against Itself* (New York, Harper, 1954), Annex 7, pp. 303–304. For the fuller testimony of Streit and late Supreme Court Justice Owen Roberts, see U.S. Senate, Subcommittee of Committee on Foreign Relations, *Hearings on the Revision of the United Nations Charter* (81st Congr., 2nd sess., February, 1950).

that the new federal union of free democracies would constitute the nucleus out of which would eventually develop a world government. In other words, the new Union would be designed to grow so as eventually to incorporate all the nations of the globe, much as the United States grew from thirteen to forty-eight states. As the architects of Atlantic Federal Union see it, pending growth into a world government, the individual members would maintain membership in the United Nations. The new Union would seek to strengthen rather than weaken that organization, to serve as a dynamic democratic nucleus which could act to enforce the decisions of the United Nations.

Freedom Divided Against Itself

In 1954, Mr. Streit advanced the further argument that the danger to freedom, peace, and the whole human species is inherent in freedom's "house divided against itself." [6] The danger is great, growing, and imminent. Conditions of freedom, Streit contended, stimulate the inquiring, inventive mind, thus uniting the world scientifically and technologically, and holding out the promise of an abundant life. Yet, politically, pursuant to notions like exclusive national self-determination, freedom has divided the world among nations. The scientific and technological machines fostered by freedom have served to unite the free peoples more and more in an Atlantic community, which can be governed either by free agreement or by force. At the same time, the political policies of free nations have been dividing free men and nations. The division is dangerous because the scientific and technological machines of freedom, created largely by liberal democratic and constitutional nations, can rather easily be acquired by totalitarian and dictatorial governments, and thus serve to equip them with the means of securing their kind of world political unity by force or conquest. This is why it is imperative for the democracies of the Atlantic community to join together in a free Union.

Needless to say, advocates of Atlantic Union were greatly heartened, in the spring of 1956, by the talk of broadening NATO beyond the predominantly military alliance that it has been.

European Union

Similar to Streit's plan for Atlantic Union, but different in the projected membership, are various proposals for European Union. They combine the regional approach to union with minimal powers, and might be said to be closer to current political reality since they are under active consideration by European governments.

Actually, there is a *Council of Europe* in existence. Created on May 5, 1949, it is in effect a European Assembly of most democracies of Western Europe. The original members were Belgium, Denmark, France,

---

[6] *Freedom Against Itself, op. cit.*

Ireland, Italy, Luxembourg, the Netherlands, Norway, the Saar (associate member), Sweden, the United Kingdom, Greece, Turkey, Iceland, and the West German Republic. The Council is composed of a Committee of Ministers, who are the Foreign Ministers of each member country; a Consultative Assembly; and a Secretariat. The Consultative Assembly constitutes a kind of primitive European parliament, since its delegates are elected by the parliaments of the various countries rather than appointed by the foreign offices. At present the Council has very limited powers; it merely debates relevant issues and makes recommendations to its member countries.

Advocates of European Union look forward, however, to the gradual transfer of power from member countries to an all-European government. The first step in the transfer involves the guarantee of political rights to all citizens of a democratic Europe, to be honored and upheld by a European Court. Here, the Council has already produced the European Convention on Human Rights, which was passed by the Consultative Assembly in November, 1950.

A second step requires the freeing of basic resources from the restrictions of national boundaries. Here, too, some success has been achieved in the Schuman Plan or European Coal and Steel Community. This plan will be treated a little more fully in a subsequent section on the "functional" approach to world organization. Similarly, agreement was reached in 1957 to establish a federal authority for nuclear energy (Euratom) and progressively to work toward a general common market in Europe.

A third step toward the development of a European Federal Union is the creation of a unified European army, a single military force, with a European Minister of Defense responsible to an all-European government. It was hoped that this army would come into being as a result of the acceptance of a 1952 treaty establishing a European Defense Community. France, however, fearful lest her national interest be jeopardized by the arrangement, refused to approve the treaty in 1954. Subsequently, a greatly modified arrangement for the co-operative defense of Western Europe was approved, without the supranational features of the defeated European Defense Community. It is known as Western European Union.

Advocates of European Union would like to see Great Britain and other European countries come into the Schuman Plan, the common market, and Euratom. In this and other ways, they hope to lay the foundations for a more comprehensive and effective European federation.

The Council of Europe, Schuman Plan, European Common Market, and Euratom are cited to illuminate the problem of the feasibility of a supranational, federal organization, for feasibility is an important factor to be considered in any debate on the nature and prospects of a new type of world organization.

Although plans for government on a regional basis may differ in details, they are in substantial agreement on the necessity of more closely uniting the democracies and/or the separate nations of Europe into a stronger whole. Most of the plans hold that a union of democracies or a united Europe can provide a nucleus for an eventual world-wide organization.

GOVERNMENT ON A WORLD-WIDE BASIS

Another plan for world federal government, which has received attention in the United States, is the proposal of the group known as the United World Federalists (U.W.F.). Whereas the Streit plan contemplates a regional grouping of democratic nations with extensive supranational powers, the United World Federalists suggest a government on a world-wide basis with more limited jurisdiction.[7] To use the distinctions made earlier in this chapter, the Streit plan is regional in scope and maximal in jurisdiction, whereas the U.W.F. plan is universal in scope and minimal in jurisdiction. United World Federalists argue that agreement on a world-wide government is unlikely unless the powers granted it are much more limited than those Streit would give his federal union of the Atlantic democracies.

United World Federalists start with the proposition that the United Nations should be the basis of any new world organization, but that it must be given governmental power in at least the area of armaments if it is to be effective in maintaining peace.

Powers to Enforce Universal Disarmament and Prevent Aggression

United World Federalists argue that peace and security cannot be obtained or maintained so long as any nation can assemble military power to threaten others. Nor will there be peace or security against aggression so long as nations must rely upon their own armed forces. Furthermore, neither unilateral disarmament nor a disarmament treaty resting on the good faith of sovereign nations can be depended upon to reduce the military power that makes aggression possible. Effective disarmament must be enforceable disarmament, and enforcement can be assured only by an all-inclusive world organization with the authority and power to guarantee to each nation security from attack by others.

To make the United Nations such an organization, certain changes must be made in the United Nations Charter:

[7] For the position of the United World Federalists, see their various policy statements and platforms. This summary of the U.W.F. program is largely based on the statement and platform adopted by the U.W.F.'s Seventh General Assembly, June 19–21, 1953. A recent book by Grenville Clark and Louis B. Sohn, *World Peace Through World Law* (Cambridge, Harvard University Press, 1958), presents a comprehensive plan for world federal government, and reflects the U.W.F. position.

1. The United Nations must be given the power to prohibit by law the right of nations to apply force or the threat of force in international affairs.

2. The United Nations must be given the power to make laws, affecting disarmament, binding on individuals and national governments. These laws would prohibit the construction or possession of armament beyond that required for internal police purposes; they would also enable the United Nations to administer an agreed schedule for universal disarmament.

3. The United Nations must be given the power to maintain adequate and effective civilian inspection and police forces to assure that world law controlling national armaments is respected.

4. The United Nations must be given the power to maintain United Nations armed services sufficient to enforce world law prohibiting aggression and to support United Nations civilian police wherever necessary.

5. The United Nations must be given the power to bring to trial in world courts any individuals or groups who violate such world law or obstruct its enforcement.

6. The United Nations must be given the power to raise dependable revenue under a carefully defined and limited but direct taxing power, with a ceiling fixed by the Charter of the United Nations.

The United World Federalists, it will be observed, do not go as far as Streit in proposing government jurisdiction over questions of trade, currency, citizenship, or human rights. This is the reason their plan is described as "minimalist," and the Streit proposals as "maximalist." The U.W.F. also maintains that regional federations of the type envisaged by Streit will tend to increase the division and tension between existing rival blocs. Consequently, a more nearly universal organization is preferred, but the new world body should obviously not bite off more than it can chew, and its powers should for some time be limited to the minimal ones necessary to prevent armed violence and guarantee the security of its members. Thus, it would be given the power to promulgate and enforce laws regarding armaments and the use of force. United World Federalists are hopeful that even the Soviet Union would see the advantage of such a world government and would join.

A Revised Structure to Administer the New Powers

Along with revision of its powers, obviously the structure of the United Nations would have to be changed fundamentally as well. The precise character of the alterations cannot now be foreseen, but the general outlines are discernible.

Initially, the General Assembly of the United Nations would have to be transformed into a legislature really capable of making laws. This would require revision of the basis for representation in the Assembly. Obviously one vote for one nation gives unreasonable power to the smaller nations; on the other hand, representation based solely on population would not fairly reflect what certain nations, like the United States, can contribute to the success of the world organization. The eventual compromise might consider such factors as economic development and educational level, in addition to population. It would be important, however, for each representative to vote as an individual, and not necessarily as the spokesman of his nation.

Another revision would transform the Security Council of the United Nations into an executive organ, with the authority and power to administer and enforce the laws of the world organization. It would then become a responsible executive body, without judicial or legislative functions. Equally important, no single nation would have the power to suspend effective administration or enforcement of the law by means of a veto.

There would also have to be established a United Nations judiciary, with the authority to interpret world law and to render judgments on it. These world courts would have to have compulsory jurisdiction over all cases and disputes arising under world law, covering both individuals and governments.

In addition, an equity tribunal would be required within the United Nations, that is, a court designed to secure remedies not available in the regular courts. It would not have compulsory jurisdiction, but its job would be the highly important one of passing upon disputes between nations or between non-self-governing territories and their administering powers, with the aim of achieving peaceful and just settlement of the disputes.

Finally, the revised United Nations Charter would provide for amendments favored by a heavily preponderant majority.

Safeguards

This strengthened United Nations would have to include safeguards for the rights of the individuals and countries comprising the new world organization. It must not weaken or destroy such rights; it must be a strictly limited world government, not a world superstate. Consequently, the revised Charter of the United Nations would have to guarantee the rights in the following manner:

1. Each nation would retain complete sovereignty to manage its domestic affairs; the United Nations would be prohibited from interfering with any nation's form of government, economic system, flag, constitution, religion, or culture.

2. The revised Charter would contain a Bill of Rights to protect individuals against arbitrary or unjust action by the United Nations, and against United Nations interference with rights and liberties guaranteed to persons by their own national and state constitutions.

3. All powers not expressly delegated to the United Nations would be reserved to the nations and their peoples.

4. The limited powers of the United Nations would be so defined in the Charter that attempts to enlarge them would be declared unconstitutional by United Nations courts.

An Expanded United Nations Program to Meet Human Needs

Although the United World Federalists would restrict the powers of the new universal organization to the control of armaments and the prevention of aggression, they recognize the equally important need for promoting peaceful change in the direction of a free, just, and prosperous world community. Consequently, they call for greater support for the work of the specialized agencies of the United Nations and for the eventual elimination of colonialism. Specifically, they urge that monies saved as a result of universal disarmament be contributed voluntarily to a world fund, to be administered by the United Nations, for economic development and rehabilitation. They hope, too, that the United Nations equity tribunal will help speed non-self-governing territories toward peaceful achievement of self-government and full membership in the world organization.

Reasonable Restraints of a Limited Government

Obviously, all nations would have to transfer to the revised United Nations some authority that they now possess. The restraints upon national freedom of action would be limited to those necessary and sufficient to achieve peace and order in the world. The United World Federalists argue that the revised organization would have no need to increase and centralize its powers, in large part because absence of an outside enemy would make it unnecessary.

The Action Program of the United World Federalists

How do the United World Federalists expect to secure the necessary amendments to the United Nations Charter? In the United States, they seek initially to arouse public opinion, which alone can successfully demand action for limited world government. Second, with broad public support, they would urge the United States government to declare the development of federal world government to be the major objective of its foreign policy. Third, with the United States supporting it, they would have the United Nations call a review conference under Article 109 of the Charter. Article 109 provides for review of the Charter. Fourth, the United Nations review conference would propose amendments for transforming the United Nations into an effective world government. Fifth, amendments to the United States Constitution, providing for U.S. membership in this limited federal world government, would be proposed and ratified. Sixth, with the amendments to the United Nations Charter ratified by the required number of nations, they would become the basic law of the world. A new world organization would have come into being!

What If a Major Nation (Soviet Union) Refused to Participate?

One of the basic problems which plagues all western plans for a new world organization is the question of the attitude of the Soviet Union. Advocates of united world federalism believe that a fundamental distinction must be made between *permissibly* going ahead without the Soviet Union *after* every possibility has been exhausted of facilitating her entry, and impermissibly ruling her out, *in advance*, on ideological grounds. This distinction divides the advocates of united world federalism and those of Atlantic federal union. In the end, the U.W.F. concede, the result may be the same: The U.S.S.R. may stay out anyhow. Nevertheless, they maintain that their approach is sound for at least two reasons. First, it holds out hope for the dim possibility of Soviet entry and co-operation. Second, it is more likely to rally the peoples of the world than the policy of the "closed door." Many who favor united world federalism also consider the U.S.S.R. not solely responsible for the present world crisis. They hold, rather, to the "equal guilt" thesis: that all major nations are equally guilty of creating the conditions of war and fear dominating our century, that the real enemy is the narrowly nationalistic conception of world affairs, which creates international anarchy.

THE FUNCTIONAL APPROACH

A third approach to the problem of world organization is described as "functional." It is based on the premise that the barriers to effective world unity can best be overcome when the peoples and nations of the world work together to meet common needs and advance mutual interests, essentially nonpolitical in nature. The needs and interests are those relating to the laborer, farmer, businessman, the little child, the expectant mother, the doctor, scientist, teacher, aviator, engineer, fisherman. The specialized agencies of the United Nations are good illustrations of such functional organizations. Their very names indicate the common functions that may serve to unite the world's peoples across national boundary lines, develop mutual confidence as a result of solving mutual problems, and promote an international network of activities, which may in practice transfer sovereignty to organs of an international community. The agencies were listed and described in the preceding chapter.

The general case for the functional approach has been well put by David Mitrany in his book, *A Working Peace System*, originally published in 1943. The book is subtitled "An Argument for the Functional Development of International Organization." The following summary indicates Mitrany's views on the general problem confronting the world, his reasons for rejecting other types of world organization, and the logic back of his belief in the functional alternative.

The General Problem

The fundamental problem of the present age, according to Mitrany, is to determine how to achieve a new and necessary international system. The system must be capable of preventing aggression and of organizing peace and peaceful change. Without destroying the valuable diversity of nations, it must also be able to achieve unity in a badly divided modern world. Logically, unity might be obtained on the basis of conquest or consent, or it might be accomplished through immediate establishment of a world state or a long period of gradual evolution. It might be secured pursuant to formal, constitutional blueprints, or according to informal, practical satisfaction of pressing international needs. In the process, however, neither deep-rooted loyalties of nationality nor modern man's ever mounting insistence upon social betterment can be ignored. National loyalties have tended politically to separate and divide men in the modern world, even if they have frequently operated to increase man's freedom within the nation-state. On the other hand, the demand for social betterment and conditions of economic interdependence have increasingly bound peoples together. In view of these patent facts of the modern world, the problem confronting mankind can be restated: how to stimulate a voluntary and progressive evolution of world society, which will preserve the valuable aspects of nationality and satisfy the legitimate needs of mankind. Here, Mitrany notes that, although there may be agreement on the general principles and ultimate aims of world organization, there is genuine dispute on the question of how to move toward it.

Rejection of the Formal, Constitutional
Approach to World Organization

From the outset, Mitrany is impressed by the difficulties of the formal, constitutional approach to a new kind of international system. He notes that significant changes within modern democratic nations have not come about as a result of formal constitutional amendment. An illustration of this point can be found in the New Deal. The United States government, under the New Deal, concentrated on meeting actual, pressing problems, without waiting for constitutional amendment or a clear and consistent blueprint of reform. Functional agencies were established and practical action taken to aid the unemployed, farmers, home owners, businessmen, depressed regions, banks, and so on. Services were provided to meet needs. The one recent attempt by the United States at direct constitutional revision—the effort to increase and liberalize the membership of the Supreme Court—was bitterly disputed and defeated. If this holds true in a country as strongly united as the United States, Mitrany inquires, what hopes are there for formal, constitutional change by nations of the world, which would move them toward a new kind of international system?

Difficulties of a League or a Regional or Ideological Union

An association of nations, like the League of Nations or the United Nations, leaving almost untouched the identity and policy of states, would be too loose an organization to do the necessary job of achieving unity in diversity. A federal system of international organization theoretically provides the cohesion lacking in a league of sovereign nations, but, in Mitrany's opinion, the basic community of interest needed for such a federal state does not yet exist on a world-wide scale. The federal system would therefore have to operate within the limits of a region or within the framework of an ideological union. However, the regional or ideological union would be defective, since it would tend to divide the world into several potentially competing units.

Continental or regional unions would not contribute to real world unity. They might bring peace within their respective areas, but they could not do so outside those areas. They would probably keep the world divided in closed territorial units: one for Europe, one for Asia, one for Africa, and so on! According to Mitrany, other shortcomings might mar these unions. For example, there would always be the danger that the most powerful member would dominate the union. Furthermore, there would be no assurance that such a self-contained union would increase prosperity within its area. Indeed, it might destroy valuable ties with the world even while creating new ties within the union. Hence, these continental or regional unions might well have an unreal unity of outlook and interest.

Ideological unions might suffer from comparable defects. A glance at a suppositious union of democratic countries yields the following dangers. There could be no guarantee of stability or cohesion among countries not uniformly democratic; there might be no agreement on what democracy means; and changes within the countries might make member countries undemocratic. Furthermore, it might become a crusading union, seeking to impose the union's standards of democracy on member nations or, indeed, on the undemocratic outside world. An ideological union, finally, might cut across certain genuine national interests, relating to questions of international trade, domestic problems, and national security.

One adverse criticism of regional or ideological unions is outstanding: They would continue to divide the world and therefore intensify the international rivalry that holds such peril for peaceful change in the world.

If other approaches to international organization must be rejected, what can be said for the functional approach?

The Functional Alternative

The advantage of the functional approach, according to Mitrany, is that it would "overlay political divisions with a spreading web of international activities and agencies, in which and through which the interests and life of all the nations would be gradually integrated." [8] International government can be effective only when it is coextensive with practical international activities. The starting point must be common needs, with momentary disregard for the presence of jealously sovereign nation-states and the absence of larger political or ideological unity. The proper approach must be experimental and practical, free of insistence upon formal blueprints and constitutional requirements.

As men and nations work together to meet practical and pressing problems—trade and shipping, health and literacy, agriculture and fishing, aviation and broadcasting, atomic research and development, among a host of others—sovereignty may be gradually transferred, in the work involved, from the participating nations to the functional agencies performing a job agreed upon. "By entrusting an authority with a certain task," Mitrany writes, "carrying with it command over the requisite powers and means, a slice of sovereignty is transferred from the old authority to the new; and the accumulation of such partial transfers in time brings about a translation of the true seat of authority." [9]

In this way, too, Mitrany maintains, the touchy question of peaceful change would be given a new perspective: [10]

> The only sound sense of peaceful change is to do internationally what it does nationally: to make changes of frontiers unnecessary by making frontiers meaningless through the continuous development of common activities and interests across them. A change of frontier is bound to disturb the social life of the groups concerned, no matter whether it comes about peacefully or forcibly. The purpose of peaceful change can only be to prevent such disturbance; one might say indeed that the true task of peaceful change is to remove the need and the wish for changes of frontiers. The functional approach may be justifiably expected to do precisely that: it would help the growth of such positive and constructive common work, of common habits and interests, making frontier lines meaningless by overlaying them with a natural growth of common activities and common administrative agencies.

The functional approach also involves a different view of equality and authority. A nation's insistence on legal equality and authority in the performance of a given function would not make much sense if the nation lacked the interest and capacity to perform the necessary function. In other words, a nation's authority in the performance of a given function

[8] David Mitrany, *A Working Peace System*, 4th ed. (London, National Peace Council, 1946), p. 14.
[9] *Ibid.*, p. 9.
[10] *Ibid.*, pp. 34–35.

would be commensurate with its responsibility in that area. In this way no country would be arbitrarily excluded from a share in authority; no nation's legal authority would be insulted. Rather, the principle of natural selection would operate to ascertain which nation would have a major or minor role in the performance of necessary functions. The major powers would undoubtedly bear the chief responsibility in matters of security; the smaller nations would be able to make contributions in areas where they possessed the requisite capacity, interest, and experience. Thus, Norway would have a prominent role in the organization of shipping, Canada in the production of nickel, Switzerland in the organization of leisure, and so on. No state would be placed in a position of general inferiority. In some functions a nation might be first, in others last, and nations might bear greater or less responsibility in a given function, as circumstances changed. Thus, claims to a share in the control of a given function would be measured by the principle of evident capacity for performance.

Again, the broad lines of the functional organization would be determined by the nature of the function, not by a formal constitution or legal blueprint. Thus, the international organization of the railway systems would clearly be continental, the European, North American, or African continents, for example, providing the logical administrative unit of co-ordination. Obviously, separate democratic, communist, or neutralist railroad systems would not make very much sense. Here, geography, not politics or ideology, would indicate the broad lines of functional organization.

Shipping, Mitrany suggests, might be organized on international or intercontinental lines. Here, all overseas states would have to co-operate in the solution of common problems. Conversely, since aviation and broadcasting would involve all countries in the world, they would have to be organized on a universal scale, with subsidiary regional arrangements to minister to local needs.

In other words, the functional approach would bypass the thorny questions of sovereignty, legal equality, and national prestige. It would emphasize common solutions for common problems. It would proceed in accord with the principle of natural selection, "binding together those interests which are common, where they are common, and to the extent to which they are common." Such a "functional selection and organization of international relations would extend, and in a way resume, an international development which has been gathering strength since the latter part of the nineteenth century." [11]

Mitrany is not unaware of the special problem of security in international organization. Security is first among the essential functions that must eventually be transferred to a new international organization. "There can be no real transfer of sovereignty until defense is entrusted to

[11] *Ibid.*, p. 40.

a common authority, because national means of defence are also means of offense and also of possible resistance to that common authority." [12]

This problem, a political one, is crucial, "for on its being solved effectively the successful working of the other activities will depend." [13] Nevertheless, security is a function too, and, however important, should not be considered in isolation from other functions. It is indispensable to the peaceful growth of an international society but of itself is incapable of producing that growth. Actually, in addition to developing the conditions that must underpin the eventual world community and state, the functional agencies may play an important role in advancing the crucial function of security. They might watch over and check the building of strategic railroads, the accumulation of strategic stocks in metals and grains, and they might even serve to check threatening aggression by the withholding of vital services from potential aggressors.[14]

The functional trend, if followed, could "grow in time into a rounded political system." [15] It would have grown gradually, by natural selection and evolution, tested and accepted by experience. It would have a cohesiveness based on mutual service and a strength rooted in free growth and successful accomplishment. Functional integration would pave the way for political integration. A functional international society, socially interdependent, economically united, would prepare for the more complete political federation, in which man could turn from preoccupation with the prevention of aggression and war, and focus his attention on the "real tasks of our common society—the conquest of poverty and of disease and of ignorance." [16]

This is Mr. Mitrany's general argument. We shall now examine a living, though limited, illustration of the functional approach in Europe.

Functional Steps Toward Unity in Europe

The European Coal and Steel Community. In this plan, a supranational High Authority pools the coal and steel resources of France, West Germany, Belgium, Luxembourg, Holland, and Italy. In these six nations the Community exercises control in all matters pertaining to coal and steel. The plan, which owes a great deal to the far-sighted thinking and dedicated service of the French economist Jean Monnet, was formulated as early as March, 1949. It was formally proposed by the French government in the spring of 1950 and is often called the Schuman Plan, after Robert Schuman, former French Foreign Minister and Premier. The Coal and Steel Community was established by treaty on April 18, 1951, and has been in actual operation since August 10, 1952. It operates under its

[12] *Ibid.*, p. 9.
[13] *Ibid.*, p. 45.
[14] *Ibid.*, p. 46.
[15] *Ibid.*, p. 51.
[16] *Ibid.*, p. 62.

own High Authority, Council of Ministers, Common Assembly, and Court
of Justice. The function of the Council of Ministers, made up of one
representative from each of the six nations, is to determine major policy.
The Common Assembly, composed of delegates elected by the parliaments of member states, serves in an advisory capacity. The role of the
Court of Justice is to settle disputes and rule on treaty violations. The
High Authority is the executive organ of the Community. The Schuman
Plan was designed to create a common or free market for coal and steel,
unburdened by trade barriers and other restrictive practices. Its central
objectives are to spur production, lower prices, and increase consumption,
thus raising the standard of living of participating nations. The ultimate
goal is to create a great free trading area in Western Europe under the
direction of a supranational authority, responsible to a genuine European
parliament and court. Its supporters hope that it will create the first concrete foundation for a European federation. That their hopes have not
proved illusory is borne out, in part, by two other treaties signed in
March, 1957—one establishing a common market, the other providing
for the joint development of another raw material, atomic energy. It
should be noted that the Coal and Steel Community (itself a relative
"baby" in the history of Western Europe) has served as a prototype for
the more recent "arrivals."

The European Economic Community (Euromarket). This plan envisages a common or free market for France, West Germany, Belgium,
Holland, Luxembourg, and Italy—and eventually their overseas territories. The elimination of tariffs or customs duties within the six-nation
bloc is to be achieved gradually, over a period of seventeen years, in order
to cushion the shocks of economic integration. Economic co-operation
will include standardization of wage rates and social security systems
of the six participating nations, and formation of an investment pool for
the development of their overseas territories. Restrictions on other aspects
of trade within the common market are also to be removed gradually—
restrictions, for example, on foreign exchange, labor, and capital. As
in the Schuman Plan, trade practices, like cartels, that restrain competition will be eliminated. Agriculture, however, will be excluded from the
full provisions of the common market. In the transitional period, member
states will adopt a common tariff against goods from outside Euromarket.
In brief, the type of economic integration envisaged is roughly analogous
to the economic integration of the states in the United States. Both the
European Economic Community and the European Atomic Energy
Community (see next paragraph) will function through the federal machinery already established for the Coal and Steel Community.

The European Atomic Energy Community (Euratom). Here again
a supranational agency has been established, this time to spur the de-

velopment of atomic energy for the mutual benefit of the same nations. A common or free market is to be created for nuclear raw materials and equipment. Joint research will be stimulated, and a reservoir of nuclear technicians will be built up and maintained to serve all six nations. The actual construction of reactors will, however, be left to individual members. Western Europe's determination to develop atomic power was strengthened by the Suez dispute, which underscored its common dependence on Middle Eastern oil.

The promise of economic integration. It seems clear that Europe has decided to achieve economic unity before it pursues political unity. Advocates of this course, like Jean Monnet, have argued that political federation will naturally follow economic fusion. The potentialities of economic union are great. United, the six countries in Euromarket alone (with a vigorous and skilled population, large potential internal and foreign markets, production of coal, steel, and electricity) can stand comparison with either the United States or the Soviet Union. If Britain, Scandinavia, Austria, and Switzerland should be added to the common market, the showing would be even more impressive. Then Europe's potential "domestic" market, 240 million persons, would surpass the individual markets of the United States and of the Soviet Union. Figure 14 reveals the economic potential of a united Europe rather dramatically.

Great Britain and European union. These factors play a part, as well, in Britain's concern for a united Europe. However, Britain has been torn between her natural attraction to a united Europe and her equally natural attraction to the Commonwealth and to the United States. Faced with this dilemma, Britain proposed a plan which would increase her participation in the economic affairs of Western Europe without jeopardizing her legitimate ties to members of the Commonwealth and to the United States. A free-trade zone would be established for the whole of Western Europe that would dovetail with the scheme for Euromarket. With Britain an active participant and customs barriers removed, a single internal market would be created for the whole of Western Europe. To fit the scheme in with her preferential tariff system for members of the British Commonwealth, Britain proposed that each zone member maintain its own tariff system with the outside world, the six nations in Euromarket to be treated as one zone member. This would mean, in effect, that Britain and the European Economic Community might have different tariff policies toward the outside world but the same policy with regard to each other in Europe.

Just as Britain's close economic ties with the Commonwealth militated against her full participation in Euromarket, so her close links with the United States and Canada in the development of atomic energy were a barrier to full "membership" in Euratom. Furthermore, Britain's attain-

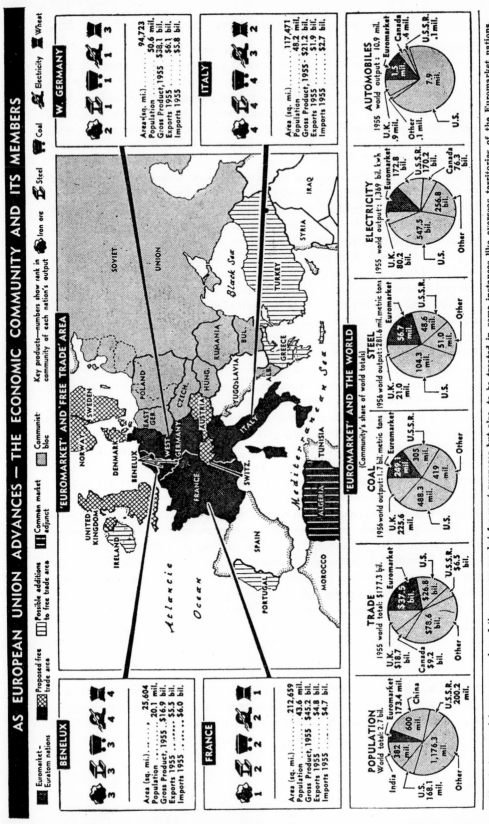

Fig. 14. The European Common Market. (*Source: New York Times*, March 31, 1957, Section IV, p. E5.)

Algeria is a special case, a member of the common market for most purposes but also to be treated in some instances like overseas territories of the Euromarket nations.

ment of the status of a hydrogen-bomb power in the spring of 1957 probably strengthened her determination not to link her atomic-power destiny more closely with Western Europe.

Nevertheless, it was Britain who urged the establishment of a general legislative assembly to co-ordinate the several military, political, and economic organizations already functioning in Western Europe: Western European Union, the Council of Europe, the Organization for European Economic Cooperation, the European Payments Union, and the North Atlantic Treaty Organization. It remains to be seen whether the significant if limited functional steps toward unity in Europe will lead to political federation. Whether regional political federation, if achieved, will make more or less difficult the achievement of a world community is also a question for the future.

SUMMARY

So far, three major types of approach looking toward a new world organization have been considered. All three would, directly or indirectly, strengthen the United Nations, but all would go beyond the present organization of the United Nations, immediately or eventually, in one important respect, the relinquishment of external sovereign power in certain areas of common concern. The functionalists look forward to a gradual transfer of sovereignty, bit by bit, in conjunction with the practical solution of mutual practical problems. Advocates of immediate world government believe that the surrender of sovereignty by nation-states need only be limited to matters related to armaments and war. Proponents of Atlantic Union, however, are convinced that the union of democracies must have power not only over security and defense but also over questions of a common market, currency, postal system, citizenship, and so on. It will be recalled, by way of contrast, that the United Nations is now based on the "principle of the sovereign equality of all its Members," internally and externally.

With representative plans for a new type of world organization set forth, together with the proponents' criticisms of each other, we now turn our attention to some major arguments that other critics of world government have made against these proposals.

ADVERSE CRITICISM OF NEW APPROACHES TO WORLD ORGANIZATION

The literature of adverse criticism of new approaches to world organization abounds in the words *Utopian, unrealistic, naïve, simple-minded, impractical, unworkable, dangerous.*

The criticism comes from American nationalists, hostile to the United

Nations or to America's allies like Britain and France. It comes, as well, from valiant defenders of the United Nations, who are fearful lest the advocacy of new ideas of world organization weaken the efficacy of the present organization. Advocates of the balance of power contend that such ideas of world organization are futile distractions, preventing concentration upon the harsh realities of the business at hand, the incontestable rivalry of nations. A more subtle kind of criticism is that which urges advocates of a new kind of world organization not to flee from present evils to others which might be worse, for instance, the possibility of a tyrannical world government. Still others remind spokesmen for a new world organization that success in eliminating war between nations may be followed by equally catastrophic civil war within the new unitary world organization. Even the Soviet Union has added its barbs of hostile criticism, with the implication that the only new type of world organization that is bound to emerge is a world union of Soviet communist states!

The Criticism of Fearful Nationalists in All Countries

Nationalists in all countries are fearful of what the surrender of sovereignty will mean to the security of the institutions and principles they hold dear. They dislike yielding power to a new and alien organization. Southerners in the United States, for example, may be concerned about the power that a new world organization might have over civil rights, affecting, as it does, their long-established way of life. In general, advocates of states' rights are disturbed by the possibility that this new world organization might interfere with the traditional liberties and powers of the states. Patriots may be disheartened by the potential dangers to American symbols, power, and prestige, and to America's uniqueness. Hard-headed realists speculate that the new organization may diminish the nation's ability to protect itself against foreign and domestic foes; that our treasure may be expended for the benefit of others, with no adequate return to the nation; that we may be overwhelmed by the tide of numbers in this world organization; that we will have sacrificed more than we have gained in participating in a new world organization. These doubts extend to regional organizations like the much discussed proposal for a united Europe. Some Americans are fearful lest a powerful united Europe loosen its ties with the United States or even become an economic, political, and military rival.

Similar fears may lead Frenchmen to hold aloof from intimate connection with a European Union, which might well be dominated by Germany or restrict French freedom of action in North Africa. Comparable worries may dissuade the British: It might disrupt the world-wide British Commonwealth of Nations. In a word, considerations of this sort carry weight with nationalists in other countries, lest their nations lose their freedom of action in matters of vital national interest.

The Criticism of Strong Supporters of the United Nations

Many United Nations supporters are apprehensive about new approaches to world organization because they feel that the efforts are rocking the United Nations boat, already buffeted by stormy weather in its courageous and perilous voyage. They urge support for the United Nations, the best international organization now existing and functioning, and call upon all men and countries to devote their time and energy to making a success of the United Nations, rather than pursuing the dream of an Utopian new world organization. It is hard enough, they feel, to make the United Nations a going concern. If its proponents divide their efforts, they may lose the bird in the hand for the phantom in the bush.[17]

The Criticism of Advocates of Balance of Power

Those who believe in relying upon the balance of power in world politics feel that it is premature to look to a new world organization for achievement of national security and well-being. As Chapter 12 has made clear, they hold that men and nations must operate in the real world of conflict and rivalry, and apply the techniques best adapted to such a world. Only when diplomacy, backed up by a realistic balance of power, has made significant headway in reducing world tensions will it be sensible to examine the possibilities of a new world organization.[18]

[17] In connection with this criticism, the views of Philip C. Jessup are of interest. See his "World Government and Mankind," in Ruth N. Anshen, *Moral Principles of Action* (New York, Harper, 1952), pp. 303–342. Jessup is sympathetic to some premises and goals of a new world organization but is doubtful as to its practicability now. He agrees that national sovereignty, "the ultimate freedom of national states to enforce their wills by the use of their power," is the root of war. Yet, he does not believe, apparently, that the evil root of sovereignty can be pulled up in one revolutionary heave, as advocated by many proponents of world government now. Jessup prefers to seek peace through the United Nations, but he clearly indicates that he does not agree with the view that, since world government at this time is impractical, verbal agitation for it should be opposed.

[18] In this connection, see the provocative views of Hans J. Morgenthau, in *Politics Among Nations*, 2nd ed. (New York, Knopf, 1954), pp. 481, 505 in particular, and Chaps. 29 and 30 in general. Morgenthau states that there "is no shirking the conclusion that international peace cannot be permanent without a world state," and "that in no period of modern history was civilization more in need of permanent peace and, hence, of a world state. . . ." He does not believe that a world state is feasible now, nor that a world state alone is sufficient to maintain peace. Yet, he concedes that, although it is now unattainable, it is still indispensable for world survival.

His way out of the dilemma is to take steps "to create the conditions under which it will not be impossible from the outset to establish a world state." "As the prime requisite for the creation of such conditions," Morgenthau suggests "the mitigation and minimization of those political conflicts which in our time pit the two superpowers against each other and evoke the specter of a cataclysmic war." He calls the method of establishing the preconditions for permanent peace "peace through accommodation." "Its instrument," Morgenthau argues, "is diplomacy." This diplomacy must be employed by statesmen prudently adhering to the realistic standard of the national interest, judiciously avoiding the temptation to impose one's national standards and will on the rest of the world, skillfully using the balance of power for what it is worth in the modern world.

Some Final Criticisms of a New Approach to World Organization

Other critics contend that a world state can only be based on a world community, which does not at present exist. Most advocates of a new world organization are putting the cart (a world state) before the horse (a world community). Emphasis is also placed on the dangers of civil war in a world state, in the absence of a world community. The conclusion follows that efforts must first be directed to creating the conditions that will make a world community possible, and then eventually a world state.

In the next section, the representative proposals for world government are examined and criticized more fully. In question form, the problems vital to this debate might be put as follows: Is a federal union of the free democracies the basis for peace and freedom now and the prototype for world government later? Or is limited world federal government now the necessary and proper approach to world organization? Or is world government now fallacious, and an obstacle to the success of the functional approach to world order?

POSITIONS
ON THE PROBLEM

1. A FEDERAL UNION OF THE FREE DEMOCRACIES IS THE WAY TO PEACE AND FREEDOM NOW AND WORLD GOVERNMENT LATER

(The following two extracts are from the testimony of late Supreme Court Justice Owen Roberts, before a Senate Committee in 1950, and from Clarence Streit, *Freedom Against Itself*.[19])

Would Reassure Our Friends

(1) Passage of our Resolution [for an exploratory convention, Justice Roberts testified] would quiet European fears of our return to isolationism, by proving we are ready to explore the possibilities of going beyond the [North Atlantic] Pact and E.C.A. . . . . Its passage will demonstrate we are no longer merely preaching federation to Europe, but are preparing to practice it with them.

[19] See note 5 for source of Roberts' testimony. The passage from Streit, which follows Roberts' testimony, may be found on pp. 220–221 of *Freedom Against Itself, op. cit.*

Would Not Divide the World into Two Camps

(2) . . . The calling of a Convention implies no division of the world into two antagonistic camps, as does the policy that *ostensibly* makes an offer to all nations—such as world federation or alliance—which all Communist nations are certain to refuse. That sort of offer tends to harden the present Communist–non-Communist division of the world. It forces every nation to choose sides formally or to formally declare its neutrality. . . . [The Atlantic Union resolution] leaves the great bulk of the nations where they are now—in between the Communist bloc and the Atlantic Pact group, but none of them [is] forced to formally take sides or position.

Would Not Mean the Loss of Popular Sovereignty

(3) Adherence to the Union involves the transfer from the United States of such powers as are given to the Union government. But it involves no loss by the United States of their other existing powers under their respective constitutions. Moreover, the citizen, whose sovereignty is basic in our form of government, loses none of his sovereignty. He exercises it. He remains at the hub of the wheel; he merely creates a new spoke; he re-delegates power to a new agent. Thereby he gains greater power and freedom, more security, less taxes and a vaster free market. Great economies are bound to result from Union. . . .

Would Immensely Strengthen Our International Position

(4) The calling of the proposed convention requires no action by the United Nations, nor would it be contrary to any provision of the Charter. . . . The Kremlin cannot veto it. Atlantic Union . . . would immeasurably strengthen the United Nations by uniting those members most devoted to United Nations aims. . . . The Union would strengthen the United Nations morally through the example of sovereign peoples uniting voluntarily. Once formed, the Union would be a member of the United Nations, and could retain the voting power now employed by its several members.

The proposed Union would inherit the position of the United States in the Inter-American Organization; and as Latin American Nations entered the Union, it would gradually replace that organization. . . . The Atlantic Pact . . . would not be affected by the Convention, but would have no further reason for existence once the Union is formed. In fact, the Union would supersede all those poisonous rich-uncle-poor-nephew stopgaps by a healthier citizen-to-citizen relationship.

Would Leave the Door Open for Democratic Membership

(5) Moreover, the Union, when formed, will keep the door open to any nation which guarantees individual liberty and popular representative government.

Would Enhance the Economic and Hence the Political Strength of Federated Democracies

(6) It [the Union] will establish a free market for 400,000,000 people. It would, in turn, afford the only important market for all other nations. It would be their best buyer of raw materials and their sole source of supply for many

manufactured goods. They [nations outside the Union] could not sell their products to Soviet Russia, nor buy what they needed from her, nor transport much to or from her. The Union would have to blunder badly to lose any of these nations to the Kremlin.

I would make crystal clear [wrote Clarence Streit] *why I find only one peaceful way to end this tension, without loss of freedom or any other disaster.* Consider:

We cannot possibly change the nature of freedom so that it will no longer foster inventions that build up our Atlantic community.

We cannot possibly change the nature of a community so that ours will no longer need some kind of government, free or unfree.

We cannot possibly change the nature of freedom's inventions so they will no longer arm dictatorship industrially and militarily.

We cannot possibly change the nature of totalitarian dictatorship so that it will no longer seek to destroy freedom and extend its rule wherever it safely can. We can prevent its attack by gaining and maintaining overwhelming power —but we must do this economically enough to avoid losing to dictatorship through an internal crash. We cannot destroy the existing dictatorship peacefully, except by creating conditions that cause it to crash internally, itself. Destruction of the Red autocracy, whether by war or without war, will not, however, change the nature of dictatorship, or keep another dictator from rising swiftly again, so long as Atlantica maintains anarchy in the world.

We cannot possibly change the nature of anarchy or of men, so that men will no longer prefer dictatorship to anarchy.

There is only one major factor in the mounting tension of our time that we *can* change without any disaster, or any loss of freedom or peace. We *can* end Atlantica's anarchy. *To change disunion into union does not require us to change the nature of anything, but merely to change our minds . . .* through foresight and reason today, instead of force and treason tomorrow. . .

We need only discard the false notion that now makes individual freedom depend on our maintaining the anarchy of unlimited national sovereignty. We need but hold to the truth, that freedom depends on free people constituting the government of a limited Union wherever a community of them comes to exist.

2. LIMITED WORLD FEDERAL GOVERNMENT IS THE NECESSARY AND PROPER APPROACH TO WORLD ORGANIZATION

(The following position on behalf of limited world federal government is drawn from the literature of United World Federalists, Inc.)

Preface to Peace: Through Law and Justice [20]

Today we know that treaties and covenants do not prevent wars.

We know that the world is again in a feverish arms race and that in all history arms races have had but one end—war.

We know that the simple desire for peace is not enough to keep the peace.

[20] This extract is taken from an U.W.F. pamphlet entitled *Suppose You Had No Cop on the Corner.*

We know that the nations, the United Nations and tens of millions of people everywhere look to us—the great, strong, prosperous United States—to end the horror and folly that is war.

We believe that America has an answer.

We believe that the American form of federal government is the most perfect form of government that man has conceived.

We believe that history proves that men of all races, colors, creeds and tongues can exist side by side, happily and prosperously, under the law and justice that is federal government.

We believe that if the United States took the lead in the effort to create such a government, the nations of the world would compete to be the first to follow.

We believe that, of all the contributions the United States has made to mankind, this could be by far the greatest.

We do not believe the creation of such a government would be without great problems but problems are easier to deal with than mass destruction and a devastated world—and finally we believe that the horror and disillusionment of another war will lead to a world of Communism and slavery. So to preserve the American way of life, the American form of government—

We believe that the United States must lead the world to peace through law and justice. UWF exists because we believe and work for this end.

The Policy of United World Federalists, Inc.[21]

Modern warfare imposes crushing economic burdens and threatens to destroy the rights, freedoms and lives of Americans and of all mankind.

As men in the past created national governments to provide the security local governments could not assure, so we must now create a limited world federal government to give all people the protection against war which is no longer within the power of national governments.

To this end, we call for the support and strengthening of the United Nations and for such amendments of its Charter as will enable it to achieve universal disarmament enforced under adequate safeguards, thus preventing aggression and making possible a world at peace under law.

The United Nations: What It Has Been Able to Do

The United Nations has many remarkable accomplishments to its credit. Among these, it helped save Iran and Greece from Russian aggression in 1946 and 1947. It brought the Arab-Israeli and the India-Pakistan wars to armistice. It settled the Netherlands-Indonesian war and ushered the Indonesian Republic into the United Nations. In Korea, it has demonstrated that aggression can be resisted by the international community. Through the World Health Organization, it has cut the world death rate from tuberculosis by fifty per cent in a few short years, and virtually eliminated from vast areas diseases which a few years ago took a heavy toll of life. It has, through the Technical Assistance Administration, lifted the productive capacity of underdeveloped areas. It has, through its many Specialized Agencies, begun the task of developing a sense of community and understanding among the nations.

[21] This policy statement is taken from the U.W.F. platform adopted at the U.W.F.'s Seventh General Assembly, June 19–21, 1953.

What It Has Not Been Able to Do

Though much has been accomplished by the United Nations, many have been disappointed by its failure to achieve international peace and security. Korea is not peace and the arms race can hardly be called security. The United Nations' failures, however, are to be assigned to the magnitude of the problems it has faced, and the limitations upon its effective action to solve them embodied in the Charter at San Francisco. Responsibility for these cannot be attached to the United Nations as such, but rather to those who created it. In the face of its limitations, the United Nations has accomplished much.

Why It Must Be Supported

It provides the foundation on which the structure of durable peace can be erected. It is already fulfilling certain specific tasks of value to men and nations which would otherwise go undone.

Irresponsible attacks on the UN, attempts to weaken or withdraw U.S. membership in the UN, schemes to drive one nation or the other from the UN, are wanton destruction of the instrument which can yet achieve the substance of men's hope for a peaceful world under just law.

The UN's weaknesses should lead us to strengthen the UN, not to abandon it. The best friends of the UN are those who work to give it the power it needs to maintain peace.

It Can Be Strengthened

While there is little the general public can do concerning the day-to-day problems of the UN, an informed public opinion could do very much to remove the limitations on effective action for world peace embodied in the present Charter.

How This Policy Strengthens American Foreign Policy

In a lawless world, torn apart by war and threats of war, attention is diverted from the goal of a United Nations able to maintain peace by enforcing law. But to concentrate only on preparation for war and to set aside the hope of peace is to lose sight of the goal. Before the achievement of a strengthened United Nations comes the advocacy of it. In that advocacy America has the opportunity to assume the moral leadership of the world, to seize the initiative from Communist imperialism and to join together in a unified front all nations truly seeking peace. This dynamic moral offensive is not only the essential first step to peace; it is also indispensable to defense against Communist aggression. The announced determination to seek the necessary amendment of the United Nations to give it power to prevent aggression will give positive purpose and direction to American foreign policy. It will make our program for defense a means to the larger end of establishing for all nations protection under law.

American foreign policy to be complete must consist of both a program for defense and a program for peace. Neither program alone is adequate. The purpose of peace is not served by inadequate defenses or failure to resist aggression. Unpreparedness in the face of Communist imperialism will be an invitation to disaster. But a defense program alone, however right the cause may be which it defends, fails to ignite the world's will to resist aggression because it offers only an arms race with the historical result of all other arms races: war.

Nor does preventive war provide a solution. To propose that the United States should seek peace by launching an atomic attack is not only wholly immoral, but such an aggressive war would alienate our allies and bring in its wake the chaos and destruction on which dictatorship thrives.

On the other hand, a program which has as its goal the establishment of peace under law will win respect for its strength and will win also the hearts and minds of men the world over.

If the Soviet Union, faced with the suicidal consequences of a continued arms race, should accept this American offer and agree to join in creating a common structure of security under enforceable law, then the necessary changes in the United Nations will be achieved and the threat of armed aggression removed from the competition between differing ideologies and systems of government.

Our best and only hope of enduring peace is universal world law and the governmental agencies through which it can be justly administered and promptly enforced. If, in spite of our best efforts, this hope is not realized in time and war again is to be our lot, then our purpose in that war must be to build the world federation that alone can give meaning to the sacrifices victory will cost.

If security against aggression is achieved under enforceable world law, the United States and other nations would be freed from many compulsions caused by fear of aggression and each would thus regain the initiative in the use of its sovereign control over its own concerns.

Conclusion

We reaffirm [declares the 1953 U.W.F. platform] our conviction that peace is not merely the absence of war, but the presence of justice, of law, of order, in short of government. We wholeheartedly support the United Nations and believe that its members must transfer to it sufficient authority to enable it to maintain law and order at the world level.

3. WORLD GOVERNMENT NOW IS FALLACIOUS—THE WAY TO WORLD ORDER IS BY WAY OF THE FUNCTIONAL APPROACH

(The following position is taken from an article by N. A. Pelcovits.[22] Mr. Pelcovits is currently Chief, External Research Staff, Office of Intelligence Research and Analysis, Department of State. The extract presented here is a reprint of an article he wrote before joining the Department of State, and is not a new piece written since. Consequently, it does not necessarily reflect the position of or have the approval of the Department of State.)

Ever since the events at Hiroshima and Nagasaki convinced the intellectual multitude that the political ways of modern man are obsolete, a frantic search for the formula of perpetual peace has possessed campus and platform. Time is short and the danger to civilization, indeed to human survival itself, so immediate that it is small wonder that the thirsty thousands mistake the mirage of world government for the oasis of perpetual peace.

[22] The full article "World Government Now?" originally appeared in *Harper's Magazine*, November, 1946, pp. 396–403.

Plans proposed by the high-minded people who are currently engaged in drafting blueprints for global peace are morally so unassailable and logically so irrefutable that converts to a new political theology can be forgiven for exhibiting righteous intolerance toward the skeptic. The truth, after all, is so inescapable when it arrives with the blinding flash of revelation. War, they say, is caused by anarchy or the "absence of government" in the relations between nations. Clashing sovereignties, which know neither law nor restraint, can be curbed only by the creation of a world government enforcing world law. It is an all or nothing proposition. The primary political task of the atomic age, therefore, is the drafting of a world constitution acceptable to the peoples of the earth.

. . . While admitting that the step they advocate is radical, enthusiasts disregard the revolutionary implications of the move and reduce complexity to a simple problem in deductive reasoning. Thus, the "Appeal to the Peoples of the World" issued by the Rollins College Conference last March was presented in the ordered form of a statement of principle and a syllogistic argument. The principle: "There can be no absolute guarantee that peace will be maintained so long as any nation has the sovereign right to decide questions of war and peace for itself," because peace "is not merely the absence of war but the presence of justice, law, order—in short, government." The argument then noted that the United Nations, as a league of sovereign states, could not prevent conflict or establish justice until it had been transformed into world government. The immediate political task, therefore, was the calling of a General Conference under Article 109 of the Charter to draft a world constitution.

The sheer simplicity of the argument is so appealing, the solution offered so economical, the cause in which it is advocated so noble, that it is no wonder that men of good will are signing up in wholesale numbers. Nor is it surprising that opponents shrink from challenging the faith. To do so labels one as a blind reactionary bogged down in the outworn concepts of ichthyosaurian politics and unwilling to face the facts of atomic life. But the time has come for skeptics to inject a few doubts. For the fallacy of World Government Now is so overwhelming that its adherents must soon realize that they are being led a merry chase down a blind alley.

. . . The World Government Now craze might thus be dismissed as politically innocuous were it not also possessed of the dangerous doctrine that World Government Now means World Government First. Immediate, hard issues of international life can postpone solution until the "primary" task of establishing a world federation has been accomplished. True believers express prophetic impatience with skeptics in the State Department who continue to haggle over the lesser issues of power politics.

. . . Peace cannot be achieved by a syllogism which is based on fantastic premises, discredited by elementary political science years ago. The prophets of World Government Now have been getting away with their sleight-of-hand by effectively concealing three Grand Errors. The first of these is the error commonly made by neophyte students of political science: that you can pass a law to stop almost everything, including sin. This view stems from a topsy-turvy misconception of the way governments are made. Reduced to its barest elements, the chain of distortion takes the following path: Constitutions establish governments. Governments, in turn, pass laws to stop people from fighting each other and to persuade them to settle their differences in friendly fashion. Resultant law and order encourage people to cooperate and live as one big, universal, happy family. Nothing could be more absurd. Except for short periods under dictatorship the process is exactly reverse. Through common living and common loyalties a community forms, establishing common habits and rules of behavior. It is out of this *social* order that political authority and government arise. Constitution-making is the last step.

Error number two may be labeled the devil theory of sovereignty. This assumes that if you do away with the right of sovereign states to wage war, by delegating that right to a "higher sovereignty," you do away with war. The shadow of sovereignty is mistaken for the reality of power. For, as the history of civil strife demonstrates, the sovereign right to make war is hardly a prerequisite of battle.

Closely related is the third major error, that war is a lawsuit fought with bombs instead of briefs. World government, it is argued, will establish effective tribunals for the settlement of "disputes" which lead to war. But war is rarely so much a dispute over justice as a conflict of interests. War, like politics, is an attempt to determine by pressure who gets what, where, when; it is an attempt to change the status quo.

. . . Are conditions ripe for the adoption of World Government Now?

They are not. The Greeks had a word for the type of thought-process employed by World Government Firsters to convince us that only a suitable constitutional formula is required to ensure global law and order. They called it *hysteronproteron,* which Webster defines as "the fallacy of explaining a thing by that which presupposes it and so inverting the natural order of reason." This fallacy is implicit in the three Grand Errors noted above, which now require fuller analysis.

1. *Men make a government by drawing up a set of rules called a constitution which serves as the foundation of law and order.*

Only in the looking-glass world of make-believe can this feat be accomplished. Constitution-making is always the end of a process, never the beginning. Political science is based on the truism that society precedes the state. In laymen's terms this simply means that men must live together, form common habits, and cooperate on the functional level before government can be instituted among them. Through cooperative living plus common habits and loyalties men come to feel and act as though they belong together. This community, as the sociologists call it, may codify its standards of behavior, refine its administration, and set down in a constitution what it will recognize as political authority. Constitution-making is the final step in establishing a regime of law and order. Only where basic law and order already function can men sit down to draft a constitution with any chance of success.

If this is true then the primary question of world law and order is not whether world government is desirable. Nor is the primary argument that without World Government Now we will perish in the international jungle. There is a previous question: do we now have a world community? If not, how can we best encourage its growth? For without community, constitution-making is a noble but vain endeavor.

That we're all in the same boat does not prove the existence of a world community. Neither does the fact that in space-time Moscow is only a day's travel from Chicago, nor that a decision taken on the Potomac may intimately affect the livelihood of a peasant on the Ganges. Still less can we convince men that they are brothers by frightening tales of Hiroshima. These are all pressing reasons for accelerating the growth of a world community. We can no longer afford to postpone functional solutions of such global problems as world famine, world aviation, world living standards, world education, world atomic energy control. But we can never force the birth of a world community by "inverting the natural order of reason." We are a long way from a world constitution.

. . . To bolster the argument that the world is ripe for constitution-making, no more misleading analogy has been offered than the experience of the United States in 1787. It is the trump card played at every debate. But to compare the contemporary state of international relations with that of the states under the Articles of Confederation is willful nonsense. By the time the convention met in Philadelphia the states had fought a revolutionary war as a united force and under a single command; they possessed a common cultural heritage, common language and tradition and habits and law. Interstate trade, though subjected to some obstructions, was relatively free. Moreover, the colonists had never lost their common nationality and citizenship. There were no immigration barriers between New York and Connecticut, nor did a Virginian who moved to Philadelphia feel even remotely in need of naturalization. The separate states enjoyed neither tariff autonomy nor independent conduct of foreign relations. The inhabitants of each state were "entitled to all the privileges and immunities of free citizens in the several states."

The wild comparison arises partly from a misconception of what the delegates at Philadelphia set out to do in 1787. An accurate reading of history will show that they did *not* create a government, let alone build a social order and community where none existed before. They did not even form a union. The Convention performed the much more modest task of *perfecting* a union already in existence. No constitution can do more than that.

2. *Clashing national sovereignties are responsible for war. Merge them into the higher sovereignty of a world government and the sole cause of war will be removed.*

This error, too, can best be exploded by recalling certain facts about the birth of the United States. The American Revolutionary War resulted in the splitting of a sovereignty. It was a civil war which started with rebellion against the central authority in London. There was war despite the fact that the American colonies were united with Britain in a "higher sovereignty"; despite the fact that sole war-making authority rested with the Crown, which represented that higher sovereignty; despite the fact that no organized force was initially at the disposal of the rebels; and despite the fact that the revolution was definitely against the constitutional law which obtained in the colonies in 1775. According to the folklore of World Government Now, such an occurrence should have been impossible.

"The only cause of war," Adler maintains, "is anarchy. Anarchy occurs wherever men and nations try to live together without each surrendering their sovereignty." How then explain the impossible fact that men who were living together under a single sovereignty in 1775 found themselves engaged in war with each other during the next eight years? If anarchy can occur within a sovereignty, then global unification under a world constitution is hardly the clue to global peace.

. . . Advocates of World Government Now skirt around the issue of civil war, but its prevalence is directly germane to any discussion of the subject. For we are entitled to be skeptical about the efficacy of their prescription as a war-remover when the history of civil strife demonstrates that the "surrender of sovereignty" to a central constitutional authority cannot ensure law and order. Sovereignty, then, is *not* the key to war and peace. The establishment of a superstate will not automatically dissolve the conflicts which lead to war. . . .

Nor has civil war been an incidental part of history. From the middle of the tenth century, Europe suffered a centuries-long civil war to determine whether Pope or Emperor would inherit the sovereignty of Rome. The French Wars of Religion which lasted throughout the latter half of the sixteenth century, like the English War of Roses a hundred years previously, were struggles over the internal exercise of power. England fought another civil war in the seventeenth century to determine, according to the historian H.A.L. Fisher, "whether the true seat of sovereign authority lay with the Crown or Parliament." Americans need hardly be reminded that the Constitution, which even foreign statesmen hailed as the most perfect instrument of its kind, did not stand the test of a house divided.

That is always the test. Not the perfection of a constitution, but the degree of basic unity within a house, a society, or a state determines peace. Ever since the depression of 1930 threatened the stability of democratic regimes, political scientists have remarked on the truism that democratic government cannot survive unless its people agree on fundamental social issues. Where, as in the case of Germany in 1932, of Spain in 1936, of China in 1946, as of the United States in 1860, there exists a profound cleavage on such issues, loyalty is split and constitutional authority ceases to have any real meaning. The result is either civil war or dictatorship or both. Lincoln's profound observation on the condition of domestic peace is no less valid for world peace.

3. *War is a lawsuit fought with bombs instead of briefs. World government alone can provide an effective world court to settle disputes since it will be backed by a world police force.*

Closely related to error number two, this one assumes that sovereign states tote their own six-shooters on the frontier of international politics merely because law-enforcement machinery is lacking. Nations have "recourse to war" for the settlement of disputes because international law is imperfect, international courts lack jurisdiction, and there is no sheriff to enforce their judgments. Each nation thus serves as its own justice of the peace.

This error leads to the absurd conclusion that Hitler attacked Poland because of a "dispute" over territorial and population rights; that Pearl Harbor resulted from a "dispute" over a just settlement for the Pacific area; that the present tension between East and West stems from a difference over the proper interpretation of rights under the Yalta and Potsdam agreements. What is the reality? All war, civil and international, is a conflict over interests, not a substitute for litigation. War is an instrument of policy and an attempt to change the status quo, not to define it. War is not an appeal to the rules of the game but a forced reshuffling of the deck and re-distribution of the chips. Conflict, of course, need not issue in war; differences can be resolved, compromised, arbitrated. But the solution lies not in delegating the war-making power to a world authority. Making war illegal for nations and legal only for the world federation is destined to be a vain endeavor. No one has ever been known to ask for an advisory opinion on whether it is legal to go to war.

Those who delight in discussing whether international law is "law" at all tend to raise an eyebrow over the practice of nations in refusing to submit to international tribunals issues regarded as "nonjusticiable." States, it is pointed out, never arbitrate questions involving "vital interests." This is so, but it has nothing to do with the "weakness" of international law or with the fact that it is not a complete code of laws. The reason is simple enough: the issues in-

volved concern differences over policy, not the definition of established rights.
. . . When the issues are important enough, law cannot prevent people from
fighting.

Given these three Grand Errors it is clear that the constitutional formula
of World Government Now can solve nothing. It cannot create government,
much less bring about a social order with any prospect of stability. So long as
fundamental global problems remain unsolved there can be no basis for the
world community which must precede world government. The beginning of
wisdom will come with the realization that world order is a complex problem
which can be solved only, piece by piece, on the functional level. Global solutions on that level will weave the fabric of world administration into a design
for world order. Constitution-making comes last.

The test, I repeat, will be on the functional level. Plans for atomic energy
control, for example, must be judged not on their punitive aspects but by the
degree of effective control they delegate to a world administrative agency over
the sources and uses of atomic energy. Well-meaning internationalists who are
now capering down the primrose path of world government could do infinitely more for the cause of world peace by mobilizing their political strength
behind the proposal of . . . the Food and Agriculture Organization of the
United Nations to establish an international ever-normal granary. The plan
would set up a World Food Board with authority to store food, stabilize food
production and prices, and allocate surpluses so as to prevent famine. This
is but one example in a long list of projects which deserve priority support over
constitution-making. There is the suggestion to set up an International Petroleum Authority; the need for implementing the recently-constituted World
Health Organization; the arduous tasks facing the . . . International Refugee
Organization; and dozens of other attempts to solve global problems on the
functional level.

It is through such instruments of world cooperation that the laborious beginnings of a world community will become real. One World is the recognition
of a problem, not the description of a fact. "Blue-prints for global peace" must
wait on the evolution of a world order. To be able to time the introduction of
a world constitution will take the genius for political timing which present-day
enthusiasts for World Government Now appear woefully to lack.

QUESTIONS

1. What is the logical appeal of a new world organization? How sound is the
logic of the appeal?

2. Upon what points are the advocates of a new type of world organization
in agreement? In disagreement?

3. Outline the essential features of the plan for a federal union of the
democracies, as presented by Mr. Clarence Streit. What are its strengths and
weaknesses?

4. Outline the essential features of the plan for government on a world-wide
basis, as set forth by the United World Federalists. What are its strengths and
weaknesses?

5. What is the Council of Europe? The Schuman Plan? The European Common Market? Euratom? Does the history of such ideas help to demonstrate the
feasibility or unfeasibility of a new world organization? Explain.

6. Contrast David Mitrany's functional approach to world government with the "regional" approach of Clarence Streit's federal union of the democracies and with the "universal" approach of the United World Federalists. Be sure to indicate similarities as well as differences.

7. What rebuttal might advocates of a new world organization make to the arguments adverse to world government made by N. A. Pelcovits and others?

8. Which of the practical obstacles to the achievement of world government do you think is the most difficult? Explain.

9. Which of the three positions in the last section of this chapter is the most convincing? Why?

10. What do you think should be the role of the intelligent and patriotic citizen with regard to movements looking toward the achievement eventually of a new world organization?

SELECT BIBLIOGRAPHY

ADLER, Mortimer J., *How to Think about War and Peace* (New York, Simon and Schuster, 1944). A clear, analytical, cogent presentation of the case for world government. Treats, in turn, the problem, possibility, probability, and practicality of peace. Maintains that the only cause of war is anarchy. Recognizes the obstacles to peace but feels that these can be overcome over a long period of time.

BRYSON, Lyman, and others, eds., *Foundations of World Organization: A Political and Cultural Appraisal* (New York, Harper, 1952). Consists of short papers on such topics as "Social Forces for World Organization," "Experience of Non-governmental and Governmental Organization in International Co-operation," "Philosophical and Religious Bases for World Organization." Represents the perspectives of a number of different disciplines.

DE RUSETT, Alan, *Strengthening the Framework of Peace* (London, Royal Institute of International Affairs, 1950). An admirable, brief study of current proposals for amending, developing, or replacing present international institutions for the maintenance of peace. Summarizes proposals within the present structure of the United Nations, international force proposals, functional approaches to world organization, proposals for world federal government, and proposals for the unification of Europe. Points out differences between and similarities among plans. A very helpful starting point for the beginning student.

MANGONE, GERARD J., *The Idea and Practice of World Government* (New York, Columbia University Press, 1951). Deals with the theory and progress of world government; the relationship of justice, international law, and the world community; and democracy and world government. Contains a helpful bibliography.

MITRANY, David, *A Working Peace System*, 4th ed. (London, National Peace Council, 1946). Contains a cogent argument for the functional development of international organization. Warns against the dangers of primarily political approaches to international organization.

MORGENTHAU, Hans J., *Politics Among Nations*, 2nd ed. (New York, Knopf, 1954). Holds that the world state is theoretically sound but practically impossible now because of the absence of a world community. Looks with favor upon the functional approach to world organization. Believes that we must first mitigate dangerous power struggles, using a wise diplomacy to advance a policy of peace through accommodation. Adversely critical of those who would base our foreign policy upon abstract moral principles that overlook the prudent safeguarding of the national interest. Select bibliographical references on the problem of the world state and world community are given on pp. 578–579.

NIEBUHR, Reinhold, *The Nature and Destiny of Man*, Vol. 2 (New York, Scribner, 1943). See pp. 284–286, "Justice and World Community," for a brief but penetrating criticism. The author's adverse criticism of idealistic plans for world government appears in his *The Children of Light and the Children of Darkness* and *The Irony of American History*. He is equally critical of balance-of-power pessimists and imperialistic cynics.

REVES, Emery, *The Anatomy of Peace* (New York, Harper, 1945). An early best-selling manifesto on behalf of world government. Sharply and bitterly critical of narrow nationalism and the sovereign nation-state. Attacks the fallacy of internationalism, of self-determination of nations, of collective security. Maintains that peace necessitates a legal order to regulate relations among men beyond and above the nation-states.

SCHUMAN, Frederick L., *The Commonwealth of Man* (New York, Knopf, 1952). An inquiry into power politics and world government by a partisan of federal world government. Deals, respectively, with the way of violence, the vision of man, peace by conquest, the new Caesarism, peace by treason, peace by planning, peace by war, and peace by contrast.

STREIT, Clarence K., *Freedom Against Itself* (New York, Harper, 1954). The most recent book by the energetic and eloquent author of *Union Now* (1939), *Union Now with Britain* (1941), and co-author of *The New Federalist* (1950). Emphasizes that the federal union of the Atlantic democracies (the feasibility of which is supported by the great American example of federal union) is required primarily by the very nature of freedom itself, and would be required even if the Kremlin no longer sought to divide and rule the free, to develop depression among us, to win the world by revolution and war.

U.S. Congress, Senate Subcommittee of the Committee on Foreign Relations, *Hearings on the Revision of the United Nations Charter* (Washington, D.C., Government Printing Office, 1950). These hearings in the 81st Congress, 2nd session, contain a mine of valuable information, pro and con, relative to revision of the United Nations Charter, Atlantic Union, World Federation, and other plans. Frequently very illuminating questions and answers on key points occur. See also the invaluable and comparable hearings in 1955, *Review of the United Nations Charter*. The 1955 hearings in the 84th Congress, 1st session, which contain a helpful Index (Part 13), were concerned with proposals to amend or otherwise modify existing international peace and security organizations, including the United Nations.

APPENDIX

APPENDIX

PREPARATION OF A "POSITION PAPER" ON SOME CURRENT PROBLEM OF AMERICAN FOREIGN POLICY

NATURE AND PURPOSE OF THIS PROJECT

One of the best ways of integrating one's knowledge of world affairs is to prepare an analysis of some international problem, together with a recommended line of policy for the solution of it. Putting oneself in the position of a government official in the Department of State, for example, who has to formulate American foreign policy, is an extremely realistic way of studying and understanding that policy.

As the concluding exercise in this study of world affairs, therefore, it is suggested that a policy paper be prepared, comparable in substance and method to the policy papers which might be prepared within the Department of State. It should deal with some current problem of American foreign policy, and should cover (a) a definition of the problem; (b) an analysis of the background of the problem; (c) a discussion of alternative policies which the United States might adopt in dealing with the problem; and (d) a recommendation of the specific policy that seems best designed to cope with the problem.

Within the Department of State, a policy paper—or position paper, as it is sometimes called—is usually drafted first by a committee of officials in the lower or middle echelons of the Department who have the most direct interest in the problem under consideration. When the paper has been approved by this committee, it is referred to the top officials in the Department of State and to the Secretary of State for a decision.[1] The purpose of the paper is to

[1] Final decisions on major foreign policy problems are not usually made by the Secretary of State alone but by the President of the United States. Before making such

provide the Secretary of State and his top associates with the necessary information and background on all possible policy alternatives, in order to help them make the wisest foreign policy decision for the United States.

In preparing such a paper, the reader should therefore try to put himself as completely as possible in the position of a Department of State committee which has been asked to prepare a policy recommendation for the Secretary of State or the President. Considering all relevant aspects of the problem—historical, political, economic, psychological, technological, military—he will quickly find that he is applying the interdisciplinary approach to which frequent reference has been made in this book. Although he will not, of course, have access to the type of classified or confidential information available to government officials, his study will not be unduly restricted, nor will the value of his experience be reduced in preparing a policy recommendation. A very high proportion of government intelligence, perhaps 90 per cent or more, consists of research and analysis based on nonconfidential materials available in any good library. The important function is the careful study of this information and the intelligent use of it in examining all implications of the various policy alternatives under consideration.

SUGGESTED OUTLINE

In order to assure some consistency and uniformity of organization, it is suggested that the paper be organized in the following manner:

Title

State the title in question form.
Example: What Should United States Policy Be Regarding the Unification of Germany?

A. Statement of the Problem

This should be a concise statement of the foreign policy problem under consideration. Usually three or four sentences will suffice.

Example. If German unification is the topic, the problem might be stated as follows:

"Since the end of World War II, the Soviet Union and the western powers have been unable to agree on the terms for the reunification of Germany, thereby leaving unresolved what is perhaps the most critical current problem of Europe. Whether German unification can be accomplished without a heightened danger of communist infiltration, or whether any western concessions on such points as neutralizing Germany or restricting German rearmament should be made in an effort to reach a compromise agreement, are some major unresolved aspects of the problem. The United States is interested in any possibility of breaking the stalemate on German unification, and the problem

decisions, the President obtains the advice of other key executive departments and agencies involved in foreign affairs, such as the National Security Council, Central Intelligence Agency, United States Information Agency, Department of Defense, Treasury Department, Department of Commerce, Atomic Energy Commission, and the Export-Import Bank.

now is to determine whether progress in this direction is more likely to result from maintaining the present American policy or from making certain modifications in it."

B. Background of the Problem

This should be a reasonably detailed account of how the problem originated and developed. It should indicate the main factors contributing to the issue, and list the principal events or actions that have taken place. If major proposals have been previously discussed for dealing with the problem, appropriate reference should be made to them. The viewpoints of the major governments interested in the problem might also be relevant. The purpose of this background statement is to provide the necessary information on which an intelligent discussion of policy alternatives can be based. It should be approximately five or six pages in length. It should include footnotes to indicate sources of the main points of information.

Example. With the problem of German unification again as an illustration, the background statement might appropriately cover such points as (1) the basic postwar agreements on the division of Germany; (2) an explanation of Germany's political, economic, and potential military significance in Europe, together with the reasons why both the Soviet Union and the western powers have felt that Germany could not be allowed to come under the domination of the other side; (3) a summary of the major proposals regarding German unification that both sides have advanced since 1946; (4) the reactions or replies of the various governments to these proposals; (5) an explanation of German official and public-opinion views on unification; (6) an analysis of the current positions of the different governments and the chief points of disagreement at present.

C. Alternative Policies

At least three alternative policies should be presented for dealing with the problem under consideration. These should be proposals the United States might be reasonably expected to adopt, that is, they should be proposals that a United States official might reasonably defend as being in the best interest of United States security and welfare. (See the discussion of national interest, pp. 44–47.) The arguments pro and con regarding each alternative must be presented and analyzed. The effects and implications of each alternative should be indicated. Footnotes should be used to indicate sources of main ideas or arguments. This section will normally be five to six pages in length.

Example. In the case of German unification, such alternative policies as the following might be suggested, with a pro and con analysis for each alternative:

1. The United States should continue its present policy of insisting on free, impartially supervised elections throughout Germany, with the right of any freely elected German government to decide its own future policies on such questions as NATO membership, rearmament, or neutralization.

2. In an effort to secure Soviet acceptance of the principle of free elections throughout Germany, the United States should agree to support the neutralization of Germany.

3. In an effort to secure Soviet acceptance of the principle of free elections throughout Germany, the United States should agree to merge the NATO alliance with the East European security system (Warsaw Pact) and form a regional all-European security pact under Article 51 of the United Nations Charter. A united Germany would be a member of this all-European security system.

D. Recommended Policy

This concluding section should indicate the policy it is recommended that the United States adopt. The reasons for making the recommendation should be given, together with the reasons why various alternative policies do not seem desirable. This final policy recommendation may be one of the alternative policies discussed in Section C, or it may be a combination and synthesis of two or more alternatives. If it is one of the alternatives already presented, it is not necessary to repeat in full the arguments in favor of the policy. A brief summary will suffice.

FOOTNOTES

Notes should be numbered consecutively, and may be placed either at the bottom of each page or on a separate page at the end of the paper. They should generally conform to the following style:

Books
Harry B. Price, *The Marshall Plan and Its Meaning* (Ithaca, 1955), p. 45.

If the following footnote also refers to the same book, it is not necessary to repeat the author and title, but simply to write *Ibid.*, p. 75. If, after a different reference has been listed in a subsequent footnote, the Price book were again to be cited, the reference could be as follows: Price, *op. cit.*, p. 75.

Periodicals
John H. Kautsky, "The New Strategy of International Communism," *The American Political Science Review*, June, 1955, p. 478.

Newspapers
New York Times, March 20, 1957, p. 5.

Documents
U.S. Congress, *A Decade of American Foreign Policy, Basic Documents, 1941–1949*, Senate Document 123, 81st Congress, 1950, p. 26.

GENERAL REFERENCES

The following list of references may be helpful in gathering information on the general background of various foreign policy problems:

Readers Guide to Periodical Literature. An index to periodical articles.
International Index to Periodicals. Similar to the *Readers Guide* but includes
  reference to some foreign periodicals and to some of the scholarly journals.

New York Times Index. An index to all articles in the *New York Times.* Very useful sometimes in checking details or locating public speeches and documents.

Facts on File. An excellent index and summary of all main current events, year by year.

Public Affairs Information Service. An index to books, pamphlets, articles, and government documents on various topics in public affairs. Very useful guide, especially for finding references to documents and similar studies.

Council on Foreign Relations, *The United States in World Affairs.* Annual surveys of major developments in U.S. foreign policy.

Royal Institute of International Affairs, *Survey of International Affairs.* Annual survey of all major international problems.

World Peace Foundation, *Documents on American Foreign Relations.* Annual series of documents on events of the year. Since 1952, the volumes have been published by the Council on Foreign Relations.

Royal Institute of International Affairs, *Documents on International Affairs.* Annual series.

United Nations Yearbook. Annual report on all U.N. activities. Excellent, comprehensive accounts of all issues that have come before the U.N.

Clyde Eagleton, and others, *Annual Review of United Nations Affairs.* Not so detailed as *United Nations Yearbook,* but volumes for recent events are more quickly published.

United Nations Review. Monthly periodical on current U.N. activities.

Foreign Policy Bulletin. Biweekly analysis of selected major problems of international affairs. Objective. Issued by the Foreign Policy Association, 345 East 46th Street, New York 17, N.Y.

Foreign Policy Association, *Headline Series.* A series of booklets on a wide range of international problems. Objective and popular in style. Approximately six are published each year.

Index

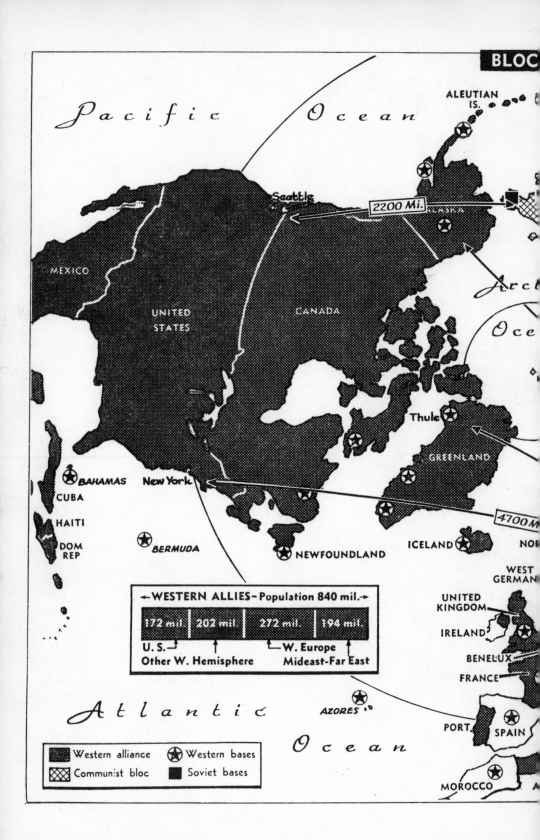

BLOC

Pacific Ocean

ALEUTIAN IS.

Seattle

2200 Mi. ALASKA

Arc

Oce

MEXICO

UNITED STATES

CANADA

Thule

GREENLAND

BAHAMAS

CUBA

New York

HAITI

DOM REP

BERMUDA

NEWFOUNDLAND

ICELAND

4700 M

NOR

WEST GERMAN

UNITED KINGDOM

IRELAND

BENELUX

FRANCE

← WESTERN ALLIES – Population 840 mil. →

172 mil.	202 mil.	272 mil.	194 mil.

U.S.┘   ↑   └ W. Europe   ↑
Other W. Hemisphere   Mideast-Far East

Atlantic

AZORES

Ocean

PORT.   SPAIN

	Western alliance		Western bases
	Communist bloc		Soviet bases

MOROCCO